Acclaim for Allen C. Guelzo's

ROBERT E. LEE

"Guelzo not only covers new ground with the incredible depth and breadth of his research, he does an exemplary job of showing how history should be written, keenly aware of historical context, contemporary values, and the space between them. . . . Reading more histories like these would be a good start to dealing with our country's racist past and the ways it permeates into the present day." —*New York Journal of Books*

"Guelzo's timely biography expertly scrubs off 150 years of political and cultural patina accumulated since the renowned general's passing to reveal a tragic humanity. . . . Guelzo's formal yet enjoyable writing style evokes the period without getting lost in it." —Associated Press

"Injects learning, subtlety, and even compassion into a debate that has more often been characterized by ignorance, simplemindedness, and sanctimony." —*The Washington Free Beacon*

"Evenhanded and insightful. . . . Deeply researched and elegantly written, this nuanced portrait captures Lee's 'ambiguous place in American history.' " —*Publishers Weekly*

"The award-winning Civil War historian offers a fresh assessment of Robert E. Lee. . . . A fine biography of a flawed American icon." —*Kirkus Reviews*

"Guelzo has written the definitive biography of Robert E. Lee for our time." —Michael Lind, author of *What Lincoln Believed*

"Guelzo confirms his place in the top rank of Civil War historians with his masterly biography. . . . Well-researched, well-written, and captivating, it will stand as the definitive single-volume life for decades to come. Guelzo's judicious comments on Lee's 'crime and glory' might be a good place for America to start healing her present-day wounds."

—Andrew Roberts, author of *Churchill: Walking with Destiny*

"At once bold and balanced. . . . Backed by impressive research, honed on mature and evenhanded judgment, and presented with the eloquence of a master craftsman, *Robert E. Lee: A Life* will please many, anger a few, and inform everyone who takes it up."

—William C. Davis, author of *Crucible of Command: Ulysses S. Grant and Robert E. Lee—the War They Fought, the Peace They Forged*

"Allen C. Guelzo has written exactly what the nation urgently needs right now—an example of mature thinking about complex, flawed people who took difficult actions in contexts not of their making or choosing. In today's blizzard of facile, overheated, and grandstanding judgments about the past, this unsentimental biography illustrates the intellectual responsibility that the present owes to the past."

—George F. Will

Allen C. Guelzo

ROBERT E. LEE

Allen C. Guelzo is a senior research scholar in the Humanities Council at Princeton University and the director of the James Madison Program's Initiative on Politics and Statesmanship. He is the author of several books about the Civil War and early nineteenth-century American history. He has been the recipient of the Lincoln Prize three times, the Guggenheim-Lehrman Prize in Military History, and many other honors. He lives in Paoli and Gettysburg, Pennsylvania, and is at work on a book about Abraham Lincoln and the American experiment.

allenguelzo.com

ALSO BY ALLEN C. GUELZO

Reconstruction: A Very Short Introduction

Redeeming the Great Emancipator (The Nathan I. Huggins Lectures)

Lincoln: An Intimate Portrait

Gettysburg: The Last Invasion

Fateful Lightning: A New History of the Civil War & Reconstruction

Lincoln Speeches (editor)

Lincoln: A Very Short Introduction

Abraham Lincoln as a Man of Ideas

Lincoln and Douglas: The Debates That Defined America

The New England Theology: From Jonathan Edwards to Edwards Amasa Park (editor, with Douglas A. Sweeney)

Lincoln's Emancipation Proclamation: The End of Slavery in America

Abraham Lincoln: Redeemer President

Edwards in Our Time: Jonathan Edwards and the Shaping of American Religion (editor, with Sang Hyun Lee)

Holland's Life of Abraham Lincoln (editor)

For the Union of Evangelical Christendom: The Irony of the Reformed Episcopalians

Edwards on the Will: A Century of American Theological Debate

ROBERT E.
LEE

ROBERT E. LEE

A LIFE

Allen C. Guelzo

VINTAGE BOOKS
A Division of Penguin Random House LLC
New York

FIRST VINTAGE BOOKS EDITION 2022

The title page image of Stratford Hall originally appeared opposite page 41 of Robert E. Lee's edition of Henry Lee's *Memoir of the War in the Southern Department of the United States* (New York: University Publishing, 1870).

The Library of Congress has cataloged the Knopf edition as follows:
Names: Guelzo, Allen C., author.
Title: Robert E. Lee : a life / Allen C. Guelzo.
Description: First edition. | New York : Alfred A. Knopf, 2021. |
Includes bibliographical references and index.
Identifiers: LCCN 2020056283 (print) | LCCN 2020056284 (ebook)
Subjects: LCSH: Lee, Robert E. (Robert Edward), 1807–1870. | Generals—United States—Biography. | Generals—Confederate States of America—Biography. | Confederate States of America Army—Biography. | United States—History—Civil War, 1861–1865—Campaigns. | United States Army—Biography. | Slavery—Virginia—History—19th century. | Lee family. | Custis family. | Virginia—Biography.
Classification: LCC E467.1.L4 G84 2021 (print) |
LCC E467.1.L4 (ebook) | DDC 335.0092 B—dc23
LC record available at https://lccn.loc.gov/2020056283
LC ebook record available at https://lccn.loc.gov/2020056284

Vintage Books Trade Paperback ISBN: 978-1-101-91222-5
eBook ISBN: 978-1-101-94621-3

Author photograph © Sameer Kahn, Fotobuddy
Book design by Michael Collica

vintagebooks.com

Printed in the United States of America
10 9 8 7 6 5 4 3 2

To the memory of the grandmother I scarcely knew,

Ruth Bloomenthal

(1902–1961),

but who blessed me exceedingly

I said, in writing a life, a man's peculiarities should be mentioned, because they mark his character. Johnson: "Sir, there is no doubt as to peculiarities: the question is, whether a man's vices should be mentioned. . . ." [W]hen Lord Hailes and he sat one morning calmly conversing in my house at Edinburgh, I well remember that Dr. Johnson maintained, that "If a man is to write A Panegyrick, he may keep vices out of sight; but if he professes to write A Life, he must represent it really as it was:" and when I objected to the danger of telling that Parnell drank to excess, he said, that "it would produce an instructive caution to avoid drinking, when it was seen, that even the learning and genius of Parnell could be debased by it." And in the Hebrides he maintained, as appears from my Journal, that a man's intimate friend should mention his faults, if he writes his life.

—James Boswell, *The Life of Samuel Johnson, LL.D.* (1791)

Oh, we were always honorable—Robert Lee, Jackson, Albert Sidney Johnston, A. P. Hill—but we served venal men and a vile enterprise. How many lives would have been spared had we not lent ourselves to the defense of a repellent cause like slavery?

—James Lee Burke, *In the Electric Mist with Confederate Dead* (1993)

Whence did I come by this readiness to give way, though with a murmur, this weak yielding, though after rebellion and a protest? . . . This wavering, this dissonance . . . has done me infinite harm in my life, and has not even left me with the faint comfort of recognizing that my mistake was involuntary, unconscious. . . . I saw the absurdity of the movement and its impotence, the indifference of the people, the ferocity of the reaction, and the pettiness of the revolutionaries. . . . How many misfortunes, how many blows I should have been spared in my life, if at all the crises in it I had had the strength to listen to myself. . . . The reason for my quick compliance was false shame, though sometimes it was the better influences of love, friendship and indulgence; but did all this overcome my power of reasoning?

—Alexander Herzen, "M. Bakunin and the Cause of Poland" (1862)

My experience of men has neither disposed me to think worse of them or indisposed me to serve them; nor in spite of failures, which I lament, of errors which I now see and acknowledge; or of the present aspect of affairs; do I despair of the future. The truth is this: The march of Providence is so slow, and our desires so impatient; the work of progress is so immense and our means of aiding it so feeble; the life of humanity is so long, that of the individual so brief, that we often see only the ebb of the advancing wave and are thus discouraged. It is history that teaches us to hope.

—Robert E. Lee to Charles Marshall, in Marshall's *Address to the Lee Monument Association* (October 27, 1887)

With the best of the young men dead, the country ruined,
And the sourness of Military District no. 1,
The War was an after-image, a dominant lightning
To dazzle the stunned eyes of a generation.
But Lee in his college office in Lexington,
The man beyond criticism, spoke reconciliation.
Slavery at least was gone. Over yet one more century
As the wounds heal up, the flaws start slowly to fade.

—Robert Conquest, "The Idea of Virginia," *Collected Poems* (2020)

Contents

ROBERT E.
LEE

Prologue: The Mystery of Robert E. Lee

This book began in 2014, in what now seems like almost another world, with a single question: How do you write the biography of someone who commits treason? The question is complicated, because (as Paul Murray Kendall wrote in *The Art of Biography*) the usual task of the biographer "is to perpetuate a man as he was in the days he lived—a spring task of bringing to life again, constantly threatened by unseasonable freezes." What my question suggests is that there may be some lives that we hesitate to perpetuate, and among the reasons for that hesitation must surely be treason.

In the case of Robert Edward Lee, this turns out to be an even more serious hesitation. Being a Yankee from Yankeeland, it has always seemed to me that the treason Lee committed was aggravated by the nature of the cause for which he committed it—the protection of legalized human slavery—and that rankles me to the sole of my abolitionist boots. I was, literally, catechized at my grandmother's knee in the righteousness of the Union war (she had caught the enthusiasm herself as a girl in Philadelphia's George Clymer School, when white-haired veterans of the Union Army would make their annual Decoration Day visit to explain the real meaning of the war and excoriate the Confederate traitors), and it would take no great struggle for me to capture Lee in a squinting and cynical view. Yet no one who met Robert Edward Lee—no matter what the circumstances of the meeting—ever seemed to fail to be impressed by the man. His dignity, his manners, his composure, all seemed to create a peculiar sense of awe in the minds of observers. From his earliest days as a cadet at West Point, through twenty-five years as an officer in the U.S. Army's Corps of Engineers and six more as a senior cavalry officer, and then as the supreme commander of the armies of the Confederacy, Lee was the model of gentility and propriety. John Brown Gordon, who served under Lee through the Civil War until the end at Appomattox, thought Lee was the pattern of "modest demeanor" and "manly decorum." Abraham Lincoln remarked that a photograph of Lee showed that Lee's "is a good face; it is the face of a noble, noble, brave man." Not even Ulysses Grant could escape the sense of being upstaged by Lee at Appomattox. "He was a man of much dignity, with an impassible face," Grant wrote in his *Memoirs,* "dressed in a full uniform which was entirely new" and "wearing a sword of considerable value," while Grant was self-conscious of "my rough travelling suit, the uniform of a private with the straps of a lieutenant-general" sewn on. "I must have contrasted strangely," Grant admitted, "with a man so handsomely dressed, six feet high and of faultless form."[1]

These impressions appear so consistent, and over so many years, that it has been easy to conclude that dignity, manners, and composure simply *were* the man, that there was (as Douglas Southall Freeman insisted at the end of his four-volume biography of Lee) "no mystery" at all to Robert E. Lee. Or, as Burton Hendrick wrote (in *The Lees of Virginia*), that "Lee's character" was ruled by a "great simplicity," or that (in the words of an even-more-worshipful biographer, Clifford Dowdey) Lee "could rest totally . . . in very simple things." Even those close to Lee (like his staffer Armistead Lindsay Long) were convinced that "his character was perfectly simple; there were in it no folds or sinuosities."[2]

However, this picture of straightforward, well-nigh angelic serenity sits uneasily beside moments when cracks and inconsistencies in that fabled serenity appeared. For instance: Lee worried constantly and insistently about money, even though he had married into one of the most prominent families in the District of Columbia—that of George Washington Parke Custis and his wife, Mary Fitzhugh Custis, who owned the palatial estate they called Arlington, perched Palatine-like on the Potomac bluffs overlooking the capital city and staffed with a small army of slaves. In fact, according to the will he filed before going off to fight in the Mexican War, Lee had actually inherited a decent sum from his mother, Ann Carter Lee, and had invested it with enough success to have acquired a portfolio worth $38,750 (almost $1.2 million in 2020).[3] It made no difference. When he left for Texas in 1855 to become lieutenant colonel of the 2nd Cavalry, he still insisted on managing the family's money affairs, even though the rest of the family was living sixteen hundred miles away at Arlington.

Other kinds of cracks opened under pressure. Trained as an engineer, and the director of a series of demanding coastal engineering projects (from controlling the silting up of the St. Louis waterfront to the construction of

Fort Carroll in Baltimore harbor), Lee was at his happiest with a draftsman's notebook in hand. But when matters spilled out of the kind of control that T squares and equations can impose, Lee grew impatient, contemptuous, and, on one significant occasion, violent. When his father-in-law died in 1857, Lee was named executor of the Custis estate, which, to his surprise, required him to superintend the emancipation, within five years, of all the Custis slaves at Arlington and two other Custis-owned properties.

Lee could not hurry to execute this emancipation because the will also mandated that a $10,000 legacy be paid to each of Lee's four daughters. Because the properties had been for years run haphazardly by old Custis, Lee would need to turn them into engines of efficiency to pay the required legacies. That, he did with an engineer's sense of precision. But the Custis slaves did not share his interest in making Arlington and the other places profitable; they believed that the Custis will had, in fact, emancipated them at once, and in 1858 three of them—two men and a woman—acted on that belief and fled to Westminster, Maryland, where they were apprehended and returned to Arlington.

Lee had all three whipped; by one account, he took the whip in his own hands and flayed them himself. Afterward, he was so appalled at his own rage that he could not admit the full extent of what he had done, even to his son Custis. What exacerbated his guilt was the fact that Lee actually owned only one slave family himself, inherited from his mother, and regarded slavery as "a moral and political evil," which, however, he was content to leave in the hands of God to resolve. He funded the expatriation of slaves from Arlington who agreed to resettle in the American Colonization Society's West African outpost of Liberia and in 1862 completed the emancipation of the Custis slaves (which he was obligated to do by his father-in-law's will) and then freed his own (which he was not).

Robert E. Lee's anxieties, his impatience, and his inconsistencies have, since the publication of Thomas L. Connelly's melodramatic recasting of Lee's historical reputation in *The Marble Man: Robert E. Lee and His Image in American Society* (1977), been seized upon as a triumphant contradiction of the Lee who so impressed his contemporaries, civilian and military.[4] But casting Lee in *contradiction*—as *either* saint or sinner, as *either* simple or pathological—is, in the end, less profitable than seeing his anxieties as a *counterpoint* to his dignity, his impatience and his temper as the match to his composure.

To begin to understand the mystery of Robert E. Lee is to begin with three large-scale factors, lodged deep in the man's personality, all three rooted in the early trauma inflicted by one of the more remarkably dysfunctional families of the early republic. Through the Revolution, the Lees of Virginia had been one of the first of American families, presiding over large properties on the Northern Neck of Virginia. The four Lee siblings who straddled the Revolutionary years—Richard Henry, Francis Lightfoot, Arthur, and William—were described by John Adams as "that band of brothers, intrepid and unchangeable . . . [who] stood in the gap in defense of their country, from the first glimmering of the Revolution . . . through all its rising light, to its perfect day."[5]

But something in the succeeding generation of Lees snapped, and nowhere was the snap louder than in the case of Henry Lee, Robert's father. A graduate of Princeton in the same student body as James Madison, Henry Lee served George Washington so effectively as a cavalry leader that he won the nickname Light Horse Harry. And in the glow of the Revolution, Light Horse Harry captured not only the hand of his cousin Matilda (and her family's estate, Stratford Hall) but the governorship of Virginia. After that, Light Horse Harry disintegrated. His ardent Federalism antagonized Virginia's Jeffersonians; his harebrained investment schemes bankrupted him.

After Matilda's death, he attempted to recoup his fortune by marrying a Virginia Carter, Ann Hill Carter. But he burned through her cash, too, and after he spent a stint in debtors' prison, the sadder but wiser Ann Carter Lee demanded that her family—which now numbered three sons (including Robert) and two daughters—move to more manageable quarters in Alexandria. But Light Horse Harry could not shake his penchant for disaster. After being beaten within an inch of his life in an Anti-Federalist riot in Baltimore in 1812, he decamped the following year for the safety of the West Indies. Robert never saw his father again. He was six years old.

Light Horse Harry only returned to America, fatally ill, in 1818, barely making landfall in Georgia before dying and leaving Robert to grow up, in practical terms, fatherless. "There is," wrote the literary critic Leon Edel, "no hurt among all the human hurts deeper and less understandable than the loss of a parent when one is not yet an adolescent," and Robert E. Lee offers us a textbook case in the truth of that saying.[6] Until he achieved fame in his own right in 1862, people invariably referred to Robert as the son of the famed Light Horse Harry. But *he* never did, except in his application letter to West Point, when he needed the glamour of Light Horse Harry's name to secure an at-large appointment. He did not visit his father's grave until the winter of 1861–62, even though his first posting out of West Point, at Cockspur Island, was only a few miles away. He was, instead, his mother's son, becoming the de facto head of household in Alexandria. He would, in other words, fulfill the role his father had abandoned; he would sacrifice himself in order to perfect the imperfections Light Horse Harry had visited on the Lees.

The pursuit of redemptive perfection lies behind much of the "marble model" that met so many people's eyes, and it was Lee's determination to not be Light Horse Harry that fired his impatience and, in later years, his ferocious outbursts of temper at his own and others' imperfections. That did not mean that Robert would *enjoy* the shackles and demands of perfection, and it came as a shock to Ann Carter Lee when in 1824 Robert announced his desire to leave her home in Alexandria and attend West Point. She would have been more disturbed still if she could have sensed how much Robert, for all his uncomplaining self-sacrifice, longed to be free and unencumbered of her as much as of his father.

The problem with the longing for independence is that it does not guarantee security, and security was precisely the most damaging subtraction Light Horse Harry made in Robert's life. So, as much as Robert Lee longed to be his own man, he was also aware that the independent man could very well be the impoverished, lonely, neglected man, and he did not want that either. One of the major attractions of a career in the U.S. Army was its guarantee of lifetime employment security; for the tiny cadre of officers who commanded the pre–Civil War Army, there was no retirement system, and once in many stayed in, and at paid rank, until their last breath. The Army was not generous, and promotion was agonizingly slow, but it was one of the few professions in the pre–Civil War republic that was secure. When his older brother Charles Carter Lee tried to persuade him to leave the Army and develop the land in Hardy, Patrick, and Shenandoah Counties they had inherited from their father, Robert declined. (And it was just as well that he did, because Carter Lee's development schemes came to fully as little as their father's.)

Matrimony was yet another path to security, and by marrying Mary Anna Randolph Custis, the sole surviving child of George Washington Parke Custis, he won himself a permanent home at Arlington for the next thirty years. The difficulty was that the security represented by the Custis marriage and Arlington did not sit very easily beside Lee's yearning for independence. His Custis in-laws made no secret of their desire that Robert leave the Army and take up permanent residence at Arlington, where he would become, in effect, the Custises' majordomo. But Lee had no desire to abandon the Army merely to become a glorified overseer for the Custises. Despite his very real affection for his mother-in-law, Mary Fitzhugh Custis, Lee regarded his father-in-law as a well-intentioned incompetent whose mismanagement of Arlington and two other Custis properties on the Pamunkey River was almost legendary. It is a measure of how ambivalent a symbol Arlington was for Lee that seven months into the Civil War, when Arlington had been lost to Union occupation, Lee dismissed the estate's loss and turned his attention to the possibility of acquiring another property—nothing less than his onetime boyhood home, Stratford Hall. He might have found security in attaching himself to the Custises, but he yearned for the independence of being a Lee, and nothing symbolized that more than Stratford. And perhaps it was no coincidence that two months later Robert E. Lee finally paid his father's grave on Cumberland Island a long-delayed visit.

Robert E. Lee was not a profound thinker: his compulsive letter writing betrays little evidence of reading beyond the demands of his profession. But he was a clear thinker, and much of that thinking oscillated within the poles he had set up for himself of perfection, independence, and security. That was particularly true as the Confederacy's most successful and influential soldier. Although Lee spent almost all of his prewar career in the U.S. Army constructing fortifications, dredging harbors, and managing civilian laborers, and only commanded troops under fire for the first time when he took charge of the company of Marines that captured John Brown in 1859, Lee saw more clearly than any other Confederate leader that the South could not survive a long-drawn bout with the North. Southern armies must move across the Potomac and there persuade Northerners, either by battle or by simple occupation, to agree to peace and Southern independence. He would attempt this twice, in 1862 and 1863, and was ready for a third attempt in 1864 when Grant's Overland Campaign struck that option away.

This strategy, which some admirers characterized as "audacity," was for Lee merely logic. Lee's modern critics have railed against what they decry as his obsession with Virginia at the expense of the rest of the Confederacy. But Lee understood that in the pursuit of both independence and security the Confederacy could lose Tennessee, Mississippi, Alabama, even Georgia, and still win; losing Virginia meant losing almost all the resources that kept the Confederacy going. And he dreaded nothing more than being forced into a siege of Richmond, because Richmond was itself the key to Virginia. With Richmond would go Virginia and then the Confederacy—which, in 1865, is exactly what happened. Lee had foreseen it all and understood the war's denouement as a failure to meet the standard of perfect commitment that independence and security required.[7]

Yet this was not the final chapter for Robert E. Lee. In the summer of 1865, he was made the unlikely offer of the presidency of Washington College, in faraway Lexington, Virginia. Almost as unlikely, he accepted, and in the final five years of his life he managed to achieve the resolution of the impulses to perfection, independence, and security he had spent a lifetime seeking. The trustees of the college were congratulated on acquiring a figurehead, but Lee made *them* the figureheads and turned the nearly bankrupt college into a major Southern institution, nearly outstripping even the University of Virginia. And in this college, he would finally find the independence to run matters as he saw fit, the security he sought for himself and his family, and perfection in what he could demand of his students.

Perhaps, in retrospect, we can say that Robert Lee should have shrugged off the shadow of Light Horse Harry; perhaps he should have left the Army and built a real estate empire in western Virginia; perhaps he should have become the handsome but aloof family overseer of Arlington and let the Civil War and the taint of treason wash past him. But he did not, and the forces that had made him what he was in the past governed the extraordinary skill with which he managed Confederate military affairs. They did not, however, make him a happy man. That only came at the end, in Lexington. But it was, for him, a perfect end.

CHAPTER ONE

The Garden Spot of Virginia

Leave the sprawl of the national metropolis behind and drive south into Virginia on the crowded superhighway that leads to Fredericksburg. Turn east, though, at Fredericksburg and follow the old King's Highway, where the land stretches to the tree lines on either side, fragrant with hay and wheat and corn. There are few houses at the roadside, only occasional farm stands hawking fresh produce, and small horse farms with white fences reaching up to the road's edge. Old names appear on gray historical wayside markers—Lamb's Creek, King's Charter—and the ground has the feel of a flatness that should roll away forever to the left or right.

This, of course, is a deception. As it moves east, the highway is actually bisecting a long, narrow peninsula, the Northern Neck of Virginia, a formidable, tall plateau with cliffs that fall down sharply either to the swan-shaped estuary of the Potomac River on the left or to the Rappahannock River on the right. In the War of 1812, British warships boldly stalked along the Potomac shore of the Northern Neck, landing parties of marines and sailors to burn farms and plantations; fifty years later, the Rappahannock shore was the line that for two years separated Union occupation from tenacious Confederate defense. After twenty miles, the four-lane passes out of King George County and enters Westmoreland County, and narrows to a two-lane road where spindly pine trees with enormous high crowns crowd down to the verge. The horse farms become more numerous, but the houses more weather-beaten and isolated. Fifteen miles farther, a marker points toward the Potomac and the birthplace of George Washington, and finally, five miles more, the trees suddenly fall back on either side, and a sharp turn at a pristine white clapboard Anglican church brings you, after a mile, to a gatehouse set amid "cedars, oaks and forest poplars."

Slip past the gatehouse, under the dark, thick shade of hickory, tulip, and holly trees, and suddenly, emerging in the opening distance, is Stratford Hall, what Myron Magnet was moved to call "a fanfare in brick," a proclamation of the superiority of design and intelligence over a building material not always noted for spectacular architectural statement. Wood had long been the principal building resource for the Neck. Brick moved Stratford far in advance of its peers. And such brick: hot-fired Flemish bond to give it sheen, laid in checkerboard style on the basement story, light-colored headers and stretchers alternating with the darker bricks. "There is, we presume, no structure like it in our country," gushed a national newspaper in 1848. Three centuries ago, this was built to be the home of Thomas Lee, and it was in a very real sense Lee's bid to be considered the greatest of the Lees of Virginia, and the Lees the greatest family of the Neck's Potomac shoreline.

From thy south shore, great stream of swans,
Came the great Lees and Washingtons.[1]

But Stratford, like the Neck itself, is full of appearances that hard realities often belie. It was not Thomas Lee's fortune that built Stratford so much as that of his wife, Hannah Ludwell. And the ninety-foot-long house is actually only a one-story affair, built over a spacious basement, its enormous row of sixteen-over-sixteen windows all around the house creating an illusion of grandeur and height, resembling in layout a very squat and exaggerated capital H. But the central hall is a magnificent showpiece, twenty-nine feet square with a seventeen-foot tray ceiling. Eight enormous chimneys, vaulting upward in two quadrangles like towers, shoulder the task of proclaiming the glory of the Lees, while fine brick "dependencies" stand watch at each corner, flanked by two formal gardens and a six-bay stable.[2]

Thomas Lee died in 1750, only ten years after the house's completion. It would remain in the hands of succeeding Lees for three brief, and increasingly incapable, generations, until 1822. What would make Stratford worth remembering, and in time worth preserving with the most startlingly meticulous care as an American shrine, was that on January 19, 1807, it became the birthplace of the one member of the family every Virginian would recognize more readily than any Virginia leader after Washington, an individual revered so steadfastly across the Old South that one artist, Clyde Broadway, could portray him as the third person in every Southerner's historical version of a holy trinity—Robert Edward Lee.[3]

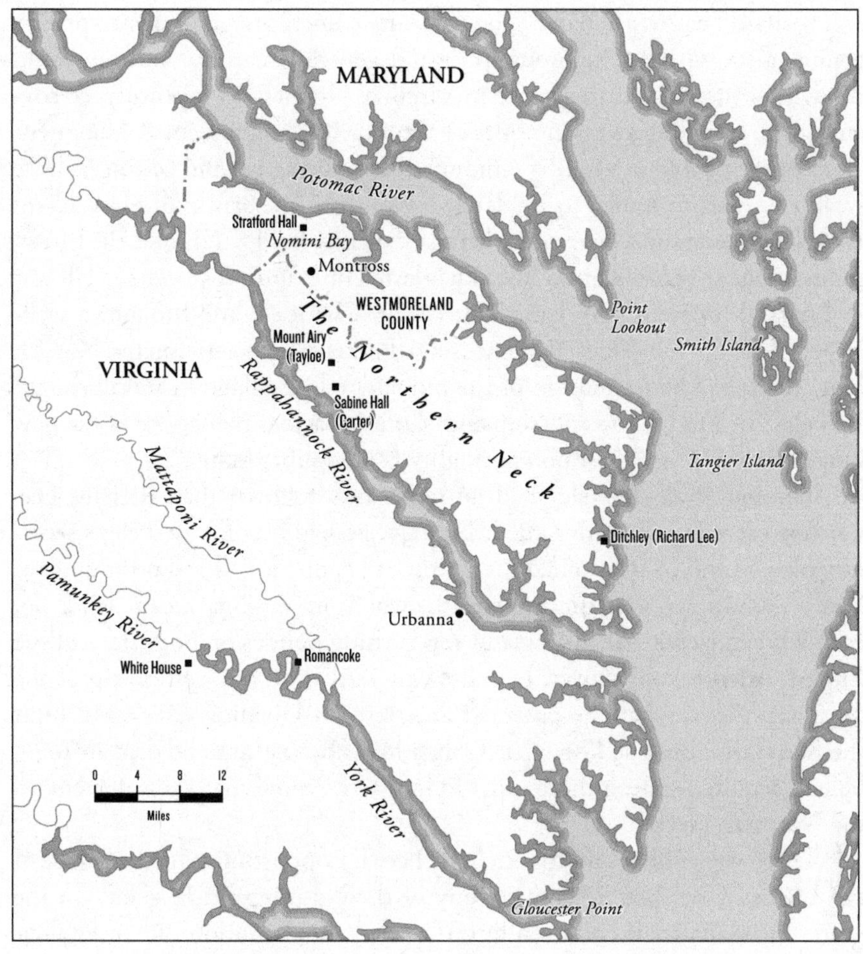

—

There is no way to pinpoint the arrival of the original Lee in Virginia apart from placing it generally in 1640. Richard Lee was probably the younger son of a family of Shropshire gentry who, with no fortune before him in England, turned his hand to finding one in the New World. This was not the most fortuitous moment for a gentleman's son to swagger off to Virginia. The Virginia colony had been founded as a monopoly corporation, only to founder on the shoals of bad planning, decimating diseases, an Indian massacre, and an overall mortality rate approaching 65 percent of all its immigrants. King James I then assumed direct royal control of the colony and proceeded to appoint governors whom the Virginia settlers preferred to resist and occasionally overthrow.[4]

Richard Lee "was a man of good stature, comely visage, and enterprising genius, a sound head, vigorous spirit and generous nature," and he would need all of those assets to survive in Virginia. "Ignorance, ingenuity, & covetousness" were the governing rules of Virginia life, and it seemed "the intencions of the people in Virginia" amounted to nothing beyond getting "a little wealth . . . and to return to Englande." Not until the arrival of Sir William Berkeley in 1642 did a governor with a sufficiently hard hand force the fifteen thousand or so colonists into line. That lasted only until 1652, when civil war in England toppled King James's successor, Charles I, and brought a well-armed fleet up the James River to send Berkeley into retirement. Not for long, though. The restoration of the monarchy in England in 1660 brought Berkeley back to his governorship and Virginia back to the service of the new king, Charles II, its "most potent mighty & undoubted king."[5]

Through it all, Berkeley had no more loyal follower than Richard Lee, nor one more faithfully rewarded. By 1649, he had become Berkeley's secretary of state and in 1651 joined the governor's council. Political position gave him an advantage in acquiring wealth, which in Virginia meant land. So, even while the civil war in England was turning politics on both sides of the English Atlantic topsy-turvy, Lee shrewdly settled on the western tip of the Northern Neck, where he patented an estate on Dividing Creek and built the house that became known as Cobbs Hall. By the time he died in 1664, he had acquired sixteen thousand Virginia acres, more than half of them on the Northern Neck.[6]

There was, unhappily for Richard Lee, no opportunity in the midst of the English Civil War to confirm any of these dealings in England. In the years when Charles II had been forced to eke out a penurious life in French-supported exile, his only hope of fanning the embers of loyalty in his band of followers was the lavish pledges he made in the form of proprietary land grants in America. There was, however, no one at the right hand of the youthful exile to correct him when he awarded the entirety of the Northern Neck to seven of his most devoted followers.[7]

When, to the general surprise of Europe, Charles II was actually invited by a disheartened Parliament to reclaim his throne, the king's proprietors found that entrepreneurs like Richard Lee had already claimed title to much of the Neck and were understandably resistant to conceding it. Nor could Lee in particular be dispossessed on the easy ground that he had been untrue to the monarchy. A series of unpleasant negotiations ensued between 1669 and 1680 that finally confirmed the Northern Neck as a proprietorship in the hands of Lord Thomas Culpeper, but with maddeningly generous exceptions for those who already claimed property there. When Culpeper died in 1689, the proprietorship passed into the hands of Culpeper's relative by marriage

Lord Thomas Fairfax, whereupon the haggling over who owned what on the Neck resumed, to the point where Fairfax heartily wished "we had neaver medeled with them."[8]

The Lee family's solution to this threat was to go to work for the Fairfax family. The first instinct of Richard Lee's heirs had been to fight for his original titles. But Richard's grandson Thomas Lee thought better of this. In 1713, when the Fairfax family grew dissatisfied with the revenues being passed to them through the hands of their existing agent, Robert "King" Carter, they turned to Thomas Lee, who served them, to the mutual satisfaction of both Lees and Fairfaxes, until 1747.[9]

As his reward, Thomas Lee built a comfortable gentleman's country seat (and land office) on Machodoc Creek, which he named Mount Pleasant. When it burned down in January 1728, Lee replaced it with a still grander project on 1,400 acres along the Potomac that he named Stratford, purportedly in honor of an earlier Lee family estate in old Shropshire. He had expanded Stratford to 4,800 acres by 1750, and at its zenith it would embrace 6,600 acres, with a wharf for receiving and hauling cargoes, a warehouse, and a gristmill. Imposing family portraits would begin to line the paneled walls of Stratford's central hall, bands of musicians would trumpet the beginning of balls from the quadruple chimneys, and Stratford's master would preside "in great state."[10]

There was, in fact, a good deal for the Lees to trumpet. Richard the Emigrant's second son—also named Richard, but known as "the Scholar" for his bookish inclinations—married into the Corbin family, and the Corbins had a large role in steering the Fairfax agency into Thomas Lee's hands. Thomas himself did well in the marriage mart, marrying Hannah Ludwell in 1722 (whose grandfather Philip had also been a loyal supporter of Governor Berkeley and even married Berkeley's widow). So did his brother Henry, who developed a parallel establishment to Thomas's Stratford property farther up the Neck at Freestone Point, which he named Leesylvania (and where he made the acquaintance of the young George Washington, the manager of his brother Augustine's estate at Mount Vernon). But the apex of the Lee dynasty lay in the formidable array of sons born to Thomas and Hannah at Stratford—Philip Ludwell Lee (who inherited Stratford), Thomas Ludwell Lee, Richard Henry Lee (who was allowed to carve out a plantation of his own, Chantilly, from the Stratford property), Francis Lightfoot Lee (who parlayed his family connections into Virginia politics and married into one of the Neck's other great families, the Tayloes of Mount Airy, on the Rappahannock side), and Arthur Lee and William Lee, who were both packed off to England for an education and life in finance and law.[11]

These advantages were fully matched by the Lees' energies. Richard

Henry Lee and Francis Lightfoot Lee both served in the Continental Congress at the outbreak of the American Revolution and are the only brothers to appear as signers of the Declaration of Independence. Arthur Lee would turn into an outstanding diplomat in Spain and France (Samuel Johnson would regard him suspiciously in London for being "not only a *patriot* but an *American*"), and William Lee would represent American interests in the German states and Austria. Above all, it was Richard Henry Lee, "a tall, spare man" (as John Adams described him) who hid the left hand he had maimed in a shooting accident in a black silk glove, who would offer the climactic resolution in the Continental Congress in 1776: "That these United Colonies are, and of right ought to be, free and independent States, that they are absolved from all allegiance to the British Crown, and that all political connection between them and the State of Great Britain is, and ought to be, totally dissolved." Lee's resolution, in turn, would become the core around which Thomas Jefferson would write the Declaration of Independence.[12]

The Northern Neck sparkled under the smile of the Lees, and not the Lees only. The Princeton College graduate Philip Vickers Fithian described it as a "most delightful Country; in a civil, polite neighbourhood." If Virginia was considered "the garden of America," the Northern Neck was "the garden spot of Virginia . . . possessing a very fertile soil, easily renovated by the marl which everywhere underlies it." The Neck was home to nearly 6,900 taxpayers by the 1780s. The majority were landless tenants, while the average landholdings of all but 1 percent of the rest amounted to little more than 300 acres. But the Lees, at Stratford, at Leesylvania, and at Dividing Creek, were securely in the top bracket of the Neck's wealth. They shared that pinnacle with several other Virginia dynasties on the Neck—the Tayloes at Mount Airy and Landon Carter at Sabine Hall, both of whose properties faced the Rappahannock, and Robert Carter's Nomini Hall, and the Turbervilles at Hickory Hill, the nearer neighbors of Stratford and of Richard Henry Lee's Chantilly.[13]

Much of the Lee wealth on the Neck was tied up in slaves, because none of the Lees had ever actually delved for their own bread on the land they engrossed with such unrelenting energy. The Lees, Tayloes, and Carters never owned fewer than 50 slaves each across the decades of the eighteenth century, while Robert Carter owned 345 slaves, John Tayloe 173, and George Turberville 68. Thomas Lee had, at varying times, owned between 60 and 100 slaves at Stratford, and as late as 1782, 83 slaves worked for Thomas Lee's successors there.[14]

But these grandees were not necessarily prospering on their land. Although Virginians had made early fortunes in the seventeenth century through tobacco, the demand for the "Indian weed" declined throughout the eighteenth century, as had the nutrients in the soil of the Neck that supported it. Few people in England, complained Richard Henry Lee in the 1760s, understood "how much labour is required on a Virginean estate & how poor the produce." Increasingly, the great plantations turned to growing wheat, fodder, and pork for export to the West Indies, where they could be fed to the slave and animal populations of the sugar islands whose vastly wealthier owners declined to waste arable sugar lands on growing food. Even more annoying, the West Indies trade was managed not by the planters themselves but by Scots and the factors whom they posted to the Neck, as ships from Glasgow, London, Bristol, and Whitehaven called at plantation landings along the Potomac and Rappahannock and bore off the Neck's produce to feed other mouths. As they did, the white population of the Neck began to uproot, first for the Piedmont and the Shenandoah Valley, then still later for Kentucky and Tennessee.[15]

However humbling the realization that they were becoming little more than a cog in the imperial sugar system, the nabobs of the Neck insisted nonetheless in living in the grand style of English gentry. They built grandiloquent houses, of which Stratford was only one example. (John Tayloe's Mount Airy, which was built at approximately the same time as Stratford, featured marble floors, mahogany paneling, and a French cut-glass chandelier.) At Stratford, opposing sets of wide doors off the central hall looked out either to the large oval driveway that bore visitors to its outdoor stairs or toward the Potomac, where the green haze of Maryland could be glimpsed in the distance. And they did not mind lording it over tradesmen, merchants, and lesser farmers. Philip Ludwell Lee "stalked" into George Fisher's English Coffee House in Williamsburg with "an arrogant, hauty carriage" and made it clear to Fisher not only that he regarded himself as "a Person of no mean Rank or Dignity" but that he expected Fisher to "resign the lease I had taken" of the coffeehouse "to him . . . and that if I did not, I should surely repent it."[16]

They raised their sons to prize honor, style, manners, pride, and reputation, seasoning their drinking, wenching, gambling, swearing, and horse racing with an elegant hauteur. Debt was a way of life, but it was cast in the glow of arrogance and entitlement rather than humility. "I can hardly remember a time when I did not owe sums larger than my credit might seem to be worth," admitted the Anglican parson Jonathan Boucher, who briefly served a parish on the Neck. "All I have to offer in vindication of it is, that . . . determined always to raise myself in the world, I had not patience to wait for the slow savings of a humble station; and I fancied I could get into a higher, only by being taken notice of by people of condition; which was not to be done without my making a certain appearance." And they continued to import slaves—more than 6,000 between 1727 and 1769—so that John Tayloe III's slave force at Mount Airy increased to 370 by 1792. And no wonder, because slave owning fed their sense of superiority. "Such amazing property . . . blows up the owners to an imagination . . . that they are exalted as much above other Men in worth & precedency."[17]

But the Northern Neck's landed elite were spitting into a rising wind. In the 1760s, the deluge of Protestant religious revival known as the Great Awakening, which had engulfed large parts of Europe, England, and New England, now spread its thunderous clouds over Virginia and the Neck, and with subversive force. From its founding, Virginia had countenanced only the legally established Church of England, and the church's liturgical formality discouraged "the unreasonable exercise . . . of indiscreet Acts of publick Devotion" and "the inventing and using new religious Ceremonies, other than are prescribed or in use in the Place where we live" as "one sign of Hypocrisy." But by the 1760s, evangelical Protestantism, especially in the form of Baptist exhorters and missionaries, was invading the Neck, establishing in 1778 the Neck's first Baptist congregation at Morattico Hall in Richmond County. Just how dire a challenge the Awakening could be to the squirearchy of the Neck could be heard in the denunciations by the Awakeners of the Anglican establishment as "arbitrary and tyrannical" and in the behavior of new converts who, "prostrate on the floor," passed through the fires of grace with a topsy-turvy inversion of the great planters' behavior in "screams, cries, groans, songs, shouts, and hozannas, notes of grief and notes of joy." They now had a manner of their own, and a divine authority to throw back at the flustered parsons.

Nor would it stop there, because a convert willing to dismiss the local Anglican parson as a spiritual impostor might not hesitate at denouncing the squire, or the governor, as a political despot, to be resisted with the same zeal. If "the *Anabaptists*" could suppress "pleasure in the Country" in the name of "ardent Pray'r; strong and constant faith, & an entire Banishment of *Gaming, Dancing,* & Sabbath-Day Diversions," then the entire social system of the Neck was in danger. That included slavery, especially after Robert Carter of Nomini Hall announced his conversion, testifying "that Jesus Christ is the Son of god; that through him mankind can be saved only," and proceeded in 1791 to begin emancipating his slaves as an act of religious devotion.[18]

And then, on the heels of Awakening, came revolt. As much as the phalanx of Thomas Lee's sons provided invaluable leadership to the American Revolution at home and abroad, the Revolution also brought disruption to the Neck, and not just from British marauders prowling along the wide Potomac estuary. "I could have wished that ambition had not so visibly seized so much ignorance all over the Colony as it seems to have done," complained

Landon Carter of Sabine Hall to George Washington in 1776. Virginians like Washington and the Lees might talk with glittering eyes of independence from Britain. But the only independence Carter was hearing was "a form of Government that, by being independent of the rich men, every man would then be able to do as he pleased." In the old days, "such rascals would have been turned out; but now it is not to be supposed that a dog will eat a dog."[19]

Not even the Lees could expect the old deference, no matter how important their contributions to the Revolutionary cause. "Look around you," Richard Henry Lee raged. "The inundation of money appears to have overflowed virtue, and I fear will bury the liberty of America in the same grave. . . . Do you anywhere see wisdom and integrity and industry prevail either in council or execution?"[20] The answer he expected was no; the answer given by yet another Revolutionary Lee was—at least for a while—the exact opposite.

"I have the melancholy news to inform you," wrote Henry Lee of Leesylvania to his cousin William Lee, one of the sons of Thomas Lee, "of yr Brother Col. Phil's death, who died at Stratford of a nervous Pleurisy on the 21st of last month and had left Mrs. Lee his widow Very Big with Child."[21]

This was indeed bad news for William Lee, though not necessarily for his cousin Henry. The late Philip Ludwell Lee was the oldest son of the redoubtable Thomas and became master of Stratford upon his father's death in 1750, where it "became a very grand place." His death at age forty-eight in 1775 had taken him enough by surprise that he left no will, leaving Stratford to be haphazardly managed by his widow and his two surviving daughters, Flora and Matilda.[22]

That became the cue for Henry Lee III to sweep into Matilda's life. Henry Lee was the great-great-grandson of Richard the Emigrant, and his grandfather Henry I was the younger brother of Stratford's Thomas Lee and the owner of Leesylvania, a 3,500-acre estate perched on the Potomac shore far upriver above Stratford. Even so, the Lees of Leesylvania did not have the wherewithal of their Stratford cousins, and so when Henry Lee III was born in 1756, there was no likelihood of sending him to England for an education. Henry III would have to be content with a more domestic education—Princeton College, in New Jersey—rather than Oxford.

A provincial education dampened nothing in Henry's appetite for learning, which he manifested with surprising glee. "Your cousin Henry Lee is in College and will be one of the first fellows of this country," reported William Shippen of Philadelphia, a cousin by marriage, to Richard Henry Lee. "He is more than strict in his morality; he has a fine genius and is too diligent." A career in law would probably have beckoned to Henry had not the Revolution erupted after his graduation in 1773. He was at once caught up in the enthusiasm of the struggle, abandoning the study of law for a "commencement in the study of Mars," and quickly vaulted into the saddle as a captain of dragoons.[23]

He also quickly displayed a thirst for daredevil risk taking, being "intrusted with the command of outposts, the superintendence of scouts, and that kind of service which required the possession of coolness, address and enterprise." He caught George Washington's eye after being surprised, along with ten troopers, "by two hundred British light horse" at one of the outlying posts protecting the American encampment at Valley Forge in January 1778. Lee "assured the dragoons under his command" that if they stood with him and refused to surrender, "he should consider their future establishment in life as his peculiar care," and animated by that promise, they successfully fought off the British ambush. Washington urged him to join the band of promising young officers—Alexander Hamilton, Henry Laurens, the Marquis de Lafayette—whom Washington was gathering around him as aides. Lee declined. Despite the "high sense of gratitude I feel for your Excellency's approbation of my conduct," Lee thirsted for action. "I am wedded to my sword," and he frankly avowed that "my object in the present war, is military reputation." Far from taking offense at this cheekiness, Washington replied that this only strengthened "my good opinion of you." Instead, he allowed Lee to organize an "independent partisan corps" of cavalry and then an all-arms "legion" of infantry, cavalry, and artillery to strike at isolated British cantonments and forts. When Lee boldly raided the British fort at Paulus Hook in August 1779, he was rewarded by the Continental Congress with a gold medal and promotion to lieutenant colonel. He had become "Light Horse Harry."[24]

Lack of self-confidence was never Harry Lee's flaw. "I feel an assurance of brilliant success," he wrote, "and no human exertion will be wanting" under his command. But he also displayed signs of darker, more erratic impulses. The Paulus Hook adventure was bitterly criticized by other officers as a useless display of bravado. "Major Lee has performed a most gallant affair," wrote a sympathetic general, Nathanael Greene, "but can you believe it, he has been persecuted with a bitterness by his Countrymen, that is almost disgraceful to mention." When his troopers captured a deserter, a corporal, in July 1779, an infuriated Lee had the corporal's head cut off and set up in camp to frighten other waverers. This time, even Washington rebuked Lee, for fear of "a bad effect both in the army and in the country." Others resented Lee for preening as a superpatriot and dismissing other officers as half hearts who tolerated "an enemical disposition or even luke warmness, to the independence of America." Finally, in 1780, Washington sent Lee south to the Carolinas, as much to get him out of the way of other officers who were "already extremely jealous of the superior advantages and privileges" Lee enjoyed as Washington's pet as to assist Nathanael Greene in retrieving the disastrous situation that prevailed there in the wake of the American defeat at Camden.[25]

Lee served Greene brilliantly in the Carolinas campaign and endeared himself as much to Greene as he had to Washington. Much of the fighting there was really a war of detachments, and Lee excelled in it. Light Horse Harry became "*the eye*" of the southern army, and Greene extolled him as the officer to whom "I am more indebted . . . than to any other for the advantages gained over the enemy in the operations of the last campaign." At the critical battle at Guilford Court House, one North Carolina militiaman remembered seeing "Lee of the horse, just as the general engagement was coming on," riding "along the lines of the American Infantry . . . in a great rage for battle." Yet, even here, Lee showed no signs of curbing his impulsiveness or his gift for antagonizing his peers. He "seldom failed to disgust the state and militia officers, whenever he was called upon to serve with them." When, in conjunction with Francis Marion's South Carolina partisans, Lee's Legion captured Fort Motte on the Congaree River, Marion had to restrain Light Horse Harry from hanging captured Tory militiamen who had been accused of atrocities. Lee shot back with the customary Lee hauteur, blaming the Georgia and South Carolina militia for setting the moral bar so low. "They exceed the Goths & Vandals in the schemes of plunder & iniquity," Lee countered in June 1781, and all "under the pretense of supporting the virtuous cause of America."[26]

The surrender of the British army at Yorktown in October 1781 did not bring all of the Revolution's fighting to an end, but it did mean the end of the warfare Lee loved the best—"where the mind was always on the stretch"—and in February 1782 he resigned his commission. Nathanael Greene pleaded with him to stay. You are "one of the first Officers in the world," Greene argued. "No man in the progress of the Campaign had equal merit with you." But Light Horse Harry's resentment over the "ill-natured insinuations" of his fellow officers rankled far beyond any repair even Greene could provide. Besides, he had other conquests in view. Sometime in the spring of 1782, Harry Lee, "attended by his military servant," rode through "the grove of maples" that shielded Stratford from the roadside view and was "welcomed with joy" by his nineteen-year-old cousin, Matilda Lee, the "Queen of Stratford." She married him in April. As Greene had said of Lee, "For rapid marches, you exceed Lord Cornwallis and everybody else."[27]

No one had ever doubted that Harry Lee could be as charming as he was headstrong, and he now proceeded to turn his charms to political advantage.

Two of the Stratford Lees sat in the national Congress formed by the Articles of Confederation in the mid-1780s, and Harry Lee followed them in November 1785, taking on a full calendar of responsibilities. Like the Revolutionary militia, Light Horse Harry found the confederation's state governments undisciplined and self-seeking, and the Confederation Congress a weak pleader for useful action. He helped author a report that criticized the lackadaisical attitude of the states in failing to dispatch enough delegates to Congress to ensure a quorum; he pressed for the organization of the Northwest Territory (including its prohibition of slavery), and he urged independent spending for "all such Stores, equipments, and supplies as may be requisite for the military service." Finally, in August 1786, Lee was part of the Grand Committee that recommended "such Amendments to the Confederation, and such Resolutions as may be necessary to recommend to the several states for the purpose of obtaining from them such powers as will render the federal government adequate to the ends for which it was instituted." A year later, the fruit of his efforts would blossom in the new federal Constitution written by a national convention in Philadelphia.[28]

Harry Lee's political service was not entirely an exercise of unsullied patriotism. Lee was eager to create a fortune for himself, and there seemed to be no shorter path to that fortune than speculation in land. Investments in "such hazardous & perishable Articles as Negroes, Stock, & Chattels" can "be swept off by innumerable distempers, & subject to many accidents and & misfortunes," warned George Washington. But, added Lee's old commander, "an enterprising Man with very little Money" could invest "at very low rates" in "the rich back Lands . . . in the New Settlements upon [the] Monongahela" and then sell them "in the course of 20 yrs" for stratospheric profits. The problem was obtaining even that "very little Money," because foreign bankers and investors balked at lending money to Americans whose affairs were disordered by states that laid tariffs on one another's goods and judges who cheerfully dissolved lenders' obligations in favor of local debtors.[29]

The new federal Constitution would, Lee was confident, override the impediments put in speculation's path by state restrictions and state judges. So, when the Constitution was sent to the states for ratification, Lee won a seat in Virginia's state ratification convention, and there led as daring a charge in debate as he ever had on horseback against the new Constitution's principal critics—Patrick Henry, George Mason, and his own gout-stricken kinsman and neighbor, Richard Henry Lee. For nine days, the debate roared onward, until finally, by an 89-to-79 vote, the Virginia convention delivered what turned out to be the new Constitution's key ratification vote. And as his reward, Light Horse Harry was elected to the Virginia legislature and, in 1791, as the state's governor.[30]

That would prove, unhappily, to be the summit of Lee's political career, apart from one resultless term in the federal Congress in 1799 to 1801. The Anti-Federalist critics of the Constitution remained a powerful and unreconciled force in Virginia politics, and they soon coalesced around Thomas Jefferson, whom Lee had already antagonized by criticisms of Jefferson's record as Virginia's wartime governor. Lee made still more enemies in 1794, when he sprang to the summons of his old commander (and now president) George Washington to bring the Virginia militia northward to suppress the Whiskey Rebellion in western Pennsylvania. The Pennsylvania rebels had substantial sympathy in western Virginia for the resistance they showed to the imposition of a federal excise tax on whiskey, and Lee did himself no favors by loudly proclaiming his suspicion that Anti-Federalist Virginians were "banditti," planning a general uprising against national authority. He earned a major general's commission for his labors, and the Whiskey Rebellion collapsed. But in Virginia, his victory made Lee "an object of the most virulent enmity of a certain political junto," and in December 1794 the Virginia legislature disapprovingly elected Robert Brooke, a Jeffersonian, to the governorship.[31]

Lee met with severer disappointments in his dreams of landed wealth. He fully expected to inherit 10,000 acres from an elderly and childless Lee uncle, Richard the Squire, but the uncle remarried in 1786 at age sixty and uncooperatively fathered five children. Lee's father, Henry II, left him the largest part of the Leesylvania property. But the house at Leesylvania went to Henry II's widow and thereafter to the second oldest of his sons, Charles Lee, and in a significant reservation of judgment about his eldest son's financial wisdom Henry II named Light Horse Harry's four younger brothers as executors. Nor did Light Horse Harry do much better at Stratford. In 1782, the trustees of Colonel Phil's estate finally arrived at a plan for equitably dividing the Stratford property by granting 1,800 acres to his widow, Elizabeth Steptoe Lee, and reserving the remaining two-thirds of Stratford for her two daughters, Matilda and Flora. Elizabeth obligingly removed herself and Flora from the scene by marrying Philip Fendall in 1780 and moving to Alexandria, which ought to have left Light Horse Harry free to become the master of the remainder of Stratford simply as Matilda's husband. But the Revolution had wrought major changes in Virginia's inheritance laws, and Matilda retained title to both the original parcel bought by Thomas Lee on the Potomac cliffs and the brick mansion he had built there.[32]

That did nothing to dissuade Light Horse Harry from using whatever persuasions he could muster to induce Matilda to sign away piece after piece of Stratford as collateral for western land speculation. Like George Washington, Lee was convinced that the Potomac River was certain to become the great commercial superhighway of the continent, aided by a system of canals that would channel the Potomac's waters deep into the Virginia interior and eventually allow them to be linked with the Ohio River and the broad stretches of the west beyond the Appalachians. Like Washington again, Lee became an investor in the Potowmack Navigation Company, and bought more than 200,000 acres in his own name along the Potomac route where he hoped to build the town of "Matildaville" and sell off town lots at fabulous profits. "Men who can afford to lay a little while out of their money," Washington wrote to another protégé, the Marquis de Lafayette, "are laying the foundation of the greatest returns of any speculation I know of in the world." Lee could not have agreed more enthusiastically. It was proof that "difficultys vanish as they are approached."[33]

But they did not vanish. Through the money he lavished on his own land purchases, then lent to others to invest themselves, Light Horse Harry Lee probably laid claim to more than a million acres, some in North Carolina, some in Georgia, but most in western Virginia. With John Marshall (the future chief justice) and his brothers, Harry invested in a 150,000-acre domain in northwest Virginia; with Benjamin Lincoln, the Revolutionary general, he bought into an enormous 250,000-acre development in the Ohio River valley. From them all, it is not likely that he ever realized one cent of return, much less retrieved any of the capital he threw away on them. Matildaville was never built; the canals to the Ohio were never completed; and his creditors had begun to wonder whether Harry Lee's zeal had come unhooked from reason, or at least "propriety" and "honor." As early as 1785, he was coming up short of cash and begging the indulgence of Richard Henry Lee on "matters of money." By 1792, even Washington had grown alarmed at Lee's recklessness. No one, said Lee's former commander, had "a better head and more resource." The trouble was that Lee also had "no economy."[34]

Matilda Lee saw what was coming earlier than most. She gave birth to five children, beginning with a short-lived son, Nathanael Greene Lee, in 1783, another short-lived son, Philip Ludwell in 1784, a daughter, Lucy, in 1786, and a third son, Henry IV, in 1787. Over those years, she reluctantly consented to selling portions of the Stratford property to fund her husband's investment schemes, but in 1790, pregnant with her fifth child and seriously ill, Matilda drew the line and signed a trust, with two Lee cousins as executors, that passed what was left of Stratford into her two surviving children's hands once they came of age—and beyond her husband's control. Matilda gave birth, and then died on August 16, 1790, followed by the child, amid Harry's wild lamentations. "The ways of Providence are as inscrutable as just," Washington wrote to him on August 27, and so "it becomes the children of it to submit with resignation & fortitude to its decrees as far as the feelings of humanity will allow and your good sense will."[35]

Lee toyed for some time with abandoning both Stratford and Virginia and accepting a commission in the new French revolutionary armies. "Bred to arms," he explained to Washington, "I have always since my domestic calamity wished for a return to my profession." Washington talked him out of it, thereby paving the way for Lee to exchange "the rugged and dangerous field of Mars for the soft and pleasurable bed of Venus" by remarrying, this time to Ann Hill Carter, the great-great-granddaughter of Robert "King" Carter and the oldest child of the second marriage of Charles Carter, the master of Shirley Plantation, on the James River.[36]

This was an odd alliance, dynastically speaking, because the Carters had been rivals of the Lees, both for the favors of the Fairfax family on the Northern Neck and over the ratification of the Constitution. Ann Carter was also seventeen years Henry Lee's junior and her father's carefully sheltered favorite. But in 1791, Lee was enjoying his high roll as governor of Virginia, and on June 18, 1793, Lee and Ann Carter were married in the drawing room at Shirley. This was not without serious reservations on the part of Charles Carter, whose will in 1804 prudently bestowed on the couple not Carter lands or money but a trust fund that was to remain securely in Ann's name, "free from the claim, demand, hindrance or molestation of her husband, Genl. Henry Lee or his creditors."[37]

Ann soon learned how well-founded her father's reservations about Harry Lee were. "In the short space of a fortnight," recalled her cousin Maria Farley, "she awoke to a life of misery," as every loose Carter penny she could beg from her family "was soon thrown away upon his debts contracted previous to marriage." By 1797, Light Horse Harry's fiscal house of cards was beginning to collapse inward, starting with the bankruptcy of the Philadelphia financier Robert Morris, his partner in the North American Land Company. He began selling "a great deal of property at half price to make up the heavy losses to which the failures of R. Morris . . . & others exposed me" while issuing promissory notes to satisfy other creditors. He persisted in the belief that "property like mine must be in great demand." It wasn't, and what's worse, much of what he had bought in the exuberant hurry of the 1780s turned out to have multiple claims of ownership. By 1805, Lee's creditors would take only cash, because "all titles of land held under Genl. Lee may be supposed as precarious."[38]

As his credit disappeared, so did his protectors. Nathanael Greene died in 1786 on his plantation on the Georgia coast, depriving Lee of one of his firmest friends from the Revolution. Nor could Washington, in these later days, always be counted upon. When the post of secretary of war fell vacant in 1795, there was some discussion inside Washington's cabinet about Lee as the next secretary. But despite Lee's "ample military talents," the damning conclusion was that "this appointment would doubtless be extremely unpopular; it would be disapproved by the enemies of the government, without acquiring the confidence of its friends." Worse, Washington himself died in 1799, and even though Lee delivered one of the most eloquent eulogies in American history—that Washington had been "first in war, first in peace, and first in the hearts of his countrymen"—all pleas thereafter for a federal job fell on deaf ears. The federal government had passed in 1801 into the hands of Thomas Jefferson and Lee's virulent Anti-Federalist enemies. "I see the nation entering upon its darkest days," Lee moaned to Alexander Hamilton. Jefferson "has been vindictive and petty . . . and has, behind my back, sneered at the financial misfortunes that have befallen me." Meanwhile, the circle of land around Stratford shrank to just 236 acres. In the spring of 1809, rather than admit bankruptcy (and lose what was left), Lee surrendered to the Westmoreland County sheriff and was imprisoned as a debtor, first in the county jail in Montross and then in Fredericksburg.[39]

Ann Lee was by this time the mother of five more junior Lees—an infant who died in little more than a year, a daughter, Anne Kinloch, and three sons, all of whom she defiantly named for her Carter relatives: Charles Carter Lee in 1798, Sidney Smith Lee in 1802, and finally, in 1807, Robert Edward Lee. She was, at the same time, compelled to play stepmother to Henry's two surviving children by Matilda, Henry IV and Lucy, a task made all the more disagreeable in 1808 when Henry IV came of age and, according to his late mother's trust, became the legal master of Stratford. Not that young Henry harbored any eviction animosities toward Ann. But Ann had had enough of living on Light Horse Harry's sham titles, and that included life under a roof she could no longer reasonably think of as her own. In 1810, after Light Horse Harry's brothers had scraped together enough money to pay off the most pressing of his debts, he returned to Stratford to find Ann determined to leave the Neck once and for all for Alexandria. "Mr. Lee constantly assures me his intention is, to live with his family, after his release from his present situation," Ann informed a relative. But Stratford was not "the part of the world I wish to fix in," and she told her husband bluntly that she was "reserving to myself the right of choosing my place of residence afterwards." That would not be Stratford. "Was I in your place," she wrote to a cousin in Philadelphia, she would "readily dispense with communications from old Westmoreland."[40]

As soon as Light Horse Harry was free, the family packed up what was left of their possessions and departed for Alexandria. It would be only the first of many sad farewells in the life of Robert Edward Lee.[41]

CHAPTER TWO

The Making of an Engineer

The Revolution was not gentle to Virginia. The last three years of the war saw destructive British raids and invasions, and British interdiction of American trade on the high seas deeply depressed an economy that had already been slipping from its apex earlier in the eighteenth century. The postwar years were worse, as American exports and per capita income slid grimly downward, in some places by as much as two-fifths. "I think this country was never more distressed," moaned one Virginia merchant to his English partner. New postcolonial inheritance laws allowed fathers to divide their property among multiple sons, and thus save the younger offspring from penury, but it also shrank the once-great holdings of the Carters, Fitzhughs, Turbervilles, Randolphs, and, of course, Lees. The religious prop of the gentry, the Church of England, was stripped of its legal standing by the Revolutionary state legislature, losing income from taxes and from public lands and slicing the number of active parishes from 107 to just 40; the Church of England only barely survived as an organization by reconfiguring itself, in sharply reduced circumstances, as the Protestant Episcopal Church.

On the Northern Neck, "the country was in an impoverished and depressed condition," and "many of the best and most thrifty settlers, unwilling to live in such constant peril and alarm, sold their lands, at greatly reduced prices, or left them without tenants." Some of the great families diversified: the Tayloes at Mount Airy not only began planting wheat, corn, oats, rye, peas, and potatoes but built three ironworks and several taverns and stores. Even the august Philip Ludwell Lee, before his death in 1775, began converting Stratford from the production of tobacco to the cultivation of wheat, corn, and barley, four fisheries, and a small quarry. Those who did not diversify either sank sadly out of view or turned their faces westward.[1]

"What has become of, or who owns, those mansions where were the voluptuous feasts, the sparkling wine, the flowing bowl, the viol and the dance and the card-table, and the dogs for the chase, and the horses for the turf?" asked a plaintive William Meade (who would soon enter the ministry of the Episcopal Church and rise to become its bishop of Virginia). "What has become of the old Episcopal families, the Skipwiths, Wormleys, Grymeses, Churchills, Robinsons, Berkeleys, and others? . . . I am told, and I believe it, that the whole of that county was at one time in possession of some few of these old families, and that now not a rood of it is owned by one of their name, and scarcely by one in whom is a remnant of their blood."[2]

The world of Ann and Light Horse Harry Lee contracted even more than most, first to a rented two-story house on Cameron Street in Alexandria, and then to another belonging to one of Ann Lee's cousins, William Henry Fitzhugh, at 607 Oronoco Street. These were not ungenerous quarters. The Oronoco Street house, built in 1795, was "large & commodious," with fifteen rooms and 7,800 square feet of living space, plus "a good Garden." (Washington had occasionally dined there when visiting the Fitzhughs.) But compared with Stratford, both Oronoco Street and Alexandria were daily reminders of how far Light Horse Harry and his family had fallen.

Alexandria itself was originally a land grant dating back to Governor Berkeley's time. It was not until the 1730s that it began to sprout warehouses, a ferry across the Potomac, and a small village known as Belle Haven, and not until another decade had passed before the town was surveyed into lots and acquired its grander name. It became, as one French tourist wrote in 1792, "a great commercial town . . . admitting the largest ships to anchor near the quay" and passing along the produce of "an immense extent of back country, fertile and abounding in provisions." (This included a vigorous traffic in slaves, who were housed in transit at a large barracks on the north side of Duke Street; its owner, Franklin and Armfield, would become the largest slave-trading company in the country.) Its doorways and house facades were stamped by Federal and Greek Revival architectural patterns, and its single greatest building was the soaring Episcopal church, Christ Church, with its pepper-pot steeple and the brass plaque proudly marking the pew George Washington had used. The decision of the new national Congress to establish the federal capital across the Potomac only exalted Alexandria's business expectations, and in 1801 the town was absorbed into the new District of Columbia.[3]

But commerce held no charms for Light Horse Harry. In the eyes of the onetime master of Stratford, Alexandria could only have appeared

. . . mean, the people poor,
The same dull scene went constant o'er,
No change, except approaching cold,
Which there in frozen fetters hold
The bold Patomak in its chain
Of ice, approaching near the main.

During his months in debtors' prison, he hatched the plan of writing his memoirs of the Revolution, anticipating great revenues from the sale of the book. He claimed that "this work was begun in a degree as soon as we heard of the death of General Greene" in 1786, and when it was published in Philadelphia in two volumes, Lee hoped "that it will take a great run." True enough, it was widely read and reviewed, and even praised by *The American Review of History and Politics* as worthy of "lively interest and unabated solicitude." But it generated little in the way of profit and much in the way of hatred from Thomas Jefferson, whom Harry freely criticized in its pages.[4]

Instead, the family lived on the proceeds from the trust fund that Ann's father, Charles Carter, had created for her. Harry, however, could not resist playing with fire, this time political fire. The year after the Lees moved to Alexandria, Jefferson's handpicked successor in the presidency, James Madison, following the lead of Jeffersonian "War Hawks," plunged the Republic into the ill-considered War of 1812. Lee had managed to quarrel with Madison as well as Jefferson, and good Federalist as he professed to be, Light Horse Harry duly opposed the war. Worse, in July 1812, while supposedly on business in Baltimore for the promotion of his memoirs, he allowed himself to be talked into providing protection for a Federalist newspaper editor, Alexander Contee Hanson, who had already been chased out of town once by a Jeffersonian mob and who feared the mob would be back again. Stirred by the prospect of offering his soldierly expertise in defense of "the liberty of the Press," Lee helped Hanson arrange the barricading of the editor's house—just in time for the mob to finish its work. Unlike the feisty junior cavalry officer he had been at Valley Forge, Lee recommended surrendering and accepting the promise of the local militia of a safe escort to the local jail. But the mob was no more intimidated by the jail than by Light Horse Harry. On July 28, they returned to the attack, overrunning the jail, killing one of Hanson's other Federalist protectors, bludgeoning and slashing Lee as "the d——d old tory general," and even attempting to blind him by tipping hot candle wax into his eyes. Lee survived, "black as a negro" from multiple wounds and bruises, "his clothes torn and covered with blood from tip to toe."[5]

Light Horse Harry spent the next six months recovering from "the extraordinary Atrocity of the unpunished Baltimore mob." Limping into

Christ Church in Alexandria, he frightened a small girl who remembered that "his bright penetrating look was made a terror to me" because of the surrounding swath of "white bandages that bound his brow and others passing over his head and chin."[6] He convinced himself that he required a warmer, happier climate to speed his return to health and strength, and in May 1813 he left for the West Indies. This put distance between himself and not only vengeful Jeffersonians but also his remaining creditors, who were still hounding him for unpaid bills.

He wandered, homeless, through the Caribbean—Barbados, Cuba, the Windward Islands—living off charity and sympathy, always promising to return as soon as his health was permanently restored, always offering charming letters of encouragement and advice, especially to his oldest son, Charles Carter Lee, who was now preparing to enter Harvard College with the support of Ann's brother William. "My eldest boy," wrote the absentee father, "has been from the hour of his birth unchangeably my delight." He claimed to have his next-oldest son, Smith Lee, "ever in my thoughts," and wrote to him, "I long to get a thorough knowledge of you."

In the spring of 1818, he left Nassau, hoping finally to return to Virginia. But he was too feeble to make it. He was put ashore at the first American landfall the ship could make, which turned out, in one last turn of good fortune for Harry Lee, to be the Cumberland Island property of Nathanael Greene's daughter. Two weeks later, he died, without ever having again seen Virginia, his wife, or his youngest son, Robert.[7]

Henry Lee III was sixty-two when he died, but Virginia had already left him far behind, and in more ways than just commerce. Virginia was now part of a republic that knew no prelates, no landed nobility, no hereditary monarchs, and the mob that assaulted Light Horse Harry in Baltimore was indicative of a new political culture in which the lower orders no longer yielded an instinctive deference to the high mightiness of an earlier generation of Lees. Anyone who imagined that the new Constitution would ensure "that the representatives will generally be composed of the first class in the community" awoke to the unwelcome surprise that politics, as Benjamin Rush complained, fell no longer naturally and effortlessly into the hands of men of quality but into "the young and ignorant and needy part of the community."

In just the same way that evangelical religion had assaulted the hierarchy of Virginia Anglicanism before the Revolution, consumer exchange replaced patronage as the sinew of the social order, and social status became a mere temporary rung on which any ambitious white man could place his foot. "Every tradesman" became "a Merchant, every Merchant is a Gentleman, and every Gentleman one of the Noblesse." The American, as Hector St. John Crèvecoeur explained in 1782, "is a new man, who acts upon new principles" and has passed from "involuntary idleness, servile dependence, penury, and useless labour . . . to toils of a very different nature, rewarded by ample subsistence." There would still be "gentlemen," but the word would no longer define the few who had no need to labor with their hands, in distinction from many leather-apron men and farmers; it would instead become merely a synonym for someone of sincere or kindly manners. Similarly, there had been mobs before, in colonial times, but they had been directed and targeted by their betters, who managed their violence at a discreet distance; the mob that nearly destroyed Light Horse Harry was a different affair entirely, democratic, spontaneous, and headless.[8]

If Virginians of ancient birth wished to live as gentlemen, they would have to do it not by hauteur and honor but by a new bourgeois code of gentility. "It is a common phrase among the rich . . . that a man (naming him) was born a Gentleman," warned *The Virginia Gazette,* but to "talk of a man's being born a Gentleman is as inconsistent as to say he was born a fiddler, and with a fiddle in his arms." The mark of the gentleman had once been his participation in society balls, horse races, cockfights, and fish feasts. "Taste and Politeness" were measured in the old days by "so much Elegance in Dress, Furniture, Equipage, so much Musick and Dancing, so much Fencing and Skaiting, so much Cards and Backgammon, so much Horse Racing and Cockfighting, so many Balls and Assemblies, so many Plays and Concerts that the very imagination of them makes me feel vain, light, frivolous and insignificant."

In the new republic, Americans would guide themselves by an entirely different set of standards, "Strength, Hardiness, Activity, Courage, Fortitude and Enterprise." Or, as Catharine Maria Sedgwick distilled it into one word, "manners": "There is nothing that tends more to the separation into classes than difference of manners. This is the badge that all can see." And the relationship between classes would be marked by *respect* rather than deference; leadership would be marked by *humility* and *reticence* rather than the assertion of power; virtue would be demonstrated through *perspective* and *resilience,* not honor and style; even bodily movement would unstiffen, and frock coats and trousers would replace skirted coats and knee breeches. Politeness would supplant dueling and argument; courtesy would take the place of childish impulsiveness. "The old barriers are down," Sedgwick announced. "Talent and worth are the only eternal grounds of distinction."[9]

This gentility might express itself in the study of moral goodness, the reading of history and biography, modesty, politeness, cheerfulness, delicacy and sensibility in conversation, unostentatious material competence, and voluminous self-revealing letter writing and diary keeping. And despite the demands of the evangelicals for repentance, abasement, and humility in their converts, the genteel style soon converted the revivalists, too, by setting out refinement and decency as equally acceptable goals for a Christian public. Above all, competence (a non-flamboyant economic style that was content with sufficiency and shunned excess) and independence were the great goals. No longer were braggadocio, arrogance, and swagger to be tolerated as the special behavior of social superiors; one and all, in Virginia's fading shadow, would be judged and governed by the rule of the genteel.[10]

And even though she was the offspring of the mighty Virginia Carters, the genteel ruled Ann Carter Lee, too. Frugality came as a necessity, because, as she plainly told Robert's brother Carter at Harvard, "we have no alternative—We cannot borrow money, because we cannot repay it; the interest of our money being only sufficient for each years expenditure." Hence, no more freewheeling debt mongering: she urged on him "that noble independence of spirit, which would cause you to blush at incurring an expense, you could not in justice to your family afford." And though she never swayed from her allegiance to the Episcopal Church, even the Episcopal Church in Virginia took on a strongly evangelical tinge that contrasted smartly with the High Church snobbery that prevailed among the holdover colonial Episcopalians in New England and New York and that Ann Lee absorbed as her own. She was "singularly pious" and determined that Robert and his siblings should be, too. "You must repel every evil," she lectured Robert's brother Smith Lee, "allow yourself to indulge in such habits only as are consistent with religion and morality." Light Horse Harry preferred to think of his wife's piety as shaped by the same sort of featureless deism that formed his own, based on "love of virtue . . . not from fear of hell,—a low, base influence." But as in so many other misestimates of Ann Lee, Harry was wrong again. "Pray fervently for faith in Jesus Christ," Ann urged her children, because "he is the only rock of your salvation, and the only security for your resurrection from the grave."[11]

Like all the Lees, Robert had been born unremarkably into the fold of Virginia Episcopalianism, and though no record of his baptism has survived in the records of the Episcopal Diocese of Virginia, it is likely that he was baptized at Stratford and imbibed the rudiments of Episcopal Christianity at Christ Church while growing up in Alexandria. With his oldest brother at Harvard, and Smith Lee determined to gain an appointment in the Navy, Robert became the domestic runner and manager for his mother and his two sisters (the second sister, Catharine Mildred, was born shortly after the family relocated to Alexandria). It was Robert who "carried 'the keys,' attended to the marketing, managed all the out-door business, and took care of his mother's horses." When his mother was ill—as she was increasingly after the move to Alexandria—it was Robert who ordered up the family's shabby brougham "and would then be seen carrying her in his arms to the carriage, and arranging her cushions with the gentleness of an experienced nurse." One of the flock of Lee cousins in Alexandria remembered that Robert became legendary for "his devotion to his Mother, and the great help he was to her in all her business and household matters." Years later, he would describe himself simply as "my mothers outdoor agent & confidential messenger."[12]

Certainly it was a devotion Ann Carter Lee needed, because the income from her father's trust gradually diminished over the years. Dividends paid by the Bank of Virginia fell from a modest $1,440 per annum in 1812 (perhaps $25,000 in modern equivalents) to as little as half that after Light Horse Harry's death, while another $1,000 a year was paid in dividends from the Potomac Bank. In the waning days of Light Horse Harry at Stratford, the Lees had been surrounded by more than thirty African American slaves; after Alexandria and after Light Horse Harry was dead, there might have been only six, and at least three of those seem to have been hired out to generate income. Ann Lee could scrimp in other ways, spending large parts of the year on the circuit of her relatives' plantations, at Shirley, where the Carters maintained a school Robert could attend, at Chatham, on the Rappahannock, and even at Stratford, where his half brother, Henry IV, now presided. There, the boy could grow into adolescence on the land where he had been born, becoming "very fond of hunting" and sometimes following "the hounds on foot all day."[13]

Nevertheless, necessity continued to pinch. After Light Horse Harry's departure, Ann Lee was forced to move yet again, to a house around the corner from Oronoco Street, on North Washington Street, which had been owned by her late brother-in-law; she would then move back once more to Oronoco Street in 1820. But if necessity pinched too greatly, there was as a last resort the vast network of Carter and Lee cousinage in Alexandria upon which Ann Lee could fall back, chief among whom was Edmund Jennings Lee, the younger brother of Light Horse Harry and the mayor of Alexandria from 1815 to 1818, and her Alexandria benefactor, William Henry Fitzhugh, who opened doors to her at the Fitzhugh farm of Ravensworth, outside Alexandria. The Fitzhugh clan had married into not only the Carters but also the Washingtons; William Henry Fitzhugh's sister, Mary Lee Fitzhugh, had married Washington's only surviving step-grandson, George Washington Parke Custis. Meanwhile, Jennings Lee and his son Cassius Francis Lee (who would bear a striking resemblance in later life to his cousin Robert) became the pillars of Alexandria's Episcopal society at Christ Church; they lived nearby at the corner of North Washington and Oronoco Streets. They were, all of them, case-hardened Federalists "of the Washington school" who "opposed . . . the rise and domination of" Thomas Jefferson's Democratic Party, convinced that the Democrats were "that party which has consummated the ruin of the most glorious Republic the sun ever shone on."[14]

Growing up in Alexandria, Robert would remember the humiliation the town endured during the War of 1812—the looting of Alexandria by British warships in the Potomac in 1814, the impotent potting of the Alexandria militia's artillery at the British warships in the river, the tame surrender of the town in the mayor's office, and the burning of the public buildings in Washington by Admiral Sir George Cockburn on August 24, in retaliation for the destruction of the Canadian town of York. But he would also remember a happier moment, ten years later, when the aged compatriot of his father from the Revolution the Marquis de Lafayette stopped in Alexandria on his valedictory tour of the United States and paid a personal call on Light Horse Harry's widow. He would also remember fondly his education, which began at the Alexandria Academy, a school that offered free tuition for the offspring of Revolutionary veterans. His first teacher was "an Irish gentleman," William B. Leary, and it is likely that he was under Leary's tutelage from 1820 (when he was thirteen) to 1822. "A Man is of little importance in society without education," Ann reminded her son. "You will regret in after-life, if you neglect to lay in a store of knowledge now." Leary was likable and diligent and put Robert through the paces of "all the minor classics in addition to Homer & Longinus, Tacitus & Cicero," and complimented him for his work in "Arithmetic, Algebra & Euclid." It must have come as a surprise to both Leary and Robert's mother when, sometime in 1823, Robert announced that he desired to attend the U.S. Military Academy at West Point, and thus follow in the professional footsteps of his father, as a soldier.[15]

West Point, however, would require more than a head full of Greek and Latin, and for the next year Lee was shifted to a school next to his old home on Oronoco Street, where a Quaker and student of astronomy, Benjamin Hallowell, presided. Hallowell's school was new, and Hallowell himself laid down only two rules for its management for his young male students: "Be good boys" and "Learn all you can" (it was a simplicity that Lee would imitate forty years later in a similar situation). But Hallowell's classes soon became a roaring success, drawing between eighty and a hundred boys as boarders and as day students.

Lee surprised himself and Hallowell by turning into "a most exemplary student" in mathematics. Half a century later, Hallowell could still remember how he had assigned Lee some "very complicated" diagrams in conic sections, which Lee "drew . . . with as much accuracy and finish, lettering and all, as if it was to be engraved and printed." The one person who had no enthusiasm for Robert's decision for West Point was Ann Lee. "How can I live without Robert?" she wailed. "He is both son and daughter to me." She would have been more disturbed still if she could have sensed how much Robert, for all his uncomplaining gentility, longed to be free and unencumbered. "I thought & intended always to be one & alone in the World," and from the day he reported on the parade ground at West Point in June 1825, he would strive to be.[16]

Robert E. Lee was a compulsive letter writer, most of them multipage epistles, many of them written on the same day as two or three others, and all in a fine, spidery cursive that he signed "R. E. Lee." No letters remain from before his seventeenth birthday, though; it was not until February 24, 1824, that his earliest surviving effort as a letter writer occurs, and it arrived on the desk of Secretary of War John Caldwell Calhoun as part of Robert Lee's application for admission to West Point. "Having just heard that it was always agreeable to you to receive from every applicant for a Cadets Warrant, a statement of his age, studies, &c. made by himself, I take the earliest opportunity of sending you the following"; what comes after is a listing of Lee's reading, which included "Caesar, Sallust, Virgil, Cicero, Horace, and Tacitus" in Latin, along with Xenophon and Homer in Greek, and finally the most critical for his purposes at the military academy, "Arithmetic, Algebra, and the first six books of Euclid."[17] It was correct, proper, and undemanding. He wished to be noticed but did not strain to be more than noticed. He had already absorbed the finesse of the genteel.

No one of Calhoun's generation, or from Calhoun's state of South Carolina, would have needed much of an introduction to a son of Light Horse Harry Lee. But as secretary of war, Calhoun was then the single individual who (apart from the president) held admission to the military academy in his hands, and Lee's relatives had been careful to make as polite an impression as possible on young Robert's behalf. Arrangements for personal interviews with both Calhoun and President John Quincy Adams had been followed by letters from William Henry Fitzhugh; Robert's half brother, Henry; Robert's teachers, Leary and Hallowell; and eight members of Congress. All of them touted "the revolutionary services of the father."[18]

Yet Robert's own letter contained an odd lapse. He misdated his birth, giving it as January 29 (it was actually January 19) and placing himself in his "eighteenth year." The muddle over the birth year might have been the fault of Ann Lee. In the Lee family Bible, where she recorded the births of her children, Robert's birth year was first given as 1806, then corrected at some point to 1807, and that might have generated a confusion that it took years to correct. What was more peculiar was that January 29 was the birthday of Light Horse Harry.

There is no record of Calhoun's eye being snagged by these oddities, and Robert Lee's next letter, written five weeks later, is a brief and formal acceptance of his "appointment to the station of a Cadet in the service of the United States."[19] The slipup in the birth year must have soon been rectified, because Lee could not in fact be formally inducted into the Corps of Cadets until the summer of 1825, after he had turned eighteen.

The army of the United States during the Revolutionary War (which Light Horse Harry would have known as the Continental Army) ceased to exist as soon as Congress, under the Articles of Confederation, could disband it. Only one company of Continentals was kept in existence after 1784, and that was merely to guard the Army's warehouses at West Point, on the Hudson River.[20] Too many Americans imagined that temporary citizen militias were the real heroes of the Revolution, and the Constitutional Convention in 1787 had to overcome some eloquent paranoia about the threat of "standing armies" before its new Constitution allowed Congress the power to "raise and support Armies" and "provide and maintain a Navy." Even then, the new Constitution's Congress only authorized the recruitment of a single regiment of infantry and four artillery companies. It was not until the threat of war with France in the 1790s that Congress was finally forced to consider the needs of a real army, with a working military staff, and a new plan for fortifications to protect the American coastline.[21]

Meeting those needs would require what George Washington described as "Academies, one or more, for the Instruction of the Art Military . . . particularly [in] those Branches of it which respect Engineering and Artillery," where some expertise in mathematics, physics, and chemistry was required. West Point recommended itself as the most obvious locale for such an "academy," and in 1798 the secretary of war, James McHenry, urged that the post be expanded into "A Regular Military Academy" that featured instruction in mathematics, geography, "natural philosophy" (physics), chemistry, mineralogy, architecture, and drawing, with the fundamental aim "to form Engineers."[22]

Even then, political suspicion hovered darkly over both the newly founded Army and its academy, especially because both had been hatched under the aegis of a Federalist president. When Thomas Jefferson took the presidential oath in March 1801, it would have surprised no one if he had pulled down the Army's new scaffolding entirely. Instead, Jefferson decided to spare the

Army, but rinse out as much of its Federalism as possible. He appointed as the academy's first superintendent Jonathan Williams, a doughy—but reliably Jeffersonian—Army engineer, and authorized a Corps of Engineers to be based at West Point. But the academy remained small and ineffectual until 1817, when President James Monroe appointed Sylvanus Thayer the academy's chief officer.

Cold, polite, thorough, Thayer created an academic revolution at West Point. Taking the French École Polytechnique as his model, Thayer not only introduced a rigid code of discipline, class rankings, and a demerit system to measure cadet conduct but rewrote the academy's four-year curriculum to emphasize for entering cadets the mastery of French (as the language in which the foremost military literature was written), algebra, and geometry, and then to progress over the ensuing three years through a formidable thicket of analytic geometry, topographical drawing, physics, and chemistry. No one had any doubt that Thayer, this "grave, courteous and dignified man . . . in his full Colonel's uniform," was "competent in all branches of knowledge," and it became his mission "to bring order out of the chaos that prevailed when he took charge at West Point." Through Thayer, "the institution . . . acquired a wide and honorable reputation, and is deservedly in favor with the people and the government."[23]

Almost nothing in Thayer's curriculum set the student-cadet to the study of battlefield tactics or grand strategy. Partly, this was because battlefield tactics were defined by the limitations of nineteenth-century weaponry, which handed soldiers muskets whose effective range barely exceeded 140 yards. On those terms, tactics involved little more than the maneuver of close-packed bodies of infantry into close firing distance to an enemy, followed by a short rush by whichever side could first fix to their muskets their wicked-looking steel bayonets and drive an intimidated enemy into retreat. Drill manuals covered that aspect of war making nearly as well as the technology allowed, and open-air drill at the academy was the real education in tactics. But the other reason why there was such a paucity of instruction in warfare itself, especially on a large scale, was the assumption that a republic like the United States would never resort to violent conquest, such aggression being "contrary to the true spirit of the Constitution of our country, and in opposition to all our republican institutions." What American soldiers needed to learn were the lessons not of subjugation and annexation, in the style of Napoleon Bonaparte, but of homeland protection, conducted mainly through fortification, and that meant an education in engineering.[24]

Newly minted cadets would find themselves facing what amounted to a curriculum not in warfare but in building things. Cadets like Albert Church (who entered the academy a year ahead of Lee) would arrive at West Point by packet boat on the Hudson River from New York City and would spend their first summer on the parade-ground plain overlooking the river, mastering the intricacies of close-order drill. But from then on, the high road led to mathematics and, after two years, to the glories of engineering—roads, bridges, wharves, fortifications. Preliminary examinations in arithmetic, writing, and reading would cull the least likely cadets (Church recalled that twenty of the one hundred in his entering group fell to first exams) and paved the way for instruction in drawing "and problems in Engineering." By their third year, cadets would be ready to tackle elementary physics and in their fourth and final year pursue a capstone course in fortification building. Only in this last year would they spend any classroom time on military law and the Constitution, and the only textbook resembling an instruction in tactics was the new Army drill book, *General Regulations for the Army,* prepared in 1821 by an ambitious and determined officer for whom Robert E. Lee would develop a near-fatherly reverence, Winfield Scott.[25]

Skill in conventional fortification building was the ultimate goal of Thayer's curriculum. But along the way, cadets had to master most of what was then the newly emerging profession of civil engineering—the management of roadways, irrigation, drainage, flood control, tunnels, canals, and so forth—so Thayer and his faculty inadvertently found themselves presiding over the most advanced engineering education to be had in America.[26] And because the Army laid only the most minimal service obligations on the academy's graduates, West Pointers were surprisingly well equipped to abandon the drudgery of army life for a profitable career in civil engineering as soon as they could decently resign. By 1838, more than a hundred West Point alumni were at work as civil engineers; by 1860, almost a quarter of the academy's graduates had gone into private civil engineering practice. It might rankle the academy's Board of Visitors to discover that West Point's graduates were so eager to abandon the Army for civilian careers. But the Army's loss was the engineering profession's gain. West Point–educated engineers founded rival engineering schools and programs at Harvard, Yale, Columbia, and the University of Michigan and stimulated the creation of Norwich University in Vermont in 1819 and the Rensselaer Polytechnic Institute at Troy, New York, which awarded its first engineering degree in 1835. When the American Society of Civil Engineers was formed in 1852, eleven of its fifty-two members were academy alumni.[27]

The heavy tilt of the academy's curriculum toward engineering served a number of other purposes as well. In the first place, the highest-rated graduates were commissioned into the Corps of Engineers, turning the Corps into a small cadre of brainy technicians who prided themselves on their superiority to lesser graduates who ended up in the artillery, the infantry, or (later) the cavalry. Having the Corps of Engineers as the apex of American military respectability, in turn, reinforced the tendency of the American military profession to think of its primary mission in defensive terms. It also helped to ward off unappeased critics of professional military education by showing how West Point bestowed "greater public benefits" than the critics imagined by putting its graduates to work "in constructing canals, roads & bridges," which are "always in demand," and "constant and profitable employment."[28]

Above all, the heavy emphasis on engineering nudged the academy and its graduates into a convergence with the rising star of western politics, Henry Clay. The debacle of the War of 1812 had convinced Clay that the American republic had no chance of survival unless it shook off its Jeffersonian slumbers and threw itself energetically into the same sort of industrial and commercial development that had made the British Empire a world power. That would require a massive investment in an infrastructure system of "internal improvements" that would connect American producers with larger national and world markets. "I would see a chain of turnpike roads and canals from Passamaquoddy to New Orleans, and other similar roads intersecting the mountains, to facilitate intercourse between all parts of the country, and to bind and to connect us together," Clay announced, and that made engineers into Clay's most interested admirers.

This apostasy from Jeffersonian orthodoxy would eventually force Clay out of Jefferson's old Democratic Party and into a new breakaway political party, the Whigs. But Clay's Whigs would find a congenial audience at West Point for a program "in developing the capacities of the country for internal improvement, and in building up works which belong exclusively to the department of political economy." Among those Whiggish engineers would be the heir of one of Jefferson's most prominent political victims.[29]

The vision of West Point that opened to Robert Edward Lee's eyes when he made the long ascent by "a narrow, steep and ill-conditioned cart-road" to the parade ground—"the Plain"—overlooking the Hudson River in June 1825 was not inviting. The academy comprised only four principal buildings: two long, multistory dormitories known unimaginatively as the North Barracks and South Barracks; a smaller two-story classroom building; and a mess hall shaded by six stout elms (with "a cadet garden . . . barns and outbuildings, the bakery, and the sutler's store"). Beyond that, there were only the stone cottages of the faculty and staff and a scattering of stables, a tavern, and odds and ends of artillery and their storage sheds, plus the ruins of the Revolutionary-era Fort Clinton.

Lee would spend most of June on "the Plain" itself, sleeping under tents and learning by rote the interminable sequence of basic drill maneuvers that constituted the manual of arms, the school of the soldier, and the school of the company. On June 28, he passed the basic entrance examination (which "the student regarded . . . largely as a matter of luck"), and on September 25 he took the prescribed oath to "observe and obey the orders of the officers appointed over me, the rules and articles of war, and the regulations which have been or may hereafter be established for the government of the Military Academy."[30]

His class, when it finally graduated in 1829, would contain only forty-six cadets. Twenty-three of them would take the earliest opportunity and, before the tenth anniversary of their graduation, resign from the Army to become civil engineers (except for the three who became lawyers, and the two who became Episcopal clergymen). Fourteen would die before the outbreak of the Civil War in 1861; nine, in addition to Lee, would serve in the war, and of that number three would join Lee in serving the Confederacy. Only one, though, would be of any distinction besides Lee, and that would be Joseph Eggleston Johnston, from Richmond, who was the son of one of Light Horse Harry's Revolutionary troopers. There would be others of future note for Lee in the classes before and behind him: Jefferson Davis, one class ahead; Albert Sidney Johnston, a senior classman as Lee was entering; William Nelson Pendleton, a year behind Lee.[31]

Lee did not have any noticeable difficulty in making himself shine academically. His name appears third for "Mathematics and French" in the "fourth class" in 1826 and inches up to second a year later for "Mathematics, French, and drawing." But what really drew attention was the steadiness and dependability of his conduct, which passed without a single demerit. The adolescent who had organized his mother's pinched existence so carefully transitioned easily into making his own existence a matter of noticeable orderliness and precision. He caught Superintendent Thayer's notice as readily as his father had caught Washington's and by the end of his first year at the academy had been appointed cadet staff sergeant and a teaching assistant in mathematics. The next year, Lee was promoted to cadet adjutant, the highest rank a student could hold in the Corps of Cadets. "He is much pleased with his situation at West Point," Ann Lee reported, "and has advanced rapidly, never having received a mark of demerit, and being assistant professor of mathematics, which appointment gives him $10 per month in addition to his monthly allowance." By the time he graduated, he had hoarded more than $100 of his pay, rather than (in the case of so many other cadets) finishing his schooling in debt.[32]

Robert's parsimony pleased and relieved Ann Lee. What stood out most in the memories of those who had been students with him at West Point, however, was his almost unbearable gentility. Joseph E. Johnston remembered that Lee "was full of sympathy and kindness, genial and fond of gay conversation, and even of fun, that made him the most agreeable of companions." But the fun never strayed over the line of the ribald. He might have been, as William Nelson Pendleton remembered, "on the whole the handsomest young man I ever saw," but there is no record or witness whatsoever of dalliance with women. "His correctness of demeanor and language and attention to all duties, personal and official," were preternatural. Where Light Horse Harry had been all impulse and drama, Robert was self-restraint and correctness.

The words that most seemed to capture Lee were "dignity" and "agreeableness." Johnston thought Lee's "dignity as much a part of himself as the elegance of his person" and "gave him a superiority that every one acknowledged in his heart." Pendleton agreed: "There was always about him . . . a dignity which repelled improper familiarity." Lee "was a great soldier and a good man," one of his junior officers would later admit, "but I never wanted to put my arm around his neck and kiss him as I used to want to do with Joe Johnston—never." But this was not the dignity that had once marked the Lees of the Northern Neck with the hauteur of planter aristocrats. Pendleton also saw in Lee "a genial courtesy and joyous humor . . . that rendered him a charming companion." "He was the only one of all the men I have known," Johnston added, "who could laugh at the faults and follies of his friends in such a manner as to make them ashamed without touching their affection for him."[33]

It was Lee's determination to be agreeable that softened any resentment dignity could have generated. Jefferson Davis could not remember "an occasion on which there was not entire harmony of purpose and accordance as to means" between himself and Lee—which, given Davis's legendary capacity for touchiness and argument, was saying a great deal. But agreeableness exacted a price from Lee. It fostered an inclination to avoid personal conflict with people, something Jefferson Davis noticed when he remarked that he had never seen "in my life . . . the slightest tendency to self-seeking" in Lee. That might give him high marks for the sort of unselfishness that his mother had depended upon, but it came at the cost of waiting on the decisions of others, even of playing for safety, especially with those in authority. If Robert Lee had wished to draw a wide line between himself and the memory of Light Horse Harry, he could not have used a more successful pencil.[34]

Curiously, one of the few books that Lee borrowed from the academy's diminutive library was his father's memoir of the southern campaigns of the Revolution (although the motive might have been little more than curiosity; it was a new edition of the memoirs edited by Robert's half brother, Henry, and published in early 1827). Not surprisingly for a son of a Federalist martyr, Lee also spent time with the three-volume Williams and Whiting edition of *The Works of Alexander Hamilton* (containing "an improved edition of *The Federalist*"). Almost everything else in Lee's library list, however, was strictly related to class work, from Sir John Leslie's *Geometrical Analysis, and Geometry of Curve Lines* (which Benjamin Hallowell had recommended to his pupils) to James Atkinson's classic *Epitome of the Art of Navigation.* The only military studies that snared his interest were Machiavelli's *Art of War* (in the 1815 translation "by a Gentleman of the State of New York") and Charles de Warnery's *Anecdotes et pensées historiques et militaires* (1781). Oddly, Warnery's *Anecdotes* contained the unusually aggressive warning that generals who fight safely never win anything, "while the man who thrusts risks only the losing of his thrust; but by continually returning to the charge, he may once succeed." It was a counsel that Warnery, a cavalry officer, might have used to describe Light Horse Harry. It would be a long time before anyone thought of applying it to Light Horse Harry's son.[35]

CHAPTER THREE

Marriage and the Third System

Lee would, by regulation, spend two years at West Point before being allowed a furlough, so it was not until the summer of 1827 that he was granted permission to return home for a visit. Home, however, was no longer Alexandria. Ann Lee was in poor health and had moved across the Potomac to a house at 3322 O Street in Georgetown the year before to live with Lee's older brother Carter and sister Mildred.

Not that Carter offered the most luxurious quarters for either his mother or his siblings. Charles Carter Lee had enjoyed nearly all the advantages that Ann and Light Horse Harry had been able to bestow on their progeny, including a Harvard education, but he had made vanishingly little of them. At Harvard, he had distinguished himself by a hail-fellow bonhomie that earned him membership in the Hasty Pudding Club, and a certain literary flair that garnered both the Bowdoin Prize and the Boylston Prize. When he graduated in 1819, he stood second in his class and set up a law practice in New York City. But the practice fizzled, and Carter moved back to the District of Columbia to start another, which barely paid his bills and left him reliant on increasingly unwilling handouts from his mother's relatives. ("I am very, very sorry that Carter wants money," grumbled William Henry Fitzhugh, who had paid Carter's Harvard tuition. "Let the dog make some.") Robert's other brother, Sidney Smith Lee, was even more of a social charmer than Carter and had wangled a commission in the Navy that would see him promoted to lieutenant in 1828. None of this pleased Ann Lee, though, who peppered Smith with letters complaining "extremely that you never write to me."[1]

Far more dismaying was the nemesis that overcame Robert's half brother, Henry, the master of Stratford Hall. When young Henry married a wealthy heiress, Anne Robinson McCarty, in 1817, it appeared that the unhappy fortunes of the Stratford Lees might finally be turning in profitable directions. But in the summer of 1820, the daughter who was born to this second Henry-and-Ann(e) dynasty at Stratford died from a fall down Stratford's unforgiving front stone staircase, and Anne McCarty Lee went into a tailspin of depression and addiction. Anne's nineteen-year-old sister, Betsy, came to Stratford to minister to her distressed sibling, but instead found herself in the embraces of Henry, who soon impregnated her. By Virginia law, Henry Lee had managed simultaneously to commit both adultery and incest; worse, Henry had assumed the guardianship of Betsy's affairs, and the account books soon showed that he had been helping himself to her trust funds. Betsy's stepfather intervened, and after a lengthy legal imbroglio Henry Lee—now snickeringly referred to as Black Horse Harry—was forced to sell Stratford out of the Lee family forever. Henry and Anne struggled to rebuild their lives by moving to France in 1829, where Henry died in 1837, "persecuted unrelentingly by my enemies and still more unrelentingly neglected by my friends."[2]

This might as well have been said collectively about Light Horse Harry and all his progeny—except for Robert. "The first time I remember being particularly struck with his manly beauty and attractive manners," recalled one of his multitude of Alexandria cousins, "was when he returned home, after his first two years at West Point." In his cadet-gray uniform and white buttons, "I heard his beauty and fine manners constantly commented on." Once again, he was his mother's "devoted" son and took charge "in all her business and household matters" and of his sisters. But he was old enough now, at age twenty, to begin thinking about the shape of a life of his own, something that took on more focus that summer as he and his youngest sibling, Mildred, began calling frequently on yet another Fitzhugh relative, Mary Anna Randolph Custis of Arlington.[3]

Arlington was the creation of George Washington Parke Custis, whose father, John Parke Custis, had been one of two surviving children of Martha Washington's from her first marriage. When she remarried in 1759, to George Washington, "Jackie" was only four. But he grew to manhood willful and capricious, unpleasantly surprising his mother and stepfather by marrying and then buying, from a paternal inheritance, a large property on the south bank of the Potomac that nearly bankrupted him. "I am afraid Jack Custis, in spite of all of the admonition and advice I gave him . . . is making a ruinous hand of his Estate," Washington grumbled. He took no part in his stepfather's

Revolution until the very end, when he joined Washington as an aide at Yorktown. But, unlucky to a fault, "Jackie" contracted a fever and died in November 1781, leaving two small children to be raised by the Washingtons. One of them was George Washington Parke Custis, who would spend the rest of his life reminding people that he was the step-grandson of the first president.

When he came of age, the younger Custis transformed his father's Potomac investment into an estate that he ran with no more common sense than had his father. He named it Arlington (the name of the original Custis property on the Eastern Shore of the Chesapeake), and when the new national capital was laid out immediately across the Potomac in the 1790s, Custis began construction of an appropriately grand house of his own at Arlington in 1802. Building first one wing to the north, then adding a south wing in 1804, Custis finally united the entire structure behind an enormous front portico and eight great Doric columns that peered grandly down from bluffs over the Potomac at the infant capital, its muddy streets, vacant lots, and undistinguished buildings. By contrast with the capital, Arlington, gushed one admirer in 1853, appeared as the epitome of classical grace, "modeled after the Temple of Theseus, at Athens, sixty feet in front, and twenty-five in depth," with "a fine park of two hundred acres" in front, and in back, "a dark old forest, with patriarchal trees . . . covering six hundred acres of hill and dale."[4]

Yet there was always something about Custis, and Arlington, that was longer on show than substance. The Doric portico dominated the vista of the Potomac, yet the house behind the portico was surprisingly small, with a footprint of only thirty-five hundred square feet. The great columns were actually wood, covered with cement and painted to give the impression of marble; the walls, which at first gave the look of cut stone, were simple hard stucco. Something similar was true of Custis himself. On paper, George Washington Parke Custis was one of the wealthiest men in northern Virginia; in addition to Arlington, he inherited Washington and Custis family properties at Romancoke and White House on the Pamunkey River, along with nearly two hundred slaves. Yet his real interests wandered from pillar to post. He dabbled in raising sheep "of the improved breed," only to have the prospects for harvesting a superior American wool peter out by 1811; he dabbled in real estate speculation, trying to sell lots for a town he would name Mount Vernon, but that failed, too; he dabbled in politics, as a Federalist, and lost; he dabbled in painting historical depictions of Washington's victories that showed no special skill.

Custis's chief success was in marrying Mary Lee Fitzhugh, one of the Alexandria Fitzhughs who had taken so deep an interest in the wandering Lees. Like Ann Lee, "Mrs. Custis was remarkable for her simplicity and piety," with "an entire . . . freedom from ostentation," wrote a neighboring clergyman, and was a lively advocate for the chief institution of evangelical Episcopalianism, the Virginia Theological Seminary, which adjoined the Arlington property. Her husband, by contrast, was a putterer, "social in disposition and affable to all who visited Arlington," but "you would with difficulty be convinced he was the adopted grandson of George Washington."[5]

Mary Anna Randolph Custis was their only child, and it was the Fitzhugh connection that seems to have brought Robert Lee and Mary Custis together as teenagers, both at Arlington and at the Fitzhugh property at Chatham, across the Rappahannock from Fredericksburg. They were, technically, cousins, but only by a long chain through the Fitzhughs to the Carters. When, exactly, this acquaintance blossomed into romance is difficult to ascertain, because neither left any lengthy record of their courtship, but it would be at least safe to date the beginnings of serious interest to Robert's first summer leave from West Point in 1827, when Mary was eighteen.

Henry Stuart Foote, who had just begun a law practice in Virginia and would eventually make himself notorious as a would-be defector from the Confederate Congress, was bowled over by her charms. "No one, I am confident, has ever beheld a more placid and winning face," Foote remembered, and no "young lady" had a more "sound and vigorous intellect." Those who knew her better were less certain about Mary Custis's intellectual appetites. She loved "the beautiful with an artist's passion," but "her heart was as unworldly and artless as a child's"—qualities that did not necessarily augur well for the wife of a professional soldier. What she was unquestionably, however, "was the heiress expectant of two of the largest estates that Virginia could then boast," and that could outweigh any number of other deficits.[6]

For the moment, "that all-admiring & admired one Mr Lee" (as Mary described him before his return to West Point at the end of August) would have to be admired by her from afar. "He is so much occupied in the duties of his profession that he has but little time for the frivolous affairs of the heart," she pouted. "They are always *light* with him you know." The fall of 1827 brought Robert Lee to his third year at West Point and though another brief vacation in the summer of 1828 fanned the flames of his interest in Mary Custis still further, it also fed anxiety over the steady disintegration of his mother's health and household. Carter Lee was still struggling to make a success out of his law practice in the District, but Carter's real attentions were turning, unprofitably, toward writing poetry. One sister, Anne Kinloch Lee, had fled the claustrophobia of their mother's demands in 1825 by marrying a Baltimore Episcopal clergyman, William Louis Marshall, who would soon turn to law and build a successful career as a lawyer and judge; the other sister, Mildred, would find herself courted by another lawyer, Edward Vernon Childe, whom she married in 1831. None of them proved as domestically devoted as Robert had been. (Carter and Mildred, Ann Lee complained, "both, do very little else than read; so you will know how the family affairs are conducted, when you consider that I am too much of an invalid to take the part in the management of them, that I formerly did.") Soon enough, Mildred and her husband would move to Paris, and as if to put all the trauma of the Lee family's history behind her, she would never return.[7]

If any of this weighed on Robert Lee's spirits, his academic performance in his fourth and final year at West Point showed no signs of it. He barely missed top academic standing in the class of 1829, just twenty-nine points (out of two thousand) behind the top scorer, the New Yorker Charles Mason. But this was more than enough to ensure the offer of a coveted commission in the Corps of Engineers, and upon graduation Lee took the oath that would bind him as a brevet (or temporary) second lieutenant and soldier of the U.S. Army:

> *I do solemnly swear or affirm (as the case may be) to bear true allegiance to the United States of America, and to serve them honestly and faithfully, against all their enemies or opposers whatsoever, and to observe and obey the orders of the President of the United States of America and the orders of the officers appointed over me, according to the articles of war.*[8]

Graduation that June also meant another leave to go home, but this time his arrival would be shrouded by death. Ann Lee's health had gone from bad to worse, with only temporary improvements, and Robert returned to Virginia to find his mother bedridden at the Fitzhughs' Ravensworth. "My health," Ann Lee admitted, "has declined very much within the last two years, and I never calculate on living longer than from one season to another." At once, Robert stepped back into his old role of maternal nurse. "In her last illness he mixed every dose of medicine she took, and he nursed her night and day," and if he "left the room she kept her eyes on the door till he returned. He never left her but for a short time." But the advance of her disease, which was probably tuberculosis, knew no remission, and she died on July 26, aged fifty-six. She was buried at Ravensworth, but Robert could not bring himself to attend the interment, instead pacing "to and fro the floor of her bedroom in inconsolable grief."[9]

The brevity of her will, which was probated in September, was a testimony to how far the Lees had fallen. Ann's daughters came first: Anne Lee Marshall was to inherit "my maid servant, Charlotte, and her child, together with Kaziah, William and Betsy," along with "my set of white tea china, my wardrobe, two of my best tablecloths & one half of my family napkins and wearing apparel." Mildred would inherit the coachman, Nat, plus "my carriage and horses, *beaureau,* piano," and the rest of the tablecloths, napkins, and clothes. What was left of her Carter trust fund would be divided into shares of $10,000 each for Anne and Mildred, with William Henry Fitzhugh to serve as trustee. Everything else—and what that entailed was not specified—was "to be divided in equal portion between my three sons, Charles C. Lee, Sidney S. Lee & Robt E Lee." That was all. Significantly, among the four witnesses were William Henry Fitzhugh and his wife, Anna, and William Henry Fitzhugh's sister, Mary Lee Fitzhugh Custis of Arlington.[10]

Lee would, however, not have long to mourn. On August 10, his first orders arrived from Brigadier General Charles Gratiot, the chief of the Corps of Engineers: "Brevet 2nd Lieut Robert E Lee of the Corps of Engineers will, by the middle of November next, report to Major Samuel Babcock of the Corps of Engineers, for duty at Cockspur Island, in the Savannah River, Georgia."

"Wherever the standard of freedom and independence has been or shall be unfurled, there," promised John Quincy Adams, will America's "heart, her benedictions, and her prayers be." Americans would not, however, be making any active efforts at export. "She is the well-wisher to the freedom and independence of all. She is the champion and vindicator only of her own." That task would be best served by the construction of fortifications, especially to defend America's vulnerable port cities, and that was the labor to which West Point had bent Robert Lee's training. It soothed congressional budget makers, too, that fortifications, with long material lives and minimal manpower requirements in peacetime, were less expensive than paying for the vast and costly paraphernalia of nineteenth-century militaries. "When once constructed," one report assured Congress, "they require but little expenditure for their support," and "can never exert an influence dangerous to public liberty."[11]

Congress's first effort at creating a system of protective fortifications was characteristically feeble. Earthen walls, braced with timber and embracing leftover heavy artillery from the Revolution, were erected to cover the water approaches to thirteen important ports along the Eastern Seaboard. But the earthworks easily eroded, and after serious rumblings of war with the British were felt in 1807, Congress nervously authorized the construction of a new and more powerful "second system" of fortifications, with brick rather than earthen walls and laid out in European style with star-shaped bastions to repel land attack, as well as heavy guns, sited in protective masonry casemates, to fend off hostile warships. Although Second System fortifications like Baltimore's Fort McHenry stood up well to the pounding of the Royal Navy during the War of 1812, they did little to prevent the British from landing the infantry that occupied Alexandria or that burned Washington. So, in 1817, an even more ambitious "third system" of eighteen new coastal fortifications was inaugurated, constructed entirely of brick masonry, with multiple tiers of casemates and artillery arranged in a five-sided pattern.[12]

Planning was one thing, execution another. Without the threat of war on the horizon after 1815, the creation of the Third System forts slowed to a maddeningly halting pace. One of the largest Third System fortifications, Fort Monroe, was begun in 1817 and designed to secure the entrance to the Chesapeake Bay, but the fits and starts of congressional appropriations delayed its completion until 1837; the most famous Third System fortification, Fort Sumter in Charleston harbor, began construction in 1829 and was still unfinished when the Civil War broke out in 1861.

It was not just a matter of money. The Corps of Engineers, which would carry the burden of designing and building the forts, might have been the most elite branch of the Army, but it was also the smallest, comprising, off and on, only two dozen officers and no permanent enlisted personnel. Not only were the existing engineering officers thinly stretched to provide guidance for Third System projects, but they were forced to rely on civilian contractors and workers, and occasionally even military prisoners. Above all, construction of the Third System fortifications required more complicated design ingenuity than inland fortifications, roads, or bridges. Third System projects needed to take account of wave heights, beaches, and breakers, the behavior of tidal estuaries, seasonal water fluctuations, and the long-reach effect of distant lakes and rivers flowing down past military construction sites that often had to be built in pile-driven salt marshes and even (in the case of Fort Sumter) artificial spits of rubble.[13]

Lee's orders from Charles Gratiot sent him to the mouth of the Savannah River and a triangular marshy flat known as Cockspur Island that divided the river just as it flowed into the Atlantic. There, ten miles downstream from the bustling town of Savannah, with its 7,500 inhabitants, the Corps of Engineers began work on a multitiered Third System fortification under the eye of Major Samuel Babcock, a forty-four-year-old Massachusetts-born engineer from the pre-Thayer era at West Point. When Lee arrived there by coastal schooner in early November, he found that Babcock had been able to do little more than sketch out preliminary plans for a five-sided masonry fort (with its apex pointed seaward) and several small shoreline artillery emplacements, begin hiring civilian (and enslaved) workers, and arrange for the quick construction of the laborers' quarters on the island. No rockets' red glare or bombs bursting in air over Cockspur Island; instead, Lee was assigned to finishing a small wharf and "raising embankments, cutting ditches . . . building houses of all kinds & descriptions for all conceived."

Babcock was not impressed by his new assistant: Lee was "active and intelligent," but, Babcock sniffed, "in a measure inexperienced." Nor was Lee impressed with Babcock, especially after Babcock insisted on siting the wharf on the east face of the island, where Lee was sure it would be washed away by autumnal hurricanes. "How disagreeable it is to have anything to do with such a man," Lee complained, "and the more so, as I am confident the system he has pursued of carrying into effect the proposed operation here, is entirely wrong." What was more annoying, Babcock dumped a number of unwanted administrative tasks into Lee's lap, including the thankless job of serving as chief supply clerk and "acting assistant commissary of Subsistence of the Post." At the same time, Lee worked all through the spring of 1830 on preparations for ground breaking for the new fortification, only to have Major Babcock call a halt to the work in the summer, partly because of his plea for a medical leave on the advice of Savannah's "most eminent Physicians" and partly because of the near approach of hurricane season.[14]

This at least gave Lee an opportunity to return on leave to Virginia, where his chief goal would be the engineering of his romance with Mary Custis. Once his mother's death had freed him from his heavy sense of obligation to her, he was intoxicated with the prospect of letting his fancy run free in "confused sentences about beauty." After "so many years in the habit of repressing my feelings, I can now scarcely realize that I may give vent to them, and act according to their dictates." The freedom of his leave in 1830 was spent in the customary round of relatives' visits to the Fitzhugh places at Ravensworth and Chatham, and the Carters at Kinloch and Woodstock in the Piedmont. By the end of the summer, this pilgrimage had brought him to Arlington, and it was there that he proposed to Mary, after a dramatic reading aloud from Sir Walter Scott.

It was clear that she already regarded him as "him who I love." But it was not quite so clear to George Washington Parke Custis that Robert Lee was the man to whom he could conscientiously see his daughter married. Whether from Custis's own predilection for dithering over decisions, or from a darker hesitation at the soiled reputation of Lee's father and half brother, or simply from a fear that a junior lieutenant with no great material prospects in this world would attach himself to the Custises like some impecunious barnacle, the master of Arlington balked at giving his paternal blessing to the engagement. Robert might well consider himself "engaged to Miss Mary C.," but he admitted to his brother Carter that while "she & her mother have given their consent . . . the Father has not yet made up his mind." That meant that any wedding would "not be till next Spring"—to which Robert inserted the qualifier "if there is one."[15]

As the year waned, love was compelled to pause, because Lee was due to return to Cockspur Island in early November. What he found there, in the wake of the seasonal "Gales," was disheartening: the housing whose construction he had supervised had survived intact, but "nearly all the embankments were broken down, ditches filled . . . and what was worse than all the wharf which cost us so much time & money is destroyed," just as he had predicted. Not that Babcock would be around to accept responsibility. The ailing major was in Philadelphia, "nor did the packet from Philadelphia . . . bring any intelligence of his movements." (In fact, Babcock was dying, his wife had left him, and he would live only until June of the following year.)

In Babcock's place arrived Joseph F. K. Mansfield, an 1822 West Pointer who assumed command at Cockspur Island on January 21, 1831. Mansfield had his own opinion of Babcock's work, which he promptly threw to the winds, and ordered Lee to commence a new "Survey and Plan of the Island," after which "commencement of the body of the work will immediately be examined, fixed and take place." The survey revealed what Lee had suspected all along, that the site Babcock had originally chosen for the fort was too spongy to support serious construction. But in Mansfield's mind, the solution would require more expertise than Lieutenant Lee could lend. In March, the veteran Captain Richard Delafield was dispatched to Cockspur, which now saddled Lee with two taskmasters instead of one. "I have been dreadfully harassed by these two men, who call themselves Engineers," Lee grumbled. "Will you believe that they are still at it . . . with 'Lee give us a sketch of that.'" Like so many other Third System fortifications, the Cockspur project would not be completed for another fifteen years—when, as Fort Pulaski, it would once again, but only briefly, come under the command of Robert E. Lee.[16]

The work at Cockspur Island taxed everything Lee had learned about coastal engineering. "We have cut a canal ½ mile long through the Island," he explained to Mary Custis:

> *Embanked the exposed side, wharfed all around the end to about 200 ft. in order to secure it. Constructed a wharf nearly 300 ft in length. Built three houses. Laid out the Fort & made an Embankment all around it, 8 ft. high, 6 ft. at top & 20 ft. at bottom, in case of storms. Made machinery of different descriptions, and among the rest, Screw Pumps, pile drivers, Cranes tread Wheels &c. &c. Made the necessary surveys, soundings, drawings. Kept in steady employ 150 men & upwards, for all of whom we have to lay out their work, whether it be in wood or on the ground.*

It also bored Lee. "To be out early & late urging a set of poor creatures to the top of their strength to erect that, of which the next tide will destroy half, & perhaps all," was not what he wanted to see in his future, and for the first time notions of resignation from the Army twitched in his head. "Had I felt when with you, as I do now," he wrote to Mary Custis, "I believe I should almost have refused to come." He was made even more unhappy by the arrival of Nat, his mother's old slave coachman, on Christmas Day 1830. There is no record of how closely Lee might have been attached to Nat as part of the Lee household in Alexandria. He had been willed by Ann Lee to Mildred. But Nat was old and sick, and because Mildred was about to marry Edward Vernon Childe, she wished on her brother what she had no desire to keep for herself, and "after a long & boisterous passage of 25 days," Nat arrived at Cockspur, weak and coughing from the tuberculosis that killed him that spring.[17]

Lee found amusement and hope in only two sources, one being his letters to Mary Custis and the other being the Mackay family of Savannah, to which he escaped whenever opportunity beckoned. Jack Mackay, the son of a Savannah merchant, had been Lee's classmate at West Point, only three months younger than Lee and six places beneath him in academic standing, and "the friend which I love above all things." Mackay's first posting as a second lieutenant in the artillery had been, conveniently, to the Oglethorpe Barracks in Savannah, and under the widow Mackay's pointed roof on Broughton Street the two newly commissioned lieutenants swam effortlessly into the stream of Savannah society, which "has been quite gay so far in dinners, dances &c." Society included Jack Mackay's five glamorous sisters. "They were blessed creatures," Lee remembered, and he was "so taken up with" them "that I could make myself agreeable to no one else."[18]

For all of their charms, Mary Custis was in no real danger of losing him to the Mackays. Robert Lee had spent most of his childhood in a world where women held a central place, both as rulers and as servants. Ann Lee had made the decision to leave Stratford; Ann Lee had assumed the role of matriarch after Light Horse Harry's departure and dominated Robert's early life. Hence, his relationships with women would always be happier, more cozy, and more uninhibited than those in the masculine world, where genteel propriety and dignity would rule his behavior. "No one enjoyed the society of ladies more than himself," Mary wrote years later, and the letters he wrote to Mary that winter from Georgia sparkle with the same flirtatious teasing that filled his days with the Mackays. She was "My sweet Mary" and "My Sweet Cousin," and he "would even now give the world if you were here, on this desolate and comfortless Island." In his imagination, he "could almost hear you speak and read, and laugh," and he had no other desires than "to read to you, walk with you, ride with you."

She had desires, too, although those now included a determination that her future husband should embrace the same evangelical Virginia Episcopalianism to which she and her parents subscribed. Before his departure for Cockspur, she promised to send him a New Testament, and she extracted a pledge from him to read it, "especially on the Sabbath." He humored her, although it was not much more than humoring. West Point had done nothing to water whatever religious seeds had been planted in Lee's soul as he grew up in Christ Church, Alexandria; it was, as many other cadets discovered, "a hard place to practice religion," and the Army as a whole had a reputation for discouraging anything in the way of holy zeal. So he read the New Testament Mary sent, but dutifully rather than piously. "I found my eyes were running over verse after verse, while my mind was far otherwise engaged," he admitted. He even "followed your wishes exactly & went to Church" in Savannah on Christmas Day, "& listened to the sermon." Still, she should not "expect miracles in my case," and he hoped she would be willing to "leave something to time, and more to opportunity . . . and so seek that I may find."[19]

Lee was delighted to learn in April that his father-in-law-to-be had at last given his "approbation" to the wedding, and when orders arrived in March, transferring Lee to Fort Monroe, planning for a June ceremony at Arlington shot ahead. "The day has been fixed," he wrote to his brother Carter, who had returned to New York after the breakup of Ann Lee's Georgetown home and was making a second try at a law practice there, "& it is the 30th June." He planned to wear his "uniform coat on the important night," and he assigned Carter the job of having a New York tailor make a new pair of white dress trousers to match. Remember, he added with his usual precision, "the *white* pantaloons must be in character."

Like many a groom, he admitted, "I begin to feel right funny when I count my days." But he had a particular anxiety at the prospect of becoming George Washington Parke Custis's son-in-law, "especially when I consider the novel situation in which I shall be placed." He had no permanent home outside the Army. Mary, on the other hand, was as wedded to Arlington and her parents as she would be to him, and nothing would delight her more than for Robert to resign his commission and live with her, happily ever after, on the blessed heights above the Potomac. Certainly Arlington would make for easier living than coastal swamps. But if he yielded to that impulse, the likeliest result would be for Robert Lee to be sucked into the orbit of the Custises, with himself cast as Arlington's junior squire and his father-in-law's general factotum. If old Custis worried that the fortuneless lieutenant of engineers would become a burden on Arlington, he needn't have been concerned. Robert Lee had lived long enough under his mother's thumb to find no cheer in living under his father-in-law's. (If anything, Custis would soon enough regret that Lee *hadn't* resigned from the Army and joined him at Arlington.)

For the moment, Fort Monroe resolved that question for both of them. Lee would still be the junior engineering officer at what remained the largest of the Army's Third System fortifications. But his superior would be Captain Andrew Talcott, ten years Lee's senior but newly wed himself and an ingenious inventor of a method of determining latitude by observing the zenith distances of stars. "Capt. Talcott . . . is a man of a first rate mind, of great acquirement, & gentlemanly feelings," Lee exulted, "& one in whose society I can derive much profit, as well as pleasure." Moreover, Lee's principal task would be the construction of a new fortification, Fort Calhoun, on an artificial shoal known as the Rip Raps, flanking the ship channel formed by Hampton Roads and guarded by Fort Monroe, and there Lee would have more latitude for self-oversight. "This is a very pleasant Post," he wrote to Carter, "& I have charge of Ft Calhoun . . . on the other side of the Channel." Whether Mary would find it pleasant was another story. But he set out, even before the wedding, to convince Mary that it would be perfectly agreeable to set up housekeeping there. It might not be Arlington, he conceded anxiously, but "there are very good quarters over at the Rip Raps & we might live there."[20]

Even the wedding itself generated some nervous flutters. Lee had been unsure down to the end of May whether he could obtain leave from Fort Monroe, and Mary's mother came down with "chills" in mid-June. The evening of the wedding brought on showers that drenched the presiding clergyman, Dr. Reuel Keith, the Virginia Theological Seminary's founder and a particular friend of Mary's mother, on his way to Arlington. The "tall and slender" Keith "had to change his dress, and Mr. Custis supplied him with garments ill-befitting so tall a man, for Mr. Custis was short in stature, so that there was something ludicrous in the Doctor's appearance." At least, as Lee explained afterward to Andrew Talcott, "there was neither fainting nor fighting, nor anything uncommon which could be twisted into an adventure."

Keith had no lengthy sermon to preach, although the "few words" he did utter as a charge to the newly married couple were serious enough, in evangelical fashion, to make Lee feel "as if he had been reading my Death warrant," and he noticed in Mary's hand "a tremulousness . . . that made me anxious for him to end." But everything proceeded without greater trouble, and Lee actually confessed to feeling no "more excitement than at the black Board at West Point." He did not expect to return to Fort Monroe until the beginning of August, and in anticipation of Mary's new role of wife he had ordered a "new bedstead" in Alexandria, to be shipped down the Potomac in time for their arrival at Hampton Roads. The newlyweds would take up residence in a second-floor two-room apartment in the officers' quarters near the south postern gate.[21]

The Lees had scarcely returned to Fort Monroe before Southampton County, forty miles southwest of Hampton Roads, erupted in the most ferocious slave uprising in the new republic's history. A slave preacher, Nat Turner, "began to receive the true knowledge of faith" in visions of blood falling "in the form of dew" and in May 1828 "heard a loud noise in the heavens" which announced that he must "fight against the Serpent, for the time was fast approaching when the first should be last and the last should be first." An eclipse of the sun in February 1831 was Turner's signal to prepare an insurrection, and a second eclipse in August provided the trigger for the uprising. In a two-day rebellion that eventually recruited seventy slaves for Turner's band, Turner killed more than sixty whites—men, women, and children, without discrimination—before hastily organized white militia surrounded them and crushed it, equally without discrimination. Turner eluded capture until October, but eventually eighteen of his slave allies and one free black were hanged, while others were sold out of state.[22]

The artillery companies that garrisoned Fort Monroe were mobilized for action, but by the time they were ready, the Virginia militia had already poured its own vision of blood onto the rebels, and as an engineering officer nothing necessarily required Lee's services. Lee was busier trying to calm nervous white reactions to Turner's revolt. Writing to his mother-in-law, he blamed Turner's "religious assemblies, which ought to have been devoted to better purposes," for the outbreak, and downplayed the actual scale of the uprising. "There are many instances," he reassured her, of slaves "defending their masters," while "the whole number of blacks taken and killed did not amount to the number of whites murdered by them."[23]

Some of Lee's indifference to the Turner uprising was calculated as a balm for soothing his in-laws' nerves. But another part of it was rooted in the sense of distance he felt from slave owning himself. When Ann Lee died in 1829, no slaves were named as part of the vague "remainder of my estate," which was to be divided among Robert and his two older brothers. Still, this "remainder" probably included at least one un-itemized slave family in Ann Lee's estate, because Robert would mention, almost in passing, in a letter to Carter Lee in 1835, "Mrs. Sally Diggs" and "Mrs Nancy Ruffin & her three illegitimate pledges," who "are all of the race in my poss[ession]." Beyond that, he had little direct connection to slave owning.[24]

On the other hand, Robert Lee certainly benefited *indirectly* from slave ownership. The bulk of the workforce at Fort Monroe were black slaves, hired out by their owners, or free blacks, because "Blacks in this Country are mostly Labourers, & Mechanics white." He also had another hand in slavery through the Custises, who owned a vast slave workforce at Arlington, White House, and Romancoke. Lee might not have felt much incentive to acquire slaves in his own name, but the personal needs slaves served were more than met through the Custis slaves, who would provide the bulk of Mary's "goods & chattels" at Fort Monroe and attend the family's summer vacation peregrinations to visit various relatives as part of "a squad of children, Negroes, horses, and dogs."

Not that the Custises were themselves easy-minded about slavery. As in so many other things, G.W.P. was notoriously lax in managing his enslaved laborers, leaving them an unusual amount of "opportunity for gossip and idleness and greater temptation and inducement to appropriate the small proceeds of their labor to themselves." And like many elite Virginia slave owners, the Custises took the opportunity of slavery's steady drain toward the southwestern states to profess their distaste for the "peculiar institution"—although without necessarily doing anything about it. Custis even described slavery as a "vulture" that gnawed at the "vitals" of Southern society and "the mightiest serpent that ever infested the world," while Custis's brother-in-law, William Henry Fitzhugh, had scheduled the postmortem emancipation of his own slaves. Custis publicly favored colonization as the best solution to ending slavery, but neither G.W.P. nor his son-in-law showed any interest in immediate emancipation, nor did they oppose in any public way the fanatical turn in Southern thinking generated by the Turner uprising toward claiming slavery to be a positive good, to be defended at all costs—including, if necessary, at the cost of the American Union.[25]

Lee had a more immediate problem in coping with his new wife. She tried to persuade Robert to bring her mother to Fort Monroe to manage the new housekeeping arrangements, and when Mrs. Custis wisely declined, Mary tried to persuade him to induce his sister Anne to join them from Baltimore. Moreover, he discovered that Mary "is somewhat addicted to laziness & forgetfulness in her Housekeeping." Certainly, "she does her best," but "in her Mothers words, 'The Spirit is willing but the flesh is weak.'" For her part, Mary found the cramped quarters at Fort Monroe a trial. "It is so public you can never go out alone," she complained to her mother, nor was there a chaplain on post to hold regular services. She waited only three months at Fort Monroe before planning an extended return to Arlington for the Christmas holidays. "I am a wanderer on the face of the earth," she wrote—except at Arlington, where "the past and the future" could alike be "disregarded."[26]

The Army was not nearly so indulgent with Robert. He accompanied Mary on leave to Arlington for Christmas, but left by himself at the end of January to recommence work on Fort Calhoun. Much of it descended into the same routine he had managed on Cockspur Island, only now he had to act as general contractor, designer, supply supervisor, personnel manager, and disciplinarian. "We are going on at the Rip Raps as usual," he reported to Andrew Talcott. He signed contracts for pork for the workmen and hay for the mules ("both good and cheap") and for "iron piping" at "3½ cts per lb." A sutler and "Post Bakery" were set up temporarily in "the interior of [the] Casemates . . . and the railing of Bridge Front 6 is to be put on." There were labor troubles to resolve and "we have been obliged to Suspend operations on [the] Ramparts for want of Force." A drunken officer "appeared on parade perfectly intoxicated & was Sent to his Qrs. & arrested." Unusually high tides "broke over the dyke around the Marsh & made two large breaches." Curbstone had to be "procured . . . 6" thick (not less) & from 2' to 5' long, & 14" or more deep—allowing 175 lbs to a cubic foot." He needed "at least Six more masons" to add to a workforce of ninety-two "Labourers" at Fort Monroe and "at [the R[ip] R[aps] 26," alongside "20 or 30 Blacks [who] arrived from Smithfield . . . for the works at this place." None of this was made easier by the decision of President Andrew Jackson, now in his second term, to adopt Fort Calhoun as his summer vacation retreat and demand that "it *must* be finished in two years, or in other words, during *his* administration."[27]

Mary did not join him at Fort Monroe until June, leaving him to enjoy bachelorhood as best he could in the company of another West Point classmate, Joseph Johnston, whose artillery company had been posted to Fort Monroe at the height of the Turner scare (and whose "improvident & Spendthrift" bills Lee found himself managing). He was exasperated when he learned that she did not plan on returning to Fort Monroe "till the last of May," and he was equally perplexed when he learned that she proposed to bring as many as four slaves from Arlington with her. Still, "it will not do to try conclusions with these Custis women," Lee would eventually decide. "They always come out best," like "the vixen in the family, whose husband had tried in vain to conquer her." Besides, Mary had an inarguable excuse for delay this time: she was pregnant with their first child (who had probably been conceived over the Christmas holidays, appropriately for Mary, at Arlington) and was happy to take her time journeying back to Fort Monroe. When she did, she gave birth on September 16 to a boy who could be given no other name except that of his maternal grandfather—George Washington Custis Lee.

Far from indulging any reservations, Lee rejoiced at the prospect of fatherhood, as though becoming a father himself offered yet another chance to fill the gap left in his own life by the disappearance of Light Horse Harry.

"I have an heir to my Estates!" he trumpeted in a letter to his brother Carter, "Aye, a Boy!" who was "quite large fat & hearty" and who was born "without giving his mother notice of his approach & earlier than was expected."[28]

Lee's reference to "my Estates" was intended as sarcasm, but it might not have been read that way by Carter. All through his life, Robert E. Lee would harp incessantly on his poverty to any listener, starting with Mary, whom he did not mind telling was spoiled by the abundance in which she had grown up. "Your dear Mother will be for giving you everything she has; but you must recollect one thing, and that is, that they have been accustomed to comforts all their lives, which now they could not dispense with," Robert wrote reprovingly. The life she would lead with him would be different, and "we in the commencement ought to contract our wishes to their smallest compass and enlarge them as opportunity offers." And yet Lee was not exactly penniless. Buried within the vagueness of his mother's will about dividing the remainder of her estate was an inheritance of just under $10,000 (the same portion bestowed on each of his sisters) that he was already investing through the aid of John Lloyd, a prominent Alexandria merchant who had married one of Robert's multitude of cousins.[29]

What also lay unmentioned in Ann Lee's will were the remnants of the lands Light Horse Harry had bought so optimistically in western Virginia in the 1790s and went to debtors' prison to avoid surrendering. Among the prizes to be divided equally among Charles Carter Lee, Sidney Smith Lee, and Robert Lee were seventeen thousand acres scattered across Hardy, Patrick, and Shenandoah Counties (plus about two hundred acres' worth of small in-parcels in Fairfax County). When in late 1831 Carter turned away from practicing law for good, he decided to try land speculation and moved himself to a two-story forest cabin, forty-five miles west of Warrenton, Virginia. Among his projects was the creation of the White Sulphur Springs Company, organized to build a resort around a natural hot springs "usually known by the name of Howard's Spring," plus a gristmill and an ironworks. But a more ambitious project was to persuade his brothers, Smith and Robert, to leave the Navy and the Army and join him in realizing the immense good fortune that had eluded their father.[30]

"Such lands! Such lands!" Robert marveled as Carter began unrolling his schemes for the development of the Hardy County properties. The prospect of setting up independently of both the Army and his Custis in-laws beckoned to Lee's anxieties, and it was especially "tempting to a newly married couple." Lee was all too well aware that advancement in the Army would be a slow and tedious affair: the average time to his next rank, first lieutenant, was eight years, and it would take ten more for him to make captain, twenty to make major, and that was without any mishaps. He was not sure that "being an indifferent Engineer," he could easily turn into a planter, but he could at least "take the Mule & cattle Department under my sole superintendence" as a sort of "Scientific *Drovier.*" He would, of course, have "to persuade Mary to go out." But "perhaps the charms of your Establishment may win me from Uncle Sam." Certainly he could at least make an inspection of the potential of the Hardy lands. "Should you be out there this winter & I can get off from here, I will pay you a visit, & together we can reconnoitre the whole concern."

There was, nevertheless, a note of caution in Robert's interest, because this was precisely the sort of thing that had brought about Light Horse Harry's ruin. By the summer of 1832 (and just before little Custis Lee's arrival) he was proposing a division of the properties "into Northern, Middle & Southern districts," but less with the idea of ensuring equal portions among the three brothers than with making sure that he would have a free hand in managing his own portion. "When the land is surveyed & divided," he expected, "each mans part will be wholly to itself."[31]

Soon enough, Robert began to suspect that the whole project for the western Virginia properties was a pipe dream after all. "I have executed the deed you sent," he wrote in April 1832, and was surprised to "find there set down 70,000 acres in Patrick Cy." He was puzzled also that Carter was now claiming title to "land in Harrison, too . . . where did that come from." He was still hoping to "come in the winter . . . & perhaps I may induce Smith to accompany me & we shall have quite a cosy time together in your cabin." But the trip never took place, and Robert's enthusiasm waned as Carter's letters began to fill up with queries about expensive equipment for various projects that Robert knew would likely never turn a penny of profit. Carter proposed an investment in a "machine" for "getting out shingles"; Robert promptly downplayed it as a fast road to bankruptcy:

> *The only machine I can hear of about here for getting out shingles is a large one that was erected in the Dismal Swamp by a man who thought he was going to make his fortune & the whole apparatus of which (worked by steam) cost $5000. It worked beautifully & turned out a great deal & yet the poor Fellow was obliged to run away & leave his machine standing in the Swamp, which does not say much for its profitability.*

Finally, he called a halt to Carter's visions. Much as he "would take great delight in foraging over that Country with you by my side & on the back of my pretty little mare," Carter's land speculations seemed too unstable for Robert's anxieties. "I notwithstanding must stick to Engineering," Robert wrote, something which, in a revealing comparison, he likened to being married to Mary Custis. The Army was his place, "for better, for worse, as we say in matrimony," and he would have to "relinquish such . . . prospects" as western Virginia offered "to Bachelors like yourself."[32]

Admittedly, the Army offered thin living, poor pay, and slow promotion, but it at least offered lifetime tenure. Lee's annual salary as a second lieutenant in 1833 came to only $1,113.40, while civil engineers in private practice could earn anywhere from double to six times that amount, but he also received housing, food, and other allowances, and in times of financial panic Lee's income would remain stable, while his civilian counterparts could see their business fall into an abyss. For every West Pointer who used the academy's engineering curriculum as a springboard into a successful civilian engineering practice between 1830 and 1860, there was another who, like the North Carolinian Alfred Mordecai, concluded, "I think it will be better for the present to 'hold fast to that which is good,' even if not the best."[33]

No one should have known more about the consequences of those risks than the sons of Light Horse Harry, but in this case, it was Robert who had read the signs accurately. Carter never made any serious money out of western Virginia, even though he continued to pester Robert about joining him. "The description you give of . . . the prospects of the increased value of the property are very flattering," Robert wrote ten years later, when Carter begged for cash to fund still more development schemes, but "it is the very kind of property that requires a large outlay before any profit Can be realized." Not only did Robert claim to have no such money, but even if he had, sinking it into Carter's schemes would be akin to "the purchase of a lottery ticket." In 1847, the brothers sold out their interests in western Virginia, leaving only Carter to hold on to stock in a few hotels and the one speculative success he could boast, a medicinal spa and hotel at White Sulphur Springs. And Robert stayed at Fort Monroe.[34]

But not for long. As much as he assured Mary that he was perfectly content at Fort Monroe, and that "there cannot be a more natural or more pleasing field" for an engineer's work, he also confessed to Carter that "there is nothing new here nor ever will be." Mary insisted on repeated returns to Arlington, taking little Custis with her and leaving Robert feeling deserted. "My Sweet little Boy, what I would give to See him! The house is a perfect desert without him & his Mother & there is no comfort in it." He was even more candid about his restlessness with Andrew Talcott. "As much as I like the Location . . . and as fond as I am of the Company of some of the Offrs & of Some persons in the neighborhood . . . yet there are so many of the *disagreements* connected with the duty that I should like to get to another Post." Congress, he complained to Jack Mackay, showed no interest in "promoting modest merit in the person of you and I," and he warned his "glorious Jack" that his "situation" was "full of pains" and "one from which I shall modestly rebel on the first fitting opportunity."

Lee, however, had no clear idea of what such a "fitting opportunity" constituted. As it was, old G. W. P. Custis was beginning to reverse himself and ply Robert with suggestions that would tie him to the Custis family's affairs, asking him on one occasion to visit and report on the small Custis property of Smith Island, in the Chesapeake Bay, and on another to parlay with G.W.P.'s overseer at the Pamunkey River plantations. And Robert's mother-in-law, Mary Fitzhugh Custis, was even more pressing in her pleas to her husband to "withdraw Robert from his present professions and yield to him the management of affairs."[35]

And then the ground shifted. On October 24, 1834, he was ordered by the Chief Engineer, Charles Gratiot, to leave Fort Monroe and join Gratiot's own staff at the War Department in Washington. For Mary, it would mean they could live permanently at Arlington, but for Robert, the twenty-seven-year-old second lieutenant, it meant a dizzying vault into the very center of the Army's life.

CHAPTER FOUR

Mission to the Mississippi

"You may suppose a situation in W[ashington] will be particularly agreeable to me," Lee wrote to Andrew Talcott a week after the orders transferring him to the Chief Engineer's office arrived. After all, Lee was a mere second lieutenant of engineers who sat at twentieth, out of twenty-six, on the Corps of Engineers' seniority list, and here he was on the Chief Engineer's own staff. Actually, Talcott might have had every reason for thinking otherwise, because Andrew Jackson was steering Washington into its last and most climactic political battle just as Lee was arriving in the capital. Jackson, the newest version of a Jeffersonian Democrat to occupy the presidency, had fought his way free from sexual scandal involving his Secretary of War, John Eaton, then run roughshod over the Supreme Court in forcing the removal of the five "civilized" Indian tribes from Georgia and Alabama, and finally quashed the attempt of a South Carolina state convention (led by John Calhoun, who had once served as Jackson's own vice president) to nullify federal tariff legislation within the state.[1] Jackson was now about to pick his most monumental fight with Nicholas Biddle, the president of the republic's central bank, the Second Bank of the United States, and Washington was likely to become an uncomfortably warm spot for anyone who did not espouse the Democratic faith according to Andrew Jackson.

Unlike the Custises and the Lees, Jackson had no patience with banks or any other instruments of commerce and development, and in 1832 he declared war on the bank by vetoing the congressional bill that renewed its charter. Biddle and the bank fought back, calling in loans, driving up interest rates, and squeezing merchants and investors until they squealed in pain to

Andrew Jackson. "This worthy President thinks that because he has scalped Indians and imprisoned Judges he is to have his way with the Bank," Biddle retorted. "He is mistaken." But Jackson wasn't. The unbending president told desperate merchants and financiers to "go to Nicholas Biddle. We have no money here, gentlemen. Biddle has all the money." And through 1834, public opinion turned on Biddle, until by 1841 he and his bank (operating with a charter issued by the Commonwealth of Pennsylvania) slid into bankruptcy.[2]

Serving as the assistant to the Chief Engineer gave Lee a box seat to witness these turmoils, because the Chief Engineer's office was part of the War Department headquarters and shared the same block occupied by the Executive Mansion and the Treasury Department. But Lee himself was careful to offer no political opinions of his own. "I never mention politics," he told Jack Mackay, shortly before the move to Washington. Still, anyone with the slightest acquaintance with the Lees understood the revulsion they felt for Andrew Jackson. Carter Lee wished "morally speaking to send the old dotard to the penitentiary for seven years," and after Henry Clay called the Whig Party into formal organizational life in 1834 to oppose Jackson, Carter cheerfully joined in with anti-Jacksonian campaigning of his own.[3]

Robert Lee had more reason for discretion, and more than enough business on hand to occupy his attention as the senior of Charles Gratiot's two chief clerks (the other being George Washington Cullum). "Mr. Lee is so closely confined to his office," complained Mary Custis Lee, "that he is scarcely allowed the leisure of the Sabbath." It would be Lee's task to arrange the payment of junior clerks, deliver messages, requests, and reports to members of Congress, and oversee contracts—work that he soon discovered he had no aptitude for whatsoever. "I abhor the sight of pen and paper," he admitted, "and to put one to the other requires as great a moral effort as for a cat to walk on live coals." (This distaste for paperwork stopped with office matters; Lee's own personal correspondence continued in an uninterrupted flood.) Still worse was the everyday witness he had to bear to the Jacksonian contempt for the Army. "Oh we have been horribly, shamefully treated," he complained to Jack Mackay, "and this treatment has been quietly concurred in, if not connived at, by those who ought to have defended us." Rather than moving up, Lee appeared only to have moved over.[4]

What took some of the edge off Lee's boredom was the personal relationship that matured between him and his chief, Charles Gratiot. Gratiot was born in St. Louis (while it was still ruled by Spain) to a French-speaking fur merchant's family; his father was the first presiding judge appointed for St. Louis once President Jefferson had secured the purchase of the Louisiana Territory in 1803, and the son was one of the first cadets appointed by Jefferson to West Point. "Brilliant and cultivated," Gratiot had already made captain by

1808, vaulted up to major by 1815 on the basis of his service in the War of 1812, planned and supervised the construction of Fort Monroe, and entered on the task of Chief Engineer as a colonel and brevet brigadier general. He was "a man of the first professional achievements," the sort who did not suffer fools gladly, and "accustomed to having his instructions and commands respected and executed"—which was exactly the sort of man Robert Lee aspired to be. Gratiot quickly became for Robert Lee the first of a series of substitute fathers to fill up the vacuum left by Light Horse Harry. It was to Lee that Gratiot delegated the delicate task of providing documents and data to "some of my acquaintances in the Senate & House" whenever "a new Army Bill" came up for debate. Gratiot's patronage, in turn, saved Lee from several other postings that would have been substantially more demeaning or dangerous—the removal of the Creeks, Chickasaw, and Cherokee, and the bloody Second Seminole War in Florida.[5]

Lee's Washington appointment also allowed him to make Arlington his home and the Chain Bridge over the Potomac his commuting route. "I am obliged to spend the most of my time in W[ashington]," he wrote to Carter, where he was "constantly occupied till near four," but then "I . . . most generally go to A[rlington]." He had hoped originally to rent a house in Washington itself, but the Bank War had made the cost of living in the capital exorbitant, and life across the river at Arlington much more sensible. "I tried to get a house when I first came up, but could find none coming within the purviews of a 2nd Lt.," he wrote to Carter. "There is no such thing as selling property in the District." The "Corporations are all Broke. Taxes are enormous, & People have no money." He would use Mrs. Ulrich's boardinghouse at the corner of Fifteenth and G Streets as a temporary overnight in bad weather, and there he could enjoy the camaraderie of Army friends—especially Joe Johnston—who had been posted to Washington. But permanent residence in Washington was out of the question.

Besides, Mary Lee could never have tolerated being so close to Arlington and her parents and her familiar platoon of slaves without actually living there. And no sooner had Robert and Mary made the move to Washington than Mary conceived their second child, who was born on July 12 and named Mary (whether for her mother or grandmother was not clear; Lee would simply call her "Daughter" to keep the expanding number of Marys at Arlington identifiable). Living anywhere but Arlington, and with two small children, was beyond discussion, and it became even more so when Mary Custis Lee developed a severe postpartum infection—the doctors called it "Rheumatic Diathesis"—which kept her bedridden for more than four months.[6]

Not that life at Arlington lacked attractions for Robert Lee. "The Country looks very Sweet now," he wrote to Andrew Talcott in the spring of 1836, "and the hill at A[rlington] Covered with verdure, and perfumed by the blossoms of the trees, the flowers of the Garden, Honey-Suckles, Yellow jasmine, &c. is more to my taste than at any other season of the year." His new daughter was "the brightest flower" of them all, and his mother-in-law, Mary Fitzhugh Custis, became as much a substitute for Ann Lee as Charles Gratiot had for Light Horse Harry. "She was to me all that a mother could be," Lee would reflect in later years, "and I yield to none in admiration for her character, love for her virtues, and veneration for her memory."[7]

Lee found his father-in-law more of a trial. "The Major"—G.W.P.'s honorary militia title, which nettled Lee to hear Custis use, being himself only a lieutenant of engineers—"is busy farming," he wrote to Carter. "Busy" was sardonic: "His *Corn*field is not yet *enclosed or ploughed*—but he is *rushing* on *all he Knows.*" The old man had tried his hand that April at a Sir Walter Scott–ish play about thirteenth-century Scotland that he called *Montgomerie; or, The Orphan of a Wreck.* It ran for four nights. And so, as Lee wrote, "Montgomerie *failed.*" (Indeed it did. "A more vapid, tedious, and uninteresting production never wearied the patience of an audience" was the estimate of one Washington critic.) Meanwhile, one of Custis's six amateurish history paintings, *The Battle of Trenton,* "has been exhibited in the Capitol" and met with more or less the same response. It "attracted some Severe animadversions from the Critics, which he says were levelled at his *Politics*!!!"[8]

Lee increasingly dreaded the prospect of being pulled so deeply into the orbit of Arlington that he might never escape. So it was with a certain measure of relief that after seven months in Washington, he was ordered by Gratiot to accompany Andrew Talcott on a surveying expedition to fix the state boundary between Ohio and Michigan. Both states were originally part of the Northwest Territory, ceded by Great Britain to the United States at the end of the Revolution, and the boundary line between what became Ohio and Michigan was supposed to have been drawn near 41° latitude. But there were varying interpretations of just where this line lay, and there was enough difference in subsequent maps and legislation to create a 468-square-mile strip to which both states angrily laid claim. The governors ordered out militia, survey parties were harassed, and in 1834, Congress finally put a heavy foot down and ordered a commission to settle the matter. Gratiot dispatched Andrew Talcott to perform a preliminary survey later that year and in the spring of 1835 sent Talcott back, with Lee as his assistant, "to resume at once the survey of the boundary line of Ohio."[9]

The expedition was hardly a lark. "Our present abode may have many beauties," Lee wrote from tiny Turtle Island, at the western end of Lake Erie, "but to me they are as yet undiscovered & shall remain nameless, as I cannot find it in my heart to utter aught against a place with so plaintive & Sentimental a name." Everything "savours marvellously of Bilious Fevers, and Seems to be productive of nothing more plentifully than of *Moschitoes* & Snakes." But he certainly did savor the five-month escape the surveying provided from the blandness of bureaucratic Washington and from the smothering embrace of Arlington. And he showed a rare moment of unconcealed irritation when a beseeching letter from Mary caught up with him at Detroit, urging "my immediate return" and proposing that he "endeavor to get excused from the performance of a duty." Lee erupted in a rant of scolding:

> *Do you not think . . . that I rather require to be strengthened & encouraged to the full performance of what I am called on to execute, rather than excited to a dereliction, which even our affection could not palliate, or our judgment excuse? . . . In your calmer moments, I am sure you would not have me . . . plainly shew to the Dept: that I am one of those fair Weather Gentlemen whose duty & pleasure must go together; or that if I should be called on to sacrifice the latter, I cannot be trusted to ~~perform~~ execute the former—Again with what face could I ask to leave a party, the fewness of whose numbers renders the duty now too laborious.*[10]

And so it went on for several more unthinking pages.

It came as a great shock for Lee to discover, once he returned to Arlington in October, that Mary had indeed been continuously and seriously ill since the birth of little Mary in July and, to make the discovery worse, had been moved for recuperation to the Fitzhugh estate at Ravensworth, where his mother had died. Not until the spring of 1836 did Mary Lee's health finally seem to be stabilizing, and even then she came down with mumps. And so once again Lee began morosely contemplating a resignation from the Army, this time driven by the fear that "Mary's health was so bad" he would be forever marooned in his Washington desk job. His only consolations were his promotion, in the fall of 1836, to first lieutenant—a step so minor that it only exacerbated his feeling that he should be looking "to bid an affectionate farewell to my dear Uncle Sam"—and the birth in 1837 of a second son, who was named for his old sponsor, William Henry Fitzhugh (but who would always be known by the family nickname Rooney).[11]

But once again, General Gratiot came to the rescue.

The Mississippi River and its vast spread of tributaries—the Ohio River, the Missouri River, the Red River, the Arkansas River—was the central nerve of North America, and whoever could control it and use it, down to its mouth at New Orleans, would be the real owner of the continent. The triumph of the American Revolution brought the United States to the eastern bank of the Mississippi, but it took years of unpleasant negotiating with Spain and France, and finally the Louisiana Purchase in 1803, to secure uncontested control of the river.

Using it turned out to be even more difficult. Although military and commercial settlements had already begun to spring up along its 2,300 miles—St. Louis, Memphis, Baton Rouge—the river itself was vast and unpredictable, varying from violently channeled rapids where thundering torrents of water made the boldest river navigator shiver to near-turgid swamp where the soil-thickened water eased down lazily to the Gulf of Mexico. Unpredictable spring floods could raise the river's level by an astonishing thirty-eight feet.

At the time of Jefferson's purchase, water traffic on the river amounted to little more than barges, keelboats, rafts, pirogues, and flatboats, and in a good year ten to twenty 100-ton barges called at St. Louis, at the river system's midpoint. Then, in 1811, a steam-powered 450-ton paddle-wheel boat, optimistically named *New Orleans,* puffed its torturous way from Pittsburgh, down the Ohio, to the mouth of the Mississippi. The trip took two and a half months, and the *New Orleans* never pushed faster than eight miles an hour. But it could carry many times the commercial load of the rafts and barges, and unlike the flatboats and keelboats it could turn around and breast the Mississippi's current for a trip upstream, making possible a complete circuit of the entire river highway between New Orleans and Pittsburgh. "What a prospect of commerce is held out to the immense regions of the west, by the use of these boats!" drooled *Niles' Weekly Register.* By 1834, 230 steamboats were nudging up to St. Louis's wharves every year, and the city's population had sprung from fewer than a thousand to more than six thousand.[12]

But the river still posed unforgiving obstacles: underwater snags, swiftly formed sandbars, siltage around levees, rock ledges, and unpredictable currents. St. Louis was particularly troubled by "the extremely difficult navigation" along its waterfront, especially because by 1825 two sandbar islands had surfaced in the Mississippi there, which looked like the end of the world for the St. Louis economy.[13] The first of these, Duncan's Island, appeared on river maps in 1796, lying at the foot of St. Louis's southern limits; the other, known at first as Island No. 3 and then as Bloody Island (for the frequency with which duelists chose it as their murderous venue), was more dangerous because it was growing in size and gradually diverting the main channel of the Mississippi to its eastward, Illinois-facing side. Inevitably, the island's St. Louis–facing side would silt up and transform St. Louis into a useless inland town.[14]

St. Louis turned for relief to the federal government, but a federal government presided over by Andrew Jackson showed little interest in a project with the Whiggish look of an "internal improvement." But the city had a friend in its native son Charles Gratiot, and in 1836, Gratiot commissioned the federal superintendent of western river improvements, Henry Miller Shreve, to survey the St. Louis problem. Shreve was an old river hand and understood that problems in water at one point are usually caused by problems in water a great distance away. So it was with St. Louis. One hundred and seventy miles to the north, the Mississippi narrowed into an eleven-mile-long gorge known as the Des Moines Rapids, bounded by bluffs "one hundred to two hundred and fifty feet above the water," bottomed by rock, and descending twenty-two feet along the distance of the gorge. The problem the Des Moines Rapids posed for St. Louis was the way it funneled the river into a torrent that, when it had finally broadened and slowed on its way down to St. Louis, dropped its waterborne cargo of sand and affluvia on St. Louis's doorstep to form Duncan's and Bloody Islands. Anything that cured St. Louis's problem with the islands would have to begin at the rapids, and the rapids would be a project just on their own.[15]

Shreve was optimistic about dealing with the rapids and the islands; he was not optimistic about its costs, and horrified the mayor of St. Louis and his council by projecting a $50,000 price tag for deepening the rapids and clearing its effluvia downstream. Mayor John Fletcher Darby had only $15,000 to offer; Congress grudgingly appropriated another $15,000, then added $35,000 more. Darby hoped that Gratiot would come out to St. Louis and supervise the work personally, and Gratiot relented sufficiently to spend two weeks in St. Louis, "going up and down the river on both sides, talking with pilots and steamboatmen." But Gratiot had other plans. By the terms of the General Survey Act of 1824, Congress had authorized the use of Army engineers on civil projects, and after assuring Darby he would "send us a competent man," Gratiot went back to Washington and began describing the need for "a skillful engineer on the upper Miss[issippi] and Missouri."

Robert Lee volunteered himself. He had "a desire to see this country," he explained, but even more, he was "heartily sick of the duties of the office and wished to get away." The orders sending him to St. Louis were issued on April 6, 1837, with Gratiot enthusiastically assuring Lee that "there is no such Country as Missouri, and no one equal to the Upper Miss." Little Rooney was born less than two months later, and by July, Lee was on his way to St. Louis, where he arrived on August 5. He went alone and with apparently few qualms about leaving Mary and the children behind. "I shall leave my family in the care of my *eldest Son,*" he joked to Talcott, "who will take them over the Mountains Somewhere this Summer, and his Gdmother along with them."[16]

St. Louis would be Robert Lee's first on-his-own venture as an Army engineer. There were other federal government personnel nearby—the Army's

Jefferson Barracks had been established in 1826 and was home to both the 1st U.S. Infantry and the newly organized 1st U.S. Dragoons—and a federal land office, staffed by civilian appointees. But for the projects in view, Lee would be entirely in charge, with the assistance of only one other engineering officer, a newly graduated West Pointer named Montgomery Meigs (who would find his senior officer, as his peers at West Point found him, the model of the genteel: "noble and commanding" but also aloof, "one with whom nobody ever wished to take a liberty").[17]

The planning began even before his arrival in St. Louis. He traveled first north to Philadelphia, with vouchers in hand for the purchase of surveying instruments, and then west to Pittsburgh, and by an Ohio River steamboat to Louisville. There, Lee consulted with Henry Shreve and signed contracts for two barges for hauling stone and a small steamboat, the *Pearl,* to tug them to St. Louis. Fresh from the center of political warfare in Washington, Lee could not restrain a sniff of condescension, telling John Lloyd (his banker in Alexandria) that St. Louis was the "dirtiest and dreariest city I have *ever* been in." He particularly assured Mary that there was nothing about "St. Louis or its inhabitants" that she would miss. "The Scenery on the Mississippi river . . . is monotonous and uninteresting," and "no inhabitants on either Side excepting a few embryo *Cities,* Save wood cutters and their families."[18]

Lee's mood was not improved by having to wait for the arrival of the boats and the slowness with which orders for ordinary tools were filled in St. Louis. "I have been here ten days and not a single thing ordered, simple as they are, and consisting of leveling Staics, measuring rods, tin cones for signals etc etc are yet done," he complained to Carter. "They are powerful at a promise, but don't mention the fulfillment." When the barges and the *Pearl* ("very pretty in shape and model") finally arrived from Louisville, Lee decided that because the Mississippi was still at an unusually low level—"Still 8 or 10 feet above low water level"—he would head immediately for the Des Moines Rapids and use the low water to facilitate a survey of the rocky riverbed there. He expected that "we shall be fully two weeks in getting up to the heads of the rapids."[19]

Once there, Lee, Meigs, and a crew of a dozen hired civilian workmen settled into a pleasantly rough routine. Even with "bad weather, successive rains, the rapid current and the blind, intricate and crooked channel," he enjoyed being on his own and in sole charge of his little crew. You would laugh, he wrote to Carter, at "the hungry, tired, wet, well-bearded set" his little brother commanded, "these fourteen with bacon and bread in hand picking their location for the night on the puncheon floor of an uninhabited log cabin." His attitude even softened enough to admit to Carter that above St. Louis "the Country changes its character altogether and the river is filled with Islands which gives great beauty and Softness to the Scenery." He wrote to Jack Mackay, "This is a beautiful country, and must one day be a great one." And he extolled "the Soil" to Carter as "magnificent and to the eyes of the uninitiated nothing can be finer. . . . At the upper rapids I dug down 3½ feet into the Soil and could see no difference—An entire mass of Black light mold that you could cultivate with your feet. . . . The accounts they give of their crops are enormous and surpass any belief."[20]

Lee and his party were back in St. Louis by October 8, now devoting their attention to the Bloody Island problem. After six weeks of "making surveys, preparing drawings, and planning the manner of doing the work," Lee concluded that the solution was comparatively simple: build a dam from the northern tip of Bloody Island to the Illinois shore. This would deflect the main channel of the river back between Bloody Island and St. Louis and "throw the great body of the river into the Missouri channel." Adding a dike along the western side of Bloody Island would further push the current midway between the island the city and bring "a greater volume of water to bear upon the bar and head of Duncan's island," and eventually wash that away, too.

On the other hand, if the solution was simple enough, building the solution was not. The dam would have to be 594 yards in length "and its height 5 feet above the low water level," and the "length of the dike as laid down" would need to be "1,000 yards." Even more formidable would be the expense. Henry Shreve, by Lee's reckoning, had hugely underestimated the cost of redirecting the river channel at St. Louis, which Lee pegged with typical precision at a staggering $158,554. Deepening or widening the channel at the Des Moines Rapids would take another heart-stopping $189,629, and if Congress wished to do a thorough job and authorize redirection of the Rock River Rapids, still farther upstream, they should expect to spend another $154,658. Lee finished his report to Gratiot on December 6, and because the oncoming winter would shut down the beginning of any work, he discharged the workers, sent the *Pearl* back to Louisville, and took himself back to Arlington. Considering that he had already spent half of the original appropriation on "S[team] Boat, Stone Boats, Pile Drivers, &c.," it was entirely possible that he might never be back.[21]

But after a great deal of congressional huffing about the "enormous appropriations" for "this business of making harbors," an omnibus harbor improvements bill was approved, and on March 25, 1838, Lee was on his way once again to St. Louis, via Baltimore, Philadelphia, Pittsburgh, and Cincinnati, with start-up funding of $50,000. This was not without increasing pressure from his in-laws to give up the Army altogether and "locate ourselves at Arlington." But Lee begged off as politely, if not quite as candidly, as possible.

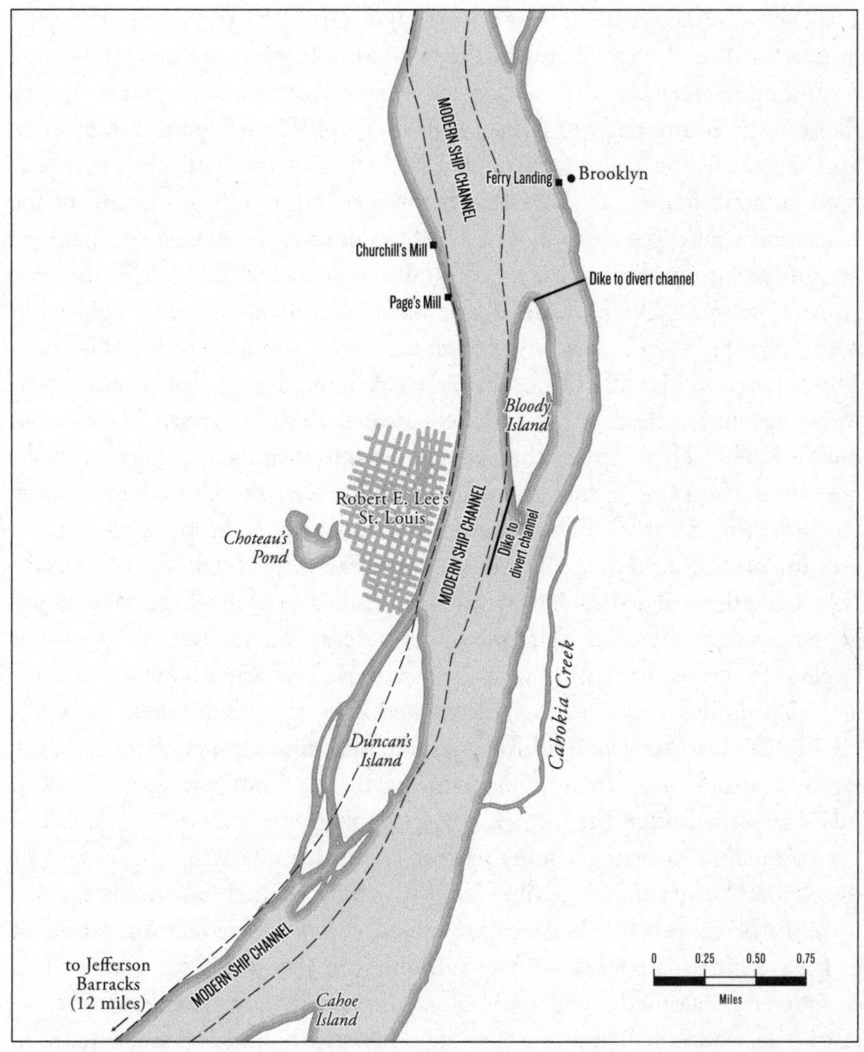

"If our own interest or welfare was alone our concern, I am certain . . . I Should not have Sought to have left Wash[ington]." But, he insisted, it was a question of money. He could not afford to give up his Army salary. So, it was "my duty to make a Sacrifice . . . and advance myself in my profession and be thus enabled to give our dear Children Such an education and standing in life as they could wish." And to make the point of his "sacrifice" for their "education" more clear, he decided to take his two boys, Custis and Rooney, along with their mother, with him on his return to St. Louis. "Daughter" Mary would remain at Arlington with her grandmother.[22]

—

The Lee entourage (with at least one Arlington slave, Kitty, to act as the boys' minder) had reached St. Louis by the beginning of May. Lee had established a working partnership with a German-born architect and engineer, Henry Kayser, who immigrated to Missouri in 1833, and Kayser found rental space for the Lees in the house at Vine and Main Streets that had until that year been home to Missouri's onetime territorial governor William Clark (of the Lewis and Clark Expedition). The Lee boys quickly discovered companions in another family sharing the Clark house, that of Dr. William Beaumont, an Army surgeon who performed landmark experiments in human digestion with Alexis St. Martin, a survivor of an accidental shooting to the abdomen. The doctor and his wife, Deborah, endeared themselves to Robert and Mary, while the junior Beaumonts and Lees turned the old governor's mansion upside down. "They convert themselves even into steamboats, ring their bells, raise their steam (High Pressure) and put off," Lee wrote, amused, to Andrew Talcott's wife, Harriet. "They fire up so frequently, & keep on so heavy a pressure of steam, that I am constantly fearing they will burst their boilers."[23]

Lee's principal assistant this time would be an older officer, an artillery lieutenant named Horace Bliss, along with Henry Kayser. Because the water levels at St. Louis that spring were "11 feet above low-water level and continued high until September," Lee dispatched Bliss and a contingent of workmen to the Des Moines Rapids to prepare blasting a deeper channel in the rapids' bedrock "for S[team] Boats during the stages of low water," and in July, Lee joined them there to supervise the work on the new channel. But the Mississippi then unaccountably rose twelve feet, delaying the cutting of the channel until mid-September, after which he worked frantically to complete the blasting before the weather closed it down. The fall of the river at least gave him the chance to begin driving the two thousand piles he had contracted for along the line of the Bloody Island dam, in double rows, "from 12 to 17 feet into the bed of the river" and filled with sand and stone quarried "for that purpose out of the City quarry at South St. Louis."

On October 16, however, the first ice formed on the river surface, followed by "a charming snow storm," and Lee reluctantly discharged the workforce at both locations. But he had the satisfaction of seeing the Bloody Island dam begin to do its work of washing away the west face of the island and deepening the navigable water at the St. Louis wharves. And he had the even greater satisfaction of receiving word of his promotion, at long last, to captain, courtesy of General Gratiot, on July 7.[24]

But life in St. Louis had not made Lee any less restless and dissatisfied. "The lower class are a swaggering drowsy Set," Lee informed his mother-in-law, "careless of getting work except occasionally for which they get high wages," while "those of the higher order . . . are . . . engrossed in business in which here it Seems their pleasures all consist." He decided now that "all my *Schemes* of happiness" depend on "retiring to some quiet Corner among the hills of Virginia where I can indulge my natural propensities without interruption." But, as he explained, once more, to his mother-in-law, this could not happen so long as he was so mired in poverty. If he had "*$20,000* a year to put everything in Apple-free order . . . then mother we could all live together, enjoy the daily expansion of our little children and witness their improvement in knowledge goodness and beauty." But not until then.

If the "one great Cause for my *not* putting these schemes into execution arises from the want of *Money*," he also had no notion of where an income like that would be found. He confessed to Andrew Talcott that "I should have made a desperate effort last Spring" to leave the Army and that he really was "waiting, looking and hoping for Some good opportunity to bid an affectionate farewell to my Uncle Sam." The problem, as he recognized, was that security did not sit easily beside aggressive career shopping. "I seem to think that Said opportunity is to drop in my lap like a ripe pear," he admitted. Nevertheless, he persisted in believing that it was "remarkable that a man of my Standing should not have been Sought after by all these Companies for internal improvement." It seems never to have occurred to Lee to go looking for those companies and opportunities on his own, or that the coastal engineering projects that had consumed his career thus far were of little interest to the infinitely more lucrative inland projects of railroads, real estate, and bridges.[25]

St. Louis had certainly done nothing to enchant Mary Lee, either. "My dame and little Lees are with me," Robert assured Jack Mackay, and though "it is rough country to bring them to I acknowledge . . . they smooth it to me most marvelously." But in truth, Mary Lee longed for Virginia, and even if "the soil here is like a rich alluvial deposit," Mary "would rather a thousand times over live in Old Virginia or somewhere near it." She struggled to play teacher to Custis but found it "very hard to induce him to sit down to his lessons." And Rooney was "an unsettled brat" who strained her patience whenever "Kitty is washing" and unable to watch him. Her husband merely laughed off their antics: "Boo [the family nickname for Custis] & Rooney with four of their little playmates have been keeping such a laughing, bawling, jumping rumpous and a rioting around me that I hardly know what I have written," Robert scribbled to Carter Lee, "and Mr Rooney is at this moment jerking the cover of my table with one hand and cracking me over the head with the broom with the other."

That might have amused the father, but not the mother. Through the summer Mary was "rather low & weak" and "affected by lassitude," and when she realized in September that she was pregnant again, there was no question but that a return to Arlington must be in order. But, Mary complained, "in this country it is impossible to travel by land with young children & the navigation is all closed," and in fact the Lees would not make it back to Arlington until the middle of May 1839—barely in time for the fourth Lee child to be born on June 18 (and named for Lee's mother, but known simply as Annie).[26]

While marooned for the winter in St. Louis, Lee was shocked to learn of the downfall of Charles Gratiot. The patrician Chief Engineer had crossed the purposes of the Jacksonians one too many times, and he had left himself vulnerable by claiming extra compensation for "work, labour, care, diligence and responsibility by him," and for using Corps of Engineers personnel to perform personal surveys for his own interest. On December 6, 1838, the administration of Jackson's successor, Martin Van Buren, declared that Gratiot had misappropriated $31,056, then filed suit for recovery, and finally dismissed Gratiot both from his post as Chief Engineer and from the Army.

The news fell upon Robert Lee like a rock. "The rumor which has reached me of this distressing event, I could not before credit, nor can I even now realize its truth," Lee wailed in a letter to Gratiot on December 23. The charges against Gratiot were simple proof of the perfidy of the Democrats, who treated the Army's officers "without any regard to their rights as men or Priviledges as Soldiers, a Situation which I cannot think was intended by the Constitution of the laws of the Country." Perhaps not, but it taught Lee a vivid lesson about soldiers who steered too near the shoals of political controversy, a lesson that he would see demonstrated even more dramatically a decade later and that would leave a mark on him for the rest of his life.[27]

At the moment, though, the Gratiot scandal set Lee to wondering whether the St. Louis river work would also fall victim to Democratic schemers. "The funds for the Harbor are all exhausted," he wrote to Horace Bliss, "and as far as I Could judge at this distance of the disposition of Congress towards this class of Works, I am not over sanguine of the favors of the next." Nevertheless, Lee had hardly returned to Arlington in May 1839 before orders sending him back to St. Louis were received. He was on the road west on May 25, even before his newest child was born.[28]

He did not consider the outlook bright. He warned Horace Bliss at the Des Moines Rapids that they would have to "confine the operations to the worst points" and "excavate the Channel to the proposed depth but to limit its width to 90 feet for the present." In St. Louis, winter ice jams had punctured the Bloody Island dam, and Lee was forced to divert his energies to repair work. Still worse, disgruntled property speculators on the Illinois side of the river saw Lee's project as the end of their hopes that Bloody Island would snuff out St. Louis and open up the river's economic prospects to the wharves of Alton and Quincy, and in August they filed suit in Illinois's Second Circuit Court to block any further work by Lee on the river. The injunction was not lifted until October 7, by which time Lee had moved up to the rapids and left Henry Kayser to finish driving a new series of piles. At least, in the limited time he had been able to direct more work, "the head of Duncan's Island is entirely removed, and there is now 15 feet water where it was formerly dry at the same stage of the river."

But money remained the chief difficulty. The war Andrew Jackson waged in 1832 on Nicholas Biddle and the Second Bank of the United States succeeded not only in destroying the bank but in triggering a massive economic recession, the Panic of 1837, the year that Jackson left office. The funds Congress expected to lavish on improvements up and down the Mississippi River fell lower than the river itself. Lee had already been forced in 1838 to go cap in hand to St. Louis's board of aldermen to raise $15,000 from their pockets to keep his "operations for the improvement of the harbor" going. When the winter weather closed down operations yet again, he departed for Arlington, delegating Henry Kayser to "act for me." He "felt so elated when I again found myself within the confines of the Ancient Dominion that I nodded to all the old trees as I passed, chatted with the drivers and stable-boys, Shook hands with the landlords, and in the fullness of my heart . . . wanted to kiss all the pretty girls I met."[29]

Gloom—his own and other people's—followed him. "After being here a day," he wrote to Kayser, "I was sent for to my Sister in Baltimore"—Anne Kinloch Marshall—"who was in the deepest distress" over the death of her younger son, a "beautiful little boy about the age of Custis" whom she had named for Robert. "While playing before the door," the child "was run over by a loaded dray and his head entirely *crushed* by the wheel." They buried the boy at Ravensworth, beside his grandmother, and Robert sent his brother-in-law William Marshall money "to get a locket, ring, or pin to contain the lock of hair of dear little Lee." But Anne Marshall would never be the same afterward, "suffering under the hands of Surgeons & her mind suffering from every thing."

Hardly a week passed before new miseries arrived, this time from France. His scapegrace half brother, Black Horse Harry Lee, had died in Paris in 1837; by 1840, his widow, Anne McCarty Lee, was out of money and enlisted her nephew Richard Stuart to beg support from her dead husband's three half brothers. Robert Lee's response was polite but self-protective. Black Horse Harry's behavior, as much as Light Horse Harry's, had made fiscal insecurity the Lee family's chief inheritance, and he was certainly in no mood to throw life rings to the people who had burned the final bridge the Lees had to Stratford. "You are probably Aware that my income exceeds but little that of a Captn in the Army," he explained to Stuart, while "that of my brother Smiths is about the Same, and my brother Carters depends so much on his Success in business that it would be hard to say what Sum he could certainly calculate on." The best he could suggest was that he, Smith, and Carter might be able to send her $100 a year for the next few years. He wanted Stuart to understand that "I have been led by a sincere desire to promote as far as is in my power the happiness of one that is Still dear to me." But he was angrier when he wrote to Carter. "It seems vain to rely on her Support in Paris upon you, Smith and myself," and he frankly suggested that perhaps Stuart should bring her back from France and care for her himself. There would, however, be no such need. Anne McCarty Lee would die in France in August 1840.[30]

By the time Lee set out for his fourth posting to St. Louis, it was clear from the political situation that he would have nothing to do this time except tend to minor repairs and liquidate the boats, equipment, and other government property he had acquired over the previous three years. "I wish I could give you some idea of future prospects," he wrote to Horace Bliss, but "every thing is uncertain and it is useless to Speculate in the dark." He was relieved to discover "that Duncans Ild. has been worn away Some." But he warned Henry Kayser to "reduce the expenses as low as possible," because it was not likely Congress would renew even the minimal funding that had been dribbling their way. "Cong: has not touched on the App[ropriations] yet," and he did not expect in the end that "they will give anything for the Civil works. It is my opinion that if the Citizens of St Louis think that by Carrying out the present plan the Harbor Can be permanently improved they had better make arrangements to execute it themselves."

The flatboats, keelboats, and cranes were to be sold, and Deborah Beaumont was advised that because Lee's family would not be accompanying him, "if any furniture is in her way or at all troublesome, just to dispatch to the Auctioneer." Otherwise, there was little for Lee to do in his official capacity but write out his final summary of the river work. "The few works remaining under this Dept," he complained to Jack Mackay, "are for the present *dished.*" "No progress," he reported in October, "has been made . . . in improving the navigation of the rapids." However, he insisted that the dam "from the foot of Bloody Island confines the water to the Missouri shore and directs the current against the head of Duncan's Island," just as he had originally designed, leaving at least "the harbor" of St. Louis "in a good condition."[31]

One thing that did occupy Lee's attention was investment. Lee never ceased to believe that nothing but the Army stood between him and poverty, even if it meant leaving his sister-in-law to look out for herself. Yet, at the same moment, his interest in investing the vague amounts he had inherited through his mother was oddly vivid. He was scrupulous in making sure interest and dividends from the Bank of Virginia's branches in Winchester and Norfolk were paid; he contested bills submitted by a doctor for treating "Mrs. Lee & children"; and he appointed one of the Biddle family to manage investments in the Philadelphia, Wilmington & Baltimore Railroad and a Richmond lawyer to invest $1,327.85 in the stock of the James River & Kanawha Canal Company. He even played with the idea of "wishing to make a grand Speculation" in Missouri real estate, both in St. Louis town lots and in "some fine land in Rock Island County" above the Des Moines Rapids, and he wished his Alexandria banker, John Lloyd, could "transport Some of your houses in Alexa to this place," where "they would all rent from $800 to $1000 per year."

As the misery of the Panic of 1837 wore off, Missourians were clamoring to borrow, and "the best paper in this City" was going for usurious rates "as high as 7 per cent per month." With "quantities of goods . . . daily arriving and departing," merchants, Lee remarked hungrily, could clear as much as "$80,000 in a year." And Henry Kayser, whom Lee had put in charge of the sale of the river project property, gradually became Lee's deputy for personal investments in and around St. Louis. "Suppose you see if you can . . . negotiate a draft . . . payable in 2 to 4 months," he proposed to Kayser, "I should prefer the Am[erican] Fur Comp." Kayser eventually guided him into buying "bonds of the City of St. Louis," and for years after leaving St. Louis, Lee continued to use Kayser as his financial agent for investing "some $3000 that I do not know what to do with" in Missouri state bonds.[32]

And yet Lee could not nerve himself to take any step that would free him from the Army and turn him into a high-rolling entrepreneur. The lure of speculation had destroyed his father, and done nothing but uselessly burn up years of his brother's life, and he could not bring himself to follow in what might only turn out to be the same path to genuine poverty. "The more comfortably I am fixed in the Army," he wrote to Andrew Talcott's mother-in-law, "the less likely I Shall be to leave it." Whatever disappointments army life had dealt him as he approached his fifteenth year in uniform, the world outside that uniform seemed more and more strange, and the only familiarity he enjoyed beyond his family existed within the circle of the Army. "The friendship & kind consideration of my brother officers I have always enjoyed & it is this that has so far retained me in the service," he would later claim to Carter Lee. And with four children to look after, the knowledge that his commission was as close to a sinecure as American life offered was becoming more and more an issue. "The little Lees are increasing rapidly," he informed another relative, Hill Carter, and "have large mouths & backs that require to be filled & covered."[33]

—

Lee's forebodings about life outside the Army were cushioned by the man who succeeded Charles Gratiot as the new Chief Engineer of the Army, Joseph Gilbert Totten. Born in Connecticut in 1788, Totten bore some unusual similarities to Lee. Totten's mother died when he was three, and his father, Peter Totten, left the boy in the care of an uncle, Jared Mansfield, while the elder Totten went off to the West Indies. Mansfield was one of the first appointments to the faculty of West Point in 1802, and young Totten went with Mansfield as one of the first cadets, "a flaxen-headed boy of fourteen years of age." Totten was commissioned into the Corps of Engineers, served in the War of 1812, and played a major role in designing and building the fortifications of the Third System until, in December 1838, he was appointed to succeed the disgraced Gratiot. Unlike Lee (and Gratiot), however, Totten was entirely the scientific professional, publishing experimental papers "on common mortars, hydraulic mortars, and concretes" and "various materials used in the construction of casemate embrasures" and devoting "his spare hours to Natural History, paying much attention to the Mollusca of the Northern coast of the United States."

Lee made his first acquaintance with Totten during the leave he enjoyed after his third posting to St. Louis, during the winter of 1839–40, when Lee was once more assigned to temporary duty in the Chief Engineer's office. He took an immediate liking to Totten, "a first rate officer as well as man," and Totten seems to have been sufficiently impressed with Lee that he suggested sending Lee to West Point as an instructor rather than back to St. Louis. Lee demurred. He had no gift for "imparting . . . knowledge, and in making a Subject agreeable to those who learn." But when Lee returned from St. Louis for the last time in mid-October 1840, Totten had a New York assignment ready for him anyway—not to the faculty at West Point, but as post engineer at Fort Hamilton, guarding the narrows that shielded what had, by 1840, become the most populous city of the Republic.[34]

Fort Hamilton began life as a battery of artillery, thrown up hastily during the Revolution on the western tip of Long Island to close off access to the narrows at the mouth of New York's harbor. Between 1825 and 1831, a Third System fortification, named for Alexander Hamilton, was constructed there. Supporting Fort Hamilton and forming the middle wedge of the harbor defenses was a smaller fortification on an artificial island in the narrows, Fort Lafayette, and a network of earthen embrasures on the eastern shore of Staten Island known as Battery Hudson and Battery Morton.

Construction, however, was one thing, active use another: for the next ten years, Fort Hamilton was garrisoned only off and on by a single company of the 4th Artillery, and for a brief while in 1838 the senior officer on-site was an assistant surgeon. Totten, however, was determined to make Fort Hamilton and its neighbors fully operational. He wanted Battery Hudson expanded to accommodate an additional thirteen guns (to make up a full complement of fifty artillery pieces) and Battery Morton expanded by ten guns, with another twenty-seven designated for Fort Hamilton. Lee's assignment would be to rebuild washed-out walls and casemates, construct furnaces for heating solid shot (to set wooden warships afire), and expand the capacity of the forts for their new armament.[35]

Lee arrived at Fort Hamilton in April 1841 after a brief tour in the Carolinas to report on the condition of fortifications on the southern Atlantic coast. He discovered at once that no one possessed a set of plans for the trapezoid-shaped fort and the two Staten Island batteries, and so everything had to be itemized and evaluated, right down to the "screw holes in [the] Barbette gun tracks" at Fort Lafayette. Once he had taken the full measure of the forts' condition, he had to convert himself (as he had at Cockspur Island and Fort Monroe) into a general contractor for their repair, which included everything from hiring workmen to ordering and shipping materials to acting as on-site supervisor. He would also compose polite letters of complaint to the senior artillery officer at Fort Hamilton, brusquely noticing that "for more than a week past . . . some one is in the habit of turning into the Fort field every day & night a white cow belonging to the garrison" and asking that the cow be gotten out of the way of the working parties.

Cows notwithstanding, in July 1842, Lee was able to report to Totten that the reconditioning of Battery Hudson "was finished with the exception of laying six traverses, the stone for which is daily expected," that "the barbette wall" at Fort Lafayette "has been raised to the required height" and was ready for its artillery to "be mounted at any time," and that the interior of Fort Hamilton had been "replaced by a brick pavement laid in cement & mortar" and "is ready for its guns." Then, a year later, a hurricane struck New York, tearing off the northwest parapet of Fort Hamilton "along one-half its length" and causing "extensive slides . . . at many points"—all of which Lee would have to rebuild. By 1845, Lee had reconstructed the southeast wall, raised new officers' quarters, upgraded the enlisted men's quarters in the fort's casemates "as regards health, comfort, and accommodation," and was planning to rebuild the east wall and "construct a permanent wharf."[36]

The work was simultaneously consuming and dull. On the other hand, it excused him from other duties he dreaded more. In 1842 Bernard Moore Carter, the unhappy husband of Robert's other half sibling from Light Horse Harry's first marriage, Lucy Grymes, died. In his will, Bernard Carter quixotically named Robert and Carter Lee as his executors. But Robert wanted no more to do with this new reminder of the darker-horse side of the Lee clan than he had two years before with Black Horse Harry's widow, and he was happy to plead that "my whole time is engrossed by my duties" in order to beg out of the executorship. (He was almost relieved to make the same excuse for his brother: "I have not seen my brother Carter for more than a year," and the last Robert had heard, Carter was "in the lower part of VA," still chasing the chimera of the Hardy County lands.)[37]

One major consolation for Lee was the arrival of Mary Lee and the children in the summer of 1841. He went out of his way to convince her that Fort Hamilton "is healthy" and "open to the sea," the country on the western end of Long Island is "fertile and well-cultivated & there are quantities of handsome Country seats in all directions," as if to assure her that it would all remind her of Arlington. A house he had an eye to rent was, he admitted, "out of repair," but "a nice Yankee wife would soon have it in order," and Mary would certainly do no worse than that. Beyond that, "you can get every thing you desire in N. York." She should not, he hinted, expect to bring slaves from Arlington. "I receive poor encouragement about Servants & every one Seems to attend to their own matters." This might have been a realistic assessment of life in a free state, but it was not the best of news for Mary, who had just given birth at the end of February to their fifth child, Eleanor Agnes Lee. Even Robert ruefully admitted that this baby's "approach, however long foreseen, I could have dispensed with for a year or two more." Nevertheless, by the summer, the full entourage of Lees had arrived at Fort Hamilton. Robert loosened his purse strings enough to buy "a very nice little carriage" in which to trot around so that the family could "occasionally ride to N. York on a visiting or shopping expedition" (where Robert was convinced "I shall be ruined" by Mary's penchant for "bargains & remnants").[38]

The metropolis afforded all the diversions St. Louis lacked. There were elaborate garrison reviews to be staged, with one visitor, Elizabeth Oakes Smith, marveling at the "wonderful display of movements on the part of horse and rider" and flattered by Lee, "a most elegant man, quite the ideal of a military hero . . . who received me with something more than military courtesy . . . bending his clear handsome eye upon me." In 1844, President John Tyler visited New York to inspect the facilities at the Brooklyn Navy Yard, and all the officers from Fort Hamilton turned out to greet him (good Whig to the core, Mary thought "the procession a rather poor one & there seemed to prevail among the crowd but little enthusiasm"). Tyler also took the opportunity to marry Julia Gardiner, "accomplished, beautiful, interesting, an heiress," at the Church of the Ascension. That December, Gaetano Donizetti's *Lucrezia Borgia* had its U.S. debut at the American Theatre, where the Lees saw Rosina Pico and Eufrasia Borghese in the lead roles.

No one seemed to enjoy Fort Hamilton more than the Lee children, who like other small children at Army installations easily became the center of attention for officers and enlisted men alike. That did not prevent two near disasters. Little Annie, who had been born with a raspberry-colored facial birthmark (which Lee hoped she could "veil if not eradicate" by cultivating "the purity of and brightness of her mind"), ran the point of a pair of scissors into an eye and partially blinded herself. Eight-year-old Rooney, "a large hearty fellow that requires a tight rein," escaped the rein long enough in November 1845 to make the acquaintance of a crank-powered straw cutter in the post stable that "took off the end of the fore and middle fingers of the left hand." The post surgeon tried to reattach the severed parts, but with no success. Lee was distraught for fear that Rooney would "lose his fingers" entirely "and be maimed for life." The boy survived with little more than minor disfigurement, but Lee wailed in distress "how two have been punished for their inattention & disobedience. One with the loss of an eye, another with the amputation of two fingers."[39]

Lee also found new sources of controversy to dread. The Episcopalianism of the Diocese of Virginia remained the bastion of evangelical Episcopalianism's peculiar balance of fervent Protestantism and "low church" simplicity in liturgy, vestments, and church architecture, especially during the tenure of William Meade as diocesan bishop. By the time Robert Lee arrived in New York, this evangelicalism had become a power to be reckoned with throughout the Episcopal Church, from New England (where two talented evangelical bishops, Alexander Viets Griswold and Manton Eastburn, held sway) to Ohio, when Bishop Philander Chase established an evangelical outpost at Kenyon College, and it was certainly the religious marker of Lee's wife and in-laws. But by the 1840s, there was also a powerful countermovement at work in the Episcopal Church, aimed at rolling back the evangelical tide. Sometimes known as the Oxford Movement from its English origins with John Henry Newman and Edward Bouverie Pusey, the movement adored ritual and proclaimed a Catholic rather than a Protestant theology.[40]

When the Lees took up full-time life at Fort Hamilton, the family became attenders at the nearby St. John's Church, one of seven Episcopal parishes in Brooklyn and almost entirely populated by "the garrisons of Forts Hamilton and Lafayette." Robert, even though he had never undergone the Episcopal rite of confirmation (as he should have in his teens) under the hands of Bishop Meade, was duly made a member of the parish's ruling vestry. However, the bishop of the Episcopal Diocese of New York, Benjamin Onderdonk, was notoriously sympathetic to the Oxford Movement, and soon enough Lee was dogged at St. John's by "efforts . . . to draw him out" on ritualism, on Oxford, and on Newman and Pusey, "but without success, for he always contrived in some pleasant way to avoid any expression of opinion." Henry Hunt, a junior artillery lieutenant at Fort Hamilton and an Episcopalian himself, had the good sense not to tempt Lee for a response—and therefore got one. "I am glad to see that you keep aloof from the dispute that is disturbing our little parish," Lee told Hunt. Still, he added, "I must give you some advice about it, in order that we may understand each other." "*Beware,*" he said, with deadpan seriousness, "*of Pussyism!*" Pussy? A kitty? Or was it "Pusey"? "*Pussyism* is always bad and may lead to unchristian feeling," Lee announced with poker-faced humor, "therefore beware of *Pussyism!*" The whole performance was intentionally "ludicrous," and Lee kept the question at bay thereafter by shaking his head gravely every time he encountered Hunt: "Keep clear of this *Pussyism!*"[41]

Money anxieties created more clouds in Lee's mind than religious ones, although in the usual contradictory way. Henry Kayser continued to manage his Missouri investments, regularly reporting on the "safe & profitable" dividends and interest he and his brother Alexander collected for Lee, and his Army pay as a captain now was pegged at $1,817. But Robert also convinced himself—and tried to convince others—that "it was as much as I could do to make both ends meet this year & I am anxiously looking for the dividend of the VA Bank to enable me [to] Square off all scores." Carter made a last bid to persuade Robert to put money into developing their western Virginia land; Robert would only reply that there was nothing he could do. "My pay seems to decrease as my children increase," he moaned. As increase they did: a third son, Robert E. Lee Jr., was born in October 1843, and a seventh child, named for his long-vanished sister, Mildred, debuted in February 1845 (and earned the endearing nickname Precious Life).

Once again, Lee debated leaving the Army. Totten tried to appease his restlessness by appointing him to the examining board for West Point in 1844, then made him a member of the Board of Engineers for Atlantic Coast Defense and detailed him for work in Washington during the winter months so that Mary could retreat each Christmas to Arlington. But Washington desk work gave him little satisfaction. Just as it had under Charles Gratiot, the Corps of Engineers spent its time lobbying, cajoling, and jockeying with politicians, trading suggestions for infrastructure projects in their districts for votes on military appropriations. "Could you see my list of correspondence upon Whigs, Democrats, Congressmen and Officers," he wrote to Jack Mackay, "you would not wonder at my horror at the sight of pen, ink, and paper, and with what perfect disgust, I pick up my hat between 4 and 5 p.m. with the firm determination of doing nothing till next morning, except to go home, eat my dinner, play with the little Lees, & rest."

None of Totten's gestures reached the heart of Lee's insecurities. Finally, in the summer of 1845, he frankly asked Totten for a transfer out of the Corps of Engineers. "In case of an increase of the Mil: establishment at the next Sess of Cong: I would desire a transfer to the new forces with promotion," he wrote, in a strange mix of despair and overconfidence about an increase in rank. Especially "in the event of war with any foreign government I should desire to be brought into active Service in the field with as high a rank in the regular army as I could obtain & if that Could not be accomplished without leaving the Corps of Engineers I should then desire a transfer to Some other branch of the Service, & would prefer the artillery."[42]

Which, on the surface of things, seemed absurd. The United States had not gone to any sort of war with anyone but hapless tribes of Indians—the Sauk and Fox, the Seminole—in more than thirty years. And then, unpredictably, Lee got his wish. War—with Mexico.

CHAPTER FIVE

Ruling the Aztec Sky

"What means this war?" demanded the *New-York Tribune* on May 13, 1846, the day President James Knox Polk signed the bill he had asked Congress to provide two days before, an "Act providing for the prosecution of the existing war between the United States and the Republic of Mexico." The answer given by the *Tribune* was not amusing: "It means that, so far as our Government can effect, the laws of Heaven are suspended and those of Hell established in their stead." It means

> *that we are to exhaust our Treasury, multiply Taxes, incur Public Debts, and mortgage the sweat and blood of honest labor for untold years to come. It means security, quiet and gladness are to be driven from Earth and Ocean, and their places usurped by Butchery, Rape, devastation and Horror . . . and the world recede toward the midnight of Barbarism.*[1]

No sign of any such impending cataclysm surfaced in any of Lee's correspondence, which was one mark of how determined he was to avert his eyes from the unpleasantness of politics. Nevertheless, cataclysm was in the air, and actually had been for longer than Lee had been in the Army. The immediate issue was the expansion of the United States westward across the North American continent to the Pacific, which meant collision with the northern American lands of the Republic of Mexico. But the underlying matter was slavery, and whether slavery would be allowed to accompany that expansion and claim a place in the American future. Few of the framers of the Constitution in 1787 had expected slavery to survive for more than a few decades. "As population increases poor laborers will be so plenty as to render slaves useless," reasoned Connecticut's Oliver Ellsworth. Slavery was ebbing away in the United States, so that "slavery in time will not be a speck in our Country."[2]

What the framers at the Constitutional Convention had not anticipated were two developments which tore away that easy assumption. The first was President Jefferson's unexpected acquisition of the vast Louisiana Territory, which diverted the energies of a coastal republic into the development of the western American landmass. The second was the Industrial Revolution, whose technological innovations—from the cotton gin to power looms—made the American South's slave-grown cotton the most desirable single commodity in the Western world. Both of these erupted together in February 1819, when Missouri became the first piece of the Louisiana Purchase to petition Congress for admission to the Union as a state. New York's congressman James Tallmadge offered an amendment that would ban any future importation of slaves there and required a plan for the gradual phaseout of whatever slavery presently existed. Southern slaveholders responded with threats of secession if Tallmadge's addendum was adopted. Dismayed at the aggressiveness of slavery's rebound, Northerners just as vehemently replied that "if a dissolution of the union must take place, let it be so!" It took nearly a year, a new Congress, and a compromise crafted by Henry Clay to dissolve the hardened oppositions, until in 1821 Missouri was admitted as a slave state, but with the express proviso that no further slave states above the line of Missouri's southern border (along the latitude of 36°30') would be permitted in the Louisiana Purchase.[3]

On a map, that left only a remarkably small portion of the Louisiana lands open to slave development and even less room for dissension. But the map was a deceiver. In the North, resentment at slaveholding's aggressiveness now began to harden, and opposition to slavery's extension began to generate, at the fringe, demands for its complete and immediate abolition. The map also had no way of predicting how slavery might try to outflank the 36°30' compromise. From the 1820s through the 1830s, American immigrants poured into the Mexican province of Texas, many of them with slaves in tow. When, in the mid-1830s, the Mexican government grew alarmed at the rising tide of *norteamericanos* in Texas, the Anglo-Texans rose in revolt and created their own independent Republic of Texas—with slavery legalized. The Texans' prevailing desire was to attach themselves to the United States. But the U.S. economy sank under the Panic of 1837, and there was little political will in Washington to assume Texas's debts from its brief revolution against Mexico, especially when the federal government passed for the first time into the hands of the Whig Party and a Whig president, William Henry Harrison.

Nor was the Mexican government willing to turn an entirely blind eye to Texas independence, and Mexico made it clear that any gesture by the United States to annex Texas would be treated as a provocation for war.

Unhappily, President Harrison (who Democrats predicted "will be an abolitionist of the first water," which he was not) died of pneumonia only a month after taking office in 1841 and was succeeded by a vice president, John Tyler, a Virginia Democrat who had been selected as Harrison's running mate in a quixotic attempt to demonstrate the bipartisan goodwill of Whig politics. Tyler threw aside any restraint on the idea of annexing Texas, and although he managed to achieve the annexation only over ferocious Whig opposition, and only in the final days of his administration, Tyler set the stage for his Democratic successor in the presidency, James K. Polk, to incorporate Texas into the United States in July 1845. The Mexican government denounced the annexation as a "monstrous novelty," made more monstrous by a messy disagreement over whether Texas's southern boundary was the Nueces River (as claimed by Mexico) or farther south at the Rio Grande. Such novelties bothered James K. Polk not at all. As a slaveholder and protégé of Andrew Jackson's, he was committed to a dream of slave expansion, and if Mexico stood in the path of that expansion, so much the worse for Mexico. Polk stridently claimed the Rio Grande as the Texas boundary and sent an "Army of Observation" to Texas under a weather-beaten Louisiana slaveholder, Zachary Taylor, to enforce the Rio Grande boundary. "Our force is altogether too small for the accomplishment of its errand," one of Taylor's officers complained. But it was large enough to act as bait for a Mexican attack so that President Polk would "have a pretext" for announcing a state of war. Polk got exactly that on April 25, 1846, when Mexican troops ambushed one of Taylor's patrols at Rancho de Carricitos and proceeded to engage in bloody skirmishes at Palo Alto and Resaca de la Palma. On May 11, Polk sent a message to Congress, asking for troops and authority "to meet a threatened invasion of Texas by Mexican forces."[4]

Polk got the war he wanted, but not the general enthusiasm for it he might have expected. "There is no aspect of right and wrong of which we can claim the benefit in the controversy," raged the former president John Quincy Adams. Polk had nothing else in view in provoking a war with Mexico than "to dismember Mexico, and to annex to the United States . . . several of her adjoining Provinces on this side [of] the Continent and the Californias on the other side," and all for the purpose of planting slavery there, outside the restrictions of the Missouri Compromise. When Polk submitted a request to Congress on August 8, 1846, for $2 million to pay the war's bills, the Pennsylvania congressman David Wilmot added an amendment—"Provided, That, as an express and fundamental condition to the acquisition of any territory from the Republic of Mexico by the United States . . . neither slavery nor involuntary servitude shall ever exist in any part of said territory"—which in turn moved the Mississippi senator Jefferson Davis to promise that Wilmot's amendment "is . . . a matter that will agitate the country from one end of it to the other."[5]

War with Mexico presented a more self-interested perspective to the gaze of the military professionals of the Army, and especially to Robert E. Lee. "The smiling face of peace has been changed for the grim visage of war," Lee wrote just weeks after the first clash along the Rio Grande. "There is nothing but preparation for battle: The sharpening of Swords, the grinding of bayonets & equipping for the field, occupy all thoughts & hands." But not Lee's. Lee had, after all, never commanded troops in action, or even near action. What's more, he was in the wrong place at Fort Hamilton, because fighting along the Rio Grande was already in motion, and he was uneasy that the entire affair might be over before he could have a hand in it. "I had expected to have joined the army in Mexico," Lee wrote unhappily from Fort Hamilton in July, "but the battles . . . on the Rio Grande so tipped the Scales in our favour in that quarter" that he was instead assigned "to make ready this place & New York for the reception of the English," in case Great Britain showed any inclination to intervene.[6]

Finally, on August 19, 1846, the long-coveted orders to join the army in Mexico arrived. He wrote a will, made dispositions with his brokers to redirect his investment income to Mary (who would move with the children back to Arlington), and settled his professional accounts at Fort Hamilton with the Army's paymaster general. Even then, however, Lee's prospects seemed clouded with apprehension. "I have broke up my house at Ft H[amilton] & sold out, horses & all, but as I could give but one days notice of the sale, every thing went very low," he complained to Carter Lee. "After leaving Mary enough to put the two boys to school, for their clothes etc I fear I have not enough to take me & my servant to the Army; & purchase my horses." Furthermore, his orders were not to join the main American force under Zachary Taylor, which was already thrusting deep into northern Mexico, but a "Centre Division of the Army, under Genl [John E.] Wool," which was still assembling at San Antonio. "I am the last man ordered, every one is ahead of me & I am hurrying on to endeavour to reach San Antonio," Lee wrote. "I have but little hope of accomplishing anything, or having anything to accomplish."[7]

Lee played catch-up with Wool as best he could, taking ship to New Orleans, and from there embarking for Port Lavaca, on the Texas coast, where Wool himself had landed on August 2. Wool's expedition grew to be a mixed bag of "one battery of field artillery of six guns, to which were added two small pieces captured from the Mexicans by the Texans, and manned with volunteers; one squadron of the 1st and one squadron of the 2nd Dragoons; one regiment of Arkansas horse; three companies of the 6th U.S. infantry, with which was incorporated one independent company of Kentucky foot and two regiments of Illinois infantry." Wool had successfully "organized this almost chaotic mass into an efficient and well-drilled army" at San Antonio, but almost nothing in the way of maps was available, making the Texas countryside "but little understood," and Wool's handful of engineer officers "were almost literally compelled to grope our way, and, like a ship at sea, to determine our positions by astronomical observations."

Lee did not reach Wool's 2,800-man column until September 21. But when he did, he riveted everyone's attention by bringing with him one of his father-in-law's Washington relics—George Washington's portable mess chest. "Revolutionary knives & forks were passed around the table with much veneration," Lee wrote to his wife, "& excited universal attention." Two days after Lee's arrival, Wool's column marched out of San Antonio, headed for the Rio Grande. It was an easy and careful march, across "country . . . high and broken, and the road for more than a mile quite precipitous, when it suddenly changes to a beautiful open and rolling prairie, covered with a luxuriant growth of sweet and nutritious grasses." Reconnaissance and "the astronomical observations" necessary for determining positions were performed by the four engineers already attached to Wool's staff. Lee's responsibilities were confined mostly to selecting campsites, bridge building, and road improvement—especially roads, because "the utility and importance of possessing good roads is . . . an object worthy the attention of the Engineers of all countries"—and supervising a company of thirty pioneers.[8]

They crossed the contested Nueces River on October 3 and the Rio Grande on October 12 on a pontoon bridge "transported to this place in wagons." By Christmas, Wool—and Lee—had managed to penetrate as far south into Mexico as Saltillo without having encountered more than a rumor of the Mexican army under the mercurial adventurer Antonio López de Santa Anna. "We have met with no resistance yet," Lee wrote to Mary from the Rio Grande. Although there was still more "whetting of knives, grinding of swords, and sharpening of bayonets ever since we reached the river . . . the Mexicans who were guarding the passage retired on our approach."[9]

It was just as well, because the contingent of mounted Texas volunteers who attached themselves to Wool's column became notorious for "straggling along, day after day, some reaching camp long after nightfall, inviting attack by their looseness of array, and scorning the commands of superior officers." But Wool succeeded in reaching Saltillo without the loss of a single man on the march, and with that same eye to caution he soon selected Lee to serve as his staff engineer, and Lee's name began to appear more and more in connection with Wool's care in reconnoitering. By January, Wool had made him his acting inspector general.[10]

That might have been all that Lee got out of the war but for two movements quite beyond his control. The first was President Polk's political jealousy of General Zachary Taylor, whose modest victories were already "giving great uneasiness to the administration" and leading to discussions about a presidential bid by the old planter-general. "These officers are all Whigs and violent partisans," Polk spluttered, and in November 1846 he turned to the Army's general in chief, Winfield Scott (known less obligingly as Old Fuss and Feathers), and authorized Scott to execute a plan Scott had presented on October 27 to stage an amphibious landing at Veracruz and march an army inland to Mexico City along the old route taken three centuries before by Hernando Cortés and thus "conquer a peace." Scott was actually even more partisan a Whig than Taylor, and just as mistrusted by Polk for his "inordinate vanity." But for the moment, Polk wanted anyone who was not Taylor to win the war, and Scott was the likeliest choice. To accomplish that, however, Scott estimated he would need 20,000 regulars, a need Polk would try to meet by stripping away large elements of Zachary Taylor's army. Along with them would come Robert E. Lee.[11]

There is nothing to suggest that Lee and Winfield Scott had been closely acquainted before the war, apart from having served together on West Point's Board of Visitors in 1844. But almost from the day of his arrival in mid-January at the Scott expedition's rendezvous on the Brazos River, Lee was tagged to join Scott's personal staff, along with his boss and mentor, Joseph Totten, the acting inspector general Ethan Allen Hitchcock, and Scott's son-in-law (and military secretary) Captain Henry L. Scott. Lee still feared that his appetite for improvement and promotion would go unsatisfied. "I have done no good," he lamented in a letter to his mother-in-law. "Still here I must remain ready to perform what little service I can & hope for the best."

But gradually his spirits began to rise. Scott was planning the most unusual method of attacking Veracruz—an unprecedented joint Army-Navy operation to land his infantry under the noses of the Mexican garrison and its towering harbor fortification, the Castle of San Juan de Ulloa—and when his forces began their landings in custom-built surfboats on March 9, 1847, "we met with no opposition, not a single gun being fired," and "before ten o'clock that night upward of ten thousand men, with stores and provisions for several days, were safely deposited on the beach."[12]

The foremost surf boat nears the land;
It grounds. Out dash the dauntless band. . . .
Now raise the starry banner high;
Rally, close up, crowd around and stand by;
Our eagle rules the Aztec sky.[13]

Lee's first tasks, however, remained ordinary: reconnoiter the perimeter of the city's defenses ("near enough to see their guns & batteries quite distinctly"), select sites for setting up artillery to bombard the city, and supervise their construction "in the chapparal . . . not far from the city walls." After a demand for the city's surrender was presented and refused, Scott opened a sustained bombardment on March 22, borrowing six heavy naval guns for a land battery specially designed by Lee to crown the explosive pounding of the city. Lee was pleasantly surprised to encounter his naval brother, Sidney Smith Lee, working the guns and, while he "felt fearful of your being shot down," was relaxed enough around his brother to ask if "you through any of your comrades" could "get me a bottle or two of claret and one of brandy and four colored shirts." After three days, Lee reported, "the Castle Battery has been silenced," and later that afternoon the Mexican garrison asked for terms. Scott appointed Lee one of the commissioners "to arrange terms of surrender" and then to make "a perfect draft" of the castle "for the information of our own Government."[14]

Scott was determined from the first to make an example of decent treatment of the Mexicans, and in an effort to assure them that the conquest of Veracruz would not be seen as a Protestant triumph over Catholicism, he ostentatiously attended Mass in one of the city's undamaged churches, with his staff in tow. Scott sat on the only bench in the church, along with Lee and other staffers, including the artillery lieutenant, Henry Hunt, from Fort Hamilton. To the mystification of Scott and the others, a variety of lit candles were thrust into their hands, and it became apparent that Scott and his officers were expected to join the "array of priests in gorgeous vestments" in "a Church procession." Hunt was perplexed and turned to Lee, whose "dignified, quiet appearance looked as if the carrying of candles in religious processions was an ordinary thing with him." Helplessly, Hunt "touched Captain Lee's elbow," and as they passed the altar, Hunt whispered, "What is it?" Lee "gave me a rebuking look," but then wryly whispered back, "I really hope there is no *Pussyism* in all this." His face remained straight, but Hunt could see that "the corners of his eyes and mouth were twitching in the struggle to preserve his gravity."[15]

Scott was not minded to extend his stay in Veracruz; he was determined to get his forces moving into the interior uplands along the old National Road into the Mexican interior before warmer weather brought yellow fever along the coast. Organizing his infantry into three divisions—two of Regulars under David Twiggs and William J. Worth, and a division of volunteers under Robert Patterson—Scott set off on April 12 toward Xalapa and the Sierra Madre Oriental. As the ground rose, so did Scott's reliance on Lee, especially because Scott had sent Chief Engineer Totten with the official dispatches announcing the capture of Veracruz back to Washington on board the steam frigate USS *Princeton.*

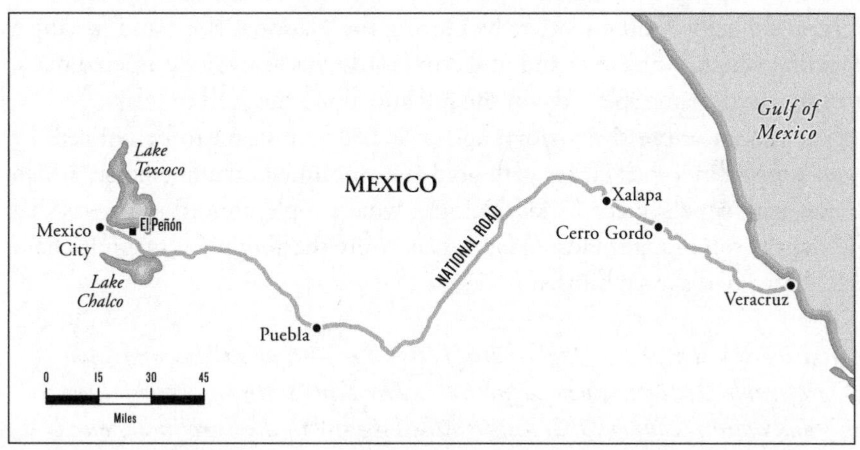

Forty-eight miles above Veracruz, steep gorges ran down on either side of the National Road near the town of Cerro Gordo, and there Santa Anna, fresh from a bruising defeat at Buena Vista by Zachary Taylor, arrayed 12,000 soldiers in a forbidding defensive position overlooking the road. It was, Lee wrote a week later, "remarkably strong."

> *The right of the Mexican line rested on the river at a perpendicular rock, unscalable by man or beast, and their left on impassable ravines; the main road was defended by field works containing thirty-five cannon; in their rear was the mountain of Cerro Gordo, surrounded by intrenchments in which were cannon and crowned by a tower overlooking all—it was around this army that it was intended to lead our troops.*[16]

Scott turned to Lee as a scout "for the purpose of discovering a route by which the Jalapa road could be gained." And not only for scouting: "at the head of a body of pioneers," Lee was charged with opening the goat tracks around the gorges to make "a passable way for light batteries," snaking so close to the Mexican positions that he was nearly captured by Mexican sentinels. Once Scott was satisfied that "further reconnaissance" by Lee was "impossible, without an action," he launched a long, looping flank attack around the left of the Mexican positions at Cerro Gordo. Lee was detailed to guide Twiggs's division to the attack, aiming to overrun the Atalaya hill on the morning of April 17. Once in possession, "the indefatigable Captain Lee" then superintended, "with the aid of picket ropes," the dragging of "one twenty-four pounder gun, and two twenty-four pounder howitzers . . . up to the crest of the height, and placed in battery." The next morning, Lee was in front again, guiding Twiggs's lead brigade under Colonel Bennet Riley "across a ravine swept by the Mexican batteries," capturing an exposed Mexican battery, and finally ending matters by cutting the National Road and forcing a mortified Santa Anna to abandon Cerro Gordo, his army "a disordered mass, running with panic speed down the hill and along the road to Jalapa."[17]

It was an impressive victory, and in it Lee had meant to be noticed; he was "dressed in a shell jacket with gold lace, mounted on a fine horse, which he sat with superb grace." Maddeningly, what people noticed most was that he was the son of Light Horse Harry. Lee, wrote the Virginia surgeon Richard McSherry, had shown himself

> *a worthy son of . . . "Light-horse Harry Lee"—that gallant and indefatigable partisan cavalry officer. . . . The same untiring watchfulness, and dashing courage, that distinguished the sire in the Carolinas showed itself in his son of the same metal, though in a more scientific arm of the service, among the hills and plains of Mexico.*

Winfield Scott, more perceptively, praised Lee in his own right. "I am compelled to make special mention of the services of Captain R. E. Lee, Engineer," Scott wrote to the secretary of war:

> *This officer, greatly distinguished at the siege of Vera Cruz, was again indefatigable, during these operations, in reconnaissances as daring as laborious, and of the utmost value. Nor was he less conspicuous in planting batteries, and conducting columns to their stations under the heavy fire of the enemy.*

Lee, for his part, experienced none of Light Horse Harry's martial elation. Veracruz had been a comparatively bloodless affair, conducted at the sort of unbloodied distance an engineer could appreciate, "a battle of the pick axe & shovel"; Cerro Gordo was Lee's first introduction to line-against-line infantry combat, and the specter of it frankly unnerved him. "You have no idea what a horrible sight a battlefield is," he wrote to his teenage son, Custis. And to Mary, he added, "The papers cannot tell you what a horrible sight a field of battle is, nor will I, owing to my accompanying General Twiggs's division in the pursuit, and being since constantly in the advance."[18]

Scott's army was jubilant at the Cerro Gordo victory and praised Scott to the clouds. Robert Anderson, who was then a captain in the 3rd U.S. Artillery, rejoiced to hear "the strongest expressions of admiration and implicit confidence expressed towards, and in him," even that Scott was "one of the greatest generals of the age." Santa Anna, however, showed no sign of wilting, so Scott pushed on to Xalapa by April 20, pausing to allow volunteer regiments with expiring enlistments to depart and resuming his advance to Puebla on May 10 (which surrendered five days later). At Puebla, he waited for ten weeks for reinforcements to reach him from the coast, which allowed him to reorganize his forces into four divisions. Pointedly, he ignored directives from Washington to live off the land and insisted that "all articles obtained . . . be fairly paid for." His supply lines were too long and vulnerable to risk alienating the Mexicans' countryside and turning them into *guerrillas.*[19]

Meanwhile, "the services of Captain Lee were invaluable to his chief," wrote Raphael Semmes, then a naval lieutenant serving as a volunteer aide to William Worth. Semmes was especially struck with Lee's "talent for topography" because "he seemed to receive impressions intuitively, which it cost other men much labor to acquire."[20] Lee would need every bit of that gift, because when Scott resumed the advance on Mexico City on August 5, he found that Santa Anna had fortified the eastern approaches to the city at El Peñón Viejo even more strongly than at Cerro Gordo. Scott hesitated to lavish the lives he would need to dislodge the Mexicans from El Peñón. But on August 12 and 13, Lee conducted a sweep below El Peñón around Lake Chalco, which he discovered would allow Scott to approach the city from its more lightly defended south side and "leave the fortifications at the Pinion to the right." That was enough for Scott: "Captain Lee's reconnaissance today has settled the route of advance in General Scott's mind. He is going southward of Chalco."[21]

That did not mean that the Chalco route was without perils of its own, and it was there that Lee would acquire his most outstanding laurels from Scott. Once Scott's army made its swing around Lake Chalco, it would arrive at the Acapulco Road, which led northward across the Churubusco River into Mexico City. Santa Anna had posted a small covering garrison astride the Acapulco Road at the hacienda of San Antonio. But rather than launching a headlong assault at San Antonio, Lee proposed yet another flanking movement to the west that would allow Scott to force the Mexicans out of the San Antonio position. To do so, however, Scott would have to shift all the way to Contreras on the San Angel Road, and, unhappily, yet another Mexican blocking force had been posted at Padierna.

Between San Antonio and Padierna lay a fifteen-square-mile bed of ancient volcanic lava, scored by huge blocks of black basalt, known as the *pedregal.* Assuming that the *pedregal* was impassable for military purposes, Santa Anna left the *pedregal* itself uncovered. But Lee, out on reconnaissance on August 18, was convinced that a "mule path" that crossed the *pedregal* could be widened to allow the passage of artillery, wagons, and cavalry and allow Scott to reach the San Angel Road *behind* Padierna. "General Scott was at once determined to gain the San Angel road, and then move round to the attack of San Antonio in rear," and Lee was dispatched, with sappers and miners, three lieutenants (Pierre G. T. Beauregard, Gustavus W. Smith, and John G. Foster), and five hundred infantrymen in working parties, to make the "mule path" workable for horse, foot, artillery, and wagons.[22]

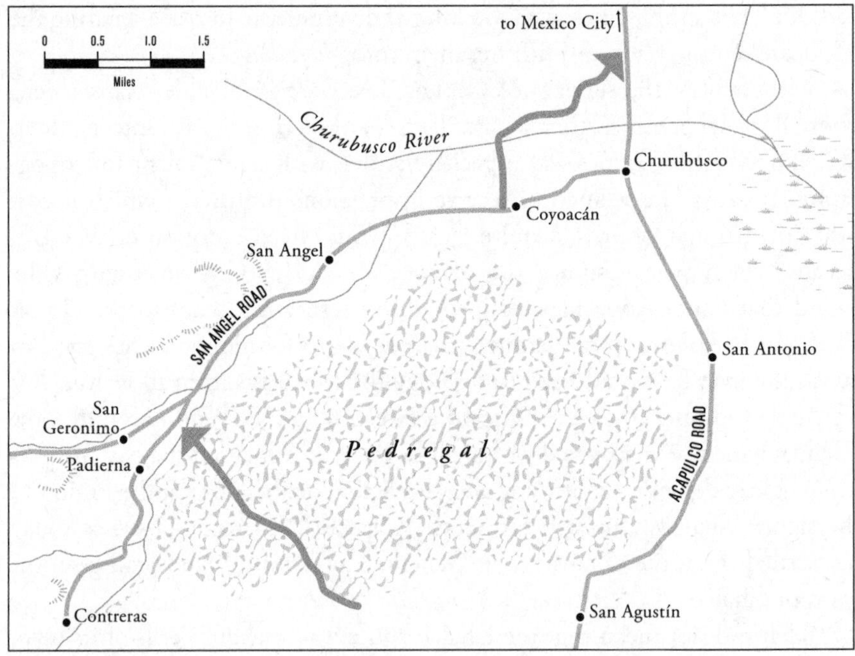

Beginning "on the morning of the 19th" the road was pushed forward "over a ridge of lava" and through "the barren and rocky waste, and over ditches filled with water, and lined with maguey [cactus] and prickly pear," until, by noon, "the Divisions of Genls. Pillow & Twiggs with their field batteries were enabled to reach" a point within range of Mexican artillery on the western side of the *pedregal.* Lee then went forward with Twiggs's skirmishers "& Selected the best route for the Artillery through the impracticable field of

Lava through which our route lay." He emerged on the far side of the *pedregal* and found a position "opposite the Village of San Geronimo" that would cut off the Mexican blocking force on the San Angel Road "by the rear." To ensure that the Americans would not themselves be cut off, Lee recrossed the *pedregal* that night, through sheets of rain and "flashes of lightning," to report to Scott and request reinforcements.[23]

Scott did not have much to spare: Lee "was therefore directed to return, and to Collect any Troops or Company I might find in front of the Enemy position"—which meant the 9th U.S. Infantry, four companies of the 12th U.S. Infantry, "and a few Riflemen & sappers that had been lost or detached from their Companies"—and crossed the *pedregal* yet again "a short time before daybreak." On the morning of August 20, the two brigades that made up Twiggs's division were just preparing to strike the Mexicans on the San Angel Road when Lee returned with his rounded-up reinforcements—his third crossing of the *pedregal* in twenty-four hours. Lee's hodgepodge battalion "made a very timely and spirited movement for the purpose of diverting and distracting the enemy" who, "finding himself attacked on two Sides . . . soon gave way in all directions, abandoning his artillery, 22 pieces, his packs, [and] ammunition."[24]

Scott was exultant, pursuing the fleeing Mexicans up to Coyoacán on the San Angel Road. As he did, Lee wrote, "the greeting of General Scott by the troops after the action, on seeing the success of all his plans, was loud and vociferous":

> *It must have shaken the "halls of the Montezumas." . . . The army has implicit confidence in him, and apprehend nothing where he commands. He sees everything, and calculates the cost of every measure; and they know and feel that their lives and labor will not be uselessly expended. During the day, we took 2,700 prisoners, eight generals, thirty-seven pieces of artillery, and ammunition enough for a whole campaign. Their defences were completely turned and their plans upset. We could have entered Mexico that evening or the next morning at our pleasure, so complete was the disorganization of their Army.*

Scott returned the compliment. "In none of the actions that took place during his campaign in Mexico," conceded the Democratic lawyer and potboiler historian John Stilwell Jenkins, "was the old war spirit of General Scott . . . more fully aroused than on this occasion." Scott greeted Pierre Beauregard with the nearest Old Fuss and Feathers had ever offered as public affection—"Young man, if I were not on horseback, I would embrace you"—and he showered praise on the engineer officers: "If West Point had only produced the Corps of Engineers, the Country ought to be proud of that institution." Even the rankers in the infantry regiments were impressed and wondered "why some of our engineer officers were not killed in the different reconaissances and actions . . . for they were always foremost."[25]

But it was Lee—"the gallant and indefatigable Captain Lee, of the engineers . . . as distinguished for felicitous execution as for science and daring"—who won the highest praise. Scott lauded the crossing and recrossing of the *pedregal* as "the greatest feat of physical and moral courage performed by any individual, in my knowledge," and he would later tell the U.S. senator and attorney general Reverdy Johnson that "his success was largely due to the skill, valor, and undaunted energy of Robert E. Lee." And the praise was showered not only by Scott but also by Twiggs's brigade commanders on Lee as an "engineer officer, in whose skill and judgement" they "had the utmost confidence."[26]

Scott was now only nine miles from Mexico City, and a dismayed Santa Anna quickly regrouped his forces around the bridgehead village of Churubusco in one more attempt to hold Scott at bay before he could cross the Churubusco River. Scott dispatched Lee again to "reconnoiter the rear of San Antonio," and when he found the Mexicans abandoning San Antonio as well, Scott turned all of his divisions toward an attack on Churubusco. While William Worth's division drove straight at the village and the fortified Franciscan convent of San Mateo, Lee was sent with a flurry of directives from Scott:

> *He gave me several orders during the day; one to reconnoitre the rear of San Antonio, and report the strength of the enemy's position. I heard him give instructions to General [Franklin] Pierce to move with his brigade to the rear of Churubusco, and make an attack at that point. He directed me to conduct the brigade to that point, and subsequently directed me to conduct the rifle regiment and a company of dragoons to the support of General [James] Shields.*

Shields ran into Santa Anna's reserve infantry at the Acapulco Road, and Lee put his own hand in by guiding a battery of howitzers under Lieutenant Jesse Reno, "who very promptly brought the pieces to bear upon the head of Their Column with good effect." The bridge defense at Churubusco collapsed before the 3rd and 5th U.S. Infantry, and the triumphant Americans spilled across the Churubusco River, some of the dragoons chasing the Mexican *soldados* along the Acapulco Road almost to the outer fortifications of Mexico City, where Lee himself "reconnoitered the Piedad and San Antonio Gate."[27]

Santa Anna now bought time by begging for an armistice on August 24, ostensibly to allow American and Mexican negotiators to begin peace talks, but in reality to allow him to call up every last conscript he could summon. While the other "engineer officers had suspended their reconnaissances," Scott kept Lee on the move to observe whatever Santa Anna might be up to. When "it had been learned that the Mexicans were completing some heavy guns at their Foundry" at Molino del Rey, just outside the city, Scott canceled the armistice and, on September 8, attacked and captured Molino del Rey in a fierce fight that cost Worth's division 116 killed and 665 wounded, then moved under the shadow of the last barrier to the gates that led into the Mexican capital, the citadel of Chapultepec, the home of Mexico's *colegio militar*.[28]

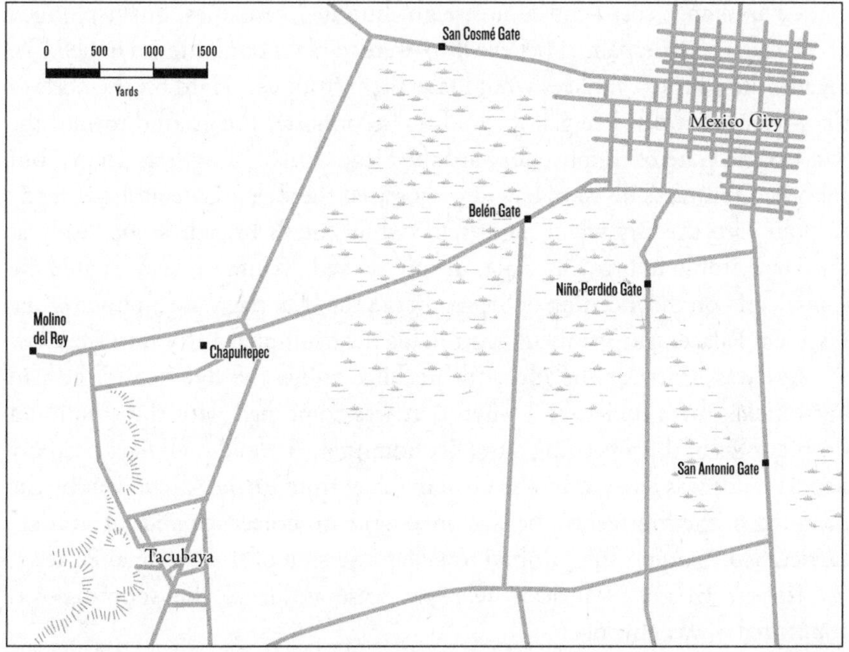

This time, Scott kept Lee close at hand, and together they spent three days scouting the city gates of Belén (at the southwest), Niño Perdido, and San Antonio (along the south rim of the capital) for the best approach. On the eleventh, Scott called a council of war to "consider the best mode of threatening and attacking the city," but in the end he determined to hit the city from the west (despite Lee's counsel to the contrary, "so expressed to General Scott, at his invitation"), and that meant a direct attack on Chapultepec. Scott planned to batter "the frowning hill of Chapultepec" first with his artillery, and it was Lee who, one more time, was assigned to lay out three batteries to breach the citadel (despite Lee's reservations about "whether our guns could do more than demolish the upper part of the building"). The next afternoon the first of the batteries opened fire. Scott was ready to launch the attack that afternoon, and it was Lee who dissuaded him, saying "that perhaps, upon the whole, the attack might better be delayed until next morning, as I feared there would be hardly time." All three batteries were ready to begin together on the morning of September 13, and after two hours of bombardment—"so slowly and deliberately that they could not believe we were in earnest"—Lee signaled "that the attacking columns would move to the assault of the hill." All through the attack, Lee worked directly with Scott that day, "employed by the Genl in Chief in Executing his directions & bringing him information of the Events of the day, until the works of Chapultepec were carried."[29]

Chapultepec cost Scott almost eight hundred casualties, but it plunged Santa Anna into despair. "I believe if we were to plant our batteries in hell," he raged, "the damned Yankees would take them from us." Hard on the heels of the Mexican retreat, Lee galloped off to "reconnoiter the ground toward the San Cosme Gate & to move forward the Siege Guns & Engineer Train." But John A. Quitman's division had already seized the Belén Gate and was ready to pour into the city when night fell, "while Riley's brigade stood ready at the San Antonio to break in if opportunity served." Santa Anna evacuated the capital, and on the morning of September 14 the U.S. flag was run up over the National Palace, and Winfield Scott made his triumphal entry into the city.

Lee was nearly at the physical breaking point: the day before, he had been nicked by a bullet, and when that was combined with the strain and sleeplessness of the preceding days, Lee admitted, "I could no longer keep my Saddle [and] was relieved by the Genl in Chief from further duty." But by the morning of the fourteenth, he was once more on horseback and "at sunrise" carried Scott's orders to Quitman to take possession of the National Palace.[30]

Robert E. Lee's Mexican War—at least as far as the shooting was concerned—was now over.

From the vantage point of five decades, Lew Wallace (who served in Mexico as a second lieutenant in the 1st Indiana Volunteers and went on to become a Civil War general and the author of *Ben-Hur*) thought the memory of Mexico seemed like a dream of paradise. "There is not one of us to whom the service in Mexico is not a recollection surpassing in interest the most brilliant operation" of the Civil War. "Mexico was a strange land to us all, and full of novelties" that "charmed us irresistibly," and Wallace was confident that "every soldier who made the march . . . would like once more to go over the route and see the country and people again."[31]

To the American occupiers of Mexico City in the fall of 1847, the immediate impressions of Mexico were more sobering, especially once the enthusiasm of victory had worn off. Scott had conducted an astounding campaign, while the cost in American lives seemed almost negligible. But sniping and vandalism directed at the American occupiers were rife, and Scott quickly imposed martial law on Mexico City, "denouncing such warfare after the city had been fairly surrendered, and threatening the destruction of houses, and the execution of the occupants, wherever it was sanctioned or allowed."[32]

Scott's army now settled into an unexpectedly long period of occupation as the politicians and diplomats turned to what became uncertain negotiations over the future of Mexico and the United States. President Polk had never bothered to conceal his hope that, once the Texas boundary question was finalized at the Rio Grande, a war with Mexico could produce "the acquisition of California and a large district on the [Pacific] coast." But with Mexico militarily prostrate at Scott's feet, a more ambitious agenda began to emerge, sparked by Polk's secretary of state, James Buchanan, who now proposed annexation of the entire Republic of Mexico. The rush to annex "the whole of the Mexican territory now in our possession," in turn, fitted neatly under the popular rubric of a "manifest destiny" to create "a more perfect Union; embracing the entire North American continent."[33]

Lee never used the term "manifest destiny" in his letters, but the concept lay underneath all the public excuses for the Mexican War. Its principal apostle was Polk, and its prophet was the Democratic journalist John L. O'Sullivan, whose *Democratic Review* announced in 1845 that it was "our manifest destiny to overspread the continent allotted by Providence for the free development of our yearly multiplying millions." This destiny conveniently coincided with the grasp of slavery for more and more land for slave agriculture, and it quickly expanded its scope to include both Mexico and the Spanish-speaking Caribbean. "It seems to be settled that Spain is at best but a tenant for years in her colony" in Cuba, predicted William Henry Hurlbert. "From these propositions it has been deduced that Cuba must soon become a member of our great and glorious confederacy," bringing its slaves with it. Thereafter, "the natural increase in slaves would," argued Thomas Clingman, "justify the extension of our territory, until we should occupy . . . Mexico . . . and ultimately Central America and the West Indies islands."[34]

The Whigs, whether the prominent ones like Henry Clay or those like Lee who dwelt in the shadow of the Whig Party, were too preoccupied with internal improvements and commercial development to have much enthusiasm for any "manifest destiny" to expand American territory. "It is much more important that we unite, harmonize, and improve what we have than attempt to acquire more," Clay wrote in 1843. The annexation of Texas never even made it, as an issue, into the 1844 Whig platform. But the Whigs, even if they resisted notions of expansion by force, were not proof against softer notions of cultural empire. Gamaliel Bailey's resolutely Whiggish *National Era* resolutely denounced the Mexican War as the stalking horse of "manifest destiny" for the expansion of slavery, but he also believed that Mexico would prove an inhospitable climate for slavery and that the Mexican states could be invited, one by one and voluntarily, to join the American Union. There really was an American destiny, avowed *The American Whig Review,* not of conquest, but of cultural superiority. "We have indeed a new world," but one of an "astonishing heterogeneousness of races, perfectly blended into one," possessing "an ideal form of government," shaped into "a wonderful theatre of mercy and love" by the "great Ruler of events" to promote the "unexampled triumph of the principles of justice, humanity and religion." Not armies, but the uncontested superiority of American culture would irresistibly subdue Mexico, "insensibly oozing into her territories, changing her customs, and out-living, out-trading, exterminating her weaker blood."[35]

Robert E. Lee would not have necessarily disagreed with *The American Whig Review* or *The National Era.* But the degree of his regard for "manifest destiny" varied over time and place, and especially during the tedious months of occupation that followed the surrender of Mexico City as the Polk administration not only prolonged the peace negotiations in the interest of annexing larger and larger chunks of Mexican territory but turned and devoured Winfield Scott in an undisguised attempt to eliminate a potential Whig presidential candidate. Although Lee initially looked on the Mexican War as an opportunity for personal self-advancement rather than territorial expansion, he could not help admiring the Mexican coast at Tampico, "& if it depends upon my vote, it will never fall back to Mexico." And as Scott swept toward the conquest of Mexico City, Lee's exuberance over Mexico blossomed. "It is a beautiful country," Lee wrote two weeks after the surrender of Mexico City, "rich, fertile, temperate & healthy after leaving the coast." The problem was with the people and "the power & iniquity of the [Catholic] Church." It was bad enough, Lee complained, that this "miserable populace" is "idle, worthless & vicious"; they made matters worse by "desultory shots from the house tops & corners of streets" that provoked "our men" into "killing some 500 of the mob & deserters from their Army, who had not the courage to fight us lawfully."

It will, Lee concluded, be necessary "to overrun the country & drive them into the sea," and "at once," then replace them with a more racially preferable set of colonists. "Open the ports to European immigration. Introduce free opinions of government & religion." He had little doubt it could be done, too. "By occupying this capital & firmly holding the line to Vera Cruz, &

some of the adjacent provinces, we can with less men & at a less expense, exert a greater influence & greater control over this country, than by taking any other line or position whatever." Or so it seemed at first. The Mexican population showed little eagerness for dispossession, and several years later Lee would recall an attempt by "a Mexican . . . with a lasso in his hand" to waylay him as he was "riding out for his health." Lee "took out his pistol and held it on his saddle, so that it could be seen by the Mexican," and the would-be assailant instead "passed with a courteous greeting." But the incident illustrated how the longer Scott's army remained in Mexico City, implementing some dream of manifest destiny, the more cut off it was liable to become in reality.[36]

Not that Scott or Lee could do much about it, because the peace negotiations seemed to be heading nowhere. President Polk dispatched his first peace commissioner, Nicholas Trist, to Mexico just after Veracruz in hopes that Trist could bring the war to a negotiated end before Scott could win any further victories. Instead, Trist struck up a surprisingly cooperative partnership with Scott, and Polk angrily ordered his recall. Before Polk's orders reached Trist, the industrious negotiator had opened talks with the Mexican government (which had by that point deposed Santa Anna), and on January 31 commissioners appointed by the civilian government of Mexico accepted a preliminary agreement and forwarded it to a temporary civilian capital at Querétaro. What they agreed to was not generous to the Mexicans: the United States would annex all Mexican territory north of the Gila River and all of California except the Baja, and set the Texas boundary firmly at the Rio Grande. But the treaty stopped far short of the demands Polk's cabinet was making for "All Mexico," and it was signed on February 2 at Guadalupe Hidalgo. More dithering ensued over an armistice that would actually end hostilities, which did not take effect until March 6, 1848.[37]

On the American side, Polk was infuriated with Trist's negotiations, and all the more so because the Whigs had regained a majority in Congress in the 1846 elections and would now itch to ratify Trist's treaty. A copy of the treaty arrived from Mexico on February 19, and after two days of hesitation Polk sent it on to the Senate—just in time for a fatal stroke to cut down John Quincy Adams on the floor of the House (he died on February 23) and delay all legislative action until the beginning of March.

The longer the treaty was delayed, the less enthusiasm Lee felt for Mexico. So far, he had "been preserved by a kind Providence from a thousand dangers," but "alas still there is no prospect of peace, & every one seems at a loss to know what is to be done next. You can scarcely realize so far off the misery this war has occasioned . . . & we can as yet see no termination." Steadily, loneliness and ennui sapped Lee's interests in annexation. Scott assigned him sumptuous quarters in the National Palace and kept Lee "engaged at the drawings of the Mexican defences around the City of Mexico & . . . occupied in plotting the Works at the Separate points in case they sh. be called upon to move with portions of the Army to finish them hereafter." Lee was also "taken up entirely in Constructing Maps of the Roads to Cumanaca, Toluca, Morelia, Guadalajara . . . and the mining Regions in their Vicinity." And from time to time, Scott took his staffers on scenic outings. But none of it compensated for the isolation of a foreign country or the uneasy sense that he had no right to be there in the first place. Lee teased his daughter Agnes with the hint that he had found a surrogate for her in the daughter of one of the European expatriates resident in Mexico City, "a nice little girl here, rather Smaller than you were when I parted from you, named *Charlollita.*" But surrogate children really did little to erase his mounting homesickness. "Your Papa," he admitted, "thinks Constantly of you & longs to be [with] you more than he Can Confess."[38]

Lee finally concluded, "War is a great evil. It brings much individual as well as national suffering. The sight of every battle field has made my heart bleed." The pursuit of any conquests beyond what Trist had negotiated was a mistake. "The friends of peace in this Country Say that a treaty has been Signed by Mr. Trist & the Mexican Commissioners & been forwarded to Washington," he wrote to Mary Custis Lee in February 1848. "The boundary is Said to be the Rio Grande as far as the head waters of the Gila, then that river to the Pacific, Giving us Texas, New Mexico & California." These "are certainly not hard terms for Mexico," and certainly not a jot more "than I would have taken before the commencement of hostilities." But more annexations would be worse than pointless. "I do not wish any part of the thickly populated Country. The inhabitants would prove an injury to us & I feel would be like Ireland to England." He simply wanted the whole business wound up. "The further prosecution of the war holds out only a prospect of evil to Mexico, without promising much real good to us. Therefore the Sooner it is closed the better for both."

If anything, what Lee now discovered was a sense of shame at having been part of the war at all. "It is true," he conceded, that we "bullied" Mexico. "Of that I am ashamed, as She was the weaker party." The battles had been fought honorably enough; it was the politicians who disgusted him. The Mexicans he had come to know are "aware how entirely they are beaten & are willing to acknowledge it" by conceding the annexation of Texas and surrendering the provinces of California and New Mexico. But the wrangling of the politicians had become so noxious that Lee wondered if it wouldn't be better to give it all back to Mexico, even "to compel her to take it back."[39]

—

Carter Lee had heard from "officers returned from Mexico" that "Robert's is the most enviable reputation in the army." But little of that took tangible form. As of September 13, 1847, Lee was promoted three times—from captain to major, from major to lieutenant colonel, and thence to colonel—but only as brevet (or honorary) promotions. For all purposes of pay and seniority, he remained in the U.S. Army Register what he had been since 1838, a captain of Engineers. "I cannot Consider myself very highly Complimented by the brevet of 2 grades," he wrote in high annoyance to his father-in-law.

Annoyance quickly became pettiness. Double brevets, he complained, had been "bestowed on two officers at Palo Alto," yet Lee had "never Seen an Officer yet present at the engagement, that thought they deserved more than one." Quickly, the grievance list got longer. He was all too aware that "Lt [John Charles] Fremont"—despite his erratic conduct in California during the war—had been "advanced 3 grades from a Lt of Topog[raphical] Engrs to a Lt Col. of Rifles," while his old West Point classmate Joe Johnston had vaulted from "a Lt to Lt. Col. of Voltigeurs." Even Zealous Tower, one of his lieutenants in the Engineer detachment, who began the war as a lowly second lieutenant, was brevetted first lieutenant for Cerro Gordo, promoted to full first lieutenant for assisting Lee in the crossing of the *pedregal,* and brevetted captain for Churubusco and finally major for Chapultepec.

On those terms, Lee thought—and with some encouragement from "Genl Twiggs in an official letter to Genl Scott, which has fallen under my eye, & endorsed by Genl S"—that he deserved "two brevets for the battles of Cerro Gordo" alone. As it was, "if I performed any Services at Vera Cruz, or at the battles around this Capital, they will go for nought." Prickling with self-pity, Lee presumed "that their Services exceeded mine, which I know to be Small." His father-in-law attempted to assuage Lee's disappointment with the gift of one of George Washington's swords, but what Lee craved was recognition, not consolation.[40]

Lee thought he saw in this neglect the hidden hand of President Polk's hostility to Whig officers. Andrew Jackson's "favourite Son, as the Newspapers term our present President," had struggled to gain control of the Army appointments system, and Lee was not the only officer who believed that Polk was reserving promotion for (as Robert Anderson termed it) "a score of men whose sole recommendation is that they or their friends have proved faithful in *their* worship of the President's party." But these suspicions paled beside the wholesale outbreak of political war after the fall of Mexico City between Polk and Winfield Scott—into which Robert E. Lee found himself unwillingly dragged.[41]

The fiasco began with Gideon Pillow, a Tennessee lawyer and favorite of Polk's who commanded Scott's Third Division. Pillow was a political blowhard who had already irritated Scott by submitting after-action reports that wildly overstated his role in the capture of Mexico City. When Scott tersely ordered Pillow to rewrite the reports, an acrimonious exchange of letters began, and in September, Pillow upped the ante by publishing a letter in the New Orleans *Daily Delta,* signed "Leonidas," claiming that Pillow, and not Scott, had been the real genius behind the Mexico City campaign. Scott replied by issuing a general order to the Army on November 12, reminding every soldier that it was a breach of Army regulations for subordinates to publish articles on Army operations without the consent of their superior, and adding that the shenanigans of "half a dozen officers" were bringing into disrepute the standing of "all honorable officers who love their country, their profession and the truth of history."[42]

Far from this settling matters, William Worth, a long-service Regular who commanded Scott's First Division and whose personal (and hitherto cordial) relations with Scott ran all the way back to their days in the War of 1812, interpreted this as a criticism of *him,* because the "Leonidas" letter had singled Worth for special praise. Worth accused Scott of conduct unbecoming an officer, and Scott put both Worth and Pillow under arrest. The arrests, however, raised the sympathetic eyebrow of President Polk, who dismissed the charges against Pillow and Worth and ordered Scott relieved of command on January 13, 1848, and hauled before a court of inquiry.[43]

Lee was aghast at Scott's treatment. Two weeks after Scott turned over command of his army to William O. Butler, Lee wrote to Smith Lee that "these dissensions in camp . . . have clouded a bright campaign." Not only was Scott the "great cause of our success," having led "us forward to this Capital & finally brought us within its gates," but the entire affair was putting the structure of the Army's command discipline in jeopardy, and especially in such a nakedly political context:

> *It is difficult for a Genl to maintain discipline in an Army composed as this is, in a foreign country, where the temptations to disorders are So great, & the chance of detection So slight. He requires every Support & Confidence from his Govt: at home. . . . To suspend a Successful Genl in Command of an Army in the heart of an enemy Country, to try the judge in place of the accused, is to upset all discipline, to jeopardize the safety of the Army and honour of the Country, & violate justice.*

It was enough to renew all his doubts about the worth of an Army career, and he warned Smith that he could "never advise any young man to enter the Army":

> *He is cut off from all hope of preferment. He performs all the tedium & drudgery of the Service, & no matter how well he may have performed his duties & prepared himself for the Service, as Soon as the opportunity occurs for which he has been preparing, waiting & laboring, a Sett of worthless, ignorant, political aspirants or roués, are put over his head, who in spite of themselves, he has to lug on his Shoulders to victory.*[44]

What aggravated Lee's irritation was that Lee himself was now called as a witness for the prosecution *against* Scott. On August 22, 1847, Lee had written a lengthy letter from Tacubaya, describing the crossing of the *pedregal* and the fighting at Churubusco, echoing praise for Scott's handling of the fighting, and sent it to Catlyna Totten, the wife of Joseph Totten. Lee would explain that it "was written to a member of Colonel Totten's family, and was not intended to be made public, but was to advise him of the substance of our operations." The letter, however, went instead "to the office of" the Chief Engineer, and Totten's assistant, Captain George Welker, passed the letter to the Washington *Daily Union* along with other official papers, where it was published on the editorial page on September 20, 1847. Lee's letter to Catlyna Totten now became a stick with which Pillow proposed to beat Scott, because it was easy to make Lee's letter look like nothing different in substance from Pillow's own "Leonidas" letter; hence, Scott's arrest of Pillow was an exercise in personal and political hypocrisy.[45]

From there, Lee's name was splashed incontinently through the newspapers. "I have read in the N.Y. Courier & Inquirer . . . a long article in reference to the Subject matter of dispute between Genl Scott & Genls Pillow & Worth, in which my name is very unceremoniously introduced to Substantiate Certain Statements there made," he wrote to Mary's aunt Anna Maria Fitzhugh in April. The reporters made "it . . . appear from the Article that I had either furnished the data, or offered myself as evidence of their truth." Lee shrank from nailing his political colors to the fragile mast of his Army career, shuddering at the memory of what politics had done to Gratiot and was presently doing to Scott. "I considered it a great outrage for any one without my Consent thus to lug me in the public papers. It is a Species of notoriety for which I have an aversion."[46]

The Scott inquiry sat in Mexico City through April 21, when it adjourned and Scott prepared to leave Mexico and his army for Veracruz and New York.

> *The Court of Inquiry closed its session about 3 P.M. on Friday [April 21]. It was somehow found out at night that the Genl intended leaving next mor'g. The street in which his Qrs: were was thronged with Officers till a late hour hoping to get sight of him. His staff were down at the gate, doing all they could to repress their efforts to go up. Some few could not be restrained. In the morg, there was a recurrence of the scene, with the hope of seeing him enter his carriage. As he drove along the street all were uncovered . . . & entering on the causeway, there was a long row of Officers on horseback who had been waiting to give him a parting salute. As he drove by, it was done in silence, neither party being able to speak, & the murmur of prayers for his safety & happiness was all that could be heard.*

Lee would gladly have left with him. "The discontent in the Army at this State of things is great," he wrote to his father-in-law, and Lee wished "I was out of the Army myself. . . . If I return, I shall make a strong effort to leave it."[47]

But no permission to join Scott was forthcoming. "Genl Butler Says if he was to allow all to leave the Country, who have applied, he Should have no Army left." Lee sent the transcripts of the inquiry's sessions to G.W.P., tactfully adding that Custis should treat "the papers Containing the proceedings of the Court" as confidential. "I do not think it necessary to Caution you against publishing anything I may write, for you know I only intend the expression of any thoughts for yourself." It was not for another month that Lee finally learned that Congress had at last ratified the Treaty of Guadalupe Hidalgo, and that, once it was returned to Querétaro, "a vote was taken in the [Mexican] Chamber of Deputies on the general passage of the Treaty of Peace & carried in the Affirmative by 48 votes to 36." The next day, he issued orders for the engineer detachment to "collect all the property appertaining to the Engineer Company" and prepare to march down to Veracruz. He arrived at the coast on June 6, oversaw the embarking of his detachment on board the brig *Helen,* and then took the steamer *Portland* for New Orleans on June 9. Twenty days later, he was at Arlington.[48]

Mexico was finally over for Robert E. Lee, although, like most wars, never entirely over. He would always consider Scott's campaign the model of all military operations, and he admitted to Jerome Napoleon Bonaparte (the American nephew of the French emperor) in 1855 that he had, as a soldier, seen "nothing to give me . . . much pleasure since the Capture of Mexico." He would continue to fantasize about leaving the Army and just as frequently chase after the rumor of promotion "for anything above a captaincy." And he would comment upon, and criticize, various historical treatments of Scott's campaign, especially commending his former subordinate Isaac Stevens for giving "credit to the two great Captains of the War"—Taylor and Scott—"to whom the Country is mainly indebted for its victories which has been denied them by others."[49]

As a soldier, Lee absorbed several vital lessons that would have large parts in the roles he would play thirteen years later. First, Scott's campaign from Veracruz to Mexico City set an example, forcibly similar to what he had once read in Warnery's *Anecdotes,* about taking the offensive, even if the numbers were unfavorable. Whatever offensives cost in casualties, they made up for in keeping the initiative firmly within one's own hands. Second, Scott was a model for how to treat the civilians in the path of war with a respectful and easy hand and thus minimize discontents and insults that could be inflamed into guerrilla warfare. Third, Scott's campaign gave a clear preference to the services of West Point Regulars, trusting them with wide discretion in executing orders and keeping the volunteers and amateurs on a short leash. "Truly this Mexican affair is a glorious thing for West Point," Lee boasted to John Mackay. "Every one must See the difference between the commencement of the present war & the last, & every one must acknowledge that this difference is caused by the difference in the officers." Last, the unhappy results of Scott's political conflicts with the Polk administration underscored a lesson already learned from Charles Gratiot about the need to stay out of the public political glare and put up with the misbehavior of politically volatile subordinates as quietly as possible.[50]

For the moment, these would be lessons Lee would keep to himself. Despite the hope of Robert Anderson that "Capt. R. Lee, U.S. Engineers, will write a Military Memoir," he would write no recollections of the Mexican War. In return, the Mexican War would, in a fashion, forget Lee. Whatever the praise showered on him by Scott and other commanders in the field, most of the contemporary histories of the Mexican War—Charles Peterson's *Military Heroes of the War with Mexico* (1848), Jonathan Buhoup's *Narrative of the Central Division, or Army of Chihuahua, Commanded by Brigadier General Wool* (1847), Luther Giddings's *Sketches of the Campaign in Northern Mexico* (1853), and the *Complete History of the Late Mexican War* (1850)—make no mention of Lee at all.

"The Lees you say are 'not popular,'" wrote the Virginia historian Nathaniel Francis Cabell to Carter Lee in March 1859. It was all politics, Cabell assured Carter Lee. The Lees do no "more than share the odium which in these democratic days is the lot of most of those who have the misfortune to be descended of an honorable and honoured ancestry unless they will turn traitors to their principles & memory." Take your brother Robert as an example, Cabell added. "Of your brother—the gallant soldier—& his signal services, I have heard from those who appreciated them highly; & if he has not received justice from his country, I hope it will not be finally withheld, & that he will yet rise above all the efforts of his detractors." He would, of course, but not in any way Cabell could have imagined.[51]

CHAPTER SIX

To Serve as a Model for the Mighty World

The world to which Robert E. Lee returned in the summer of 1848 would never be the same, nor would Lee himself. There had long been in Lee a gentle strain of "quaint humor," a puckish teasing that ranged from the "Mercy, Miss Molly, how many questions you have asked" of his early letters to Mary, to his sly mockery of "Pussyism."[1] That would, from what was now his forty-second year, almost completely disappear from the man, and a sadder, slower, less hopeful consciousness would begin to prevail. He appeared to acquaintances to be "remarkably well" after the fury of the Mexican campaigns, but "his hair is getting pretty well grizzled," and he was more conscious than ever, now that his oldest son, Custis, had reached the alarming age of sixteen, that "it behooves me to walk very straight, when this fellow is already following in my tracks."

There were other reasons for the darkening hill Lee seemed to be climbing. His old friend Jack Mackay died in Savannah on May 31 of tuberculosis. The obituary that appeared in the Savannah papers could have been written by Lee himself: "His native city has never seen one of her younger sons pass from the cradle to the grave more honored, more esteemed, more deeply regretted. As a soldier, as a son, a brother and friend, he was possessed of all those qualities which engage the affections and command respect, admiration and confidence." The war also struck glancing blows at Lee's vast kinship network. William George Williams, the father of Mary's cousin Martha Custis Williams (whom Lee affectionately nicknamed Markie), had been killed in Zachary Taylor's capture of Monterrey in 1846, and Lee ensured that his sword belt was retrieved and sent to her. Charles Gratiot still lived, but as an obscure clerk in the Government Land Office in St. Louis. Andrew Talcott had left the Army a decade before and drifted out of Lee's life and into railroad construction in Mexico. Charles Carter Lee had finally given up on both law and land and, while Robert was in Mexico, married a wealthy widow, Lucy Penn Taylor, and settled into the life of a gentleman farmer on her plantation, Windsor Forest, in Powhatan County.

More bewildering was the strangeness his two-year absence had imposed on his family. He arrived at Arlington on horseback—he missed a carriage that had been sent for him at the Washington rail station—to be greeted by surprise and delight from Mary, his in-laws, his children. The surprise and delight were not always easily mixed. "Some of the older ones gaze with astonishment & wonder & seem at a loss to reconcile what they see, to what was pictured in their imaginations." They "seem to devote themselves to staring at the furrows in my face and the white hairs in my head," he wrote to Smith Lee the next day. The younger ones barely recognized him at all, nor he them. Lee bent down to scoop up his youngest son, Robert junior, only to be told that he was embracing not Rob but the child of a houseguest, four-year-old Armistead Lippitt. ("I remember nothing more of any circumstances connected with that time, save that I was shocked and humiliated," Rob wrote years later.)[2]

It did not raise Lee's spirits, either, to learn that as soon as the Treaty of Guadalupe Hidalgo was finished, the first impulse of President Polk was to call for the demobilization of the Army, beginning with the regiments Congress had authorized for the war. A week after Lee's return to Arlington, Polk sent a special message to Congress, deploring the fate of "people of other countries, who live under forms of government less free than our own" and who are condemned to "support large standing armies in periods of peace." The war afforded no reason "why we should enlarge our land forces and thereby subject the treasury to an annual increased charge," because "such armies are not only expensive and unnecessary, but may become dangerous to liberty." The Army knew how to translate that. "The army is done for," complained one lieutenant. "It is as dead as a doornail, and . . . every young officer who possibly can will leave it in disgust and contempt."[3]

At the outbreak of the war, spending on the Army had ballooned to $4.049 million, with another $140,000 set aside for West Point and $1 million for fortifications; by the end of the fighting, Army spending had soared to $18.9 million. Polk's vision for a peacetime Army would slash military spending by half, to $9.5 million for the Army and just $607,000 for fortifications. The one hope that might stay the ax was the election of a new president in the fall of 1848, because Polk did not intend to reach for a second term. When the Whigs nominated Zachary Taylor, Mary Lee was delighted. "He is the best man to reconcile all parties," she wrote, and, as a military hero himself, the best to keep the Democrats from dissolving the Army completely, and she hoped her family "is moving Heaven & earth for the Whigs." But Taylor's election did not prevent the continuing shrinkage of the Army budget, to $6.2 million in 1850, or give a significant increase—only $53,000—to the Corps of Engineers for "Fortification, and other works of defense."[4]

Lee and the Corps of Engineers would have no choice but to suffer with their reduced means, something that Lee had to confront almost as soon as he returned to Arlington, because Joseph Totten at once assigned him to "special duty" in Totten's office in the War Department. This allowed him once more to live at Arlington and commute into the District of Columbia. But the arrangement could only be temporary. "We are always expecting to be deprived of [him]," Mary complained, "as he will probably be obliged to go North & then to Florida on Engineer duty. So you see there is no perfect bliss on Earth."[5] But "Engineer duty" would actually land him closer to home than she thought. For almost half a century, Fort McHenry had been the only protective fortification that shielded the inner harbor of Baltimore; in 1847, the War Department proposed construction of a new Third System fortification at the outer mouth of the Patapsco River, and on September 13, 1848, Lee was assigned to begin work there, surveying, blueprinting, and constructing a three-tiered, brick-and-granite, 225-gun hexagon to be known as Fort Carroll.

Lee made his first plan of Baltimore harbor in the fall of 1848, dividing time between a brief look at the harbor and an assignment to the Corps of Engineers' visitation board, an assignment that took him on an inspection tour from Boston to Florida. Not until April 1849 did he settle into the Baltimore work, renting a house owned by one of his Carter relatives, William Fanning Wickham, for himself and his family at Madison Avenue, a block west of Mount Calvary Episcopal Church. This placed the Lees less than half a mile from where his sister Anne Lee Marshall lived on St. Paul's Square (at what was then 7 Courtland Street) with her husband, William Louis Marshall, whose law practice had lifted him to the post of state's attorney. Another Lee cousin, Zaccheus Collins Lee, had a law office nearby, and Lee's naval brother, Sidney Smith Lee, now in command of the USS *Princeton,* was able to call in 1852. There was a school for Rob on Mulberry Street, and three servants (William and Elza Benke, and Frances Smith, who appear in the 1850 census as "mulatto" and who were probably hired, because none of those names tally with the list of Custis slaves).[6]

Fortification construction returned Lee to the work with which he had begun his career as an engineer at Cockspur Island and Fort Monroe. Fort

Carroll was to be built on a tidal shoal at the mouth of the Patapsco River, where it would command the principal ship channel into Baltimore harbor. Preliminary work in 1848 had already built up a three-acre artificial island, and it became Lee's task to construct 1,200 feet of temporary wharfage at the island for lighters and scows, drill a 195-foot artesian well, and begin driving more than eight hundred 12- to 15-foot wooden piles into the island to support the fort's walls with a steam pile driver he designed himself. "Powered by an engine of six horse-power, and lifting a hammer or ram weighing 2300 pounds, huge piles are driven in the most expeditious manner, to the depth of 45 feet below low water mark, the hammer giving about 200 blows per hour." He also had to supervise "a machine for sawing off the piles," a "dredge machine for leveling the surface of the shoal," and even a "diving-bell, for examining the foundation and working under water," along with a crane and a storehouse. "My days are spent pretty much at Fort Carroll," he explained to Markie Williams. "My thoughts are engrossed with driving piles & laying stone; & my imagination is exercised in the construction of cranes, Diving bells, Steam Pile drivers &c."[7]

Although the Madison Avenue house was cramped by Arlington standards—a three-story, three-bay brick town house whose rooms were "hardly big enough to swing a cat in"—the Lees managed to make "a most agreeable set" there. Rob Lee, in particular, remembered that his father was "a great favourite in Baltimore," and as a seven-year-old he never forgot the impression made on him "when he and my mother went out in the evening to some entertainment"—including Jenny Lind's recital at the Front Street Theatre in December 1850, with arias by Bellini and Rossini—and his father would dress "in full uniform" with "the golden epaulets and all." From time to time, Rob would tag along with his father to the construction work at Fort Carroll, catching a city omnibus to the inner harbor and then being rowed out with his father in "a boat with two oarsmen." For a young, impressionable boy, secure in his father's "gentle, loving care . . . his bright talk, his stories, his maxims and teachings," everything about life in Baltimore made "these days . . . very happy ones for me." It was everything Robert E. Lee should have had from his own father.[8]

But there were also family and professional concerns swirling through his father's life that Rob was too little to comprehend. Lee went down with a fever in the summer of 1849, and judging from the quinine he took for it, this was probably malaria. He felt strong enough to embark on yet another inspection tour in August at the behest of Joseph Totten, only to suffer a relapse in New York, recover, and then fall ill again, finally ending up at Cozzens Hotel at West Point until he was finally restored. His sister Anne Marshall had never rebounded emotionally from the death of her younger son ten years before and was so physically enfeebled that "she is now consequently without the use of either [hand], and cannot even feed herself." (It could only have added one more difficulty that Mount Calvary Church, the Marshalls' home parish, turned out to be a vigorous outpost of precisely the ritualistic "Pussyism" Lee deplored.)

Mindful that his oldest son would turn eighteen in 1850, Lee began plying his old chief, Winfield Scott, for a recommendation to President Taylor that would smooth Custis's application to West Point, and in March 1850, Custis was selected as one of ten presidential at-large appointments to the academy. He was just in time: four months later, President Taylor suddenly died. Lee mourned "the death of our good President." Taylor, unlike his Democratic predecessors, had been "too truthful to dissemble; Too firm a politician to serve a party; Too pure a patriot to neglect his Country! Too honest to favour individuals at the expense of right."[9]

Lee accompanied his son on the journey to the summer encampment that would be the teenager's introduction to the academy. "When I bid him adieu," Lee wrote to his mother-in-law, "he seemed for the first time to realize the full force of his separation from us all, & the convulsion of his countenance indicated the grief at his heart." But he was less interested in assuaging Custis's grief than in exhorting his son to self-discipline and application. "Between us two let there be no concealment," he urged Custis. "I may give you advice and encouragement and you will give me pleasure." He was just as worried for Annie and Agnes (now aged eleven and nine), who were under the eye of their grandmother at Arlington and the tutelage of a governess, Susan Poor. "I particularly desire," Lee wrote to his mother-in-law, that his daughters learn to "write a good hand, & to be regular, orderly, & energetic in the performance of all their duties."[10]

The work at Fort Carroll settled into the routine of yet one more coastal engineering project. Baltimoreans praised the new fortification as testimony to "the finest abilities in Col. Lee, than whom a more excellent appointment could not have been made." But Lee was not nearly so enchanted. "Times are pretty dull in B.," he wrote to Custis, but "we hammer on lustily." Through the heat of the summers, Mary fled to Arlington, leaving her husband with "no Mim, no children" and feeling as though "I might as well be a pile or a stone myself laid quietly at the bottom of the river." There was "but little amusement in the ev[ening]s," apart from "killing moskitoes & watching kittens playing with their tails."

He was drafted for two more inspection tours by Totten, to New England and New York, and experienced a brief alarm when Custis and two of his West Point roommates were accused of concealing alcohol in their room. Custis vehemently denied responsibility, and even more vehemently refused the offer of his entire class to pledge total abstinence as a strategy for averting Custis's dismissal. Eventually, the superintendent, Henry Brewerton, merely chided Custis by assessing eight demerits against him, and a cascade of relief washed over Custis's father. "I was delighted at the contradiction in your last letter of that *slanderous* report," Lee wrote to Custis. "I could not believe it before . . . & supposed it must have been greatly exaggerated." Still, the incident cost him a deeply quiet worry. "The consequences even of that slight deviation were so serious . . . that I often felt deeply for you and your parents," Custis's grandmother wrote to him from Arlington in October 1851, "especially your Father who had doubtless expected you to come out like himself *blameless.*" Or at least not like his own father, Light Horse Harry, *blameworthy.* And yet, Lee held his agitation within himself. "He never once adverted to the subject in my presence."[11]

The incident did, however, produce one odd moment of self-revelation from Robert E. Lee. He was particularly pleased that Custis had refused the offer of his class to share some of the burden of the accusation, because it accorded with one of the emotional passions that guided his life. "I am fond of independence," Lee wrote to Custis. "It is that feeling that prompts me to come up strictly to the requirements of law and regulations. I wish neither to seek or receive indulgence from anyone. I wish to feel under obligation to no one."[12] There still lurked and lunged within the man the desire to stand apart, and alone, not to be known as Light Horse Harry's son or a Custis son-in-law, or anything else but himself.

And yet, when Lee was approached by the largest opening of independence yet proffered to him, he turned it down.

Narciso López de Urriola was the head of a New York–based junta of Cuban exiles who were intent on using the United States as the platform to launch an expedition to overthrow Spain's colonial rule of the island. López was not particular about the allies he recruited. They included notorious proslavery expansionists who cynically encouraged López, hoping to use the end of Spanish rule as an opening for annexing Cuba as a new slave state. But López needed at least a core of professional military men for his plans, and he approached officers who made names for themselves in Mexico, starting with William Worth and the Mississippian Jefferson Davis. Worth blew hot and cold over the López plan; Davis refused outright, but not before suggesting that López recruit Lee "to be their leader in the revolutionary effort in that island." (Henry Hunt was one officer who picked up rumors that López was making overtures "in which the pious Capt. Lee figures conspicuously.")

But Lee only listened to López, who "offered him every temptation that ambition could desire." He consulted Jefferson Davis, who had by then been appointed to fill the vacant Mississippi U.S. Senate seat, and then declined.[13]

He had taken the measure of manifest destiny in Mexico, and it sounded no more charming to him when Cuba was proposed as the target. López went ahead with his Cuban invasion anyway in 1851, was easily defeated by Spanish authorities, and just as easily executed.

Independence, yes, but not at the expense of security. Except, of course, that security was what was already beginning to evaporate all around Robert E. Lee.

David Wilmot's wickedly troublesome proviso, banning slavery from any territory the United States would acquire from Mexico, was tacked onto one congressional bill after another, only to be firmly pruned away every time. Abraham Lincoln, then serving a solitary term as the solitary Whig congressman from Illinois, remembered voting for the proviso "at least forty times." And no wonder: "throughout the entire northern portion of this country," declared the New York representative Martin Grover, "the charge was iterated and reiterated that" the Mexican War "was undertaken on the part of the Administration" of James K. Polk, "aided by the South, for the purpose of extending the area of slavery" by outflanking the restriction placed on slave expansion by the Missouri Compromise.[14]

Nevertheless, Wilmot's proviso surprised Polk, both because Wilmot was a Democrat and because Polk had what he imagined was a reasonable answer to the question of what to do with the so-called Mexican Cession, which was simply to extend the 36°30' line of the Missouri Compromise to the Pacific. Northerners sniffed that this was exactly the trouble: extending the Missouri Compromise line merely allowed the Cession to be a handy way of dodging the original intent of the Missouri Compromise, to *restrict* the spread of slavery. For Southerners, however, Polk's plea was entirely too soft. The man who had become the paladin of pro-slavery orthodoxy, John Calhoun, rose in the Senate in February 1847 not only to deny that Congress had any authority to restrict the introduction of slavery into any territory acquired from Mexico but also to argue that no restrictions ought to have been imposed on the Louisiana Purchase, either. "Congress, as the joint agent and representative of the States of this Union, has no right to make any law . . . that shall deprive the citizens of any of the States of this Union from emigrating, with their property, into any of the territories of the United States"—with "property" clearly meaning "slaves."

That, in turn, was countered by an entirely different theory, formulated first by Michigan's U.S. senator Lewis Cass and then taken up by the Illinois senator Stephen A. Douglas: take all jurisdiction over the question, whether for or against slavery, out of the hands of Congress and transfer it to the territories themselves, letting the settlers in those territories decide on their own whether they would legalize slavery. Congress should limit itself "to the creation of proper governments" for the territories and then let them "regulate their internal concerns in their own way." This notion of "popular sovereignty" had a deceptively democratic twist to it. But it ran hard into the Whig wall erected by Zachary Taylor when he assumed the presidency in 1849. Although a slaveholder himself, Taylor would not "permit a state made from" the Mexican Cession "to enter our Union with the features of slavery connected with it," and at Taylor's prompting the onetime Mexican province of California applied directly for admission to the Union as a free state.[15]

It fell to Henry Clay, the architect of the Missouri Compromise thirty years before, to present to Congress yet another compromise to avert disunion. Clay's Compromise of 1850 was an "omnibus" proposal, with something to bribe the cooperation of all factions: admit California as a free state, adopt "popular sovereignty" as the rule for organizing the rest of the Mexican Cession, and soften the rejection of Calhoun's all-or-nothing pro-slavery doctrine by writing a stronger fugitive-slave recapture law. For once Clay's compromise magic failed. Calhoun, dying of tuberculosis, denounced the compromise and warned that if it passed, "the Southern States . . . cannot remain, as things now are, consistently with safety and honor, in the Union." President Taylor just as adamantly refused to bless the compromise, threatening to meet disunionists with armed force and hanging "them with less reluctance than he had hung deserters and spies in Mexico." By the summer of 1850, Clay's "omnibus" lay in ruins.

But then, on July 4, 1850, Taylor attended ceremonies at the Washington Monument, listening in the broiling Potomac sun to a series of orators, climaxing with "a patriotic and eloquent address" by none other than Robert E. Lee's father-in-law, George Washington Parke Custis, who "touchingly and delicately"—and relentlessly—apotheosized "a box containing earth from the great monumental mound in Cracow, in Poland, reared to the memory of the brave Kosciusko, which had been presented . . . to the Board of Managers of the Monument Society, and a portion of which was placed on the Washington block by Mr. Custis, to enter into the cement which should bind the stone in its place and form a part of the monument to the Pater Patriae." And on and on. The whole business was not finished until four in the afternoon, and afterward Taylor gratefully wolfed down iced cherries and cold milk at the Executive Mansion. They were probably tainted by cholera. The next day, Taylor felt unwell; four days later he was dead.[16]

Taylor's demise was a gift to Clay's compromise package. Taylor's successor, Millard Fillmore, endorsed Clay's proposals, and Stephen A. Douglas, displaying for the first time his extraordinary gifts of political charm, split the "omnibus" into separate bills, constructed differing coalitions behind each of them, and managed to slip each of them through Congress. "The difference between Mr. Clay's Compromise Bill & my . . . Bills was a wafer," Douglas cheerfully admitted. Not that the nation seemed to care. "One thing is certain, that every face I meet is happy," wrote a jubilant Washingtonian. "All look upon the question as settled, and no fears are felt in relation to the movements in either the South or North." In Baltimore, Lee's lawyer-cousin Zaccheus Collins Lee sighed in relief that "the question of union & disunion seems to be settled, at least for the present by the compromises and I think the agitation to the North can not disturb it." The day after the final bills passed, *The New York Herald* triumphantly announced, "There is universal rejoicing here by the passage of the . . . bills by the House. The whole difficulty is considered at an end and a better and more fraternal feeling prevails. . . . A new epoch begins from this day."[17]

Ironically, the apparent success of the Compromise of 1850 was actually its undoing, for the compromise was really only an appeasement that inflated the South's sense of what it could demand. Horace Mann declared the compromise to be "heart-sickening. The slaveholders have overthrown principles, and put them to rout as Napoleon did armies." The territories of Utah and New Mexico were organized on the popular sovereignty principle, "with or without slavery, as their constitution may prescribe at the time of their admission" to the Union, and so effortlessly that it seemed to Stephen A. Douglas that popular sovereignty might be the charm that would unlock the organization of the remaining bulk of the Louisiana Purchase north of the old Missouri Compromise line.

However, it turned out to be one thing to apply "popular sovereignty" to territories that hadn't even been U.S. possessions at the time of the Missouri Compromise; it was quite another to lay hands on what lay north of the sacrosanct 36°30' line—the vast stretch of land known simply as Kansas and Nebraska—and replace the ban on slavery there with an utterly laissez-faire formula like popular sovereignty. And when, in 1854, Douglas boldly browbeat his congressional colleagues into passing a Kansas-Nebraska territorial bill on the basis of "popular sovereignty," the lid blew off everything.[18]

Northerners had been willing to let the Mexican Cession slide under the rubric of popular sovereignty because few of them believed that either Utah or New Mexico would prove welcoming geography for plantation-style slavery, and fewer still believed that either would be ready for statehood anytime in the foreseeable future. Kansas and Nebraska were different. They were prairies, not deserts, and they would fill up swiftly with land-hungry farmers, and if they ever once passed into the hands of pro-slavery settler majorities, the balance of political power in the Union would be irretrievably altered.

We "were astounded by this measure," Abraham Lincoln remembered. "But we rose, each fighting, grasping whatever he could first reach—a scythe, a pitchfork, a chopping ax, or a butcher's cleaver," and heaved themselves into the fight against slavery's extension. Northern Democrats turned on their Southern colleagues, accusing them of selling out to a "Slave Power" that nursed conspiratorial ambitions for turning all of the United States into a legalized slave empire.

"The thing is a terrible outrage, and the more I look at it the more enraged I become," confessed Maine's U.S. senator William Pitt Fessenden. But that did not stop pro-slavery and antislavery settlers from pouring into Kansas, bent on grasping for control by sheer numbers. Or if not by numbers, then by violence. Eye was given for eye, tooth for tooth; the Kansas territory became "Bleeding Kansas," with more than fifty political murders making it seem as though "murder and coldblooded assassination were of almost daily occurrence."[19] Then, in May 1856, a wild shadow crossed over the sun in the form of the abolitionist John Brown, who deliberately executed five pro-slavery Kansans at Pottawatomie Creek in retaliation for what he imagined was a bloody pro-slavery attack on the free-state settlement of Lawrence.

In that shadow, Brevet Colonel Robert E. Lee sat, silent.

With the approach of the 1851 Christmas holidays, Lee took the family back to Arlington. They left Baltimore on a bitterly cold Christmas Eve, so bitter that snow piled up on the tracks and delayed the departure of their train for an hour. George Washington Parke Custis met them in Washington with "Daniel and the old carriage horses," and together they trekked across the Potomac to Arlington. The children were restless with anticipation for the next day, and on Christmas morning six-year-old Mildred (Precious Life) "drew the prize" among the Christmas presents "in the shape of a beautiful new doll." The tables groaned with "the turkey, cold ham, plum-pudding, mince-pies, etc., at dinner," and on the twenty-eighth (as he wrote to Custis), "Your mother, Mary, Rooney, and I went into church" in Alexandria. But the weather continued frigid. "I do not recollect such weather," Lee wrote to Custis, "since the winter of 1835," the year of the Great Freeze that iced over rivers in Georgia and northern Florida. A week later, Lee had to report that fourteen-year-old Rooney "is quite sick & will not be able to travel," and measles soon made its appearance among the young Lees.[20]

Lee could not stay to nurse them. By mid-January, he was back in Baltimore to resume work on Fort Carroll, and with illnesses laying low the house slaves as well, Mary had to play "nurse & chamber maid too." By the time the family caught up with him in Baltimore in mid-February, Rooney was still suffering from "a little cold in my head." But recuperation brought no relaxation of Lee's anxiety for his offspring. He bore down heavily on Custis at West Point: "Do not dream. It is too ideal, too imaginary. . . . Look upon things as they are. Take them as you find them. Make the best of them, Turn them to your advantage." Again, Lee wrote to Custis, urging him, "You must press forward in your studies. . . . You must be No. 1. It is a fine number. Easily found & remembered. Simple & unique. Jump to it fellow."

He exhorted his mother-in-law to press Annie and Agnes, too, who were still under the tutelage of Sarah Poor at Arlington, since failure on their part would inflict agony on him. "If they knew how I love them, how I feel through them, I know they would spare me much I now suffer & all I apprehend." By contrast, Mary Lee's view of her children was sunny and untroubled. "Custis is . . . doing very well so far not a single demerit," she reported blithely (the demerits for alcohol smuggling would not catch up to Custis until later), while "Daughter" Mary has "grown so much she is quite a woman in appearance tho' just 15." As for the rest of her brood, "We begin to feel quite patriarchial with our sons & daughters growing up around us."[21]

They were now about to enter into a vastly different realm of patriarchy. On May 28, orders arrived from Joseph Totten, on the authority of the secretary of war, Charles Conrad, instructing Lee "to transfer the operations now under your charge . . . to Lieut. [William] Whiting, in order that you may proceed to West Point . . . and on the 1st of September next relieve Capt. Brewerton of the Superintendency of the Military Academy, and of the command of the post of West Point." Lee was bewildered. He had brought the construction of Fort Carroll to the point where the foundation work was complete, a parade ground had been laid out and sodded, and the first course of casemates was being finished, and now he was being yanked away to an utterly different assignment. And even though the academy was still the domain of the Corps of Engineers, Lee was far from confident that he had either the temperament or the interest to become the presiding officer of a collegiate institution. Besides, he would overlap his own son's senior year at the academy, with complications and embarrassments that no one could foresee, and take command just as his brother Sidney Smith Lee was sending his own son Fitzhugh Lee to the Point.

Thirteen years before, when Totten had first assumed the role of Chief Engineer, Lee had balked at a proposal from Totten to join the faculty at West Point: "So far as I know my own inclinations they would never prompt me to volunteer for such Service, the duties of an Instructor being very foreign to my taste and disposition." In his long years with the Engineers, he had never been expected to command any large body of soldiers; the workforces he had managed at Fort Calhoun, on the Mississippi, at Fort Hamilton, and in Baltimore had all been civilians, free or enslaved. Even in Mexico, he had operated mostly as Winfield Scott's eyes and ears, with only a handful of junior Engineer lieutenants to assist him. Now he had the prospect of commanding a battalion of cadets and faculty (with the latter's civilian dependents) made up of high-spirited collegians and military-education pontiffs rather than ordinary rankers and worn-down company officers, and the prospect did not suit him. "I learn with much regret the determination of the Secretary of War to assign me to that duty," Lee replied hastily. Did he have no choice in the matter? "If I be allowed any option in the matter, I would respectfully ask that some other successor than myself be appointed to the present able Superintendent." Totten waved the plea away.

He "had never undertaken duty with such reluctance," Lee grumbled. When his former lieutenant from Mexico days, Pierre Beauregard, gingerly wrote to congratulate him, he was in no humor to feel honored. "You are right in your conjecture of my not being pleased at being ordered to W.P.," Lee lamented. "I know too well the thanklessness of the duty, and the impossibility of either giving or receiving satisfaction." The truth was that he had no experience for such command: "I have been behind the scenes too long." Nor did the superintendent have the sort of authority with which he could cloak himself. "The Supt. can do nothing right and must father every wrong." But as plainly as he had begged "that some other be appointed in my place . . . I have been told it cannot be done." So to West Point he would go. "But," he promised Beauregard, "I shall get away from it as soon as I can." On July 31, he formally turned over command of Fort Carroll to William Whiting and designated James Eveleth, a clerk in Totten's office, as "my lawful agent" to hire out his Arlington valet, Philip Meredith, "& to exercise such authority, control, and direction over him as may be necessary as well as for his protection, safety, & well doing."[22]

As Lee ascended to the old familiar parade ground—the Plain—above the Hudson, he was not entirely surprised at the vista that spread before him. He had been to West Point on various bits of Army business at several times in the twenty-three years since he graduated. Still, his eye could not have helped but be struck by the physical changes the academy had undergone. Hardly a single building he had known as a cadet was still there. The two barracks buildings that had stood in 1829 were gone, replaced by a four-story L-shaped barracks, completed in 1851 on the south side of the Plain, featuring steam heat and iron bedsteads. A "Library Building and Artillery Laboratory" had been built, along with "the improvement of the Chemical Laboratory" and "many acquisitions to the Drawing department." A new mess hall was ready for use just as Lee arrived, while under Henry Brewerton's superintendency, the Plain was regraded and new roads leading up from the river docks and Cozzens Hotel had been constructed.

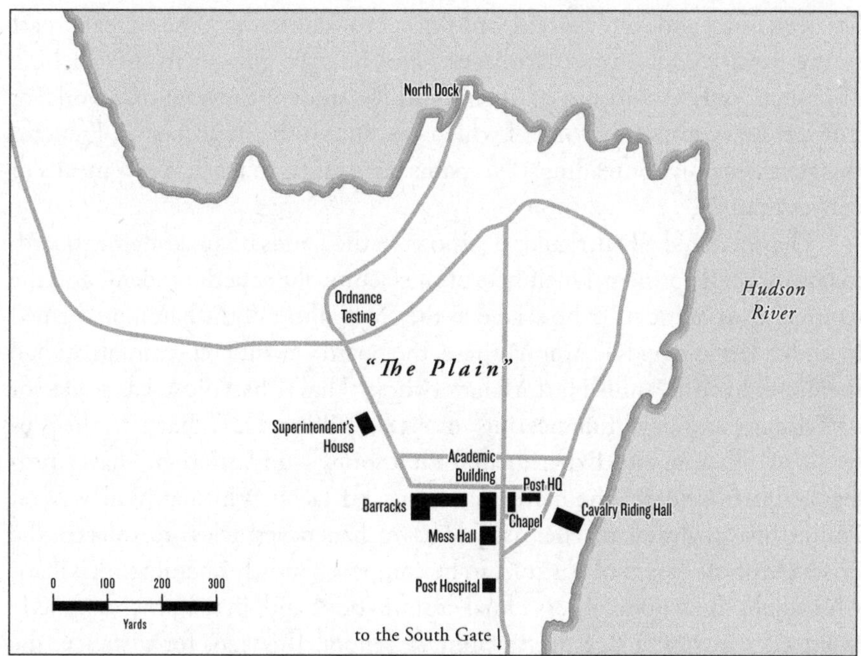

There were also new personnel. The "Company of Sappers, Miners, and Pontoniers" created by Congress in 1846 to provide the Corps of Engineers (which until then had been an officers-only organization) with a permanent battalion of enlisted men and noncommissioned officers were now on hand at West Point to offer practical demonstrations to cadets, as were "a sergeant and five dragoons" from the Army's two regiments of dragoons who were in charge of "the introduction of exercises in Riding at the Academy." Above all, the Mexican War had given the entire academy a new bounce of self-confidence. Politicians might complain that "West Point is too aristocratic," wrote Robert Anderson from Mexico, "but, thank God, every battlefield attests the steady valor of her pupils; there has been no faltering, no wavering among them."[23]

Some things, however, had not changed at all from Lee's day, and most of those concerned the curriculum. Sylvanus Thayer had succeeded more grandly than he might have hoped at fashioning West Point into an engineering school, and even though Thayer resigned his superintendency (in a spat with President Andrew Jackson) only four years after Lee's graduation, the curriculum's overwhelming emphasis on engineering had barely shifted at all. Thayer "rightly believed that a military education must be founded on a mathematical training and knowledge, hence he gave in that course that prominence, which they have ever retained," wrote Albert Church, now professor of mathematics. It seemed to Thayer a waste of effort to "do that which has been often and vainly attempted since, crowd into this time a greater part of the literary course of our colleges," and he gave ground to the teaching of French "only as a means of opening to the student the scientific works of Europe, every important one of which was sure to be published in French." But that was only for reading. "No pains were taken to teach it as a means of conversation."[24]

Thayer vested all curricular decisions in the hands of an academic board, to consist of the principal members of the faculty, the superintendent, and the commandant of cadets (who served as the chief officer of the battalion formed by the cadets as a body). Among these, the board's faculty representatives had the upper hand: Dennis Hart Mahan (whom Thayer had picked as professor of "Military and Civil Engineering" in 1832), William H. C. Bartlett, the professor of "Natural and Experimental Philosophy" (and another Thayer protégé); Albert Church, the mathematician; and Jacob Whitman Bailey, West Point's first professor of chemistry. Thayer had nevertheless to tolerate the existence of the Board of Visitors, to be composed mostly of eminent civilians who would show up to observe final examinations and, in the process, quietly assert civilian supremacy over a military school. (In 1826, for instance, the Board of Visitors comprised thirteen individuals, including a future governor of North Carolina, a member of Congress from Rhode Island, a deputy attorney general of Pennsylvania, the professor of chemistry at Dartmouth College, and a Philadelphia bank president; Lee himself had served on the board in 1844 while at Fort Hamilton.) Their annual reports would presumably quiet any political anxieties that West Point was breeding a nest of potential Napoleons, bent on overturning the Republic, and thus "spread over the U.S. 'liberal views' of the Academy."[25]

What they spread were complaints that the engineering curriculum bulked too large. In 1828, the Corporation of Yale College released a widely read report that vigorously asserted the primacy of the liberal arts—and especially the classical languages, Latin and Greek—as "the foundations of a correct taste," the basis for "those elementary ideas which are found in the literature of modern times," and "the most effectual discipline of the mental faculties." And almost on Yale's cue, all through the 1830s and 1840s the civilian visitors frequently complained that "the course of instruction" at West Point was not suitable to "a full development" of the cadets' "aptitudes" and recommended curricular expansions to include literature, history, and languages. "In the West Point instructions, science, either abstract or practical, receives the prominent attentions," complained *The Quarterly Christian Spectator.* But that "leaves certain mental faculties in the back-ground" and results in leaving "the military students . . . behind the civil" in "largeness of views, symmetry of powers, and maturity of useful, practical qualities of mind." The academy's Academic Board fired back in 1843: yes, "a thorough course of mental as well as military discipline" was necessary to teach the future officers of the Army "to reason accurately, and readily to apply right principles." But the existing curriculum of "mathematical and philosophical study . . . is by far the best calculated to bring about this end."[26]

The solution, proposed by Joseph Totten in 1852, was to expand the term of study at West Point from four to five years, to accommodate history, languages, and geography. This was promptly vetoed by the secretary of war. But 1852 was an election year, and the election brought a new president, Franklin Pierce, who in turn appointed a new secretary of war, Jefferson Davis, and Davis endorsed Totten's plan. An expanded arts curriculum would prepare "the cadets better to comprehend the higher branches of mathematics and natural philosophy." Robert E. Lee, as the new superintendent, would be Totten's man to implement the new curriculum. In fact, he would be Totten's man to run whatever aspects of the academy Totten was interested in—which was virtually all of them.[27]

Robert E. Lee discovered just how little latitude existed for his own judgment as superintendent from his first week at West Point. Cadets were not permitted to keep cash, "and such adventitious aids to popularity were therefore eliminated"; thus, Lee had to disclose to Totten that on September 3 the New Jersey Democratic congressman Rodman Price had sent his cadet nephew (and adopted son) Rodman Lewis a check for $50, which Lee appropriated and entered as a credit for Lewis on the academy's books. A month later, Lee had to notify Totten that Lewis had "left his quarters in Barrack yesterday Morg. & has not been heard of" and then followed that up with notices of Lewis's "discouraged" return, second disappearance, and return again on October 11. "I have no excuse to offer for his conduct & in consideration of his having repeated his offense & broken his arrest," Lee added, and with evident relief, he felt "compelled to recommend he be dismissed the service." (Lee was premature in his relief: Lewis's congressional uncle appealed to the outgoing secretary of war for his nephew's reinstatement, and Lee was forced to write an unenthusiastic letter to the uncle, welcoming Lewis's return if he "will earnestly apply himself to be more diligent in his studies & attentive to his duties.")[28]

On it went. Totten had to be informed when five cadets needed the Chief Engineer's permission "to receive the articles" sent from home that Lee listed:

a writing desk and stationery, "shirts & drawers," uniform collars. The disappearance without leave of a distant relative of Lee's, "Cadet Richd. H. Lee Jr.," had to be explained to Totten, and a series of letters written itemizing young Lee's return and holding over for court-martial. (Cadet Lee saved his relation any further grief by turning in a resignation when his father showed up for "the purpose of taking him home.")[29]

In addition to itemizing the peccadilloes of the cadets to Totten, Lee had to submit for Totten's approval the appointment of adjunct military instructors, get Totten's approval of the proof sheets for a new printing of the academy regulations (and then nag Totten repeatedly when Totten failed to reply), submit plans for the construction of a "Cavalry Exercise Hall & stable," and make a survey for a new wharf on the Hudson, all the while warning that there were no funds left for "Forage for Artillery & Cavalry horses." And every month brought a report to Totten on the expenditure of funds.[30]

The incessant bureaucratic begging annoyed Lee. He did not mind telling Jerome Bonaparte "of my regret at leaving Baltimore." He was determined to "administer [the academy] to the best of my ability" but "shall relinquish that charge with more cheerfulness than I felt reluctance in undertaking it." His daily routine, which began at seven in the morning, was filled with "an hundred interruptions," and he complained to Bonaparte after less than a year in office that "my health is failing fast," and "the sooner I get away from [the academy] the better."[31]

Just as wearisome were the parents of cadets, especially those like Rodman Price who had significant political wires to pull. (Price continued to plague Lee with complaints about the "injustice" done his nephew, until Lee tartly informed him that "no one has had more consideration extended to him than he.") Although Lee dismissed John P. Sherburne for acquiring a whopping demerit total, in addition to having "missed recitations on 14 days," Sherburne appeared in Lee's office in the post headquarters facing the Plain with instructions from the secretary of war to reduce the demerit total and readmit him. Lee refused—"the members of the Academic Board" had agreed that "in their opinion [he] would not be able to succeed" academically, entirely aside from the demerits—but he took the precaution of sending a copy of his letter to Totten. (Sherburne eventually wangled a commission anyway in 1862 and appears on the post–Civil War Army List as a major.)[32]

And there were still sadder cases, when Lee had to report on the illnesses and deaths of cadets. Elias Coryell had been sick since arriving at West Point in the summer of 1854, and Lee warned his father, an influential Pennsylvania Democrat, that "there is little probability of his being able to continue at the Academy." (There wasn't; he died the next year.) Charles W. Frank developed typhoid, and when "he expired at the Cadet Hospital," Lee could only offer his grieving father, Alpheus, "my sincere sympathy in your deep affliction" and a clumsy proffer of religious consolation "by reflecting on his gain" in eternity. What Lee did *not* report to parents (but did to Totten) was the gonorrhea contracted by four new cadets almost as soon as they had arrived at the academy.[33]

The hardest case, however, concerned his own nephew Fitzhugh Lee, who was from the first the wild inverse of his sedate cousin Custis and who entered the academy just as his uncle was moving to West Point. Custis knew better than to risk embarrassing his superintendent father, whose perfect "eye is sure to distinguish him among his comrades & follow him over the plain," and in 1854 Custis graduated gloriously at the head of his class and went, like his father, straight into the Corps of Engineers as a second lieutenant. (In yet another echo of his father, he would be assigned in 1856 to the completion of Fort Pulaski, on Cockspur Island.) Nephew Fitzhugh, however, was a free spirit. "He is so full of mischief," wrote his thirteen-year-old cousin, Agnes Lee, in the journal her governess had directed her to keep, "he is always getting into trouble."[34]

He certainly was. His uncle had been in the superintendent's office for little more than a year before Fitzhugh was arrested, along with four other cadets, returning from a drinking spree at five in the morning, with "spirituous liquors in their possession" and "in citizens dress." Lee knew all too well what the situation called for—"dismissal from the service"—and he applied to Totten to convene "a Genl. Court Martial for their trial." Promptly, the members of Fitzhugh Lee's class deployed the tactic intended to save his cousin Custis, and that was to take the pledge as an entire class not to commit any similar offense. Lee "considered this kind of convention between the authorities and the corps irregular." But then he weakened and advised the new secretary of war, Jefferson Davis, that "experience has shown the happiest results from these specific pledges." Davis did not agree, and the case went to court-martial.

Fitzhugh eventually slipped past with only minor punishment. "Fitzhugh Lee, our first cousin, got into a scrape," wrote Agnes Lee, in an adolescent mixture of disapproval and admiration, but his worst punishment seemed only to be "walking post." He did not, however, learn from his escape. Eight months later, Fitzhugh Lee was again "found absent from camp," and once again the uncle-superintendent recommended "trial by a Genl. Court Martial." Once more, Fitzhugh's classmates stepped forward to offer a class pledge, once more the uncle-superintendent referred the matter to Totten, and once more Fitzhugh was let off by Jefferson Davis, who this time accepted the class pledge. No wonder, when Davis visited West Point that year, he "was surprised to see so many gray hairs" on Lee's head. "He confessed that the cadets did exceedingly worry him," and the portrait Robert Walter Weir, the academy's drawing instructor, painted of him in 1855 confirms it. "The expression of strength peculiar to his face is wanting," Rob observed years later, "and the mouth fails to portray that sweetness of disposition so characteristic of his countenance."[35]

Lee's great consolation at West Point was the pleasure of gathering his family around him. Mary Lee followed her husband to West Point from Arlington in the fall of 1852, bringing with her "Daughter" Mary (now seventeen), Rooney (fifteen), Rob (nine), and Mildred; Annie and Agnes would remain at Arlington to finish their tutoring for another year. (Regulations limited Custis's visits that first year to Saturdays; that the superintendent was his father made no difference.) The superintendent's house was at "the centre of a row of houses"—the faculty cottages—"facing the plain" on its west side, and "built of stone, large and roomy." Mary Lee went to work on the garden, begging "any seed you have" from her mother at Arlington and "taking all of the flowers out of the green house & putting them in the grounds."

Lee arranged to buy "a very pretty Carriage for *four Sitters,* two seats, of medium build" with "a folding top," and together there were rides and hikes to the top of the fourteen-hundred-foot Crow's Nest, overlooking the academy, with Lee riding his favorite horse from Mexico, Grace Darling, and Rob on a white mustang pony Lee named for Santa Anna. "We rode the dragoon-seat," Rob remembered, using the French-style long forward leg filling the stirrup, body erect in the saddle, and jumping any obstacles leaning well back on the horse's hindquarters. It was gorgeous country for riding. "West Point is a beautiful place," Agnes Lee admitted when she finally arrived there in the fall of 1853. "Our house is quite large and convenient. We have a fine garden with a pond in it & several meadows. There is quite a nice greenhouse with a splendid lemon tree in it."[36]

The house became the theater of an almost endless round of entertaining. There were "cadet suppers" every Saturday evening and dinners for visiting dignitaries, from the Mexican general Manuel Robles Pezuela (as one of Santa Anna's engineering officers during the Mexican War, he and Lee had both fought at Cerro Gordo; he was regarded by the French minister to Mexico, Alphonse Dubois de Saligny, as "the only general and the only honorable man, in the country," but he would be executed for betraying his country to the French intervention of 1861) to Sherrard Clemens (a first cousin of Samuel Langhorne Clemens who had briefly been a cadet himself, but turned to politics and returned to West Point as secretary of the Board of Visitors in 1854) to Winfield Scott (for whom Lee obligingly ordered "a salute," a tour of the buildings, and dinner at the superintendent's house "with such of our natives as I can collect").

The cadets had no social organizations of their own apart from "a literary society called 'The Dialectic,'" but Lee made a point of attending the society's annual fall oration, and the officers and faculty improvised "an amateur orchestral club" to play Beethoven and Schumann chamber music. The high point of the year was always New Year's Day, when "from morning till night the house was filled by officers & cadets" and "dinner was dispensed with by most of us while 'sweets' of all kinds supplied its place." And occasionally, there would be an event of such drama that the whole academy was swept up into it, as in May 1854, when a total eclipse of the sun "scattered" cadets "all over the plain with pieces of smoked glass, each his own astronomer, begriming his face and hands."

For Lee's teenage daughters, flirting with handsome cadets at these events was intimidating—"I have met a great many cadets," Agnes confided to her journal, "but it frightens me so, I am so dreadfully diffident"—and exhilarating. "Daughter" Mary, as the oldest, attracted serious attention from a cadet, James Ewell Brown Stuart, who hailed from the old Lee territories in western Virginia. Stuart was attracted by Mary's "beauty and sprightliness," and she presented him with a small pencil portrait showing a woman holding a child in her lap, attended by an angel with a cross. (Mary's mother seems to have hoped that something would come of this, because she sent Stuart "a bouquet" and made herself "my most particular friend among the ladies.")[37]

At every event, Lee played faultlessly the genteel host. At a dinner to welcome the new bride of the French instructor H. Robert Agnel, Lee seated the wife of the French-born captain Theophile D'Oremieulx at the table in view of "four silver jardinières," or wine coolers. Laura D'Oremieulx was the granddaughter of Oliver Wolcott, a governor of Connecticut and Washington's second secretary of the treasury, and she was startled to remember that her grandfather "had left one exactly like them to her mother." Yes, Lee replied, without even slightly breaking the social tempo. "These four are the rest of the set. . . . I inherited four and the other two Washington presented, one to General Hamilton, the other to Governor Wolcott." But Lee could impress people even with the smallest gestures. Laura D'Oremieulx remembered that "in a snow storm" in 1853 she had been struggling "on my way to market" and found Lee catching up to her and "saying: 'Going to buy your little beefsteak, Mrs.——, so am I, and will you allow me to offer you my arm.'"

Yet Lee "did not ostentatiously stoop from his high estate to elevate a suppliant." He governed by politeness, sensibility, and refinement, like Tennyson's King Arthur:

The realms together under me, their Head, . . .
A glorious company, the flower of men,
To serve as model for the mighty world.

When Erasmus Keyes, who would become Winfield Scott's military secretary, struck up a conversation with Lee on "all subjects relating to the Union and the dangers that threatened it," Lee patiently heard out Keyes's "ardent Northern sentiments, and treated them with a candor and fairness altogether unusual with his fellow Southerners." John M. Schofield, who graduated seventh in his class in 1853 and would himself later become superintendent of West Point, recalled Lee as "the personification of dignity, justice, and kindness . . . the ideal of a commanding officer." The mother of one cadet who described Lee as a "marble model" found, on meeting Lee, that he was actually "very human kind, calm and definite." Even William Whitman Bailey, the ten-year-old son of the academy's chemistry professor, remembered Lee as "a most heroic figure." Clean-shaven, "with the exception of a mustache," Lee was young Bailey's "boyhood ideal of Washington, Bruce, Wallace, and those I loved and admired most in my books." He was the personification of the genteel, "expert in figure, gracious in countenance, and urbane in manner."[38]

And yet the anxieties for security never left Lee, even here. Not every cadet who saluted him properly appreciated his stiff enforcement of discipline, and during the preliminary summer encampment of 1854 rowdy cadets were heard singing songs "decrying the merits of Old Bob Lee—and stating his cruelties to cadets." The superintendent's house was the finest home Lee had ever enjoyed, apart from Stratford, long ago, and Arlington. Yet it would never really be his, any more than the others had been, and in a few unspecified years he would have to move on to—what, exactly? Nothing he could do seemed to wean his wife or his children from their affection for Arlington and the Custises. "Where am I?" Agnes asked her journal. "Really at West Point," but "I long for Arlington my previous Arlington my own dear home. . . . Thou art an old & tried friend; as for this place I know nothing about it."

Nothing underscored the family's ties to Arlington more dramatically than when, on April 21, 1853, Mary Fitzhugh Custis was felled by a stroke and died two days later. "Her illness was short," Lee wrote to Markie Williams. "One day in the garden with her flowers, the next with her God," and at the end she was only able to murmur the Lord's Prayer and wonder, almost from a distance, "how terribly" her daughter "will be shocked when she hears this." She was. Mary Lee at once departed for Arlington, only barely arriving in time for her mother's funeral on the twenty-seventh; the following Sunday, the rector of Christ Church, Alexandria, Charles B. Dana, held up Mary Fitzhugh Custis's example in his sermon, "setting forth some of the excellent traits of her character, and actions of her life, and exhorting others to an imitation of her virtues." Robert would not catch up with Mary until July, when the annual examinations were past and he could bring little Rob and Mildred with him.

The stream of condolences and visitors was almost endless, including President Franklin Pierce. "I was much occupied with my own & Mrs Ls distress at the death of her mother & consequent events," Lee later wrote to Jerome Bonaparte. Those "consequent events" included the care of George Washington Parke Custis, who was almost helpless with grief. "Poor grandpa," Agnes Lee wrote, weeping, "I can hardly think of his agony. He knelt by her bedside & implored God to spare her." For weeks after, Mary attended on her father, "who has been very ill," and by the time Lee had to return to the academy at the end of August, they had all agreed to bring his seventy-two-year-old father-in-law back to West Point with them. It was, at first, a restorative for the frail old man, who "seems cheered & interested by the new scenes around him." But the pull of Arlington was inexorable. "I fear," Lee conceded to Markie Williams, "that he will soon tire of the monotony of our life & wish to return to his home." And when he did, the argument that "the Major" required the ministrations of the Lee family there full-time would be almost unchallengeable.[39]

Lee's fears about the Arlington vortex were not exaggerated. "I do not like to think of leaving Arlington now," wailed Agnes Lee, "I love it more than ever," especially because "Grandma's remains" were buried on the grounds and "I can visit them whenever I want to" and "carry flowers & place them on her grave." When Lee arrived at Arlington that July, "Daughter" Mary and Annie were both scheduled to be confirmed at Christ Church, Alexandria, by Bishop John Johns, the newest evangelical bishop of Virginia, and almost in submission to the piety of his mother-in-law Lee impulsively decided to join his daughters in being confirmed.

This was an odd moment in Lee's life. Strictly speaking, Lee ought never to have been admitted to communion without confirmation at any earlier point in his life, and yet, until age forty-six, there seems to have been no motion on his part to be confirmed, even though he had been prepared for confirmation by Bishop William Meade "when he was a boy in Alexandria." Partly, this was a marker of the indifference into which confirmation had sunk as a ritual of the Church of England and the Episcopal Church at the end of the eighteenth century. But only partly: Episcopal evangelicalism reversed this indifference and made confirmation, as a conscious and devout embrace of Christian doctrine, into virtually a third sacrament. "It is a solemn and public assumption and establishing of a covenant which you are presumed to have previously made with God . . . in his own ordinance of baptism," declared

Stephen H. Tyng, the formidable rector of St. Paul's Church in Philadelphia, one of the bastions of evangelical Episcopalianism in the North. "It must have been inwardly and spiritually made, in your new birth of the Spirit." So, instead of being indifferent, Episcopalians now became intimidated by it, fearing to repeat with insufficient sincerity the words of the confirmation rite in the Episcopal prayer book.

At this point, however, Lee set these hesitations aside, as if finally determined to reach out to the God whom his mother-in-law "so fervently adored & earnestly served." Even so, he did not reach far. The children of the fatherless are particularly vulnerable to religious uncertainty, and Lee would always retain that uncertainty. Toward the end of his life, he would admit to Mary that "he wished he felt sure of his acceptance" with God. She reassured him that "all who love & trust in the Savior need not fear," but "he did not reply."[40]

The counterpoise to Arlington was West Point, where Totten had more than enough engineering and academic work to occupy Lee's attention. Totten had long viewed West Point as the ideal proving grounds for measuring "the effects of firing with heavy ordnance from casemate embrasures," and Lee as the ideal officer to execute the testing. Two "embrasure-targets" had been built just before Lee's arrival in the summer of 1852, and both came under Lee's supervision for experiments and analysis of their mortar and concrete, and "the effect of solid shot from guns of large caliber" on their "outer edges and the flaring surfaces." There were observations to be recorded, tables to be drawn up, and further directions from Totten to be followed for additional experiments. The tests indicated that the day of solid masonry fortifications, especially the Third System forts used to protect American harbors, was fast passing away under improvements in naval gunnery and ammunition. "A casemated battery having large embrasures" could not "be served at all" if, for instance, a reasonably large warship "has gained a position, within a short distance, and opened her fire of small canister balls."[41]

Lee also had his hands full as Totten's agent for expanding the academy curriculum, and with all the uncertainty that involved. Lee did not receive final authorization, through Totten, from Secretary Davis for implementation of the new five-year plan until July 1854. At once, "the practical difficulties" of creating "certain branches of the English Course" appeared from the Academic Board, which balked at committing the academy to a full-fledged introduction of "the higher branches" of the new curriculum. Finally, they extorted a compromise: because the new entering class in 1854 would be the largest on record—103 had been accepted—47 of the new cadets would enter on the old four-year course; the rest, mostly younger, would begin a new five-year program. This would avoid the awkward possibility that the three existing classes would all graduate in 1855, 1856, and 1857 and leave an entire year without a graduating class before the first five-years would graduate (in 1859), because the incoming four-years would provide a graduating class for 1858. More important, the arriving five-years would take on new courses in English, geography, and world history and serve as the test cases for the new curriculum; if it failed, they could revert to four years of the old curriculum without any loss.

By the end of the year, Lee was at last ready to submit a new report on textbooks for the five-years' first courses, which included Salma Hale's multi-edition *History of the United States of America* and an Americanized edition of Georg Weber's *Outlines of Universal History from the Creation of the World to the Present Time* prepared by Harvard's Francis Bowen. But he was not confident about the possibilities even after all the backing and filling, and he conceded that the faculty, truculent to the end, "may prefer some other mode of its organization."[42]

His sense of unfulfillment seeped through his correspondence, personal as well as official. Despite his brevet rank of colonel, he was still stalled at the *real* rank of captain, and there was not much prospect within the closed precincts of the Corps of Engineers that any senior officers were planning to vacate a spot he might fill. When his brother-in-law Edward Vernon Childe brought Lee's fifteen-year-old nephew on a surprise visit from Paris, Lee was delighted with Edward Lee Childe's precocity and in equal measure downcast when measuring his own meager accomplishments against their past promise. "To you life is new & light, & you can naturally look forward with anticipation of joy & pleasure," Lee wrote to young Childe.

> *To me looking at the future from the past, it brings feelings of apprehension & resignation. We do not therefore see things with the same eyes, nor do the same circumstances produce in us the same feelings. Happy is it that it is not so, & may all your anticipations be realized & all my hopes be fulfilled.*

When John Livingston, the editor of the *American Portrait Gallery,* a four-volume biographical encyclopedia, approached him about including him in its "sketches of eminent Americans," Lee demurred. "I fear the little incidents of my life would add nothing to the interest of your work, nor would your readers be compensated for the trouble of their perusal"—but he would buy the set for the academy library.

The longer he stayed in place at West Point, the more restless he seemed to become, something his children were the first to notice. The Saturday evening cadet dinners were not intended to be "very exquisite," but Agnes Lee observed that her father insisted that everything "be just right for Papa's scrutinizing eye." Even Rob, at ten years old, remembered that Lee made a fetish of being "punctual" and on Sunday mornings would "appear some minutes before the rest of us," ready to proceed to the academy chapel, and "rallying my mother for being late, and for forgetting something at the last moment." If she strained his patience, "he was off and would march along to church himself, or with any of the children who were ready." (It never occurred to her husband that Mary Lee's slowness might be due to some other cause than forgetfulness.) Young Rob had a room to himself for the first time, but his father "made me attend to it, just as the cadets had to do with their quarters in barracks and in camp," even to the point of "inspecting it."[43]

The longer he stayed at West Point, the more he lamented a life spent in the Army, or at least life in the Corps of Engineers. When Markie Williams's brother, Orton, made noises about entering West Point, Lee urged her to discourage him. "I can advise no young man to enter the Army," he wrote. "The same application, the same self denial, the same endurance, in any other profession, will advance him faster & farther." But Lee set his own worst example, not only because of his own halfhearted efforts to leave the service, but because he already had one son in the Army, and the next oldest, sixteen-year-old Rooney, was soon chafing for his own chance to enter West Point. This time, unlike with his older brother, Custis, Lee was having none of it. "The tears stream down Roonys cheeks, when I tell him of the almost insuperable difficulties to his procuring an app[ointmen]t to W.P.," not to mention "my disapprobation of his application," but Lee refused to do anything to advance an appointment for him. It was painful to watch: "I remember last summer when he used to stand watching dress parade he would involuntarily exclaim, 'O if I was only one of them.' "

In Rooney's case, his father's will prevailed, and in the fall of 1854, Rooney was packed off to Harvard, where his uncle Carter had graduated in 1819. But Rooney did so "with a heavy heart," Lee admitted to Jerome Bonaparte. "He said no one knew how sorry he was to leave W.P. & all hope of being a Cadet." Despite this demonstration, the military bug continued to bite the Lees: "Even Robt—thinks he can be nothing but a soldier!"[44]

What Lee did not realize, even as he accompanied Rooney to Harvard, was that his own time at West Point was about to close, and not only as superintendent of the academy, but as a captain of Engineers.

CHAPTER SEVEN

The Unpleasant Legacy

Agnes Lee was "returning from Mr. Agnel's with our French books" when a voice called out, "Miss Lee, Miss Lee." It was Lieutenant Edward Stockton, Professor Bailey's assistant, and he could not contain his excitement. "Do you know," he shouted, "your father is Col. Lieut-Colonel in one of these new regiments?" Stockton was holding a newspaper—probably *The New York Herald,* which contained this announcement on March 5—with the notice that the U.S. Senate had authorized a windfall promotion of sixteen Army officers. Among those "to be Lieut. Colonel"—a real lieutenant colonel, not merely a brevet—was the name "R. E. Lee, Captain Engineers." By the time Agnes walked through the front door of the superintendent's house, the post surgeon, John Cuyler, was already "informing Mamma."[1]

Surprise though this was to Agnes, it was probably no shock to her parents. The Mexican Cession added more than 525,000 square miles to the United States, from Texas to California, and secured Texas's boundaries at the Rio Grande. It added with these new lands the burden of governing and policing enormous stretches of arid, thinly populated territory, where fiercely independent bands of Indians had hunted, traded, stolen, and flouted both Mexican and American law from Kansas to central Texas for decades. This was no country for infantry. But the Army had only three mounted regiments, two of dragoons and one of mounted rifles, all created in the 1830s and the latter devoted mostly to guarding settlers on the Oregon Trail. Infantry would have to do.

Winfield Scott began agitating for an expansion of the Army's presence in the Mexican Cession as early as 1853, with two new light cavalry regiments to handle most of the work. Congress was no happier at the prospect of paying for more soldiers than it had been in Mexican War days, and especially the expense of cavalry, which meant a sizable investment in horses and training, as well as new recruits. "To govern a country well, where intelligence predominates over selfishness and interest, I think the smaller the army is better," objected one senator. "If you increase it, it will never get less." But in the summer of 1854, a detachment of the 6th Infantry under an inexperienced West Pointer named John Lawrence Grattan was handily annihilated by Brulé and Oglala Sioux near Fort Laramie, and after that there was no more talk about the adequacy of the foot soldiers for Indian warfare. When Jefferson Davis made his first report to Congress as secretary of war in 1854, he endorsed Scott's proposal for the two new cavalry regiments, to be staffed by promoting existing Army officers, and an authorization bill was passed on March 3, 1855. The next day, Davis issued his list of promotions for the new units, and among the sixteen designated for promotion and assignment was R. E. Lee.[2]

Agitation for these coveted new ranks had been going on for as long as Congress had debated the new regiments. The Texas legislature had loudly pressed Albert Sidney Johnston, a West Pointer from 1826, as colonel for one of the cavalry regiments, and Jefferson Davis "had known him from boyhood and . . . esteemed him as highly as any man living." Joseph E. Johnston, Lee's old classmate from West Point, began plying the adjutant general, Samuel Cooper, with pleas for a post in the new regiments as soon as he learned of the possibility of their creation.

There is nothing in Lee's correspondence that indicates any similar agitation, and the appointment announcement, as it appeared in the Pierce administration's house organ, the Washington *Daily Union,* was surprisingly lackluster: "R. E. Lee, the daring soldier and accomplished engineer, conspicuous on so many fields during the war with Mexico, will hardly be deemed unfit to be intrusted with the honor of his country's flag." But Lee's record in Mexico and his work at the academy impressed Jefferson Davis fully as much as it had Winfield Scott. "He came from Mexico crowned with honors, covered by brevets, and recognized, young as he was, as one of the ablest of his country's soldiers," Davis said. And Scott did not hesitate to endorse him in the most dramatic terms: "If I were on my death-bed tomorrow, and the President of the United States should tell me that a great battle was to be fought for the liberty or slavery of the country, and asked my judgment as to the ability of a commander, I would say with my dying breath, Let it be Robert E. Lee." In reality, Lee would be acquiring nothing quite so grandiose—the lieutenant colonelcy of the new 2nd Cavalry—but the promotion certainly meant that he would, finally, vault upward in real rank by two grades. Just as pleasing, assignment to one of the new regiments would open an easy and dignified door out of West Point.[3]

The difficulty for Lee was that after a quarter century of service in the Corps of Engineers he would have to leave the Corps and join an entirely different branch of the Army. Nor was that the only hesitation: in the 2nd Cavalry, he would be serving directly under Sidney Johnston, Jefferson Davis's favorite, as colonel and be responsible, as he had never been before, for the command of troops under fire, and horse soldiers at that. "I assure you," Lee wrote to George W. Cullum, who commanded West Point's enlisted engineer detachment, "my separation from the Corps of Engrs is attended with bitter regret." Still, on his present trajectory in the Corps of Engineers, he was unlikely to win real promotion to major (as opposed to mere brevet promotion) until he was in his fifties, or make colonel before he was seventy. And if he refused this opportunity, everyone would remember that he had declined a promotion, and another one might never be offered; or worse, by refusing an appointment, he would be told frankly that he needed to resign. That would leave him with no real alternative, at age forty-eight, but to surrender to Arlington, to his widower father-in-law, and to final loss of anything even remotely resembling independence. "I confess my preference in time of peace for Engr duty over that of Cavalry; But so long as I continue an Officer of the Army, I can neither decline promotion or service."[4]

The worst of all these considerations was that the 2nd Cavalry would be posted to central Texas, on the Brazos River. Under no circumstances could he imagine transporting Mary and the five children who were still under his eye to what Frederick Law Olmsted discovered Texas to be in the 1850s, a desolate land of "broad prairie, reaching, in swells like the ocean after a great storm, to the horizon" and "the dwarf mesquite and its congeners," a land where "we did not see one of the inhabitants look into a newspaper or a book," full of "overworked" women with "thin faces, sallow complexions, and expressions either sad or sour," and slavery so grinding that "the consciousness of a wrong relation" was assuaged only by "a determination to face conscience down, and continue it." Agnes Lee understood that "Papa is glad to leave here & of course likes promotion." But he could not hide from his fourteen-year-old daughter that he "doesn't like giving up the Eng. Corps," and liked even less the need "to break up & leave us for those western wilds." At least, he explained to Markie Williams (Mary's cousin who had moved to Arlington to supervise the house after Mary Fitzhugh Custis's death) "the change from my present confined & sedentary life, to one more free & active, will certainly be more agreeable to my feelings & serviceable to my health."[5]

The household "commenced to pack & sell everything we could lay our hands on." Lee sent his official acceptance of the appointment on March 15, submitting his final accounts to Totten on April 3. Finally, on April 15, a week after Easter Sunday, in a driving rain, the entire family crowded down to the south dock amid cadets giving "a very sweet serenade" and the band playing "'Home sweet Home,' 'Carry me back to Old Virginny' & others." There was a brief stopover in New York City and then a train to Baltimore and a brief visit with Anne Lee Marshall and her husband. ("Aunt Anne was looking very badly," Agnes noticed. "She can only move her head . . . & she only uses one arm a little. She hasn't been out of bed since October.")

They arrived in Washington on the twenty-first, where Lee left them to report to the War Department. But Mary and the children continued on to Arlington, dashing "around the garden fence" to be greeted by G.W.P. and Markie Williams. It had been exactly two years, Agnes wrote, since "my precious Grandmamma's death . . . my first real grief."[6]

Lee's most pressing task with the 2nd Cavalry would be organizing it, because the entire enlisted strength would have to be recruited from scratch. At least he and Sidney Johnston would have the advantage of an experienced cadre of junior officers, most of them promoted or appointed from elsewhere in the Army, to help. The regiment's two majors, William J. Hardee and George Henry Thomas, were both West Pointers: Hardee had seen mounted service with the 2nd Dragoons in Mexico and in Texas and had even written a textbook on tactics, while Thomas had been in Mexico with the 3rd Artillery and was the artillery instructor at West Point when Lee arrived there in 1852. Earl Van Dorn, the senior of the company captains, was another West Pointer who had marched with Scott up to Mexico City and won two brevets in the process. Impetuous to a fault, Van Dorn "was among the first to scale the wall" at Chapultepec "and with his sword to cut his way into the citadel."

The other captains included four more West Pointers—Edmund Kirby Smith, who had also collected two brevets in the Mexico City campaign as an infantry lieutenant, James Oakes of Pennsylvania, the New Yorker Innis Palmer, and George Stoneman—but also three civilians who had served in Mexico as volunteers and were now being handed commissions as Regulars: Albert Brackett of Indiana; Theodore O'Hara, who had served as Gideon Pillow's quartermaster in Mexico and barely escaped the debacle of Narciso López's Cuban expedition in 1851; and Charles Travis, the son of the ill-fated commander of the Alamo. The oldest of the captains, Charles J. Whiting, was a West Pointer but had resigned in 1836 and spent almost twenty years building railroads and teaching school.[7]

Lee spent only a whisper of time at Arlington before departing for Louisville, Kentucky, where he would coordinate the activities of the new captains in recruitment—Van Dorn in Alabama, Oakes in western Pennsylvania, O'Hara in Kentucky, Palmer in Maryland, Travis and Brackett in Indiana—of both men and horses. "You civilians do not know what work is," he wrote to Carter. He had "spent 2 days in Washington," just "endeavouring to get the addresses of the different officers of the Regt, & to get them relieved of their duties." But in little more than a week, Captain Oakes "opened his unit rendezvous" in Pittsburgh, and Van Dorn was collecting recruits "at the fort at Mobile Point," and by July, Lee had moved to St. Louis for a complete assembly of the new regiment at the Jefferson Barracks, "nearly 600" strong.

They were by no means the cream of anyone's crop. A large portion were immigrants "from all parts . . . of other countries" who only wanted government-paid passage to the west, where they could desert. Others were refugees from poverty or the law, and "there is much sickness among them." "Yesterday at *muster,*" Lee wrote to Mary, "I found one of the late arrivals in a dirty, tattered shirt & pants with a white slouched hat, & shoes, his only garments." Lee suggested that he at least wash and mend his threadbare garments, but the recruit objected that "he had nothing else to put on." Lee pointed him to the Mississippi riverbank and proposed that he clean up there while watching "the passing steamboats . . . & then mend" his clothes. He did, and the next morning "he . . . stood in the position of a soldier . . . his toes sticking through his shoes; but his skin & solitary two garments clean. He grinned very happily at my compliments."[8]

Nothing, however, gave him more unease than the family he had left behind. "What I value more than anything else," he wrote Mary, is "the society of you & my children." His visit to his "prostrated & afflicted" sister Anne in Baltimore was so depressing that he assigned "Daughter" Mary to care for her. Rooney had finished his first year at Harvard, fifty-sixth out of ninety-one freshmen, and "I fear not satisfied, or making the most of his opportunities." Annie and Agnes were to begin at the Virginia Female Institute in Staunton—"one of the salubrious regions of the state"—and "labour at their French, & music & try to progress in Mathematics & English"; young Rob was to start at the Reverend Edward R. Lippitt's school in Alexandria; and all of them must "conduct themselves so, as to gain the friendship of their schoolmates, & the admiration & esteem of their teachers."

He had worries and advice for everyone. "Do not be out much in the hot sun, or night air, or allow the children," he wrote to Mary again in August. "I fear you will all be sick." There were directions to be given about the upkeep of Arlington so that "the place dear to their affections" is "properly preserved." And, he might have added, because management of Arlington was increasingly beyond the grip of G.W.P. "Attend to all his wishes & wants," Lee advised, but do not let him "stay down at the farm late in the evg, & indeed not too much in the day." And "get some respectable farmer, in whom he could repose confidence, to manage his farm for him."[9]

The Jefferson Barracks, "beautifully situated upon the Mississippi river, about ten miles below the city of St. Louis," featured "barracks of hewn stone . . . in the shape of a hollow square" and a parade ground "which is handsomely graded, and from the river presents a fine appearance." It was the Army's largest training facility and the original home of its two dragoon regiments, and though Lee had been aware of it during his postings to St. Louis in the 1830s, his work as an engineer on the Mississippi River kept it beyond his everyday horizons. Now, however, the Jefferson Barracks became his school as a cavalry officer, "superintending the drilling of recruits" and "making them police themselves, their quarters & grounds." The outdoor labor refreshed him, and by the beginning of September he could write to Mary, "I was never in better health than I am now." As he told one junior officer, he "was always fond of horses and liked the [cavalry] service for the outdoor life." He would certainly have enough of horses: more than eight hundred of them had to be purchased for the regiment and apportioned to the regiment's ten companies by color, grays to Company A, sorrels to Companies B and E, bays to Companies C, D, F, and I, roans to Company K.

The human material for riding them wore a less charming aspect. The "raw recruits" were "soon sick of the service," and "passing steamers" offered "great . . . facilities . . . for escape." (All told, 329 of the recruits would disappear before the regiment reached Texas.) Deserters who were caught were not treated kindly. Sidney Johnston's wife, Eliza, who had lived with her husband in Texas before the Mexican War and had no illusions about its challenges, was still shocked to see "6 of my husbands men . . . whipped, and . . . drummed out . . . with shaven heads marched round the garrison to the tune of poor old soldier." At least Lee found the Episcopalian post chaplain, John Fish, to be an earnest man, "plain & practical . . . & without conceit or pretensions." But Fish had a large circuit of posts and missions to serve, and it was not until September that Lee was able to go "to church for the first time since my arrival." Lee himself was pulled away by demands to serve on courts-martial, one of them as far away as Fort Leavenworth and the new Fort Riley, in the Kansas Territory.

Nevertheless, by the end of October, the 2nd Cavalry had assembled 696 troopers, and on October 27 the new regiment set off, trailed by twenty-nine wagons, seven ambulances, and the wives and children of a surprisingly large number of the officers and enlisted men, in converted ambulances with "seats" that could be folded down to form "a good bed upon which to sleep." Their path would take them through southern Missouri, across the Ozarks and the "Indian Territory," to which the Cherokee, Choctaw, Creek, and

Chickasaw tribes had been exiled by Andrew Jackson, and Captain Brackett noted that "many a grim old warrior watched" the regiment unforgivingly "as it passed along on its journey." They would finally cross the Red River into Texas on December 15.[10]

Lee was not with them on this trek, his court-martial duties having been extended from Fort Riley to the Carlisle Barracks in Pennsylvania in January, followed by yet another court-martial assignment at West Point. He sandwiched an extended visit to Arlington between these assignments and found that his uneasiness about G.W.P.'s loosening hold, not only on Arlington, but on his two other properties at White House and Romancoke on the Pamunkey River, was all too well justified. He wrote in alarm to one of his Carter relatives to alert him that old Custis's property manager, Francis Nelson, was robbing G.W.P. under his nose. "Many of his debits, or charges against Mr C are not supported by vouchers at all, or the vouchers are not in the proper or necessary form." Between courts-martial, he hired the clerk of the Hanover County courts to investigate Nelson's accounts. But more than that was

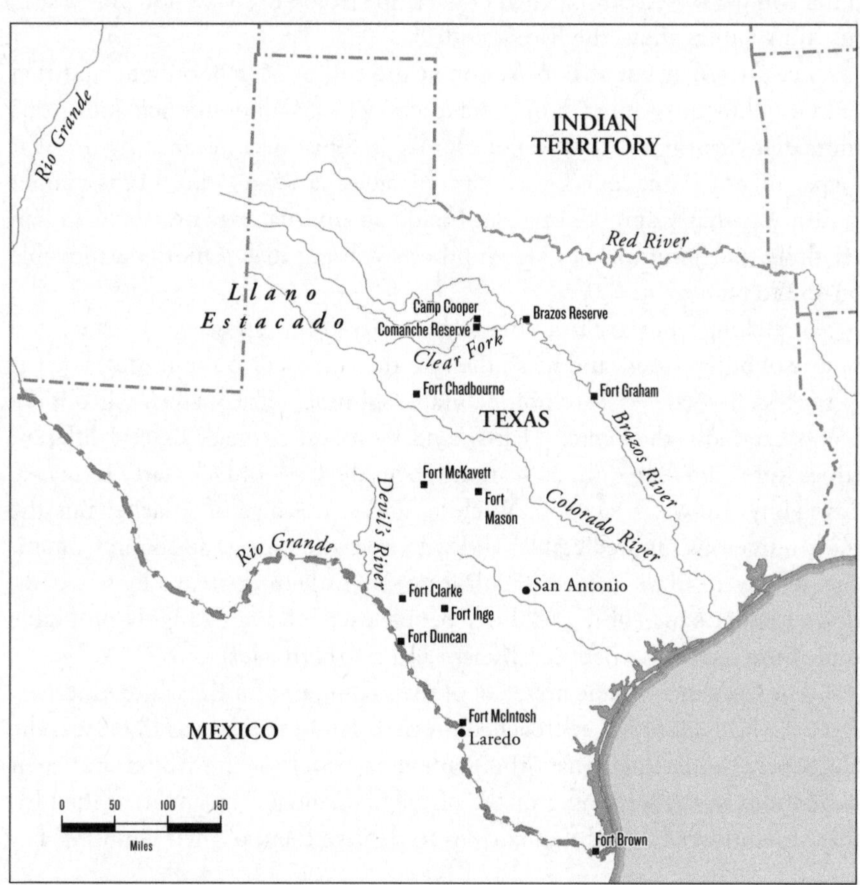

impossible to do: "It will be necessary for me to repair to Texas." In mid-February he was on his way by sea to Galveston, and from thence to Indianola and San Antonio.[11]

His regiment had meanwhile reached Fort Belknap, the northern edge of Texas's string of eight protective Army posts, just after Christmas 1855. There, the regiment was split into two battalions, four of the companies under William Hardee heading thirty miles west to the Clear Fork of the Brazos River to set up a new post (to be named Camp Cooper, in honor of the Army's adjutant general, Samuel Cooper), while the remaining six companies followed Johnston 150 miles south to Fort Mason, which would serve as the regimental headquarters. The two battalions would then be parceled out to occupy other posts along the barrier forts vacated by the Regiment of Mounted Rifles, who were being reshuffled to the New Mexico Territory. Two companies from Hardee's battalion at Camp Cooper under Captain Van Dorn erected a new camp to fill in the space between Camp Cooper and Fort Mason. Two companies of Sidney Johnston's battalion would remain at Fort Mason, while the other companies were dispatched down a line from Fort Mason to Fort Clark, just thirty miles above the Rio Grande.[12]

Lee arrived at last at Fort Mason at the end of March, only to find that Sidney Johnston wanted him to take charge of Camp Cooper. Johnston's immediate reason was that Major Hardee had just been recalled by the War Department for duty as commandant of cadets at West Point, but the larger reason was that Camp Cooper sat beside an unusual experiment in Indian relations, and Johnston needed an officer with as much seniority as possible on-site to manage it.

Stretching westward from the 2nd Cavalry's line of posts was a dreary, dry prairie of buffalo grass and mesquite that the Army's 1850 survey described as "a treeless, desolate waste of uninhabitable solitude." The Spanish called it the Llano Estacado (the Staked Plains), and by rough estimate sixteen different tribes were represented there—among them the Caddo, Delaware, Tonkawa, Tawakony, Kiowa, Kickapoo, Wichita, and scatterings of Apache. But the most numerous, unpredictable, and wily were the Numic-speaking Comanche, who were all the more difficult for being little more than a loose federation of raider bands of ten to thirty people each who ran a highly profitable trade in stolen horses between Kansas and northern Mexico.[13]

The Comanche made no secret of their contempt for the white American settlers who relentlessly encroached on their lands. As early as the 1830s, the Comanche understood that "the gradual approach of the whites and their habitations to the hunting grounds of the Comanches" meant "that the ultimate intention of the white man was to deprive them of their country." For that reason they "would . . . continue to be the enemy of the white race," and they proved it by staging three large-scale raids into the white settlements in the 1840s. The solution Secretary of War Davis proposed for corralling these nomads was similar to what had been imposed on the tribes in the Indian Territory, and in 1854 the Texas legislature authorized the creation of two "reservations," one of them sited fifteen miles south of Fort Belknap and comprising 37,000 acres, and a smaller one for the Comanche on the Clear Fork of the Brazos River, forty-five miles west, and embracing 18,000 acres. It would be the responsibility of Camp Cooper and Robert E. Lee to watch over the Comanche reserve, both to keep its approximately four hundred residents from slipping away for a profitable romp through the *rancheros* and to keep infuriated Texans from staging retaliatory massacres.

The opinions of the Comanche's federal guardians were mixed. In Washington, officialdom believed that "most, if not all, the aggressions, complained of against the Indians may be traced immediately to the improper encroachments by white men on Indian rights." Along the line of the Army posts in Texas, however, the Comanche in particular were regarded as "devils" and "savages . . . in the worst sense of the word," and the unwritten word was "to take no prisoners; to spare no one; to listen to no terms of peace until the race is cowed by their punishment." It did nothing to ease the racial hostilities in the air that the two reservation supervisors on the Clear Fork, Shapley Ross and John Baylor, had long records of Indian fighting and regarded their charges as "wild restless and discontented" and easily lured by their unsettled Comanche brethren to the north "in their excursions to Mexico, and the frontiers of Texas."[14]

Lee made his first official acquaintance with the Comanche three days after arriving at Camp Cooper in April 1856. Katum'seh, the spokesman for the reservation band, who had achieved fairly remarkable progress as farmers, called on Lee. It was an unpromising start, "very tedious on his part & very sententious on mine." Katum'seh was "a fine-looking man . . . full six feet high, with a dark red bronze complexion," dressed "in corduroy leggings and buckskin moccasins . . . an old, torn, greasy, checkered cotton coat, and a sixpenny straw hat." Lee wanted Katum'seh to understand from the first that he "hailed him as a friend" but there were limits that had to be observed. Friendship would prevail only "so long as his conduct & that of his band entitled him to it." Otherwise, substituting condescension for gentility, Lee "would meet him as an enemy, the first moment he deserved it."

The next day, Lee thought better of condescension and "returned his visit, & remained a short time in his lodge." But sympathy did not sprout in its place: Katum'seh cheerily informed Lee that "he had six wifes," and Lee was put off by the "paint & ornaments" that made the Comanche "more hideous than nature made them, & the whole race extremely uninteresting." Another "head chief" who had fallen ill called for "a big Medicine Man" from the whites. Lee and an orderly rode over to see him but were barred at the door of the lodge by a demand that Lee "disrobe before presenting myself before the august patient." Lee had no intention of surrendering propriety to a Comanche, until he "ascertained" that what was wanted was the removal of his "cravat." That he could do, and more: he unbuttoned his uniform coat and revealed his "blue check shirt," which won admiring approval—and still more condescension from Lee. "I see more of them than I desire, & when I can be of no service, take little interest in them."[15]

Life in Camp Cooper did not offer many more elevated distractions. Lee was relieved to find that "the country is fertile & rolling, lightly timbered, & the deer & antelope luxuriate in the abundant grass." Still, he admitted, "we are far beyond civilisation." He wrote a whimsical letter to Mildred, now eleven, describing the hens he had brought with him "in a coop behind my wagon" so that he could have the luxury of eggs. He had to build "a house of twigs" on stilts for them because "there are so many reptiles in this country that you cannot keep fowles on the ground." The Army's inspector general, Joseph F. K. Mansfield (whom Lee had first encountered twenty years before at Cockspur Island), toured Texas to report on the Army's installations and found Camp Cooper to be nothing more than a tent city, "an open camp in winter & poor water in summer & dry seasons." Both "officers and men & horses" had no other stabling than "at the picket rope," while the troopers were "deficient in clothing of all kinds . . . boots and shoes most wanted." And yet, Mansfield thought, "the post is very well commanded by Col. Lee & in good discipline." "Target firing" was kept up with Colt revolvers and Maynard carbines to train the men, and Lee had worked them up to "platoon drill," in which "they had progressed extremely well."[16]

Sidney Johnston was not, however, content for the 2nd Cavalry merely to mount guard along the line from Fort Belknap to Fort Clark. He had long believed that "to give peace to the frontier, and that perfect security so necessary to the happiness and prosperity of communities, the troops ought to act offensively and carry the war to the homes of the enemy." So, as early as February, Johnston dispatched Captain Oakes and Company C in pursuit of horse raiders; the next month, Captain Brackett and Company I ran down a band of twenty-five Lipan Apache on the Guadalupe River. Oakes was out again in May on the trail of a party of Comanche on the Concho River. And finally Lee, with four companies of the 2nd, was ordered in June to chase Comanche on the Brazos. The pursuit lasted forty days and 1,600 miles and netted Lee nothing. The only action fell to Captain Van Dorn, whom Lee had sent on a separate scout and who ran a Comanche band—all of four warriors—to earth on June 30.

"We visited the Hdwaters of the Wichita, & Brazos Rivers" and "in five separate columns . . . swept down the vallies of the Concha, the Colorado & the Red Fork," Lee reported, but "we could find no indians & all traces of them were old." It had been a grueling expedition, and he spent the Fourth of July "under my blanket elevated on four sticks driven into the ground, as a sun shade," enduring an "atmosphere like the blast from a hot air furnace." Nevertheless, he hadn't forgotten to remember the Fourth and all it stood for, and "my feelings for my country were as ardent, my faith in her future as true, & my hopes for her advancement as unabated, as if felt under more propitious circumstances."[17]

Those circumstances were anything but propitious in that summer of 1856, and for the first time politics began to intrude into Robert E. Lee's letters in a serious way. Lee was a technician, not a man of ideas. His reading, even as superintendent at West Point, had been made up of professional and military material—Louis-Gabriel Suchet's *Memoirs of the War in Spain, from 1808 to 1814,* Jared Sparks's biographies of the American revolutionaries, John O'Brien's 1846 *Treatise on American Military Laws, and the Practice of Courts Martial* (which came in handy during the courts-martial he sat during 1855)—and a handful of books borrowed from the academy library on "domestic architecture" (which might have been intended for Mary's daydreams about Arlington). This made him a more bookish officer than most of his contemporaries, but only by comparison.[18] Though the few hints he scattered through his letters over the years on politics clearly point to the Whigs, he had little to say that could be seized upon as advocacy. There is no evidence, at least from his own mouth, that he even voted.

But in 1856 he could not turn his gaze from the violence in Kansas, or from the vain efforts of the politicians to stanch the bloodletting of proslavery and antislavery factions there. Franklin Pierce, who won the 1852 presidential election for the Democrats by an easy 214,000 votes (out of 2.9 million), squandered all the goodwill he brought with him into office by his mishandling of affairs in Kansas, and in June 1856 the Democratic Party dumped him as its candidate. "The Kansas outrages are all imputable to him," complained one Washington insider, "and if he is not called to answer for them here, 'in Hell they'll roast him like a herring.'" His substitute was James Buchanan, a colorless Pennsylvanian who had successively sat in both the House and the Senate, the cabinet and the diplomatic corps without being "known to deliver a single speech remarkable either for eloquence, for potential reasoning, or for valuable practical illustration" but who had the single advantage of being sympathetic to the Southern slaveholders who now led the Democratic Party by the nose.

The Whigs were unable to draw a bead on this soft target, for the Whig Party was in the process of disintegration. After repeated defeats at the polls, "I have got tired of officiating as a sort of hoop to the democratic barrel!" erupted Truman Smith, the Whig national chairman, who promised he would "never again lift a finger to put the Whig party in power." As early as 1854, Northern Whigs had concluded that "the only question available is Freedom against Slavery," and that would mean that "many will seek new party connections." The most formidable of those new connections was the Republican Party, a coalition of antislavery Whigs, anti–Kansas-Nebraska Democrats, a scattering of nativists, and even a handful of abolitionists. Whig diehards struggled to nominate Millard Fillmore in 1856 as a last desperate Whig response to Buchanan. But Fillmore was overshadowed by the new Republicans' nominee, John Charles Frémont, an ardently antislavery celebrity who carried eleven states—all Northern—and registered an impressive 1.3 million votes. Buchanan still won, by nearly 500,000 votes, but it was the death knell of the Whigs. Fillmore carried only Maryland.[19]

From his distant perch in Texas, the 1856 election filled Lee with political foreboding, and for the first time it showed in detail. He directed Mary to obtain a subscription for him to the resolutely Whiggish *Weekly National Intelligencer* to keep up on the political news, and once the voting began on November 4, he was beside himself to have tidings of the results. Not that he expected Whig success. "I saw no hope of Mr. Filmores election," he admitted. But he would prefer Buchanan to Frémont, because Buchanan would be more likely to avert a national collision of North and South over slavery and ensure "that the Union & Constitution is triumphant." He was almost surprised at the degree of his relief when the news of Buchanan's election finally arrived. "Mr. Buchanan it appears, is to be our next President," and Lee looked to Buchanan "to extinguish fanaticism North & South, & cultivate love for the country & Union." Two weeks later, when more newspapers brought him reporting on President Pierce's final annual message to Congress, he felt "assured, that the Govt: is in operation, & the Union in existence." Pierce "condemned the idea of organizing in these United States mere geographical parties, of marshaling in hostile array toward each other the different parts of the country, North or South," and just as frankly condemned "associations . . . inflamed with desire to change the domestic institutions of existing States."[20]

That left Lee "much pleased," and for the first time he allowed himself to sketch for Mary the outlines of a political position on slavery. Pierce had been right, he thought, to condemn "the systematic & progressive efforts of certain people of the North, to interfere with & change the domestic institutions of the South." Northerners might talk, as the Republicans did, about merely containing slavery in the Old South, but their real goal was complete abolition, and under their breath the object of containment was to asphyxiate it. "The consequence of their plans & purposes are . . . clearly set forth, & they must be aware, that their object is both unlawful & entirely foreighn to them and & their duty." The outright abolition of slavery, Lee believed, would result in national suicide and "can only be accomplished by *them* through the agency of a civil and servile war."[21]

But, Lee insisted, it was the violence of the abolitionist solution that alarmed him, not a love for slavery itself. "In this enlightened age, there are few, I believe, but what will acknowledge, that slavery as an institution, is a moral & political evil in any country." Like his Custis and Fitzhugh relatives, Lee entertained no illusions about the "positive good" of enslaving other human beings. ("He had never been an advocate of slavery," he later claimed.) But he had convinced himself that the "greater evil" of slavery was "to the white" rather "than to the black race"; hence, it was up to the whites to decide when enough was enough. Besides, Lee argued, "the blacks are immeasurably better off here than in Africa, morally, socially & physically," and their "painful discipline" as slaves will "prepare & lead them to better things."[22]

Among the "better things" slaves might expect was a return to Africa. Both the Custises and their son-in-law were members of the American Colonization Society, and Mary, after her mother's death, remembered that she had wanted "all the slaves enabled to emigrate to Africa." In 1855, Lee bought Mary a life membership in the ACS and offered sponsorship for any of Arlington's enslaved families "who were willing to go" to the ACS's West African colony of Liberia. A few did, and from them, Lee would later insist, he had received "the most affectionate letters." Mary herself maintained an informal Sunday school at Arlington for slave children, teaching them (in quiet violation of Virginia law but mostly to satisfy her own sense of a white woman's obligation to lesser beings) to read in "a little school house" in the woods.[23]

If emancipation was indeed the future, it was a future, and a place, conveniently removed to a substantial distance. "How long their subjugation may be necessary," Lee concluded, "is known & ordered" only "by a wise & merciful Providence." Because it took "two thousand years to convert but a small part of the human race" to Christianity, Lee would not be surprised if "the final abolition of human slavery" took a correspondingly lengthy period to implement.

Why the abolitionists could not see the need for gradualism puzzled and annoyed Lee. Legally and constitutionally, "the abolitionist . . . has neither the right or power of operating except by moral means & suasion." The hectoring that filled abolitionist newspapers and speeches would accomplish no more than any other "kind of interference with our neighbors when we disapprove of their conduct." If the opponents of slavery "mean well to the slave," Lee declared, they will get no closer to their goal by creating "angry feelings in the master." The "final abolition of human slavery is onward, & we give it the aid of our prayers & all justifiable means in our power," but it is a process that cannot be rushed and "will sooner result from the mild & melting influence of Christianity, than the storms & tempests of fiery controversy."[24]

Through this cloud of pious wishes, there is no glimpse of Lee's thinking his way through the contradiction slavery posed to the American founding, or to the natural rights of the enslaved, beyond a polite acknowledgment of slavery as an "evil." Slavery was, for Robert Lee, an abstraction; its three and a half million victims were personally invisible, despite their presence all around. And now that Pierce's message and Buchanan's election somehow guaranteed that the "angry feelings" over slavery would subside, American life could resume its gradual and painless movement toward some distant resolution of the embarrassment of slavery that did not press very mightily on Robert Lee.

At least Lee recognized slavery as an embarrassment that would one day have to be released, an admission that would have infuriated white Southerners who preferred to tout slavery as the "best condition" for "those human beings intrusted to our charge." He simply had no plan for that release and felt no urgency about improvising one. His indifference to the follies of a slave economy and its jagged violation of natural rights was a cruelty in self-disguised velvet, and for the next three and a half years the politics of slavery would subside into the background of Lee's thinking as suddenly as they had erupted.[25]

Lee had other preoccupations as the calendar turned to 1857 and he turned fifty. He spent much of the winter sitting on one court-martial after another, trailing across Texas from Brownsville to San Antonio to Indianola. In his absence, Lee's companies at Camp Cooper gradually constructed wooden barracks so that they could have a roof over their heads and so that he would no longer be compelled "to look to my tent" every time there was "a dust storm raging." But Lee would have little enough time to enjoy them. In July, Sidney Johnston was recalled to Washington, where he would be given charge of a bizarre expedition to quell resistance to federal authority in the Mormon settlements in Utah. Command of the 2nd U.S. Cavalry now devolved on Lee, and the new secretary of war, John B. Floyd, ordered Lee "to San Antonio, to take command of the Regt." Beside Camp Cooper, San Antonio and its population of thirty-five hundred would seem almost metropolitan, and Lee would be able to "rent me a little house" and "enjoy the bathing" in the San Antonio River. In August, he half seriously suggested that Annie and Agnes come for a visit: "Two strong minded American women can . . . easily wend their way here."[26]

His other children were just as much on his mind. He wanted Rob to move on from Lippitt's school in Alexandria to St. James College, Bishop William Whittingham's school in Hagerstown, Maryland, and in preparation he warned Mary not to let Rob "touch a novel." Fiction "will teach him to sigh after that, which has no reality." He should instead cultivate "industry & frugality"—virtues Lee's own father painfully lacked—and "be prudent, before he is liberal, & be just before he is generous." Which was, of course, a more elegant way of encouraging Rob to follow in his own father's parsimonious footsteps. Mildred—"my *precious Life*"—was lectured about not angering God "by your neglect": "Be careful of your conduct. Do not even *wish* for what you ought not to have or do, but try hard to be a truly good, as well as wise girl, & rigidly obey your Mother."

On none of them did he expend more worry than on Rooney at Harvard, in his "tight frock-coat, silk cap, and kid gloves of an undergraduate." Henry Adams would pin a negative immortality onto Rooney in *The Education of Henry Adams* some sixty years later, picturing Rooney as "the most popular and prominent young man" in his freshman class, a member of the Hasty Pudding Club and the Psi Upsilon fraternity, and yet, for all the popularity, a chicken-brained oaf, "ignorant" and "childlike" and "helpless before the relative complexity of a school." Adams was being cruel, but as Rooney embarked on his second year at Harvard, this was exactly what was worrying his father. "It is time he began to think of something else besides running about amusing himself," Lee complained. "He thinks entirely of his pleasures, & not of what is proper to be done."

Actually, what Rooney was thinking about was the same thing he had sighed after at West Point—a commission in the Army. No, his father intervened, "my experience has taught me to recommend no young man to enter the service." Rooney was unconvinced, and inattentive to studies in which he had no interest. "I hope he is doing well," Lee wrote, but Rooney wasted too much time partying, and "I more frequently hear of him away from than at his college." Rooney's spendthrift ways also reminded him dishearteningly of "that disposition from both branches of his family" to let money slip through their fingers like water. Lee had almost made up his mind to relent and seek a civilian commission for Rooney once he graduated, when the news arrived from Mary in June 1857 that Winfield Scott "without consulting us" had offered Rooney a lieutenant's vacancy in the 6th U.S. Infantry. "Your information of Rooneys appointment to the Army, was entirely unexpected," Lee replied to his wife. And it might be for the best, after all, Lee conceded. But he should still "prepare himself for his station & not . . . trifle away his time. . . . A soldier's life I know to be a hard one."[27]

Lee worried almost as much about his own money as Rooney's. Although his carefully hoarded investments generated more income than his Army salary, he had no confidence that Mary could manage it. He insisted on writing checks on his Alexandria bank from Texas for Mary to deposit for cash and the children's school bills, all the while chiding her to "be very particular dear Mary when you deal in money matters," to get help from William Louis Marshall, and to "keep a memorandum book & set everything down." Nothing made his stomach sink faster than the thought that Mary would fail to manage some transaction properly and thus cause people to "think I am endeavouring to swindle" them (as some other prominent Lees had done).

He was just as anxious to avoid *being* swindled. The Ohio Life Insurance and Trust Company locked the doors of its New York office on August 24, a failure that triggered a cascade of financial collapses and ushered in the worldwide Panic of 1857. When he picked up the news through "the last New York papers," Lee nervously ordered his wife to leaf through the certificates at the Alexandria bank to see whether two "small printed certificates" were "Ohio Life & Trust Compy" issues; "if so, it may be requisite to do something with them." (He was relieved when Mary was able to tell him that "the two Ohio bonds" were "*State* Stock & not of the *trust* Compy.")[28]

It was not just Mary Custis Lee's financial acumen he mistrusted. Over the years, his reluctant interventions in her father's affairs at Arlington, White House, and Romancoke had convinced him that management of the properties had to be put securely into other hands, and he frankly apprised G.W.P. that someone else was going to have to run his accounts for him. Within months, it was clear that matters were even worse than he feared. Father Custis "has more need of money than I have & will require all his friends I fear, to meet the balance" of the bills run up by his former manager. Lee eventually hoped that Mary could "get your father to leave Arlington for a season," perhaps taking him "to the mountains" or even (in the spirit of his suggestion to Annie and Agnes) spending "the Winter with me." They could "roam about Texas, or you could all remain here."[29]

The invitation sat oddly beside his continuing gloom over life in the Army. He stayed in touch with the sister of his old friend Jack Mackay, updating her on his adventures in Texas, but also cautioning her not to let her son "enter the army—It is a hard life," and so lacking in upward professional mobility that "he can never rise to any military eminence. . . . I think he had better become a good farmer, & get a sweet wife." Not that Lee himself knew the slightest thing about farming, but the image of an idyllic pastoral retreat of some undefined sort had increasingly become a fantasy escape for him. "I like the wilderness," he insisted. It appealed to his yearning for independence, and as much as he complained to Annie of his loneliness at Camp Cooper, "solitude seems more consonant to my feelings & temperament." (Years later, he would still daydream about having "some little quiet house in the woods where I can procure shelter and my daily bread.") And he might not have much choice. He was alarmed to read "in a stray number of the New York Times" calls "to disband all these new Regiments and save the Treasury millions," which would leave him unemployed and mostly unemployable, and for a brief moment he considered launching a scheme to secure a new appointment, perhaps as inspector general of the Army.[30]

What he nearly missed in his bevy of concerns was the first stumble of Mary Custis Lee into the debilitating grasp of rheumatoid arthritis. There was no technical name for the disease in the 1850s beyond simply rheumatism, but rheumatoid arthritis was, and is, more than simply aches and pains; it was, and is, a systemic failure of the body's immune system in which the body's infection defenses turn and attack the lining of the joints—hands, fingers, feet, knees, ankles—inflaming and swelling them and causing a rising cacophony of pain, misery, and exhaustion. Unchecked, the cartilage is worn away, and joints can become hideously gnarled and deformed. It is a slow, clever disease, probably genetic but possibly bacterial, often beginning in the hands and easy to dismiss as temporary. It tends to strike women three times more often than men, usually after the age of thirty—which means that it occurred somewhat late in the case of Mary Lee—but is nonetheless destructive in its long-term reach. There is still no cure. It is, as one English therapist in the 1750s described it, "a most stubborn distemper, and has baffled all the professors of Physick that ever have appeared in the World. The cause lies too deep for any Medicine or Method yet known." In the 1850s, its principal treatment was heat—warm "sulphur" baths, "Medical Galvanism," scrub brushing.[31]

Mary Lee's first symptoms probably arrived just before the Lees left West Point, and they began to appear more steadily in Lee's letters soon after his arrival in Texas in 1856. "I have been much grieved to learn of your sufferings from rheumatism," he wrote in dismay that July, although he expected that "each letter" from her "would have brought me information of your restoration to health." They didn't, and Lee began to "fear it must be bad." Mary admitted as much in September: she could hardly walk, and Robert should consider himself "fortunate . . . that you have not got me in your tent at present." In the fall, Mary began her first round of treatments in the mineral baths at the Warm Springs Inn in western Virginia (thirty miles west of Staunton).

Lee was hopeful she would "find relief from the waters." But he soon enough learned that "your visit to the Springs has not restored you to health as I had hoped," and as much as she tried to reassure him that she suffered "more from inconvenience than from pain," it gradually dawned on him that "there is little amendment of your disease, or improvement in your comfort," nor was there likely to be. Navigating the stairs at Arlington became increasingly difficult. "I generally take my breakfast in my room," Mary wrote to Robert, "& after I have arranged all my work for the day, come down stairs and remain until bed time."

Robert was tempted to apply for leave. "I wish indeed I could be with you," he wrote at the beginning of 1857. But he took no actual steps to return to Arlington, because he knew of nothing "I could do for your relief." Nor did Mary encourage him. "I almost dread his seeing my crippled condition," she wrote to a friend in February. And so he preferred to believe "that your painful malady may be so much ameliorated this winter, as to leave you entirely in the Spring." But at the back of his mind lingered the concern that her debility would eventually "compel my separation from the Army, Unless I can get some position nearer home, or upon the general staff."[32]

He could have told her, for whatever scant comfort it offered, that there were deeper sorrows all around them. In June 1857, before leaving Camp Cooper for San Antonio, one of the troopers' children, "a bright little boy," died, and "for the first time in my life" Lee found himself, as the senior officer present, obliged to "read the beautiful funeral service of our Church over the grave, to a large & attentive audience of soldiers." Three weeks later, one of his troop sergeants lost "as handsome a little boy as I ever saw," and Lee was called "to read the funeral service over his body . . . for the second time in my life." It was almost too much for him: "I hope I shall not be called on again," because as much as he could convince himself in Christian terms that "it is far better for the child to be called by its Heavenly creator into his presence, in its purity & innocence," it depressed him to see how "it so wrings a parents heart with anguish."

Death struck even closer to home for Lee. His youngest sister, Mildred, had been in Paris with her husband, Edward Vernon Childe, for more than twenty years. There, she created a Tuesday evening salon of fellow expatriates and French Americanophiles who included Jean-Jacques Ampère, Prosper Mérimée (whose novella *Carmen* became the source for Bizet's opera), and Alexis de Tocqueville, who "admired the vigor and clarity of her mind, the soundness of her judgment." But she died, suddenly, in the summer of 1856, a death Tocqueville called a "catastrophe . . . which fills me with despair and horror." It was hardly less so for her brother. The news "came upon me very unexpectedly," and even "though parted from her for years," he still held her "vividly . . . in my imagination." It gave him some consolation that "her remembrance of me in the last moments of life" was "sweet . . . beyond expression." But it also reminded him of mortality: "May we all so live that we too can with joy yield up our lives as a sacrifice of obedience to the will of our creator & say his 'will be done.'"[33]

Reflecting on that mortality should have better prepared Lee for an even more deafening surprise: "the decease" on October 10, 1857, of "the venerable GEORGE WASHINGTON PARKE CUSTIS the last of the members of the family of WASHINGTON."[34]

Old Custis seemed unusually depressed and listless that fall. He planned "an excursion" to the National Agricultural Fair in Louisville, Kentucky, in September, along with former president Franklin Pierce and James Buchanan's vice president, John C. Breckinridge, but was forced "to relinquish this design." He began to have trouble breathing, and by October 3 "he was so ill" that he took to his bed. The shortness of breath only got worse, turning into pneumonia—a general "congestion of the lungs." By the eighth, it was clear he was dying. "He seemed to be aware of his approaching end," Agnes Lee wrote sorrowfully in her journal. "Often he spoke as if his death was near at hand & would ask God to bless him."

His decline gave Mary time to gather Annie, Agnes, Mildred, Markie Williams, and, as the end neared, the Reverend Charles Dana of Christ Church. (A telegram had been sent to Rooney, who arrived just hours too late.) Shortly after midnight on the tenth, the breathing grew shallower and then "suddenly ceased—quietly, peacefully as an infant he passed to his rest." His lengthy obituary in the *National Intelligencer* claimed that "he died in communion with the Protestant Episcopal Church." As it turned out, G.W.P. (almost like his son-in-law) had never been confirmed, and so "had never taken the holy communion." But serious as the neglect of confirmation was in evangelical eyes, it could still be forgiven in his case because "he knew the only way to be saved was through the blood of Jesus Christ."[35]

Robert E. Lee learned of his father-in-law's death by telegraph and by mail on October 21 and left San Antonio, with leave granted by the secretary of war, three days later. For all that he knew, the settlement of old Custis's estate might be the final release from his dependence on the Army, and he wrote to Sidney Johnston, "I have at last to decide the question I have staved off for twenty years, whether I am to continue in the army all my life, or to leave it now." Along with Bishop Meade, Robert Lee Randolph (a Fitzhugh and Carter relative), and George Washington Peter (his nephew), Lee had been named one of the executors of Custis's will. Curiously, the other executors "wish me to act alone." He quickly discovered why. G.W.P.'s estate was in disarray.

Despite the rumors in the newspapers that "Mr. C.'s fortune is worth $250,000, without any debts or incumbrance," Lee found that in his long Texas absence Arlington was "in ruins & will, have to be rebuilt." Creditors of various shapes, smiling, threatening, "are pouring in on me, not in large amounts, but sufficient to absorb my available funds." The swindles Lee suspected G.W.P.'s overseer at White House and Romancoke of perpetuating were even worse than he imagined, leaving "no inventories of the property, many debts unpaid, over a thousand dollars of which, have been recently presented to me." Just by a rough estimate, Lee feared it "would require about $10,000 to put this place in order," not to mention the "labour, economy & devotion to the object" that would be demanded.

That, however, was not the worst of it. In his will, which Custis drew up in 1855, "my Arlington House estate . . . containing eleven hundred acres, more or less, and my mill on Four-Mile Run, in the county of Alexandria, and the lands of mine adjacent to said mill, in the counties of Alexandria and Fairfax" were bequeathed not to Robert and Mary Lee but to G.W.P.'s oldest grandson and namesake—George Washington Custis Lee. White House, the original Washington property on the Pamunkey River, was to go to Rooney; the other Pamunkey River property, Romancoke, was to go to Rob. Mary, at least, was to have a life interest in Arlington; her husband would receive only G.W.P.'s "lot in square No. 21, Washington city." Otherwise, Robert E. Lee was entirely cut out of the Custis estate.

He would, nevertheless, still have to bear its burdens as executor, and those burdens were not light. The will required the payment of a cash legacy to each of Custis's "four granddaughters, Mary, Ann, Agnes, and Mildred Lee," each to the tune of "ten thousand dollars." The money for this would come, Custis had predicted, from the sale of Smith Island and a scattering of properties in Stafford, Richmond, and Westmoreland Counties, topped up from the ordinary revenue generated by "the lands of the White House and Romancock." (No explanation was offered for what Rooney and Rob were to do with these "lands" in the meantime.) How those proceeds were to be guaranteed while the newspapers were filled with the tidings of "the wretched financial difficulties of the country" was anyone's guess, but Custis made the guarantee even more perilous by the will's last provision. In a gesture imitating George Washington, Custis directed the emancipation of "my slaves . . . to be accomplished in not exceeding five years from the time of my decease."[36]

Lee allowed himself a moment to pay a dutiful tribute to his father-in-law. "I grieve to find his chair empty & his place vacant," he wrote to Mary's venerable aunt, Anna Maria Fitzhugh. "I miss every moment, him that always recd me with the kindness & affection of a father." But it was as though the ancient mistrust of Light Horse Harry, spun like a web by Philip Ludwell Lee, by Charles Carter of Shirley, and even by old G.W.P. himself at the time of his daughter's engagement, had descended on the one Lee who had struggled all his life to live down his progenitor's erratic reputation. The will was, in effect, a gigantic vote of no confidence in Robert, and yet it was tied to an expectation that Robert would cooperate in taking charge of administering that vote.

The provisions of the will were so appalling that when the will was probated on December 7, 1857, a horrified Custis Lee immediately offered his humiliated father "the deed relinquishing . . . all right and title to Arlington, the Mill, adjacent lands, personal property &c bequeathed" by his grandfather. Robert E. Lee merely shook his head. "I am deeply impressed by your filial feeling of love & consideration," he wrote back, but "Your dear Grdfather distributed his property as he thought best, & it is proper that it should remain as he bestowed it." He could not tolerate the thought of whispers that he had pressured his son into a forfeiture; if he could not be the master of Arlington, he was certainly not now going to be mastered by it. He had placed himself as a boy at his mother's whim because his father was nowhere to be found; he would sacrifice himself yet again to show that he possessed the integrity so many other Lees had lacked. He would build up Arlington, but he would do it because Mary would want that as "the place of her birth and the graves of her parents"; he would make it produce the legacies, because his daughters deserved them; and he would emancipate the slaves, once they had generated the wealth needed for the legacies. After that, he had no plans.[37]

Getting to that point, and in just five years, would call up all the resourcefulness and all the determination that twenty-five years as an Army engineer had developed in him. "The new duties devolved upon me" caused him great "uncertainty as to the best course to pursue," because (despite the fantasies about peaceful retirement in the Virginia countryside) "I feel more familiar with the military operations of a campaighn than the details of a farm," he confided to Anna Maria Fitzhugh, and he admitted to his distant cousin Edward Turner in the Shenandoah Valley that "I am no farmer myself."

Nor was he going to be able to move quickly: Smith Lee and his wife came down from Philadelphia (where Smith had assumed command of the Philadelphia naval shipyard), and Edward Vernon Childe with his motherless offspring all "claimed their share of my company" for December. The weather turned miserable, snowing hard for Christmas and staying "disagreeable, raw, rainy" through January. It only got worse in February and March, with snowstorms so severe that ice floated in the Potomac "for several miles," and on March 4 the Potomac was completely frozen over "from shore to shore." In spite of the weather, Lee set off on a tour of the Pamunkey River properties, hiring a new overseer for White House. There, he started work on "some corn houses, a barn & some negro quarters, which were much wanted," and at Romancoke "commenced at once upon the mill, the Negro quarters & fences" and ordered fertilizer from Baltimore "as I wished to lose no time to commence the endeavour to restore the land."[38]

But it was Arlington that would tax his patience to the limit. Dramatic steps were needed both to "arrest the dilapidation of the house" and to move the farming operations back to profitability. This, he admitted, was going to wear "down my purse." The stable roof was ready to fall in; the overseer's house needed rebuilding; the stucco on the house exterior was crumbling; all that remained of his father-in-law's experiments in livestock were thirty-two cattle, sheep, and hogs, and he was forced to borrow a worthwhile "pair of oxen" from Edward Turner for plowing in the spring of 1858. The mill on the grounds would have to be repaired, which he expected to cost another $800, and a new shaft for the mill obtained. But he set to work, ordering a new survey of the property ("from what I hear . . . the neighbors are trespassing on the property"), planting "a good crop of corn," spending "$831 in strengthening the teams, & about $200. in necessary implements," and purchasing "lime & guano" to the tune of $500 "to put on this land this year" in hope that it would generate a newly increased crop and "profit the next."

At the same time, there were constant interruptions for the patriotic celebrations G.W.P. had been so fond of sponsoring at Arlington—the Steuben Monument Festival, the St. Matthew's Sunday School Picnic benefit, the Ryland Chapel "excursion." Lee always resented the way "the whole place will be exposed to the depredations of the public" by these partiers, but felt duty-bound to play host when "the friends of the late G.W.P. Custis availed themselves of the occasion to visit the mansion." And also, because he was still a serving officer, he was not exempt from assignments to courts-martial and boards of inquiry, including at West Point. But by the end of 1858, he could report that "the mansion house & stable" had been resurfaced and reroofed, "the mill & overseers house are completed," and "the masonry of the barn is completed." Only "an early frost" kept him from doing more. As young Rob remembered, "In a very short time the appearance of everything on the estate was improved."[39]

Lee himself was less sure. "I have not accomplished all I wished," he wrote to Custis after the weather finally broke in the spring of 1859, "still I have ameliorated some things." But by the summer, he was willing to admit to Custis that he had managed "to clean up on the hill" and "polish up your mother's habitation, and to prepare for you an acceptable home." New crops had been sown—"the rye is secured, and we are getting in the hay"—and he was encouraged enough to hope that "we shall make fair crops of everything" at Arlington and at least "an average one" at White House. The one thing that was beyond his power to improve was Mary Custis Lee's arthritis. When he returned from Texas in the fall of 1857, she had only been able to get around the house with the help of crutches and canes; travel outside the house could only be done by carriage.

At times, Robert hoped he saw improvement in her condition and told Custis Lee that "she walked with less difficulty," even though "her joints appear very stiff." She tried new therapies, "taking the cold bath all winter." Robert thought this was a "fearful experiment," yet it seemed to reduce "the swelling from her feet, ankles &c. & relieved her of nearly *all* pain." But the relief was temporary. By the summer of 1858, Robert was once again carrying her to "the springs"—the Shenandoah Alum Springs in Mount Jackson for "its medicinal waters," the Hot Springs in Bath County. "Your poor mother is a great sufferer again," Lee advised his son the following spring, "& I think as bad as when I first returned from Texas," and after another month he "really" began "to despond of her recovery and fear she will never be entirely relieved." When Rooney married Charlotte Wickham (a granddaughter of the Carters') at the same Shirley plantation on the James where Robert's parents had been married sixty-six years before, Robert had to make the journey alone.[40]

The unpleasantness of these responsibilities paled beside the mushrooming embarrassment that resulted from his dealings with the Arlington slaves. The elder Custis, burdened with his own private guilt over slavery, had been "an easygoing master, requiring little of his slaves"—especially because it was rumored that over the years he had fathered fifteen of them. By the time of his death in 1857, most of the forty-two adult slaves at Arlington were planting and plowing as much for themselves as for G.W.P. "They have their comfortable homes, their families around them, and nothing to do but consult their own pleasure," old Custis explained to Markie Williams when she came to live at Arlington in 1853. They were, as Mildred Lee sniffed, "much fonder of play, than work"—something that might have been said of Mildred, too.

Lee saw the slaves from a different angle: his task was to make the Custis properties profitable again, both for the sake of his three sons and for the legacies the Custis will bound him to pay to his daughters, and the engines of that profitability would be the Custis slaves. Privately, Mary doubted whether this could be accomplished "in double five years." Not Robert. He would emancipate them at the end of the five-year term specified in the will. But he also wanted those legacies paid, and one of his first actions as executor in the spring of 1858 was to seek guidance from the Alexandria County Circuit Court and then the Virginia Supreme Court, in order to sort out the will's self-contradictions. For instance: "How are said legacies to be raised," he queried, "and for what period will the charge for that purpose continue on the lands and negroes of the White House and Romancoke estates?"

Lee's fixation on making the Custis properties produce those legacies quickly generated dismay among the enslaved population at Arlington, who understood the Custis will to mean that "they were then free" and not obliged to work at all. A sensational report, "whispered around Washington," appeared in the Boston and New York papers, alleging that the dying Custis had called "they of the Arlington House" to his "deathbed" and "told them that he had left them, and all his servants, their freedom." Worse, it was rumored, the Custis heirs, headed by Mary Lee's cousin John Augustine Washington, were suppressing the will to conceal its provisions.

Lee at once leaped to the attack in a letter to the *Alexandria Gazette.* John Augustine Washington "is not one of the heirs, and has no interest in Mr. Custis's estate"; moreover, Custis's will "is on record in his own handwriting" in "the Alexandria county court." Any speeches Custis made to "his assembled slaves" were "not known to any member of his family . . . during the brief days of his last illness."[41]

It is a sign of how edgy the disposing of the Custis will had made him that this incident became the occasion for Lee to appear, for the first time in his life, intentionally in public print over his own name. What the letter did not disclose was that Lee had created a great deal of his own trouble by going about the business of mobilizing the Arlington slaves entirely as though it *were* a business. He made the tone-deaf decision that there were more slaves at Arlington than the reconstruction of the place required and began hiring them out—"three of the men, & five of the girls"—to generate cash for the legacies. "Among them is Reuben [Bingham], a great rogue & rascal whom I must get rid of some way." He took no account of how this would effectively split up slave families, the enslaved people's worst nightmare, and in short order several of them "whom I have hired out in Alexa[ndria] returned the first day." Several others tried to turn the hiring-out strategy to their benefit by disappearing into the slave population of Washington, claiming that they were "at service with my consent."

As he persisted in his plans to make Arlington turn a profit, they, just as persistently, resisted. "Reuben, Parks & Edward, in the beginning of the previous week, rebelled against my authority," Lee wrote angrily to Rooney in May 1858. "They refused to obey my orders, & said they were as free as I was." Lee eventually "overpowered them" and had them lodged in one of Alexandria's slave pens until he could find a lessee willing to hire them. And, as Mary Lee confessed, only "the merciful hand of Kind providence & their own ineptness I suppose prevented an outbreak."[42]

Lee could not comprehend why the demands he was making did not earn the understanding, even the cooperation, of the Arlington slaves. But they didn't, and his frustration at their obstinacy boiled over in the spring of 1859 when three of the Arlington slaves—Wesley Norris, his sister Mary Norris, and their cousin George Parks—"determined to run away." They made it as far as Westminster, Maryland, only a few miles from the free-state border of Pennsylvania, when they were stopped and imprisoned. Two weeks later, they were shipped back to Arlington, where Lee had to pay the costs for their rendition. His fabled self-control teetering unsteadily, Lee demanded of the three why they ran away. Because, they replied, "frankly . . . we considered ourselves free."

This was not the first time Lee had been obliged to pay for the recovery of fugitives from Arlington. But on previous occasions, he had been acting on behalf of old Custis, not himself. Parks and the Norrises were a direct challenge to his integrity as executor of the will and to the financial future of his daughters, and finally Lee's gentility cracked and fell away. "He then told us he would teach us a lesson we would never forget," ordered the three "stripped to the waist," and directed the Arlington overseer, John McQuinn, to give the men "50 lashes each" and twenty to Mary Norris. McQuinn balked and "had sufficient humanity to decline," so Lee turned to Richard Williams, the Arlington constable who had brought the fugitives back, and had him perform the whipping, while Lee demanded he "lay it on well." Even with the administration of this "lesson," Lee wasn't having them back at Arlington, and even if he had wanted them, Mary Lee was even more incensed than her husband at how "discontented and impertinent" they were. The men were taken instead to the Hanover County jail and eventually hired out as laborers on the Orange and Alexandria Railroad and shipped from there to Alabama; Mary Norris was packed off to an "agent" in Richmond to be hired out.[43]

To Lee's mortification, a vivid denunciation of the whipping promptly appeared in the *New-York Tribune* on June 24, sandwiched between lurid accounts of a Pennsylvania kidnapping and the Buchanan State Department's surrender of naturalized immigrants to military conscription in their home countries. This time, the place of the whipping was identified as Arlington's "barn," and Lee was accused of having personally "stripped" Mary Norris and then "administered . . . thirty and nine lashes to her" himself. Lee made no rebuttals. A week later, he wrote to Custis Lee (now posted to Fort Point in San Francisco harbor), gingerly wondering whether "you have been told that George Wesly and Mary Norris absconded some months ago, were captured in Maryland, making their way to Pennsylvania, brought back, and are now hired out in lower Virginia." He said nothing about the whipping, except to acknowledge that "the *N. Y. Tribune* has attacked me for my treatment of your grandfather's slaves." He added, cryptically, "I shall not reply."

But he could not bring himself actually to deny that he had done what the *Tribune* described, and it is difficult to avoid the conclusion that when his fury had cooled, he was sickened at himself, as much for the damage done to his own self-image as for the cruelty inflicted on the three fugitives. In that moment, he had reverted to Light Horse Harry, spiking a deserter's head on a pole. Your grandfather, he told Custis, "has left me an unpleasant legacy," and it is tantalizing to wonder whether it was not G.W.P. but another grandfather who was peering out from the recesses of his memory. If ever there was a moment when Robert E. Lee wished himself free from that legacy, that estate, those slaves, and everything else that earlier generations had foisted on him, this was it.[44]

He could wish all he liked. That legacy was not going to disappear from Robert Lee's life, for on the morning of October 17 a national fury over slavery broke in a paroxysm of violence over Lee's head, and the head of the entire American republic.

CHAPTER EIGHT

I Will Cling to It to the Last

The work of renewing Arlington went slowly, especially after the whipping incident. "I am getting along as usual, trying to get a little work done and to mend up some things," but "I succeed very badly," Lee lamented to Rooney in the summer of 1858. Work during the winter went even more slowly and "is much behind hand." He was called away repeatedly to serve on a variety of examining boards in Washington, which "consumes most of the day," although that gave him an opportunity to see his brother Smith, who had moved from the Philadelphia Navy Yard to the Navy Department building in the District.

By the following spring, the recovery was again so far behindhand that he was compelled to apply for an extension of his leave from Texas. It was granted; even more, Winfield Scott now broadly suggested that Lee "enter his Staff as Military Secy." Lee declined. The uppermost thought in his mind was to "arrange" the "business devolved upon me by the will of Mr. Custis" and then "join my Rgt." But standing in the way of that escape was the will's requirement that the Custis slaves be emancipated. Almost as though he wished to wipe away the memory of the whipping, he explained to Scott that "justice to the negroes require[s] that this should be accomplished as soon as possible"—although "soon" would be shaped by the need for the slaves to produce enough of a profit to fill up his daughters' legacies.[1]

At least Lee was relieved that "there was no military news." Sidney Johnston's expedition to suppress the Mormon disturbances in Utah fizzled peacefully, because the Mormons wisely declined to confront the U.S. Army. Rooney Lee's 6th U.S. Infantry had been part of Johnston's expedition but after several resultless months was moved on to San Francisco, where he was able to link up with his older brother, Custis. "I am delighted at you two being together," their father wrote, "and nothing has occurred so gratifying to me for the past year." (Even then, he could not resist chiding Rooney when he learned "that you smoke occasionally.")

He was even happier when he learned that Rooney, newly married to Charlotte Wickham, had decided to resign the commission he had yearned after for so many years and settle with Charlotte at White House, the old Custis property on the Pamunkey, and take the renovations of White House and Romancoke off his father's hands. Even Custis was now looking for a transfer to fill a pending vacancy in the Chief Engineer's office in Washington, where (to his father's relief) "you would then be near your mother . . . & carry on the work of the farm" while he returned to Texas. Perhaps the dreary affairs of Arlington and the Custises would have a speedy and happy ending after all.[2]

But not without one bloody interruption.

On the morning of October 17, 1859, Lee was out in the Arlington fields, supervising slaves in harvesting the fall rye crop, when "a mounted soldier" cantered up, saluted, and handed Lee a note from Secretary of War Floyd, ordering him to report at once to the War Department, over in the District. When Lee arrived there, he found Floyd in a barely suppressed state of panic. Early that morning, John W. Garrett, the president of the Baltimore and Ohio Railroad, had frantically forwarded to President Buchanan telegrams received through Baltimore from the conductor of an eastbound train that was briefly stopped around 1:30 a.m. in Harpers Ferry, Virginia, where the federal government maintained an arsenal and one of its two weapons-manufacturing and refitting armories (the other was in Springfield, Massachusetts). The station at Harpers Ferry was in the hands of armed men, and the longer the train was blocked there, the more it became apparent that they were occupying the armory and the arsenal as well.[3]

The leader of the robbers, or strikers, or whatever they were, eventually gave the train permission to proceed at dawn. By then, the conductor figured out that the interlopers were 150 "armed abolitionists," led by a man named "S. C. Anderson," who "have come to free the slaves and intend to do it at all hazards" and to arm poor whites who were similarly aggrieved with the slave system. When the train reached Monocacy, Maryland, the conductor telegraphed the news to his incredulous supervisor in Baltimore. "Why should our train be stopped by Abolitionists and how do you know they are such?" came the confused response. A furious reply shot back: "My dispatch was not exaggerated. . . . I have not made it half as bad as it is." In fact, he estimated there were fifteen hundred more "abolitionists" descending on Harpers Ferry. The supervisor finally relented and telegraphed Garrett, who in turn fired off a warning to the commandant of the Maryland militia, to Virginia's governor, Henry Wise, to President Buchanan, and to Secretary Floyd.[4]

Southerners had lived under the specter of a slave insurrection ever since Nat Turner. But though they talked endlessly of how abolitionist agitation would somehow trigger such a nightmare, surprisingly little thought had ever been given to how to meet it, and nowhere was less thought apparent than in John Floyd's War Department. The Maryland and Virginia state militia could be summoned, but a terrified Buchanan embargoed all the news coming into his hands "for fear of a rise at Washington." And not without reason, because there were no federal troops in Washington, or nearer than Baltimore or Fort Monroe, apart from the Marines at the Washington Navy Yard.

As Floyd cast around urgently for any forces he could divert to Harpers Ferry that morning, one of Lee's former students at West Point, Lieutenant James Ewell Brown Stuart, strolled into the War Department for an appointment with Floyd. Stuart, the onetime admirer of Lee's daughter Mary, had been posted to the 1st Cavalry in Kansas, where he divided time between near-fatal skirmishing with the Cheyenne and negotiating with the radical abolitionist John Brown for the release of captured Missouri militiamen. Stuart was now in Washington on leave and called on his old commandant "several times" at Arlington. But his real mission was to patent a new "stout brass hook" that would allow a mounted trooper to shift his saber from his belt and attach it to his saddle, and he expected to sell the invention to the secretary of war.[5]

Instead, he found the War Department teeming with frantic rumors that "the Harpers Ferry armory was in the possession of a mob of . . . over 3000 men" bent on "a servile insurrection." Stuart at once volunteered himself for duty and then remembered that his former commandant was just across the Potomac at Arlington, on leave, and suggested that he and Lee be sent up to Harpers Ferry "to render any service." By the time Lee could be brought over to the War Department and briefed on the situation, Floyd had already ordered the Marines from the Washington barracks—just one company of ninety men and two howitzers under Lieutenant Israel Greene was available—and three artillery companies from Fort Monroe to head by train to Harpers Ferry. Lee was to take command of them as soon as he could catch up, and Stuart would serve as his assistant.

Stuart "had barely time to borrow a un'f. coat and a sabre," and Lee hadn't time even for that (he would have to go in civilian dress and a top hat, although at some point a sword was procured for him). Floyd equipped Lee with an emergency proclamation by the president and commandeered an express B&O locomotive for Lee and Stuart to catch up with the Marines, and the two flew along the track in the cab of the locomotive with only the engineer and fireman for company. They finally rendezvoused with the Marine company and several companies of Maryland militia on the Maryland side of the Potomac from Harpers Ferry near midnight of the seventeenth and gingerly pushed their way over the railroad bridge into the town.[6]

The town was a lawless pandemonium. The raiders occupied the armory and arsenal on the night of the sixteenth and sent parties into the surrounding hills to take several prominent slaveholders—including Lewis Washington, a cousin of Mary's and great-grandnephew of the first president—hostage. But there had been no spontaneous uprising of slaves, much less of poor whites, and instead armed civilians set up a rough cordon of pot-shotters who killed several of the raiders and forced the rest of them to back into the arsenal grounds, where they finally barricaded themselves and their hostages into the brick barn that housed the arsenal's emergency fire engines.

As word spread, a gaggle of militia companies from the surrounding farms and towns hurriedly descended on Harpers Ferry to reinforce the snipers, and together they eventually surrounded the arsenal, cutting off any retreat. On paper, as many as ten companies from Maryland and Virginia showed up; in practice, wrote a Marylander, "four-fifths of them were under no command," and "men who were intoxicated were firing their guns in the air, and others at the engine house." They had expected the raiders to surrender as soon as they showed up; instead the militia "beat a confused retreat" to cover, where they picked off any of the raiders in exposed positions. Virginia's governor, Henry Wise, deputized a local militia officer, Robert Baylor, to assume command, but had no hope of controlling much beyond his own company of Charles Town Guards, and very little appetite to stage a full-scale assault on the arsenal.

It was raining lightly when Lee, Stuart, and the Marines crossed the railroad bridge and set up their own cordon around the arsenal. There, Lee carried out "a rapid reconnaissance of the grounds, and gathered what was reliable from the many contradictory accounts of the state of the insurgents." It was the Lee of Cerro Gordo and the *pedregal* again, only with this difference: for the first time in his life, Lee would actually have to command federal troops under fire.[7]

The insurrection Lee found was more pathetic than catastrophic. Instead of a "mob" of "over 3000 men," he could estimate that "the original party consisted of not more than twenty white men and five free negroes." Of these, perhaps a dozen raiders remained in the engine house, plus their hostages, and if it had not been for his fear "of sacrificing the lives of some of the gentlemen held . . . as prisoners in a midnight assault, I should have ordered" an attack "at once." He never bothered to distribute Buchanan's emergency proclamation. Instead, he waited for daylight and prepared a terse little ultimatum for the raiders, demanding "the surrender of the persons in the armory buildings" and promising that if they "will peaceably surrender themselves . . . they shall be kept in safety to await the orders of the president."

Lee made one polite deference to local authority; if the ultimatum was refused, either Edward Shriver, the senior Maryland militia officer in Harpers Ferry, or Baylor and the Virginia militia could have the honor of leading an assault. They both hastily declined. "These men of mine have wives and children at home," Shriver stammered. "You are paid for doing this kind of work." That satisfied Lee. At seven o'clock on the morning of the eighteenth, he had Baylor's militia form up in ranks around the arsenal "and clear the streets of all citizens and spectators," then took Stuart, Lieutenant Greene, and a storming party of twelve Marines to within hailing distance of the engine house, with a second group of twelve Marines in reserve.[8]

Stuart "was deputed by Col Lee to read" the surrender demand "to the leader" in the engine house. This "leader" had been identified by the townspeople as Isaac Smith, a long-bearded Northerner who had arrived in Harpers Ferry in July under the pretense of looking for business opportunities. Lee did not seriously expect Smith or his much-reduced band to accept his demand "to surrender immediately," so when a refusal was given, Stuart was to step aside, "wave my cap," and the Marines would "rush up and batter the doors & capture the insurgents." The Marines would use bayonets only; otherwise, there was too much risk of shooting the hostages in a melee.

Stuart stepped up to the barred double door of the engine house, while Lee watched from forty paces away, and called to Smith that he "had a communication for him from Col Lee." The door opened a crack for Smith to peer out, and Stuart at once recognized that the man who had been alternately called Anderson and Smith was in fact John Brown, whom he remembered from his Kansas negotiations. "You are Osawatomie Brown, of Kansas?" Stuart choked out in surprise. "Well, they do call me that sometimes, Lieutenant," Brown drily replied.

Brown had no intention of yielding to Lee's terms, and so after a few minutes of pointless argument Stuart stepped aside and waved his cap, the door slammed shut, and Lieutenant Greene and his Marines sprang forward with sledgehammers and fixed bayonets to force their way in. Braced by Brown, the double door would not give under the blows of the sledgehammers. But Greene "caught sight of a ladder, lying a few feet from the enginehouse," and he had the Marines pick it up "as a battering ram." Two blows from the ladder and the planking of the doors began to come off its frames, leaving a hole just wide enough for Lieutenant Greene to duck through. One Marine private, Luke Quinn, was fatally wounded, but Greene and the rest swarmed in, bayoneting two of Brown's raiders and wounding Brown. None of the hostages were harmed; Brown and four of his men were taken alive.[9]

The capture of the engine house. Robert E. Lee is the figure fifth from the left, holding a sword but still in civilian dress. (*Frank Leslie's Illustrated Newspaper,* November 5, 1859)

Lee cleared the engine house and had the dying Marine, along with Brown and one of his wounded raiders, carried to the arsenal paymaster's office. Brown's wounds turned out to be superficial, and Lee telegraphed John Floyd that though Brown "has three wounds . . . they are not considered by the surgeon as bad as first reported." The crowds of civilians surrounding the arsenal suddenly found their courage, and only "the steadiness of the marines" kept a spontaneous lynching from occurring. Lee, however, could not keep the politicians from intruding. Governor Wise arrived shortly after the cap-

Governor Wise's interrogation of John Brown. Robert E. Lee is third from the left. (*Frank Leslie's Illustrated Newspaper,* November 5, 1859)

ture of the engine house, "ready to weep" in exasperation when he found that "Virginia volunteers had not captured" Brown "before Col. Lee arrived."

Soon, Wise was joined by still more Virginia politicians—Alexander Boteler, Charles Faulkner, Senator James Mason (a relative by marriage to Smith Lee), the state's attorney, Andrew Hunter—and even Ohio congressman Clement Vallandigham, who had been on a train carrying him home when it was stopped at Harpers Ferry by the action at the engine house. After Lee's apprehensive warning that "he would exclude all visitors from the room if the wounded men were annoyed or pained thereby," they proceeded to interrogate Brown for three hours.

They did nothing, however, to assist Lee when he learned that Brown had cached weapons and papers in a farmhouse across the river (he could persuade the Virginia militia to help Stuart investigate only with some difficulty). The next day, a wild report that more of Brown's raiders had appeared five miles to the north forced Lee to send Stuart in pursuit of what turned out to be an empty rumor. By Wednesday, October 19, Lee was able to free himself from responsibility for Brown by sending him and the other prisoners to the Jefferson County courthouse in nearby Charles Town. The next morning, he left for Washington for "a protracted interview with the President and Secretary of War."[10]

But Lee could not be rid of John Brown that easily. The white South went frantic over the news, seeing in Brown a specter bigger with terror than Nat Turner, that of whites like themselves providing direction and leadership for a slave insurrection, an inversion of racial loyalty even more unnerving and unpredictable than a murderous uprising of racial fury. "The Southern people have heretofore disregarded the ravings of Northern fanatics, because they believed such madness to be merely of pecuniary speculation," wailed the *Richmond Enquirer,* but Harpers Ferry "shows that the Northern people mean more than words." How long will it be, the *Enquirer* asked, "before the Abolition fanatics of Cincinnati may seize Newport, in Kentucky"? For the moment, "the aid of the Federal government was near Harper's Ferry, and was in hands faithful to the Constitution, but another year may place that in the hands of our assailants, and . . . urge on and strengthen the hands that murder our families and pillage our property." In Harpers Ferry itself, Lee's departure "increased the general consternation, and the citizens are . . . endeavoring to organize companies for general defence."[11]

Curiously, Northern opinion recoiled from Brown, too—at first. *The New York Herald* swiftly pointed its editorial finger at "the black republican party," and Republicans wailed that Brown's raid, and the failure of Virginia slaves to rally to it, would be the stick slaveholders would use to beat the entire antislavery movement into silence. Even William Henry Seward, the emerging front-runner for the Republican presidential nomination in 1860, reluctantly denounced Brown's raid—"this attempt to execute an unlawful purpose in Virginia by invasion, involving servile war"—as an "act of sedition and treason" and branded Brown himself as "misguided" and "desperate." But from the moment Brown was put on trial in Charles Town for treason against Virginia, the old raider put on such a display of messianic willingness for crucifixion that embarrassed Northerners turned to praising him as a secular saint. "Harper's Ferry," proclaimed the Boston abolitionist Wendell Phillips, "is the Lexington of to-day," and Brown was "the brave, frank, and sublime truster in God's right and absolute justice." The Massachusetts lawyer John Andrew attacked Brown's "hurried trial" as "a judicial outrage" and raised $1,300 for Brown's defense costs; a mass meeting in Boston's Tremont Temple "realized four hundred dollars for John Brown's family."

Virginia, notwithstanding, found him guilty on November 2 and sentenced him to hang. The North listened to his last impassioned address to the court—"Now, if it is deemed necessary that I should forfeit my life for the furtherance of the ends of justice, and mingle my blood . . . with the blood of millions in this slave country whose rights are disregarded by wicked, cruel, and unjust enactments, I say let it be done"—and lauded him as a martyr.

The shadows of his stormy life that moment fell apart;
And they who blamed the bloody hand forgave the loving heart. . . .
And round the grisly fighter's hair the martyr's aureole bent![12]

Lee struggled to find a middle way of thinking about Brown that avoided both Southern paranoia and Northern exaltation over Brown's martyrdom. He was relieved that the Virginia militia would take charge of Brown's execution on December 2 in Charles Town and irked when Secretary Floyd sent him, not very willingly, back to Harpers Ferry on November 30 with four companies of artillerymen from Fort Monroe to guard against any last-minute interventions by shadowy Northern banditti. Lee refused to believe that Brown was anything more than sound and fury, signifying nothing, and he wryly described to Mary how he busied himself "posting sentinels & picquets to ensure timely notice of the approach of *the enemy.*" Despite the frantic ravings and protestations of the politicians, North as well as South, Lee insisted in a letter he wrote four days after Brown was hanged that there was nothing worth regarding seriously in Brown's raid, except to say, "*Poor fly, he done buzz,* as the crazy man said." And he was annoyed, even as the militia companies that had attended the hanging in Charles Town slowly disbanded and "are returning daily, almost hourly to their homes," to be surrounded by an unrelenting clamor of alarms of fresh invasion by Brown's sympathizers. "Last night I was informed that 1400 men were on their way to meet us." Lee listened, "went to bed . . . & find this mor[nin]g they did not arrive." He fully expected that by December 14 "these young soldiers" from Fort Monroe "will have to return to their oysters at old Point, without their breakfast or the sympathizers."[13]

Lee would nevertheless find himself lionized for his role in the capture of Brown as "the distinguished Col. Robert Lee . . . this gallant Virginian," and presented with a sword by the Virginia legislature "for his . . . gallant conduct at Harper's Ferry." He had, declared the *Richmond Enquirer,* become "universally regarded as the Chevalier Bayard of the age." When the U.S. Senate assembled on December 5 for the first session of the Thirty-Sixth Congress, James Mason was on his feet at once to demand an inquiry into the Harpers Ferry attack, and Lee was notified that "my testimony will be required" by the inquiry committee and "to hold myself in readiness to attend its call." At almost the same moment, the Committee on Military Affairs of the Virginia General Assembly, which had been authorized to renovate the state arsenal and purchase $500,000 worth of weapons, asked Lee to "attend their deliberations for the organizing & arming the militia of the State."

None of this swarm of adulation seemed to Lee to be in the slightest measure justified by the scope of the Harpers Ferry affair. Lee calmly declined the Virginia military committee's invitation and was happy when the Senate committee called him for only five minutes of questioning by Mason on January 10 (although the committee spread his entire report to Secretary Floyd across the pages of their published proceedings). He shared the middle-of-the-road skepticism published by a Wheeling newspaper:

> *What are the facts of the case? The news is telegraphed to all quarters of the Union as being a "negro insurrection," and forthwith the excitement become as intense as if a hostile army had landed in Chesapeake Bay, and were marching straight on Washington. . . . The upshot of the affair is that by the time the wretched Brown and his twenty men meet their fate, full a thousand troops, with artillery, are collected on the spot, though there has really been no negro rising whatever, and the sole enemy is a score of lunatics armed with Sharp's rifles, and shut up in a loop-holed house.*[14]

It came almost as a relief to learn that the overall military commander of the Department of Texas, David Twiggs, having picked a monumental quarrel with Secretary Floyd and survived a court-martial at the secretary's vengeful hands, had taken a leave of absence in December. And because it was widely assumed that Twiggs had "resigned his command," Lee was appointed in his place on December 14. He did not object. In October, Custis Lee was promoted to first lieutenant and reassigned to Joseph Totten's staff in Washington, all of which meant that he could live at Arlington and look after the gradual refurbishment of the property and the eventual payment of his sisters' legacies, as well as keep a watchful eye on Mary Lee's steady surrender to the grasp of rheumatoid arthritis. Rooney and his bride (who were now expecting their first child) were already ensconced on the Pamunkey, and young Rob, at age sixteen, was being firmly pointed toward entrance at the University of Virginia.

"Custis & Fitzhugh being both on the spot, & able to attend to the general welfare, as well as their individual interests," Lee wrote cheerfully to Anna Maria Fitzhugh in February 1860, "relieves me of a weight of care," and he was confident—perhaps wishfully so—that they would be "better able to attend to their Mother & Sisters than I am, and do more for the general good." Rooney and Charlotte were particularly "pleased with their location, & the latter was as much engrossed with her house, as the former was with the farm," and he added a curious note of appreciation that the slaves at White House and Romancoke were "undergoing a rapid Course of instruction"—he did not say *instruction* in *what*—"as they had been largely elevated from the hoe & plough."[15]

When Lee finally departed Arlington for Texas on February 10, he could escape the unwelcome burden of G.W.P.'s will, the resentful reluctance of slaves who believed they were entitled to freedom *now,* and the disheartening spiral of remission and return of Mary Lee's crippling arthritis. In Texas, perhaps, the specter of John Brown could be escaped as well. He was, of course, wrong.

He was off early on the morning of February 10, while "the Household is all asleep," and reached New Orleans in just three and a half days, where typically he stopped to dispatch a directive to Custis to do "whatever you may determine best for the farm, house, mill, etc." By the twentieth, he was in San Antonio, where he issued orders assuming command of the Department of Texas.

Little had been quiet during the two years he had been gone. Comanche raids had shot upward—nineteen skirmishes with Comanche bands marked

1857, and twenty Comanche raids followed in just the first month of 1858—and they drew no line, either, at stealing horses from their brother Comanche on the reservation on the Clear Fork. This easily convinced white settlers that the reservation was providing cover for the raiders, and the garrison at Camp Cooper had to turn out to prevent the rabid John Baylor from leading 250 armed men into the Comanche reserve. The Texans took their anger instead to the state governor, the veteran of Texas independence Sam Houston, and in 1859 both of the Brazos reservations were closed and their fourteen hundred inhabitants moved north of the Red River into Indian Territory. Meanwhile, the 2nd Cavalry, under the temporary command of Major George Thomas, was dispatched on a campaign in the fall of 1859 to shut down the raiding. Lee's wayward nephew, Fitz Lee, who had been posted to his uncle's regiment in 1858, very nearly got himself killed when a Comanche arrow pierced his right lung.[16]

But in 1860, a new challenge materialized from across the Rio Grande. A former Mexican officer, Juan Nepomuceno Cortina, presided over a sprawling *ranchero* across the river from Brownsville. His family had once owned property on both sides of the Rio Grande, and Cortina set himself up as the champion of displaced Mexicans angered by aggressive encroachments by American settlers and by land swindles by American lawyers. The Americans, Cortina asserted, were "flocks of vampires, in the guise of men" who "came and scattered themselves in the settlements, without any capital except the corrupt heart and the most perverse intentions." They form, "with a multitude of lawyers, a secret conclave . . . for the sole purpose of despoiling the Mexicans of their lands and usurp them afterwards."

The real trouble began in July 1859, when Cortina intervened in Brownsville to prevent the arrest of a former employee and ended by shooting Brownsville's sheriff. Cortina eluded a posse sent in pursuit and in September returned to Brownsville, raised the Mexican flag, killed five people on a death list he had prepared, then slipped back across the river. The Mexican government promised to take action against Cortina, but on the Mexican side of the river, in Matamoros, he was hailed as a hero, and a hastily recruited militia company from Brownsville failed to do more than exchange some useless fire with men whom Cortina had recruited as his own private army.[17]

Weapons, money, and volunteers from disgruntled Mexicans now arrived in Cortina's hands, and soon Brownsville began to imagine itself as the new Harpers Ferry. "What great difference is there between the outlawry of Opossum Brown, or whatever his name is, and that of Juan Nepomuceno Cortina?" raved the *San Antonio Daily Herald*, which frankly surmised that Cortina's raid was "the result of an organized system of fanatics of the John Brown stamp." In November, the Texas Rangers were dispatched to Brownsville, where they promptly lynched one of Cortina's allies, then crossed the Rio Grande into Mexico, where Cortina neatly ambushed them. The Cortinistas now swarmed across the river, robbing and burning, until five companies of the 1st and 8th U.S. Infantry and two companies from the 2nd Cavalry under Major Samuel Heintzelman were finally sent to restore order. But Cortina himself remained at large, crossing and recrossing the Rio Grande in a series of hit-and-run raids.[18]

Lee arrived in San Antonio to the applause of Texans who saw him as the hero of Harpers Ferry and "an accomplished gentleman and a finished soldier," and just the man to deal with Cortina. The demands of Texans that the Army come "to the defence and rescue of our fellow-citizens" were mounting, and Sam Houston, who made no secret of his interest in establishing an American protectorate over Mexico, was vaguely threatening President Buchanan that "circumstances may impel a course on the part of Texas which she desires to avoid." (Houston might have sanctioned one "filibuster" promoter to approach Lee in the hope that Lee would be "willing to . . . pacificate Mexico"; Lee declined.)

The first orders Lee received from Washington on February 24 instructed him to "put a period to the predatory operation . . . of Cortinas and his followers on American soil." With what, though? The constant pursuit of Comanche and Kiowa raiders meant that "the troops are always out" and "the Cav[alr]y horses are nearly worn out and sometimes drop dead on the trail." Moreover, the War Department gave him no authority to cross the Rio Grande in pursuit of Cortina; at best, he was authorized only to send official letters of protest to the Mexican authorities from the Texas side of the river. Nevertheless, Cortina could not be ignored, and less than a month after arriving in San Antonio, Lee, accompanied by "but a single Compy of Cav[alr]y," was on the road to the Rio Grande, hoping that "if I can hear of the whereabouts of Mr. Cortinas, I will endeavour to pick him up."[19]

Lee reached the Rio Grande, only to find that "all the alarms about Cortinas at that place were false." Through April, he scoured the valley of the lower Rio Grande with both infantry and cavalry. But even though "I hear various reports about Cortina," the man himself had disappeared "into the interior and was 135 miles off." Lee was reduced to submitting a protest letter to the governor of the Mexican state of Tamaulipas, asking him to "cause to be dispersed any bands within the States under your jurisdiction, having for their object depredations upon American soil." When the Mexican military commandant at Matamoras tartly replied by pointing out that the Americans had violated Mexican sovereignty fully as much as Cortina had American, Lee diplomatically turned the complaint into a compliment for the Mexican resolve to "pursue and punish Cortinas and his followers."

Lee found the Mexican authorities more reasonable to deal with than the Texans and so "vastly civil & polite that it is impossible to quarrel with them." But he did not expect anything to be done by them, and he certainly had no intention of plunging blindly into the Mexican interior "with broken down horses," in "barren, mountainous" terrain, in pursuit of Cortina. When rumors of Cortina's return to the Rio Grande began to fly in May, Lee took them seriously enough "that I laid a plan to take him by surprise," if only to show "that it is not entirely safe to approach the river too near." But the Cortinistas would not be back until long after Lee was gone, in 1861, and only for a brief time. After that, Cortina's attention would be consumed with opposition to the French occupation of Mexico and the ongoing convulsions of Mexican politics, until his death under house arrest in 1894 in Mexico City.[20]

Which suited Lee very well. "You know I am a great advocate of people staying at home & minding their own affairs," and he had more than enough in San Antonio to keep him peaceably occupied through the summer of 1860. At the end of April, he began reorganizing the deployment of the Army's Texas-based infantry and cavalry, parceling out two companies of the 8th Infantry to the Ringgold Barracks, another company to Fort McIntosh, and four companies of his own 2nd Cavalry to Brownsville. He also handed down a particular bit of praise for Samuel Heintzelman's "great prudence and ability" in the pursuit of Cortina, all the while hoping that the end of the Mormon confrontation in Utah could bring two more regiments to Texas to deal with the Comanche troubles. In 1857, the Army experimented with introducing thirty-three camels from Egypt as the basis for a new mounted unit that could traverse the western deserts, and in June 1860, Lee arranged for twenty of the camels to be used by "an exploring expedition to a rough corner of the upper Rio Grande." Otherwise, he was preoccupied with "the various wants & applications" of the department and assuring irritable Texans (starting with Sam Houston) that "at this time there are no disturbances on this frontier & that I hear of the presence of no banditti on either side of the river."

He was slightly cheered by the news, in June, of the promotion of Sidney Johnston to command of the Department of the Pacific, because that might "move everybody . . . one round up the long ladder of promotion." But not Lee. His old friend from West Point Joe Johnston wangled an assignment as the Army's quartermaster general, with a brevet promotion to brigadier general, and Lee stiffly conceded, "My friend Col Joe Johnston is a good soldier & worthy man" for the promotion. But it was evident that Johnston owed his good fortune to his close family connection to Secretary of War Floyd, and Lee privately suspected "that it never was the intention of Congress"—merely the favoritism of Floyd—"to advance him to the position assigned him by the Sec[retar]y." Meanwhile, David Twiggs boldly announced that he now intended to return from leave and resume command of the Department of Texas by the end of the year, thus bumping Lee from departmental command back to command of the 2nd Cavalry.[21]

At least in Texas, Lee continued to earn high marks, even among the most impatient Texans. Although Lee was critical of the "exuberant sympathy of our people with filibusterers & protectionists," the commandant of the Texas Rangers, John Salmon Ford, was impressed by Lee in spite of himself, and on precisely the terms that might have drawn a rare self-congratulatory smile from Lee:

> *Colonel Lee's appearance was dignified without hauteur, grand without pride, and in keeping with the noble simplicity characterizing a true republican. He evinced an imperturbable self-possession, and a complete control of his passions. To approach him was to feel yourself in the presence of a man of superior intellect, possessing the capacity to accomplish great ends and the gift of controlling and leading men.*

Another Texan watched him observing a squad of new recruits at drill and came away thinking that Lee "seemed a column of antique marble, a pillar of state—so calm, so serene, so thoughtful, so commanding . . . and I said involuntarily to myself: 'There stands a great man.' " He mixed easily and serenely with San Antonio society. When he attended a soiree hosted by Richard McCormick, the governor's secretary, he coaxed the teenage Kate Merritt to play the piano, even leading "me to the piano" and standing beside her, thanking her "in the most gracious terms, and when supper was announced he took me in to supper." He was, she remembered, "one of the most charming and gracious gentlemen I ever met."[22]

But privately, the dreariness of departmental administration and the separation from his children wore him into new ruts of depression. He had no sooner returned to Texas in February than he was complaining to his twenty-one-year-old daughter, Annie (who was becoming the favorite confidante among his offspring), of "my distress at parting with you all, & my longing desire to see you again." These "departures grow harder to bear with" as the years rolled on, he wrote to Mary, even as he reproached himself for "useless repining." He lamented bitterly to Anna Maria Fitzhugh that he had suffered for too long from "a divided heart . . . & a divided life. . . . My military duties require me here, where as my affections & urgent domestic claims call me away."

It was not Arlington that called to him, but his children and wife, yet they were as fully devoted to Arlington as he was to them. "I long to see you," he wrote to Annie, and thought that "if I had one of my daughters to keep house for me, I could be set up." But his daughters regarded "dear dear Arlington" as "my home of joy," and Mary Lee turned her increasingly immobilized attentions to the publication of an edition of her father's *Recollections and Private Memoirs of Washington,* with her own memoir of G.W.P. in which Arlington almost became a third parent, "a place of frequent resort to many of the eminent and good of this and other countries." Lee had never been able to supplant Arlington in the hearts of those whom he loved, and thanks to G.W.P.'s will Arlington would always have a life for them apart from any control he could exert. The rivalry this created was, in his mind, "one cause of the small progress I have made on either hand [in] my professional & civil career."[23]

Lee struggled to resign himself to what he now had to assume was the twilight of his Army years. "We must . . . lay nothing too much to heart," he wrote to Mary, in a letter that was supposed to console her for the stealthy onslaught of her disability but that had as much to say about himself. "Desire nothing too eagerly, rejoice not excessively, nor grieve too much at disasters." He could always have taken the course of resignation from the Army, but that would only land him back at Arlington, and even as he received letters from Annie extolling "the trees & hills at A[rlington]," he gently pushed away any suggestion that he return there for good. "I do not think my presence would add anything to their appearance," he replied, in a peculiar mix of regret and self-pity, "& it is better that I am away."

When Annie pressed the suggestion again in August, he calmly but firmly told her that it would be far easier if "you will come out here. . . . I will endeavor to make you as comfortable as possible. I have a nice little pony on which you can accompany me in my ev[enin]g rides, & a commodious travelling wagon that can carry you wherever I go." There was no point in his returning to Arlington. He was, and always would be, a stranger there. "You know I am much in the way of everybody & my tastes and pursuits did not coincide with the rest of the household"—and certainly not with the Arlington slaves. "Now I hope everybody is happier."[24]

This did not prevent Lee from dispensing his usual ladles of patrimonial advice. To Custis and Rooney, he warned "never exceed your means." Mildred, now fifteen, must "learn & improve herself . . . that she may have the enjoyment of doing good & of being appreciated by the wise & virtuous in the world." "Dear little Agnes" has to develop "a great deal of patience in this world & a great deal of waiting upon events." Young Rob needs "to learn to write a good hand." And while he coaxed Mary to take care of herself, he also warned Custis to keep an eye on his mother's spending habits. She "from time to time will be wanting a little money," but he should be prepared to corral any excessive expenses, "as she is always wanting to do a little shopping." Not even Mary's edition of G.W.P.'s Washington memoirs escaped his urgings for improvement. "You might," he wrote, "encourage the publisher to issue another edition" and take that as an opportunity to "make some improvement in the text, & add to the illustrations," and especially "cut and retain the remarks of the various papers."[25]

The one unalloyed delight Lee had in 1860 was the birth of Rooney and Charlotte's first child, an eight-pound baby boy whom they named for his grandfather. The debut of the first grandchild was epochal enough that Mary, even with her arthritis, made it down to White House, rejoicing "at another baby in the house," and Charles Dana of Christ Church made the steamboat journey from Alexandria to perform the baptism. But even this new Robert Edward Lee could not quite pull Lee out of his despond. As much as he congratulated Rooney "at his prosperous advent," Lee could not suppress the dreary anticipation that "this promising scion of my scattered house" will somehow "resuscitate its name and fame," as though the shade of Light Horse Harry were still smothering it. He might even "do his part to supply the deficiencies of his Gr[an]dfather," which was Lee's way of signaling how little he imagined he had accomplished in that direction.

Lee no longer anticipated being able to do much toward those deficiencies now, in his fifty-fourth year. He began to warn Agnes for the first time in June 1860 of "rheumatism" of his own, although this was much more likely the first sign of heart disease. At nearly six feet in height, Lee was not overweight—he estimated his "respectable weight" at 155 pounds—but he was now resorting to "my spectacles" for close objects, and during his first tour in Texas he had tried to grow a beard, only to have it turn a heavy gray. "I am sure," he drily told Mary, "I am not getting young." And if he needed a reminder of that, the "rheumatism" struck again late in August. "My attack was a slight one," he informed Annie, "though you know a little in that way goes hard with me."[26]

John Brown's body was buried in North Elba, New York, on December 8, 1859, and from that moment the country proceeded to slice itself to ribbons. Whatever hope James Buchanan entertained for heading the Democratic presidential ticket again in 1860 disappeared in the debacle over Kansas and his inability to prevent the reelection to the Senate in 1858 of his chief Democratic critic over Kansas, Stephen A. Douglas. Yet, for precisely that reason, Douglas was utterly unacceptable to Southern Democrats. His challenger during the 1858 reelection campaign was the antislavery Whig turned Republican Abraham Lincoln, and Lincoln had pinned Douglas publicly during the campaign into conceding that Douglas's favorite solution—popular sovereignty—meant that settlers in the new western territories could as easily decide to ban slavery as legalize it.

Southern Democrats were incensed at Douglas's admission that under popular sovereignty enough territorial settlers could, even theoretically, bar slavery from the west. Not only did slaveholders feel a raw economic need for new territories; they fell delirious at even the vague possibility that popular sovereignty might add to the free-state column in Congress, where free territories and additional free states would end forever their dominance of national politics. Popular sovereignty, which a decade before seemed like a sensible compromise for slaveholders and non-slaveholders alike, was no longer even faintly acceptable to the South. "Congress cannot destroy the property of a citizen in his slave in a Territory," Louisiana's senator Judah P. Benjamin declared, and Stephen Douglas was now a heretic "when he assumed the power of the people of a Territory to exercise what he terms squatter or popular sovereignty."[27]

Northern Democrats like Douglas thought popular sovereignty was exactly the equitable solution North and South alike should embrace, and Douglas "had the heart of the Northern Democracy." When the Democratic National Convention met in Charleston on April 23, 1860, every expectation pointed to a Douglas presidential nomination, until eight Southern delegations walked out rather than permit Douglas to be nominated. A second convention was hastily arranged for the Front Street Theatre in Baltimore in June, only to run aground even more furiously over Douglas, with more than a third of delegates walking out and, this time, withdrawing to Baltimore's Mechanics Hall to nominate their own pro-slavery presidential candidate, John C. Breckinridge. Douglas had to be acclaimed by what remained of the Front Street Theatre convention, which ensured a fatal split of the Democratic Party and that Breckinridge and Douglas would "aim, specially and primarily, to defeat the other."

And then, to dim Democratic prospects still further, a third political convention, under the banner of the hastily contrived Constitutional Union Party, nominated an old Whig, John Bell of Tennessee, for the presidency. Bell's nomination guaranteed only that neither Breckinridge nor Douglas could expect much from the slaveholding states of the upper South, where Whiggism still had nostalgic sympathizers. By contrast, when the Republicans gathered in Chicago in May to nominate their candidate, they enthusiastically united on choosing Douglas's old nemesis Lincoln. At best, there was some fleeting hope that these divisions would "carry the election into the House of Representatives." What was more likely was that Bell, Breckinridge, and Douglas would only succeed in shivering the Democratic vote into three impotent pieces and allow the election of the first avowed antislavery, anti-extension Republican to the presidency.

With the power to control the entire mechanism of federal patronage in Lincoln's hands, Southerners could only imagine the Republican president slyly posting to every federal job in the South antislavery appointees who would feel no compunction whatsoever about encouraging more John Browns to take their chances, or using patronage to seduce the loyalties of Southerners who hungered for political patronage salaries more than slaves. The election of Lincoln had only one attraction for the slaveholding states: it would convince the fainthearted that the handwriting was on the wall and that it was time to leave the American Union. The "extremists," reported *The New York Times,* "are delighted at the prospect . . . which will give them an opportunity to rally the South in favor of dissolution" and "plunge the cotton states into revolution."[28]

From his lonely perch in San Antonio, Lee beheld the fracturing of the Democratic Party—and the ease with which Southern Democrats talked about disunion as a result—with the same incredulity with which he had treated John Brown. It was essential to his own relationship to slavery to believe that slavery was fundamentally evil, but an evil that was wasting away on its own, and it neither justified Brown's raid nor deserved the sacrifice of the Union. Mary agreed. "My unsuspecting mind," she recalled, refused to embrace "the possibility of the dissolution of that Union so long our boast & pride & to maintain which we would even *then* have gladly laid down our lives." With the Whigs a dead letter and the Democrats a suicidal one, politics once more bobbed ominously to the surface of Lee's letters, beginning less than two weeks after the Baltimore convention debacle. In a letter to one of his 2nd Cavalry officers, Earl Van Dorn (a Mississippian who might have discreetly sounded out Lee on political matters as a fellow Southerner), Lee admitted that the "news of the Baltimore convention" chilled him. But he laid the blame on Douglas and hoped that "Douglass would now withdraw & join himself & party to aid in the election of Breckinridge"—not so much because he loved Breckinridge and his fire-eating disunion supporters as to ensure that "Lincoln be defeated."[29]

Lee said no more on politics until the election actually took place on November 6. Immediately, the legislature of South Carolina authorized the calling of a state secession convention, and on December 20 the Carolinians declared their participation in the Union at an end. They were joined in quick order by Mississippi, Georgia, Florida, Alabama, Louisiana, and eventually Texas. From department headquarters in San Antonio, Lee watched the secession tide creep closer and closer. "The lone star is floating all over this state," he noticed irritably, as the Texas state flag began replacing the Stars and Stripes. The local San Antonio newspaper endorsed John Bell's Constitutional Union Party and announced itself as promoting "the Conservative Union sentiment." But as Lincoln's victory loomed, the town was filled with meetings that "labored hard to establish the idea that each State was an independent nation" and "that Lincoln's election would be sufficient cause for disunion." Northern Texas ran wild with rumors of a new John Brown–style slave uprising; newspapers published crazed reports that "the North has gone overwhelmingly for Negro Equality and Southern Vassalage! Southern men will you submit to this degradation?" Governor Houston tried to stave off a rush to secession by refusing to convene the legislature. "If an attempt is made to destroy our Union, or violate our Constitution," Houston swore, "there will be blood shed to maintain them." But in December, even Houston's opposition unwillingly crumbled. A secession convention was rapidly authorized, and just as rapidly voted to withdraw Texas from the Union on February 1.[30]

Lee's incredulity now turned to apprehension. At the most personal level, the screams for secession would certainly derange the economy, and his own finances with it. "The political troubles of the country," he warned Custis, "will curtail my resources," and he urged Custis "to see what means you will have for the expenses of the house & farm." On the national stage, the secession melodrama would, if successful, almost certainly force some kind of dissolution and reconstruction of the entire Union. And there were plenty of such schemes in play. The young Henry Adams, far away in Washington, heard the seceders talk about seizing Washington itself, then inviting "the northern States" to a restructuring "of the Union on terms which should suit the South" (and which would exclude New England but include New York City and California). Virginia's governor, John Letcher, opened the state legislative session on January 7 by predicting that "when disunion shall come, we will have four organizations, independent and distinct": New England and New York would form one new confederacy; Pennsylvania, the Northwest, and the border slave states would form another; the "cotton states" would form the third; and the Pacific coast the fourth. What Virginia would do was at that moment beyond his ken. Even the old general Winfield Scott believed that a breakup of the Union into "new Confederacies, probably four," might be inevitable (although he added that "there is good reason to hope" that this would happen "without one conflict of arms, one execution, or one arrest for treason," and once the secession passions had cooled, negotiations could then begin a process of rebuilding the Union). Perplexed, Lee could only promise Custis, "If the Union is dissolved, which God in his mercy forbid, I shall return to you."[31]

Lee had a brief glimmer of hope in the pleas for restraint made by President Buchanan in his last official message to Congress on December 3. But it was only a glimmer, and that was doused by the reappearance on December 13 of David Twiggs in San Antonio. A Georgian and a slaveholder, Twiggs did not hesitate to assure Lee that "the Union will be dissolved in six weeks"; after that, there would be no more U.S. Army, and Twiggs would "then return to New Orleans." Lee, packing his bags for Fort Mason and the headquarters of the 2nd Cavalry, shook his head in disbelief. If Twiggs was right, "I should not take the trouble to go to Mason," but leave for Virginia at once.

He clung to the hope that "the wisdom & patriotism of the country will devise some way of saving it," and "I will cling to it to the last." The slaveholding states might have reason to complain of "the aggressions of the North" and Lincoln's avowal that as president he would oppose the extension of slavery into the territories (the territories, Lee reasoned, were after all "the common territory of the commonwealth," just as John Calhoun had argued a decade before, and Lincoln had no authority to exclude slaveholders from them). But the behavior of "the cotton states" was wholly beyond any justification, and he was worried that "their selfish & dictatorial bearing" would make life for Virginia miserable "should she determine to coalesce with them." He had scant patience for the slaveholders' argument that the Constitution was only a compact from which the states could legally secede at will. To one of his Carter cousins, Lee bleakly insisted that "secession . . . is revolution"—a radical break with the Constitution—and will be followed by "war at last and cannot be otherwise."[32]

But if war and not reconstruction of some sort was the likeliest result of secession, on what side would Robert E. Lee find himself? Would there even be a side? Even as the Texas legislature was authorizing its secession convention, Lee wrote despairingly to Markie Williams that "a fearful calamity is upon us." He still could not believe that "our people will destroy a government inaugurated by the blood & wisdom of our patriot fathers, that has given us peace & prosperity at home, power & security abroad, & under which we have acquired a colossal strength unequalled in the history of mankind." For his part, he wished "to live under no other government" and to have "no other flag than the 'Star Spangled banner.'" But if that government was now going to disappear, then the only alternative was to "go back in sorrow to my people & share the misery of my native state, & save in her defense there will be one soldier less in the world than now."

The convening of the Texas secession convention only increased the churning of his fears. "Secession is nothing but revolution," he repeated to Custis on January 23 and to Rooney six days later, and he poured contempt on the idea that the Union "was intended to be broken by every member of the Confederacy at will." He had been reading Edward Everett's brief new *Life of George Washington,* and reading it filled him with the conviction that "the framers of our Constitution never exhausted so much labor, wisdom, and forbearance in its formation" only for the purpose of erecting a temporary dalliance. In the same terms Abraham Lincoln would use, Lee insisted that the Constitution "was intended for 'perpetual union' . . . and for the establishment of a government, not a compact." Secession was "anarchy . . . and not a government." Even worse, he wrote to Rooney, "in 1808 when the new England States resisted Mr. Jeffersons Imbargo Law & the Hartford Convention assembled, secession was termed treason by a Virga statesman. What can it be now?"[33]

He would have that conviction tested sooner than he thought. On February 6, three representatives of the Texas secession convention met with David Twiggs in San Antonio to negotiate the surrender of federal military property in the state. Twiggs easily agreed to turn over forts, supplies, and equipment and on February 18 ordered all federal troops in Texas to abandon their posts and proceed to Indianola on the coast for transportation. The San Antonio garrison, humiliated and enraged at Twiggs's betrayal, insisted on marching out in full-dress uniforms and with band blaring.[34]

Lee paled at the rumors of Twiggs's betrayal, and even as the secession convention was severing Texas's ties to the Union, he began quietly testing the loyalty of the garrison at Fort Mason and whether they would rally behind him and "defend his post at all hazards" if the secessionists attacked. As he warned Samuel Heintzelman, the Texans would not get Fort Mason or its stores "without fighting for them." But on February 13, Lee received preemptory orders directly from Washington: he was "relieved from duty in this department, and will repair forthwith to Washington and report in person to the General-in Chief." Mystified and "distressed," Lee packed at once, heading for San Antonio, only to arrive on the same day Twiggs ordered the evacuation of federal troops from Texas. The plaza was teeming with Texas Rangers who eyed with an unexpected hostility the military ambulance in which Lee had arrived (because this was the only wagon with springs and padded benches available), and he might have come to harm on the spot had not the wife of the departmental paymaster's clerk run out to warn him, "General Twiggs surrendered everything to the State this morning, and we are all prisoners of war."

This was not entirely true; there was no war, and thus no prisoners, and federal military personnel were allowed to depart freely. But Jefferson Davis, now the Confederate government's newly elected provisional president, was already preparing orders to arrest Army personnel and treat them as prisoners. "Has it come so soon as this?" Lee wondered in dismay. Indeed it had, and he took the precaution of changing into civilian dress while he waited for the next coach that would take him to the coast.[35]

That did not save him from suspicious questions. But to them all, he returned bland and inoffensive answers. "In conversations," Lee "declared that the position he held was a neutral one." He was returning to Virginia to "resign and go to planting corn," and though he "would never bear arms against the United States," he might "carry a musket in defense of my native state, Virginia," if it was assailed by some unnamed party. He was anxious enough, though, that he consigned his trunks ("seven boxes containing papers and baggage") to the care of a Texas unionist, Charles Anderson—whose brother Major Robert Anderson was at that moment commanding the last holdout federal garrison in secessionist South Carolina, Fort Sumter, in Charleston harbor.

On February 22, Lee finally arrived at Indianola, where he took passage for New Orleans. By March 1, he was at Arlington. He would never see the trunks again.[36]

CHAPTER NINE

The Decisions

Abraham Lincoln was inaugurated as the sixteenth president of the United States three days after Lee's return. There is no evidence that Lee attended the inaugural festivities, although that had always been G.W.P.'s custom. However, on March 12, Lee did yield to another custom, which brought all the serving officers of the Army resident in or near the District of Columbia to the White House for a presidential reception. Lee left no record of his impressions of the homely, stoop-shouldered Illinoisan with the broad backwoods accent. (Eight months later, Julia Ward Howe would be perplexed at Lincoln's "unusual pronunciation" of "heerd" for "heard.") But four days later, Lincoln promoted Edwin Sumner of the 1st Cavalry to brigadier general (to replace David Twiggs), and that left a colonelcy vacant at the head of Sumner's regiment that Lincoln nominated Lee to fill. Now the whispers began to thicken that Lee's recall from Texas was the first step toward making him the successor to Winfield Scott, because "Lee of Virginia" is "the only man the Army acknowledges to be fit to be the successor of Gen. Scott."[1]

Lee was summoned to a preliminary meeting with Scott "directly after his return" from Texas in which Lee asked Scott "what was going to be done." There was no talk as yet about Lee's commanding armies or inheriting Scott's office. But if there was some kind of military action in the offing, Lee "wanted to know," because if that involved coercion of Virginia, "he might at once resign." Scott, however, assured him that his recall from Texas was purely for administrative reasons—to assist in updating the Army's official *Regulations*—and Scott soothed Lee's anxieties by showing him "letters" from both Lincoln and William Henry Seward (in his new role as secretary of state) indicating that "a peaceful solution would be attained," and so Lee went back to Arlington "much relieved."

Meanwhile, Virginia's legislature authorized the calling of a state secession convention to weigh appeals from the seven seceding states to join the new Southern Confederacy they had organized in February. Lee made no further comment on secession, but Mary did, hotly asserting that "those who have been foremost in this Revolution will deserve & meet with the reprobation of the world either North or South, for having destroyed the most glorious Confederacy that ever existed." If Virginia was to play any role, she hoped it might be to act as a mediator and "obtain the mead promised in the Bible to the *peacemakers.*"[2]

Still, for a month thereafter, the situation stalled, with the standoff in Charleston harbor over Fort Sumter becoming the theater of national agony. The new Confederate government effectively sealed off Major Robert Anderson and his garrison from resupply or reinforcement with a ring of artillery emplacements around the harbor, but hesitated to do more. Lincoln likewise hesitated to rush to Major Anderson's rescue. His cabinet counseled against it, understanding all too well that any provocative gesture from Lincoln would trigger an equally provocative response from the Confederates that would leave no practical alternative to civil war. That, in turn, might stampede the remaining slave states—and especially Virginia—into the arms of the Confederates. Hopefully, desperately, Lincoln played for time, knowing that the longer the Confederates waited on him, the less substantial the secession strategy looked. He even offered to trade an evacuation of Sumter's garrison for the dismissal of the Virginia secession convention, which up to this point had done little except talk and wait.

But Lincoln also had to reckon with the rising impatience of Northern public opinion and the Northern governors, who demanded action. Lincoln proposed a compromise: he would resupply Fort Sumter, but only with food and medicine, not weapons or reinforcements. To the Confederacy's provisional president, Jefferson Davis, this meant little more than running out a clock he could not afford to leave running, and on April 12, Confederate artillery began a bombardment of the fort. Major Anderson and his beleaguered garrison held out for two days, until their supplies were exhausted, and then surrendered. The next day, citing the authority of the federal militia acts, Lincoln called on the remaining states of the Union—including Virginia—for 75,000 militia to suppress "combinations too powerful to be suppressed by the ordinary course of judicial proceedings."[3]

The militia callout was the moment of crisis for Virginia. The Virginia secession convention was bitterly divided between a hard core of secession sympathizers and a larger but less certain unionist majority, much of which was drawn from the western part of the state. On April 4, the convention decisively voted down a secession resolution, and it was this vote that gave Lincoln the hope that he could swap an evacuation of Sumter for a dissolution of the convention. But it stayed in session all the same, still debating whether "we shall be expected to rush off like a flock of sheep, right into the embrace of the Southern Confederacy," or "remain in the Northern free-soil Confederacy," or even create a "middle confederacy" formed by "a tier of friendly States between the slaveholding States and the States of the extreme North and North-west." There was little enthusiasm for embracing the seceders, and if the Confederates planned to seize the national capital by marching across Virginia, Virginians would stop them. One defiant western delegate, Jubal Early, declared that "the idea of marching an army from the Confederated States through our borders to Washington . . . will be promptly resisted." But after the fall of Fort Sumter, the call upon Virginia for its militia to join in a movement against the seceders swung the convention the other way, and on April 17 a secession ordinance was adopted, 88 to 55. And yet the deed was not entirely done. The secession ordinance would have to be put to a statewide referendum on May 23, and in the meantime disgruntled western Virginia unionists met in Clarksburg to organize their own convention in Wheeling on May 13.[4]

Robert E. Lee would not have the luxury of waiting on the referendum. On Thursday, April 18, he was summoned to a meeting with Francis Preston Blair, the veteran Washington political operative whose extended family was in "control of Mr. Lincoln's administration." The message specified a rendezvous at the Washington town house of Montgomery Blair (Francis Preston Blair's son and Lincoln's new appointee as postmaster general) at 1651 Pennsylvania Avenue. There, Blair, with the blessing of Lincoln, asked Lee whether he would "take command of the army" Lincoln was calling into being and serve once more under Winfield Scott as the overall general in chief.[5]

At least seven contemporaneous descriptions of this interview—one from Montgomery Blair in 1866, one from the then secretary of war, Simon Cameron, three from Lee himself between 1868 and 1870, and one each from Mary Custis Lee and Francis Preston Blair in 1871—exist. They are by no means consistent with one another. The earliest of these accounts, from Montgomery Blair, positions Lee as a reluctant but unapologetic defender of Virginia, and for the sake of Virginia (but not for secession) Lee declines to take command of troops that could conceivably be used to invade the Old Dominion:

General Lee said to my father, when he was sounded by him, at the request of President Lincoln, about taking command of our army against the rebellion, then hanging upon the decision of the Virginia [secession] convention, "Mr. Blair, I look upon secession as anarchy. If I owned the four millions of slaves in the South, I would sacrifice them all to the Union: but how can I draw my sword upon Virginia, my native State?" He could not determine then; said he would consult with his friend General Scott, and went on the same day to Richmond, probably to arbitrate difficulties; and we see the result.[6]

In 1868, Simon Cameron, who would certainly have been privy to any decision to put Lee in charge of federal forces, painted a much darker, treasonous picture of the Blair meeting (though without using Blair's name), insisting that Lee, not Blair, had initiated the April 18 meeting, and with a view to usurping Winfield Scott:

General Lee called on a gentleman who had my entire confidence, and intimated that he would like to have the command of the Army. He assured that gentleman, who was a man in the confidence of the Administration, of his entire loyalty, and his devotion to the interests of the Administration and of the country. I consulted with General Scott, and General Scott approved of placing him at the head of the Army. The place was offered to him unofficially, with my approbation, and with the approbation of General Scott. It was accepted by him verbally, with the promise that he would go into Virginia and settle his business and then come back to take command. He never gave us an opportunity to arrest him; he deserted under false pretenses. I should have arrested him in a moment if I had had a chance at him, and I have always regretted that I never did get that chance. . . . I think he behaved worse than any of the men who acted so treacherously to the Government.[7]

Lee's own versions of the meeting came as angry responses to Cameron's *j'accuse,* the first in an interview with William Allan one week after Cameron's charges. Furious at Cameron's claim, Lee "stated . . . all the circumstances connected with his resignation from the old army." Winfield Scott had recalled him from Texas, ostensibly to have him "revise (in connection with others) the army regulations," but in reality to have Lee on hand as the situation over secession deteriorated. Lee, however, warned Scott at the time that there was at least one thing he should not expect, that Lee "could not go on duty against the South." But Scott assured him that "there would be no war."

It was not until April 18, when he was summoned to the meeting with

Francis Preston Blair, that it became clear that "Mr. L. and Cabinet wanted Gen Lee to be Commander in Chief in [the] field." So far as Lee knew on the morning of April 18, the Virginia secession convention "remained in secret session," so it was still possible for Lee to imagine that Virginia would not secede, would not join the Southern Confederacy, and military confrontation with the seceder states would be unnecessary. Blair's offer suggested a very different direction, that force would be used on the secessionists and would require a commander in the field to direct it. Blair was "very wily and keen," appealing to Lee's "ambition" and his place as "a representative of the Washington family." But Lee was dubious about coercing the seceders, so even as he "deprecated War" and "said as far as the negro was concerned he would willingly give up his own (400) for peace," he would refuse Blair's (and Lincoln's) offer.

On the same day as the Allan interview, Lee wrote to the Maryland senator Reverdy Johnson (who had challenged Cameron's veracity on the floor of the Senate) with a second account of the Blair meeting. He energetically denied that he had ever "intimated to any one that I desired the command of the United States Army," much less to Blair. The meeting with Blair had been at Blair's invitation, "and as I understood at the instance of President Lincoln," and Lee had made it clear that "though opposed to secession and deprecating war," he "could take no part in an invasion of the Southern States." This was not, however, because he necessarily took the side of the seceders but because he expected that "some way would have been found to save the country from the calamities of war." Lee reiterated that last detail in an interview with William Preston Johnston in 1870 in which Lee insisted that the most important influence on his decision had been Winfield Scott's assurances that there would be no war. "General Scott was induced to believe that pacification was intended by Mr. Lincoln and Mr. Seward," and Scott in turn had tried to convince Lee "that Mr. Lincoln would recede."[8]

Francis Preston Blair dictated his own recollection of the April 18 interview with Lee in 1871, and it conformed almost entirely to Lee's refutation of Simon Cameron. The elder Blair wanted it understood that he had acted at Lincoln's bidding, not Lee's. "The matter was talked over by President Lincoln and myself for some hours on two or three different occasions," and both "expressed themselves as anxious to give the command of our army to Robert E. Lee." But Blair, acting only as an intermediary, was cautious of approach, intending the discussion with Lee to be not so much an offer as an effort to "sound General Robert E. Lee, to know whether his feelings would justify him in taking command of our army." For the first time, a go-between was mentioned: Lee's cousin Major John Fitzgerald Lee, the judge advocate general of the Army, who "sent him a note at my suggestion."

If Blair's original approach to Lee was cautious, in the meeting he was more direct, and he plainly told Lee that "President Lincoln . . . wanted him to take command of the army." Lee's reply at first sounded encouraging, because Lee professed to be "devoted to the Union" and "would do everything in his power to save it, and that if he owned all the negroes in the South, he would be willing to give them up and make the sacrifice of the value of every one of them to save the Union." The sticking point was Virginia, because "he did not know how he could draw his sword upon his native State"—although at that moment neither Blair nor Lee could have known anything for certain about Virginia's decision. Blair remembered the interview as a long one, lasting "several hours." Significantly, at the end, Blair believed that Lee remained undecided and asked for time to consult with "his friend General Scott." Blair agreed to the delay, and Lee "left the house." The next Blair heard, Lee had been met "by a committee from Richmond" and "went with them," although even then it was only "to consult the Virginia convention as to some mode of settling the difficulty." (The elderly Francis Preston Blair did not correct his son Montgomery's misapprehension that Lee "went on the same day to Richmond," but he left standing Montgomery's understanding that Lee went there with the intention of "probably to arbitrate difficulties.")[9]

What emerges from the welter of reminiscences of the Blair interview are three things: first, Blair was authorized by Lincoln to make a serious command offer to Lee on April 18, which Lee refused; second, Lee made it clear that his refusal had nothing to do with defending slavery but rested entirely on his reluctance to take responsibility for operations that would require him to invade the South and perhaps even oppose "his native State"; third, and oddest of all, his decision was motivated in large part by assurances that there would be no war after all, especially if he had a hand in resolving "difficulties." The third of those propositions makes no sense in the light of the second: if Lee believed there would be no conflict—that "some way would have been found to save the country from the calamities of war"—then there should have been no risk in his mind that he would have to conduct any kind of hostile campaign, and certainly not against Virginia, and the golden prize of his professional life would fall neatly into his lap. There is also a question about Lee's invocation of "his native State," because the Lees, however prominent they had been in Virginia life, were mostly nationalists, Federalists, and Whigs. Moreover, Virginia had not, strictly speaking, been Lee's native state for most of his life. His youth, from the time the Lee family moved to Alexandria, had been spent within what were then the boundaries of the District of Columbia (Alexandria County would not be retroceded to Virginia until 1846), and his professional responsibilities had scattered him for thirty years from Texas to New York. Arlington was his home but not his property, and its facing across the Potomac River toward the Capitol was a constant reminder of where the Custises always saw their loyalties residing.

The key to reconciling these oddities lies in the second meeting Lee had on April 18, and that was with Winfield Scott, in the Army's headquarters building around the corner from the Blair house. It is one of the more startling omissions in Scott's 1864 autobiography that he made no mention at all of this interview with Lee; there are copious mentions in the book of Lee's service to Scott in the Mexican War, but not a word about the offer of command of the Union armies in 1861.[10] There are, nevertheless, three eyewitness accounts of the interview, starting with Lee himself, in a follow-up letter to Scott on April 20. It is a spare letter, thanking Scott for "more than a quarter century" of "uniform kindness and consideration" but informing the old general that with the news on April 19 of Virginia's secession vote he not only could not take command of federal forces but would resign his newly bestowed colonel's commission in the 1st U.S. Cavalry. "Save in defense of my native State, I never desire again to draw my sword."[11]

The two other witnesses were more expansive. Erasmus Keyes, who became Scott's military secretary after Lee declined the job in 1857, related (in his 1884 memoir) how Lee, "just arrived in Washington from Texas," had come unannounced "to pay his respects to the commanding general." (Keyes had collapsed in memory the six weeks between Lee's return "from Texas" and the interview of April 18, but it is clear that it is the April 18 meeting that he was describing, because "the two Virginians remained alone together nearly three hours.") Keyes admitted that Scott remained completely closemouthed about "this occasion," even "painfully solemn," leaving Keyes to piece together on his own the substance of the conversation. Still, Keyes "surmised" that Scott had "offered to retire from the service and give Lee the command of the Federal army," which is not quite the arrangement Blair described. What is unusual is Keyes's understanding that Scott "desired to see him at the head of a Union force" for the purpose of averting war rather than making it, "to keep the peace and to prevent civil war, which they equally abhorred."[12]

Edward D. Townsend, who was then serving as an assistant adjutant general on Scott's staff, was also a witness to Lee's call on Scott (like Keyes, Townsend did not claim to have been part of the interview itself). Townsend has Lee returning to Arlington from Texas, but without reporting to Scott, and provoking the general to declare that "it is time he should show his hand." A summons is thus sent, not by Blair or a Blair representative, but by Townsend himself, suggesting Lee "call at the general's headquarters." Lee does so (although Townsend misdates Lee's arrival to April 19), and Scott and Lee proceed to a frosty exchange in which Scott confronts Lee with the demand for not *one* but *two* decisions, that Lee "frankly declare" his "intentions" about accepting command and that if that first decision is *no,* then to make a concomitant decision, to resign his commission. And "if you purpose to resign, it is proper you should do so at once." Lee then makes a remarkable plea for understanding, based on the legal vulnerability of the Lee family's Virginia properties, which were still being administered by Lee as G.W.P.'s executor. "General, the property belonging to my children, all they possess, lies in Virginia. They will be ruined if they do not go with their State. I can not raise my hand against my children."[13]

In Townsend's account, the encounter is formal to the point of chilliness. By contrast, an anonymous account that appeared at the end of April in the *Alexandria Gazette* made the Scott interview regretful, claiming that Scott "would rather have received the resignation of every general officer than Col. Lee." And another anonymous description that appeared in a brief note in *Household Journal* four months later has Scott begging Lee, "For God's sake, don't resign Lee," only to have Lee respond, "I am compelled to; I cannot consult my feelings in this matter." Finally, "while the tears were coursing down their cheeks," they were "too full of feeling to find utterance for one word."[14]

Once the Scott interview is integrated with the Blair meeting, a reasonably clear picture of Lee's motives in making the first of what will become three decisions begins to emerge. Robert E. Lee might have been a Virginia-less Virginian, in terms of his actual connections to the Old Dominion, but he had deep family ties to Virginia, and it is consistently *family* and not *politics* that enters into his explanations to Blair and Scott about *Virginia.* From birth, Lee inhabited a thick network of cousinage, including at least eighty other individuals and a lifetime of peregrinations from one extended-relative estate to another. Many of these relations had been the rescuers of Ann Carter Lee and her helpless offspring after Light Horse Harry Lee's death. It was this fabulous skein of Carters, Fitzhughs, and other Lees, to whom Lee was knit by remembered obligations, that was the real Virginia Lee could not bring himself to oppose.[15]

But family does not explain everything in Lee's decision, because a number of Lee relatives—John Fitzgerald Lee, the judge advocate general whom Francis Preston Blair remembered as his messenger for the April 18 meeting, Samuel Phillips Lee, a commander in the Navy—stayed with the Union. Both his brother Smith and his son Custis were still undecided. Instead, considerations of family intersected for Robert E. Lee with the obligations of property, for with a Virginia secession anyone living at Arlington would be placed in a precarious position. Perched on its bluff over the Potomac, Arlington provided a perfect platform for artillery that could rebuff attempts by the gathering militia to cross the Potomac and even make the entire federal capital untenable. A reporter for *The New York Times* warned that "Arlington Heights . . . command every building and every foot of ground in Washington." And voices in Richmond were calling for "the construction of earthwork batteries on the Va. heights overlooking & commanding Washington—to be defended from assault by musketry until heavy artillery can be mounted."[16]

If Lee had decided to cooperate with Blair, Scott, and Lincoln and taken charge of the federal forces being summoned to Washington by Lincoln's April 15 proclamation, he would have had to face the prospect that Arlington might be commandeered by Virginia forces in the event of a Virginia secession, and probably be beyond any later legal recovery by U.S. courts. It is this that throws into unexpected color the plea overheard by Edward Townsend during Lee's interview with Scott: "General, the property belonging to my children, all they possess, lies in Virginia. They will be ruined if they do not go with their State." Or, what was just as true, they would be ruined if Lee did not cooperate with the Virginia secessionists, and Robert Lee was not about to throw away his children's inheritance, much less to do so in any way that harked back to Light Horse Harry's (not to mention Black Horse Harry's) destruction of an earlier Lee inheritance.

The possibility of an Arlington seizure also figured in the thinking of the Lee to whom Arlington technically belonged, Custis Lee. "That Arlington estate over the river is mine," Custis Lee agonized to his West Point classmate (and future Union general) William Woods Averell. "I would give it in a moment and all I have on earth if the Union could be preserved in peace," but if secession was Virginia's decision, then he would have no choice but to "go with my State," and Averell "left him leaning on his elbows on the mantelpiece with his face buried in his hands." Arlington, even at this point of ultimate challenge, managed to elbow its way into Robert E. Lee's calculations, and in the long struggle between Arlington and his yearning for independence Arlington was still winning.[17]

On the other hand, if he cooperated with a Virginia secession movement, he would certainly save Arlington and the other Custis properties from Virginia confiscation for his children. That would, of course, not protect them from *federal* occupation and confiscation. But the key factor in play here was the assumption that in fact there would be no such occupation. John Baldwin, arguing in the Virginia secession convention against taking military action, reminded Virginians that "there was and is no military necessity of an intended attack upon the State of Virginia, unless that military necessity has been created without authority or law." "The idea is secession," explained the *Alexandria Gazette* on April 19, while Lee was in the throes of his decision, "and then consultation with the Border States afterward." (Two years into the war, the Anglo-Austrian observer FitzGerald Ross "was surprised to learn from conversations with politicians here, how very little it had been expected in the South that secession would have been followed by war.")[18]

To save Arlington and the other Custis properties for his children, and to dodge a betrayal of the broad web of his relations, Lee's best path, once the news of Virginia secession became public in Alexandria on April 19, lay in neutrality, especially after his meeting with Scott the day previous. That would require him to make a second decision—to resign his commission, because he could not, consistently with the Blair offer, refuse to obey orders that might destroy his family's future and still remain a U.S. officer. But in this crisis, it would become easy for Lee to convince himself that such a resignation would open the door to an even greater role in saving the country—in Montgomery Blair's words, "probably to arbitrate difficulties." And the path to that new role, and a third decision, would present itself within forty-eight hours.

Robert E. Lee rode home, after his meeting with Scott, over the Long Bridge, stopping first at the Navy Department building for an "earnest consultation" with Sidney Smith Lee. He did not actually return to Arlington "till late in the evening." In Alexandria, the notice board of the town's *Gazette* was tacked full of news bulletins from the secession convention in Richmond.

He went down into Alexandria the next morning, April 19, "to pay a bill" and there found extras about the Virginia secession ordinance, along with proclamations from Governor Letcher and the mayor of Alexandria being read on every street corner by "an interested and excited, and yet entirely decorous crowd." He did not share their enthusiasm. "I must say," he remarked unhappily to the merchant he was paying, "I am one of those dull creatures that cannot see the good of secession."[19]

Good or not, he was unwilling to take a hand in suppressing the Virginia secession movement, and that could only mean the end of his career in the Army. For all the years when he had toyed with farewells to "my Uncle Sam," he had never imagined that this would be the actual trigger. He returned to Arlington knowing that he had no alternative to making his second decision and yet fighting it as he had fought for thirty years against it.

In accounts Mary Lee gave years later, Lee reenacts a kind of Gethsemane, spending the night of April 19–20 in the throes of depression, sleepless, weeping "tears of blood," asking "to be left alone for a time," pacing "his chamber above," where he was "heard frequently to fall on his knees and engage in earnest prayer for divine guidance" as he passed through "the severest struggle of his life." There was still some glimmer in his mind that "matters might be accommodated without recourse to arms" and without a resignation from him. But cups in Gethsemane never pass.[20]

Mary Lee might have been a little too eager to cast her husband's decision as a rehearsal of Christian agony. His own recollection in 1868 was that the resignation letter, a one-sentence affair addressed to Secretary of War Cameron ("Sir: I have the honour to tender the resignation of my commission as Colonel of the 1st Regt of Cavalry"), was composed some time after the Scott interview but was "kept . . . by him another night," because the letter itself is dated the twentieth. The announcement of his resignation was made to his family on Saturday, April 20, after a breakfast visit by "two gentlemen of Alexandria" (one of them a Fitzhugh relative, the wealthy merchant Henry Daingerfield, who had brought news of pro-secession riots in the streets of Baltimore the day before). He called the family "into his private room, where . . . we found him seated at his table," explained the resignation decision, and then read to them a copy of a second letter, written to Winfield Scott and explaining his reasons for resigning (this letter he had already sent off by an Arlington slave, Perry Parks). "I suppose you all think I have done very wrong," Lee explained, "but it had come to this, & after my last interview with Gen. Scott I felt that I ought to wait no longer." Whatever his agonies overnight, he appeared on the morning of the twentieth to be at last at peace with himself, "calm collected, almost cheerful."[21]

The appearance was deceptive: the covering letter he had written to Winfield Scott to accompany a copy of his resignation must have cost him dearly, simply to judge by its contents. He asked Scott to read the resignation letter and "recommend" it "for acceptance," half apologizing for not having "presented" it "at once" after their interview on the eighteenth, but for "the struggle it cost me to separate myself from a service to which I have devoted the best years of my life, & all the ability I possessed." But the real pain lay not in the farewell to the Army so much as in the farewell he was giving to the last of the father figures he had followed in that career—Gratiot, Totten, and now Scott. "To no one Genl have I been as much indebted as to yourself for uniform kindness & consideration," and in what was the clincher for the fatherless boy who would now once again be fatherless, and by his own hand, he added, "It has always been my ardent desire to meet your approbation." For that reason, "I shall carry with me to the grave the most grateful recollections of your kind consideration, & your name and fame will always be dear to me."[22] When one reads that, it is difficult not to think that Mary was wrong: the real Gethsemane was in his letters.

Nor was Lee finished with writing difficult letters, one of them intended for his invalid sister, Anne Kinloch Lee Marshall, in Baltimore. He knew that

Anne Marshall would have no good words for secession, or for any action her younger brother took that didn't stare it down. Anne and her husband had long since parted with any sympathy for slavery or secession, and William Louis Marshall appears in May 1860 as one of the handful of slave-state Republican delegates (alongside old Francis Preston Blair) who attended the Republican National Convention and nominated Lincoln for the presidency. "I am grieved at my inability to see you," Lee began, and "abhor myself more than ever for not having visited you." He began explaining what she surely already knew, that "the whole South is in a state of revolution, into which Virginia, after a long struggle, has been drawn." Quite candidly, he admitted that there was "no necessity" for Virginia's secession. Yet, "with all my devotion to the Union, and the feeling and loyalty and duty of an American citizen, I have not been able to make up my mind to raise my hand against my relatives, my children, my home." Not *against Virginia,* and certainly not for slavery: just as Edward Townsend had heard him explain, "against my relatives, my children, my home."

And yet, with equal candor, he knew he could never convince her of the merits of what he was doing. "I know you will blame me," but he promised, "I shall love you till death & you will be as dear to me as ever." He only hoped that "you must think as kindly of me as you can, and believe that I have endeavoured to do what I thought right." Which she did not. Anne Marshall died in 1864 without ever communicating with her brother again; her surviving son, Louis Henry Marshall, would serve in the Army his uncle was now leaving.[23]

Then there was another, easier letter, to Smith Lee. Robert could be briefer to Smith, because he had already learned from talking to Smith just forty-eight hours before that Smith was leaning in the same direction. He merely notified Smith that "the question . . . has in my own mind been decided." After the Blair and Scott interviews, he knew he was "liable at any time to be ordered on duty which I Could not Conscientiously perform," and rather than wait until such orders forced his hand, "I had to act at once." But he had no illusions about the implications of this second decision. What Virginians called secession was, quite frankly, "the ordinance of revolution." With *revolution,* he proposed to have no involvement, if he could help it. From this point, "I am now a private citizen, and have no other ambition than to remain at home," followed by what had become almost a scripted line: "Save in defense of my native State, I have no desire ever again to draw my sword."[24]

Finally, Lee had at least two other explanatory letters to write: one to a cousin, Roger Jones, a lieutenant in the Mounted Rifles who had pressed him for advice on what to do (and who eventually remained with the Army), and one other that appeared, anonymously addressed, in *The New York Times* in August 1861. "I must side either with or against my section of country," Lee once again explains. "I cannot raise my hand against my birth-place, my home, my children."[25]

What was not clear, though, was what Lee would do next. The implication of his letters was that he had no *next* clearly in mind.

The possibility of a third decision materialized while Lee attended Christ Church, Alexandria, with his daughter Mary on Sunday morning, April 21, where he "was followed by the crowd, & buttonholed in the street, as if their faith was pinned on him alone." Alexandria had been a unionist town, and elected a unionist to the state secession convention, and Mary remembered that no one "wanted secession, and were waiting to see what Colonel Robert E. Lee would do."

The likeliest answer was that he would do nothing. By resigning from the Army, Lee needed only to do *that* and sit out the ensuing conflict as a neutral. And at least ten other Southern officers who, like Lee, resigned their commissions rather than assume responsibility for subduing secession decided to do exactly that. (Major Alfred Mordecai was a North Carolinian, a Whig, and a slave owner, but like Lee he was no slavery partisan and would certainly raise no hand against the Union, despite a direct offer from Jefferson Davis; Mordecai's solution was to request assignment out of the way of war, to California, and when this was refused, he resigned and became a railroad engineer in Mexico.) After Sunday services, Lee huddled with his closest Lee cousin, Cassius Francis Lee, who lived across Oronoco Street from where Lee had grown up. Cassius Lee "was a strong union man, and for some hours they discussed the condition of the country." Cassius's eleven-year-old son recalled his father using "all his influence to dissuade Col. Lee from taking any part in the war, and when he left it was with the understanding that he would resign from the U.S.A[rmy] and remain at Arlington, a neutral in the conflict."[26]

But a simple resignation might not be enough to dissuade Virginia secessionists from demanding something more from Lee—cooperation—and then punishing a refusal by laying hands on Arlington. And almost on cue that Sunday afternoon, "a delegation of gentlemen . . . from Richmond" arrived at Arlington and then, finding him gone, pursued him into Alexandria "on a mission to persuade him to place his sword at the service of his State."[27]

The "delegation" that appeared on Lee's doorstep had been authorized by the secession convention in Richmond on April 20 to persuade "efficient and worthy Virginians . . . in the army and navy of the United States to return therefrom, and to enter the service of Virginia." Its informal head was Judge

John Robertson, acting as a "special messenger" from Governor John Letcher, and Robertson had in fact already made an overture to Winfield Scott, as a Virginian, in a meeting on April 19. (Scott rebuffed him with "astonishment" because "he was devoted to the Union and would do all in his power to preserve it.") It might have been from Scott that Robertson learned of Lee's resignation, because the judge wired news of it to Governor Letcher on April 20 and received Letcher's sanction to "see Lee and invite him to Richmond."[28] Robertson asked to meet with Lee that evening at Arlington and gave Lee what he later called the first news "officially" about the Virginia secession ordinance; the judge now asked Lee to meet with him in Alexandria on the morning of the twenty-second and travel thence to Richmond.[29]

Bafflingly, Lee agreed. This third decision, unlike the previous ones—to decline command and then to resign from the Army—seems to have been made without consulting anyone, almost impulsively. The young Cazenove Gardner Lee, "standing on our front steps," was startled on the morning of the twenty-second to see "the Arlington Carriage past" on the way to the Alexandria train station "and Col. Lee put his head out and waved his hands adieu, and said good by I am gone." On the other hand, this departure for Richmond might not necessarily have been as unusual as it seemed, first, because Lee had been solicited by Virginia state authorities for military advice after the Harpers Ferry debacle, and, second, because it was still unclear what Virginia secession would mean. There was no indication yet that, even after seceding, Virginia would join the Southern Confederacy, and a good deal of fear remained that secession might set off a "servile war" of the sort dreamed of by John Brown. Virginia might very easily follow its own path, perhaps in conjunction with other border states, and in the end act as some kind of agent of national reconciliation and reconstruction.

But Robertson's delegation from Richmond was not coy about its mandate, which involved more than inviting Lee to bestow useful advice. "It is probable that the Secession of Virginia will cause an immediate resignation of many officers of the Army and Navy from this State," declared the *Alexandria Gazette* on April 20, with perhaps more inside knowledge that it wanted to reveal. "We do not know, and have no right to speak for or anticipate, the course, of Col. Robt. E. Lee." Still, added the *Gazette* hopefully, "if he should resign his present position in the Army of the U.S. we call the immediate attention of our State to him as an able, brave, experienced, officer:—no man his superior in all that constitutes the soldier, and the gentleman—no man more worthy to head our forces and lead our army." By the day of Lee's departure, the *Gazette* was certain that "Col. R. E. Lee, of Virginia, one of the most accomplished and estimable officers in the service of the United States," will have "the command of the forces of this commonwealth tendered to him."[30]

Before secession, this would have been unusual but not illegal, any more than it would have been illegal to have accepted any other position in the Virginia state government. After secession—after Virginia had attempted to rend the legal bonds that attached the Old Dominion to the constitutional Union and was prepared to use force to make that rending permanent—this would be treason. And yet the gauze of uncertainty that overhung the events following Sumter, as well as Lee's own silence, keeps that judgment teetering, if only because "before" and "after" did not follow immediately. Lee's impression (as he related in 1870 to William Preston Johnston) was "that pacification was intended by Mr. Lincoln and Mr. Seward" and "that Mr. Lincoln would recede" from outright confrontation with Virginia. Lincoln fed this understanding by assuring Reverdy Johnson (the same Johnson to whom he would describe his decisions) that the militia called out by his proclamation were designed "to defend this capital. . . . I have no purpose to invade Virginia, with them or any other troops, as I understand the word *invasion.*" And that notion persisted even in Lee's post-resignation explanatory letters: "I should like, above all things, that our difficulties might be peaceably arranged," he insisted, "and still trust that a merciful God, whom I know will not unnecessarily afflict us, may yet allay the fury for war."[31]

By accepting an invitation to take a role in determining Virginia's military response, Lee might actually be in the perfect position to ensure that peace would be the result rather than war and save the Custis properties from molestation by either federal or Virginia authorities. This certainly seems to have been what Cassius Francis Lee expected in the wake of his after-church conference with his cousin on April 21. Putting Lee "in command of the Virginia troops," Cassius Lee hinted, "might lead to a peaceful settlement of our difficulties." Citing other Virginians, Cassius Lee wrote to Robert to urge his cousin to understand that he would be in a position to "bring about, at least, an armistice, preparatory to a National Assembly for peaceful settlement of our troubles." After all, "Virginia from her geographical position . . . has it in her power . . . to come in as mediator, rather as an umpire & settle the question." In such a role, Robert E. Lee would "be a leader in this matter" and "have an honor never reached by Napoleon or Wellington."

If Lee's behavior on the trip to Richmond is any indication, he certainly aspired to no recognition as a conquering hero. William Wallace Scott would remember more than half a century later that Lee's train was stopped at Gordonsville by "enthusiastic calls for 'Lee,' 'Lee.'" But Lee appeared only briefly "on the rear platform of the coach, dressed in citizens' apparel . . . dark hair with eyes to match, a short mustache without a single strand of grey," and declined to make any speeches. "He simply bowed to the crowd, said no word, re-entered the car, and the train passed on."[32]

Lee's arrival in Richmond late on April 22 introduced him to a very different world from Alexandria and disabused him of any idea that counsels of sweet reason were likely to prevail there. The Stars and Bars flag of the Confederacy and the palmetto flag of South Carolina were on display all through the city. "Cannons were fired, bells rang, shouts rent the air, the inhabitants rushed to and fro to discuss the joyful event," remembered Sallie Ann Brock, and a stranger blundering into Richmond "would have imagined the people in a state of intoxication or insanity." Militia units paraded through the streets "with very full ranks, and were drilled and inspected on the Square, in squad, company and battalion drill," while private funds "for the benefit of the families of the volunteers in the State's service" were established. Both the armory at Harpers Ferry and the Gosport naval yard at Norfolk had been seized by Virginia militia, and the clamor grew louder for Virginia to attach itself to the Southern Confederacy. "Virginia did not secede to assume an attitude of distrustful isolation," trumpeted the Richmond *Dispatch*. So, "why is not Virginia at once united with the Confederacy"? Jefferson Davis had already sent his vice president, Alexander Stephens, to Richmond to nudge Virginia into abandoning all appearance of neutrality and joining the Confederacy, and John Floyd, the onetime secretary of war who had sent Lee to Harpers Ferry, arrived in Richmond to discuss arrangements for "raising a brigade of 1,500 men in Southwestern Virginia."[33]

Lee stepped off the train into the midst of this bedlam to be met by Judge Robertson and the state adjutant general, William Richardson, who escorted him to the five-story Spotswood Hotel on Main Street, where "an immense crowd of citizens congregated anxious to pay their respects." He met with Governor Letcher, who informed him that one of the ordinances adopted by the secession convention had provided for the appointment of a "commander of the military and naval forces" of the state, with the rank of major general. Would Lee accept it? This was the brink on which he had been balancing for three days, and now he fell over onto Virginia's side. Letcher informed the convention of Lee's acceptance at its evening session, and the convention immediately confirmed it, inviting Lee to attend the convention's sessions the next day, April 23, at noon. Mayor Joseph Mayo and a crowd of "citizens repaired to the Spotswood House to serenade Col. Lee." But Lee did not appear. "He was," Mayo hastily explained, "consulting" with Governor Letcher "as to the proper measures to be pursued."[34]

Lee was at the state capitol promptly before noon the next day and entered the main hall, escorted by the chair of the state military committee. The convention stood to receive him, and the president of the convention,

John Janney (ironically, a former Whig and unionist who had once urged the abolition of slavery on the legislature thirty years before), greeted him with a carefully rehearsed speech of welcome that began by hailing Lee as the son of a former governor of Virginia whose voice "we may almost yet hear" as an echo and "whose blood now flows in your veins." Virginia was the home "of heroes and statesmen," he droned on, little imagining what images any invocations of Light Horse Harry—"your own gallant father"—were likely to arouse in Lee's mind.

Lee's response was "clear, distinct, full volumed" but also brief and almost unenthusiastic. He was "profoundly impressed with the solemnity of the occasion," although he would confess that he "was not prepared" for it and "could have much preferred had your choice fallen on an abler man." But he accepted "the position assigned me by your partiality"—*partiality?*—and pledged that he would "devote myself to the service of my native State," adding one last time his favorite line: "in whose behalf alone will I ever again draw my sword." There was a polite smattering of applause, and then the convention moved on to an introduction of Alexander Stephens.[35]

Thus did Robert E. Lee pass through his third decision, a decision in which he irrevocably, finally, publicly turned his back on his service, his flag, and, ultimately, his country. All of this was done for the sake of a political regime whose acknowledged purpose was the preservation of a system of chattel slavery that he knew to be an evil and for which he felt little affection and whose constitutional basis he dismissed as a fiction. (If we can judge by a comment retailed years later by a member of the convention to John S. Mosby, Lee was dubious about secession even as he accepted secession's commission, telling John Critcher of Westmoreland County as he waited to be introduced to the convention, "I hope we have seen the last of secession.")

It would, in the end, cost him nearly everything that he thought, by these decisions, he was protecting. That the decisions had occurred in separate stages make them resemble a kind of sleepwalking. But awake or asleep, he would spend the balance of his life in their glare. Meanwhile, a new militia company, the Lee Guard, was advertised in the Richmond *Dispatch.* The next day, in Syracuse, New York, "a man named Lee" was mobbed for distributing "a South-side treasonable article." His name had already acquired consequences of its own.[36]

CHAPTER TEN

This Is Not the Way to Accomplish Our Independence

In Richmond, the announcement of Lee's commission was greeted with jubilation. "General Lee, son of Light Horse Harry Lee, has been made general in chief of Virginia," exulted Mary Chesnut, the wife of the former U.S. senator James Chesnut. "With such men to the fore we have hope." Northern newspapers were quick to predict that Robert Lee would lead Virginia's forces straight up to the Potomac, bombard Washington from Arlington, and invade Maryland.

Realistically, however, those forces were unprepared to do anything of the sort, and no one knew that better than Lee. Richmond "looked like a camp" when Moxley Sorrel arrived there a few days after the fall of Fort Sumter, and especially "full of officers in their smart uniforms." John Beauchamp Jones, who would serve for the next four years as a clerk in the new Confederate War Department, wrote in his meticulous diary, "Martial music is heard everywhere, day and night and all the trappings and paraphernalia of war's decorations are in great demand." By May 3, 48,000 Virginia Volunteers had crowded forward, ten thousand of them alone in Richmond, where a drill field was laid out and named Camp Lee (in honor of Light Horse Harry, not his son). But gilt epaulets do not an army make, and Lee's first task as "commander-in-chief" of all Virginia forces was to bring the glittery prewar mess of the state's militia, with their ill-matched and ill-sorted military equipment, into something that could function as, and not just resemble, a defense force.[1]

Lee officially assumed command "of the military and naval forces of Virginia" in a terse, one-sentence general order on April 23 and at once set about creating a staff and finding offices for it. Although the Virginia legislature provided for a statewide militia system of four divisions, little of this force existed apart from local militia companies whose chief purpose seemed to be showy parades and well-inebriated musters. No overall organizing staff existed, even after the John Brown scare. So, within his first week, Lee had to set up quartermaster and commissary departments for equipping and feeding the volunteers and put administrative help to work in office space in the imposing Italianate Customs House on Main Street, vacated by former federal officials. (He would eventually move them to Mechanics Hall at Ninth and Bank, which he leased at the end of May and began converting "into suites of offices.")

He did not have many familiar faces to choose from. He appointed as his adjutant general (and de facto chief of staff) Robert Selden Garnett, who had served Lee during his West Point superintendency as commandant of cadets, and as chief clerk Thomas W. White, a court clerk from Alexandria. But as quartermaster general, Lee had little choice but to pick a hotel owner from Staunton, Michael Harman, and as commissary general a onetime regimental quartermaster, William Lewis Cabell (who had to take out want ads in the Richmond papers to recruit clerks). Lee also imported 185 cadets from the Virginia Military Institute (along with one of their instructors, Thomas Jonathan Jackson) to take charge of the training at Camp Lee.

He acquired his most important staffer through Francis H. Smith, the commandant of the Virginia Military Institute, who recommended the twenty-two-year-old Walter Herron Taylor as an aide and secretary for Lee. A VMI graduate, Taylor was pulled out of the volunteer company in which he had enlisted and "assigned to duty at General Lee's headquarters." Meeting Lee for the first time in the dining room of the Spotswood Hotel, Taylor was impressed by Lee's "graceful and dignified carriage . . . bright and penetrating eyes, his iron-gray hair closely cut, his face cleanly shaved except a mustache . . . every inch a soldier and a man born to command."[2]

With this tiny support, Lee had to supervise recruitment at twenty-three enlistment points throughout the state, "Gen. Lee" having "a *carte blanche* to call out as many volunteers as he pleases." He would provide direction to the state convention, which was still sitting as Virginia's practical legislature, about creating a reliable railroad network for "military operations within Virginia," and then issue orders forbidding local officers to commandeer the rail lines whenever they felt like it. He would take the train to Norfolk and then to Manassas Junction to supervise the construction of fortifications. And there was always paperwork, which he enjoyed no more now than at other times in his career. "He did not enjoy writing," Walter Taylor noticed, "indeed, he wrote with labor, and nothing seemed to tax his amiability so much as the necessity for writing lengthy official communications."

He was easily overwhelmed. At Norfolk, he found that the U.S. Navy had scuttled the steam frigate *Merrimack,* and he ordered it refloated and dry-docked, but an artillery battery he ordered built at Sewell's Point was easily blown to bits by a federal gunboat. Lee, looking out from Sewell's Point toward Fort Monroe (where he had been an engineering lieutenant thirty years before), complained "that a battery should have been built here long ago" and reprimanded Virginia officers there for fraternizing with truce parties from across Hampton Roads, where he had once built up the pilings for Fort Calhoun. He could not get recruiting officers to send in timely reports, but he was also unable to keep them from handing out "arms, accouterments, and ammunition" on demand. He was so short-tempered over the sprawling, undisciplined camps around Manassas that when he was "vociferously called on for a speech at Orange Court House," he would only tell the raw levies that "he had much more important matters on his mind than speech making" and "advised all who were in service to be drilling, and those who, for good reasons, were not, to attend to their private affairs and avoid the excitement and rumors of crowds, &c."[3]

Lee still hoped that there would be no war, and that he could keep hotheaded Virginians from provoking one until less hasty counsel could prevail, and either arrange a peaceful breakup of the Union or fashion some reconstruction of it that could blot the slavery controversy from view. He assured Cassius Francis Lee that "no earthly act would give me so much pleasure, as to restore peace to my Country"; his plan was simply to "resist aggression & allow time to allay the passions & reason to resume her sway." In his first day of command, he wired Philip Cocke, who had just been appointed by Governor Letcher as a brigadier general in charge of the militia forces in and around Alexandria, advising Cocke that "it is not considered probable that the U.S. troops will occupy the Virga shore opposite Washington." Hence, Cocke should do nothing that would provoke such a movement and "the troops in Alexa should be quiet & prepared & the movements in Washington be observed without attracting attention."

The next day he sent a similar message to Daniel Ruggles, Cocke's counterpart on the Rappahannock. "You will act on the defensive," Lee reiterated, and "allay popular excitement as far as possible." When the veteran Richmond lawyer James Lyons volunteered to serve on Lee's staff, Lee thanked him but hoped that somehow "all good men" like Lyons "would not be involved in the Calamities of War." He ordered VMI's impenetrable Colonel Jackson to break off training at Camp Lee and proceed to Harpers Ferry to ensure "the safety of such arms, machinery, parts of arms, raw material, &c., that may be useful." But when, two weeks later, Jackson decided to preemptively occupy Maryland Heights, on the north side of the Potomac, Lee ordered him back to Harpers Ferry. "Confine yourself to a strictly defensive course," Lee instructed him. "You know our limited resources, & must abstain from all provocation for attack."[4]

Enough of the peacemaker attitude was on display that complaints about Lee soon blossomed in Virginia. "No one admires Genl. Lee more than I do," wrote Albert Taylor Bledsoe to Jefferson Davis on May 10, "but I fear he is too despondent. His remarks are calculated to dispirit our people. I have heard such remarks myself and energetically dissented from them. . . . I fear he does not know how good and how righteous our cause is." When Dabney Herndon Maury "reported to the governor and to General Lee," he was surprised "by the grave and anxious aspect of General Lee," and even Walter Taylor thought Lee was the rare Confederate who "expressed his most serious apprehensions of a prolonged and bloody war." Overexuberant Southerners began glancing over their shoulders at Lee. "Have conversed with General Robert E. Lee," reported an informant for the Confederate secretary of war, LeRoy Pope Walker. "He wishes to repress the enthusiasm of our people" and seemed to "favor temporizing." One of Mary Chesnut's South Carolina "notables" whispered that "Robert E. Lee is against us—that I know," and another predicted that "General Lee will surely be tried for a traitor."

And no wonder: John D. Imboden reported on the situation at Harpers Ferry to Lee on May 2 and heard nothing but gloom from his lips:

> *He desired to impress me . . . with the gravity and danger of our situation. . . . Growing warm and earnest, he said: "I fear our people do not yet realize the magnitude of the struggle they have entered upon, nor its probable duration and the sacrifices it will impose upon them. The United States Government," he said, "is one of the most powerful upon earth. I know the people and the Government we have to contend with. In a little while they will be even more united than we are. Their resources are almost without limit. Their army . . . will be commanded by the foremost soldier of the country, General Scott. . . . And above all, we shall have to fight the prejudices of the world, because of the existence of slavery in our country."*

And almost in echo of that warning, Winfield Scott was still recommending that Lee be approached in Richmond as a possible peace broker. "Go see Robert E. Lee," Scott told one self-appointed peace delegation on May 1. "Tell him for me, that we must have no war, but that we must avert a conflict of arms until the 'sober second thought' of the people can stop the mad schemes of the politicians."[5]

But there were other moments when any prospect of peace seemed to Lee to have vanished. The surrender of Sumter had whipped Northern hostility to the South to a frenzy. In Chicago, "ten thousand men of all religious creeds and party affiliations" met in the Wigwam (the same convention hall where Lincoln had been nominated for the presidency eleven months before) and uncovered their heads to take a solemn oath from Judge George Manierre that "I will faithfully support the constitution of the United States. . . . So help me God!" In New York City, on April 20, "the streets were thronged with a surging mass of people" estimated at "more than one hundred thousand" to hear speaker after speaker at Union Square announce that "the hour for reconciliation is past," never to return until "the flag of Sumter . . . is avenged." The fury across the North, Lee feared, was becoming such "against the South that it may not be in the power of the authorities to restrain them." As early as April 26, he began advising his wife to expect some sort of federal incursion and occupation. Very gingerly, he broached the unthinkable subject: that Mary might have to abandon Arlington and seek refuge elsewhere. She should not rely on the customary wisdom that "the presence of a lady" on the property at Arlington "would tend to ensure respect toward the place from both contending parties." He was "very anxious about you, you have to move, & make arrangements to go to some point of safety which you must select."[6]

Mary's first response was disbelief. "I have lived 7 of the happiest years of my life in the North, and have admired its institutions, its energy, its progress," she wrote to a friend, and could not believe that Northern soldiers and politicians would dream of forcing her away from her majestic and beloved home, where both her parents were buried, where her children had grown up and spent every day that their father's duty or their schooling had not required them to be elsewhere. Rather than abandon Arlington to the "military despotism now at Washington," she would prefer to "most gladly lay" where "my dear parents are both . . . low in their graves." Instead, she turned "more than usually" to tending "my flowers & garden," while Custis continued "attending to his Engineer duties." There was a brief scare on April 25, when Orton Williams (Markie Williams's brother) bolted across the Long Bridge to warn Mary that federal troops were preparing to occupy Arlington the next day and that "she must pack up all you value immediately . . . & send it off very early in the morning." But the scare came to nothing, and Mary went back to dreaming.

Robert, however, kept plying her with letters, imploring her to leave. "Make your preparations quickly, to be ready for an emergency," he wrote again: let John McQuinn, the Arlington overseer, "prosecute work on the farm" while Mary packed up the Washington relics—"the plate, &c."—and sent them to her aunt Anna Maria Fitzhugh at Ravensworth. Have Custis "secure my package of private papers from the Br[anch of the] Farmers Bank of Alexandria" and send Perry Parks from the Arlington slaves to Richmond so that he could "have some one with me." She refused. Instead, she wrote to General Scott, begging from him "all the protection you can in honor afford." On May 11, Robert wrote again, now more urgently: "You had better complete your arrangements and retire from the scene of war. It may burst upon you at any time."[7]

Finally, inch by inch, she relented. Custis resigned from the U.S. Army on April 27 and readied himself to join his father in Richmond. Without Custis nearby and able to walk only with the help of crutches, Mary began to fear for her two daughters still at home, Mary and Agnes, and on May 8 she packed them off to Ravensworth. (Mildred was at school in Winchester; Annie was at White House, helping Rooney and Charlotte with the new baby; young Rob was in his first year at the University of Virginia, although even there he was busily organizing a student military company.)

The rumors now began flying rapidly that "the government troops are to take possession of these heights in a few days" and (as she wrote to Mildred) turn Arlington into "a field of carnage." She finally began directing the Arlington slaves to crate up "our silver & valuables" and shipped two trunksful of them to Richmond while packing her father's Washington relics into the attic. Robert continued to hector her. He even tried to shock her out of her lassitude by warning her, "Do not put faith in rumors of adjustment," and added some extra stimulus by telling Mary to "make your plans for several years of war." At last, on May 19, she gave in and left Arlington for Ravensworth "in a state of mind almost phrensied," but still wedded to the delusion that "in a few weeks I should return." She never would.[8]

His shock advice was more nearly correct than he could have wished. By the middle of May, events were galloping far away from any likelihood that Virginia could be steered toward reunion negotiations. The Virginia convention voted to attach the Old Dominion to the Confederate States of America on May 7, and on May 22 the provisional Confederate Congress, meeting in Montgomery, Alabama, voted to reconvene in Richmond in July, thus making Richmond the new capital of the Confederate States. Meanwhile, on May 23, the statewide referendum on secession confirmed what everyone had expected: secession triumphed at the polls, 132,201 votes to 37,451 (even as the western counties went three to two against).

The vote, in turn, triggered precisely the descent on Arlington and Alexandria Lee had feared. On May 24 "about five o'clock" in the morning, "the forces of the United States consisting of a regiment of Michigan volunteers, a regiment of New York Zouaves, the New York Seventh Regiment and a detachment of U.S. Artillery with ten field pieces entered this city under command of Col. [Orlando] Willcox." Federal cavalry also crossed the Potomac at Leesburg and stopped the local trains. "A temporary camp had been formed a few miles from Arlington, at which some six hundred troops were stationed."

For the moment, Arlington itself was spared. The commandant of the New York militia, Major General Charles Sandford, declared martial law and set up his headquarters in three tents erected on the south side of the house, but the occupying troops had their hands full with establishing control over Alexandria and its outlying region and did no greater damage than shoot John McQuinn's "chickens and rabbits and scared his wife." Sandford "was courteous in taking possession of the house," and even asked "whether the family of Gen. Lee was there, and to offer a guard if so."[9]

"We all trust our dear home will be uninjured," Agnes wrote to Mildred, "but it is almost too good to hope if men are to occupy it." She was right. At once, the Arlington slaves began to look out for themselves, either by slipping over the river to Washington and disappearing facelessly into the capital's African American population or by reverting to the patterns of the old Custis days, tending their gardens and selling the produce to Union occupiers to suit themselves. Mary Lee, who left the mansion's keys with her slave housekeeper, Selina Gray, expected that she would be able to send messages and orders through her slaves back and forth to Arlington. Not under Sandford's martial law regime, though, and for the first time it seems to have dawned on Mary that Arlington might be lost. "It never occurred to me Gen'l Sanford," she wrote in fury, "that I could be forced to sue for permission to enter my own home & that such an outrage as its military occupation to the exclusion of me & my children could ever have been perpetrated."

But it was. When Major General Irvin McDowell succeeded Sandford in command of the federal forces gathering on the south side of the Potomac on May 28, McDowell promised to "have all things ordered that on your return you will find things as little disturbed as possible." Soon enough, though, McDowell moved into the house itself and strung a telegraph line from his desk in the house to Winfield Scott's office in Washington. Uninvited guests, including Mary Todd Lincoln, made curiosity visits. "The Arlington estate," reported *The New York Times* in June, is "a noted but dilapidated one. . . . All the pictures have been taken from the frames and carried away by Mrs. Lee, but the frames remain against the wall." The improvements Robert Lee had labored to install fell quickly into decay. "Arlington House, the seedy palace of a Virginia Don," sneered Theodore Winthrop, an officer in the 7th New

York, is "disposed to crumble" and suffers from "a certain careless, romantic, decayed-gentleman effect, wholly Virginian." When Custis Lee's old friend William Averell was posted to Arlington as a staff officer in July, he found "the grassy slopes and open woodlands of Arlington occupied with tented troops," encamped in "heedless disregard of fences and shrubbery."[10]

In Richmond, Robert Lee had more issues than Arlington crowding upon him. Virginia's admission to the Confederacy placed "the whole military force and military operations, offensive and defensive," of the commonwealth "under the chief control and directions of" Jefferson Davis as "the President of [the] Confederate States." Four days later, Lee was assigned "control of the Forces of the Confederate States in Virginia," but that amounted to little more than coordinating traffic until Davis and the Confederate government could assert their oversight of Virginia affairs. Davis himself arrived in Richmond on May 29, and along with him came an influx of Confederate volunteers from Georgia, Tennessee, and Alabama.[11]

There was more confusion in store for Lee. "Yesterday I turned over . . . the command of the military & naval forces of the State," he wrote to Mary, and he admitted that after that he did "not know what my position will be." Perhaps he could somehow retreat back into the neutrality he had once imagined as his likeliest choice and "retire to private life." But retire *where*? Arlington was now occupied by federal troops. Ravensworth was out of the question: it was too close to the federal occupation in northern Virginia, and in any case Lee urged Mary to begin thinking of leaving Ravensworth to avoid "personal annoyance to yourself." A month later, he was still complaining that "he did not know where he was."

On June 15, he submitted a comprehensive report to Governor Letcher on the steps he had taken to prepare Virginia's defenses, and it resembled nothing so much as the sort of final summary he had submitted many times before, prior to moving on. "Since the transfer of the Mil: operation in Virga. to the authorities of the C.S.," he lamented to Mary, "where I shall go I do not Know." Yet, until something more organized in the way of the Confederate government was operating in Virginia, he felt obliged to stay in place and give as much direction as he could to Virginia's military affairs. "If I can be of service to the State or her cause, I must continue." By midsummer, rumors were flying "that Lee had left the secession army in disgust, and that he was anxious to regain his old post in the Federal army."[12]

It was Jefferson Davis who, as before when he promoted Lee to the 2nd Cavalry, came to Lee's professional rescue. Davis and his family took up temporary quarters in the Spotswood Hotel along with Lee, and Davis soon came to rely on Lee for advice about the dispositions of Virginia's defenses and the best deployment of new Confederate troops as they arrived in Virginia.

Davis awarded Lee the rank of brigadier general in the regular Confederate Army (although what that meant exactly was unclear, because the Confederate troops descending on Virginia had been recruited on the old Mexican War basis as *Volunteers,* not as part of a *Regular* Confederate army) and then on June 12 nominated Lee and four others to the newly created grade of full general (although actual confirmation from the Confederate Congress would not come until the end of August). Even then, Lee found himself ranked, by seniority, below two others: Samuel Cooper, who had been the adjutant general of the old Army and who had resigned from it in March, and Lee's onetime commander in Texas, Albert Sidney Johnston, Davis's favorite.[13]

Lee hoped he could escape the tedium of desk work by taking "the field as soon as certain arrangements can be made." But Davis kept him in Richmond, supervising ("200 tons of Gun metal" needed transfer to Richmond), organizing (the creation of a city militia in Richmond "for the defense of the city"), and advising. Especially advising, which mostly meant counseling Davis to keep Confederate forces in Virginia on the defensive. This, wrote the War Department clerk John Jones, "will be severely criticized, for a vast majority of our people are for 'carrying the war into Africa' without a moment's delay." That impatience overlooked how carefully Lee had laid out a defensive system around the railroad junction at Manassas, "some two miles in extent, zigzag in form, with angles, salients, bastions, casemates," and backed up by a "similar formation . . . 14 miles further on." But no one seemed interested in Lee's defensive advice. When Davis, asserting his new authority over the war front, installed Pierre G. T. Beauregard (Lee's junior engineering lieutenant in Mexico) as commander at Manassas, Beauregard quickly began designing offensive schemes. In mid-July, Beauregard sent the voluble James Chesnut as his emissary to Davis and Lee with a plan to reinforce the small army he commanded at Manassas with the Confederate forces occupying Harpers Ferry (under Lee's old classmate Joseph E. Johnston) and then "move rapidly forward on Fairfax Court House," attack Irvin McDowell's federal troops around Alexandria, "and thus exterminate them or drive them into the Potomac." Lee was unimpressed. If Johnston left Harpers Ferry, he would not have enough troops to leave behind to secure the armory, and federal forces across the Potomac would occupy it. Worse, McDowell's troops would "fall back on their entrenchments"—which included Arlington—and bring up reinforcements "in numbers sufficient to regain the superiority of numbers."[14]

To their surprise, it was McDowell who seized the offensive a week later, lumbering down to Manassas with an enthusiastic but poorly organized army of 35,000 Union Volunteers, militia, and Marines. McDowell attempted to skirt the fortifications Lee had ordered and outflank Beauregard by crossing a tributary of the Occoquan Creek known as Bull Run, to the west of Manassas Junction. Johnston's troops hurriedly evacuated Harpers Ferry (which was then occupied, as Lee had feared, by federal troops under Robert Patterson). But Johnston arrived just in time to fend off McDowell's attack, and together Johnston and Beauregard hounded McDowell's army into a humiliating retreat back to Alexandria and Washington.

Generously, Lee wrote letters of congratulation to both Beauregard and Johnston for the Bull Run battle, praising the former "for the skill, courage, and endurance displayed by yourself" and telling the latter that "I almost wept for joy at the glorious victory achieved by our brave troops" and "the brilliant share you had in its achievement." Personally, though, he grieved at being tied to Davis's apron strings. Bull Run "was a glorious victory" in which he "wished to partake . . . but the President thought it more important I should be here." But just as generously, he waved away any personal interest. "I Could not have done as well as has been done" and for the result "care not by whom it is done."

Perhaps, after all the uncertainty, it could turn out that he *had* made the right decisions, that peace would now prevail, that the interrupted world at Arlington could soon resume. That, certainly, was what Mary hoped. Whatever the victory at Bull Run meant to her husband, she wrote happily to Annie, "We may possibly get to Arlington."[15]

But Abraham Lincoln had no intention of admitting defeat. Two days after the Bull Run debacle, he directed that "the forces late before Manassas . . . be re-organized as rapidly as possible, in their camps here and about Arlington," and if Union troops were stymied in northern Virginia, "let the forces in Western Virginia act."[16]

Those forces were already on the move. Four days after the Virginia state convention adopted its secession ordinance, disgruntled convention delegates from Virginia's western counties issued a call for their own secession from Virginia, with a convention to meet in the Ohio River town of Wheeling on May 13 "to consult and determine upon such action as the people of Northwestern Virginia should take in the present fearful emergency." Forty-two of the no votes in the secession convention had come from delegates from the forty westernmost counties, where Virginia slavery's hold was at its weakest—perhaps eighteen thousand slaves in 1860—and once the voting on the state secession referendum was finished on May 23, a second western Virginia convention assembled in Wheeling, declared the ordinance of secession "without authority and void," and elected Francis Pierpont as the governor of a "reorganized" state of Virginia. And just as they had done in Alexandria, federal troops under the command of Major General George B. McClellan crossed the Ohio River into western Virginia on May 26 "to restore peace and confidence, to protect the majesty of the law, and to rescue our brethren from the grasp of armed traitors."[17]

George Brinton McClellan was nineteen years younger than Lee, his father a distinguished Philadelphia physician and the founder of Philadelphia's Jefferson Medical College. Slickly talented, young George was admitted to the University of Pennsylvania at age thirteen and spent two unhappy years there until his father yielded to his entreaties for a military career and persuaded President John Tyler to appoint him as a cadet in the class of 1846. Like the Lees, the McClellans were conservative Whigs, sharing more political ground with Southern Whigs than with their Quaker neighbors. "Somehow or other I take to the Southerners," McClellan wrote to his brother, finding "the manners, feelings, & opinions of the Southerners" to be "far, far preferable" to the inelegant mores "of the majority of the Northerners" at West Point. He was, nevertheless, the star of the Corps of Cadets. As Erasmus Keyes remembered him, "a pleasanter pupil was never called to the blackboard," and Orlando B. Willcox remembered McClellan as "the most popular, if not most prominent, cadet in the corps," with "charming address and manners . . . void of pretension, and a steadfast friend." He barely missed finishing first in his class and was commissioned into the Corps of Engineers. The Mexican War had just erupted, and McClellan was shipped off to the Rio Grande, where he was assigned to Winfield Scott's army of invasion and found himself a junior lieutenant reporting to Robert E. Lee.[18]

After Mexico, McClellan distinguished himself as a student of warfare, serving on the three-man commission Congress dispatched to Europe to observe military affairs there at the end of the Crimean War. But he also distinguished himself as arrogant and narcissistic, constantly arguing with superiors and suffering his peers as fools. He was particularly impatient at the slowness of promotion. "I cannot stand the idea of being a Second Lieutenant all my life," McClellan grumbled, and in November 1856 he resigned his commission. "It is difficult, at first, to realize that you can decide upon important matters without referring either to the Adjt General or Secretary of War," he rejoiced, "and I feel already as if a heavy load was removed from my shoulders." He was pulled into prestige engineering and management positions, first with the Illinois Central Railroad and then with the Ohio and Mississippi. But secession reignited the glitter of military life for McClellan, and on April 23, Ohio's governor, William Dennison, appointed him to command of Ohio's Volunteers. The next month, he was promoted to major general of U.S. forces, and a week later troops under his command had crossed the Ohio, linked up with anti-secession militia units, and marched to reclaim western Virginia for the Union.[19]

These western counties formed a vulnerable flank to Confederate Virginia. Vital as it had been to stop McDowell's overland advance into northern Virginia at Bull Run, it was going to be just as necessary to parry a Union strike over the western Virginia mountains. Even before Lee's appointment to command of Virginia's state forces, Governor Letcher had been struggling to awaken recruitment and organization in the western counties, and in early May, Lee commissioned George Porterfield, a former Virginia militia officer and Berkeley County farmer, to begin organizing troops around the Baltimore and Ohio railroad junction at Grafton.

Porterfield did not meet with any rousing enthusiasm for his mission in Grafton. Instead, "the people of this region . . . are apparently upon the verge of civil war" against Virginia. Lee regretted "that you have been unsuccessful in organizing the companies of volunteers you expected," but regrets did nothing to reinforce Porterfield, and when McClellan's troops crossed into western Virginia on May 26, Porterfield abandoned Grafton and fell back to Philippi, where he hoped to concentrate enough Confederate volunteers to make a stand. He had been able to scrape together only 550 volunteers when three regiments of federal troops—one each of western Virginians, Ohioans, and Indianans—closed in on Philippi and forced Porterfield to evacuate Philippi as well. By now, it was obvious that Porterfield was "entirely unequal to the position," and in desperation Lee turned to his chief of staff, Robert Garnett, to take charge of Confederate troops in western Virginia, who were now clustered "in a miserable condition as to arms, clothing, equipment, instruction and discipline" at the strategic pass between Laurel Hill and Rich Mountain.[20]

Garnett set to work, recruiting, organizing, creating two new regiments out of the motley volunteers who had survived the ignominy of Grafton and Philippi, and pulling three other Virginia regiments to his aid. But the overall area was "thoroughly imbued with an ignorant and bigoted Union sentiment," and what was worse, he could get no cooperation from two other Confederate forces operating in western Virginia under Virginia's eccentric former governor Henry Wise and the onetime secretary of war John B. Floyd. "The two generals being hostile to each other before the war were now by no means friendly," and to complicate the picture, "their commissions unfortunately bore the same date, and each claimed the right of command." They were even less inclined to heed pleas from Lee to cooperate with Garnett. So, quite predictably, when McClellan closed in on Garnett's position at Rich Mountain and Laurel Hill in early July, Garnett's small forces were overrun.

The next day, trying to organize his retreat, Garnett was mortally wounded at Corrick's Ford on the Tygart River.[21]

The humiliating federal defeat at Bull Run a week later threw McClellan's success into absurdly high relief, and on July 22, McClellan was abruptly called to Washington to take command of the dispirited army reeling back from Manassas. The defeat at Rich Mountain and Laurel Hill generated a very different reaction in Richmond. With the death of Garnett, Davis directed Robert E. Lee to head to western Virginia and "strike a decisive blow," and on July 28, Lee left for "the North West Army." Surely, rejoiced the Confederate capital, the scion of Light Horse Harry would save western Virginia:

Who dare invade our homes and country,
Braggarts though the villains be,
We'll dose them well with shot and bullets,
To the tune of General Lee!

One Confederate officer eagerly expected that "Genl Lee" would "strike a blow in N W Va" that would open the way "to move down through Maryland and cooperate" with the victorious Confederates at Manassas "against Washington."[22]

Both Light Horse Harry Lee and his son Carter had dreamed of building a land empire in western Virginia, and Robert Lee could remember passing through western Virginia twenty years before on his trips back and forth to St. Louis. Of course, "if any one had then told me that the next time I travelled that road would have been on present errand," he admitted, a little sadly, in a letter to Mary, "I should have supposed him insane." Still, the vistas, as he took the train to Staunton in the Shenandoah Valley and then rode by horseback into the mountains, charmed him as scenery rarely did. "I enjoyed the mountains as I rode along. The views were magnificent. The valleys so beautiful, the scenery so peaceful." It moved him to one of his equally infrequent religious moments: "What a glorious world Almighty God has given us." But at once, the contrast between the beauty of his surroundings and the dismay of his task overcame him. "How thankless & ungrateful we are, & how we labour to mar His gifts." A suspicion of the futility of what he was doing attacked him. "May He have mercy on us!"[23]

Prayer of that sort was very much in order. The so-called Army of the Northwest was in disarray. Command of Robert Garnett's little force had fallen to the wholly inadequate Henry Rootes Jackson, and Lee at once replaced him with William Loring, a Mexican War veteran and the former colonel of the Regiment of Mounted Rifles. The death of Robert Garnett removed his chief of staff, so Lee moved up to Garnett's place one of the

Stratford Hall, Thomas Lee's grand project on Virginia's Northern Neck in the 1730s and the birthplace of Robert Edward Lee in 1807. Lost to the Lee family in the 1820s through the mismanagement of Lee's father and older half brother, Lee would dream in later years of retrieving ownership of Stratford. (Author's collection)

Henry Lee III (1756–1818), son of Henry Lee II of Leesylvania and father of Robert E. Lee. His record as a cavalry commander in the Revolution earned him the favor of George Washington, the governorship of Virginia, the hand (and property) of Matilda Lee and, after her death, Ann Hill Carter, and the nickname "Light Horse Harry." He fumbled away a fortune in western land investments, losing control of Stratford and exiling himself to the West Indies. (Princeton University Art Museum, Princeton, N.J.)

607 Oronoco Street, the later boyhood home of Robert E. Lee in Alexandria (then a part of the District of Columbia). Lee's parents, Light Horse Harry and Ann Carter Lee, moved to Alexandria in 1811, and Robert attended the academy operated by Benjamin Hallowell. (Author's collection)

The Alexandria waterfront in 1836. Alexandria was "a great commercial town . . . admitting the largest ships to anchor near the quay." Its strategic location for trade in slaves (depicted here by a line of slaves readied for embarkation to other points South) made it the home of Franklin and Armfield, one of the largest slave-trading companies in the United States. (Library of Congress, Washington, D.C.)

The Plain at West Point in 1828, while Robert E. Lee was a cadet. A lithograph from an original painting by George Catlin. Under the leadership of Superintendent Sylvanus Thayer, West Point became the premier institution for engineering education. Lee arrived there in 1825 and graduated second in the class of 1829, earning himself a commission in the Army's prestigious Corps of Engineers. (Library of Congress, Washington, D.C.)

Robert E. Lee in the dress uniform of a lieutenant of Engineers, by American portraitist William Edward West (1788–1857), probably painted in Baltimore in 1838, where West worked from 1837 to 1841, and where he painted portraits of numerous prominent families. (Washington and Lee University, Lexington, Va.)

Mary Anna Randolph Custis Lee (1807–1873), also by William Edward West. Mary Custis married Robert E. Lee in 1831, bringing him into the circle of the Custis family of Arlington. She and Robert had seven children; in later life, she was seriously disabled by rheumatoid arthritis. (Washington and Lee University, Lexington, Va.)

Fort Monroe is seen in front, on OLD POINT COMFORT, and in the distance, Fort Calhoun, at the Rip Raps.

Lee was assigned in 1831 to Fort Monroe, at the mouth of the James River, with responsibility for overseeing the construction of a new fortification, Fort Calhoun, on an artificial shoal known as the Rip Raps that commanded the middle of the ship channel flowing from the James River into the Chesapeake Bay. After the outbreak of the Civil War, Fort Calhoun was renamed Fort Wool to avoid any connection with John C. Calhoun, the arch-theorist of secession. (New York Public Library, New York, N.Y.)

Charles Carter Lee (1798–1871), Lee's oldest full sibling from the marriage of Light Horse Harry and Ann Carter Lee. He graduated from Harvard College (class of 1819) and tried, unsuccessfully, to set up a law practice in New York and Virginia. He enticed his brother Robert to join him in real-estate development schemes in western Virginia, also unsuccessfully. He married Lucy Penn Taylor in 1847 and settled into the life of a gentleman planter at Windsor Forest, in Powhatan County, Virginia. (Mary Selden Kennedy, *Seldens of Virginia and Allied Families* [1911])

Sidney (or Sydney) Smith Lee (1802–1869), Lee's next-oldest brother. Smith Lee (his family nickname was "Rose") was appointed a midshipman in the U.S. Navy in 1820. He rose to command the steam frigate *Mississippi* under Commodore Matthew Perry during Perry's famous commercial and diplomatic mission to Japan in 1853. He resigned from the Navy at the outbreak of the Civil War and served in the Confederate Navy. He married Anne Marie Mason in 1834; his son, Fitzhugh, served as a cavalry commander under his uncle Robert during the Civil War. (Library of Congress, Washington, D.C.)

Arlington House, built by George Washington Parke Custis, from Greek Revival plans by George Hadfield, on a bluff on the south bank of the Potomac overlooking the District of Columbia. The perspective in this lithograph by Joseph F. Gedney is skewed: it shows the Capitol dome in the rear distance, when the Capitol was in fact visible on a direct line from the Arlington's front porch. (Library of Congress, Washington, D.C.)

George Washington Parke Custis (1781–1857), Lee's father-in-law. Custis's father, John "Jackie" Parke Custis, was the stepson of George Washington, and much of Custis's life was devoted to memorializing Washington. His daughter, Mary Anna Randolph Custis, was his only child to survive to adulthood. (Library of Congress, Washington, D.C.)

Mary Fitzhugh Custis (1788–1853), Lee's mother-in-law. She was the daughter of William Fitzhugh of Ravensworth and married George Washington Parke Custis in 1804. She was a devout member of Christ Church, Alexandria, and a supporter of a variety of evangelical Episcopal endeavors. (Virginia Museum of History & Culture, Richmond, Va.)

Robert E. Lee with his second son, William Henry Fitzhugh "Rooney" Lee, in a daguerreotype made either in New York City or Baltimore while Lee was serving at Fort Carroll. The coverage of Rooney's left hand under his right may be a concealment of the damage done to his fore- and middle fingers by a straw cutter in November 1845. (Virginia Museum of History & Culture, Richmond, Va.)

Mary Custis Lee, in a daguerreotype probably made in New York City, with the Lee family's third son, Robert E. Lee Jr., born in 1843. (Virginia Museum of History & Culture, Richmond, Va.)

The St. Louis waterfront on the Mississippi River, a daguerreotype created by Thomas M. Easterly in 1848. Lee was assigned to supervise the clearance of the St. Louis wharf area and the Des Moines Rapids from 1837 to 1841. (*Lloyd's Steamboat Directory, and Disasters on the Western Waters* [1856])

Fort Hamilton was a Third System fortification on the western tip of Long Island, commanding water access to New York City. Lee was the principal engineering officer at Fort Hamilton from 1841 until 1846. (New-York Historical Society, New York, N.Y.)

Landing of the Troops at Vera Cruz, chromolithograph by Peter S. Duval, 1851. With the outbreak of the Mexican War, Lee joined the expeditionary force commanded by Gen. John Wool, and then a larger one commanded by Gen. Winfield Scott that executed an ambitious joint Army-Navy capture of Veracruz, on the Mexican coast. Lee became one of Scott's principal aides as Scott's expedition moved inland to capture Mexico City. (John Frost, *Pictorial History of Mexico and the Mexican War* [1851])

Carl Nebel, *The Storming of Chapultepec,* from George Wilkins Kendall's *The War Between the United States and Mexico, Illustrated* (1851). Lee undertook key reconnaissance missions for Scott all through the campaign to capture Mexico City. Scott particularly praised Lee for his crossing of the *pedregal* as "the greatest feat of physical and moral courage performed by any individual, in my knowledge." (George Wilkins Kendall, *The War Between the United States and Mexico, Illustrated* [1851])

Major General Winfield Scott (1786–1866), by Robert Walter Weir. Scott was the Army's senior major general at the time of the Mexican War and became one of Lee's principal patrons. (National Portrait Gallery, Washington, D.C.)

Robert E. Lee, a daguerreotype probably made by Mathew Brady in New York City while Lee was superintendent of West Point from 1852 to 1855. (Virginia Museum of History & Culture, Richmond, Va.)

Joseph Gilbert Totten (1788–1864) graduated from West Point in 1805, was commissioned into the Corps of Engineers, and rose to become the Army's Chief Engineer in 1838. He became another of Lee's patrons. (National Portrait Gallery, Washington, D.C.)

Christ Church, Alexandria, Virginia, was the Episcopal church that Lee attended as a boy, under the rectorship of William Meade, and then later with his family when living at Arlington. Lee was confirmed there in 1853 by Bishop John Johns. (Author's collection)

Edward Beyer, *White Sulphur Springs,* from Beyer's *Album of Virginia* (1858). Mary Custis Lee developed the symptoms of rheumatoid arthritis in the mid-1850s and could find relief only at a variety of hot spring and sulphur spas that dotted the mountains of western Virginia and North Carolina. (National Portrait Gallery, Washington, D.C.)

George Washington Custis Lee (1832–1913) was the oldest son of Robert and Mary Lee. He graduated first in his class from West Point in 1854 and was commissioned into the Corps of Engineers. In the Civil War, he served on the staff of Confederate president Jefferson Davis. He succeeded his father as president of Washington and Lee University, serving until 1897. (Stratford Hall, Stratford, Va.)

William Henry Fitzhugh "Rooney" Lee (1837–1891) was the second Lee son. At the outbreak of the Civil War, he was commissioned as a captain in the 9th Virginia Cavalry. He surrendered along with his father at Appomattox Court House. (Stratford Hall, Stratford, Va.)

Robert Edward Lee Jr. (1843–1914) was the third son and sixth child of Robert and Mary Lee. He enlisted in the Rockbridge Artillery and rose to the rank of captain. He was the only Lee family member to write a memoir of his father. (Private collection)

Mary Custis Lee "Daughter" (1835–1918) was the oldest of the Lee daughters and the Lees' second child. Very much the free spirit, she visited twenty-six countries over the course of her long life. (Arlington House, George Washington Memorial Parkway, National Park Service)

Eleanor Agnes Lee (1841–1873), the second Lee daughter, was courted by Orton Williams and devastated by his execution by federal military authorities as a spy during the Civil War. (Arlington House, George Washington Memorial Parkway, National Park Service)

Mildred Childe Lee (1845–1905), the Lees' youngest child, named for Lee's youngest sister. In the years after the war, Mildred ran the household at Washington College for her mother. She said of her father, "To me, he seems a Hero—& all other men small in comparison." (Arlington House, George Washington Memorial Parkway, National Park Service)

Anne Carter Lee (1839–1862) was named for Robert E. Lee's mother. She was born with a "raspberry" facial birthmark and blinded in one eye at age three by an accident with shears; no photograph of her seems to have been made. She became her father's favorite and confidante. Her death in 1862 from typhoid may have helped trigger Robert E. Lee's first major heart attack. (Arlington House, George Washington Memorial Parkway, National Park Service)

Martha Custis "Markie" Williams (1827–1899) was a great-great-grand-daughter of Martha Washington and thus a cousin to Mary Custis Lee. Born at Tudor Place in Georgetown, she became the household manager at Arlington after the death of Mary Fitzhugh Custis in 1853 and one of Robert E. Lee's favorite correspondents over the years. (Tudor Place Historic House & Garden, Washington, D.C.)

The White House, on the Pamunkey River, was originally owned by Daniel Parke Custis (whose widow, Martha Dandridge Custis, married George Washington at White House in 1759) and passed to his infant grandson, George Washington Parke Custis, in 1781. By the terms of G.W.P.'s estate, his grandson, Rooney Lee, inherited White House, but the house was burned by Union troops in 1862. A third White House, rebuilt by Rooney, burned in 1880. (Library of Congress, Washington, D.C.)

Francis Preston Blair (1791–1876), head of the politically powerful Blair family, to whom Abraham Lincoln delegated the task of interviewing Robert E. Lee on April 18, 1861, about the possibility of taking command of federal field armies. (Library of Congress, Washington, D.C.)

Lee at Fredericksburg, by military artist Henry Alexander Ogden (1856–1936), depicts Lee with a full beard, and overseeing the defense of Marye's Heights during the Battle of Fredericksburg, Virginia, on December 13, 1862. (Library of Congress, Washington, D.C.)

Another Vannerson image of Lee, one of three made later in 1864, known as the "floppy tie" images, printed and mounted here as a *carte de visite.* (Library of Congress, Washington, D.C.)

One of a series of photographs of Lee made by Julian Vannerson (1827–1875) of Richmond in 1864. Vannerson made at least two standing photographs of Lee, and then a left-profile and a near front-face image. (Library of Congress, Washington, D.C.)

The Stewart-Lee House, 707 E. Franklin Street, Richmond. Built in 1844 by Norman Stewart, it was occupied as "The Mess" during the war first by Custis Lee and other Confederate officers, and then by Mary Lee and her daughters. It is currently the headquarters of the Family Foundation of Virginia. (Library of Congress, Washington, D.C.)

Lee, flanked by Custis Lee and Walter Taylor, one of a series of six photographs made on the back porch of 707 E. Franklin soon after Lee's return from Appomattox by Mathew Brady in April 1865. (Library of Congress, Washington, D.C.)

Two of the images made by Brady show Lee standing, almost defiantly. In one of the poses, the word DEVIL had been scrawled on a brick above the chair at left but was erased in order to take the second standing pose. (Library of Congress, Washington, D.C.)

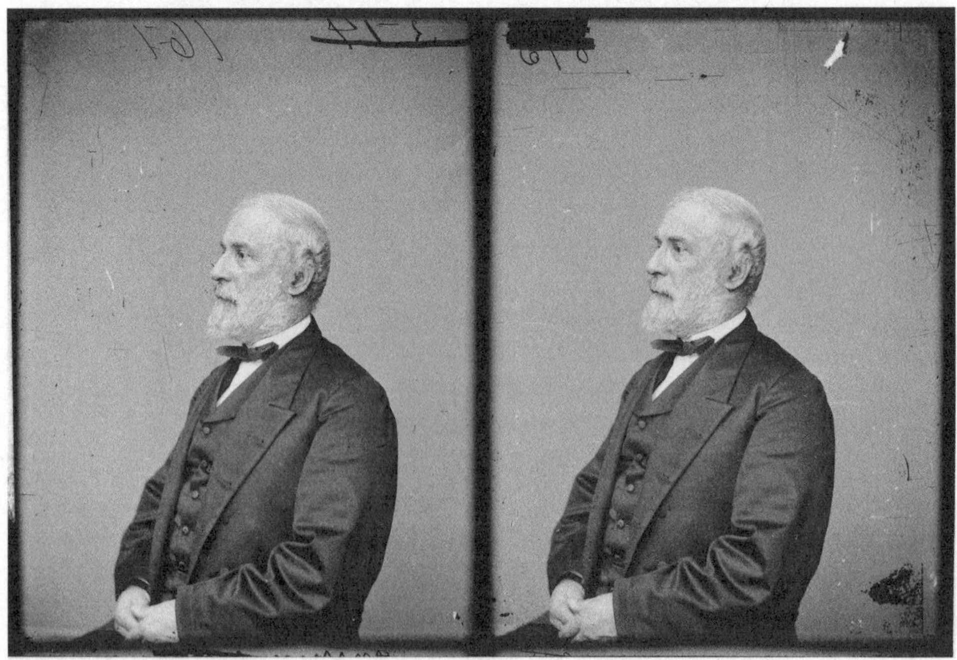

Lee as the president of Washington College, an image made by Mathew Brady at his Washington, D.C., studio in February 1866, when Lee was in the capital to testify before the Joint Committee on Reconstruction. (Library of Congress, Washington, D.C.)

Lee with Traveller, one of a pair of photographs taken in the summer of 1866 at the Rockbridge Baths by Michael Miley (1841–1918) of Lexington and Lynchburg photographer Adam H. Plecker (1840–1925). (Library of Congress, Washington, D.C.)

Lee, as photographed by Michael Miley of Lexington in 1869. The volume of requests he received for a photograph compelled him to order prints and *cartes de visite* for distribution to inquirers and admirers. (Virginia Museum of History & Culture, Richmond, Va.)

Mary Custis Lee in Lexington, where her husband rebuilt the college president's house specifically to accommodate the wheelchair to which she was largely confined. (Stratford Hall, Stratford, Va.)

This full-length photograph of Lee was made by Michael Miley after Lee's return from his sabbatical in June 1870 and was intended as a model for a bust that had been commissioned from the sculptor Edward Valentine (1838–1930). Despite the restoration he felt from the sabbatical, Lee was evidently in poor health. (Virginia Museum of History & Culture, Richmond, Va.)

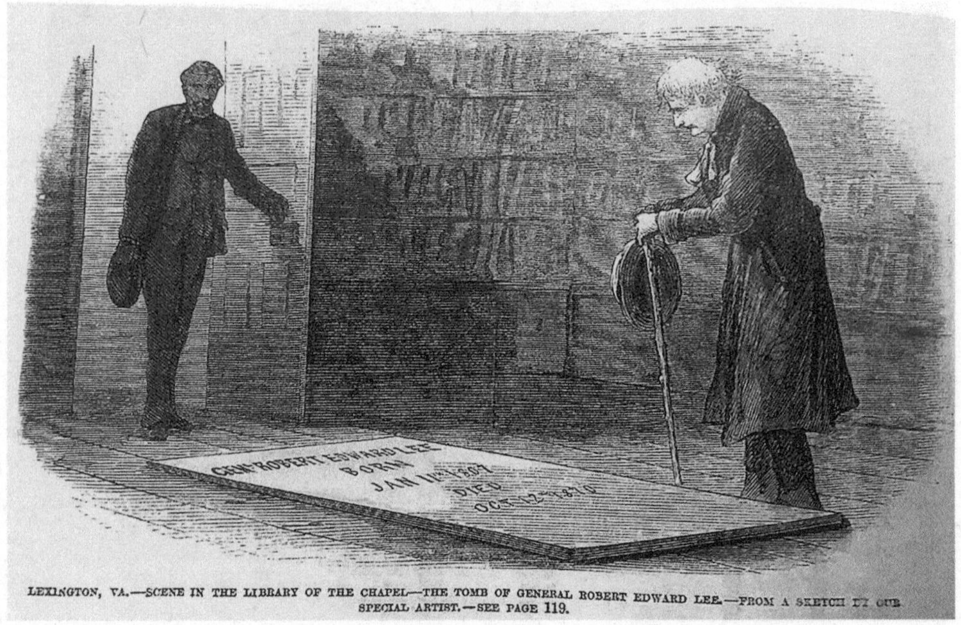

LEXINGTON, VA.—SCENE IN THE LIBRARY OF THE CHAPEL—THE TOMB OF GENERAL ROBERT EDWARD LEE.—FROM A SKETCH BY OUR SPECIAL ARTIST.—SEE PAGE 119.

Lee's original burial place in the lower level of the college chapel, from *Frank Leslie's Illustrated Newspaper*, November 5, 1870. Note the mistaken birth date. (*Frank Leslie's Illustrated Newspaper* [November 5, 1870])

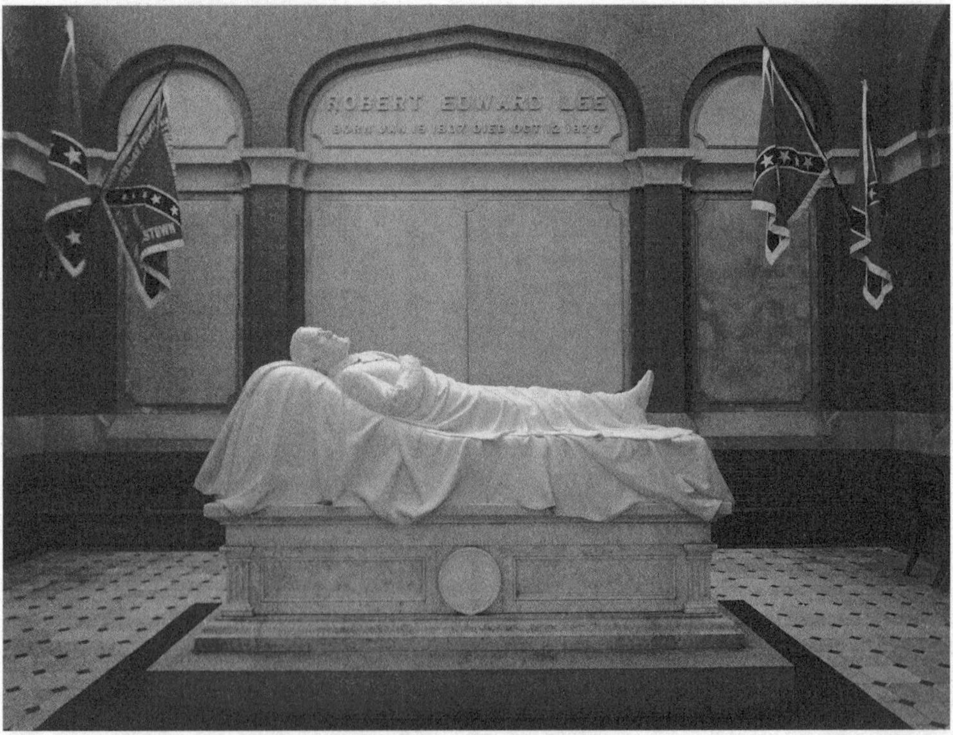

Edward Valentine's recumbent Lee monument, in the specially rebuilt apse of the college chapel (renamed the Lee Chapel). The Confederate battle flags, which were installed in 1930, were removed in 2014. Lee and his family, including Light Horse Harry Lee, are buried in a vault below. (Washington and Lee University, Lexington, Va.)

Custis relatives who had been defamed over old G.W.P.'s will, John Augustine Washington, and brought with him his Richmond secretary, Walter Taylor, the slave Perry Parks as "washerman," and Rooney, who had always yearned to be a "dragoon" and who was now a major of Virginia cavalry and "the commanding cavalry officer on the line at present."

Otherwise, the resources at Lee's disposal were meager. He himself had no particular uniform, just a suit of "blue cottonade" with "no sword or pistol, or anything to show his rank," although he kept a pair of binoculars slung "over his shoulder by a strap." Worse, "our means of transportation is limited," so "our supplies come up slowly." Already, in August, the mountain nights were cold, and it rained without end. "The incessant rains and constant travel have rendered the roads impassable, and so prevented the transportation of supplies as to paralyze, for the present, operations in this quarter." The weather, in turn, took its toll on the soldiers. "The soldiers are everywhere sick," with "measles . . . prevalent throughout the whole army."

And then there was the obstreperous Henry Wise and his never-ending arguments over seniority with John Floyd. Lee told Wise in the most peremptory fashion that "our enemy is so strong at all points that we can only hope to give him an effective blow by a concentration of our forces," which meant "that you will Join Genl Floyd," no matter how distasteful, and clear the "Kanawha District." Maddeningly, there was no guarantee that Wise would listen. Davis's commission to Lee was "one of inspection, and consultation on the plan of campaign," not direct command. So even though western Virginia was actually Robert E. Lee's first independent campaign, his authority was palsied by uncertainty.

Wise and Floyd, however, were models of loyalty compared with the indifference, even perfidy, of the mountain people. "Spies lurked around every hill," remembered Walter Taylor. "Our weakness, our embarrassments, and our every movement, were promptly reported to the enemy." On one side of the mountains, the citizens of Hardy County (where Carter Lee had once tempted his brother to move) complained to Jefferson Davis that they had been "hoping for relief from General Lee's army," but "in this we have been disappointed"; on the other side, "our citizens" were sullen unionists who betrayed news of his activities without compunction. "Our movements seem rapidly to be Communicated to them while theirs Come to us slowly & indistinctly." He was infuriated "to learn that the four companies of Vol[unteer]s in the county of Mercer" had second thoughts about the war and "declined being mustered into the service."[24]

The only factor operating in Lee's favor was the direction given by McClellan to his western Virginia forces before departing for Washington, instructing them to adopt a defensive posture. Even so, the Union troops in the Kanawha, under Jacob Dolson Cox, conveniently ignored that directive and pushed Henry Wise's little command out of the Kanawha Valley and then fended off an attempt by John Floyd to retake it. By mid-September, the Kanawha was securely in federal hands. Mercifully for Lee, William Starke Rosecrans, whom McClellan had left in control of northwestern Virginia, was friendlier to the idea of staying comfortably in place, and in early August, Lee began planning to strike Rosecrans's advance position at Cheat Mountain with the Army of the Northwest. This did not turn out to be as easy as Lee had hoped. William Loring, as the new commander of the Army of the Northwest, turned out to be fully as difficult and argumentative as Wise and Floyd, and Lee soon began conducting reconnaissance for his move, Mexico-style, by himself.[25]

This all ended badly. By mid-September, Lee had concentrated some 15,000 soldiers near Cheat Mountain. But when he launched a five-pronged attack reminiscent of Cerro Gordo on the Union defenders, orders and communications went awry and the attack fizzled. The next day, struggling to retrieve something from the failure, Lee looked for a path that would outflank the Federals, and put out reconnaissance parties all around Cheat Mountain. One of these, with Rooney and John Washington, blundered into a Union picket line, and in the fusillade of bullets Washington was shot dead. For the first time, the war had reached into the wide circle of Lee's relations and struck down one whose "intimate association . . . for some months has more fully disclosed to me his great worth, than double so many years of ordinary intercourse would have been sufficient to reveal."[26]

Lee's reputation, which had risen so kitelike since April, now twirled downward in dead air. In September, the *Richmond Enquirer* had predicted that the attack on Cheat Mountain would "stand as a monument to his fame of which any professor of the military art, however gifted or fortunate, might well be proud." Now the newspapers were tight-lipped. Lee had shown "too great circumspection," declared the *Richmond Dispatch,* and he should have understood that "ingeniously studied military evolutions or consummately arranged plans of campaign" were of little use in the mountains. "While General Lee was weaving ingenious webs of strategy about Cheat Mountain, Rosencranz was legging it down to the Gauley [River]," and the unionist state convention was planning to create an entirely new state out of the western counties.

His "reputation was suffering," and wagging heads in Richmond reported that "the people are getting mighty sick of this dilly-dally . . . scientific warfare." Even his former student and aide at Harpers Ferry, J. E. B. Stuart, who joined the Confederacy in May, admitted that "with profound personal regard for General Lee, he has disappointed me as a General." Lee made a desultory effort after Cheat Mountain to revive an offensive into the Kanawha Valley, but he could make no progress against the enmity between Wise and Floyd. When falling temperatures closed down operations in the mountains for good in mid-October, Davis mandated a reorganization of Virginia's military districts that effectively ceded control of everything in western Virginia between the Blue Ridge and the Ohio River to federal occupation. Lee returned to Richmond, a general without a command. Seeing him pass by, the Confederate War Department clerk John B. Jones thought Lee "bore the aspect of a discontented man."[27]

He had at least one small laurel to comfort him, because he had managed to stymie any serious federal advance over the Blue Ridge into the Shenandoah Valley and beyond to Richmond. But this was as much the result of McClellan's departure from the scene in July as it was Lee's planning. What was profoundly disheartening to Lee was, given the vagueness of his authority from Jefferson Davis, his inability to make Wise, Floyd, Loring, and the rest either bend to his direction or face dismissal. Nor was it just the generals. Regimental officers complained and bickered. The soldiers, too, were undisciplined and resistant to military order: "They are worse than children."

Everywhere, the people he met seemed listless and apathetic about the Confederacy. "It is so difficult," he admitted to Mary, "to get our people, unaccustomed to the necessities of war, to comprehend . . . the measures required for the occasion." For their sakes, he had already sacrificed two men—Robert Garnett and John Washington—whose deaths were hardly worth the joyless result. He almost wished himself with them. To Washington's daughter Louisa, Lee wrote, "He is now safely in heaven. . . . We ought not to wish him back." Did he ever, contemplating the image of himself reflected in the window of the railway car that brought him back to Richmond, ask himself, *What have I done?*[28]

One who had not lost faith in Lee was Jefferson Davis. "He came back carrying the heavy weight of defeat," remembered Davis, "unappreciated by the people whom he served." But in Davis's estimate, "if his plans and orders had been carried out, the result would have been victory rather than retreat." So when Lee arrived in Richmond on the Virginia Central on October 31, Davis already had another assignment in mind. A federal fleet of "fourteen large steamers and gunboats," plus troop transports, had been assembling in the Chesapeake Bay in mid-October, and rumor screamed that it was bound for the Carolina coast, to seize points there for supplying the federal naval blockade of the Confederacy. Summoning Lee to a lengthy meeting with the new secretary of war, Judah P. Benjamin, Davis directed Lee "to repair thither" and take command of a newly created military district that embraced East Florida, Georgia, and South Carolina. This time, Lee wanted clarity about his authority. "Before leaving," Davis remembered, "he said that, while he was serving in Virginia, he had never thought it needful to inquire about his rank; but now . . . he would like to be informed upon that point." And this time, Davis assured him that he would be going as "a full general" and in full command.[29]

But once again, Lee arrived only in time to play catch-up. He stepped off the train in Charleston on the morning of November 7, accompanied by Walter Taylor. Even as he did so, the federal flotilla was sweeping into the Port Royal Sound, easily silencing the two Confederate forts that defended it. Lee "proceeded immediately to the scene of action" by train that evening, only to find the islands of the sound—Hilton Head, Parris Island, St. Helena Island—already covered with 15,000 Union infantry. "Nothing could then be done but to make arrangements to withdraw," he reported to Judah Benjamin.

He set up a temporary headquarters at Coosawhatchie, upstream from the Port Royal Sound on the Broad River, and began issuing a stream of orders, banning "the sale of arms and munitions of war," ordering the disbandment of the militia so that he could "fight the invaders" with regularly enlisted "volunteers exclusively," removing artillery "from the less important points" on the coast to strengthen "those considered of greater consequence," and even appropriating a locomotive and a "special train" to allow him to move quickly over the landscape of his department. He detoured south two times to inspect the defenses of the Savannah River at Fort Pulaski (where he had driven the pilings as a newly graduated engineer in 1829), then back up to Charleston by December 14, just as the city's most destructive fire was burning itself out, and then inspected coastal batteries from Charleston down to Florida.[30]

What he discovered was as disappointing as western Virginia. Within three days, Lee realized that the entire force he could rely upon in his district amounted to fifty-five hundred men, "made up chiefly of raw troops." Worse still, the district's governors who had sent their state volunteers into Confederate service now expected them to be returned to defend the home territory and not used to defend someone else's. Georgia's governor, Joseph Brown, had already lodged a protest with Jefferson Davis about creating Lee's new district; he and the state's former U.S. senator Herschel Johnson now demanded that Georgia's Confederates be returned to protect Savannah, because "all these troops were trained at the State's expense and thoroughly armed by her." When the demands were refused, Lee rather than Davis became their target. "From the interviews I have had with Genl. Lee," wrote South Carolina's governor, Francis Pickens, "I have a very high estimation of his . . . enlightened judgement" and "high bred cultivated bearing." But he suffers from "over caution, which results from his scientific mind"—a polite way of suggesting that Lee was nothing more than an engineer—and had no taste for "guerilla dashes . . . if the enemy land in large force on our coast." Mary Chesnut acidly condemned Lee as "never hopeful" (adding, "so far his bonnie face has only brought us ill luck"), and Edmund Ruffin, the Virginia fire-eater and agricultural apostle who had pulled the lanyard on the first shot fired at Fort Sumter, denounced Lee at the end of November as "too much of a red-tapist to be an effective commander in the field."[31]

Lee's estimate of South Carolina did not rise much higher. He was dismayed at the level of self-deception on the part of South Carolinians, who thought that they could begin a war and not have to pay for its consequences, that they could indulge their customary habits and pursuits while other people were obliged to protect them, that the whole business required only a little effort, most of which was to be made by someone else. "I am dreadfully disapp[ointe]d at the spirit here," he told Custis, who had been taken onto Jefferson Davis's staff in Richmond. "The people do not seem to realize there is a war," he complained to his confidante-daughter, Annie, a month after arriving in South Carolina. He beseeched the Confederate district judge Andrew Magrath to press on the South Carolina legislature "the urgent necessity of bringing out the military strength of the State." Yet "it is so very hard to get anything done."

Lee believed that no one realized the strength the North could bring to bear on the war, nor did they seem to understand what Lee had divined by the previous summer, that Lincoln would never stop short of complete reconquest of the Confederacy. "While all wish well & mean well, it is so difficult to get them to act energetically & promptly." He complained again to Annie that "our people have not been in earnest enough, have thought too much of themselves & their ease, & instead of turning out to a man, have been content to nurse themselves & their dimes, & leave the protection of themselves & families to others." His mission was simply "another forlorn hope expedition. Worse than Western Virginia."[32]

Anyone who doubted the seriousness of the Confederacy's dilemma had to look no farther than Charleston, where (as Lee reported to Judah P. Benjamin), "the enemy brought his stone fleet to the entrance of Charleston Harbor" and sank "between thirteen & seventeen vessels" to block "the main ship channel." This Lee thought "unworthy [of] any nation" and revealed "the malice & revenge of a people" who aimed to reduce a city "to a condition not to be enjoyed." Or, if proof of Northern vindictiveness was still wanting, he could consult his own losses. Arlington, "if not destroyed by our enemies, has been so desecrated that I cannot bear to think of it."

> *Even if the enemy had wished to preserve it, it would almost have been impossible. With the number of troops encamped around it, the change of officers, &c the want of fuel, shelter, &c, & all the dire necessities of war, it is vain to think of its being in a habitable Condition. I fear too books, furniture, & the relics of Mt. Vernon will be gone. It is better to make up our minds to a general loss.*

And he expected, too, that "the bonds I hold of the Northern railroads & cities will all be confiscated" and that he would "be a pauper if I get through the war."[33]

Yet these dreary ruminations on the future were pierced by a peculiar shaft of hope, as though his losses might turn out to be a blessing in disguise. In November, he learned that Annie and Agnes had managed a visit to Stratford Hall, and the news triggered something tectonic in their father. "I am much pleased at your description of Stratford & your visit." But not merely for old times' sake. Stratford "is endeared to me by many recollections &"—here Robert Lee pulled back the curtain his dealings with the Custises had always required him to keep in place—"it has always been a great desire of my life to be able to purchase it."

He was serious. "In the absence of a home," he wrote to Mary on Christmas Day, "I wish I could purchase Stratford." Stratford Hall had not been in the hands of the Lees since his half brother, Black Horse Harry, had fumbled it away. Yet the great brick monument was still there on the Northern Neck; it was the place where Robert had been born, the place his mother returned to on her endless circuit of family visitations, the place that was incontestably the monument of the Lees. Arlington had always been the temple of the Custises, the Washingtons, the place he could never own, with its always-dancing illusion of self-rule and certainty that never came true. *Stratford.* "That is the only other place that I could go to now accessible to us, that would inspire me with feelings of pleasure & local love," Robert explained, struggling to translate fantasy into reality and forgetting all his moans about pauperdom *and* all about Mary's single-minded devotion to someplace else. "I wonder if it is for sale & at how much. Ask Fitzhugh to try & find out when he gets to Fredericksburg."[34]

But Stratford was not for sale, and even if it had been, its perch on the Potomac would have made it just as easy a target for Yankee seizure as Arlington. The contradictions in this impulse were, in a small way, of a piece with all the other unexamined contradictions Lee allowed to flow through his life; of the military life that constricted him but that he could never bring himself to leave; of the Custises, whom alternatively he loved and fled; of the Confederacy he deplored as a revolution and the unenthusiastic decision he had made to serve it. Routinely, he urged Governor Pickens (over the protests of slave owners) to conscript slaves for "works for military defense"; just as routinely, he doggedly insisted that under G.W.P.'s will the Custis slaves "must be emancipated at the close of" 1862. And perhaps not just the Custis slaves alone. Years later, he would claim to William Allan that he had "told Mr. Davis often and early in the war that the slaves should be emancipated"—not as an act of justice so much as "the only way to remove a weakness at home and to get sympathy abroad, and to divide our enemies." He had even, for the first time since Mexico, allowed a full beard to grow out, "a beautiful white beard" beneath his graying hair and mustache, although he admitted that it was more "remarked on" than "admired."

Could there ever be a reconciliation of these conflicting currents? Perhaps. And it might have begun with his daughters' visit to Stratford, for in mid-January 1862, while on an inspection tour to Fernandina, Lee stopped at Cumberland Island, one of the Georgia sea islands. Cumberland was the site of a small fortification he needed to check. But it was also where Light Horse Harry was buried, and there Lee "had the gratification at length of visiting my father's grave."

He had barely mentioned his father's name in forty years, but now something in him loosened enough that he could pay a small homage to the battered bankrupt who had deserted him so many decades before. Perhaps it was possible to stop the endless cycle of looking and looking away. "He went alone to the tomb," recalled Armistead Lindsay Long, who had just joined Lee's staff the month before, "and after a few moments of silence plucked a flower and slowly retraced his steps, leaving the lonely grave to the guardianship of the crumbling stones and the spirit of the restless waves that perpetually beat against the neighboring shore."[35]

Through the winter and into the first blush of a Charleston spring, the Union incursion into Port Royal did little more than secure its grasp of the sound, launch occasional nuisance raids up its tributary rivers, and become an experiment in self-management for the slaves on the surrounding plantations whose masters had abandoned them to their freedom. Lee redistributed troops and artillery into a handful of points that were worth defending—Charleston, Savannah, the St. Marys River—and exhorted the South Carolinians to recruit more volunteers and sign them up for the duration of the war, not just twelve months. "I have been doing all I can with our small means & slow workmen to defend the cities & coast here," he wrote to Annie. But he was conscious that "this is not the way to accomplish our independence. . . . Against ordinary numbers we are pretty strong, but against the hosts our enemies seem able to bring every where, there is no calculation."

Then, in mid-February, far to the west, a hammer-like Union blow fashioned by an obscure onetime Army captain named Ulysses S. Grant fell on two Confederate forts—Fort Henry on the Tennessee River and Fort Donelson on the Cumberland—cracking open the entire western shield of the Confederacy and forcing Jefferson Davis to contemplate a complete reordering of Confederate national strategy. "The recent disaster to our arms in Tennessee forces the Government to the stern necessity of withdrawing its lines within more defensible limits," Judah P. Benjamin warned Lee on February 24, which meant stripping Lee's district of most of the troops he commanded. But to coordinate the reordering, Jefferson Davis wanted Robert E. Lee himself. "If circumstances will in your judgment warrant your leaving," Davis wired him on Sunday, March 2, "I wish to see you here with the least delay." Lee replied at once: "I will leave Tuesday morning."[36]

CHAPTER ELEVEN

To Dash Against Mine Enemy and to Win

Jefferson Davis was inaugurated as the first full president of the Confederate States of America on the 22nd of February in Richmond's Capitol Square while "heavy rains" poured down "unceasingly throughout the day." The square was "black with umbrellas," and a special tent had to be erected "for the President to stand under" while he took the oath of office and delivered his inaugural address. "The day was an inclement one," admitted the *Richmond Dispatch,* and not just for Davis. In the west, the fall of Forts Henry and Donelson forced a mass evacuation of Nashville; that, in turn, compelled the abandonment of the Confederacy's northernmost post along the Mississippi at Columbus, Kentucky, and paved the way for Ulysses Grant and a federal army to begin moving up the Tennessee River toward the vital western railroad junction at Corinth, Mississippi. Robert E. Lee's onetime junior officer from the 2nd Cavalry Earl Van Dorn was massing 14,000 men for a desperate attack on federal troops invading Arkansas at Pea Ridge, but that would shortly end in a humiliating defeat and the effective loss of Arkansas to the Confederacy.

For a brief moment, on March 8, one of Lee's projects from his days as Virginia's commander in chief—the refloating of the wrecked federal steam frigate *Merrimack* from its scuttled grave at the Gosport naval yard in Norfolk and its resurrection as an ironclad gunboat, the *Virginia*—looked as if it might be able to gain control of the Chesapeake Bay. But the next day, a federal ironclad, the USS *Monitor,* made its debut at Fort Monroe and fought the *Virginia* to a standstill. "Recent disasters have depressed the weak and are depriving us of the aid of the wavering," Davis admitted to Joseph Johnston, whose army in northern Virginia once held positions within sight of the federal Capitol in Washington. "Traitors show the tendencies heretofore concealed and the selfish grow clamorous for local and personal interests."[1]

In the furor over the Confederacy's losses, the press paid little attention to the return of Robert E. Lee to the Confederate capital. The tide of political disappointment had instead swept over the heads of Davis's military administration, and especially over Secretary of War Judah P. Benjamin. Tennessee's congressional delegation in Richmond promptly informed Davis that "confidence is no longer felt in the military skill" of Davis's handpicked commanding general in the west, Albert Sidney Johnston, and on the same day as it passed a suspension of the writ of habeas corpus, the Confederate Congress signaled its displeasure with Benjamin by passing a bill authorizing the replacement of the secretary of war with an "officer of the Army," and guaranteeing that such officer "shall not thereby lose his rank in the Army" by assuming a civilian office.

Davis's recall of Lee from South Carolina set off speculation that Davis intended to plant Lee in Benjamin's place, and a second bill passed by Congress on March 6 created a rank of "commanding general of the armies of the Confederate States," which wise heads similarly guessed would be designed for Lee. But Davis was touchy about anything that looked like trenching on his constitutional prerogatives as the presidential commander in chief. He vetoed the second bill and filled the War Department post with a Virginian, George Wythe Randolph, on March 17. On Lee, he bestowed the anomalous assignment of "conduct of the military operations in the armies of the Confederacy" and handed him "duty at the seat of government . . . under the direction of the President." More obligingly, the Confederate Congress granted Lee a staff to consist of "a military secretary, with the rank of colonel; four aides-de-camp, with the rank of major; and such clerks, not to exceed four in number, as the President shall, from time to time, authorize."[2]

The Richmond papers hailed Lee's appointment "with great satisfaction," even as they admitted that Lee had been criticized for "too much caution." And though the appointment was described as a "commander-in-chief of the whole army," which would "have at the head of all of her military operations one man," there was nothing in this new task, when looked at closely, that appeared so grandiose. If anything, smirked *The Charleston Mercury*, it reduced Lee "himself from a Commanding General to an Orderly Sergeant" for Davis. Mary Lee, who after shuttling from cousin to cousin had finally settled at Rooney's White House plantation on the Pamunkey River, fumed that while her husband "is put in charge of the armies of the Confederacy," they had only done so because "now they have got into trouble" and without ever giving him "any credit for what he has done." The loss of Arlington still obsessed her. "I do not allow myself to think of my dear old home," she wailed to Elizabeth Stiles, "would that it had been razed to the ground or submerged in the Potomac rather than have fallen into such hands." It did nothing to soothe her anxieties that young Rob had now enlisted in the Confederate Army. "My last one Rob, you recollect now a sweet golden haired cherub has volunteered. He is just 18."

Lee himself was far from confident that he would be able to work any military miracles in an atmosphere of so little political faith. "I am willing to do anything I can do to help," he wrote to Carter, but "I fear I shall be able to do little in the position assigned me & cannot hope to satisfy the feverish & excited expectation of our good people." To Mary, he was more direct: "I do not see either advantage or pleasure in my duties." The only remotely attractive possibility was that "I shall, in all human probability, soon have to take the field," although that would likely have to be in "N.C. or Norfolk. . . . The enemy is pushing us back in all directions & how far he will be successful depends much upon our efforts & the mercy of Providence."[3]

Still, Lee set to work with as much will as he had displayed only a year before in Richmond. Lindsay Long, whom he brought with him from Charleston, became his military secretary, while Walter Taylor became one of his four aides. They were joined by two new acquisitions appropriate to the general who had once been a mathematics standout: a mathematics professor turned lawyer from Baltimore named Charles Marshall, and yet another mathematics professor from South Carolina College, Charles Venable. From the first, it was clear that Lee wanted nothing to do with paper pushing. "When the staff was first organized," Taylor remembered, "a large batch" of "routine" papers "was submitted to him every morning," and Lee dealt with them by sitting his staffers "in a semicircle" and passing out "each paper" to them "with instructions as to how it should be disposed of."

He preferred to keep his eyes above the minutiae. Already the Confederacy's rail system was in distress, with less than ten thousand miles of railroads owned by 113 different companies, many of them created and effectively controlled by Southern state governments; all of these would have to be coordinated if the Confederate armies were to be adequately supplied. The Confederate Congress had authorized Jefferson Davis to seize the South's existing telegraph lines for military service, but Davis put the management of the lines into the hands of the postmaster general, and the two primary Southern telegraph lines fought each other with as much energy as they fought the Union. Clothing supply had been unwisely placed by the Confederate Congress into the hands of states and even individual soldiers (for a fee), and there were few Southerners with the kind of large-scale managerial experience equal to the task of supplying the Confederate armies' quartermaster and commissary needs. (Quartermaster General Abraham C. Myers estimated that the Confederate armies would require the manufacture of 1.6 million pairs of shoes each year, yet Southern resources would be able to produce only 600,000.) And as Union armies tore deeper penetrations into the upper South, it would become increasingly harder for the Confederacy to round up the wagons, horses, and mules it needed for transportation. Soon enough, Lee would have no choice but to resort to a kind of black-market trade in Southern cotton with the North.[4]

In the face of these shortages, nothing exasperated Lee more than the continuing reluctance of Southerners to make the sacrifices the war was demanding. "The Confederate Congress and a great part of the Southern people, encouraged by their representatives and by the press, were eager to adopt any theory that promised relief from the threatened danger other than recognition of the fact that their only safety lay in the vigorous use of the whole military resources of the country," remembered Charles Marshall. Davis had spent much of the first year of the war resting in the confidence that a "show of force" all along the Confederacy's northern borders would dissuade "the Northern people" from "supporting the war." The disasters of the early spring of 1862 had destroyed that confidence, but without replacing it with any corresponding energy in the South's response. Too many other Southerners now predicted that it was perfectly sensible to "decoy the enemy into the interior, and then to cut them off as were Braddock, and Burgoyne, and Cornwallis, and Ross, and Packenham, and our own troops in the everglades of Florida."

Nor did Lee find in Jefferson Davis or Joe Johnston the qualities that would stimulate a corrective urgency. Walter Taylor might admire Davis's "knowledge of constitutional law and familiarity with the principles of representative government," but those who had to work with him found Davis to be "a slow, very slow worker," fond of "endless tedious consultations which yield no results" and produce "a total absence of vigor." As for Joe Johnston, Lee could not understand why his old West Point friend and fellow Mexican War veteran allowed a Confederate army to sit passively behind the Potomac. Western Virginia, the Carolinas, the loss of Arlington—these were Lee's Rubicon, and they convinced him that there was nothing to be gained any longer by defensive thinking. He was being mastered by the conviction that the "policy for gaining our independence was to concentrate all our troops & fight a great battle with everything at stake—or if possible to have made it a war of invasion & aggression," and now he could not fathom why Southerners were so unwilling to give the effort their all.[5]

If Lee could not summon Southern enthusiasm with a carrot, he would do it with a stick. In late March, "all leaves and furloughs, from whatever source obtained," were canceled, and when one commander from western

Virginia complained that "the prospect of calling volunteers" there "is so unfavorable," Lee frankly advised him to "call out the militia" and fill up the Virginia Volunteer regiments with them, whether they liked it or not. But even the Confederate Volunteer service was a problem, because the Confederacy's provisional Volunteer army had been recruited in 1861 for only a year's service and that year was nearly running out. Lee's solution was national conscription, on the European model. At the end of March, Lee directed Charles Marshall "to prepare a draft of a bill for raising an army by the direct agency of the Confederate government," rendering the entire white male population of the Confederacy "between the ages of eighteen and forty-five" liable for "the service of the Confederate States for the duration of the war."

This was, Marshall said, "inspired by General Lee's views of the real nature and object of the war on the part of the Southern people." Naturally, the proposal called out the most strident political alarmists; even Virginia's John Letcher protested that conscription would amount to "the most alarming stride towards consolidation that has ever occurred." But despite the howls that conscription "abrogates 'State-rights,'" Robert E. Lee had never put much stock in states' rights in the first place, and on March 28, Davis laid Lee's proposal before the Confederate Congress. After two weeks of dawdling, they passed it.[6]

Even with this, it all might be for nothing. Hardly had Lee arrived in Richmond than Joe Johnston initiated a massive withdrawal from his lines in northern Virginia. Johnston had discussed with Davis a tactical withdrawal to more defensible positions around Manassas Junction as early as mid-February, but nothing prepared Davis for what turned out to be an immediate and wholesale abandonment of northern Virginia on March 7 by Confederate forces, all the way to "the south bank of the Rappahannock River." Davis would later claim to have been "in the dark as to your purposes, condition and necessities" and sharply criticized Johnston for "such a sudden movement." Even Lee was flummoxed by Johnston's pell-mell retreat. "It is not the plan of the Government to abandon any country that can be held," Lee fumbled to explain to Theophilus Holmes, "and it is only the necessity of the case, I presume, that has caused the withdrawal of the troops to the Rappahannock."

But there was worse still waiting to collapse. On April 6, Albert Sidney Johnston, having scraped together an army of 40,000 Confederates, pounced on Ulysses S. Grant's army as it lay encamped near Shiloh Church, by the Tennessee River crossing at Pittsburg Landing. It was a desperate gamble, and it nearly succeeded, as Sidney Johnston's hastily assembled army drove Grant's unprepared army almost into the river. But Johnston was killed by a bullet that severed an artery in his leg, and the steam ran out of the Confederate attack, and the next day Grant recovered all the ground that had been lost. Four days later, on April 11, Fort Pulaski was pounded into surrender by the U.S. Navy, and two weeks afterward a federal naval flotilla shot its way past the Mississippi River defenses of New Orleans and put the Confederacy's principal port under federal control. "We need not say that this is an unexpected and heavy blow," although the *Richmond Enquirer* said exactly that on April 28. There was now "no alternative but utter ruin and eternal infamy."[7]

"An awful day awaits us," wrote the War Department clerk John B. Jones in his diary. But, Jones added, there was Robert E. Lee—"a Christian gentleman as well as a consummate general"—and Jones believed that Lee was making "fully known to the President his appreciation of the desperate condition of affairs." What good that would accomplish, however, seemed to be diminishing rapidly, and nowhere was that more open to the eye than on the waters of the Chesapeake Bay.

When George McClellan arrived in Washington on July 26, 1861, fresh from the only Union military successes, he set about at once to reorganize and reinspire the humiliated Union Army that had dragged itself back from its defeat at Bull Run. The militia units were sent home, floods of new three-year volunteers were organized into brigades and divisions, a new chain of fortifications was thrown up around Washington (and beyond Alexandria and Arlington) to protect the federal capital, and the reborn army he had created was equipped with a new, Napoleonic title, the Army of the Potomac. He also schemed shamelessly to undermine old Winfield Scott, who finally conceded that his authority had evaporated in the light of McClellan's glitter. Scott resigned on November 4. Two weeks later, McClellan staged what almost amounted to a celebration of his own grandeur, in a "great review of 50,000 men" for "the President, the Secretary of State," and other dignitaries, "Regiment, Brigade, Division, one after another" passing by Lincoln and McClellan "as if the line was endless."[8]

Lincoln was less happy with the plans McClellan had in mind for using his grand army. The president cheerfully admitted that he was no master of strategic theory, apart from a few books he had borrowed from the Library of Congress. His most abiding interests were in a determined offensive down the Mississippi River valley (to reopen the lifeline of western agriculture) and in a straight-through overland campaign to break apart the Confederate logjam at Manassas Junction and destroy Joe Johnston's army in a single climactic battle. What he got instead from McClellan was a sophisticated but complex plan for "a strong movement . . . on the Mississippi" but also into eastern Tennessee, while in the east McClellan proposed to bypass Manassas entirely by relying on the Union Navy's control of the Chesapeake to transfer his Army of the Potomac by water to Urbanna, on the Rappahannock River, and capture Richmond without a bloody overland confrontation.

"An essential feature of the plan of operations will be the employment of a strong naval force, to protect the movement of a fleet of transports intended to convey a considerable body of troops from point to point of the enemy's sea-coast," McClellan explained in August 1861. This, after all, was the strategy Scott had used at Veracruz and the British and French armies had pursued in the Crimean War, and it certainly seemed less costly than a head-to-head collision somewhere around Manassas. But as 1861 turned coldly into 1862, Lincoln grew less tolerant for such tender-edged plans. He mandated a reorganization of the Army of the Potomac, regrouping McClellan's divisions into larger *corps d'armée* and promoting several of McClellan's nonadmirers to their commands, and at the end of January issued a direct order for "an expedition for the immediate object of seizing and occupying a point upon the railroad southwestward of what is known as Manassas Junction."[9]

McClellan grudgingly yielded to Lincoln's directive. But when the Army of the Potomac finally rumbled into motion toward Manassas Junction in early March, it found the entrenchments McClellan had so feared were empty, evacuated by Joe Johnston's retreat to the Rappahannock. McClellan, even more apprehensive of flinging his army at Confederates protected by the Rappahannock, now pressed for his water route even more strongly, only substituting the lower James River as the target, and the Union-held toehold at Fort Monroe as the deposit point for his army. Lincoln relented, happy to get any movement out of McClellan, and on March 17 the Army of the Potomac embarked on a fleet of 389 vessels from Washington for the James River. By April 2, McClellan was setting up his headquarters at Fort Monroe and preparing to move up the wide James Peninsula toward Richmond, just sixty miles away. But through it all, the unpleasantness that had grown up between Lincoln and McClellan was already being noticed, and McClellan for his part was happy just to get away from Washington, "that sink of iniquity."[10]

All told, McClellan landed a gargantuan army of 121,000 men at Fort Monroe, leaving some 18,000 in the Washington fortifications and another 35,000 in his old western Virginia department under the onetime Republican presidential hopeful John Charles Frémont to keep up pressure on the meager rebel forces there and in the Shenandoah Valley. Lee was aware of the threat posed by McClellan's expedition almost as soon as it had cleared Washington, and anticipated that Johnston would probably abandon the Rappahannock River, too, and "to repair immediately to this city." To oppose McClellan on the James Peninsula, the Confederates had only 13,000 men under the flamboyant but untalented John Bankhead Magruder, most of them parked in a ragged series of fortifications, built by a scratch army of "negro servants from different plantations" put "to work upon the fortifications" that stretched across the peninsula from the old Revolutionary War battlefield at Yorktown, along the Warwick River, to Mulberry Island.

"Assuming that the enemy will advance up the Peninsula to Richmond," Lee warned Magruder, the Federals would be able to use Navy gunboats to slip up either side of the peninsula on the James and Pamunkey Rivers and outflank "the line of your land defences." On March 28, Davis and Lee reluctantly authorized Johnston "to commence the movement of your troops to this place" and then take overall command on the peninsula. But when Magruder suggested abandoning Yorktown as well, Lee sharply drew the line. There was still a chance that the Yorktown line could be held, especially if Magruder dammed the Warwick River and turned it into a protective moat.[11]

After nearly a month, Lee seemed to have been proven right. McClellan convinced himself, from reading captured Richmond newspapers and listening to exaggerated intelligence assessments, that he was facing "probably not less than one hundred thousand (100,000) men & possibly more" at Yorktown, while minimizing reports of his own force to "about eighty five thousand." Rather than risk a frontal attack, McClellan moved slowly up the peninsula from Fort Monroe and commenced a cautious siege of Yorktown and began crying for reinforcements to be stripped from the Shenandoah and the defenses of Washington. "Every engineer officer as well as others wonder why McClellan doesn't order an immediate assault," complained a staffer in the Army of the Potomac's Third Corps. But McClellan believed, "I am avoiding the faults of the Allies at Sebastopol & quietly preparing the way for a great success."

Joe Johnston had little interest in defending the peninsula, frankly proposing to "abandon the peninsula" entirely. In a meeting with Lee and Davis in Richmond on April 14, Johnston claimed that he had no more than 77,000 men to face the Federals on the peninsula and no confidence that the Warwick line could be held whenever McClellan was finally ready to attack. Moreover, a fresh federal infantry corps under the ill-starred Irvin McDowell (the nonhero of Bull Run) had been released from Washington in response to McClellan's pleas and was already advancing on Fredericksburg on the Rappahannock. "Should the attack on Yorktown be made earnestly, we cannot prevent its fall," Johnston advised Lee on April 27. And five days later, just before McClellan was ready to unleash a spectacular hurricane of artillery fire on Yorktown, Johnston pulled his army back toward Richmond.[12]

Johnston fought a small-scale rearguard action at Williamsburg, retreated eastward along the Williamsburg Road, and crossed the Chickahominy River at Bottoms Bridge, only twelve miles east of Richmond. The naval yard at

Norfolk fell to a federal expedition, and the now-homeless Confederate ironclad *Virginia* had to be blown up, which Lee thought "produced such profound sensation that all personal Considerations are Smothered." Johnston's army, arranged informally in three divisions and reduced to no more than 55,000 men, with a minuscule brigade of cavalry under Lee's onetime favorite, J. E. B. Stuart, and fifty-six pieces of artillery, distributed itself along Richmond's poorly improved fortifications for what could only have seemed to any onlooker as a last stand. Relentless spring rains "and constant use had churned" the roads "into liquid red mud" and turned the fields into morasses. But McClellan's Army of the Potomac relentlessly oozed eastward, trailing the retreating Confederates toward the Chickahominy River crossings.

In Richmond, "the anxiety of all classes . . . is now intense. . . . Even General Lee does not escape animadversion, and the President is the subject of the most bitter maledictions." Demoralized stragglers, "hungry and worn," trailed into the city, threw "themselves on cellar doors and sidewalks, [and] slept heavily, regardless of curious starers that collected around every group." The panicked Virginia state legislature passed defiant resolutions about fighting "to the last extremity," even as Confederate government officials began boxing up papers in crates marked "Lynchburg" and "timid persons . . . began to convert every thing into cash at ruinous rates of discount." Jefferson Davis, unhappy with Johnston's decision, called out newly conscripted recruits from "camps of instruction" in North Carolina. At the other extreme, Davis's brother Joseph urged him to "constantly think of your exposed condition" and at least send the Confederate president's wife "& the children to the interior." (Davis at last relented and sent them to North Carolina on May 6.)[13]

Lee begged Mary to do likewise, except that Mary's journey brought her closer to Richmond instead of away from it. Still situated at Rooney's home at White House ("a small, neat cottage of modern style, with gothic windows, pointed gables and little balustrades"), Mary ignored her husband's certainty that White House was too conveniently situated with a wharf on the Pamunkey for the Federals not to occupy it as a supply hub, and Lee predicted as early as April 4 that they "will land at the White House." Nevertheless, Mary dallied there until May 11, when a federal transport tied up at the wharf. She then moved to a less conspicuous house on a neighboring plantation, Criss Cross, with Annie and Mildred. But Union soldiers followed her there, too. A week later, federal cavalry searched Criss Cross, and although she was assured that she would be "properly protected," one Union surgeon did not find "our reception . . . very gracious." She did not hesitate to defiantly remind "the General in Command" that "all the plate & other valuables have long since been removed to Richmond & are now beyond the reach of Northern marauders," so there was nothing to satisfy their larcenous impulses. But the real pinch she felt was the loss of the White House slaves, "either by going to the enemy, or by staying home idle, & in quiet rebellion."

Even more annoying to Mary, fugitive slaves from other plantations found their way to Union shelter at White House, and one Philadelphia reporter noticed that they were exchanging their cheap master-issued clothing for Union uniforms, "some of them completely, others partially," so that "the slaves of the rebel Lee are much better clothed now than when he was here to look after their wants." Despite the futile raging of Rooney's overseer that "he would cut them to pieces, the slaves . . . now all obey everything a soldier tells them" and supplied the occupiers with "corn cake, eggs, fresh herring, & salmon." No one was dreaming any longer about the promised emancipation still waiting in the execution of G.W.P.'s will. "They felt, on the arrival of the Union Army, that their chains were broken."

Restlessly, and despite her crippling arthritis, Mary moved again, this time to Edmund Ruffin's plantation, Marlbourne, until that, too, was occupied. There were rumors that "Mary Lee and two of her daughters have been captured by the Yankees and are held as hostages for two Federal Officers." But Mary was only "captured" because she had nowhere else to go, and at length Robert arranged, under a flag of truce, for Mary and her two daughters to be escorted to McClellan's headquarters, and thence through the federal lines to Richmond and her husband.[14]

No one should have interpreted this as a signal of defeat on Lee's part. In mid-May, even as Davis suspected that "Richmond was to be given up without a battle" by Johnston, Lee waved away any notion of more retreats. "Richmond must not be given up—it shall not be given up," he protested with "deep emotion." As he tracked the Army of the Potomac's movements up the peninsula, he urged Joe Johnston to pay attention to the disruption McClellan would likely experience as he tried to cross the rain-swollen Chickahominy. "Should his march be across the Chickahominy his passage between that river and the James may furnish you with an opportunity," he wrote on May 17. And in case Johnston had any hesitation about numbers, Lee labored fiercely to draw away coastal garrisons from the Carolinas and organize the new legions of conscripts until Johnston had as many as 94,000 men ready, in at least some fashion or other, for duty around Richmond. McClellan proceeded to oblige both of them on May 30 by crossing the Chickahominy with two of his corps, the Third and Fourth (both of them commanded by former Lee associates, Erasmus Keyes and Samuel Heintzelman), and splitting an existing corps to create the Fifth Corps (which McClellan placed under the command of his political favorite, Fitz-John Porter). While the Third and Fourth Corps crossed the Chickahominy, the remaining three corps of

McClellan's army sat on the north side of the river, waiting to join hands with Irvin McDowell's corps as it moved down from Fredericksburg.

The Chickahominy was normally a sluggish, swampy ooze that eventually fed into the James River. But it was now swollen with spring rain, so if Johnston moved quickly, before McDowell arrived and the other three federal corps could cross the Chickahominy, he could attack and crush the Third and Fourth Corps on the south side of the river and then turn with every advantage to the destruction of the remainder. "The flood of the Chickahominy would be at its height," Johnston remembered, "and the two parts of the Federal army completely separated by it." But Johnston's planning for the blow was clumsy. He alternated between plans to attack the two isolated corps of Keyes and Heintzelman on May 31 and wondering whether he ought to strike the three federal corps on the north side of the river, and only changed his mind back to attacking Keyes and Heintzelman when he learned that McDowell's corps had been recalled to Fredericksburg. Even Lee now had forebodings, holding Johnston's hand "a long time" and admonishing "him to take care of his life."

Lee's intuitions were true to the mark. Johnston's divisions—commanded by Magruder, James Longstreet, and Daniel Harvey Hill—nearly managed to come disastrously apart as they sloshed over the soggy bottomlands toward Keyes's Fourth Corps near the crossroads of Seven Pines. But Johnston's attack carried itself over the Federals' defenses by sheer momentum, and by the end of the day the Confederates could reasonably have been said to have won something of a victory. Then, as darkness fell, Johnston was wounded, first by a spent bullet in the shoulder and then by splinters from an exploding shell that hit him in the chest and leg, "breaking three of his ribs" and bringing him to the ground. Johnston would survive, but his wounds would put him out of action until mid-November. His second-in-command, Lee's old engineering subaltern Gustavus W. Smith, was so overwhelmed by the responsibility thrust on him that the next day reinforcements from McClellan's Second Corps forced the Confederates to hand back what little they had won.

Jefferson Davis, who rode out from Richmond to observe the battle, had no intention of allowing Smith to take over the defense of the city. The next day, June 1, Davis played the last hand he had in the game. "The unfortunate casualty which has deprived the army in front of Richmond of its immediate commander, General Johnston, renders it necessary to interfere temporarily with the duties to which you were assigned in connection with the general service," Davis wrote in orders to Lee. "You will assume command of the armies in Eastern Virginia and in North Carolina, and give such orders as may be needful and proper."[15]

By the beginning of June 1862, Lee had acquired much of the appearance he would carry through the war. Now at age fifty-five, he was still "an unusually handsome man" and struck Moxley Sorrel, serving as one of James Longstreet's division staffers, as a "noble, unostentatious figure." His uniform pattern was simple: "My coat is of grey, of the regulation style and pattern, and my pants of dark blue . . . partly hid by my long boots." The coat was actually little different from any "gray sack coat with side pockets" worn by "a business man in cities," and in the Carolinas "his dress bore no marks of his rank, and hardly indicated even that he was a military man." His collar insignia were even more curious. Confederate uniform regulations allowed general officers to wear three embroidered gold stars, surrounded by a wreath, with gold braiding on the coat sleeves. Yet, from the first, Lee wore only the three stars—the insignia of a colonel—and kept that pattern in every photograph taken of him during the war, from 1863 onward. Any question about this peculiarity was waved away with an appropriate self-deprecation. "Oh, I do not care for display. And the truth is, that the rank of colonel is about as high as I ever ought to have gotten."

Perhaps: or else, the unadorned stars represented the rank he had last achieved in the old Army, and he did not want anyone assuming he had gone south merely to get a general's wreath. He was even more self-deprecating about "my ugly face." He was again "clean-shaven, except a closely-trimmed mustache which gave a touch of firmness to the well-shaped mouth," having shaved off the beard he had grown in western Virginia and the Carolinas. But in the ensuing weeks we would grow another beard "as stiff and wiry as the teeth of a card." He never regarded it as permanent. When one of Mary's relatives urged him to "take it off as soon as the war is over," Lee agreed: "When the war is over, my dear L., she may take my beard off, and my head with it, if she chooses." No wonder, he playfully surmised, "our enemies . . . shoot at it whenever visible to them . . . so unattractive is it."[16]

They had not, at least, shot at him at Seven Pines, even though (like Davis) Lee rode out to observe the battle and met the wounded Johnston as his old classmate was carried to the rear. The next morning, with Davis's authorization, Lee issued his first order, assuming direct command of a field army for the first time in his life. He expected "the cordial support of every officer and man" in Johnston's army, and he continued the use of the name Johnston had given to the army in mid-March—the Army of Northern Virginia. All the same, he did not come to this command without some very different ideas of what he wanted to do, and primary among them was his refusal even to consider the abandonment of Richmond. "He frequently spoke . . . to the effect that if the siege of Richmond were once undertaken by an army too strong to be beaten off, the fall of the place would be inevitable." And with it, the Confederacy itself might as well be given up. If "the Confederate army retired from that region" and fell back "towards the North Carolina Line," mused Charles Marshall, "the whole Southern border of the United States . . . would have been relieved of serious apprehension," and that would have released all of the federal troops committed to the Washington garrison "for aggressive movements against us." Although Virginia was only one of the eleven breakaway states that formed the Confederacy, it had nearly 20 percent of the Confederacy's white population and 17 percent of its banking capital and produced a third of its industrial goods and 40 percent of its wheat. Richmond held the Confederacy's principal "depots and arsenals . . . and through Richmond" Lee's army "had its chief means of access to sources of supply further south."[17]

That was the message he impressed on Johnston's division commanders when he summoned them to a meeting at a farmhouse on the Nine Mile Road, a short distance from Seven Pines. Their first talk was, given the disparity in the numbers between the Confederates and the Army of the Potomac, about abandoning the Army of Northern Virginia's current position "for one nearer Richmond which was considered more defensible." This Lee dismissed out of hand. He was "determined to hold the position," and he waved away all talk about McClellan's superior numbers. "Stop, stop," Lee erupted. "If you go to ciphering, we are whipped beforehand." Rather than more retreating, "Genl. Lee expressed the determination to try and wipe the enemy out when he again meets them."

To do so, however, required four actions from Lee. First, he needed to know the general topography of the Chickahominy bottomlands, and for that he dispatched the Army's chief engineer, Walter Stevens, to survey "the country in the vicinity of the line which our army now occupies, with a view to ascertaining the best position in which we may fight a battle." Second, once he had a clearer idea of the Chickahominy region, he summoned the "jovial, rollicking" J. E. B. Stuart and dispatched his twelve hundred cavalrymen (which included at this moment Rooney and his rambunctious nephew Fitzhugh Lee) on a raid behind McClellan's right-flank corps on the north side of the Chickahominy to determine how well supported the Federals might be there. Stuart not only discovered the Army of the Potomac's Fifth Corps dangling unconcernedly beyond the Chickahominy, still expecting the arrival of McDowell's corps from Fredericksburg, but managed to turn his raid into a mad race around the entire Army of the Potomac, returning unscathed to Richmond three days later.

"The achievement of General Stuart," exulted the Richmond *Dispatch,* "seems to have been one of the most brilliant of the war," and even Fitzhugh Lee chuckled at the prospect of Confederate cavalry transformed into "a noble

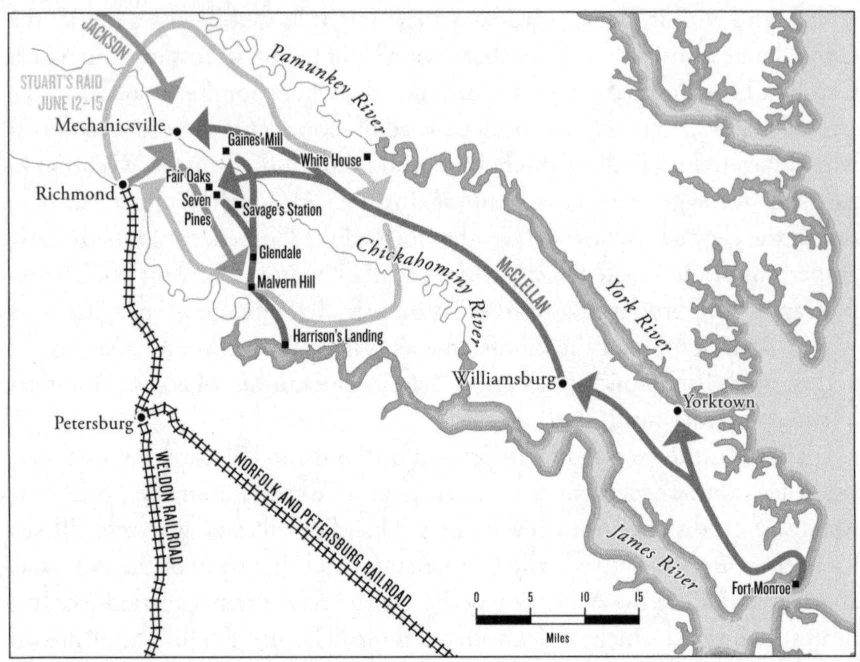

band of circuit-riders." Robert Lee was more low-key. Writing to Rooney's wife, Charlotte, he gently deplored Stuart's tendency to deal "in the flowering style." But the raid would have the strategic benefit of forcing McClellan to siphon off more troops to guard his rear-echelon communications and supply depots.[18]

Anyway, he added, Stuart "was a good soldier," and getting good soldiers into place was his third task. Lee swiftly retired Gustavus Smith and dissolved his division while reshuffling thirty regiments into new commands, reorganizing his artillery, and diverting 17,000 more men from garrisons as far away as the Carolinas. He added two brigades to the division of a testy, sparrowlike Virginia major general named Ambrose Powell Hill, added yet another brigade to the division commanded by James Longstreet, and restructured the division of the slow-footed John Bankhead Magruder. All told, he would now have six divisions at his disposal, close to 92,000 men. He also rearranged and expanded his staff, bringing on board Robert Chilton, whom he had known from Texas days, to serve as chief of staff, and A. P. Mason as his adjutant general. But his most monumental decision concerned a Confederate general with whom he had only so far communicated at a distance—Thomas Jonathan Jackson.

No more unlikely pairing of Civil War commanders would come to pass than Jackson and Lee. Born in 1824 by the West Fork River in western Virginia, Jackson belonged to the rough-hewn, self-made Scots-Irish of the western mountains, and he acquired in his twenties a deeply tinged Presbyterian Calvinism that stood at a substantial distance from Lee's polite Low Church Episcopalianism. Jackson, observed one officer, "has no social graces but infinite earnestness" and "belongs to the class from which Cromwell's regiment was made." Unlike Lee, Jackson struggled through West Point, graduating seventeenth in the class of 1846. Commissioned just in time to see action in the Mexican War, he commanded a battery section on the causeway to Chapultepec and won a brevet promotion to major. But he was also dour of temperament, strangely hypochondriac, and so prone to quarrel with his superiors that in 1851 he left the Army and joined the faculty of the Virginia Military Institute as an instructor in "natural and experimental philosophy." There, he became known as the most awkward and least liked of the VMI faculty; to other officers, he could seem as "crazy as a March hare." With Virginia's secession, Jackson was ordered to take charge of Harpers Ferry and within a few weeks found himself commanding a brigade of Virginians. He held his brigade so firmly in place at Bull Run that he won the enduring nickname *Stonewall,* and in the fall of 1861 he was handed the responsibility of keeping the Shenandoah Valley from being overrun by the same federal forces that had already occupied western Virginia.[19]

Lee's earliest notice of Jackson was not complimentary: in May 1861, he ordered Jackson to pull back from the Maryland shore of the Potomac to avoid antagonizing Marylanders. A year later, all that had changed. In January 1862, Jackson launched an unsuccessful but aggressive campaign to recapture northwestern Virginia and in March was forced to abandon the lower end of the Shenandoah after a botched battle with Union forces at Kernstown. Despite the lost ground, Jackson never stopped peppering Richmond with plans for more offensive maneuvers in the valley, something that caught Lee's eye as a refreshing change from the helplessness and indifference that seemed to prevail in other Confederate councils. Lee began shipping him modest reinforcements, and in mid-April he urged Jackson to move down the valley to induce McDowell to remain immobile at Fredericksburg.

Despite having fewer than 20,000 men on hand, Jackson whirled into action, turning back one federal column on May 8 and lunging down the valley and overrunning Front Royal on May 23 and forcing the Federals to abandon Winchester and the rest of the lower valley on May 25. Jackson even turned over once more the idea of crossing the Potomac. But the news that fresh federal troops were closing in behind him caused him to break off any advance, elude his pursuers, and then turn and defeat not one but two attacking forces, under John Charles Frémont and James Shields, at Port Republic on June 8–9. Jackson's rule was "always mystify, mislead, and surprise the enemy, if possible; and"—borrowing a leaf from the Mexico City campaign—"when you strike and overcome him, never let up in pursuit so long as your men have the strength to follow; for an army routed, if hotly pursued, becomes panic-stricken, and can then be destroyed by half their number." The rule worked. Stung with embarrassment, the Lincoln administration suspended further reinforcements for McClellan on the peninsula and pulled Irvin McDowell's corps away from Fredericksburg to become the nucleus of a new federal army that would clear Jackson from the valley. Which was exactly what Lee had hoped for, because McClellan would thus be left on the peninsula, looking for an appearance from McDowell that would never come.[20]

What refreshed Lee even more was that Jackson's aggressiveness was not limited to the valley. Using Alexander Boteler (the former federal congressman who had witnessed Lee's capture of Brown at Harpers Ferry) as a back channel, Jackson assured Lee that "with God's blessing" he "will be able to baffle the enemy's plans here with my present force." But if there was some way "my command can be gotten up to 40,000 men a movement may be made beyond the Potomac, which will soon raise the siege of Richmond and transfer this campaign from the banks of the James to those of the Susquehanna."

This was music to Lee's ears, which had had their fill of indifference and whining about the burdens of the war. (When plantation owners on the south side of the James River complained about "impressment" details sent out to confiscate their grain for the Army of Northern Virginia, Lee unsympathetically replied that while he was "opposed to the whole system of impressment," the best way to avoid it was to "do all in your power to encourage the production of subsistence by the farmers.") To win the war, the Confederacy would have to strike as quickly and as hard as it could, catching the Northern behemoth in the early rounds of the fight and scoring a surprise knockout before the North's full strength could be brought to bear.

Stonewall had said much the same thing: "We cannot stand a long war . . . a protracted struggle would wear the South out." Jackson "believed that we had but one hope, and that was to press the Federals at every point, blindly, madly, furiously." Lee could not have agreed more. "After much reflection," Lee wrote to Jefferson Davis on June 5, "I think if it was possible to reinforce Jackson strongly, it would change the character of the war." The place to do that would be on Northern soil, where a Southern army on the loose could so demoralize Northern political will that the voters and the politicians would compel Lincoln to open negotiations with the Confederacy. "Jackson could in that event cross Maryland into Pennsylvania"; at the very least "it would call all the enemy from our Southern coast & liberate those states."[21]

Here be rules. I know but one—
To dash against mine enemy and to win.

But Lee could not even begin to make such plans while McClellan was on his doorstep. "He must help me to drive these people away from Richmond first," Lee told Boteler. Lee could not do that, however, until he was certain he had created a sufficiently deep cordon of defensive works protecting Richmond's east face. To this "line of earthworks around the city of Richmond," Lee devoted "immense care and labor." And so, while Jackson in the valley and Stuart on his raid garnered jubilant praise from newly ebullient Virginians, Lee appeared to be doing nothing but directing engineering operations of the sort he had conducted in the Carolinas, creating a "line of earthworks . . . extending from the Chickahominy . . . across the Charles City Road and beyond." This earned a swift and contemptuous backlash, especially when Lee insisted that white soldiers as well as the usual legions of enslaved blacks be issued picks and shovels. He waved away the complaints. "Our people are opposed to work," Lee wrote to Davis. "All ridicule & resist it." Yet "it is the very means by which McClellan has & is advancing." But the complaints persisted. Charles Marshall heard mutterings that "General Lee was merely an engineer, and that the troops under him would be more familiar with a spade than a musket," and Moxley Sorrel heard "some in the army . . . speak of him as the 'King of Spades' who would never allow us to show fighting."[22]

The civilians joined in, forgetting (if they ever knew) the engineer who had crossed and recrossed the *pedregal.* Edward Porter Alexander, who had been on Johnston's staff, read wild railings in the *Richmond Examiner* that "spades and shovels were the only implements Gen. Lee knew anything about." "Gen. Lee takes command in person," complained Catherine Edmondston in her diary. "I do not much like him, he 'falls back' too much," and his apparent fondness for entrenchments earned him the derisory nickname "old-stick-in-the-mud." (Across the lines, George McClellan dismissed Lee in the same way, writing to Lincoln that Lee is "personally brave" but "is likely to be timid & irresolute in action.") Porter Alexander was tempted to join the naysayers, until one of Jefferson Davis's staffers, Joseph Ives, stopped him and prophesied, "Alexander, if there is one man in either army, Federal or Confederate, who is, head & shoulders, far above every other one in either army in audacity that man is Gen. Lee, and you will very soon have lived to see it. Lee is audacity personified."

Audacity, yes, but always audacity by calculation, not impulse. Audacity, because there was no other solution. So, Lee watched as McClellan licked his wounds from Seven Pines, brought up ponderous siege artillery, and did nothing to secure the dangling federal right flank beyond the Chickahominy. On the day Stuart returned from his raid, Lee ordered Stonewall Jackson to begin moving his troops out of the valley, being "careful to guard from friends and foes your purpose and your intention of personally leaving the Valley" so that he could fall without warning on the unguarded Federals from behind. It worked better than he could have imagined. "There are some vague rumors about the approach of Stonewall Jackson's army," wrote John B. Jones in his diary, "but no one knows anything about it, and but few believe it." They should have. One week later, on Monday afternoon, June 23, Jackson walked in the front door of Lee's headquarters on the Nine Mile Road.[23]

CHAPTER TWELVE

The Savior of Richmond

By the time Jackson arrived, Lee already had his plan in readiness. He assembled his division commanders, now including Jackson, and "told us he had determined to attack the federal right wing" on the north side of the Chickahominy. To do this, he would have Jackson's division, assisted by Powell Hill's division, fall on the Army of the Potomac's unprepared flank above the Chickahominy, while Longstreet's and Daniel Harvey Hill's divisions crossed the Chickahominy and hit the Federals from in front, at Mechanicsville. The Army of Northern Virginia's remaining six divisions would hold the Richmond defensive lines, with Magruder's and Benjamin Huger's divisions making "such demonstrations" as to distract the attention of McClellan and the rest of the Army of the Potomac. At best, the surprised Federals would simply abandon their hold north of the Chickahominy and regroup somehow; even the most minimal achievement north of the Chickahominy would force McClellan to bend his right flank backward, to shield the supply bases on the York and Pamunkey Rivers that Stuart had discovered to be unprotected. Either way, Lee's plan would wrench the entire Army of the Potomac back from Richmond.[1]

And then, in what would become one of Lee's most characteristic gestures in command, he "said he would retire to another room to attend to some office work, and would leave us to arrange the details among ourselves." He did not intend to manage the battle over the shoulders of his division commanders. As he later explained to the Prussian military observer Justus Scheibert, he would "plan and work with all my might to bring the troops to the right place and at the right time," but from that moment "it is my generals' turn to perform their duty." (This was an old Napoleonic dictum, and it had picked up force in the North Italian War of 1859, when the Austrian army had tried to maneuver en masse and failed to bring more than a fraction of its strength to bear at Solferino; Scheibert's master, Helmuth von Moltke, would use this principle to devastating effect in the Austro-Prussian War in 1866.)

This risked a great deal on the competence of his division commanders, a quality that had not been noticeable in the Army of Northern Virginia to this point. Even with the preliminary work of Walter Stevens, Lee's staff lacked "accurate maps . . . of the country for miles around Richmond" and had only the dimmest ideas of "every approach to that city likely to be attempted by the enemy." Daniel Harvey Hill was issued a map by Stevens with all the details "in regard to everything within our lines," but only "a red line" to mark the north side of the Chickahominy. But Lee had done enough reorganizing to convince himself that the Army might be ready after all, and the addition of Jackson, who had operated magnificently on his own initiative in the valley, seemed to be the clinching detail. Written orders, confirming these directions, went out from Lee's chief of staff, Chilton, the next day.[2]

Even so, the wheels nearly came off, and much of the blame for it belonged to Jackson. Exhausted by the long marches from the valley, Jackson was not ready to launch his attack until June 26, by which time McClellan had become suspicious that something was up and began gingerly skirmishing along the Richmond entrenchments. Jackson's only communication with Powell Hill arrived that morning, to say that he was still eight miles away, and by three o'clock, anxiously assuming that Jackson should be in position by that point, Hill and his division crossed the Chickahominy and struck the federal Fifth Corps at Mechanicsville. Fearful that Hill had sprung the trap too early and would allow himself to be repulsed and Jackson isolated, Lee became "restless with the look of a man with fever," with "necktie or cravat" askew. He decided "to allow the attack" on Mechanicsville "to proceed, in order to prevent troops being moved from it against Jackson." But Jackson never appeared, and Hill's attack went in, head down, and was in short order hacked to pieces, and the Army of Northern Virginia had little to show for its long-planned assault on the twenty-sixth beyond 1,400 dead and wounded.[3]

This should have gone down as a sharp defeat for Lee. Yet the attack caught the Federals off balance, and during the night of June 26–27 the Union Fifth Corps fell back to a new line east of Gaines' Mill. Rumors of Jackson's approach alarmed McClellan, who imagined that some innumerable host was about to swallow up his entire right flank. He ordered the destruction of his supply points and inched the entire Army of the Potomac down toward a safer position on the James River, where federal gunboats could provide shelter.

All the while, McClellan veered unsteadily between claims that the "victory of today [is] complete & against great odds" and accusations that he had lost his opportunity to capture Richmond "because my force was too small," the responsibility for which he shamelessly unloaded onto the Lincoln administration. "If I save this army now, I tell you plainly that I owe no thanks to you or to any other persons in Washington. You have done your best to sacrifice this army." Lee, of course, could not have known this, though what he could not have avoided knowing was that McClellan had more than enough troops on hand to launch his own counterattack directly on Richmond's slender defenses. Yet Jackson must certainly be close by, he believed, and the attack should certainly be renewed. On the morning of June 27, Lee sent Walter Taylor off to find Jackson and pull him into the battle, and then, following Longstreet's division, Lee finally found Jackson himself at Walnut Grove Church.[4]

Lee wasted no time on recriminations. He wanted a general attack at Gaines' Mill, with Jackson sweeping around the Federals' right flank to hit them from the rear. Powell Hill once again lunged to the attack; Jackson once again failed to appear. Late in the afternoon, Jackson finally materialized on the Old Cold Harbor Road, where Lee once again rode to meet him. "Ah, General, I am very glad to see you. I had hoped to be with you before." That was as much a rebuke as Lee had inclination for. "That fire is very heavy," Lee said, as the noise of Powell Hill's attack drifted around them. "Do you think your men can stand it?" The reply was precisely what Lee wanted to hear: "They can stand almost anything! They can stand that." And by sundown, Jackson was finally in action, and the Confederates had cracked the Union defenses, driving McClellan's troops beyond the Chickahominy.[5]

The fighting at Gaines' Mill on June 27 cost the Army of Northern Virginia even more dearly than Mechanicsville had, possibly as many as 8,000 killed and wounded. But the Army of the Potomac was now in full retreat toward the James, burning its vast supply dumps (and torching Rooney's home at White House) and ponderously slouching southward across the White Oak Swamp. "All their fortifications were carried in the most brilliant manner & turned against them," Mary Lee exulted. "We took Mechanicsville, the rail road & the telegraph wires & have pursued them for 15 miles."

There had been enough loss and disorganization caused by the two battles at Mechanicsville and Gaines' Mill to have justified a lengthy pause by the Confederates. But here a lesson learned from Mexico City surfaced, that of pressing a retreating enemy until it tumbled into disarray, for no matter how much dislocation an attacking army was suffering, a retreating enemy was bound to be in worse shape still. "The enemy was this morning driven from his strong position behind Beaver Dam Creek," Lee reported to Jefferson Davis on the twenty-seventh, "and finally after a severe context of five hours, entirely repulsed from the field." And with scarcely a pause, he added, we "shall renew the contest in the morning." That included the divisions of Benjamin Huger and John Magruder, who had been holding the Richmond fortifications. If McClellan "should diminish his forces in front of you or show a disposition to abandon his works you must press him."[6]

On the twenty-eighth, Lee sent Stuart on a second scout along the Pamunkey to determine where McClellan was heading, and the next day he informed Jefferson Davis that because McClellan was evacuating everything along the York and Pamunkey Rivers, "his only course" must be "to make for the James River & thus open communications with his gunboats and fleet." It might be possible, given McClellan's disorderly state, to force him into a full-scale battle that, in such a condition, could easily end in the surrounding and capitulation of most if not all of the Army of the Potomac. This time, he gave the lead in the pursuit to Magruder and Huger. But Magruder's approach was gingerly, and Jackson once more unaccountably failed to show up, and the result was a short and pointless firefight at Savage's Station between Magruder and the Union Second Corps (under old Edwin Sumner) on June 29.

Lee was bitterly disappointed, upbraiding Magruder for having "made so little progress today in the pursuit of the enemy. . . . We must lose no more time or he will escape us entirely." But the next day turned out no better: Magruder fought a stiffer action at Glendale, in the White Oak Swamp, but Jackson was again mysteriously absent, and Lee was left to lament, "Could the other commands have co-operated in the action the result would have proved most disastrous to the enemy." Still, the Army of the Potomac continued its tail-between-the-legs retreat. That was no consolation to Lee, who raged uncharacteristically that he could not find officers who would carry out the directives he gave or who could see the strategic opportunities he could see. "Yes," Lee replied disgustedly when one of Jackson's brigade commanders remarked that it looked as if McClellan might make it to the James, "he will get away because I cannot have my orders carried out."[7]

And now, as he had at Cheat Mountain, Lee allowed his frustration and temper to overwhelm his judgment. By July 1, McClellan had selected Harrison's Landing on the James River as the Army of the Potomac's new base, and to cover their concentration there, McClellan parked the Fourth and Fifth Corps, supported by several divisions from the Second, Third, and Sixth Corps, and eleven batteries of artillery on a large 130-foot-high plateau known as Malvern Hill (only a few miles above Shirley Plantation, where Lee's parents had been married), with their backs to the James and Union gunboats in the river.

Impatient at this formidable roadblock, Lee insisted on launching a frontal attack. He first threw Magruder's division at the Federals on Malvern Hill, then Huger's, and then Daniel Harvey Hill's. "General Lee expects you to advance rapidly," read the orders Lee dictated for Magruder. "Press forward your whole line." Which Magruder did. The result was suicidal. Fitz-John Porter, commanding the Fifth Corps, watched "the havoc made by the rapidly bursting shells from guns arranged so as to sweep any position far and near." Never before, wrote a Confederate artilleryman, "had we experienced such fire. Shell and shot seemed to pour over in one incessant stream." The senior surviving officer of the 3rd Alabama saw "6 men shot down while carrying the colors forward, the seventh bringing off the field after the fight a portion of the staff, the colors being literally cut to pieces."

Finally, when one of Jackson's brigades was ordered up, Stonewall intercepted them and asked their commander what they were doing. "I am going to charge those batteries, sir," he replied. "I guess you had better not try it," Jackson laconically replied, and that was the end of the attempts. The next day, McClellan abandoned Malvern Hill and squeezed into the safety of prepared defenses around Harrison's Landing. The series of battles that would become known simply as the Seven Days was over.[8]

"These brilliant results have cost us many brave men," Lee reminded the Army of Northern Virginia in a public letter on July 7. Taken together, the Army of the Potomac suffered 1,700 killed, 8,000 wounded, and 6,000 missing over the course of the Seven Days. Lee, in his report to Jefferson Davis, estimated Confederate casualties much higher: 2,800 killed, almost 14,000 wounded. McClellan issued a desperately self-congratulatory report to Abraham Lincoln, claiming that "we were not beaten in any conflict." But few believed him. Among several of his own generals, McClellan was scorned as "a political fool, and a military traitor, weak at both." Four days later, Lincoln himself came down to Harrison's Landing by steamboat to inspect the results and saw something very different, including McClellan's defiant resolve that he "was fighting for my country & the Union, not for abolition and the Republican party." The strength of McClellan's Democratic political allies forbade Lincoln to cashier McClellan on the spot. But from that point forward, Lincoln was determined that McClellan would never get another chance to command, and in August he hatched a scheme that drew away McClellan's army from under him, piece by piece, and transferred them to a new army he was creating in northern Virginia under a presumably more aggressive general from the west, John Pope.[9]

The Seven Days turned Richmond into a charnel house. The tavern keeper Gottfried Lange thought that "my pen is too weak to describe the great lamentation that had befallen the city." Sallie Putnam grieved that "we lived in one immense hospital," where in street after street "every family received the bodies of the wounded or dead" and "sickening odors filled the atmosphere, and soldiers' funerals were passing at every moment." Still, the capital had survived. Daniel Harvey Hill and his division "returned to our old camp near Richmond, with much cause for gratitude to the Author of all good for raising the siege of that city and crowning our arms with glorious success." And above all others, it was Robert E. Lee who floated upward to the very pinnacle of public adoration. "And now a great paean of gratitude went up to General Lee," recalled Constance Cary Harrison, "acclaimed as the savior of Richmond from destruction, the supreme leader to whom all eyes turned for protection from our foe." From now on, promised the *Richmond Dispatch,* "his name is as immortal as history can make a man."

And, as Lee might have feared, they at once began to congratulate themselves that all danger was past and all need for exertion was ended. "Lee has turned the tide, and I shall not be surprised if we have a long career of successes," rejoiced the War Department clerk John B. Jones. "I am inclined to believe that England and France, after having heard the true statements of the fights before Richmond, will certainly take some measure to put an end to this terrible war," one South Carolina soldier predicted.[10]

Lee gave himself little room for exuberance. He was lionized by Richmond society as "the head of the Lee family." But when one of Richmond's grandes dames flew "into ecstasies of pleasurable excitement" at the prospect of luring Lee to one of her soirees, "he remonstrated—said his tastes were of the simplest." He only wanted a "farm"—the farm fantasia again—"no end of cream and fresh butter—and fried chicken. Not one fried chicken or two—but unlimited fried chicken." Lee impressed the diary-keeping Mary Chesnut as "so fine looking" that "no fault" was "to be found if you hunted for one." And yet Chesnut found Lee's brother Smith the more entertaining decoration for capital drawing rooms; Robert's genteel facade seemed only to conceal some secret. "I know Smith Lee well," Chesnut wrote. "Can anybody say they know his brother? I doubt it. He looks so cold and quiet and grand."[11] *A marble model.*

Some of that aloofness was the product of circumstance: Lee had many other things on his mind. He personally reconnoitered the Harrison's Landing defenses in the same way he had once dared the *pedregal,* "in full sight of the Federal sharpshooters," utterly absorbed "in his work . . . with his glasses to his eyes." On July 7, he pulled the Army of Northern Virginia back from the James to the original fortifications his men had dug the month before and created a thirty-mile protective perimeter that ran from Mechanicsville to below the James. Although McClellan showed no sign "of either ascending or crossing the [James] river at present," Lee remained apprehensive that once the Army of the Potomac had recovered its wind, McClellan would "purpose to make a lodgment on the James River as a base for further operations," and if he shifted those operations to the south side of the James, he could threaten the vital bundle of railroad lines—the Weldon Railroad, the South Side Railroad, the Norfolk & Petersburg—that were the lifelines of the Confederate capital. The only way to prevent that, and to prevent yet another wearing fight for Richmond, was to turn his attention northward.

And quite conveniently, Major General John Pope and his newly created Army of Virginia provided exactly the target he needed.[12]

The Army of Virginia, some 45,000 strong, was actually an awkward welding of two Union forces in the Shenandoah that had failed to trap Stonewall Jackson, plus the redirected corps of Irvin McDowell. Pope's credentials for this command consisted of his energetic imposition of Union military occupation in Missouri, the capture of the Confederacy's Mississippi River obstructions at Island No. 10 and New Madrid in April, and—in stark contrast to McClellan—clear political sympathies with the Lincoln administration and the end of slavery. Lincoln brought him east in mid-June, took him to meet with old Winfield Scott at West Point, and then assigned him command of the Army of Virginia on June 26. This was followed on July 14 by Pope's sensational change-of-command order: "I have come to you from the West, where we have always seen the backs of our enemies." In a slap at McClellan, Pope dismissed talk of " 'taking strong positions and holding them,' of 'lines of retreat,' and of 'bases of supplies.' . . . The strongest position a soldier should desire to occupy is one from which he can most easily advance against the enemy."

This might have been taken only as a piece of amateurish bravado, had Pope not followed it up with a series of even more sensational general orders. On July 17, the federal Congress passed a sweeping new Confiscation Act, aimed at seizing Confederate-owned property (and especially *slave* property). It would not be very vigorously enforced, due mainly to Lincoln's skepticism about the new law's constitutionality. But that reluctance did not translate for John Pope. The next day, Pope issued a general order, directing his Army of Virginia to "subsist upon the country in which their operations are carried on," issuing only "vouchers" to the owners of seized property, "stating on their face that they will be payable at the conclusion of the war, upon sufficient testimony that such owners have been loyal citizens of the United States since the date of the vouchers." He then piled on still more injury by threatening, in a series of follow-up orders, that damages to "the lines of railroad and telegraph" or guerrilla ambushes along his lines of operations would be punished with fines, indemnities, house razings, arrests, and even "the extreme rigor of military law." He did not have to explain his intentions. "I have witnessed one continuous course of plundering, robbing, insulting women and destroying what could not be used," wrote an appalled Northern lieutenant to his father, a U.S. senator. "We are a disgrace to our country, and if we are whipped I shall not be sorry."[13]

Pope's orders appeared in the Richmond papers for Lee to read on July 24. Only fourteen months before, Robert E. Lee had struggled against making provocative gestures so as to leave open a path to reconciliation. But the grinding progress of the war was gradually devouring any sense of reluctance about the Confederate cause in Lee's emotions. "No civilized nation within my knowledge has ever carried on war as the United States government has against us," he complained in January (although he might well have asked himself what was to be expected in a case not of war between nations but of, as he had acknowledged to Smith Lee, *revolution*). Mary's forced pilgrimages throughout the spring, and then the destruction of White House, had only hardened his hostilities. Even his favorite horse, Grace Darling, which had been stabled at White House for safety, now disappeared and was "last seen bestrode by some yankee with her colt by her side." (Grace Darling's replacement would be a four-year-old gray saddlebred, sired by the popular Grey Eagle, with a "rapid, springy walk . . . high spirit, bold carriage and muscular strength" that Lee bought in the Carolinas and named Traveller.) "I could be better resigned to many things than that." But he would be greeted by worse tidings still: on June 30, his little grandson and namesake died, a refugee in Richmond with his mother, Charlotte.

Gradually, Lee's original dismay at secessionist nonsense was overwhelmed by his fury at Union depredations, and Pope's orders were a last straw, inflaming Lee's temper to another great outburst. "I want Pope to be suppressed," Lee wrote to Stonewall Jackson after reading Pope's orders in the papers. *Suppressed.* Not merely defeated, but ground heavily into the dirt. "The course indicated in his orders if the newspapers report them correctly cannot be permitted and will lead to retaliation on our part," and then the war would descend into a hellish spiral of all against all. Let this happen, Lee wrote in an unusual across-the-lines letter to the new Union general in chief, Henry Wager Halleck, and Pope and his officers will have placed themselves "in the position . . . of robbers and murderers" and Lee would "reluctantly be forced to the last resort of accepting the war on the terms chosen by our enemies." (It did nothing to improve his frame of mind to realize that his nephew Louis, Anne Marshall's son, had been assigned as a staff officer to the Army of Virginia. "I could forgive the latter for fighting against us," Lee wrote to Mildred, "if he had not joined with such a miscreant.")[14]

But what was he to suppress Pope *with*? On paper, the Army of Northern

Virginia should still have had 86,000 men in the ranks. But in the confusion of the Seven Days, wounded men were carted off to improvised hospitals without record, other men became lost and separated from their commands and attached to staff departments, and still others, "from the laxity of discipline in the army," simply slipped away, their thirst for war more than satisfied at Gaines' Mill, Glendale, and Malvern Hill. Due to so many "estrays," Lee could only count on finding some 57,000 men ready for any new consequences, and even then the governors of the Carolinas from whom he had stripped regiments and brigades at the beginning of the campaign were howling for the return of their troops. The Army of Northern Virginia's artillery had performed poorly during the campaign and needed reorganization. Staff work had been little better, and J. E. B. Stuart brought to Charles Venable a token of ominous things to come: a copy of Lee's orders during the Seven Days that had been picked up from the floor of a house at Gaines' Mill, lost by some careless staffer.

Once again, Lee began reorganizing. He found in the broad-shouldered Georgian James Longstreet a division commander with excellent managerial skills and an ability to muster his troops at the right place to deliver coordinated, concussive blows, and on August 19 he informally sorted the Army of Northern Virginia's divisions into two "commands," one under Jackson and the other under Longstreet. Although Jackson had performed well below the level he had demonstrated in the Shenandoah Valley, Lee had come to look on the chilly Presbyterian elder as one of his most valuable assets. (Jackson reciprocated the compliment: he told his political friend Boteler, "So great is my confidence in General Lee that I am willing to follow him blindfolded.") The same could not be said for the other division commanders in the Army of Northern Virginia, and any who failed to achieve the appropriate level of perfect aggressiveness soon found themselves heading elsewhere. Gustavus Smith was given command of the Richmond city militia, which very nearly amounted to doing nothing; Benjamin Huger went to a desk in the Confederate War Department; John Magruder was transferred west.[15]

Poised in Richmond between McClellan, inert on the James, and Pope north of the Rappahannock, Lee could not afford to do nothing, especially if doing nothing permitted Pope to effect some kind of junction with McClellan. Lee moved first, detaching Jackson and three divisions and sending them north to Gordonsville on July 19 to shield the vital junctions of the Virginia Central Railroad. Do "not attack the enemy's strong points," Lee began to counsel him, but then thought the better of it. Just as he had at their first meeting, Lee turned aside and let Jackson do the actual execution by his own lights. "I must now leave the matter to your reflection and good judgment," Lee added. "Make up your mind what is best to be done under all the circumstances which surround us, and let me hear the result at which you arrive."

He did not have to wait long. Pope lurched into action on August 2, sending one of his three corps across the Rappahannock to Culpeper. Jackson crossed the Rapidan River, below Culpeper, to challenge the Federals. He struck them at Cedar Mountain on August 9, hooking one of his divisions around the Federals' flank and forcing them to retreat. Jackson would gladly have chased them through Culpeper, had it not been for the fall of darkness. Federal prisoners being marched to the rear actually cheered Jackson in tribute as he passed them. Lee was even more delighted: "I congratulate you most heartily on the victory which God has granted you" and "hope your victory is but the precursor of others over our foe in that quarter."[16]

Which was what now seemed likely. On July 25, McClellan proposed to General in Chief Halleck the launch of a new Union campaign, this time along the south side of the James River and heading, as Lee dreaded, for Petersburg and its rail junctions. "I am sure you will agree with me," McClellan told Halleck, "that the true defence of Washington consists in a rapid and heavy blow given by this army upon Richmond." But the Lincoln administration wanted no more of McClellan's grand plans. On August 3, Halleck informed McClellan that "it is determined to withdraw your army from the Peninsula," and twelve days later the first elements of the Army of the Potomac began their march back down the peninsula to Fort Monroe.

"McClellan is really gone!" exulted Catherine Edmondston on August 20. "Evacuated his Camp & steamed down the River. . . . Not a tent or a transport in sight!" McClellan was almost the last man to leave the Harrison's Landing encampment, and one by one his corps were re-embarked on transports and then, one by one, sent off to join the Army of Virginia. By the time McClellan reached Alexandria, he was a general with only fragments of an army.[17]

Lee began to learn of McClellan's impending evacuation through newspapers and through "the report made" by an "English deserter of the embarkation of part of McClellan's army." The news started Lee in fast pursuit of John Pope, looking to strike an even larger blow at Pope before the pieces of McClellan's army could swell Pope's ranks. On August 13, Lee and Longstreet and the balance of the Army of Northern Virginia left Richmond for Gordonsville. "Lee has gone up the country to command in person," rejoiced John Jones, the War Department clerk. "Now let Lincoln beware, for there *is* danger."

Lee's initial plan had been to cross the Rapidan River by August 18 and trap Pope's three corps with their backs to the Rappahannock. But Pope, benefiting from the capture of a satchel of Confederate dispatches, now took fright that "all the Richmond force has been thrown in this direction," and he hurriedly recrossed to the north side of the Rappahannock, buoyed by Halleck's promise that the pieces of McClellan's army being called back from the peninsula would soon be on hand to reinforce him. Lee, riding with Longstreet to the top of Clark Mountain, with its lush views of the north side of the Rapidan, was irritated to discover that Pope was escaping his grasp. "From the summit," Longstreet remembered, they could see the rear of the Army of Virginia as it "approached the [Rappahannock] river and melted into the bright haze of the afternoon sun," and Lee, "with a deeply-drawn breath," put down his field binocular and said, "General, we little thought that the enemy would turn his back upon us thus early in the campaign."[18]

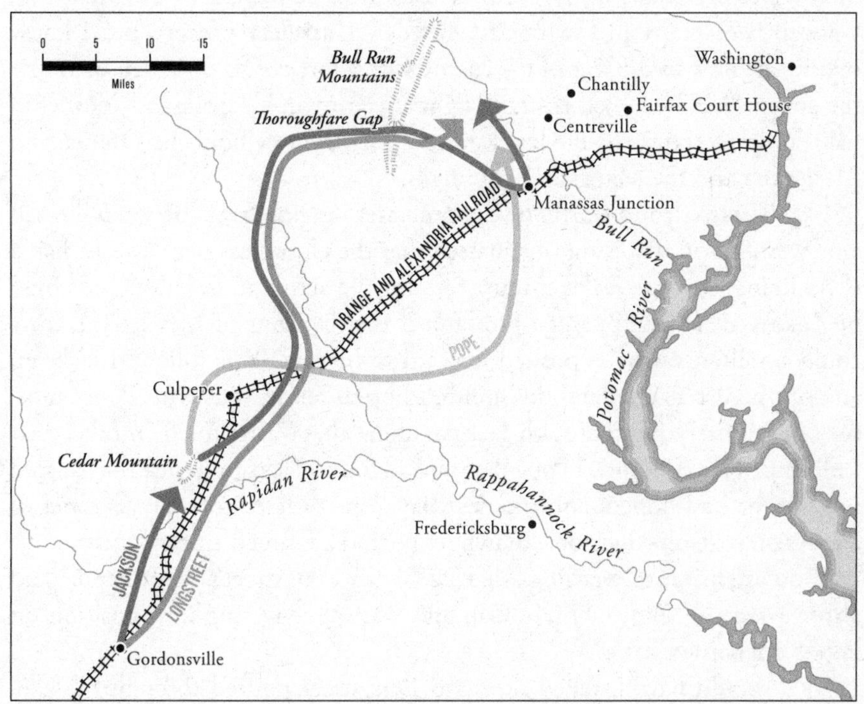

Lee did not let his disappointment fester. The Army of Northern Virginia crossed the Rapidan and then, as Pope continued to retreat, crossed the Rappahannock and moved northward, paralleling Pope's withdrawal and using the low range of the Bull Run Mountains as a shield. J. E. B. Stuart and his cavalry were sent on another winding raid, "cutting up their communications, trains, &c." and keeping Lee "informed of events." Stuart gleefully plundered Pope's own field headquarters at Catlett's Station and then tore apart the Orange and Alexandria Railroad at Bristoe Station on August 26, ranging the next day as near Washington as Fairfax Court House. (Rooney, riding with Stuart as the colonel of the 9th Virginia Cavalry, nearly captured his cousin Louis Marshall, "who escaped at the first onset, leaving his toddy untouched.")

Jackson, at virtually the same time, turned east through the Thoroughfare Gap and struck Pope's supply base at Manassas Junction, "where he allowed his troops a few hours to refresh themselves upon the abundant stores that had been captured." Exuberant rebel soldiers organized "details . . . from each company to get bacon and crackers, coffee, sugar, rice and everything else in the way of rations," recalled one of Jackson's veterans. "Long trains were switched off on the side tracks that contained clothing for Pope's army, all of which went up in smoke upon our evacuation." Jackson and his divisions then veered westward, toward the old Bull Run battlefield. "I can't tell what General Lee's plans are," wrote a Confederate artillery officer, "but I know that we are now in the rear of the enemy with a force of 50,000 men" and that the enemy "will be forced either to fight any army in his front and another in his rear, or to retreat to Fredericksburg . . . as we now hold the Orange and Alexandria and the Manassas Gap Roads."[19]

Embarrassed, and fearful of Confederates ranging freely between himself and Washington, Pope angrily guessed that the embarrassment at least had a silver lining, because Jackson must certainly be acting in isolation and could be destroyed if Pope pursued him and if the divisions of McClellan's army could simultaneously be pushed forward to his aid. Pope followed Jackson, and on August 28 a federal division heading to rendezvous with Pope stumbled into a nasty firefight with Jackson along the Warrenton Turnpike, near Bull Run. This convinced Pope that he had found Jackson in just the isolated position he had hoped, and the next day Pope ordered a ferocious series of attacks on Jackson's divisions, drawn up behind a railroad embankment. Pope paid no attention to warnings that Lee, with Longstreet's "command," had also cleared the Thoroughfare Gap and was maneuvering into position on Pope's unguarded flank.

He should have listened. Lee and Longstreet poured through the gap, and Lee's first inclination was "to engage as soon as practicable." But evening was coming on, and Longstreet preferred to "have all things in readiness at daylight for a good day's work." And that, in Lee's mind, was properly a matter for Longstreet to decide. Pope, on the other hand, confidently expected to mount a pursuit of Jackson on August 30. What he got instead was the irresistible descent of Longstreet's divisions onto his unsecured left. "General Longstreet is advancing; look out for and protect his left flank," Lee warned Jackson. But he needn't have worried. Longstreet smashed down on Pope like a hammer against Jackson's anvil. "I pushed my men forward in a pell-mell pursuit," wrote Longstreet, "and drove the enemy back, pursuing them until fully ten o'clock at night." Only a dogged rearguard stand by Pope's reserves allowed his Army of Virginia to escape almost total destruction.[20]

As it was, what became known as the Second Battle of Bull Run cost John Pope's Army of Virginia almost 14,000 casualties, plus the loss of thirty pieces of artillery. By 11:00 p.m. on August 30, the last of Pope's men crossed to the north bank of Bull Run; by the afternoon of September 1, they were streaming in disarray toward the Washington fortifications, and Jackson was urging his exhausted troops onward to Chantilly to cut them off. Only "one of the wildest rainstorms . . . ever witnessed" and a surprisingly spirited Union defense at Ox Hill prevented a complete collapse.[21]

"Gen. Lee has shown great Generalship and the greatest boldness," wrote the North Carolina brigadier Dorsey Pender after Second Bull Run. "There never was such a campaign, not even by Napoleon." And it was a marvelous victory, greater than First Bull Run, greater even than Cerro Gordo. Lee, however, had not always shown the best judgment about his own safety, any more than he had at the *pedregal* or Chapultepec. Charles Venable was unnerved, when Lee and his staff arrived at Groveton, on Jackson's right flank, to discover that Lee had gone out "on foot" to "Jackson's skirmish line" and nonchalantly reported afterward, "A sharpshooter came near Killing me just now." His cheek, Venable added, "had been grazed by the bullet." Others had not been so spared: the Army of Northern Virginia lost a thousand killed and more than five thousand wounded at Second Bull Run, and while this was less than half the damage inflicted on his Union opponents, it was still leaching away strength Lee could ill spare.

There were other losses draining his army's strength, too. Lee's soldiers had now been almost continually on the march since the end of June, outrunning their lines of supply and shedding stragglers in troops. The infantry suffered the most. "Many of our men are without shoes and all of them are very ragged," wrote Lafayette McLaws, one of Lee's new division commanders. Even soap disappeared. They were, claimed a reporter for a Philadelphia newspaper, such "a mass of . . . filthy, strong-smelling men" that "three of them in a room would make it unbearable." Worse still, Lee's quartermasters were compelled to haul "rations one hundred and fifty seven miles from Richmond," which meant that in too many cases the rations never arrived at all. "We have been marching for the last three days with nothing to eat . . . but corn and that not in abundance." So, although McLaws's division had missed Second Bull Run, almost half of his division disappeared anyway between July 20 and September 13, as absentees and wanderers rather than casualties. A sergeant in the 2nd Virginia could count only 23 of his company present for duty the day before Second Bull Run. "Riding off the road anywhere you can see parties of two & three & more settled in fence corners with green corn piled around & perhaps evidence of a meal from a stray hog or chicken." And the invisible division of black slaves who accompanied the Army's slave owners "were allowed to roam at will over the surrounding country" to find food.[22]

Yet Lee was determined to press on. Thirteen months before, the Confederacy had stood on much the same ground in northern Virginia and had done little afterward but congratulate itself. This was a mistake Lee was determined not to make a second time. The vast ring of fortifications McClellan had built around Washington gave no encouragement to the idea of besieging the federal capital. "He could do nothing more against the Yankees," he explained years later, "unless he attacked them in their fortifications around Washington, which he did not want to do." But he certainly could not stay where he was "from want of supplies and adequate transportation."

What his position did give Lee was the opening he had been hoping for since the spring, to cross the Potomac and carry the war onto Northern territory, where political disenchantment could be excited to the point that Northerners would demand an end to the fighting. He had "the possibility of ending the war and achieving the independence of this people by one short and brilliant stroke of genius, endurance, and courage." There is no indication that he had discussed this with Jefferson Davis, much less obtained Davis's sanction, and that posed a risk for Lee. Always haunting the background of his mind was the memory of what had been done so mercilessly to other soldiers he had admired so much—Gratiot, Scott—who stepped outside the boundaries drawn by the politicians. Even Pierre Beauregard, the victor of the first battle at Bull Run, had run afoul of Davis and found himself dispatched to military exile in the west, and had it not been for his wounding at Seven Pines, Joe Johnston's propensity for arguing with Davis might have led soon enough to the same result. Lee, by contrast, had deferred to Davis, cultivated Davis, and above all given Davis a deliverance on the peninsula that placed a certain amount of personal capital in Lee's hands, and he now proceeded to use it.

"The present seems to be the most propitious time since the commencement of the war for the Confederate Army to enter Maryland," Lee wrote to Davis on September 3. Both Pope's Army of Virginia and the rump of McClellan's Army of the Potomac "are much weakened and demoralized," and at the very least a move across the Potomac would "give material aid to Maryland and afford her an opportunity of throwing off the oppression to which she is now subject." He then followed with a second letter on September 4, gingerly introducing his real target: "I propose to enter Pennsylvania, unless you should deem it unadvisable upon political or other grounds." The midterm congressional elections in the North were only two months away, with other state elections scheduled even sooner. Even if he fought no battle, the prospect of a Confederate army operating unhindered on Northern soil might overthrow Lincoln's majorities in the federal Congress and force a peace.[23]

Lee had gauged his target well. Even Davis was now convinced of the need for the Army of Northern Virginia to "carry your standards beyond the outer boundaries of the Confederacy" and "wring from an unscrupulous foe the recognition of your birthright, community independence." Davis's first impulse was "to come on" and have "an interview with you . . . consulting upon all subjects of interest," but Lee quickly discouraged him and sent Walter Taylor to intercept him. There was no need for Davis to be with the Army, not to mention a good deal of residual apprehension at having politicians at his side. He spun the Army of Northern Virginia westward to Leesburg, and on September 5, Jackson's "command" splashed across the shallow fords of the Potomac at White's Ford, only twenty miles above Washington, followed by Longstreet on the seventh. Do "not be surprised to hear of our being in Philadelphia in less than three days," wrote an enthusiastic Dorsey Pender.

By the sixth, Lee was in Frederick, Maryland, and issued a proclamation to "the People of Maryland," urging them to join the Confederacy "in throwing off this foreign yoke, to enable you again to enjoy the inalienable rights of freemen . . . of which you have been despoiled." The response of the western Marylanders was decidedly mixed. This was not the same Maryland that, a year and a half before, had rioted over the passage of federal troops through Baltimore. "Some few of the people cheered us," wrote one Virginian, "but a large proportion of the people looked sullenly upon us." Passing through one Maryland town, a "Yankee school-marm" tried to annoy Lee by "singing in loud tones, 'The Star-spangled Banner.'" Lee merely "lifted his hat to her." But he candidly advised Davis not to "anticipate any general rising of the people in our behalf."

A larger surprise for Lee was the reunion of Pope's ill-used Army of Virginia with the remaining elements of George McClellan's Army of the Potomac, with McClellan himself once again in overall charge. Lee might have suspected that putting McClellan back in command violated every one of Abraham Lincoln's political instincts (privately, Lincoln suspected "that McC[lellan] wanted Pope defeated"). But Pope's mishandling of Second Bull Run made it impossible to continue the boastful westerner in charge, and the adulation of the Army of the Potomac for McClellan made anyone else but McClellan unacceptable. "He has acted badly in this matter," Lincoln complained to his secretary John Hay, "but we must use what tools we have."[24]

Not that McClellan's reappointment seriously bothered Lee. If anything pained him, it was a freak injury on the day after Second Bull Run, when Traveller bolted at a "sudden apparition" near the stone bridge that crossed Bull Run. Lee had been standing beside the horse, loosely holding the reins, and fell, spraining both wrists and breaking a small bone. For the next two weeks, his hands would have to be bandaged, his riding would be done in an ambulance, and he would not be "able to manage in pen and pencil" for himself. Beside that, McClellan seemed little more than a nuisance. "The hallucination that McClellan was not capable of serious work seemed to pervade our army," Longstreet admitted. And as far as Lee could see at Frederick, "the enemy are not moving in this direction, but continue to concentrate around Washington." Lee felt sure that McClellan, being "an able general but a very cautious one," would "not be prepared for offensive operations—or he will not think it so—for three or four weeks." Lee, meanwhile, intended to shift westward again, through the gaps of South Mountain, and "move in the direction" of "Hagerstown and Chambersburg" so that by the time McClellan got moving, the Army of Northern Virginia would "be on the Susquehanna."

To resupply his famished army in Pennsylvania, Lee would need to establish a direct route from Culpeper to the Shenandoah Valley, and then down the valley to the Potomac, and that required the evacuation or surrender of the federal garrison at Harpers Ferry. To his surprise, the federal garrisons in the lower Shenandoah, and especially at Harpers Ferry, refused to evacuate their exposed positions as the Confederates entered Maryland. "I had supposed," Lee explained, that by crossing the Potomac east of the mountains, "the enemy's forces . . . which had retired to Harper's Ferry . . . would retreat altogether from the State." They hadn't, and so on September 9 he had Robert Chilton, his chief of staff, draft a new campaign order, Special Orders No. 191, which established a new supply base at Winchester in the lower valley, then sent Longstreet's command on its way over South Mountain toward Hagerstown, and finally peeled off Jackson's command "to capture the enemy at Harper's Ferry and vicinity." Once Jackson had reduced Harpers Ferry, Lee would reunite his army and move north again. Far to the west, a reinvigorated Confederate army under Braxton Bragg was moving aggressively into Tennessee and Kentucky. Perhaps, with both of these initiatives in play, Lee began to think that "the present posture of affairs, in my opinion, places it in the power of the Confederate States to propose with propriety to that of the United States the recognition of our independence."[25]

Lee's burst of optimism was mercilessly short-lived. Over the course of just three days, McClellan set about providing a bulked-up garrison for the security of Washington, quietly dismissing Pope's senior officers, absorbing reinforcements commanded by his luxuriantly bewhiskered friend Ambrose

Burnside, and reintegrating the battered divisions and corps of the Army of Virginia with the Army of the Potomac, which he moved onto the Maryland roads in a sluggish and cautious pursuit of the Confederates. The Federals only reached Frederick by September 12. But the next morning, three soldiers from the 27th Indiana brought to their colonel a paper they had found in a field, wrapped around three cigars: it was a copy of Special Orders No. 191, and by noon it was in McClellan's hands, revealing Lee's overall plans. "Now I know what to do," he exclaimed. "I have all the plans of the rebels," McClellan jubilantly wired Lincoln, "and will catch them in their own trap."[26]

Exactly who lost Special Orders No. 191, or how, or when Lee realized that they were in McClellan's hands, has never been established with any certainty. (After the war, Lee insisted that one of J. E. B. Stuart's informants had passed the news of the Lost Orders through Stuart to Lee by the next day, which explained to Lee why McClellan was "pressing forward on the roads to Boonsborough" with such un-McClellan-like energy.) What was clear from September 13 onward was that McClellan knew where Lee's army was, and that it was in two large pieces that begged to be isolated and destroyed, in the same way Lee had nearly destroyed pieces of McClellan's army on the James River. By the afternoon of September 13, Union troops were already swarming toward the gaps in South Mountain—Fox's Gap, Crampton's Gap, and Turner's Gap—ready to pounce on Lee's unsuspecting rear guard at Boonsboro, and only frantic signaling by J. E. B. Stuart brought up enough of Daniel Harvey Hill's division to defend the gaps. Reinforced by Longstreet, the fighting for the gaps raged through the fourteenth, and under cover of darkness Lee ordered the gaps abandoned. "The day has gone against us," he concluded, "and this army will go by Sharpsburg"—due west from South Mountain, near the fords of the Potomac—"and cross the river." At one stroke, Lee's grand plans for an invasion of Pennsylvania and the end of the war appeared to be vanishing into smoke.[27]

But then, hard on the heels of that depressing order, came news from Jackson at Harpers Ferry: "Through God's blessings," Harpers Ferry had been successfully surrounded, "and I look to Him for complete success to-morrow." The next morning, the garrison surrendered, and Jackson promised that by leaving behind Powell Hill's division "until the prisoners and public property shall be disposed of," he could have his command on the road to Lee "so soon as they get their rations." Suddenly the ground shifted again. Harpers Ferry was less than twenty miles from Sharpsburg, and Jackson's reputation for hard, driving marching meant that Jackson might be able to rendezvous with Lee sometime on September 16.

"That is good news," Lee rejoiced when Jackson's courier arrived, "let it be announced to the troops," and staffers whipped Lee's troops into cheering

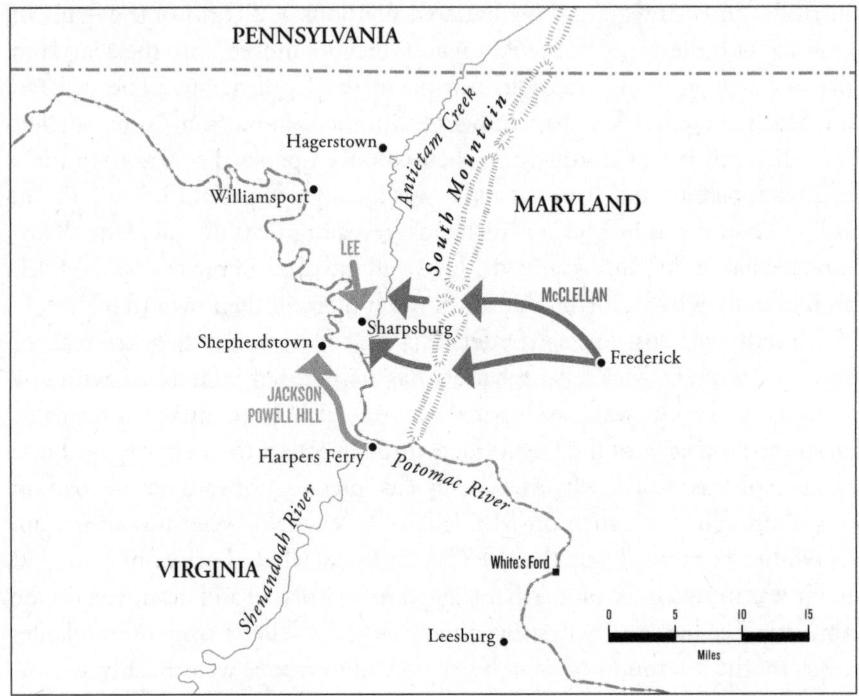

as they rode "at full gallop" from unit to unit. If McClellan took his usual time in squeezing through South Mountain, Lee might be able to have his whole army together after all, bluff McClellan into hesitation at Sharpsburg by making a determined stand on the hills overlooking the Antietam Creek, and perhaps even slip away northward to begin the chase into Pennsylvania yet again. "We will make our stand on those hills," Lee decided, and set up a temporary headquarters in "a dwelling-house on the edge of the town."

Just as Lee expected, McClellan and the Army of the Potomac now moved down into slow gear, completing his passage of the South Mountain gaps only on the morning of the sixteenth and not reaching the Antietam Creek until the afternoon. By then, Jackson's leading units were already crossing the Potomac, with Jackson himself cantering into the town of Sharpsburg to greet Lee. Lee had recovered from the wrist sprains sufficiently to be able to ride Traveller, but he still needed help to mount and an aide to lead Traveller by the bridle when he wanted to move.

"Anxious enough, no doubt he was," remarked one of Jackson's division commanders, "but there was nothing in his look or manner to indicate it. . . . If he had had a well-equipped army of a hundred thousand veterans at his back, he could not have appeared more composed and confident." Other Confederates were not so ebullient. "The route from Harper's Ferry" followed by Jackson was, remembered Walter Taylor, "strewed with foot-sore and weary men," and the dropouts reduced brigades to the size of regiments, and regiments to the dimensions "no stronger than a full company." "Lee's inferiority of force was too great to hope to do more than to fight a sort of drawn battle," wrote Porter Alexander. "Hard & incessant marching, & camp diseases aggravated by irregular diet, had greatly reduced his ranks & I don't think he mustered much if any over 40,000 men."[28]

By daybreak on the seventeenth, all but one of Lee's divisions had arrived at Sharpsburg, with the last of them, Powell Hill's division, on the road from Harpers Ferry just after sunup. Lee laid out his forces on a line running north to south, with Jackson's command covering the left flank (where thick stands of timber reached up from the cornfields around a small whitewashed church belonging to the Dunkers, a German pacifist sect). Longstreet's command extended Lee's line southward, hooking around a sunken farm lane that formed a natural entrenchment and extending down to the cemetery on the outskirts of Sharpsburg and a stone bridge that spanned the Antietam.

They did not have to wait long. By six o'clock, McClellan struck his first blow, hitting first from the north and slamming the door on any hope Lee had of slipping away toward Hagerstown and continuing toward Pennsylvania. McClellan began hammering Jackson's divisions with the Army of the Potomac's First and Twelfth Corps, even as Lee fed his new arrivals from Harpers Ferry into the fighting. Attack and counterattack raged through the cornfields, and McClellan sent yet another corps, the Second under Edwin Sumner, into the fighting. A courier brought Lee the grim tidings, but Lee merely listened impassively and counseled, "Don't be excited about it . . . re-inforcements are now rapidly approaching between Sharpsburg and the ford," and Lee himself would bring them "to his support." As indeed he did. The Federals had very nearly reached the Dunker church when Lee himself wheeled Lafayette McLaws's division into action and flung them backward.

The action then shifted, in piecemeal fashion, to the sunken lane in the center, where Lee now "rode along his lines on the right and centre" accompanied by Longstreet and Daniel Harvey Hill, gauging the wiriness of Confederate resistance. The results were not hopeful: after three hours and even more terrible slaughter, the Confederates abandoned the lane, and only an improvised line of Confederate artillery held off any further federal advance. Steadily, the life was being drained out of the Army of Northern Virginia, and just after noon McClellan's Ninth Corps (belonging to Ambrose Burnside) finally stormed the southernmost bridge across the Antietam and moved up onto the high ground opposite Sharpsburg—where Lee had virtually nothing left to oppose them, or to keep them from rolling up his battered line like

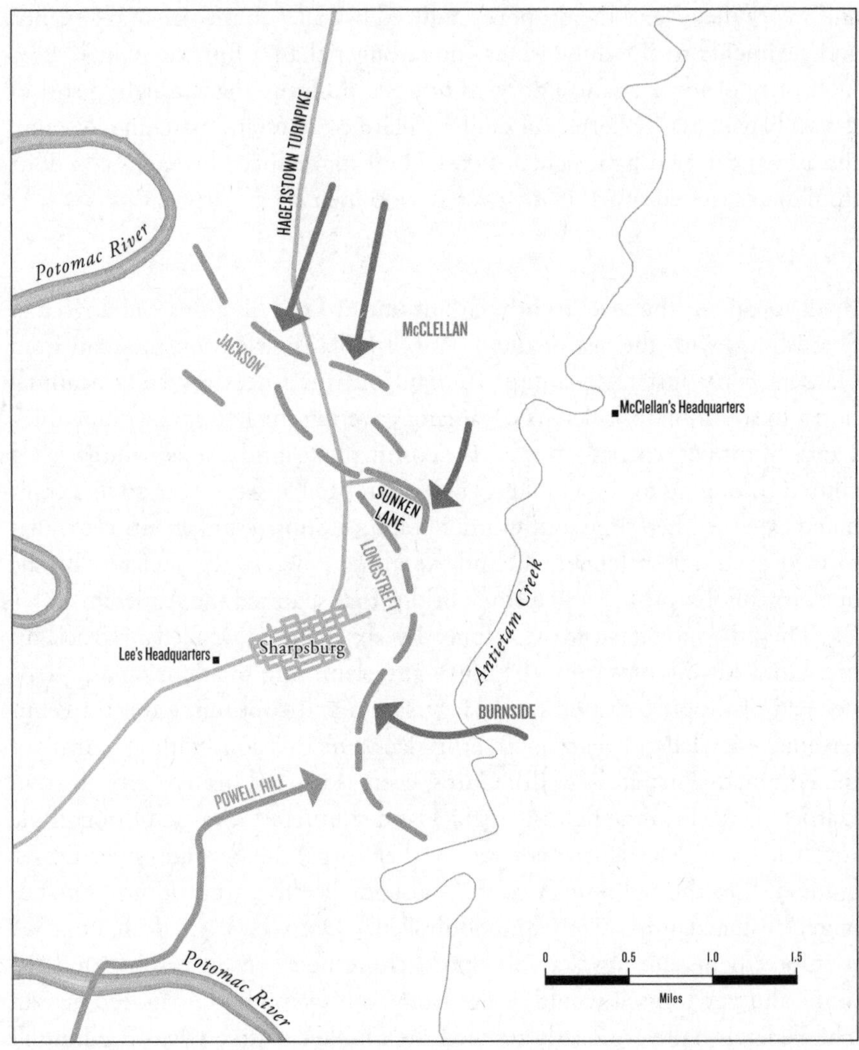

a carpet. Lee returned to the town, hoping somehow for word from Powell Hill, then rode over to "a little knoll near the road" between the town and the Potomac, where he could keep an eye open for Hill. Around him "and several of his staff" floated the wreckage of Confederate units and artillery batteries, one of them containing Lee's youngest son, Rob. At first, Lee failed to recognize his son, "his eyes passing over me without any sign of recognition." But "when he found out who I was," Rob was bold enough to ask his father, "General, are you going to send us in again?" (From almost anyone else in the nineteenth century, this would have been the opportunity for some classical exhortation to return on your shield or die fittingly and sweetly for your country; instead, a tired Lee merely replied, "Yes, my son, you all must do what you can to help drive these people back.")[29]

And then, at 2:30 p.m., deliverance. Lee caught sight, in the distance, of a dust-shrouded column moving up from the river. "What troops are those?" he asked a nearby artillery lieutenant, and the lieutenant obligingly offered Lee his telescope. Lee demurred, holding up his bandaged hands: "Can't use it. What troops are those?" The lieutenant now took his own look and reported, "They are flying the United States flag." No, Lee insisted, wrong direction. Over there: "What troops are those?" And then the reply: "They are flying the Virginia and Confederate flags." "It is A. P. Hill, from Harper's Ferry," Lee cried in relief.

Powell Hill found Lee beside the road and reported that his division was just now crossing the Potomac fords. He could not have arrived at a better moment for Lee, and at three o'clock, as Burnside confidently moved forward to begin the destruction of Lee's army, Hill's division struck Burnside's surprised Federals, sweeping them nearly back to the bridge. "We saw them advancing and supposed they were our men," wrote one Connecticut soldier, "but we soon found out the truth. Before we could form, they were upon us, and . . . our retreat was made in great confusion." At last, wrote Porter Alexander, "night put a welcome end to the bloody day." The Confederates had been "worn & fought to a perfect frazzle," but for the moment Lee and the Army of Northern Virginia were saved.[30]

CHAPTER THIRTEEN

It Is Well This Is So Terrible!

The most terrific battle that ever was fought on this continent has been going on all day near Sharpsburg," reported the *New-York Tribune,* and although it had "closed without a definite result," there were rumors that Lee and Longstreet had been killed, or that Longstreet and Powell Hill were prisoners, that "the ammunition and provisions of the Rebels have completely run out," and that everything "was favorable for a renewal of the fight in the morning."

In fact, Lee and Longstreet were quite alive, and Longstreet and Hill were not prisoners. But that was almost the only good news for the Army of Northern Virginia. Overall, Lee's army had suffered more than 2,100 killed and 10,000 wounded on September 17, approximately a third of his entire force, and that did not begin to account for the disorganization caused by holes torn in the command structure, from top to bottom, or from the sheer dislocation of battle itself. In Daniel Harvey Hill's small division, two brigadier generals were killed and three wounded; four regimental colonels were killed and eight wounded, while in the 4th North Carolina every officer was a casualty.

An hour after darkness fell on the battle, Lee called his senior officers to report to him on the road west from Sharpsburg, asking each of them in turn, "General, how is it on your part of the line?" None of the responses were encouraging. Daniel Harvey Hill bluntly told him, "My division is cut to pieces." The Texan John Bell Hood almost broke down. "I have no division," Hood faltered. "They are lying on the field where you sent them, sir." Jackson summed up the condition of his command, telling Lee that "he had had to contend against the greatest odds he had ever met" and had "lost a good many colonels killed, and several division or brigade commanders were dead or wounded, and his losses in the different commands had been terrible."

Longstreet arrived late, and in a flush of relief that Longstreet had not himself been a casualty, Lee, "coming to me very hurriedly for one of his dignified manner, threw his arms about my shoulders" and said, "Here comes my old war-horse just from the field he has done so much to save!" But Longstreet had no better comfort to offer him. The situation "was as bad as it could be; that he had lost terribly, and his lines had been barely held, and there was little better than a good skirmish line along his front." The Army of Northern Virginia, advised Longstreet, "should cross the Potomac before daylight."[1]

This was exactly what Lee did not want to hear. He had not come this far, and at this risk, without one last hope that the way northward could somehow be forced open. "I went into Maryland to give battle," Lee later explained, "and could I have kept Gen. McClellan in ignorance . . . a day or two longer I could have fought and crushed him." Even as his army sagged under the weight of the afternoon's blows, Lee had dared to query Jackson about the possibility of opening a counterattack on the right flank of the federal lines to dislodge them from the road north to Hagerstown. He would not give up the possibility now, either. "Gentlemen, we will not cross the Potomac to-night," Lee crisply informed his officers. "You will go to your respective commands, strengthen your lines; send two officers from each brigade towards the ford to collect your stragglers and get them up. Many others have come up. I have had the proper steps taken to collect all the men who are in the rear. If McClellan wants to fight in the morning, I will give him battle again. Go!" That night, the brief report he wrote to Jefferson Davis gave only the sketchiest description of the Antietam battle and closed with the bland assertion that they were "maintaining our ground."[2]

But McClellan showed nothing more than a flicker of interest in renewing the battle the next morning, and Lee did not challenge him. McClellan instead congratulated himself on having conducted "a masterpiece of art" on the seventeenth but wanted to wait for reinforcements to "make the [attack] a certain thing" before allowing the battle to "be renewed today." And when they did arrive, they seemed "too tired & too much diminished in numbers . . . to be able to do a great deal of work," and instead flags of truce went out to cover details of stretcher bearers trying to recover the wounded from both sides.

In the years after the war, a more ominous rumor bubbled up from the bloody froth at Antietam—that McClellan had used the truce to communicate by messenger with Lee, "proposing an interview between Lee and himself for the purpose . . . of arranging to end the Civil War by uniting their forces to march upon Washington and compel peace." It is hard to believe that Lee, so shy of political action, would ever have entertained such a proposition (although Longstreet would later say that "he was perfectly familiar with the McClellan letter incident"). But McClellan had already made it apparent that he considered the Lincoln administration the real problem in prolonging the war, and there had been rumors extending back to the Peninsula Campaign about unauthorized communications, under flags of truce, between McClellan's staff and the Confederate leadership. (A week after Antietam, Lincoln was so incensed by stories that McClellan "did not mean to gain any decisive victory but to keep things running on so that . . . the army might manage things to suit themselves" that he personally interrogated one of the sources of those stories, Major John Key, the brother of McClellan's adjutant, and cashiered him on the spot.)[3]

McClellan would not actually issue orders to renew an attack on Lee until later on the eighteenth and only scheduled any real movement for early on the nineteenth. By then, the Army of Northern Virginia was gone. Lee gradually concluded by early afternoon that "as we could not look for a material increase in strength . . . it was not thought prudent to wait" for McClellan to move, and "during the night of the 18th the army was accordingly withdrawn to the south side of the Potomac crossing near Sheperdstown." (This came as a relieved surprise to Longstreet, who had written out a plea for "a withdrawal to the south side of the Potomac.") Lee stood watch over the withdrawal, "sitting his horse in the stream," until the morning of the nineteenth, when one of Jackson's division commanders, John Walker, brought the last of his soldiers across the Potomac. There was a sharp little skirmish at Boteler's Ford, just below Shepherdstown, on the morning of the twentieth, and for a while it looked as though federal troops with enough energetic leadership could cross the Potomac and overrun the Confederates' artillery reserve. But Jackson pushed the Federals back, and the campaign in Maryland was finally over.[4]

Or almost over. Lee could not quite turn his eyes away from the Pennsylvania prize, moving his army westward to Martinsburg on September 20. He sent ahead J. E. B. Stuart and his cavalry to recross the Potomac farther north at Williamsport and establish a new bridgehead on the Maryland side, and on September 25 proposed to Jefferson Davis that from "a military point of view" the Army of Northern Virginia should move from "Williamsport . . . upon Hagerstown." He even recommended that William Loring's little army in the Kanawha Valley—the one he had commanded only a year before—join him in invading Pennsylvania. As late as October 7, Lee and Jackson were still poring over "maps of Maryland and Pennsylvania," convincing Jackson's chief topographical engineer, Jedediah Hotchkiss, that "no doubt another expedition is on foot."

But the case was hopeless. The Army was so short of clothing that Lee wrote a blistering letter to Abraham Myers, the quartermaster general, complaining about "the great deficiency of clothing in this army (particularly under-clothing and shoes), for the want of which there is much suffering." The straggling and pillaging were even worse, and remembering what a tight rein Scott had kept on his army in Mexico, Lee unleashed on Longstreet and Jackson a long lecture by letter on "the depredations committed by this army, its daily diminution, and the loss of arms thrown aside as too burdensome by stragglers." No shortcoming in either command missed his perfect eye, any more than had the shortcomings of his children or his cadets at West Point years before. "Roll-calls are neglected, and officers of companies and regiments are ignorant of the true condition of their commands, and are unable to account properly for absentees." He now wanted "a brigade guard" to bring up the rear of "each brigade . . . to keep up the ranks, drive up all stragglers, irrespective of commands, and all leaving the ranks."

We must, Lee demanded, "infuse a different spirit among our officers"—which was, more or less, what he had found a-begging in the Confederacy as a whole. ("There never has been discipline in the armies of the Confederacy," complained the *Richmond Enquirer,* "but instead thereof a kind of universal suffrage, which fights when it chooses and straggles when it feels like it.") It was those failings, not the long military odds, that made up Lee's mind to drop the plans for invading the North. "I would not hesitate to make it even with our diminished numbers, did the army exhibit its former temper and condition," Lee announced to Davis, "but as far as I am able to judge, the hazard would be great and a reverse disastrous. I am, therefore, led to pause."[5]

That did not prevent him from making at least one effort to inflict some form of pain north of the Potomac. While he moved the bulk of the Army of Northern Virginia back up the Shenandoah Valley to Winchester, Lee sent J. E. B. Stuart's cavalry on another long, loping raid, crossing the Potomac on October 10 and swinging up into Pennsylvania and back down to Virginia by the twelfth, riding all the way around McClellan's army a second time. The raid coincided nicely with Pennsylvania's October elections and was (said the *Richmond Dispatch*) just the thing for "frightening the Pennsylvania Yankees out of their wits," and perhaps, Lee hoped, moving "the conservative portion of that people" to "rise and depose the party now in power."[6]

Five days after the Battle of Antietam, Abraham Lincoln read to his cabinet the text of a preliminary Emancipation Proclamation that declared "forever free" more than three-quarters of the slaves in the American republic. (The final quarter he left untouched because the only constitutional justification for such a proclamation was his "war power" as commander in chief; that forced him to exclude the slaves of the border states of Maryland, Kentucky, Delaware, and Missouri for the simple reason that, having declined to join the Confederacy, they were not at war with the United States.)

The proclamation was exactly what George McClellan had warned him he must not do back in July, and what Southern slaveholders and Northern Democrats had always prophesied Lincoln would do if given half a chance. They responded accordingly. In the Confederacy, slaveholder ravings reached a pitch of hysteria not seen since John Brown. In the North, infuriated Democrats found a second political wind after their losses in the 1860 election and swore that Lincoln's Republican majority—"these wretches" and "demons of discord"—should not "be sent back to Congress to repeat their exploits." And in the fall elections, anti-administration Democrats reclaimed thirty-one seats in the House of Representatives; in Lincoln's own Illinois, Democrats recaptured control of the legislature, while in Pennsylvania the state's congressional delegation flipped from Republican to Democrat, thirteen Democrats to eleven Republicans. Most ominous of all, the governorships of New Jersey and New York switched to Democrats, which boded ill for recruiting volunteers from those states. The election was "a total rout in this state," wailed the New York lawyer George Templeton Strong. "It looks like a great, sweeping revolution of public sentiment, like general abandonment of the loyal, generous spirit of patriotism that broke out so nobly and unexpectedly in April, 1861. . . . It is a vote of national suicide. All is up. We are a lost people." Had Robert E. Lee and the Army of Northern Virginia managed to march defiantly into Pennsylvania as he had planned before the Lost Orders went astray, or even win a victory on Northern soil, the political damage could have been infinitely worse.[7]

It was not Congress, though, that weighed most heavily on Lincoln's mind. Republicans retained "a majority in the House," reasoned Lincoln's treasury secretary, Salmon P. Chase, who thought "the result not really damaging, though we shall miss in the next Congress many noble fellows." Much more worrisome was the prospect of what McClellan and the Army of the Potomac might do. Not only had McClellan not moved to reengage the Confederates at Antietam, but he had slowed all of his army's other movements to a crawl, pleading that his soldiers had been confronted by "overwhelming numbers" and that "the entire Army has been greatly exhausted by unavoidable overwork, hunger, & want of sleep & rest." He was, on the other hand, quite active in consulting prominent Democratic politicians about how he should respond to the emancipation order, and "some of those . . . on his staff . . . publicly declared that the time had come for McClellan to proclaim himself dictator."

Two weeks after Antietam, Lincoln decided to stare McClellan down personally and visit his headquarters "to satisfy himself personally . . . of the purposes intentions and fidelity of McClellan, his officers, and the army." What he saw and heard there about anti-emancipation dissension convinced him that McClellan had to go, this time for good. The day after the fall elections, Lincoln "ordered that Major General McClellan be relieved from the command of the Army of the Potomac; and that Major General Burnside take command of that Army."[8]

Lee had moved the Army of Northern Virginia out of the valley and back into the Virginia Piedmont at Culpeper when the news of McClellan's dismissal reached him. He had only one sardonic comment to make to James Longstreet, regretting McClellan's departure because "we always understood each other so well." Whether that was a description of Lee's ability to read McClellan's cautious mind, or something more oblique that ran back to the rumors of political communications, it certainly meant that Lee would have to face someone new at the helm of the Army of the Potomac, "and I fear they may continue to make these changes till they find some one whom I don't understand."

What occupied more of his attention was the need for further tightening of his army's organization. Clumps of stragglers now began to return, bit by bit making the Army of Northern Virginia "stronger than we were at Sharpsburg." The 2nd Virginia, which counted only three dozen men in Maryland, suddenly had 432 at the end of October. Not that this entirely satisfied Lee, who actively pressed state governors and legislators for new regiments "which you promised to endeavor to raise for this army. I need them much, I rely upon those we have in all tight places, and fear I have to call upon them too often. They have fought grandly, nobly, and we must have more of them." Secretary of War Randolph obliged, predicting that "we shall be able to send you . . . over 20,000 men in eight days" along with "500 conscripts, convalescents, and stragglers per diem from Richmond alone."[9]

More than just men in the ranks, Lee needed more officers who knew how to lead, train, and direct them. And they were in short supply, on both sides of the war. Less than 4 percent of Lee's regimental commanders had been professional soldiers, although a somewhat larger smattering (16 percent) had some kind of military-school education. "The secret of the whole present American War," wrote a British military observer, is that "the men on either side can be brought under fire, and when there will stand well: but they are not good enough either in morale or field movements to advance, change position, or retire." This was largely due to the sheer inexperience of the volunteer officers who "admit" that "the moment they have to manoeuvre, they get into confusion and break."

The crucial line officers of the Army of Northern Virginia (from captains to colonels) tended to be young—their median age was thirty-one—and surprisingly well educated, because roughly half of the officers at those ranks had at least some college training. They also tended to be disproportionately representative of slaveholding households—approximately half of them either owned slaves or were sons of families that owned slaves—and they behaved with a swaggeringly self-righteous confidence in the virtue of slavery. When Jackson forced the surrender of Harpers Ferry, his men bagged not only 12,000 Union prisoners but an untallied number of blacks, some free, some fugitives. These, Lee's officers eagerly picked out as slaves for themselves or just as eagerly consigned to the auction blocks in Richmond. "Many of them were never the slaves of rebels, yet all were hurried off into the interior as valuable booty," reported the *New-York Tribune.* "One shudders to think of the fate of those who shall fall into the hands of their former Rebel owners." These officers were also, for that reason, substantially wealthier than their Northern opponents: personal median wealth in the Army of Northern Virginia was six and a half times greater than that of their Union counterparts in the Army of the Potomac.[10]

These characteristics guaranteed a mentality in Lee's army that was fatally infected with ideas of personal dominance, self-indulgence, and, among the other ranks, a prickly-proud resistance to taking orders. One Georgian readily compared the routine of army discipline to "the plan of making myself a slave," because in his estimate "I have during the past six months gone through more hardships than anyone of ours or Grandma's negroes; their life is a luxury to what mine is sometimes." A Louisianan groused that his officers "are just like the owners of slaves on plantations, they have nothing to do but strut about, dress fine, and enjoy themselves; their tents are placed far away from ours, as if they were made of better clay."

This top-lofty attitude only fed Lee's frustrations with Southern disbelief in the self-denial necessary to win the war. "Without some additional power"—without the authority to reduce "incompetent officers . . . to the ranks" or impose "more stringent regulations" on the enlisted ranks—Lee argued that "the army will melt away." "Our people are so little liable to control that it is difficult to get them to follow any course not in accordance with their inclination," he admitted to Justus Scheibert. And when Scheibert "expressed frankly my admiration for the lion-like bravery of his men," Lee disagreed. "Give me also Prussian discipline and Prussian forms, and you would see quite different results!"[11]

The closest Lee had come to finding those forms and that discipline was in Jackson and Longstreet, and he successfully pressed Davis and Congress to convert their informal "commands" into official *corps d'armée* like the Army of the Potomac, with Jackson and Longstreet both promoted to the newly created rank of lieutenant general to command them. "I can confidently recommend Gens. Longstreet and Jackson in this army," he told Davis on October 2, and particularly Jackson. "My opinion of his merits . . . has been greatly enhanced during this expedition," Lee enthused. For all of Jackson's eccentricities and for all the cultural distance that lay between the rawboned Cromwellian and his genteel commander, Jackson could be "very hospitable in disposition, and welcomed warmly any guest to his tent or his table." Even more, he was one of the few Confederate officers who had exactly the win-at-all-costs energy that Lee had found so lacking elsewhere in the Confederacy. "He is true, honest and brave, has a single eye to the good of the service, and spares no exertion to accomplish his object."

He needed to say less in Longstreet's praise. In the old Army, Longstreet had been an outgoing, hail-fellow bison of a man, always at the bottom of his West Point class, always roaringly disorderly. He bolted for the Confederacy in May 1861 and like Jackson commanded a brigade at First Bull Run. He was furious at the failure to pursue the broken Federals afterward and "dashed his hat furiously to the ground, stamped, and bitter words escaped him." But the death of three children in an epidemic in Richmond in the winter of 1861 had made him "a changed man . . . very serious and reserved," to the point where one British-born staffer could not say "that my connection with General Longstreet had been pleasant to me personally." And yet it was that silent immovability that Lee came to value, and "he was like a rock in steadiness when sometimes in battle the world seemed flying to pieces."

Lee also had his pets, those of less capability whom he indulged in a singularly un-Prussian fashion far more than he should have. He had a noticeable soft spot for Powell Hill, who had staved off collapse at Antietam by his relentless march to the rescue from Harpers Ferry. Next to Longstreet and Jackson, "Genl. A. P. Hill [is] the best commander with me. He fights his troops well, and takes good care of them." He pampered his onetime aide J. E. B. Stuart, who most agreed was "a brave & brilliant executive commander," but who was also entirely dependent on Lee "to plan his expeditions, make his combinations for him, & thus ensure his success." William Nelson Pendleton, the chief of the Army of Northern Virginia's artillery, had served before the war as an Episcopal minister. But his virtues in the latter profession had not translated into competence in the former, and especially after the artillery reserve was nearly cut off at Shepherdstown, Pendleton was derided as "Old Granny" and the "Revd. General." But Pendleton had been at West Point with Lee before taking orders, and although Porter Alexander was convinced that Pendleton "was too old & had been too long out of army life to be thoroughly up to all the opportunities of his position," it was soon recognized that Pendleton "was an especial friend of General Lee." Lee kept Pendleton on his staff until the end of the war, even as he steadily reshuffled the organization of the artillery to give Pendleton smaller and smaller responsibilities.

Lee was guilty of lifting his demanding gaze above other generals' pets, too. Longstreet was "exceedingly fond" of George Pickett, whose "long ringlets flowed loosely over his shoulders" without guaranteeing that very much was operative beneath them. Longstreet "looked after Pickett" and frequently assigned his own staff to "stay with him to make sure he did not get astray." Jackson had a similar blindness to the faults of his aggressive but self-promoting division commander, John Bell Hood, and prevailed on Lee to recommend Hood's promotion to major general that October.[12]

The indulgence of such pets was both dangerous and unavoidable, because after these few the quality and character of Confederate officers fell off dramatically. "The Confederate officers were, many of them, poseurs," wrote Marietta Andrews. "They were by tradition and intention picturesque, and had they not taken themselves and each other so seriously, they might have been a little funny." Under fire, their Napoleonic bravado evaporated, and Dorsey Pender estimated after Antietam "six out [of] ten officers skulled out and did not come up until they thought all danger was over."

Outside his favorites, Lee remorselessly pared away those he regarded as the dimwits. (When it came to personnel, snorted Pierre Beauregard, "Genl Lee never had any difficulty in getting rid of any officer who did not suit him.") But not even the best of the gold-braid Confederates was free from touchy absurdities. None took themselves more seriously than Powell Hill, who quarreled violently with Jackson over Jackson's marching orders in Maryland and then retaliated by appealing directly to Lee. Lee tried to dampen the argument by endorsing Hill's appeal with the mollifying comment that whatever Hill's offense it "could not be intentional . . . from an officer of his character" and so there was "no advantage to the service" from "further investigating this matter." Neither Hill nor Jackson was satisfied; both demanded a court-martial. Lee filed the papers and let them both stew.[13]

At the other end, there were few people whom Lee despised more than the War Department's administrative bureaucrats, who consistently failed to supply the Army of Northern Virginia's necessities and thus triggered the straggling and pillaging Lee deplored. As an engineer, Lee had always been able to leave logistics largely to others, and it would be one of the weakest items among his command skills. That, together with the incompetence that marked much of the Confederate War Department's bureaucracy, turned the Army of Northern Virginia into what looked like an armed society of paupers. One South Carolina soldier wrote home in December, "I'll wager you could not tell me [at] ten steps. I am very ugly, my beard is shaggy, teeth black, clothes dirty and worn, finger nails long and black, nose little inclined to drip. . . . I am a hard looking case." Food supplies were so undependable that Charles Venable remembered the army often had no more than a day's foodstuffs in its larders, and one cheeky soldier sent Lee a letter "containing a very small slice of pork, carefully packed between two oak slips, and accompanied by a letter saying that this was the daily ration of meat," on which he would have starved had he not found the solution in "the necessity of stealing."

The medical services were even more meager. It sometimes seemed to Lee that no sooner had "conscripts and recruits" joined the Army than they went down with "measles, camp fever, &c." When an early snow fell at the beginning of November, Lee besieged Secretary of War Randolph with complaints about "our men with insufficient clothing, blankets and shoes," and was angered when he discovered that the commissary general in Richmond, Lucius Northrop, was outbidding Lee's own quartermasters for flour. By December, Lee was urging the War Department "that shoes be taken from the extortioners" and demanding "more arms." Nothing in Richmond seemed energetic but the Richmond newspapers, although, to Lee's annoyance, that energy seemed pointed mostly toward printing "early accounts of his movements," which "are taken quickly . . . to the enemy."[14]

It was easier for Lee to surround himself in the cocoon of his staff and avoid both Richmond and politicians as much as possible. By the fall of 1862, he had settled down, with all but a few exceptions, to the staff he would employ for the rest of the war: the colorless Robert Chilton as chief of staff, Lindsay Long and Charles Marshall as military secretaries, Walter Taylor as adjutant general, Charles Venable and Thomas Talcott as aides, James Corley as quartermaster general, Robert Cole as chief of commissary, Lafayette Guild as chief medical officer, the unpredictable Pendleton as artillery chief, and William Proctor Smith and Samuel R. Johnston as staff engineering officers, all of them rounded out by two companies of the 39th Virginia Cavalry as headquarters guard. The inner circle of the staff, however, were the "four majors (afterwards lieutenant colonels and colonels)" whom Lee had "carefully selected" and who "did his principal work": Taylor, Venable, Marshall, and Long.

Taylor and Marshall were the guardians of Lee's paperwork, and in an army everything marches by paper. "Every corps or independent command . . . sent daily to headquarters its package of official papers," recalled Taylor, "from the request for a furlough . . . to the notification of some activity in the camp of the enemy," and "the couriers who brought these despatches were arriving at all hours of the day and night." Taylor, who considered himself Lee's "confidential staff-officer," sorted and docketed the incoming paper and then had the unwelcome task of laying it all before Lee. Unwelcome, because Lee had lost nothing of his distaste for "office work," especially if it was heavy with "matters of detail coming from the different commands of our army" that demanded "the personal consideration and decision of the commander of the army." If Taylor brought him "some case of a vexatious character," Lee's impatience would flare up gradually, beginning with "a little nervous twist or jerk of the neck and head" and sometimes erupting in a full-fledged argument. "He is so unreasonable and provoking," Taylor raged to his fiancée in a letter. "I never worked so hard to please any one, and with so little effect as General Lee."

Charles Marshall, who handled Lee's outgoing correspondence, had only a slightly easier task, because Lee either dictated first drafts or allowed Marshall to draw up documents himself but then "weighed every sentence I wrote, frequently making minute verbal alterations, and questioned me closely as to the evidence on which I based all statements which he did not know to be correct." Looking over his colleague's shoulder, Taylor noticed that "it will be difficult to procure a dispatch written by my chief, as he scarcely ever writes them himself." And yet, for all of his frustrations, Taylor also had to say that "my Chief is the wisest and I await his word confidently." Taylor thought him "a queer old genius. I suppose it is so with all great men."[15]

And overwhelmingly, the Army of Northern Virginia agreed. "Lee has immortalized himself," wrote Dorsey Pender on the march toward Maryland. Even after Antietam, Moxley Sorrel thought the Army's "devotion for Lee and unfaltering confidence in him had never been surpassed." He had conducted the campaign that delivered Richmond, inflicted two savage defeats to the Federals at Cedar Mountain and Second Bull Run, directed the capture of Harpers Ferry, and eluded two attempts by McClellan to overwhelm the Army at South Mountain and again after the Antietam battle. "The boys never cheer him," remarked an ironic lieutenant in the 9th Alabama; instead, they "pull off their hats and worship." The soldiers now began to call him Marse Robert—adopting the slave dialect and positioning themselves as his servants, dropping all their prickly objections to being treated as "slaves," as though he were the model of the good master. Soldiers in the Army of Northern Virginia invariably "nicknamed their officers and themselves until nearly every man in the company had his sobriquet," but Lee "was always spoken of as 'Mars Bob.' "

Mars' Robert said, "My soldiers,
You've nothing now to fear,
For Longstreet's on the right of them,
And Jackson's in their rear."[16]

The irony of "Marse Robert" lay in how much Lee was, at that moment, struggling to disentangle himself, and perhaps even the Confederacy, from slavery. In every public utterance, Lee was careful to praise the Confederacy as "the noble cause we are engaged in," and he kept two of the Arlington slaves, Perry Parks and Michael Meredith, as servants on his first campaign in western Virginia and in the Carolinas. But he doggedly continued to push forward the emancipation of G.W.P.'s slaves as stipulated in the old man's will, relying on Custis's assignment to Jefferson Davis's staff in Richmond to handle the paperwork "for the people whom I wish to liberate," including "the whole list at Arlington, White House, &c." by the close of December 1862.

Not that, by that point, there were actually that many slaves left there to be emancipated. A number had been "hired on the railroad." A still larger number, like Philip Meredith, had simply drifted away to "contraband" camps in Alexandria and Washington. Meredith slipped over into the District to work as a waiter and filed for freedom after Congress passed an emancipation bill for the District in April 1862. That Philip Meredith had lived "for 30 years as a servant of Robert E. Lee" caused a minor sensation among the commissioners reviewing the filing, but he made it still more sensational by describing "frequent conversations with Gen Lee in which Gen Lee expressed regret that he owned servant & wished he was free."

When Markie Williams ventured a visit to Arlington in July 1862 to retrieve some family belongings, almost the only slave still on the grounds was the elderly gardener, Ephraim Derricks. Lee realized this meant both that the legacies G.W.P.'s will required him to pay out to his daughters were not going to come from any improved income stream generated by the properties, as he had once imagined, and that the Union occupation of northern Virginia and Lincoln's Emancipation Proclamation were rendering moot any real emancipating Lee might do. He might, in fact, have no choice but to sell "the lands at Smith's Island" and "all the land at the White House & Romancocke to pay the legacies" to the girls, which for him would always remain the prime consideration, rather than emancipation itself.[17]

Still, Lee recorded the deed of emancipation on January 2, 1863, in Richmond, "embracing all the names" of the Arlington and Romancoke slaves and suggesting a "supplementary deed" freeing any whose names had somehow "been omitted." At that moment, it is hard to imagine that if Lee had decided to balk at the whole business, any Virginia court still under the Confederate flag would have obstructed him. Yet the possibility never seems to have formed in his mind; even more, he included among the manumissions the one slave family he still owned in his name, that of Nancy Ruffin. Practically speaking, some of the Custis slaves were not actually released from bondage until late in 1863, and Lee was aware that "there is some desire on the part of the community to continue them in slavery." But this, he added, "I must resist."[18]

Robert E. Lee was now, for the first time in his life, slaveless, and largely by his own doing. What was only rumored was the hint that this was also his recommendation for the Confederate future. "After the battle of Antietam," Lee for the second time politely suggested to Jefferson Davis that, especially with the issue of Lincoln's proclamation, "the only hope left for slavery and the southern people, was an agreement to go back into the Union"—which meant that "the tenure of slave property, always precarious," was in Lee's eyes up for grabs ("absolutely a matter of lottery"). But there was no documentary evidence behind the rumors, and Lee's soldiers, in the slave-owning fashion, blissfully continued to "speak of him amongst themselves universally as 'Marse Robert' & use it as a term of endearment & affection." They believe that "'*Marse Robert,*' as the men all call him, can carry them anywhere."[19]

They would soon have the chance to test that confidence. On November 15, ten days after McClellan's dismissal, the Army of the Potomac and its new commander, Ambrose Burnside, shuddered into motion, headed for the lower Rappahannock River and the vital railroad crossing at the venerable city of Fredericksburg.

Lee's dominant anxiety in the weeks after Antietam was that McClellan, once he had refreshed the Army of the Potomac, would return to his plan for a movement on the James River, this time striking south of the James in order to elbow his way into Richmond through the back door of Petersburg. McClellan's dismissal removed one part of that concern, but not the possibility that another general might do likewise. He needn't have worried. McClellan had made the idea of another combined land-and-water campaign down the Chesapeake Bay politically toxic. The generals, Lincoln snorted in November, "have got the idea into their heads that we are going to get out of this fix, somehow, by strategy," when the only real solution would be "hard, tough fighting that will hurt somebody." That, for Lincoln, translated into a heads-down, overland campaign, straight across northern Virginia, and a forced showdown with Lee's army. Forget "the water line," Lincoln demanded. If Lee should fall back to protect Richmond, "I would press closely to him, fight him if a favorable opportunity should present, and, at least, try to beat him to Richmond on the inside track."

To bring on that smashup, Lincoln could have hardly chosen anyone more ill-fitted as a replacement for McClellan than Ambrose Burnside, something that Burnside himself was the first to admit. A longtime friend of McClellan's, but without McClellan's politics, Burnside at first seemed the right man, first to appease the disgruntled McClellanites in the Army of the Potomac's upper command echelons, and then for endorsing the Emancipation Proclamation. "He is a jolly, noisy sort of fellow," remarked a visiting English aristocrat, but "he is about the only man whom I have heard approve of the emancipation proclamation," and that was a recommendation in itself.

Burnside's reputation shone all the brighter for having led a successful campaign early in 1862 that reclaimed eastern North Carolina for the Union. But that had been a comparatively small-scale affair, and Burnside knew command of the Army of the Potomac was beyond his grasp. "I am not fit for it," he pleaded. "There are many more in the army better fitted than I am." Besides, the McClellanites would never forgive him for having supplanted their idol. But Lincoln was having none of it, and though an early winter was in the offing, Burnside was given no choice but to march. And, Lincoln added, he would "succeed, if you move rapidly."[20]

From the headquarters he established at Culpeper, Lee eyed Burnside with an element of puzzlement; Lincoln really had put up someone Lee did not entirely understand, and at first he placed Jackson's corps in the valley and Longstreet's around his own position at Culpeper as if to forestall any movement by the Federals into the Piedmont. With the return of the Maryland stragglers and the influx of the draftees Davis had promised, the numbers of the Army of Northern Virginia returned to just over 80,000 men, but guessing where Burnside might move would require him to thin them out over long distances. Stuart was ordered out "to cross the Rappahannock and feel the enemy," and Jackson was directed to "operate strongly upon his flank & rear through the gaps in the Blue Ridge" and even to strike across the Potomac "into Maryland" in order to "retard & baffle [Burnside's] designs." He was reluctant to surrender the initiative and merely adopt a wait-and-see approach. If he could, he told Custis, he would like to draw the federal army "among the mountains," and use the valley, the Blue Ridge, and its gaps to "get him separated that I can strike him to advantage." Burnside's movement eastward caught him by surprise. "His troops and trains, as far as can be discovered," were in motion, but as late as the seventeenth Lee was unsure whether that meant a descent upon Gordonsville, or still more movement eastward "to fall down upon Fredericksburg," or even to "retire towards Alexandria, to be transferred"—like McClellan—"by water south of the James River."[21]

To Lee's alarm, the first units of the Army of the Potomac arrived at Falmouth, on the north side of the Rappahannock above Fredericksburg, after only two days of swift marching through cold, mud, and rain, and Burnside himself was at Falmouth by November 19. If the army bureaucracy in Washington had moved with half that energy, the pontoon train Burnside was relying upon to bridge the Rappahannock at Fredericksburg would have been waiting for him there. It didn't. The pontoons did not arrive until nearly the end of the month, and this turned out to be a fatal gift to Robert E. Lee.

It was not until November 20 that Lee was sure that "Burnside is concentrating his whole army opposite Fredericksburg," and he began hurrying first Longstreet and then Jackson eastward to counter Burnside. He made the ride in the rain from Culpeper to Fredericksburg in the company of Rob, and from the south side of the Rappahannock River, Lee began "surveying the enemy & preparing for them." To his puzzled relief, "they seem to be hesitating." Which, because of the late arrival of Burnside's pontoons, they were, and the delay gave Lee just the time he needed to concentrate Jackson and Longstreet on a long range of hills beyond Fredericksburg. "I have determined to resist him at the outset, and to throw every obstacle in the way of his advance," Lee reported to Jefferson Davis on the twenty-fifth.

What galled Lee was his inability to do anything substantial to protect the city of Fredericksburg itself. The nineteenth century had no practical doctrine that governed street fighting, and Lee was hesitant to risk a fight in the city itself. Another consideration was Burnside's position on the heights across the river. Fredericksburg's streets and buildings crowded down to the banks of the Rappahannock and sat in the shadow of the "plateau just opposite," where federal artillery easily had their range. Lee began "moving out the women & children all last night & today," but he could offer them no shelter. "A deep melancholy, mingled with exasperation," settled on him. "It was a piteous sight," he wrote to Mary. "What is to become of them God only knows." It did nothing to preserve his equanimity that on that "plateau" sat Chatham, once the home of William Henry Fitzhugh, who had written Lee a recommendation for West Point and where he had once courted Mary Custis as a cadet on leave some three decades before.[22]

By November 27, the reason for Burnside's hesitation had become obvious. "I have learned of a large pontoon train having reached Genl Burnside." And when he heard on December 2 through "a citizen doctor who came from the other side of the river yesterday" that Lincoln was personally on hand to prod his fearful general into motion, Lee understood that "some movement of the enemy" was in the offing at Fredericksburg and sent Thomas Talcott on "a reconnaissance as far north as the mouth of the Rapidan" to identify the likeliest points Burnside would use for "throwing over a pontoon bridge."

Even so, Burnside waited until December 11, hoping that light-draft gunboats could be brought up the river to his support, before ordering his engineers to begin pushing three sets of pontoon bridges across the Rappahannock. An entire brigade of Mississippians took up open-order positions among the buildings on the Fredericksburg side of the river, and despite heavy droppings of federal artillery fire they peppered Burnside's engineers with lethal doses of sharpshooting. "The range being so short and the fire so heavy, it was impossible for the men to work," growled one Northern engineer, until finally a

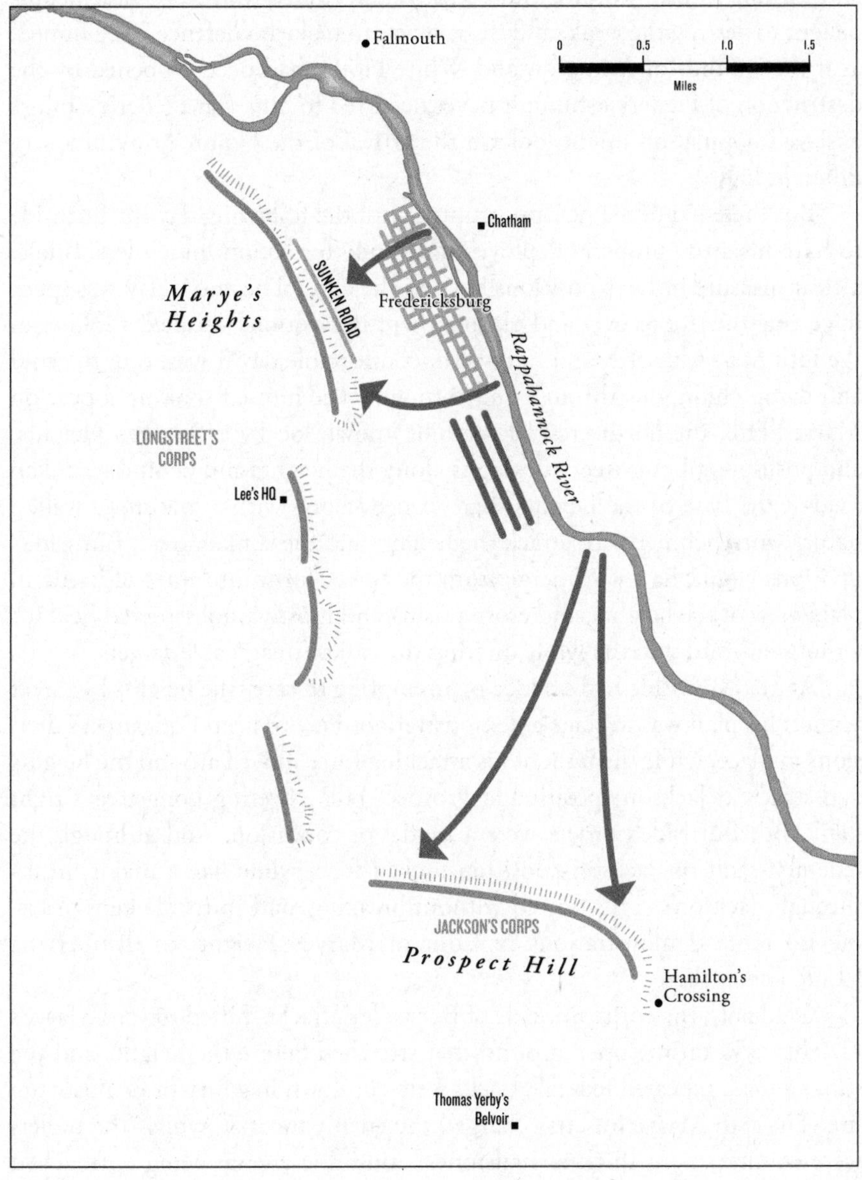

federal infantry brigade paddled itself across the river, cleared out the annoying rebels, and covered the completion of the bridges.[23]

This was only the beginning of Burnside's sorrows. "The report is that Burnside will cross the river at Fredericksburg this morning," scribbled one hasty McClellanite staffer, but "I am afraid the North will meet with a terrible blow, and will be greatly disappointed." The Army of the Potomac began crossing on the pontoon bridges on the twelfth, vengefully looting whatever in Fredericksburg had not been destroyed in the fighting the previous day and turning it into "nothing but a sacked and ruined town." ("These people delight to destroy the weak, and those who can make no defence," Lee fumed, as if the wounds of Arlington and White House had been reopened by the destruction of Fredericksburg; it never occurred to him that Fredericksburg's enslaved population might look on the arrival of the Union Army in a very different light.)

But there would be no opportunity until the following day for Burnside to have his army properly deployed and ready for action, much less to take a clear measure of Lee's positions beyond the city. "The entire day was spent in getting the troops over and placing them in position," recalled a soldier in the 12th Massachusetts, and "a most uncomfortable day it was, too, the cold and damp chilling us through and through." Lee himself took up a post on Marye's Hill, the north crest of the hills known locally as Marye's Heights, and positioned Longstreet's divisions along the heights and behind a sunken road at the base of the heights that formed, along with a low stone wall, a natural entrenchment. To attack the heights and the sunken road, Burnside's divisions would have to emerge from the town, form into lines of battle in plain view of the heights, and cross a rising and mostly unobstructed field for a thousand yards, all the while offering the easiest imaginable targets.[24]

At first, Burnside had no idea of attempting to carry the heights by direct assault; his plan was to stage a demonstration there to keep Longstreet's divisions in place, while the bulk of his attacking force moved around the heights and struck at Jackson's position at Prospect Hill, covering Longstreet's right flank. But Burnside's orders were a model of confusion. And although the federal assault on Jackson's position looked for a while like a major breakthrough, Jackson's corps bowed without breaking, and Burnside kept ordering up more demonstrations in front of Marye's Heights to distract the Confederates there.

Gradually, the entire impetus of Burnside's attacks shifted toward Marye's Heights, and on the open ground that stretched before the heights and the sunken road, repeated federal attacks were cut down in a fury of Confederate fire. The 18th Massachusetts "charged the enemy's works" while "the bullets were coming . . . as thick as hailstones." But "the enemy being entrenched behind a stone wall within very short musket range," the regiment was "dropping under their fire terribly" until "our line had become completely riddled and disorganized." For the Confederates, it was almost too easy. "At every advance we waited," wrote a soldier in the 2nd South Carolina, "until they got near us, when on knees or in stooping posture, we would rise, and fire with terrible effect—stoop, reload, and fire again." In front of the 24th Georgia, "the ground was almost covered with dead men." By the time an early winter darkness descended, Burnside had lost nearly 1,300 killed (and as many as 900 alone in front of the sunken road) and another 9,600 wounded.[25]

Lee spent the morning of the thirteenth once again performing his own reconnaissance and once more being shot at by federal pickets. "He was clad in his plain, well-worn gray uniform, with felt hat, cavalry-boots, and short cape, without sword," remembered John Esten Cooke, "and almost without any indications of his rank." When the federal advance on Marye's Heights began, Lee found a convenient position on a small eminence at the south end of the heights, passing "along his line of battle, greeted wherever he was seen with cheers." He almost defined dignity. A federal artillery shell "buried itself close . . . at General Lee's side, as he sat among the officers of his staff, but it failed to explode," and one British observer compared his "undemonstrative" manner to Lord Raglan, at the Battle of the Alma, eight years before.

He could afford dignity at Fredericksburg because, as he had explained to Justus Scheibert, he had Longstreet and Jackson to execute his overall plans; standing aloof from the details of tactical operations was what gave Lee room for the genteel assertion of serenity. Watching the twenty-four-year-old John Pelham, one of J. E. B. Stuart's artillery officers, at work, Lee remarked appreciatively that "it is inspiriting to see such glorious courage in one so young," as though he were observing cadets at the West Point blackboard. At mid-afternoon, he began to wonder if the repeated attacks on the sunken road were wearing down Longstreet's men. "General," Lee warned, "they are massing very heavily and will break your line, I am afraid." Longstreet only grinned: "General, if you put every man now on the other side of the Potomac in that field to approach me over the same line, and give me plenty of ammunition, I will kill them all before they reach my line."

Otherwise, Lee spoke little (obeying the ancient rule that it was "an ill omen to speak in hunting" but therefore, at the same time, fixing what little he said in people's minds). The only other comment his staff recollected during that day was a bitter dismissal of Burnside's stupidity in throwing away the lives of his men to so little purpose and making slaughter seem so effortless. "It is well this is so terrible!" he "murmured, in his grave and measured voice," or else "we should grow too fond of it!" This is Lee's most often-quoted statement, and all the more unusual for being so often quoted because it came from a man for whom quotables or wit were not common. At nine o'clock that night, he telegraphed an almost laconic note to Richmond: "The enemy attacked our right, and as the fog lifted the battle ran from right to left; raged until 6 p.m.; but, thanks to Almighty God, the day closed repulsed along our whole front."[26]

Lee fully expected that Burnside would somehow move again to the attack, and wired Richmond for more supplies of ammunition and ordered new entrenchments to be dug. But nothing stirred on the morning of the fourteenth, and Lee quipped to Longstreet, "I am losing faith in your friend General Burnside." Actually, it was Burnside's generals who had lost faith in him, and especially the McClellan loyalists, whose bleakest predictions had now come true. Burnside planned one last assault on the fourteenth, personally leading a charge that seemed like a gigantic, remorseful suicide pact on Burnside's part. But "nearly all disapproved of the attack which Genl. Burnside had ordered," and the unhappy Burnside relented. The next day, the Army of the Potomac withdrew across the Rappahannock, the engineers cutting the tether ropes of the pontoon bridges it had cost them so much to build only a few days before.[27]

"The great battle of Fredericksburg has been fought and won," cried the *Richmond Enquirer.* "The Yankees admit a great defeat." Surely, "the condition of affairs" must force on Northern attention "the prospects of an early peace." "Praise the Lord, O my soul, and all that is within me praise His holy name!" rejoiced Judith White McGuire. "How can we be thankful enough for such men as General Lee, General Jackson, and our glorious army, rank and file!"

Lee was no longer in the shadow of Light Horse Harry; he stood in the line of Bonaparte. "He had selected his field of battle, and had thoroughly studied it, as Napoleon had done the field of Austerlitz," crowed the *Richmond Dispatch.* "This is the tenth pitched battle in which General Lee has commanded, within less than six months, and in all of them he has been victorious." Even Union officers began paying Lee grudging tribute. "I am pretty well satisfied that . . . we have had no one to command the Army of the Potomac that was a match for Lee," admitted the 51st New York's George Washington Whitman (the brother of the poet Walt Whitman).[28]

Lee was more subdued. In his official report, he gave "great praise" to "Generals Longstreet and Jackson . . . for the disposition and management of their respective corps," and every member of his staff was commended by name for "anticipating as far as possible the wants of the troops" and "communicating orders and intelligence." But privately, he was annoyed by the "vain self boasting & adulation" of "our people." Southerners "must put forth their full strength at once," even if it meant having to "drive into the ranks, from very shame, those who will not heed the dictates of honor and patriotism." And he blamed himself for failing to anticipate Burnside's withdrawal. He expected "that the enemy" would "renew the combat of the 13th," and that led him to hold "back all that day, & husbanding our strength & ammunition for the great struggle for which I thought he was preparing. Had I devined that was to have been his only effort, he would have had more of it." At least, he wrote to Mildred, he had the consolation of knowing that "Genl Burnside & his army will not eat . . . Xmas dinner in Richmond."

In the larger context, he could not help regarding Fredericksburg as an empty victory. It only drove back a federal army; it did not force it to abandon Confederate territory. It did not undermine the Lincoln government the way a victory on Northern soil would do, and it only meant that once it had recovered its wind, the Army of the Potomac would be on the march against him once more, and he had fewer resources with which he could resist them. "At Fredericksburg we gained a battle, inflicting very severe loss on the enemy in men and material," Lee told one of Jefferson Davis's aides. But while "our people were greatly elated—I was much depressed." The truth was that "we had really accomplished nothing; we had not gained a foot of ground, and I knew the enemy could easily replace the men he had lost, and the loss of material was, if any thing, rather beneficial to him, as it gave an opportunity to contractors to make money."[29]

The gloom in his mind after Fredericksburg was darker than anything a single battle could have produced, for this second year of the war had been full of losses that bore down heavily on his spirits. In the spring, Bishop Meade, who had catechized Lee as a boy at Christ Church in Alexandria, died in exile in Richmond. Meade sent for Lee as he felt his end approaching and gave him his hand and his episcopal blessing. "God bless you! God bless you, Robert!" Meade gasped "in a voice so weak that it was almost inaudible." Meade stopped himself: "I can't call you general—I must call you Robert; I have heard you your catechism too often." One more tie to his past was now broken, one more faint token of the security he had always sought disappearing into the darkness. "Our good Bishop (Meade) died last night," he wrote to Carter, and then to Mary, "I ne'er shall look upon his like again." Another grandchild was born to Rooney and Charlotte, "a very fine pretty baby" whom they named Charlotte Carter Lee. But the baby died after only seven weeks, on December 6, and Lee was staggered. "I was so grateful at her birth," Lee wrote to Charlotte. "I felt that she would be such a comfort to you, such a pleasure to my dear Fitzhugh, and would fill so full the void still aching in your hearts"—and in his own—from the death of their son.

But the greatest blow fell on October 20. A month before, Lee had entered Mildred (now seventeen) at St. Mary's School in Raleigh, and her older sister Annie went along with her mother, Mary, who was taking the cure for her arthritis at the nearby White Sulphur Springs, operated by William Duke Jones. There, Annie, the confidante and the closest to him of all his children, came down with typhoid fever. Mary Lee summoned Agnes and Mildred to help her nurse Annie, but it was all in vain. Annie passed in and out of a coma, and after awaking to call, "Where's Agnes?" died "very peacefully and quietly."

Lee had no warning that Annie was even ill, when Walter Taylor brought him the usual morning mail, along with "the private letters . . . as was the custom." The two worked through the "matters of army routine" and he "gave his orders in regard to them," and Taylor left. A few minutes later, Taylor remembered a question he wanted to put to Lee and "with my accustomed freedom entered his tent without announcement or ceremony," only to find Lee sitting on his army cot with "an open letter in his hands." It was the news of Annie's death, delivered so matter-of-factly with the other mail that reading it struck him like death itself. "I was startled and shocked to see him overcome with grief," sitting there, mute, wounded, inconsolable, broken, Taylor remembered. "That I shall never see her again on earth, that her place in our circle, which I always hoped one day to enjoy, is forever vacant, is agonizing in the extreme," he wrote to Mary on October 26, still incredulous. He could believe she would now be in the company of "her sainted grandmother," but "beyond our hope in the great mercy of God," he could find no comfort.

Thou wilt come no more, gentle Annie,
Like a flower thy spirit did depart;
Thou art gone, alas! like the many
That have bloomed in the summer of my heart.

"Year after year my hopes go out," he cried to "Daughter" Mary in November. "In the hours of the night, when there is nothing to lighten the full weight of my grief, I feel as if I should be overwhelmed." Six months later, he was still grieving. "Old age & sorrow is wearing me away, & constant anxiety & labour, day and night."[30]

The gloom was only deepened as defeat and hardship tightened their grip on the Confederacy. The great parallel Confederate offensive in the west that fall under Braxton Bragg lunged as far north as Kentucky, only to splutter and recede after a resultless slugfest with Union forces at Perryville, Kentucky, in October. Ulysses Grant was once more on the move, this time against Vicksburg, the last Confederate citadel on the Mississippi River, while the federal Army of the Cumberland, now commanded by William S. Rosecrans, fended off one last attempt by Bragg to retrieve Tennessee for the Confederacy at Murfreesboro at New Year's.

In Richmond, the secretary of war's wife complained that ordinary household provisions were becoming scarce in the markets. "Times are getting so hard I commence to tremble for the winter," moaned Mary Randolph, a near neighbor of Mary Lee's. "Coal is scarce and provisions are dear." The War Department clerk John B. Jones managed to feed his family "four or five times a week on *liver* and rice" because "we cannot afford anything better; others do not live so well." The Virginia Central Railroad, which was so vital to supplying the needs of the Army of Northern Virginia, was wearing out from overuse and lack of repair, while new railroad projects designed to link Richmond with North Carolina and the west failed in the face of cantankerous state officials. Union officers in Virginia were shocked to find "the Villages we have passed through are the most God forsaken places," where "the people seem to have nothing to eat . . . and how they are going to get through the winter I don't know." The colonel of a New Jersey regiment agreed: "This country is sparsely settled, poorly cultivated, and the inhabitants look miserably poor. . . . The truth is: they are now starved." "In less than two years," complained Lindsay Long, "one of the most fruitful countries known was reduced to the condition of being barely able to afford a scanty subsistence" for its soldiers.[31]

After Fredericksburg, Lee considered pulling back to the North Anna River, and even sent Long and Venable to reconnoiter "the country contiguous to the North Anna River"; the Rappahannock was too easily crossed in too many places for him to cover every possible point along that line, something which Burnside's movement had demonstrated. But he could not afford to leave Burnside's army unwatched across from Fredericksburg, so he settled his headquarters tents at Hamilton's Crossing (beside the Richmond, Fredericksburg, and Potomac Railroad), put the Army into rough-hewn encampments along the heights, and, in the spirit of an engineer, began constructing "field works and rifle pits" to cover key points along a twenty-five-mile stretch of the river. He remained wary of any Union attempt to renew a landing on the banks of the James River and urged the Confederate War Department "to place the defenses of Richmond in a satisfactory state by the opening of the spring campaign."

When Secretary of War George Randolph resigned in November 1862, and was replaced by James A. Seddon, Lee's appeals to the War Department for further support—and his denunciations of Confederate apathy and self-interest—hit new highs. "If we desire to oppose effectual resistance to the vast numbers that the enemy is now precipitating upon us," Lee declared to Seddon in mid-January 1863, then there was no alternative to "the absolute necessity that exists . . . to increase the army." No one should imagine that victories like Fredericksburg were some signal for relaxation or should "betray our people into the dangerous delusion that the armies now in the field are sufficient." They were not, and there will be "blood on the hands" of the stay-at-homes while his soldiers were "enduring with noble fortitude the hardships and privations of the march and camp."

Lee was cheered by at least one result of the Fredericksburg battle, and that was the improved "calmness and steadiness with which orders were obeyed and maneuvers executed in the midst of battle" by the army, as though the Army of Northern Virginia were finally shrugging off some of the erratic behavior that had nearly ruined the campaign in Maryland and now "evinced the discipline of a veteran army." But whether he could feed and supply them was another question. Shoe shortages continued to plague the army, and finally tiring of pestering Richmond for supplies of shoes, Lee ordered all shoemakers in the Army of Northern Virginia withdrawn from regular duty and assigned to manufacturing shoes from the hides of slaughtered cattle. But he could not manufacture more food. The railroads could provide him with only half the fodder needed for the Army's horses, and even that had to be hauled seventy miles by wagon from the rail depots to the Rappahannock encampments. In February, he detached two of Longstreet's divisions, along with Longstreet himself, and sent them off below Richmond to restrain new movements being threatened by federal troops in eastern North Carolina and to relieve some of the pressure on the Army's logistics.[32]

Whatever the misgivings roiling his mind, Lee had no choice but to put on the best public face. One Virginia girl remarked on "how his hair is silvered and his brow marked with thought and care, yet what a noble, benevolent spirit looks forth from his brown eyes. What an air of dignity about his every movement." A steady stream of visitors and observers arrived to take his measure and came away charmed and impressed. A British officer on leave, Lieutenant Colonel Garnet Wolseley (who in subsequent years would emerge as Britain's most famous general, and the butt of Gilbert and Sullivan's most famous joke), tracked down Lee in September 1862 in Winchester and afterward gushed that Lee "is a strongly built man, about five feet eleven in height," and though "his hair and beard are nearly white . . . his dark brown eyes still shine with all the brightness of youth, and beam" with such "a most pleasing expression" that he could have been mistaken for "a splendid specimen of an English gentleman, with one of the most rarely handsome faces I ever saw."

Francis Charles Lawley, the London *Times*'s special correspondent in America, watched Lee through the Fredericksburg battle and wrote for the

Times "in commendation of the serenity, or, if I may so express it, the unconscious dignity of General Lee's courage, when he is under fire." And not only dignity, but wisdom: "It became more and more obvious," as the fog lifted that morning, "what a magnificent position was occupied by the Confederate army, and how wisely and sagaciously the ground had been chosen by General Lee." Another correspondent who visited Lee in November marveled that "it would seem as though the ordinary demands of human appetite were in him subordinated and subjected in presence of the imperious exactions required from his brain." Peter Alexander, who wrote for the *Southern Literary Messenger,* described Lee as "six feet in height, weighs about one hundred and ninety pounds," and possesses "rare judgment and equanimity, unerring sagacity, great self-control, and extraordinary powers of combination [concentration?]."[33]

What Lee did not let them see were his outbursts of temper at subordinates, which now became more frequent. "He did not allow any friend of soldiers condemned by court-martial . . . to reach his tent for personal appeal," remembered Charles Venable, and when "such disappointed men" elbowed their way into his presence, Lee would erupt not only at the petitioner but at Venable for not preventing the annoyance: "Why did you permit that man to come to my tent and make me show my temper?" One of Jackson's staff officers "asked an innocent question" while making a report to Lee, and Lee's response at this impertinence was so frosty that the staffer remarked, "I never felt so small in my life." Even Custis had to endure his flare-ups, reading letters from his father complaining that he was so tired of the pettiness in the Confederate Congress that he wished they would "pass a law relieving me from all duty & legislating some one in my place better able to do it. . . . I fear you will think I am in a bad humour & I fear I am."[34]

Under these burdens, something in Lee had to crack, and in March 1863 it did. He made his first visit to Richmond since the end of the Peninsula Campaign on March 13, to consult with Jefferson Davis, and stopped briefly to visit Mary for the first time in months. Mary was living with the family of James Caskie at Eleventh and Clay Streets as she tried to arrange for more permanent housing, but her arthritis had almost immobilized her. By the time he returned to his camp at Hamilton's Crossing on March 19, he was feeling seriously unwell himself, so "unwell since my return as not to be able to go anywhere." He called it a "heavy cold," mostly to allay Mary's anxieties. But it was no cold. He suffered "a good deal of pain in my chest, back, & arms" that came on "in Paroxysms . . . quite sharp." In the arcane medical vocabulary of the times, he had developed a "rheumatic inflammation of the sac enclosing the heart"—in other words, a heart attack. By March 29, word of Lee's illness was all through the Army of Northern Virginia. "Gen. Lee is sick and Gen. J[ackson] went over to see him in the p.m.," Jedediah Hotchkiss confided to his diary.[35]

He was moved on March 31 from his headquarters tent to a two-story brick house owned by Thomas Yerby a mile southwest of Hamilton's Crossing, where Lafayette Guild took charge. Guild, in turn, called on a New Orleans specialist, Samuel Merrifield Bemiss, who was serving with the army. "For over a week past he (Lee) has been sick," Bemiss wrote, "and I visit him every afternoon." But Lee continued to make as much light of it as he could. He wrote to Custis, conceding only that he was in "very indifferent health . . . weak, feverish, and altogether good for nothing," and assured Mary four days later that he had nothing more than "a violent cold."

He seemed to improve by April 5 and struggled to toss off concern by telling Mary that "the doctors are very attentive & kind & have examined my lungs, my heart, circulation . . . tapping me all over like an old steam boiler before condemning it"—which, considering the pressures he was under, was not entirely a poetic analogy. A week later, he was assuring Agnes that although "my pulse is still about 90," he was "able to ride out every day." This was not the first time he had experienced trouble with "rheumatism"—he had suffered some minor difficulty with it in the summer of 1860—but this attack was a presage of what would eventually kill him.[36]

For the time being, though, the crisis seemed to pass, only to be promptly followed by another one from across the Rappahannock.

CHAPTER FOURTEEN

In This Heathen War the Fire of God Fills Him

In December, Jefferson Davis undertook a monthlong inspection tour of the western Confederacy, addressing the Mississippi legislature, observing the Confederacy's western army (the optimistically named Army of Tennessee), speaking in Knoxville, Mobile, Atlanta, and Raleigh, and finally returning to Richmond on January 4. His intention was "to arouse all classes to united and desperate resistance." What he, like Lee, found instead were quarrels and desperate infighting among the Confederate military leadership, especially between Braxton Bragg, who commanded the Army of Tennessee, and Joe Johnston, whom Davis had only just installed as overall department commander in the west.

Just as bad, civilian morale was plunging. "The feeling in East. Tenn. and North Alabama is far from what we desire," Davis wrote to Secretary of War Seddon. "There is some hostility and much want of confidence in our strength." The relentless Ulysses Grant had mounted three major federal campaigns around Vicksburg since December, and he showed every determination to shut the fortress city up with a siege. By April, the situation in the west had deteriorated to the point that Seddon and Davis began to wonder whether the threat of losing the entire Mississippi River valley justified a proposal to Lee to peel off two or three brigades, or even an entire division, from the Army of Northern Virginia and send them west.[1]

Lee was only just recovering from his heart attack, but the idea of weakening his army to benefit the western Confederacy generated an energetic refusal. Yes, he acknowledged, "the most natural way to reinforce Genl. Johnston would seem to be to transfer a portion of the troops from this department to oppose" the Union armies operating in Mississippi under Grant and in Tennessee under Rosecrans. But they should realize that "it is not easy for us to change troops from one department to another . . . and if we rely on that method we may be always too late." He was careful not to concede that he had done that very thing by sending Longstreet and most of his corps to North Carolina, but then again, anything sent to North Carolina was much more easily recallable than troops sent across the Appalachians, and especially if he had to argue with Johnston or Bragg to retrieve them. But the more telling point for Lee was what he was already planning to do with the Army of Northern Virginia. He might strike for the Shenandoah Valley and force the Army of the Potomac to play by his rules and follow him there, away from Richmond. But the best "method of relieving the pressure upon Genl Johnston," Lee asserted, "would be for this army to cross into Maryland."[2]

Nothing that had happened since Antietam had dissuaded Lee in the least from his belief that only an invasion north of the Potomac, stunning Northern public opinion into collapse, would win the war for the Confederacy, and no such invasion would be possible if Davis and Seddon allowed troops to be drained away from the Army of Northern Virginia to prop up Johnston and Bragg. When Davis tried to insist, Lee pushed back. "On the subject of reinforcing the army in middle Tennessee," Lee carefully replied, "I . . . can arrive at no satisfactory conclusion with regard to reinforcing the troops in that department." If Joe Johnston was worried about Grant's octopus-like tentacles strangling Vicksburg, Johnston would be better advised "to concentrate the troops in his own department" and attack Grant rather than borrowing them from Virginia.

The same day, he wrote directly to Davis with even greater urgency, outlining the rationale for an offensive campaign in the east. "I think it all important that we should assume the aggressive" in Virginia "by the first of May. . . . I believe greater relief would in this way be afforded to the armies in middle Tennessee . . . than by any other method." The path to this result would lie through Northern politics. "If successful this year," Lee promised, "next fall there will be a great change in public opinion in the North." In 1864, the U.S. Congress would again be up for grabs, as would the presidency, and an uncontested occupation of Northern territory would finish the work begun by the 1862 elections. "The Republicans will be destroyed," and Northern Democrats acting as "the friends of peace will become so strong as that the next administration will go in on that basis." There were even opportunities for political mayhem as early as the fall of 1863. The governorships of Ohio and Pennsylvania were coming up for contest in October, and if they fell into Democratic hands the same way the New Jersey and New York governorships had in 1862, that central bloc of powerful Northern states might demand that

Lincoln open negotiations with the Confederacy or face the withdrawal of their state volunteers from the Union armies. For most of his life, Lee had viewed politicians as the weak pins in the fabric; this time, though, he could count on their weakness operating in his favor.[3]

But the strongest argument against dissipating Lee's forces came from the Army of the Potomac. In his misery, Burnside attempted to mount a second offensive in mid-January, only to have it flounder to a muddy standstill in the winter weather, and at the end of the month Lincoln wearily relieved him of command. (Lee's only comment was that, given the weather, "it was fortunate for the Federals that they failed to get over" the river.) His replacement was Joseph Hooker, aggressive, swaggering, rumored to be an alcoholic and womanizer, known to be an unscrupulous self-promoter and backstabber (starting with Ambrose Burnside's back). His outstanding virtue was being one of the few senior generals in the Army of the Potomac who stood unapologetically outside the circle of the McClellanites. That, however, was no guarantee that he could take in hand an army that, after Fredericksburg, appeared to have had its life and morale drained away by repeated failures. "If they don't give us McClellan or someone the army has confidence in, this army may turn into an armed mob and throw down their arms and go home. . . . I have seen a regiment so drunk that they were hard put to find 15 sober men for picket duty," wrote a disheartened soldier of the 140th Pennsylvania. By January 31, 25,363 men of the Army of the Potomac had taken French leave, some deserting at the rate of 200 a day.[4]

And yet, within three months, Hooker had worked an organizational miracle within the Army. Deserters were lured back with amnesties, other desertions headed off with a furlough policy, improved food and equipment brought into the Army's camps on the Rappahannock, and morale lifted through the invention of medals, corps badges, and battle honors for regimental flags. "I do not think it possible that such a change could have taken place for the better as has been effected," wrote a sergeant in the 2nd New Jersey. "From a dissatisfied and almost mutinous mob, we have become a good and well-disciplined army second to none." No one was more elated at this success than Joe Hooker. "I have the finest army the sun ever shone on," he chortled. "I can march this army to New Orleans." And not only was his army perfect, but so were the directions he planned to give them. "My plans are perfect, and when I start to carry them out, may God have mercy on General Lee, for I will have none."[5]

Those plans, when he delivered them to Lincoln on April 11, were not actually significantly different from Burnside's. There would be no evasive McClellan-like slips down to the James River, but rather another straightforward smash at Lee's army, crossing the Rappahannock to gain the flat country between Fredericksburg and Richmond. Hooker would differ only in where he planned to get across the river: "I have concluded that I will have more chance of inflicting a heavier blow upon the enemy by turning his position to my right," splashing across the shallow fords of the upper Rappahannock rather than trumpeting his intentions with the building of pontoon bridges.

The one hitch was that using the fords farther up the Rappahannock would land Hooker's army in a vast, gloomy forest of second-growth trees and underbrush known simply as the Wilderness. He would need to move swiftly through the Wilderness, or its narrow, shadowed roads would negate all the advantages he enjoyed by maneuver and numbers. But if he was successful, he would emerge from the Wilderness in the rear of Lee's positions west of Fredericksburg, and a surprised Lee would have no choice but to turn and fight on terms that gave Hooker a substantial edge. That satisfied Lincoln, whose only concern was that Hooker remember that the first goal was to find and crush Lee's army, not to capture Richmond. "Our prime object is the enemies' army in front of us," Lincoln reiterated, "and is not with, or about, Richmond at all, unless it be incidental to the main object."[6]

For a while, it worked. On April 27, the day Hooker's expedition began to move, Lee was still convalescing at the Yerby house and writing to Longstreet in North Carolina, asking about his operations there and "when your operations will be completed." It appeared to Lee that Hooker was moving men around "as if he intended to make an aggressive movement, but by what route I cannot ascertain." Lee did not awake to Hooker's intentions until two days later, and even then his attention was focused on a large-scale diversion Hooker arranged opposite Fredericksburg with two infantry corps. Not until that evening did Lee realize that Hooker was crossing the Rappahannock with most of his forces farther upriver.

Hurriedly, Lee ordered a division he had posted near the Rappahannock fords to fall back, "taking the strongest line you can" that would cover the rear of Fredericksburg, sending off urgent calls for Jackson to "move up . . . and take position" in Hooker's path, and ordering Longstreet to drop everything and return to Virginia. By that time, Hooker was already across the Rappahannock, three of his corps crossing at Kelly's Ford, two others at United States Ford, and plunging into the Wilderness; by the thirtieth, the leading edge of Hooker's advance had reached the Chancellor House (a tavern and hostelry that gave its name to a Wilderness crossroads, Chancellorsville), and George Meade, the commander of Hooker's Fifth Corps, was already congratulating his fellow officers. "This is splendid," Meade declared to Henry Slocum, who commanded the Army of the Potomac's Twelfth Corps. "Hurrah for old Joe; we are on Lee's flank, and he does not know it. You take the

Plank Road toward Fredericksburg, and I'll take the Pike, or vice versa, as you prefer, and we'll get out of this Wilderness."[7]

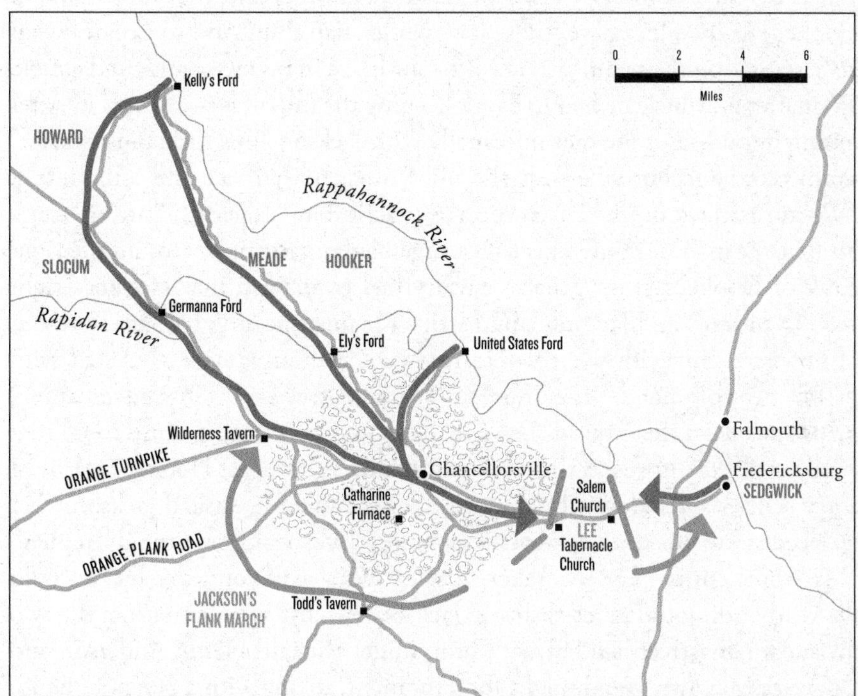

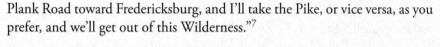

But Lee was now alive to his peril. Keeping one eye on the federal diversion at Fredericksburg, he posted one of Jackson's divisions (under the caustic Lynchburg lawyer and onetime unionist, Jubal Early) to hold the old Marye's Heights position and then turned with the rest of Jackson's corps and the two divisions left him by Longstreet to face Hooker at Chancellorsville. Hooker arrived at the Chancellorsville crossing on the afternoon of April 30 and issued his most bombastic communiqué yet: "The operations of the last three days have determined that our enemy must either ingloriously fly, or come out from behind his defences and give us battle on our own ground, where certain destruction awaits him." But when Hooker tried to press eastward from Chancellorsville to strike Lee in what he presumed was the Confederate rear, he met unexpectedly stiff opposition from Jackson, and at that moment Hooker's bombast descended to bluster, and from thence to anxiety. Hooker, said one general who had known him before the war in California, "could play the best game of poker I ever saw until it came to the point when he should go a thousand better, and then he would flunk." He now flunked, ordering Meade and Slocum to pull back to the Chancellorsville crossing and create a defensive cordon.[8]

That did not mean that Lee was delivered. He was still minus Longstreet, and he was still between the jaws of the diversionary force at Fredericksburg and the bulk of Hooker's army at Chancellorsville, and if at any moment Hooker regained his nerve, those jaws could snap shut. And so Lee did what he had done on the peninsula: keep the initiative in his own hands and attack. No matter how little he had in hand, keeping the initiative was worth it. After midnight on May 2, he met informally with Jackson "in a little pine thicket" south of Chancellorsville near the old Catharine Furnace and announced, "We must attack on the left as soon as practicable." Together, "sitting over a little fire & in close conference," Lee urged a dramatic blow around the right flank of Hooker's army. Stuart's cavalry had confirmed that Hooker's right was "in the air," and Jackson could strike the unsuspecting Hooker from out of nowhere. But with what would he make such an attack? "If I had with me all my command," Lee mused, "I should feel easy." Toward morning, maps spread on the ground, Lee and Jackson began tracing out a route that would strike the unsuspecting Federals, taking as its target Hooker's rearmost corps, Oliver Otis Howard's Eleventh Corps. When Lee asked Jackson what he needed "to make this movement with," Jackson unhesitatingly replied, "My whole corps." Lee was taken aback: "What will you leave me" to hold the road leading to Fredericksburg? Jackson was just as unhesitating: the two divisions Longstreet had left with him, under Richard Heron Anderson and Lafayette McLaws. Lee thought for a moment, toying with a pencil in hand, then told Jackson, "Well, go on."[9]

Nothing Lee had ever done conformed so closely to what Porter Alexander called "audacity" back on the peninsula, yet, even here, it was a calculated audacity, because this was exactly the sort of devastating flank attack Lee had sent Longstreet to deliver at Second Bull Run. Nor did Jackson fall in any way short of that audacity. Setting out on the morning of the second, Jackson descended like the Last Judgment on Hooker's unsuspecting flank just after five o'clock in the afternoon, and almost half of Hooker's troops folded up and ran for their lives. Whole divisions and brigades were turned into "a dense mass of beings who had lost their reasoning faculties, and were flying from a thousand fancied dangers as well as from the real danger that crowded so close upon them. . . . Battery wagons, ambulances, horses, men, cannon, caissons, all jumbled and tumbled together in an apparently inextricable mass, and that murderous fire still pouring in upon them." Had not night fallen, Jackson might easily have rolled them all the way back to the Rappahannock. The next day, Lee launched a general assault on the beleaguered federal lines around the Chancellor House, and after a solid shot nearly decapitated Hooker as he stood on the Chancellor porch, Hooker ordered a general retreat.

As the Confederates swarmed through the abandoned Chancellorsville crossing, Lee arrived to a welcome from his men that exceeded all the outward boundaries of jubilation. "The troops opened to the right and the left, and as the old Hero passed through, the line greeted him with tremendous cheers." Charles Marshall, riding with him, heard "one long, unbroken cheer, in which the feeble cry of those who lay helpless on the earth blended with the strong voices of those who still fought." In his imagination, Marshall "thought it must have been from some such scene that men in ancient days ascended to the dignity of the gods." A South Carolina soldier hailed Lee for ending "the mad career of the Federal general and sent him limping and howling back to his den on the other side of the Rappahannock River." Lee had won "another laurel which shall last as long as time itself." At that moment, Lee had achieved a plateau of glory few Americans have ever occupied, even his Revolutionary father.[10]

However mild he seems at home, nor cares
For triumph in our mimic wars. . . .
Yet in this heathen war the fire of God
Fills him; I never saw his like; there lives
No greater leader.

But the Chancellorsville victory had come at an unexpected cost. For one thing, Jackson was accidentally wounded by a volley from his own men as he attempted a reconnaissance in the darkness following his great attack. Hit twice in the left arm and once in the right hand, Jackson had to endure the amputation of his mangled arm in the wee hours of May 3. Members of his staff carried the news to Lee, "sitting under a pine tree." Any victory, Lee responded, "is dearly bought which deprives us of the services of Jackson, even for a short time," and to Jedediah Hotchkiss he "said he would rather a thousand times it had been himself." But there was nothing that indicated Jackson's wound was life threatening, and he wrote Jackson a short note repeating that "could I have directed events, I should have chosen, for the good of the country, to have been disabled in your stead." By May 7, however, pneumonia had set in. When Lee was notified that Jackson was in danger, he sent him "my affectionate regards" and assured him that while he had "lost his left arm . . . I have lost my right arm." But neither Lee nor the doctors could stem Jackson's decline, and on May 10, Jackson died. Lee's right arm was gone indeed. "I had such implicit confidence in Jackson's skill and energy, that I never troubled myself to give him detailed instructions," Lee said years later. "The most general suggestions were all that he needed." Jackson was the model of what Lee hoped for in subordinates, and he would never be replaced.[11]

Nor was Lee as exultant over the results of Chancellorsville as his soldiers. Hooker managed to extricate his dazed army from danger and safely recrossed the Rappahannock while Lee's division and brigade commanders tripped clumsily over one another in a fruitless pursuit. Porter Alexander saw him "in a temper" because "it now devolved on him to find out all about the enemy before we could move a peg." When Dorsey Pender had to report Hooker's escape, Lee's fury was volcanic. "General Pender! That is what you young men always do. You allow those people to get away." And in an echo of his complaint after Malvern Hill (and every complaint he had made about Southern indifference) he accused Pender of lukewarmness. "I tell you what to do, but you don't do it." Now he demanded, "Go after them and damage them all you can."

But it was too late. Although the Army of Northern Virginia had inflicted more than 11,500 casualties on Hooker's army, Chancellorsville had cost it almost the same number, and in a proportionately smaller army. And it was not a battle Lee had wanted to fight; like Fredericksburg, it was a triumph, but a hollow one, because ultimately it changed nothing. "At Chancellorsville we gained another victory," Lee said later that year. "Our people were wild with delight—I, on the contrary, was more depressed than after Fredericksburg; our loss was severe, and again we had gained not an inch of ground and the enemy could not be pursued." As he would later admit to Longstreet, "Even victories such as these were consuming us, and would eventually destroy us." There was only one way for the war to be won, and for everything he had lost to be redeemed, and that way pointed north.[12]

The first six months of 1863 were the nadir of the Union's confidence. Democratic successes in the 1862 elections gave them a second wind of opposition, which was then whipped into a full-blown gale when emboldened Democratic editors and orators were arrested for denouncing Lincoln, the war, and emancipation. "We must all combine to remove from power every Republican official, National, State or municipal," resolved a mass meeting in New York City. "If we were to have a Union with the South it must be because we were to meet them in a spirit of conciliation," and that included "our sacredly preserving the right of property in slaves."

The lame-duck federal Congress passed a conscription law in March that promised more recruits but also more disaffection and resistance. A much-touted naval assault on Charleston flopped, and the humiliating disasters at Fredericksburg and Chancellorsville hung more crepe around the Union cause. The news of Fredericksburg made an agonized Lincoln "wonder if the damned in hell suffer less than I do." But Chancellorsville was worse, leaving Lincoln in "the deepest depression of spirits amounting to Monomania," because he "looked upon Hooker as his 'last card.'" Unquestionably, declared Horace Greeley of the *New-York Tribune,* "the darkest hours of the National cause were those" that began at Fredericksburg, sickening "the hearts of Unionists" and strengthening "into confidence the hopes of the Rebels and those who . . . were in sympathy" with them.[13]

No one fed on this news more eagerly than Robert E. Lee, who saw in it an even better moment than the previous fall to bring the house of Northern confidence crashing down. As early as February 1863, Jackson privately directed his mapmaker, Jedediah Hotchkiss, "to prepare a map of the Valley of Va. extended to Harrisburg, Pa., and then on to Philadelphia," and camp rumors in April whispered that "we are all making grand plans . . . in favor of going straight through Md. into Penna." (If Lee's heart attack and Hooker's brief offensive over the Rappahannock had not intervened, Lee might well have launched his newest invasion of the North in the early spring.) The "central idea" of such a campaign was that "if the State of Pennsylvania were invaded" and the "capital of the commonwealth" occupied, and "a great victory gained upon her soil . . . the sentiment of the Northern people might turn in favor of peace and result in the recognition of Southern independence."[14]

To do so, however, Lee would have to win over both Jefferson Davis and Secretary of War Seddon, who interpreted Hooker's defeat at Chancellorsville as a guarantee that the Army of the Potomac would go into a long hibernation of reorganization, reequipment, and perhaps regeneraling, and thus present no active threat along the Rappahannock. He would almost have to argue against his own successes, because the case for sending reinforcements from Lee's army to the west seemed to gain greater strength from so much success in the east, especially since Ulysses Grant had now planted federal troops just south of Vicksburg and appeared to be closing in its hapless defenders. That motion was seconded by no one less than James Longstreet, who returned from North Carolina on May 8 and was beginning to cultivate ideas of an independent command for himself. As he passed through Richmond en route to Lee, Longstreet took the curious liberty of calling on Secretary Seddon and proposing that the two divisions he was bringing back from North Carolina "be swiftly moved to Tullahoma" and combined with Braxton Bragg's Army of Tennessee in order to launch a "march through Tennessee and Kentucky, and threaten the invasion of Ohio." Lee dashed those expectations, once Longstreet had reached him, by asking "me if I did not think an invasion of Maryland and Pennsylvania by his own army would accomplish the same result" as "a western forward movement," although it took some effort to persuade Longstreet that "after piercing Pennsylvania and menacing

Washington," the Army of Northern Virginia could "choose a strong position and force the Federals to attack us."

Lee was less temperate when Seddon once more pressed the western option on him. "Your proposition is hazardous, and it becomes a question between Virginia and Mississippi." Seddon should not deceive himself into thinking that Hooker would remain conveniently inert on the Rappahannock; the Army of the Potomac "will take its own time to prepare and strengthen itself to renew its advance on Richmond." The best course "would be to invade Pennsylvania, penetrating this State in the direction of Chambersburg, York, or Gettysburg." Lee would not need, he explained to his staff, "to give battle in Pennsylvania if he could avoid it." But if he did have to fight the Army of the Potomac, little in its successive flips of commanders and numerous embarrassing defeats suggested he had anything to worry about.[15]

On May 14, Lee went to Richmond to put his case personally to Davis and Seddon, and "subsequently he and the Secretary of War were long closeted with the President." He looked "thinner, and a little pale" from the heart attack and his long recovery, but after a day of haggling Lee emerged victorious. An invasion of the North must go forward, first because "army supplies had become scarce south of" the Potomac "while they were abundant north of it," and second because "he believed he commanded an invincible army, which had been so victorious in so many great battles," and a "successful campaign in the territory adjacent to Washington, Baltimore, and Philadelphia might cause the withdrawal of the troops then menacing Vicksburg" and the Mississippi. Davis continued to be bombarded by pleas from western governors for pieces of Lee's army, cries that were sharpened when, on May 18, Ulysses Grant successfully grasped Vicksburg in a tight siege. But Lee stiffened the president's resolve with the reminder that playing to the "desire for peace at the North" was the surest shortcut to saving Vicksburg and the Confederacy, and nothing would bring that to pass more quickly than an invasion north of the Potomac.[16]

Before he could do that, however, Lee would need to find a replacement for Jackson. His first instinct was to promote Powell Hill. But Hill's quarrels with Jackson had made enemies for him among Jackson's staff, and Dorsey Pender (who was commanding a brigade in Hill's division) was disturbed to discover "what a jealousy exists towards A. P. Hill." Jackson was supposed to have wished on his deathbed to be succeeded by Richard Ewell, who had been his senior division commander at Second Bull Run. But Ewell had been badly wounded there, losing a leg to a particularly painful amputation, and because he was only just now ready to return to duty, there was some question about whether he was up to its rigors. Lee decided to split the difference.

On May 23, Ewell was promoted to lieutenant general in Jackson's place, but the next day Lee recommended Hill's promotion to the same rank and informed Davis that he intended to reorganize the Army of Northern Virginia from two to three infantry corps, with each corps now to contain three divisions, and Hill and Ewell each to command one of the newly configured corps. "I have for the past year felt that the corps of this army were too large for one commander," Lee explained to Davis. The death of Jackson opened an opportunity to "remedy this evil" by giving Ewell "command of three divi-

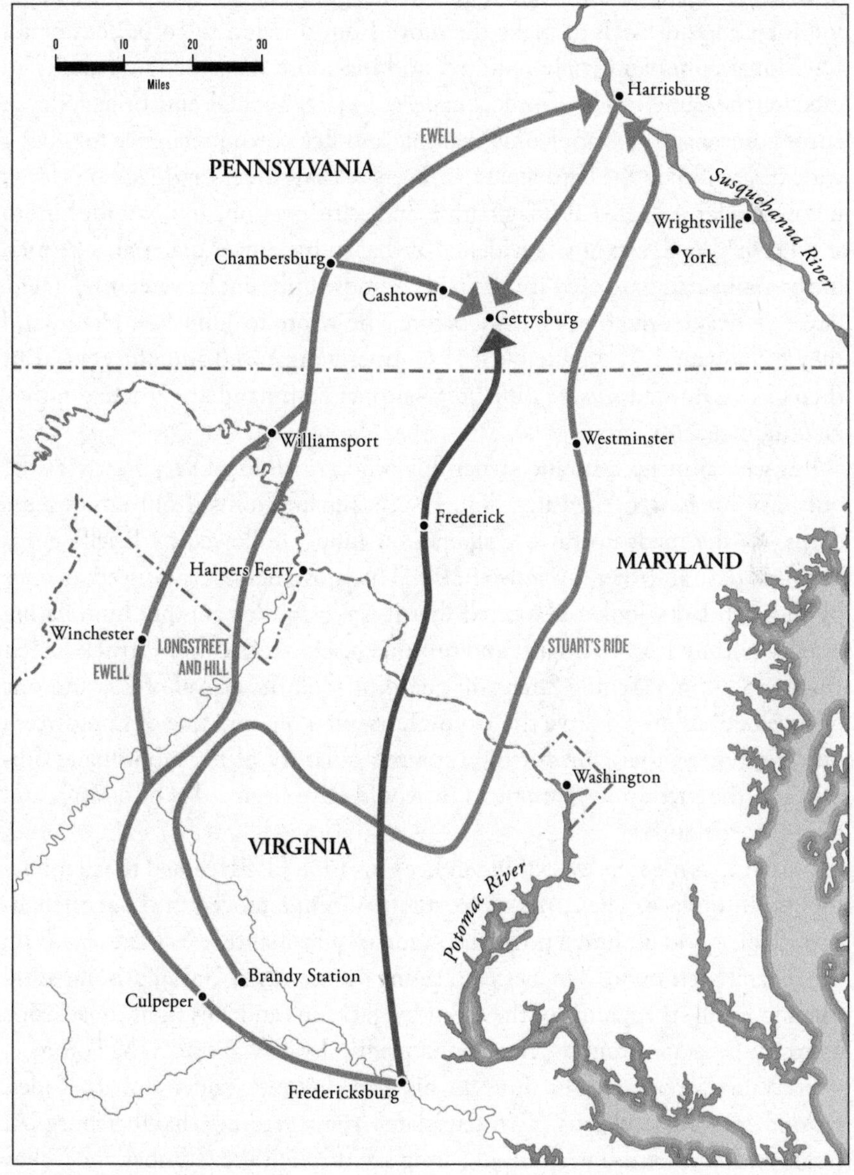

sions of Jackson's corps" and blending the remainder with "one of Longstreet's divisions" to create a new corps for Powell Hill, and thus "promote Ewell and A. P. Hill." Longstreet would retain command of the remaining three divisions of his corps. He was now ready, as Dorsey Pender believed, "to strike home and so effectually as to close the war, if possible, soon."[17]

Or so he hoped. No one understood better than Lee that Jackson was irreplaceable. And despite his recommendations for Hill and Ewell, he had been learning over the course of the past year that he did not have a deep well of military talent to draw upon, and it was going to be especially challenging for Hill and Ewell to make the move from division to corps command. Divisional command really required nothing more than the same ability to execute the same kinds of orders expected at regimental and brigade level; corps command, by Napoleonic example and Lee's own preference for giving wide discretion on the battlefield to officers at Longstreet's and Jackson's level, involved a large degree of imagination and self-direction, and, sad for him to say, Lee had not seen much evidence of that in his officer material. The men in the ranks had hardened into reliable, almost unbeatable, veterans. "There never were such men in an army before," he wrote to John Bell Hood, and they really would "be invincible if . . . properly organized and officered." But there, Lee admitted, "is the difficulty—proper commanders. Where can they be obtained?"[18]

It gave him no assurance when his officers stumbled very nearly at the outset of his long-desired invasion. Lee set his first units, from Longstreet's corps, on the roads north to Culpeper on June 3, followed by Ewell's corps the next day, and then by Powell Hill. The movement was noticed at once by Hooker. But Hooker suspected that it was a foil for another humiliating cavalry raid by J. E. B. Stuart, and on June 9, Hooker's cavalry struck first at Brandy Station, catching Stuart off guard. It took the arrival of Lee and one of Ewell's divisions to drive the Union horsemen off, and one of Longstreet's officers snorted that "but for the supreme gallantry of his subordinate officers and the men in his command, it would have been a day of disaster and disgrace" for Stuart.

After that misstep, everything in Lee's invasion plans seemed to fall miraculously into place. The Army of Northern Virginia moved into the Shenandoah Valley, and on June 14, Ewell conducted a brilliantly executed assault on the federal garrison in Winchester, bagging thousands of Union prisoners and earning Ewell "the mantle of the ascended Jackson" and "his right to Jackson's game on Jackson's ground." By the nineteenth, Ewell was across the Potomac, near Williamsport, and on June 22 his lead division, under Robert Rodes, crossed into Pennsylvania. Two days later, they were in Chambersburg. At Lee's bidding, Ewell started off in a long arc through the Cumberland Valley toward Harrisburg and the Susquehanna River, while one of Ewell's divisions, belonging to Jubal Early, headed straight eastward toward York and the vast railroad bridge that spanned the Susquehanna at Wrightsville.

By the twenty-seventh, Lee was pitching his own headquarters tent at Chambersburg, on the west side of South Mountain. Joe Hooker, meanwhile, had waited too long before realizing where Lee was headed, and now played a desperate game of catch-up in order to shield Washington from any possible designs Lee had on the capital. In the process, Hooker opened up old quarrels with Washington about who had control of what, and when he offered on June 27 to resign, Lincoln accepted without hesitation.[19]

As Union confusion multiplied, so did Confederate confidence. Lee was prepared to stay for "two months" in Pennsylvania "to subsist his army," or longer if "the way will be clear to Baltimore Philadelphia Washington and so on." But he was becoming more convinced that the Army of the Potomac would come pelting after him, stringing itself out on the roads into Pennsylvania, and setting up a climactic Union defeat. "They will come up, probably through Frederick; broken down with hunger and hard marching." He would quickly concentrate his own forces and pick off the Union pieces as they stumbled into his hands, driving "one corps back and another, and by successive repulses and surprises . . . create a panic and virtually destroy the army." His best estimate was that this would happen near the south-central Pennsylvania crossroads town of Gettysburg, where "we shall probably meet the enemy and fight a great battle." By this means, he would "attain far more decisive results than could be hoped for from a like advantage in Virginia"—nothing less, in fact, than "the recognition of our independence," because "the Federal army, if defeated . . . would be seriously disorganized . . . and it would very likely cause the fall of Washington city and the flight of the Federal government."

(Ironically, one person who did not seem to share Lee's optimism was his own naval brother, Sidney Smith Lee, who was spending his time supervising the river batteries that guarding Richmond; the Anglo-Austrian observer FitzGerald Ross thought Smith "spoke rather despondently about the coming campaign" because of "the difficulties" his brother had "to contend with—his want of mechanical appliances, pontoons, &c.; no organized corps of engineers; the dangers of exposing Richmond if he gets too far away.")[20]

The Army "is strong and in fine spirits," wrote a South Carolinian, "and has the most implicit confidence in Genl Lee." One writer for a Virginia newspaper complimented Lee on the march for his simplicity and lack of pretense as "a stoutly built man . . . with gray hair and a stiff, scrubbly gray beard . . . dressed very plainly, with not a single mark of his rank about him, wearing a black slouch hat without ornament, dark blue or black military cape, and plain gray pantaloons." This time, Lee "observed with marked satisfaction" that there was almost no straggling. Invading Pennsylvania had the soldiers' endorsement in a way the Maryland invasion the year before had never had. "The army is in splendid condition," wrote one Virginia officer, and "marches almost wholly without straggling, and is in the highest spirits." He also issued a stringent general order against pillaging, in the style of Winfield Scott and to draw a line of distinction with John Pope. But that was mostly ignored. Pennsylvania was an agricultural paradise compared with war-torn Virginia, and no straggling was needed to garner its fruits. Lee's soldiers helped themselves to the bulging contents of one Pennsylvania granary and store after another—and helped themselves to tracking down some five hundred black Pennsylvanians whom they roped and cuffed for transport and auction in Virginia slave markets. "Such a movement," predicted a staff officer for the Louisiana "Tiger" brigade, would "make the Yankees feel more sensibly the disastrous effects of the war they had inaugurated."[21]

What was missing from Lee's advance was J. E. B. Stuart and most of the Army's cavalry. Stuart had been assigned by Lee to move in tandem with the advance of Ewell's corps and screen the Army's movements from the prying eyes of federal cavalry. But, eager to redeem himself from the embarrassment at Brandy Station, Stuart and three of his cavalry brigades instead allowed themselves to be squeezed to the east, circling the Army of the Potomac yet again and crossing the Potomac far downstream at Rowser's Ford, uncomfortably close to Washington, on June 27. Out of touch with Lee, Stuart rode blindly northward to Westminster, Maryland, and would not find Lee and the main body of the Army of Northern Virginia until late on July 2.

For the eight days Stuart was galloping aimlessly in search of the Confederate army, Lee was "much disturbed" by the threat that Stuart would be cornered by superior federal forces, and increasingly nettled that Stuart was not available to screen the infantry's advance into Pennsylvania. On June 28, "with a peculiar searching, almost querulous impatience," he began badgering couriers and staffers whether they "had heard anything from Gen'*l* Jeb Stuart." Stuart, he complained, "has gone off clear around" the Union army "& I see by a [Balt*o* or N.Y.?] paper that he is near Washington." Lee was not, however, left entirely blind by Stuart's absence. Northern newspapers obligingly provided him with detailed information about the Army of the Potomac's movements, and that evening one of the Confederacy's most talented military spies, Henry Thomas Harrison, brought Lee the news that the Federals had finally crossed the Potomac River and that Lincoln had appointed as Hooker's replacement a lackluster but diligent McClellanite, George Gordon Meade.[22]

Lee at once ordered Ewell to break off his approach to Harrisburg and

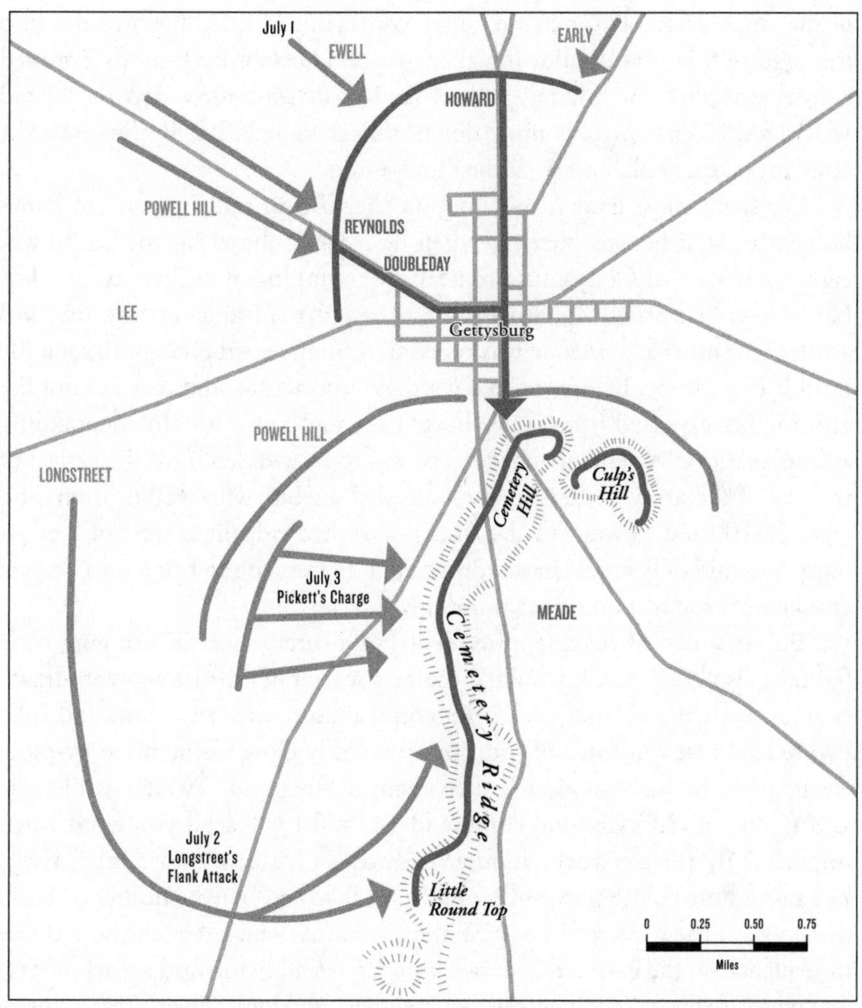

directed Powell Hill and Longstreet to move across South Mountain toward a rendezvous with Ewell near Gettysburg. "Tomorrow, gentlemen, we will not move on Harrisburg, as we expected, but will go over to Gettysburg and see what General Meade is after." The Army of the Potomac could probably count something close to 95,000 men, while Lee probably had between 85,000 and 90,000. But Lee would have the advantage of concentration, while the Federals would arrive at Gettysburg in disconnected groups, each of them easy for Lee to crush one by one.

However, to Lee's surprise, there were already Federals at Gettysburg, on the ridges west of the town, when Powell Hill attempted to march into Gettysburg on July 1. There were not many of them—a small division of Union cavalry that stubbornly disputed Hill's progress outside the town—and two of the Army of the Potomac's infantry corps. But Hill fed his brigades into the fighting piecemeal, allowing them to be knocked back by determined federal resistance. At midday, Robert Rodes's division arrived as the herald of Richard Ewell's corps, coming down from the north. But Rodes made the same mistake as Hill, and with the same results.

Lee spent most of that morning on the road in the company of James Longstreet, and he was puzzled, when he reached the village of Cashtown, eight miles west of Gettysburg, to hear the thumping of artillery to the east. No one was surprised in 1863 by the occasional spittings of rifle fire, but artillery meant that someone was meeting resistance stiff enough to take the trouble to unlimber fieldpieces and get them into action, and that was not the greeting Lee expected from Gettysburg. Lee caught up with Hill, demanding an explanation. "A general engagement was to be avoided until the arrival of the rest of the army," Lee irritably reminded anyone who would listen, and when he spurred forward to the smoke-wreathed ridgelines west of Gettysburg, he could only repeat in disapproval, "I do not wish to bring on a general engagement today. Longstreet is not up."[23]

But as much as he disapproved of Hill's carelessness in bringing on a fight, he also knew that it would "become a matter of difficulty to withdraw." Besides, with the balance of Ewell's corps almost within earshot, and only two federal corps in front of him, this was fairly close to the piece-by-piece engagement he had envisioned. Lee changed his mind. "Wait a while," he said to one of Hill's division commanders, "and I will send you word when to go in." By three o'clock, another of Ewell's divisions, under Jubal Early, had moved into place north of Gettysburg, followed by yet another of Hill's divisions on the west, and Lee gave the signal that sent them crashing down in sequence on the battered Federals, moving "steadily forward across the yellow wheat fields . . . their burnished bayonets making a silver wave across a cloth of gold." Within two hours, the Federals were in full flight through the town, only stopping to rally south of Gettysburg on a low plateau known as Cemetery Hill (where the town graveyard, the Evergreen Cemetery, had been laid out in the previous decade).

Lee watched them from "an eminence" on the west side of Gettysburg, "with the bridle rein of Traveller thrown over his right arm and looking anxiously through his field glasses." Under almost any other circumstances, Ewell's divisions should have been able to roll right over the improvised federal resistance on Cemetery Hill. But on this overcast day, twilight was coming on, the movement through the town had badly disrupted the victorious Confederate formations, and the troops themselves were exhausted from a day full of continuous marching and fighting. Lee sent one courier to Ewell with the order to "feel the enemy strongly," and then sent Walter Taylor to urge Ewell to "press 'those people' in order to secure possession of the heights"—but only if it seemed "practicable." Taylor assumed that Ewell saw no "impediment" to implementing Lee's order, which "left the impression upon my mind that it would be executed." But Ewell chose this moment to revert to the attitude of a division commander, wondering how to interpret these orders, until he finally concluded that what Lee wanted was for "him to assume the defensive and not to advance." Hill, whose carelessness had prematurely triggered the battle, decided likewise with his own corps and made no advance on Cemetery Hill. "Prudence," Hill explained, "led me to be content with what had been gained."[24]

This was not necessarily a faulty conclusion, for Hill or Ewell or even Lee. Although a division each from Hill's and Ewell's corps had failed to get into the fight, and Longstreet's entire corps was still on the road from Chambersburg, the scenario at Gettysburg had played out pretty closely to what Lee had imagined. Giving his soldiers pause to reorder themselves would put them in far better shape to occupy Cemetery Hill (whose plateau turned out to be an ideal artillery platform) and finish off its defenders and then await still more pieces of the Army of the Potomac as they staggered up to be defeated. "If the enemy is there tomorrow, we must attack him," Lee declared, and for that tomorrow would suffice.[25]

But tomorrow would not suffice. Another infantry corps from the Army of the Potomac arrived at dusk; George Gordon Meade made it to Gettysburg just after midnight, and following him far more closely than Lee anticipated were two more federal infantry corps. By mid-morning on July 2, the remaining two corps of Meade's army were at Gettysburg as well.

Lee, however, saw none of this. For once, he delegated the reconnaissance of Cemetery Hill and its environs to a staffer, Samuel Johnston, whose report assured Lee that no new federal troops were in the area. Dressed even in the midsummer heat with his "coat buttoned to the throat, sabre-belt buckled around the waist, field glasses pending at his side," Lee proposed to send Longstreet's corps on a Chancellorsville-like flank march, intending that Longstreet should swing below Cemetery Hill and then strike it from behind.

Longstreet objected. Only two of his divisions had appeared at Gettysburg by the morning of the second (his third division, commanded by the erratic George Pickett, was only just departing Chambersburg). Lee waved away the point: "The enemy is here, and if we do not whip him, he will whip us." But he allowed Longstreet to borrow a division from Powell Hill to make up the attacking force and instructed Hill and Ewell to be prepared to support Longstreet when the "warhorse" finally broke through the rear of Cemetery Hill. Even so, Longstreet was not ready to spring his assault until four o'clock in the afternoon, and by that time two fresh federal infantry corps had blocked access to the rear of Cemetery Hill, spread out along a ridgeline tapering south from Cemetery Hill (and thus acquiring the name Cemetery Ridge, even though it contained no cemetery and was little more than an up fold in the ground). Longstreet was forced to shift his line of attack to drive away these unanticipated opponents before he had any chance of rolling up to Cemetery Hill, and with only the late-afternoon daylight to do it.[26]

That he almost succeeded in smashing up the federal opposition was a tribute to Longstreet's tactical energy. "Never perhaps in all its history," not even at Chancellorsville, did Lee's men "feel the thrill of victory so vividly," wrote one Alabama officer. They "felt that the supreme moment of the war had come—that victory was with our army and we ourselves were the victors." Longstreet's divisions successfully mangled two federal corps and nearly destroyed an entire division belonging to another, and when the firing ceased at darkness, George Meade called a council of his senior officers to consider whether to abandon Gettysburg entirely. Above all, J. E. B. Stuart's long-lost and bleary-eyed cavalry finally caught up with Lee, and the Army of Northern Virginia was at last united again.

But in the process of wrecking so much of the Army of the Potomac, Longstreet had also fallen just short of capturing Cemetery Ridge. One of Hill's brigades almost overran Cemetery Ridge on its own, only to be stopped short by quick Union reinforcements, while Richard Ewell, launching a cooperating attack at Cemetery Hill (and its neighbor, Culp's Hill), fell even more agonizingly short of driving the Federals off in a rout. Lee preferred to read those results as proof that the Army of the Potomac was nearly at the end of its rope and that one more solid blow (like Second Bull Run or Chancellorsville) would splay them flat. "All we had to do was to follow them up the next day," Lindsay Long assured a friend, and a captured federal officer could not help noticing how "very sanguine of their ability to dislodge the Army of the Potomac from its position" the rebels were, that "the capture of Washington and Baltimore was considered a thing almost accomplished." And to deliver that coup de grâce, Lee had Pickett's fresh division, finally on-site and ready to land the winning punch the next day. Once again, Hill's and Ewell's corps "were to cooperate, as before, by opening with artillery & engaging the attention of the enemy as far as possible."[27]

But on July 3, the ambitious offensive Lee planned came apart in the same maddening lack of coordination that had robbed the Confederates of a comprehensive victory so many times before. Ewell's diversion was set off prematurely in the morning and dissipated by the time Longstreet was ready to send Pickett's division on its grand attack. Lee wanted to add five of Hill's brigades, and two of the brigades Longstreet had used the day before, to support Pickett and bring the total number of attackers to near 15,000. But Hill himself remained inert, and Longstreet's two support brigades jumped to the attack too late to be of any real help.

The heaviest weight of the assault would be carried by Pickett, and although Lee arranged for an hour-long bombardment of the federal position on Cemetery Ridge to silence Union artillery, Longstreet was decidedly unenthusiastic about giving the order. "General," Longstreet pleaded, "I have been a soldier all my life. I have been engaged in fights by couples, by squads, companies, regiments, divisions and armies, and . . . it is my opinion that no fifteen thousand men ever arrayed for battle can take that position." Moxley Sorrel, observing Longstreet arguing with Lee, was sure that Longstreet "did not want to fight on the ground or on the plan adopted by the General-in-chief."

It was no use. "Lee, Longstreet and Pickett rode together up and down in front of our line . . . at least three times . . . observing our assignment . . . with field glasses" and absorbed "in earnest conversation." But Lee "was impatient of listening, and tired of talking, and nothing was left but to proceed." Turning to Pickett, Lee announced, "I have reserved to your command the honor of capturing those heights"—pointing to Cemetery Ridge—"they must be taken at all hazards." They deployed, singing a hymn:

Charge for the God of battles,
And put the foe to rout.

Lee would only mutter, "The attack must succeed."[28]

The Confederate artillery opened up at one o'clock in a bombardment of the federal guns on Cemetery Hill so concentrated that farmers in Maryland "looked up to the sky in puzzlement for the source of thunder on a cloudless day." The long lines of Confederate infantry shook themselves out of the tree line opposite Cemetery Ridge and strode across the fields toward the Federals holding the ridge. "No one who saw them could help admiring the steadiness with which they came on," wrote John Cook, a captain in the 80th New York. They were like "the shadow of a cloud seen from a distance as it sweeps across a sunny field." Even as they were gouged by federal artillery fire, they swept on irresistibly, closing up the tears in their ranks. As they did, one Union artilleryman could see "gaps opened in their lines," and behind the gaps a "stream of wounded men" heading to their rear turned "from a rivulet" and "became a river."

Finally, one of Pickett's brigades punched a hole through the federal line on the ridge, and for a few minutes the fighting became an aimless mass of shooting and stabbing and clubbing around a small woodlot on the crest of the ridge. But the momentum was gone, and then the penetration was sealed, and presently Pickett's survivors "fled to the rear over dead and wounded, mangled, groaning, dying men, scattered thick, far and wide," while "officers and privates side by side, pushed, poured and rushed in a continuous stream, throwing away guns, blankets and haversacks as they hurried on in confusion toward the rear." Hill's brigades, likewise, "gave way, not in sullen retreat, but in disordered flight."[29]

Lee took up a position in the woods where Pickett's division began the attack, appearing "outwardly calm" and only betraying his anxiety by the way he was "twirling his spectacles in his hand." But as the remnants of Pickett's and Hill's men came streaming back through the thick fog of powder smoke, it became more and more painfully clear that the great attack had failed, and failed badly. A disheartened Pickett trailed back, and when he met Lee, his commander took him "by the hand" as if to soothe him. "General, your men have done all that men could do, the fault is entirely my own." But Pickett was not in a mood to be consoled, and when Lee suggested he rally the fragments of his division, "in rear of this hill, and be ready to repel the advance of the enemy should they follow up their advantage," Pickett angrily interrupted him. "General Lee, I have no division now." Lee ignored the anger, and "It is all my fault" became the message with which he greeted all of the survivors. "We met General Lee," recalled Colonel Samuel Shepard of the 7th Tennessee, "who took me by the hand and said to me: 'Colonel, rally your men and protect our artillery. The fault is mine, but it will be all right in the end.' "[30]

This was not entirely true: it was not his fault that Hill had started the fighting two days before, in spite of Lee's warnings to his corps commanders not to bring on a "general engagement"; it was not his fault that the information brought to him on the morning of July 2 was woefully inaccurate, and that there was a significant amount of federal infantry in the way of Longstreet's attack that afternoon; it was not his fault that Ewell had stopped short of Cemetery Hill on July 1 and then on the next two days failed to press home the diversions he was responsible for; and it was not his fault that Stuart was not there to screen his movements. What *was* Lee's fault was his determination to press into the battle anyway, because none of those other failures seemed to amount to much in his mind when set beside the dreadful record of incompetence the Army of the Potomac had manifested up to this point and the invincibility he attributed, if not to his officers, then to the men in the ranks.

And there is some question whether this was entirely a *fault.* Lee had actually come perilously close to exactly the success he had hoped for. A week after Gettysburg, New York City erupted in citywide riots against the new federal conscription law, and Richard Henry Dana was convinced that in the wake of a Confederate victory at Gettysburg "the Democrats would have risen and stopped the war." With the governorships of New York and New Jersey in Democratic hands, "and a [Democratic] majority in Pennsylvania, as they then would have had, they would so have crippled us as to end the contest. That they would have attempted it we at home know." Or if not outright insurrection, then certainly the collapse of the long-suffering Army of the Potomac. "Had the Army of the Potomac been whipped at Gettysburg . . . it would have dissolved," wrote one contributor to the Union Army's veterans' magazine years afterward. "Doubtless some of the . . . volunteer regiments would have held together and made some sort of retreat toward the Susquehanna," but the others would simply have deserted en masse in much the same way Napoleon's army disintegrated after Waterloo, leaving "the rebel chieftain . . . at liberty to go where and do what he pleased." Had Pickett's attack succeeded, "our army would have been cut in two, and in a few days the rebels would have occupied Harrisburg and Philadelphia, and terms of peace would have been dictated by General Lee in Philadelphia or New York."[31]

But after the failure of Pickett's monumental attack, all those possibilities disappeared, as did any hope that Lee could somehow sustain his incursion into Pennsylvania by limping off to fight another day on Northern soil. He had too little left with which to limp. The earliest reckoning of losses Lee could make put the Army of Northern Virginia's casualties at just over 20,000, including some 2,500 dead; later estimates, by William Allan, put the losses at nearly 23,000, while at least one postwar Southern calculation set them as high as 28,000. In other words, a third of Lee's army ended the Battle of Gettysburg dead, maimed, or on the march to federal prison camps. And that hardly began to take stock of the blow to the Army of Northern Virginia's command structure: of fifty generals in the army, one-third of them were casualties of some kind, starting with division commanders like John Bell Hood, whose arm was mangled by shell splinters on July 2, and Dorsey Pender, who died after the amputation of a leg on July 18. That night, Lee wearily acknowledged that "the unsuccessful issue of our final attack" made it necessary "to withdraw to the west side of the mountains," and from there to Maryland and Virginia, and gave the orders for a general retreat.[32]

The next day, July 4, Vicksburg surrendered to Ulysses Grant.

CHAPTER FIFTEEN

I Consider My Presence Here Always Necessary

The retreat was an exercise in agony for the Army of Northern Virginia. "We were drenched by a cold rain," wrote an Alabama soldier in his diary, and "several hours after day light we continued the march through mud & water ankle deep." Thousands of Confederate wounded were left behind; those who crowded the springless wagons might have wished they had been, too. "As the winds howled through the driving rain, there arose, from that awful procession of the dying, oaths and curses, sobs and prayers. . . . 'Oh, stop one minute! Take me out; let me die on the roadside.' " The news from Vicksburg further dampened soggy spirits. "Our news from the west is worse than anything from Lee," wrote a North Carolinian. "Vicksburg fell . . . and that day has been for us a day of mourning and bitterness." With Powell Hill's corps in the lead, followed by Longstreet and then Ewell, Lee retraced his path over South Mountain and then turned south to Williamsport and the Potomac, all the while fighting off harassing attacks by Union cavalry.

Lee kept up the noble bearing. A Union prisoner watched him ride "by within a few yards. . . . His long, grizzled beard was neatly arranged; his clothing was clean and faultless; his horse had been groomed and saddled with care"; and he rode "apparently cool and confident, not as one who had suffered defeat." But not even Lee could maintain his composure completely. One staffer remembered watching him as "the remnant of Pickett's Division" stumbled past, and seeing "his head uncovered . . . his face turned toward the sky with such a look of agony and consecration upon it as I have never seen."

They arrived at Williamsport, starting on July 7, only to find that the "rains . . . have so swollen the Potomac as to render it unfordable." Lee was trapped, and as he collected his battered army, he rode together with Longstreet, Ewell, and Hill "to look at ground" for an all-or-nothing stand and "determined on [a] line" on which they could fight George Gordon Meade's pursuing Federals. *The New York Herald* prophesied that Lee "is now so closely hemmed in by our superior enveloping forces that we cannot imagine how he can possibly escape a crushing disaster, whether he may try the alternative of a battle by day or an escape by pontoons by night."[1]

Except that Meade's pursuit was inexplicably lackluster. Although the Army of the Potomac's cavalry reported that "Lee's army was in an utterly demoralized condition" and Union soldiers "imagined we could see the end of the war right there," Meade moved down to Williamsport as deliberately as he dared. He was not within striking distance of Williamsport until July 12, and even then stopped to hold yet another council of war with his corps commanders to decide how to proceed. Lee's engineers, meanwhile, scoured every barn, building, and house in the neighborhood of Williamsport for wood and appropriated every sawmill along the river to construct makeshift pontoons. By the afternoon of the thirteenth, they had strung together an eight-hundred-foot-long floating causeway across the Potomac.

At the same time, the rains stopped, and the river began to fall—a foot and a half by July 12. From all appearances, "the fords near Shepherdstown and Williamsport are now practicable for infantry." So, while Meade hesitated, Lee ordered the Army of Northern Virginia to cross the Potomac under cover of darkness. "Our father, Lee, was scarcely ever out of sight" through the crossing, wrote a soldier in the 53rd North Carolina. "We could not feel gloomy when we saw his old gray head uncovered," and "when we saw him we gave that Rebel yell." The Prussian observer Justus Scheibert noticed that "the General stood here with us through the night to regulate and enliven the march, to keep all in high spirits and on the track." By the time Meade was ready to launch an attack on the morning of the fourteenth, Lee and his army had slipped over to the Virginia side of the river "without molestation." By the twentieth, they had made Martinsburg; by the twenty-fourth, Longstreet had reached Culpeper.[2]

By that time, the fury of Northern public opinion had broken over George Meade's head. *The New York Times* scathingly wrote that without a "gun fired . . . the wily rebel chieftain has crept stealthily away from under our very noses, while we were digging ditches for a line of defence." Meade, for his part, never admitted that he had been mistaken at Williamsport: "If I had attacked him on the 13th [of July] . . . it is believed by several of my officers who subsequently inspected his lines . . . that it would have been a failure." But the same hail of criticism descended on Lee and, surprisingly, with much the same response. Confederate congressmen declared that Lee, whatever his other virtues, did not possess "sufficient genius to command an invading army." Behind Lee's back, one of his brigadiers, Joseph R. Davis (the president's nephew), whispered that "there seemed to be no plan and no unity of action at Gettysburg," while *The Charleston Mercury* raged that it was "impossible for an invasion to have been more foolish and disastrous. It was opportune neither in time nor circumstances." The Southern people, mourned the *Southern Literary Messenger,* have simply "lost confidence in their rulers," and that included their "estimate of Lee."

Lee's initial reaction was a frosty silence. "Lee is at Culpeper Court House," recorded Robert Kean in his Richmond diary. "He is as silent as the grave," and any official communication is "always brief and jejune." Not completely silent, though: Lee sent eleven separate reports and telegrams to Jefferson Davis between the beginning of the retreat and the end of July. Despite his impulse, as the wreckage of Pickett's division streamed past him, to take all the "fault" on himself, Lee grew increasingly defensive as the weeks passed. His first report to Davis on July 4 merely observed that "our troops were compelled to relinquish their advantage and retire." Three days later, Gettysburg had grown to become a "position too strong to be carried," and lacking the means for "collecting necessary supplies," he had "determined to withdraw to the west side of the mountains." To others, he was even less willing to accept the idea of defeat. When Secretary of War Seddon's brother made the mistake of asking whether invading Pennsylvania had been worth the costs of Gettysburg, Lee "rose from his seat . . . with an emphatic gesture" (and a rare Shakespearean allusion), and claimed that the Army of Northern Virginia "did whip them at Gettysburg, and it will be seen for the next six months" that the Army of the Potomac "will be as quiet as a sucking dove."[3]

He was less agitated by the time he composed a summary for Jefferson Davis at the end of the month. But even there, Lee attempted to balance "our loss" (which "has been so heavy") with "the damage to the enemy," which "has been as great in proportion." He was, by then, once more willing to admit that "I am alone to blame" for Gettysburg. But in his formal report on the Gettysburg campaign (which he submitted in January), he included an oblique criticism of J. E. B. Stuart (the "movements of the army preceding the battle of Gettysburg had been much embarrassed by the absence of the cavalry"), of Longstreet (his "dispositions were not completed as early as was expected" for Pickett's assault on July 3), and even of the artillery, whose low supply of ammunition "was unknown to me when the assault took place" and left Pickett vulnerable to "a concentrated fire of artillery from the ridge in front." And in truth, Ewell and Hill *had* turned in disappointing performances at Gettysburg: Hill took little initiative at any point during the battle, while Ewell misinterpreted one order and mistimed the execution of others.

But was this their fault, or the fault of Lee's peculiar tactical philosophy of expecting corps and division commanders to take charge of the conduct of a battle, while he took responsibility only for getting them to the right place at the right time? After the war, Ewell could not "see that I should be censured" for failing to occupy Cemetery Hill at the end of the first day's fighting. "General Lee came upon the ground before I could have possibly done anything," and "after surveying the enemy's position, he did not deem it advisable to attack." Ewell was expecting a direct order before attacking on July 1; Lee gave directions that fell somewhere between opinion and recommendation, and Ewell, who was new to Lee's style of putting tactical direction into the hands of corps commanders, sat down in puzzlement. "I had frequently noticed before & have also since this occasion," wrote Ewell's stepson and aide, Campbell Brown, that "Gen. Lee's instructions to his Corps Com*rs* are of a very . . . general description & frequently admit of several interpretations—in fact will allow them to do almost anything provide it only be a *success.*"[4]

That was not the only ambiguity in Lee's reflections to Davis on Gettysburg. Lee balanced any admission of his own "fault" with the odd remark that much of that fault arose from "expecting too much" of the Army of Northern Virginia's "prowess & valour." This was similar to a comment he made in two letters written five days earlier to Mary and to Margaret Stuart—"The army did all it could. I fear I required of it impossibilities"—and both are just ambiguous enough to raise the question: Was Lee assuming blame, or shifting it, almost unconsciously, to the Army? For as much as he talked of blame for himself, it had been Lee's constant complaint since the beginning of the war that Southerners had failed to show the kind of earnestness necessary to win the war. If he had expected *too much* of them, was the fault his or theirs? He had once described the men in the ranks as unmatchable and confined his doubts to their officers. Were the rankers now in doubt, too?

It did nothing to answer that question for Lee to have to report to Davis that the Army of Northern Virginia was once more bleeding deserters. In veteran regiments like the 2nd Virginia, 61 deserted as soon as they crossed the Potomac; in the 12th Alabama, "out of a Co. of 32 men, 21 went off, with arms & accouterments"; the 13th North Carolina lost 50 men in one night. "There are many thousand men improperly absent from this army," Lee complained to Davis on July 27, and though he subsequently expected "those who straggled from the ranks" to be "now rejoining us," he urged Davis to issue some form of amnesty proclamation to draw the deserters back, and follow it with a more determined enforcement of the conscription law, minus its "former exemptions." Davis agreed to issue a "general pardon and amnesty" proclamation on August 1 if deserters returned "with the least possible delay," but the response was indifferent.[5]

None of this diminished Davis's personal confidence in Lee. Yet Gettysburg became the grounds for resurrecting the questions he and Seddon had about Lee's strategic priorities. "I have felt more than ever before the want of your advice during the recent period of disaster," Davis wrote gingerly on July 28—not because he wanted Lee in Richmond, but because he wanted Lee to admit that the situation in the west could no longer be ignored, and he broadly hinted at his intense dissatisfaction with Joe Johnston's management of affairs in Mississippi. "If he has any other plan than that of watching the enemy it has not been communicated." Perhaps Lee should consider putting his own ideas on the shelf and sacrifice himself for the good of the cause. "If a victim would secure the success of our cause," Davis added, "I would freely offer myself."

But Lee read Davis's letter in much more dramatic terms. A week later, he replied. He had been stung by the "expression of discontent in the public journals," and in such an atmosphere "the general remedy for the want of success in a military commander is his removal"—not Johnston's, but his own. "I therefore, in all sincerity, request Your Excellency to take measures to supply my place." The heart attack "I experienced the past spring" had made him "sensibly feel the growing failure of my bodily strength," so perhaps Davis should appoint "a younger and abler man than myself." This was not at all what Davis had intended, and he hastened to say so. He, too, had "to bear the criticisms of the ignorant," and he sympathized with "the effects of the illness you suffered last Spring." But Davis had no idea where he would "find that new commander," nor did he believe he could identify "some one . . . more fit to command." Lee must stay in charge.[6]

That did not mean he would necessarily stay in Virginia. At the end of August, Davis summoned Lee to Richmond to talk about a new strategy for the west and visit the fortifications of Richmond, and swiftly the rumors began to fly that "General Lee with a part of the Army of Northern Virginia is going to Tennessee" to replace Johnston and reinforce Braxton Bragg's Army of Tennessee. Lee evidently argued back and might even have persuaded Davis and Secretary of War Seddon unwillingly to sanction some new Virginia campaign for the fall, because he instructed Longstreet on August 31 to "prepare the army for offensive operations." (Longstreet, who had been corresponding privately with Seddon, was alarmed at this. "I do not know that we can reasonably hope to accomplish much here by offensive operations," he told Lee, and added, three days later, "I think it would be better for us to remain on the defensive here, and to re-enforce the west.")

But the situation in the west was on high alarm: Knoxville fell to a Union army under Lee's onetime antagonist Ambrose Burnside on September 2, and one week later the federal Army of the Cumberland crossed the Tennessee River and entered Chattanooga, which Braxton Bragg abandoned without a fight. Lee compromised. Longstreet would get his wish. On September 9, Lee ordered Longstreet and two of his divisions—Lafayette McLaws's and John Bell Hood's—to get "on the march toward Richmond," where they would entrain for Charlotte, North Carolina, and eventually for Atlanta. There, they would march north to unite with Bragg and the Army of Tennessee in northern Georgia on September 18. "Now, general," Lee said to Longstreet as they parted, "you must beat those people out in the West." Yes, Longstreet assured him, "I would not give a single man of my command for a fruitless victory."

On September 20, Lee had his second heart attack.[7]

The war had given Lee a reason for fighting. He had never had much confidence in secession as a constitutional issue, and he had no end of trouble with Southern governors aflame with states' rights enthusiasm, because that only weakened the overall fabric of Confederate resistance. He had even less use for a war in defense of slavery, and had said so to old Francis Preston Blair in the long-disappeared spring of 1861, and probably to Jefferson Davis as well. His soldiers might see themselves fighting to show "clearly that Slavery is a divine law," but not Lee. What troubled him about Lincoln's Emancipation Proclamation was not its legal unbinding of slavery in the Confederacy but its call to recruit black soldiers and the automatic assumption that it would serve as a call to slave insurrection. This, like John Pope's orders, meant a turn toward a "savage and brutal policy . . . which leaves us no alternative but success or degradation worse than death."[8]

This was the same terror—that "African slaves have not only been incited to insurrection . . . but numbers of them have actually been armed for a servile war"—which drove Jefferson Davis and the Confederate Congress to declare that the black volunteers "captured in arms be at once delivered over to the executive authorities of the respective States to which they belong" to be re-enslaved. Those who had not been slaves, according to Secretary Seddon, "should be either promptly executed" or set aside for execution after the war "to mark our stern reprobation of the barbarous employment of such inciters to insurrection with all its attendant horrors." Lincoln promptly volleyed back with a promise that "the government of the United States will give the same protection to all its soldiers, and if the enemy shall sell or enslave anyone because of his color, the offense shall be punished by retaliation upon the enemy's prisoners in our possession." The issue would not present itself directly to Lee for another year, when the Army of the Potomac began deploying black soldiers in earnest, but he would not distinguish himself—or cross the politicians—by disagreeing with Davis's policy.[9]

There were other issues, too, that fueled his bitterness over Union conduct, which seemed to diverge so wantonly and destructively from the scrupulous pattern Winfield Scott had set long ago in Mexico. (It never seems to have occurred to him that the barbarities of slavery were worth weighing in the balance, or that those barbarities and the men who excused them were precisely what he was, objectively, protecting.) In the summer of 1862, he learned that "many of our citizens engaged in peaceful avocations have been arrested and imprisoned" for refusing to take an oath of allegiance to the United States, and warned George McClellan, albeit vaguely, that he would take "retaliatory measures as the only means of compelling the observance of the rules of civilized warfare." (And, by the same token, he was sufficiently embarrassed by "the annoyance & loss which" a woman at Martinsburg "met with from stragglers of our Army" after Antietam that he wrote a personal letter to apologize.)

The sack of Fredericksburg gave him "acute grief," because "what the fire & shells of the enemy spared, their pillagers destroyed." When a Union raiding party crossed the Rappahannock below Fredericksburg, they "stole from our citizens all they could get and recrossed before we could get to them." Nevertheless, "their expeditions will serve for texts . . . for the *Herald, Tribune* & *Times* for brilliant accounts of grand Union victories & great rejoicings of the saints of the party." He described the federal occupation of the lower Shenandoah Valley in early 1863 as "barbarous" and "revolting to every principle of justice and humanity." Winchester, he told Mildred in July, "has been terribly devastated & the inhabitants plundered of all they possessed." When Hooker sent over flags of truce to recover the Union dead after Chancellorsville, Lee readily assented, snapping to Lafayette Guild that "he did not want a single Yankee to remain on our soil *dead or alive.*" (It escaped his attention that the Army of Northern Virginia appropriated some 16,000 head of cattle and 26,000 sheep from Northern farmers during the campaign, along with the free blacks who had been kidnapped from south-central Pennsylvania, and at least eight white civilian hostages from Gettysburg who would remain in detention in North Carolina until 1865.)[10]

Lee's bitterness was further stoked by a new series of personal losses. For all that Lee had written off any hope of recovering Arlington, it still came as a shock to learn in November 1863 that under the terms of the 1862 Act for the Collection of Direct Taxes in Insurrectionary Districts, Arlington was liable for $92.07 in taxes and would "become forfeited to the United States" if the tax was not paid. As it was, the federal government had by mid-1863 erected two small fortifications on the property, followed by a field hospital, and then a "Freedmen's Village" for newly emancipated slaves in 1863, with two former Custis slaves speaking at the village's dedication. But technical title to the property still remained with the Custis estate and would until it faced a delinquency hearing under the new tax legislation. It should have been no trouble for Lee to have arranged payment of the tax; even if he himself balked at paying a federal tax, there were enough Lee relatives still in Alexandria who could have paid the bill at the tax commissioners' office there.

Which they tried to do: when the commissioners' office opened in Alexandria in June 1863, Philip Fendall (a Lee cousin) and Lee's unionist brother-in-law, William Louis Marshall, collaborated to pay the tax and head off any possible auction. But the commissioners insisted that neither Fendall nor Marshall were a "party in interest," and refused the payment. An auction was duly set for January 11, 1864, and Abraham Lincoln personally authorized the commissioners "to bid in and have struck off to the United States . . . the Arlington estate, lately occupied by Robert E. Lee." The sale realized just $26,800, and because Lincoln's directive set aside Arlington for "war, military, charitable, and educational purposes," the following May the federal War Department began laying out the new "National Military Cemetery" on the Arlington grounds "to be properly enclosed, laid out, and carefully preserved." The architect of the new cemetery would be the Union Army's quartermaster general, Montgomery Meigs—who, thirty years before, had been Robert E. Lee's first assistant in building the dam to save the St. Louis waterfront.[11]

Losses of this sort soon lengthened into other disasters. Markie Williams had for years been as close as a sister to Mary Lee, and she and her brother, Orton, had lived at Arlington, where young Orton had played with Agnes, "sitting around the nursery fender telling fairy tales." Back in the balmy prewar days, Lee had persuaded Winfield Scott to commission Orton Williams from civilian life as a lieutenant in Lee's 2nd Cavalry, but Scott instead kept him on his staff in Washington. At the outbreak of the war, Williams was arrested on suspicion of passing information to the Confederates but was eventually released for lack of evidence, whereupon he promptly joined the Confederate Army. There was a common understanding within the Lee family that Orton had proposed to Agnes over Christmas 1862, he in the role of "Prince Charming and she the Sleeping Beauty." But "after a long session in the parlor," Orton "came out, bade the family good-bye, and rode away."

After Agnes turned him down, Orton, almost without thinking, proposed to another woman on the rebound. Far more erratically, he undertook a bizarre espionage foray that got him arrested, tried, and hanged as a spy in Franklin, Tennessee, on June 9, 1863. "He stepped upon the scaffold," wrote one witness, "with as much composure as though he had gone there to address the multitude." Lee was astonished, partly at Orton's folly, but more at the severity of the sentence. It was true, Lee admitted, that as a spy "his life was forfeited under the laws of war." But he believed that there was "no necessity for his death except to gratify the evil passions of those whom he offended by leaving Genl. Scott." This, he added angrily, "is in such accordance with the spirit of our enemies." Agnes "never recovered" from the shock; she kept the copy of the New Testament Orton gave her for the rest of her life.[12]

The news of Orton Williams's death was quickly overtaken by a wound much closer to Lee's vitals. Rooney had risen to command one of J. E. B. Stuart's cavalry brigades after Stuart's Pennsylvania raid in October 1862 and was wounded in the leg at Stuart's fiasco at Brandy Station (the same day that Orton Williams was hanged). The wound was a clean pass through the leg, so there was no fear for Rooney's life. He met his father as he was being carried off the field, and he "appeared comfortable & cheerful" to Lee. But he would need time to recuperate, and because White House on the Pamunkey had been torched the year before and Mary Lee was "confined" by her arthritis "to your room" at the Caskies' in Richmond, Rooney's in-laws, the Wickhams, opened up a two-room outbuilding at their home at Hickory Hill for his convalescence. This reunited him with his wife, Charlotte (who had lost two children in the four years they had been married), and with his younger brother, Rob, now a lieutenant, who was detailed as his aide. Lee was almost more solicitous for the frail Charlotte than for Rooney and assured her that "as some good is always mixed with evil in this world, you will now have him with you for a time."

Then, without any warning, on June 26, a company of the 11th Pennsylvania Cavalry descended on Hickory Hill, carried Rooney out on a mattress as their prisoner (they barely missed snatching Rob, too), and made off with him in the Wickhams' carriage, headed for Fort Monroe. The Union troopers were part of a raiding party along the Pamunkey and picked up word of Rooney's confinement at Hickory Hill while "on a foraging expedition." The 11th Pennsylvania's colonel, Samuel Spear, had been a sergeant under Robert E. Lee in the old 2nd Cavalry, and there was a delicious pleasure in seizing Lee's son from under his in-laws' roof.[13]

Lee did not learn of Rooney's capture until July 7, while still on the retreat route to Williamsport, and the news struck hard. "I have heard with great grief," he wrote to Mary, "that Fitzhugh has been captured by the enemy." He hastened to reassure Mary that "some good" would come of it, but he was even more worried about Charlotte and urged Mary to write to Charlotte and tell her "it will all come to good in the end." Rooney's capture was still clouding his mind later that day when he told a British military observer,

Arthur Fremantle, "of the raid made by the enemy, for the express purpose of arresting his badly wounded son (a Confederate Brigadier-General), who was lying in the house of a relation in Virginia."

He might have expected that Rooney would be exchanged for some equally valuable federal prisoner, or perhaps even paroled as a gesture of civility. But there were soon stories in the newspapers with a darker shadow. On April 9, two Confederate recruiting officers, William Corbin and Thomas McGraw, were arrested in Kentucky and would normally have been treated as prisoners of war. But Kentucky was now part of a federal military district, the Department of the Ohio, and so the two were instead classed as spies, tried by a military commission, and shot on May 15. The Confederate government protested the executions, to no avail, and finally responded on July 6 by having Union officers incarcerated in Libby Prison in Richmond draw lots for two retaliatory executions. The families of the condemned officers, Henry Washington Sawyer and John Flinn, at once appealed to Abraham Lincoln, and Lincoln (who had just received the news of the Army of Northern Virginia's escape across the Potomac) ordered that Rooney "and another officer . . . not below the rank of captain" be transferred to "close confinement and under strong guard." If Sawyer and Flinn were executed, the response would be "to hang General Lee and the other rebel officer designated herein."[14]

After a month of accusations back and forth, the Confederates backed down, and Sawyer and Flinn were returned to captivity with the other officers at Libby Prison. But Rooney's father was beside himself. "My grief at the intention of the enemy, as regards Fitzhugh of course, was intensified," he wrote to Custis. Retaliation, he admitted, was sometimes necessary, but "it should not be resorted to at all times, and in our case policy dictates that it should be avoided whenever possible." But he was "powerless in the matter and have only to suffer." Lee's suffering was not nearly as agonizing as Charlotte's. She had lost children and now faced the prospect of losing her husband, and the anxiety broke what slender grasp she still had on health. "I can appreciate your distress at F.'s situation," her father-in-law pleaded, "and in the lone hours of the night I groan in sorrow at his captivity and separation from you. But we must all bear it, exercise all our patience, and do nothing to aggravate the evil."

It was useless. As Charlotte swirled downward in despair, Custis tried to offer himself as a swap for Rooney, even for just forty-eight hours. He was refused. Instead, Rooney was transferred to Fort Lafayette (across the narrows of New York harbor from his father's old station at Fort Hamilton, where he had sliced the tips of his fingers as a boy) on November 15. Charlotte sickened, crying, "I want Fitzhugh, oh, I want Fitzhugh," lapsed into a coma on Christmas, and died the following day. "I loved her with a father's love," Lee mourned, "and my sorrow is heightened by the thought of the anguish her death will cause our dear son." It would take another three months before Rooney was finally exchanged, for a Union general and the two captains, Sawyer and Flinn. But even then, Mary Chesnut saw that "General Lee had tears in his eyes when he spoke of his daughter-in-law just dead." She had joined the lengthening list of private war casualties he would blame on Yankee inhumanity, and he could only hope that Charlotte "has joined her little cherubs and our angel Annie in Heaven."[15]

Maybe there had been more to his proffered resignation than an injured demand for affirmation after Gettysburg. Lee was fifty-six that summer, the oldest senior field officer in either army in the Civil War (Grant was forty-one, William Tecumseh Sherman forty-three, McClellan thirty-six, Beauregard forty-five, Bragg forty-six; Napoleon and Wellington had both been forty-five at Waterloo, Washington forty-three at the outbreak of the Revolution; only Marlborough at Blenheim had been of a similar age as Lee). He had not been exaggerating when he warned Jefferson Davis that his health was still below par, and in April, while he was still recuperating, he admitted to Mary that he felt "oppressed by what I have to undergo for the first time in my life."

During one of his visits to Richmond in the spring, the photographers George Minnis and Daniel Cowell prevailed on Lee to pose for a photograph, the first he had had taken since the West Point days. Minnis and Cowell stood Lee in an appropriately heroic pose, left arm bent so that his left hand could rest on his sword hilt, right arm clutching a folded black felt hat, the strap of his binocular case descending from his left shoulder to his right hip. In the photograph, the familiar broad face has not changed, but the eyes are tilted slightly upward, almost unfocused. A pair of seated photographs followed, both of them angled headshots, one with his uniform coat unbuttoned (and the colonel's three stars prominent), the other with the coat buttoned to the throat. In none of them does any spark of animation appear. Nor was Lee himself impressed. "My portrait I think can give pleasure to no one, & should it resemble the original would not be worth having."[16]

Religious language now came to him more often than in the past and, with it, some measure of the consolation that eluded him in so many other ways. After the first Confederate collapse in the west in February 1862, Lee urged Mary to remember that "God . . . will shield us & give us success." Because "my whole trust is in God . . . I am ready for whatever he may ordain," but he could not quite allow that God would ordain a Confederate defeat. He would even claim a modest clairvoyance, having "seen His hand in all the events of the war." He told Thomas Verner Moore, the pastor of Richmond's First Presbyterian Church, in 1863 that "it was not only his comfort, but his only comfort . . . that he had . . . God, and God alone, as his helper in that terrible struggle." The remembrance of an overarching divine protection was a pool of light in the frustration and gloom that increasingly descended around him. "My heart is filled with gratitude to Almighty God for his unspeakable mercies with which he has blessed us in this day," he wrote to Mary on Christmas 1862. Even the deaths of grandchildren could be endured if he could see them as part of a divine plan that was so full of God's mercy in other points "that I cannot repine at whatever he does."[17]

On the other hand, Lee's religion was more a matter of relief than theology. His letters speak frequently of God, but not the Christian Trinity—not Jesus, and not the Holy Spirit. When he wrote to Mildred in one of his incessant letters of moral exhortation, he told her to "gain knowledge & virtue & learn your duty to God & your neighbor," for this "is the great object of life," but he did not tell her, as her mother and grandmother had, to seek spiritual conversion and union with Christ. Only at rare moments (one of them being Rooney's exchange and release) did he refer at all "to our Lord and Saviour." True, Lee had a vivid sense of an afterlife, but it was entirely a heaven of peace and reunion rather than judgment, penance, or damnation, a place of rest rather than release from sin. When Annie died in 1862, he could think only of all the pain "she will escape in life." Charlotte, he told Fitzhugh, was "brighter & happier than ever, safe from all evil & awaiting us in her Heavenly abode."

Even sin was not so much a matter of commission as omission, a condition of imperfection in which all are entangled and which all should struggle to rise above, even if with only varying degrees of success. And, as he had often complained, there was much imperfection in the Southern people that he hoped "a merciful God will arouse us to" correct. If only, Lee wrote to Mary, "our people would recognize" the hand of God "& cease from their vain self boasting & adulation, how strong would be my belief in [the] final success & happiness to our country."

When, on August 13, he joined with Jefferson Davis in proclaiming a post-Gettysburg "day of fasting and prayer," he prefaced his general order to the Army of Northern Virginia with the very un-Lee-like declaration: "Soldiers! We have sinned." What he meant was not that Confederate soldiers had indulged in adultery, fornication, blasphemy, or any of the other cardinal offenses but that they had "cultivated a vengeful, haughty and boastful spirit" and must now "beseech Him to give us a higher Courage, a purer patriotism and more determined will." And in this, they were not unlike all the other Southerners whom Lee had railed against for their lack of full-throated dedication to the war effort. Yet, ironically, those Southerners were the first to praise him as the paladin of a sacred cause. He was (according to one admiring clergyman) "the great defender of a sacred and glorious cause, wise in council & humane in the hour of victory, trusting rather in the Providence of God than in the might of man."[18]

There was little in Lee's genteel Episcopalianism of the fire that burned in Jackson's rock-ribbed predestinarian Calvinism, where even the mailing of a letter on a Sunday could be charged as an offense against the Almighty; there was little even of the logical moral compass that Abraham Lincoln (neither a Presbyterian nor an Episcopalian nor anything else) saw in God's will, pointing to the specific actions men must take. And he never speculated on what providential sign was intended by the loss of General Orders No. 191 in Maryland, because almost any conclusion he cared to draw from that would have rocked the foundations of his leadership. But Lee had never had a father he could look to as a model for a God who safely directed even the fall of the sparrow, and he was too much the apolitical soldier to allow himself to see righteous sentences writ in burnished rows of steel. Relief would have to do for him. And he would soon need it.

The second heart attack was not as severe as the one he had suffered in the spring. Although at first it gave him "great pain & anxiety" and he could mount Traveller only with "fear & trembling," he was not bedridden, and by November he could claim that he had "been through a great deal with comparatively little suffering." The trouble was that the symptoms persisted into October, when one official, visiting Lee's headquarters at Orange Court House, was "sorry to find General Lee quite unwell from an attack of rheumatism."[19]

Not that the Army of the Potomac gave him much about which to be active. George Meade crossed the Potomac in pursuit of Lee on July 19 hoping to chase him down to Culpeper. But Meade was distracted first by the "excessive heat of the weather," then by the need to send an entire brigade to New York City in the wake of the draft riots there, and then unsettled by unprecedented news from the west. Longstreet's two divisions arrived to support Bragg just in time to deliver a staggering blow to the federal Army of the Cumberland at Chickamauga in mid-September. The Federals retreated in disarray to Chattanooga, where Bragg proceeded to fasten them in a siege that promised to starve them into surrender, a Vicksburg in reverse. To deal with this disaster, Lincoln dispatched Ulysses Grant to Chattanooga to retrieve the situation and pared off two of the Army of the Potomac's infantry corps to go west and assist him. In the meantime, as Lincoln insisted, he was "unwilling now that" Meade "should now get into a general engagement" with the Army of Northern Virginia.[20]

It thus became Lee's turn once more to grasp the initiative by making "a grand & daring flank movement and place his Army between Meade and the Potomac." On October 9, Lee crossed the Rappahannock, again heading north and retracing the route that had led him to Second Bull Run a year before. Meade just as hurriedly backpedaled, and on October 14, Powell Hill repeated his overeager mistake at Gettysburg by attacking what he thought was the Army of the Potomac's rear guard at Bristoe Station, five miles south of Manassas Junction on the Orange and Alexandria Railroad. "Guns, knapsacks, blankets, etc., strewn along the road showed that the enemy was moving in rapid retreat, and prisoners sent in every few minutes confirmed our opinion that they were fleeing in haste." Instead, Hill walked into the fire of two federal infantry corps. Two of his brigades were "badly cut up and scattered in confusion," and on the seventeenth Lee ("in no good humor") called off his advance and plodded back toward the Rappahannock. The "wasted state of the country, a wilderness & a desert with food for neither man or beast," together with the 1,300 casualties Hill had piled up, made any further movement toward the Potomac foolish.

Hill struggled to take the blame onto his own shoulders: "This is all my fault, General." But Lee dismissed it. "Yes, it is your fault; you committed a great blunder . . . your line of battle was too short, too thin, and your reserves were too far behind." But Hill was still one of his pets, and as if nothing could call back Hill's folly, Lee sighed despondently and said, "Well, well, general bury these poor men and let us say no more about it." At least Lee's "rheumatism" seemed to have improved. "Yet, I still suffer," he wrote to Mary. "The first two days of our march I had to be hauled in a wagon."

Two weeks later, Meade lumbered back to the Rappahannock in pursuit of Lee. But on November 9, an early winter snowstorm temporarily shut down operations; not until November 26 was the Army of the Potomac in motion again, only to find the way blocked by strong Confederate defenses at Mine Run. Unlike at Gettysburg, Lee insisted on doing his own reconnaissance this time, and once again he came near death—a federal shell "struck a few yards in front of him" and bounced "three or four feet over his head" without exploding. Finally, Meade called off his tapping at the Confederate positions, pulling back across the Rappahannock. "I am greatly disappointed at his getting off with so little damage," Lee wrote to Mary on December 4, "but we do not know what is best for us. I believe a kind God has ordered all things for our good."[21]

Meade glumly expected to be cashiered for not pressing ahead with the attack at Mine Run. But by that time, Lincoln had better news with which to gladden his weary mind. Notwithstanding the great Confederate victory at Chickamauga in September, the irascible Braxton Bragg managed to quarrel with Longstreet and made the unpardonable mistake of sending him off on a fool's errand to besiege Knoxville. "If Lee had been in his place with such an army we would now be chasing the shattered yankee fragments out of Tennessee," groused one of Longstreet's captains. Instead, Ulysses Grant, now in command in Chattanooga, took Bragg's diversion of Longstreet's divisions as the opportunity to strike at Bragg's siege lines on Missionary Ridge and Lookout Mountain and on November 24 and 25 drove Bragg's army away in confusion. Five days later, Bragg resigned.

There was so little confidence in Bragg, even in the Army of Tennessee, that there had been talk among Bragg's officers, even before the Chattanooga debacle, about an appeal to Lee to take charge in the west. Now Jefferson Davis put bluntly the case for Lee's going to Dalton, Georgia, to sort out what was left of the Army of Tennessee: "Could you consistently go to Dalton, as heretofore explained?" Not surprisingly, he declined. His "rheumatism," he insisted, was "still stiff & painful." More darkly, he was worried that Bragg's legacy of quarrels had poisoned the entire command structure of the Army of Tennessee so that he "would not receive cordial cooperation." But Davis seemed so much on the verge of issuing a preemptory order that when Lee left for a meeting in Richmond on December 9, he wrote to Stuart what almost sounded like a valedictory: "I am called to Richmond this morning by the President, I presume the rest will follow. My heart and thought will always be with this army." But Lee was finally able to persuade Davis to keep him in the east; instead, Lee recommended first that Beauregard be appointed to the Army of Tennessee, then that Joe Johnston take direct command, and at length Davis reluctantly chose Johnston.[22]

In the months between his arrival in Georgia on December 27 and the opening of a new campaign in May, Johnston worked a small miracle in the Army of Tennessee, rebuilding its numbers from 36,000 (after Chattanooga) to 55,000 men and restoring its morale through improved supply, mock battles, and a judicious use of furloughs. "Johnston is a great Gen[eral]," wrote one Georgian, "and our army has great confidence in him." By March, one cavalry captain enthused that "General Johnston seems to have infused a new spirit into the whole mass, and out of chaos brought order and beauty." A similar recovery took place in the Army of Northern Virginia. Finally undisturbed by their federal counterparts, the Army of Northern Virginia went into winter quarters. "Our houses were small log huts, capable of holding three or four men, and were quite comfortable," reported a sergeant in the 2nd Virginia. "Chimneys built of sticks or wood and plastered on the inside answered well.

The roof of clapboards or pieces of tents, a bed of straw . . . on pieces of split wood . . . made us quite luxurious."

In the ebb of the Gettysburg campaign, Lee's numbers had been reduced to fewer than 60,000, and the detachment of Longstreet's divisions reduced it still further, to just 46,000 by the end of the year. But a new Confederate conscription law and the tidal return of deserters and stragglers slowly rebuilt the army's numbers, while the return in April of Longstreet's men from their western adventure bulked Lee's host back up to approximately 65,000 men.

Longstreet was glad to be back, and Lee celebrated with a review of Longstreet's reunited corps on April 29. Longstreet's brief stint with quasi-independent command had not, apart from the battle at Chickamauga, gone at all well. He had quarreled with his division commanders, failed to squeeze Ambrose Burnside out of Knoxville, and disappointed his own men, who were "much afraid there is a want of energy in General Longstreet's management of a separate command." Lee, however, was delighted to have him back, and the reappearance of Longstreet's corps gave a further spurt to the renewed energies of the Army of Northern Virginia. Lee was cheered at the review with "a feeling that thrilled all hearts, ran along the lines and rose to the heavens." "Gen. Lee's old army," wrote one Virginia cavalryman, "is now generally considered to be in better spirits & health, also better armed equipped &c, than at any previous time during the war."[23]

No one had worked harder toward that end than Lee. Like Joe Johnston, he instituted generous leave policies, sent in recommendations for promotions, hectored Secretary of War Seddon and Lucius Northrop, the indolent commissary general, for fresh supplies of food, and recommended breaking up the usual policy of recruiting state volunteers only for service in regiments from their state. ("Their local character should be abolished by law," he told Jefferson Davis.) It was high time for Southerners to think nationally rather than by states or localities, and he increasingly wanted his own army (despite its regional name) to reflect that. He sent off a division under Robert Hoke to drive back the federal occupation of eastern North Carolina and would have volunteered to accompany Hoke there except that "I consider my presence here always necessary." He even chided his own planter-brother, Carter, for not growing more food for the Army. "You farmers must be very industrious & make heavy crops," he upbraided Carter in February. "You see what a distance we have now to forage, how precarious the supply must be when roads are bad & how wearing to our wagons & teams. . . . I hope by your example & precepts you will encourage our good farmers in Virginia to such exertions as will insure bountiful productions."

He was irked at Richmond's society balls and warned young Rob and his high-spirited cousin Fitzhugh Lee (who had now risen to division command in Stuart's cavalry) to give them a pass. "We have too grave subjects on hand to engage in such trivial amusements." It would be better if Fitzhugh's officers should "entertain themselves in fattening their horses, healing their men and recruiting their regiments." A far better example was being set among the enlisted men as a general revival of religion broke out during the winter months. "Almost every one seemed to become concerned" for his soul, wrote a South Carolinian. "The most ordinary preachers drew large congregations; scarcely a day passed without a sermon; there was not a night, but that the sound of prayer and hymn-singing was heard." Lee gave all of it his blessing, issuing a general order on February 7 expressing his "great pleasure that in many brigades convenient houses of worship have been erected" and ordering "that none but duties strictly necessary shall be required to be performed on Sunday." Walter Taylor even remembered "riding down the lines" of Hill's corps with Lee on a Sunday and coming "upon a collection of men engaged in Divine worship." Lee "at once halted and listened to the singing of the men" and "as the benediction was pronounced reverently raised his hat from his head" and continued riding.[24]

As a further spur to his energies, Lee had one more confirmation of Yankee perfidy at the end of February, when Union cavalry under Judson Kilpatrick led a division of the Army of the Potomac's cavalry on a wild raid against Richmond, planning "to dash into the city (which is supposed to be feebly defended by home guards and a few regulars)," free the Union prisoners held there, "grab all the" Confederate members of Congress in their path, "and then make the best of their way to the nearest, and safest, part" of the Union lines above the Rappahannock. It was a crackbrained scheme, looked at askance by Meade but blessed by the civilians in the War Department, and of course it broke up in failure without achieving any of its airy promises. (Although Lee himself had very narrowly avoided capture by Kilpatrick, because he had been on the train from Richmond to Orange Court House at almost the same hour Kilpatrick stormed across the railroad.) However, one of Kilpatrick's colonels, Ulric Dahlgren, rode his men into an ambush organized by a lieutenant from Rooney's old regiment, the 9th Virginia, and was shot dead. Found on his body were sensational orders, written on Kilpatrick's division stationery, urging nothing less than the murder of "Jeff Davis and Cabinet."[25]

The long crescendo of bloody-mindedness in the war that Lee saw beginning in 1861 and moving upward through John Pope, Orton Williams, and Rooney's hostage months now seemed to reach its apex. The Dahlgren threat, loony as it appeared in retrospect, converted normal understandings of the laws of war as they existed in the nineteenth century into simple banditry, and

Southern newspapers screamed themselves hoarse in rage. "These Dahlgren papers will destroy, during the rest of the war, all rose-water chivalry," railed an Atlanta paper. Nor was Dahlgren the only offender they accused. "The chief criminals are Lincoln, Seward, and the Black Republican crew at Washington," foamed the *Richmond Dispatch,* "men who have deliberately planned and directed the commission of one of the most gigantic crimes in the annals of human warfare." Secretary of War Seddon wanted any captured federal troopers from Kilpatrick's raid hanged, something Lee was quick to oppose, fearing for Rooney (who was still in Union hands). "I cannot recommend the execution of the prisoners that have fallen into our hands," he cautioned Seddon after the war secretary sent him copies of Dahlgren's incriminating order. "Acts in addition to intentions are necessary to constitute crime."

Nevertheless, Lee was sufficiently disturbed by the Dahlgren papers that on April 1 he sent photographed copies of Dahlgren's captured orders under a flag of truce to Meade, demanding to know whether Dahlgren's plans to assassinate Davis "and Cabinet" had "the sanction and approval of the . . . United States Government or . . . his superior officers." Meade shamefacedly denied any such authorization, and so, even more shamefully, did Kilpatrick. But it convinced Lee yet again that "if victorious, we have everything to hope for in the future," while given the evidence of the Dahlgren papers, "if defeated, nothing will be left us to live for."[26]

Lee had an added incentive that winter for concern about the safety of Richmond, because Mary Lee finally moved, in January, into a three-story redbrick Greek Revival house at 707 Franklin Street, built in 1844 by the Scottish-born merchant and developer William Stewart just off Capitol Square. The Stewarts rented the house to Custis Lee soon after he joined Jefferson Davis's staff, and the house, which was dubbed "The Mess," became bachelors' quarters for Custis and several other Lee cousins in Confederate uniform. Moving Mary (along with Mildred and Agnes) there would allow Custis to take charge of caring for his mother, although characteristically Mary took as much charge of Custis. When Mary Chesnut paid a call at Franklin Street toward the end of February, she found that "Mrs. Lee" had transformed the house into "an industrial school—everybody so busy . . . plying their needles" in knitting socks and scarves for soldiers.

The house also gave Lee a place to stay when in Richmond, even a small office on the second floor. That occurred oftener than in past years: he was there in December, in February, and again in March. But that was not as often as he could wish, because "I have as much as I can do here & more too" at the army's headquarters at Orange Court House. "I am glad you are comfortably arranged in your big house," Lee wrote to her. But her comfort was relative to the slow, relentless march of her arthritis. She had acquired a new doctor and a new regimen and suffered so uncomplainingly that Walter Taylor would urge his sister to visit Mary Lee, because "Mrs. Lee (the old lady) is very sweet and attractive." Lee urged her, "Try & take care of yourself & get well." And he instructed Agnes, "Take good care of your mother & do for her all you Can." But he was, as he told Margaret Stuart, all the same "grieved at the condition in which I found" Mary. "She is now a great sufferer. Cannot walk at all, can scarcely move."[27]

He was so much distracted by Mary's health that he barely noticed, on February 20, the death of his remaining sister, Anne Marshall, in Baltimore.

CHAPTER SIXTEEN

We Must Destroy This Army of Grant's

Even after two attempts to cross the Potomac and carry the war northward, Lee was ready in 1864 to try the same strategy. He proposed in February to move with Longstreet against "Genl Meade," forcing Meade "back to Washington," and then "invade the enemy's country." He had never looked to wage a campaign of permanent conquest above the Potomac, but he remained convinced that another lunge toward Pennsylvania would "alarm & embarrass" the Lincoln administration "& prevent his undertaking anything of magnitude against us." Much as it was "very important to repossess ourselves of Tennessee," he was certain that with proper supplies he could at least "disturb the quiet of the enemy & drive him to the Potomac." In April he was still cajoling Jefferson Davis for authority to "move right against the enemy on the Rappahannock," which he was confident would force the Army of the Potomac to "be recalled to the defense of Washington."[1]

This looked, in the late winter of 1863–64, much less promising than it had seemed in previous years. The twin victories at Gettysburg and Vicksburg, followed by Grant's triumph at Chattanooga, deflated the temporary balloon of anti-Lincoln political criticism that had mushroomed in the first half of 1863. Antiwar candidates for the governorships of Ohio and Pennsylvania both failed miserably in the fall state elections, a unionist candidate for the Kentucky governorship won a resounding victory, and a pro-emancipation majority took control of the Maryland legislature. In September, Lincoln felt confident enough to say that "peace does not appear so distant as it did," and in his annual message to Congress in December he felt sufficiently emboldened to offer a plan of "amnesty and reconstruction" for reincorporating the Southern states into the Union. By mid-January, *The New York Times* was confidently predicting that Lincoln would be renominated for the presidency, that "the crisis of the struggle is past," and that "the people" would "continue President Lincoln in office for another term." What would surely clinch victory for both Lincoln and the Union was the appointment in March of Ulysses Grant to the newly re-created rank of lieutenant general and Lincoln's invitation to Grant to come east and crush Lee's army and Confederate resistance for good. The North, as George Templeton Strong put it, could finally expect "something decisive in Virginia."[2]

Lee eyed Grant's appointment with mild apprehension. The two men's paths in the old Army had crossed only once, in Mexico, and that had not amounted to much more than being in the same room at the same time. Grant had certainly won major successes in Mississippi and Tennessee. But Lee at first doubted that Grant would have enough time to wind up his affairs in the west, assume "active duties with another army," and still be able to mount a campaign that spring. Lee thought it more likely that "the first efforts of the enemy will be directed against Genl Johnston" in Georgia, especially because "the weather and the roads" would "be more favorable for active operations at an early day" there "than in Virginia where it will be uncertain for more than a month." He soon realized otherwise. Grant assumed, along with his lieutenant general's shoulder straps, the role of general in chief of all the Union armies, but he would keep his staff and headquarters in the east, and though George Gordon Meade would remain the titular commander of the Army of the Potomac, Grant would move with Meade as though he were an admiral directing a fleet and Meade only the captain of the flagship. Although Lee at first "considered" Grant's announcement that he would attach himself to the Army of the Potomac "a stratagem to attract our attention here, while he was left unmolested in dealing us a blow from the West," Lee admitted to Longstreet on March 28, "It looks now as if Grant was really going to operate the Army of the Potomac."

Grant aimed to do even more than that. He put his principal lieutenant in the west, William Tecumseh Sherman, in charge of a direct advance on Joe Johnston and Atlanta, planned for a joint land-and-sea expedition to reduce Mobile, commissioned a third force in the western Virginia mountains under Franz Sigel and David Hunter to clear out the Shenandoah, and even planned to land an expedition, under the squint-eyed Benjamin Butler, on the south side of the James River to threaten Richmond. Grant would probably have preferred to use most of the Army of the Potomac for the James River expedition, because he saw as clearly as Lee (and as clearly as McClellan in 1862) that the Confederacy's real vulnerability was Richmond, and that Richmond's vulnerability lay below the James, through the railroad hub of Petersburg. The problem was that Lincoln would not hear of it. Landing along the James, capturing Richmond—this smacked too much, even now, of McClellanism. What Lincoln wanted from Grant was the same thing he had demanded from Burnside and Hooker, a hard, direct, overland slog at Lee's army. The idea of driving Lee "slowly back into his intrenchments at Richmond," Lincoln declared, even before Grant came east, "is an idea I have been trying to repudiate for quite a year. . . . If our army cannot fall upon the enemy and hurt him where he is, it is plain to me it can gain nothing by attempting to follow him over a succession of intrenched lines into a fortified city." Grant had no choice but to pass the same word along to Meade: "Lee's army will be your objective point. Wherever Lee goes, there you will go also."[3]

Nor did Grant take the time in executing his plans that Lee had hoped for. Riding up to the perch on Clark Mountain, Lee could observe the movements in the Union camps on the other side of the Rappahannock and Rapidan Rivers, and Lee's behind-the-lines scouts "state that great activity prevails on the Orange & Alexandria Railroad." He was now sure that "the great effort of the enemy in this campaign will be made in Virginia," and by April 20 he could see that "the enemy are all prepared to advance, packed, provisioned, and equipped, & waiting only for the ground to dry." Finally, in the wee hours of May 4, the Army of the Potomac, now numbering close to 116,000 men, quietly crossed the Rapidan and plunged into the tangled mass of the Wilderness, following the same track Joe Hooker had followed almost exactly a year before. And as before, the aim would be to strike swiftly through the Wilderness in order to reach the open country south of that bleak forest before Lee could strike them in the heavy wooded twilight overshadowing the few roads that crisscrossed the Wilderness.

They nearly succeeded. Lee's problems with supply ("The great obstacle everywhere is scarcity of supplies," he complained to Longstreet) forced him to encamp his three corps in wide separation, with Longstreet as far away as Gordonsville, and on the morning of May 5, Lee had only Ewell's and Hill's corps within striking distance. Nevertheless, Ewell hit the advancing federal columns perpendicularly, using the east-west Orange Turnpike as his funnel, while Hill drove at them on the parallel Orange Plank Road, two miles below. This was, in large measure, just what Lee might have hoped for, and as he rode along with Hill's attack column, he "spoke very cheerfully of the situation." But not all went smoothly: Lee and his staff nearly blundered into the hands of federal skirmishers, and later in the afternoon he had to personally rally men from Harry Heth's division who had become confused in the face of federal fire. Still, he remained "in fine spirits," and that night he "slept on the field" in the clearing on the Plank Road owned by the widow Catharine

Tapp and sent messages to Longstreet, urging a night march so that his corps could arrive the next morning.[4]

This time, though, instead of falling back as they had done the year before when Lee confronted them, the Federals counterattacked the next morning. Powell Hill made the careless decision to let his men rest overnight rather than improvising field entrenchments, and by seven o'clock broken pieces of Hill's brigades were streaming back westward along the Plank Road in disarray. "Our left flank," wrote the colonel of the 11th North Carolina, "rolled up as a sheet of paper would be rolled without power of resistance." As the disorganized tide of fugitives fled along the Plank Road, they passed Lee, who indignantly (and "rather roughly") demanded to know whose "splendid brigade" was "running like a flock of geese" and called vainly, "Go back, men, you can beat those people." Then up from the chaos on the road appeared the long-awaited Longstreet, who rode "some 15 yards to the left of the road" to grasp Lee's hand. "I never was so glad to see you," Lee cried, and even wept for sheer relief.

Behind Longstreet came his lead brigade, John Gregg's Texans and Arkansans, and Lee, in a rare moment of unrestrained excitement, waved his hat and "hurrahed for the Texas Brigade." Gregg's brigade deployed into line of battle, and after giving them a short exhortation—"Texans always move them"—Lee turned as though he would have joined their attack. But they responded by refusing to move unless Lee first went to safety. "Go back, General Lee. Go back. . . . We won't go forward unless you come back," and a few grabbed at Traveller to turn the horse's head around. Lee relented, and Longstreet's attack went forward, knocking the federal advance on the Plank Road back on its heels. When Evander McIver Law's Alabama brigade swept up the road behind Gregg, Lee gave them a similar benediction: "God bless the Alabamans. Alabama soldiers, all I ask of you is to keep up with the Texans."[5]

But the drama on the Plank Road was not matched by any similar energy from Richard Ewell, two miles to the north on the turnpike, who allowed an opportunity to strike a similar blow that would have cut Grant's lines back to the Rapidan to slip through his fingers. Lee urged Ewell to "make a full attack," but Ewell (as at Gettysburg) failed to "accomplish anything decisive." Worse than that, as Longstreet drove his men forward along the Plank Road, he and his staff blundered into the sights of a Virginia regiment who, in what was almost a repeat of Jackson's wounding a year before, shot Longstreet in the neck. Unlike Jackson, he would survive, but the steam went out of his attack, and night fell with the Army of the Potomac still holding the roads that led south out of the Wilderness. "I have always thought that had Longstreet not been wounded," recalled Walter Taylor, "he would have . . . forced the Federals to re-cross the Rapidan." Some of them were inclined

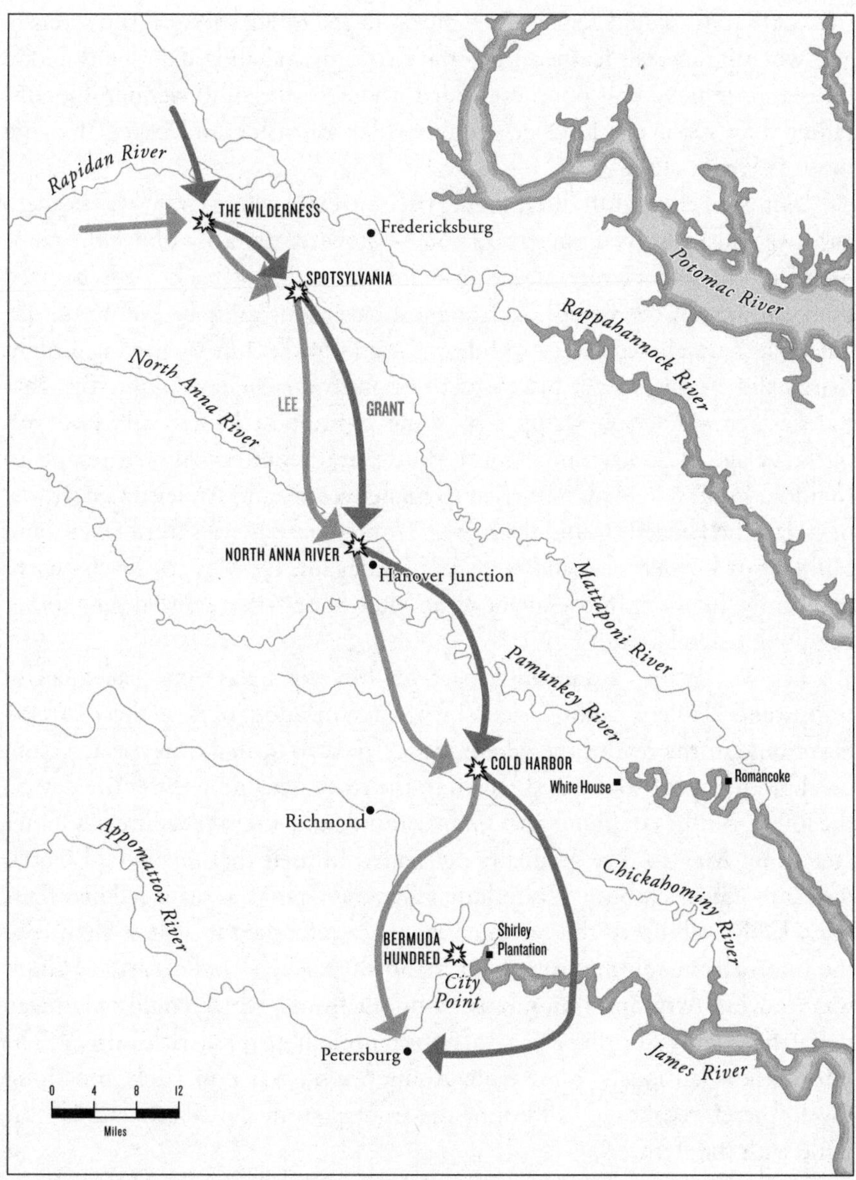

to do that anyway. "The rebels have evidently the best of the fight today thus far," groaned Congressman Elihu Washburne, Grant's strongest friend in Congress, who had accompanied the federal army thus far. "It looks gloomy enough at this time and there are long faces about the h.q."[6]

Not Grant's, however. He, too, had imbibed Winfield Scott's lesson about the virtue of the continuous campaign, and on the morning of May 7, Grant ordered the Army of the Potomac to resume its southward movement toward the open country around Spotsylvania Court House. Lee's first expectation was that Grant would renew the fighting in the Wilderness on the seventh, and when he instead learned that "the enemy has abandoned" the Rapidan fords and "removed his pontoon bridge" there, he began to wonder if Grant, rather than replaying Hooker, would replay Burnside and begin "moving towards Fredericksburg."

Not until the eighth did it finally become clear where Grant was headed, and Lee had to hurry Longstreet's corps—now temporarily under the command of Richard Heron Anderson—down a series of back roads to head them off. It was, Lee remarked, "the most hazardous thing he ever heard of," but he had no choice except to follow Grant's lead. Only by forcing a night march did Anderson get his corps to Spotsylvania before Grant. But that was enough. Anderson set up a blocking position at Laurel Hill, just west of the village of Spotsylvania Court House, and rebuffed Union attempts to shoulder him aside. As Grant tried to maneuver around Anderson's right the next day, the Federals found the newest Confederate arrivals from Ewell's and Hill's corps in their way and were repulsed again. By May 10, Ewell's corps had firmly dug itself into a salient—the Mule Shoe—that resisted yet another headlong federal assault.[7]

Lee was setting a punishing pace for himself, overseeing placement of troops and artillery, falling asleep in his new headquarters at the Harrison farmhouse in the rear of the salient "about 10 or 11 at night, to rise at 3 a.m., breakfast by candle-light, and return to the front, spending the entire day on the lines." But he could not read Grant's mind, and after the failure of Grant's attacks on May 10, Lee gradually persuaded himself that *now* Grant would retreat to Fredericksburg. "I think that General Grant has managed his affairs remarkably well up to the present time," Lee remarked to Harry Heth. But the information coming from "scouts and skirmishers" indicated that Grant was "moving Arty. and trains away from our front," which could only mean that "the enemy are preparing to retreat tonight to Fredericksburg." (The information, curiously, came from Rooney, who was now back in action.) Ewell, therefore, should "withdraw the troops" from the salient and "do the same with the Art'y."

Instead, Grant was shifting infantry, some 19,000 men, to his left for a grand smash at the Mule Shoe on the morning of May 12. William Seymour counted "*twelve lines of battle*" moving to the attack, and when they hit just before six o'clock, one of Ewell's divisions simply dissolved under the shock. Lee rode up at once to the salient, meeting the Virginians and Georgians of John Brown Gordon's division and trying to take personal command of them himself. "As he sat there on his splendid horse, his form erect, his grey head uncovered and eyes flashing with excitement, he appeared imposing and grand"—and an excellent target, as a federal shell dug into the ground fifteen feet from Lee and a musket round singed his saddle. Just like the Texans at the Tapp farm, Gordon seized Traveller's reins and told Lee to go back: "General Lee, this is no place for you. Do go to the rear. These are . . . men who have never failed—and they will not fail now." And the men took up the cry "General Lee to the rear" as they moved forward to seal off the breach. But Lee only moved on, coming up behind a Mississippi brigade and trying to give orders that the brigade commander refused to obey unless Lee stopped exposing himself.

Eventually, they barely managed to draw a new line across the base of the salient to withstand Grant's attack. But in the process, the Army of Northern Virginia suffered a disastrous 8,000 casualties, half of them prisoners; two of Ewell's division commanders were captured and two brigadiers killed. Ewell himself was virtually a casualty as he ran after fleeing soldiers "with loud curses." But it was Lee who inflicted the wound: "General Ewell, you must restrain yourself; how can you expect to control these men if you have lost control of yourself?" Ewell was astonished to find himself held responsible for the debacle of May 12, but Lee was even less willing to accept blame for the collapse of Ewell at the Mule Shoe than he had been for Ewell at Gettysburg. One of Ewell's division staff heard Lee insist that "he had been misled in regard to the enemy in our front, by his scouts, and that the fatal mistake was in removing the artillery on our line," all of which he did not mind laying on Ewell's shoulders.[8]

There was yet another casualty, this time a real one, and that was J. E. B. Stuart. The Army of the Potomac's cavalry were assigned a new commander when Grant came east, a fiery veteran of the western war, Philip Henry Sheridan. Grant gave Sheridan leave to raid around the two contending armies, and Stuart tried to stop him at Yellow Tavern, six miles north of Richmond, on May 11. Stuart barely nudged Sheridan from his tracks and was mortally wounded in a firefight. The word came to Lee on the twelfth, after the great assault on the Mule Shoe, and Lee mournfully informed his staff, "General Stuart has been mortally wounded; a most valuable and able officer." Stuart died that evening. Lee was "plunged into the deepest melancholy," withdrawing into his tent. When "one of his staff entered," Lee could only say, "I can scarcely think of him without weeping."

Years later, he would add that Stuart "was my ideal of a soldier . . . always cheerful under all circumstances, always ready for any work and always reliable." What was worse, there was no one he would seriously consider appointing in Stuart's place. The supply of hands he considered capable was getting embarrassingly short, and in the end he ordered that "the three divisions of cavalry" (one of them commanded now by Rooney, another by his nephew Fitzhugh Lee) "serving with this army will constitute separate commands and will report directly to . . . these headquarters." Stuart was thirty-one years old; it was less than five years since he and Lee had led the Marines in capturing John Brown at Harpers Ferry.[9]

Grant waited for a week, poking and prodding at the hastily thrown-up defenses around Spotsylvania. "I was afraid that Lee might be moving out," Grant wrote, and he was intent on not allowing Lee to tear loose on another reach for the Potomac. But Lee had too much reorganizing to do to worry about new offensive gestures. At both the Tapp farm and the Mule Shoe, Lee had been compelled to throw away his prized formula about moving his generals to the battlefield and letting them take charge, and with it went his fabled serenity. At least Longstreet would survive, even though he was condemned to spend months recuperating from his wound. But that did nothing to help Lee now, and he was certainly going to get nothing like help from Ewell and Hill, who had both fallen woefully below his expectations. Hill was put on sick leave on May 8, and command of his corps was given to Jubal Early; two weeks later, Ewell likewise applied for sick leave, ostensibly for the ill effects of dysentery. It never seemed to dawn on Ewell that Lee's decision to grant his request was intended as Ewell's off-ramp out of command. When Ewell felt restored enough to resume his place at the head of his corps, Lee tersely notified him that he would not be returning after all, but would instead be assigned to the defenses of Richmond. Hill would shortly be reinstated as Lee's wrath cooled and his chronic indulgence of Hill reasserted itself, but Ewell never would. A month later, Lee would even try to have Ewell reassigned to the Army of Tennessee to get him out of the way.[10]

Then, on May 19, Grant began moving again, once more southward toward the North Anna River, ten miles below Spotsylvania Court House. Lee fell back toward the North Anna on the twenty-first to stay ahead of Grant, "but in the midst of the operations on the North Anna he succumbed to sickness, against which he had struggled for some days." The strain was becoming noticeable, even to men in the ranks, one of whom noticed that "he was really a sick man." This time it was dysentery rather than heart trouble, but it made him ill enough that he could not ride, and rumors raced through Richmond that "he would have to transfer the chief command." Even Taylor was worried that Lee "c[oul]d attend to nothing except what was absolutely necessary for him to know & act upon." Sequestered in his tent with no one to whom he felt it safe to turn over command, Lee was seized by a mixture of helplessness and frustration. "As he lay in his tent," Charles Venable wrote, "he would say, in his impatience, 'We must strike them!' 'We must never let them pass us again!' 'We must strike them.' "

But when the newly restored Powell Hill moved to prevent the Army of the Potomac from crossing the North Anna at Jericho Mills, Hill failed again, this time by committing only one of his divisions and allowing himself to be driven to the south side of the river. "Why did you not do as Jackson would have done," Lee upbraided him, and "thrown your whole force upon those people and driven them back"? Grant was now only twenty miles north of Richmond, and Lee was becoming more and more anxious that Grant would crush him into the Richmond defenses. "If he is allowed to continue that course," he scolded Hill, "we shall at last be obliged to take refuge behind the works of Richmond and stand a siege, which would be but a work of time." He repeated the same fear to Jubal Early. "We must destroy this army of Grant's before he gets to the James River. If he gets there it will become a siege, and then it will be a mere question of time." But unlike Ewell, Hill stayed in command.[11]

Lee forced himself back to duty and established a formidable defensive position behind the North Anna River. But he was increasingly acting as army commander and corps commander and division commander all at once, and none of the shortness of temper this stimulated in him, together with his intestinal woes, made him easier for his staff to deal with. Venable stalked out of Lee's tent after an argument, "in a state of flurry and excitement, full to bursting," and no wonder, because he had just told Lee that "he is not fit to command this army and that he had better send for Beauregard." He didn't, because Grant did not propose giving the Army of Northern Virginia any leisure to discuss replacements for Robert E. Lee. On May 27, Grant moved again, abandoning the North Anna to shift eastward, down the Pamunkey River, crossing it at Nelson's Bridge and Dabney's Ferry, and then across the Totopotomoy Creek in the direction of the Chickahominy River.

Not that Grant had an easy time with his own campaigning. Since crossing the Rapidan, Grant had lost 40,000 men in the series of battles he had fought in May. "Exclusive of worthless bounty-jumpers and such trash," that left Grant "only about 65,000 veteran infantry." What strengthened Grant's resolve was his perception that the strain had been even greater on the Army of Northern Virginia, which was down to a total effective strength of 54,000. In addition to the death of Stuart and the wounding of Longstreet, the fighting had cost the Army six brigadier generals killed and seventeen more wounded. The increasingly merciless reach of the Confederacy's conscription laws could replace some of the manpower losses, but by the end of May the lack of coordination and élan was becoming so evident that Grant began to believe that "Lee's army is really whipped. The prisoners we now take show it, and the actions of his army show it," and Grant began to wonder if landing one more knockout blow would flatten Lee's army and bring the end of the war rushing in. He could, in that case, "crush Lee's army on the north side of the James, with the prospect in case of success of driving him into Richmond, capturing the city perhaps without a siege, and putting the Confederate government to flight."[12]

He was too quick. On May 30, federal cavalry pushed down to the crossroads of Cold Harbor, only a mile and a half from the Chickahominy, and when a mixed force of Confederate cavalry and infantry under Fitzhugh Lee and Robert Hoke failed to dislodge them, Grant rushed two infantry corps—some 30,000 men—down to the Cold Harbor Road to clear the rebels away from the Chickahominy. It should have been an easy task, but by the time the first federal arrivals were ready to attack, an entire division from the Army of Northern Virginia had arrived and dug itself in, and on June 1 the Confederates easily ripped apart a poorly coordinated assault.

But Grant was still so convinced of Confederate weakness that once he brought the bulk of the Army of the Potomac down to Cold Harbor on June 2, he could only imagine that nothing could stop them. The idea "was to attack early in the morning . . . push it vigorously, and if necessary pile in troops at the successful point from wherever they can be taken." He did not, however, launch his attack until June 3, and the delay allowed Lee to move the balance of the Army of Northern Virginia down to Cold Harbor, extend the defenses, and, in the event, tear Grant's attack into foolish and bloody shreds. South of the Cold Harbor Road, the attackers "quickly covered themselves with rifle pits or took advantage of such shelter as the broken ground afforded"; north of the road, "files of men went down like rows of blocks or bricks pushed over by striking against one another."[13]

Lee's Confederates, for their part, behaved like anything but disheartened failures. Dug in behind improvised earthworks, "the officers, with hats in hands, went up and down the line, feeling so much elated that they would strike the men over the heads and faces and shout with all the joy ever expressed at a camp-meeting by a new convert." McIver Law found his Alabama brigade "in fine spirits, laughing and talking as they fired. . . . I had seen nothing to exceed this. It was not war; it was murder." Or even worse, massacre. William Oates, commanding the 15th Alabama in Law's brigade, saw the 25th Massachusetts barreling toward him "in a column by divisions, thus presenting a front of two companies only." The Alabamians opened up "the most destructive fire I ever saw . . . I could see the dust fog out of a man's clothing in two or three places at once where as many balls would strike him at the same moment. In two minutes not a man of them was standing." Lee's men suffered 700 casualties while Grant's lost 4,500, and Lee could allow himself a moment to wonder whether, miraculously, he had managed to hold off yet another Union thundercloud, just like all the others.[14]

—

"Gen. Lee," wrote Edmund Ruffin in his diary after Cold Harbor, "said that the victory of [June] 3rd was the greatest of all that we had gained during the war." The doubts that had bubbled up after Gettysburg were long since gone, and the *Richmond Dispatch* exulted that "confidence in Lee and his army is not confined to the ranks of that army and to our fellow citizens." It included the entire Confederacy, in "every neighborhood and every family circle." Captain Charles Blackford enthusiastically agreed: "Grant . . . has lost fifty thousand men and Lee and his army are before him, full of fight and unconquerable."

Certainly, it disabused Ulysses Grant of any idea that the Army of Northern Virginia was ready to be walked over. Grant would regret the last attack at Cold Harbor "more than any one I have ever ordered. . . . As it has proved, no advantages have been gained sufficient to justify the heavy losses suffered." But with his own army wedged against the Chickahominy, Grant had nowhere left to maneuver above Richmond. To pull to his right was, in effect, to backtrack from Cold Harbor toward the North Anna. That would be a catastrophic admission of failure, and Grant, under any circumstances, was a man temperamentally averse to backtracking. He could cross the Chickahominy and fight it out with Lee on McClellan's old battlefields, but without any assurance of gaining more than he had won anywhere else south of the Rapidan. That left him no real choice but to reconfigure his whole overland strategy—cross the Chickahominy, but ignore another fight with Lee's army, and keep on moving across the James River, then the Appomattox River (its tributary), and do what he had been told not to do: capture the Confederate railhead at Petersburg and thereby force the evacuation of Richmond.[15]

This was, whether anyone was noticing, the same overall movement McClellan had wanted to employ in 1862 and an admission that the headlong slugging against the Army of Northern Virginia that the Lincoln administration had long regarded as the only politically acceptable plan had failed. Grant had always suspected that the James River and Petersburg were the real keys to Richmond and that seizing Richmond and its logistical bounty, rather than chasing Lee's army for some mythical showdown, would be the real means to bringing Lee's army to its knees. It would, in some perfect world, have been better "to get at Lee in an open battle which would wind up the Confederacy." But Lee was not offering him perfect opportunities, something that Cold Harbor demonstrated in spades. And anyway, there was no guarantee that more pitched battles might not be just what Lee wanted. "There is nothing I desire now more than a 'fair field fight,'" Lee told Powell Hill. "If Grant will meet me on equal ground, I will give him two to one odds."

Anything, in other words, to keep Grant's hands away from Richmond's neck.

So, as Grant explained, even though "my idea from the start had been to beat Lee's army, if possible, north of Richmond," the alternative had to be "to transfer the army to the south side and besiege Richmond or follow him south if he should retreat." No other Union commander could have safely made such a proposition to the Lincoln administration. But by the first week of June, Grant had paid the Army of the Potomac's dues to the overland strategy. Besides, Grant had carefully cultivated an image, ever since Vicksburg, of political harmlessness to the Lincoln administration, turning away coy suggestions from both Democrats and Republicans that he allow himself to become a presidential candidate in 1864. Lincoln would trust him. "The move had to be made," Grant wrote, "and I relied upon Lee's not seeing my danger as I saw it."[16]

Actually, Lee did see Grant's "danger." He was sufficiently recovered from his bout with dysentery to ride from point to point along the lines, "reconnoitering personally the enemy's position," and Grant's "quietude" after Cold Harbor convinced Lee that the Federals "will cross the Chickahominy." Lee hoped that, as he had done with McClellan, he could "move down and attack him with our whole force . . . in the act of crossing." Otherwise, as he warned Jefferson Davis, Grant would "endeavor to reach the James, breaking the railroads &c as he passes, and probably to descend on the south side of that river." But day followed day without any noticeable movement, dulling Lee's expectations. "No troops have left Grant's army to my knowledge," Lee reported on June 9, "and none could have crossed the James without being discovered."

Lee was also distracted by other Union movements. At the same moment, Grant's expedition into the Shenandoah Valley under David Hunter was chewing up the resources there that fed Lee's army. There was only one Confederate division in the valley, and it was handily beaten at Piedmont on June 5, leaving Hunter a free hand to occupy Lee's old base at Staunton and then Lexington, where Hunter torched the Virginia Military Institute on June 11. The Richmond papers huffed that there was little "that Gen. Hunter can do in that part of Virginia" to "contribute . . . towards the success of the movement against Richmond," but anyone could see that Hunter's position in the valley opened a direct road to Lynchburg, and Lynchburg was a direct feeder to Richmond.

Lee was reluctant to detach any of his own troops to recover the valley, knowing that if "Grant cannot be successfully resisted here we cannot hold the Valley," whereas if Grant was defeated on the Chickahominy, the valley "can be recovered." But that logic made little progress with frantic politicians, including Jefferson Davis. Lee finally conceded that Hunter "will do us great evil & in that event" he split off Ewell's old corps, only 8,000 strong and now under Jubal Early, for the valley on June 13. It was just possible that Early might be able not only to save the valley but to create the same kind of panic in Washington that Stonewall Jackson had produced in the spring of 1862 and force Grant to break off his campaign.[17]

And then, almost on cue, Grant slid into motion. On the night of June 12, the Army of the Potomac, in four huge columns, melted away from its lines at Cold Harbor, crossed the Chickahominy, and then swept down to the James, where Grant's engineers threw a massive twenty-one-hundred-foot-long pontoon bridge, using 101 pontoon boats, across the river at Weyanoke Point. Lee's "scouts and pickets" picked up Grant's movement "for the fords of the Chickahominy" by the morning of the fourteenth. Yet Lee hesitated, unsure whether Grant meant "to place his army within the fortifications around Harrison's Landing" or to get "possession of Petersburg before we can reinforce it." With only Powell Hill's corps and Richard Heron Anderson's corps at hand, he could not afford to misplace whatever shield he would use to protect Richmond.

Grant had the advantage, too, that there were already Union troops lodged on the James River—26,000 of them under the dubious oversight of Benjamin Butler on the Bermuda Hundred Peninsula. In Grant's original plans for the 1864 campaigns, Butler was to have landed on the James in May and knocked down the back door to Richmond while Grant grappled Lee along the Rappahannock. But Butler had thrown away the substantial advantage he had in numbers over Richmond's small defensive garrison and its commandant, the perennial Pierre Beauregard, and allowed himself to be bottled up at Bermuda Hundred. Butler made only token threats to cover Grant's crossing of the James, but his very position there clouded Lee's vision of what and where Grant was moving. Even as late as the afternoon of the sixteenth, when Grant already had two corps south of the James and headed for Petersburg, Lee was still plaintively asking Beauregard, "Has Grant been seen crossing [the] James River?"[18]

The same demon of hesitation that had befogged so many other movements of the Army of the Potomac saved Lee and saved Petersburg. Butler's failure to break into Richmond in May should have been a sign that the defenses of both Richmond and Petersburg were more formidable than they seemed from the small number of Confederate soldiers detailed to guard them. As indeed they were: Lee had overseen the construction of the first generation of Richmond fortifications in 1861, and an "inner line" of small bastions and artillery batteries was constructed to cover the east side of the city. An "intermediate line" was then built around the northern and western approaches to the city and then finally in 1862 an "outer line" to reinforce the eastern side, ending with a naval battery at Chaffin's Bluff on the James River (commanded, in this case, by Lee's brother Smith). Fortifications to protect Petersburg began in the summer of 1862 under the eye of Captain Charles Dimmock, with fifty-five batteries sited to cover a wide half circle with both ends tied to the Appomattox River and connected by rifle pits, trenches, and parapets.[19]

Grant's lead corps struck the Dimmock Line on June 15. It was defended by only 2,200 Confederates, but no one seemed quite capable of coordinating federal movements against them. After a series of ill-directed and fruitless Union attacks, Lee finally became convinced that "Grant's whole force has crossed to the south side of the James River," and "hurried up" the bulk of the Army of Northern Virginia into the Dimmock Line in "a free race for Petersburg." Grant had now to settle into a siege of both Petersburg and Richmond, and although he was not able to form a tight encirclement of the two cities as he had at Vicksburg, his lines wound close enough to Petersburg's vulnerable southward railroads that Lee was forced to rely more and more on wagons and turnpikes to get supplies into his army's hands, which brought matters to just the conclusion Lee had most dreaded.

Grant continued to edge his own siege lines slowly westward, cutting the Weldon Railroad in August and also probing weaknesses in Lee's lines north of the James. On September 29, Fort Harrison (one of the forts in the outer line protecting Richmond) fell to a surprise attack. This was so close to Richmond that in the city "you could see the smoke, and you could hear the cannon and rifle fire very clearly." But not even Lee's personal supervision of a counterattack could recover it. Once more, Lee forgot all about allowing his subordinates to run the machinery and tried to take charge of recapturing Fort Harrison. "With his silvery head uncovered, hat in hand," Lee reminded "the men how important Fort Harrison was to our line of defense, and that he was sure they could take it if they would make another earnest effort." But they could not, even after "cheering their beloved general." Lee "exposed himself very much in the assault, so much as to cause a thrill of alarm throughout the field," wrote the indefatigable War Department clerk John Jones, "but it all would not do." Lee could hardly have agreed more.[20]

Yet Northern public opinion did not see any of this as a cause for congratulation. "These are signs which indicate that gradually a disposition for peace is making itself felt throughout the great mass of the people of the United States," rejoiced the *Richmond Enquirer.* "The war spirit is on the wane." Grant's companion campaigns likewise spluttered with all the appearance of defeat. The expedition to capture Mobile never left New Orleans; Sherman's campaign from Chattanooga to Atlanta was frustrated over and over again by the wily defensive maneuvers of Joe Johnston and the Army of Tennessee. Above all, Jubal Early not only raised the specter of Stonewall Jackson by driving David Hunter from the Shenandoah but crossed the Potomac in July, brushed aside a Union-covering force at the Monocacy River, and lapped up to the outer ring of Washington's defenses on July 11. (Lee even meditated a plan using Early to attack the Union prisoner-of-war camp at Point Lookout and freeing 20,000 Confederate prisoners there.)

The worst embarrassment for the Federals came at the end of July. In an effort to break up the Petersburg siege, Grant authorized the digging of a spectacular 510-foot-long mine, packed with four tons of gunpowder, under the Confederate defenses. The crater the mine would blow in the Dimmock Line was supposed to offer an easy opening for a Union attack. But when the mine was exploded on July 30, an equally spectacular display of military bungling held back two divisions of U.S. Colored Troops specially trained for the assault and sent in ahead white units who milled aimlessly around the crater until the dazed Confederates cleared their wits and turned the attack into a bloody fiasco. The siege went on with no lasting disturbance.

Lee himself came up to observe the destruction wrought by the crater, irritated at "certain officers of high rank" for having failed to detect the mine and directing artillerymen who "rained a pitiless fire into the Crater." The attackers sustained almost 4,000 casualties, a suspiciously large percentage of them among the two black divisions, most of whom were probably executed after surrendering and after Lee had left the scene of the fighting. "It was the saddest affair I have witnessed in the war," Grant admitted. "I am constrained to believe that had instructions been promptly obeyed that Petersburg would have been carried with all the artillery and a large number of prisoners without a loss of 300 men." Lee, for his part, never acknowledged the massacre of black prisoners, and even though there is no evidence that he ordered or witnessed it, he also reproved none of his officers for participating in it. Like so much that governed his attitude toward slavery, he could look and still not see.[21]

Still, the challenge of dealing with black Union soldiers did not entirely go away, especially for those who survived massacre and were in Confederate hands. On the terms laid down the year before by Jefferson Davis and James Seddon, any former slaves were to be returned, through Southern state officials, to their owners. (The criteria of determining who had been a "slave" and who had been an "owner" were left opportunistically vague; in October 1864, the *Mobile Advertiser & Register* listed the names of 575 black prisoners from three of the U.S. Colored Troops regiments who had been put to hard labor on the port's defenses, and invited "the owners" to claim "the pay due them" for the use of their "property.") In October 1864, Lee gingerly proposed a local exchange to Grant; Grant promptly replied that he would only sanction an exchange if "you propose delivering these men the same as white soldiers." Surprisingly, Lee was willing to "include all captured soldiers of the United States of whatever nation and color under my control." But he could not include "negroes belonging to our citizens"—Davis and Seddon had seen to that—and Grant simply shrugged uncooperatively: "I have to state that the Government is bound to secure to all persons received into her armies the rights due to soldiers," and so no such exchange was possible. That brought Lee up to the political line, and he was not willing to cross it. As far as Lee was concerned, "there is no just cause of further responsibility" on his part.[22]

The breakdown of the exchange system, however, paid no useful political dividends for Lincoln, who now had to explain to white Northerners why thousands of white Union prisoners were dying, immobilized, in Southern prisons that had never been designed as permanent camps. Groaning under the weight of these failures, the chairman of the Republican National Committee had to warn Lincoln that the likelihood of his reelection in November was slipping away. "The tide is setting strongly against us," wrote Henry J. Raymond to Lincoln on August 22. "Were an election to be held now in Illinois we should be beaten. . . . Pennsylvania is against us. Gov. Morton writes that nothing but the most strenuous efforts can carry Indiana." Lincoln was powerless to disagree. "The people promised themselves when General Grant started out that he would take Richmond in June," Lincoln told a New York politician. "He didn't take it, and they blame me." Even the Army of the Potomac appeared to have reached past the point of exhaustion. "It was the bravest and most enterprising officers, the bravest and most enduring soldiers, who had fallen" in the Overland Campaign, wrote one senior Union staffer, and those who were left "had almost ceased to expect victory when they went into battle."[23]

Now, finally, Lee's long, wearisome plan to win the war, not by battle, but by grinding out Northern patience, seemed to be bearing fruit. On August 31, the Democratic National Convention, meeting in Chicago, nominated no one less than George McClellan as its candidate for the presidency. And though McClellan himself protested that his object, if elected, would be "the preservation of the Union, its Constitution & its laws," and not a surrender to Confederate independence, the party platform—and the party's de facto leadership—called for an immediate armistice and an end to the war, regardless of the result. McClellan, for all his talk about the necessity of restoring the Union, was not the man to resist them. "After four years of failure to restore the Union by the experiment of war," no one imagined that an armistice would end except with a complete concession to Confederate demands for independence.

Back in the early spring, James Longstreet had predicted that "if we can break up the enemy's arrangements . . . he will not be able to recover his position nor his morale until the Presidential election is over, and we shall then have a new President to treat with." That now seemed to be on the cusp of realization. Walter Taylor remembered how eagerly "the political dissensions at the North" made Lee's headquarters giddy "about everything that was calculated to have any effect upon the approaching election." Writing to his fiancée, Taylor hoped that McClellan's nomination alone "may lead to a temporary cessation of hostilities." "Lincoln and his party are now environed with dangers rushing upon them from every direction," wrote the diarist John B. Jones on August 21. "The next two months will be the most interesting period of the war; everything depends upon the result of the Presidential election in the United States."[24]

But then the political balloon burst. On August 7, Grant assigned Philip Sheridan to the Shenandoah with orders to track down and destroy Jubal Early, which he did incrementally at Winchester on September 19 and then at Cedar Creek on October 19. Jefferson Davis, fearful that Joe Johnston's endless tick-tacking in the face of Sherman's advance toward Atlanta would end with the surrender of the city (as it almost had with Richmond two years before), replaced Johnston (against Lee's advice) with John Bell Hood on July 18. (Hood was "a bold fighter," Lee warned Davis, "but I am doubtful as to [the] other qualities necessary.") Aggressive in ways Johnston would never have dreamed of, Hood threw the Army of Tennessee at Sherman in repeated—and futile—attacks in front of Atlanta in July, then slumped back into a protective siege that ended when Sherman maneuvered Hood out of the way and occupied Atlanta on September 2.

Early state voting in October now pointed to Republican victories, and although Lincoln remained anxious about the results in New York and Pennsylvania to the very end, he took the popular tally by nearly half a million votes and the Electoral College by a crushing plurality of 212 to 21. Even though Democratic candidates scored a slight increase in their overall percentages of voters over their showing in 1860, Lincoln was secure in the White House, and secure with the prospect of an increased majority in the new Congress. The best face Lee could put on the election was a dejected suggestion to Mary: "We must therefore make up our minds for another four years of war. I trust our merciful God will sustain us & give us strength & courage to bear unceasingly the chastisement & trials he may deem fit to cleanse us of our sins & make us worthy to become his servants."[25]

CHAPTER SEVENTEEN

Just as I Have Expected It Would End from the First

Thus began the winter of the Confederacy's disintegration, a bitterly cold winter in Richmond and Petersburg, with "snow from three to six inches in depth . . . constantly on the ground" and "keeping the trenches wet and muddy." In mid-December, "the snow is 2 to 3 inches deep . . . & sleet formed." On the last day of the year, "it snowed sufficiently . . . to cover the ground & weather very raw & disagreeable"; three days later it snowed again "quite heavily," and by mid-January the "vast amount of snow and rain" swelled the James River "and many of the cellars in the lower part of the city have been already inundated." By the end of January, pavements in Richmond were "almost impassable from the enamel of ice; large icicles hang from the houses, and the trees are bent down with the weight of frost."

Lee found the weather "dreadfully cold," but he nevertheless managed to be out along the lines for "a ride of over 30 miles." Once past his summer's bout with dysentery, he actually appeared "robust, though weather-worn." To a visiting British journalist in November, "Lee is more than ever a sight for gods and men . . . as cheerful to the eye and as indomitable as ever." Visiting the War Department on February 16, Lee "was in gray uniform, with a blue cloth cape over his shoulders," and though "his gray locks and beard have become white . . . his countenance is cheerful, and his health vigorous."[1]

He made his first headquarters at Violet Bank, a farm on the north bank of the Appomattox, directly across from Petersburg, which had once been owned by William Shippen—another in the wide net of Lee's cousins whose Philadelphia relatives he had once visited as a boy with his mother—but characteristically he declined to stay in the house. (Ever since taking command of the Army of Northern Virginia, Lee made a point of living and working out of a headquarters tent, although he would frequently agree to take meals at the table of a nearby householder, especially if he and his staff were occupying that householder's land.) It was to Violet Bank that the news of the July 30 mine explosion came, and it was from Violet Bank that Lee sent Venable to round up the reinforcements that closed the breach made by the mine. But after three months, Lee began to feel restless at being separated by the river from the trench lines below Petersburg, and anyway, to the discomfort of his staff, "the batteries of the enemy firing up the river had gotten the exact range of that yard" and were dropping occasional shells nearby. In mid-August, he moved his headquarters to Chaffin's Bluff to deal with threats to the lines between Richmond and Petersburg (and which culminated in the loss of Fort Harrison), and then back to the south side of the Appomattox, to Edge Hill, the farm of William Turnbull, on the west of Petersburg near the critical South Side Railroad.

He was close enough to Richmond to sit for two more photographic sessions, one with Julian Vannerson and the other with John W. Davies, but the expression in the photographs is distant, inscrutable. Curiously, he made no effort, easy though it would have been, to move into "the Mess" on Franklin Street and spend the winter with his wife. But there was just enough distance between Richmond and Petersburg to make the miles difficult to cover in an emergency, and just enough reluctance to appear that he was avoiding a share in the Army of Northern Virginia's trials. "I wish indeed I was near enough to See you occasionally," he explained to Mary, "but I Cannot be where I wish to be." Or perhaps it was simply too much to bear the trials of the war and of Mary's arthritis at the same time: she suffered a fall in August "from my crutches slipping on the polished floor," and with that "my pains have returned and the prospect of walking seems as far off as ever."[2]

There were certainly enough trials to go around. The difficulties of supply, and the number of mouths to feed, caused prices in Richmond to skyrocket and meals to shrink. The War Department clerk John Jones marked "beef (what little there is in market)" selling at "$6 per pound; meal, $80 per bushel; white beans, $5 per quart, or $160 per bushel" on January 13; the next day, he pegged flour at "$1000 per barrel" and "$1250 per barrel" by the eighteenth. The price of gold had doubled by January, and by March 1865 it took seventy Confederate dollars to buy one gold dollar.

Conditions were worse in the trenches, where Lee had to complain to Jefferson Davis that "there was no salt meat" and "neither meat nor corn are now coming over the southern roads." A month later, he complained again to Secretary of War Seddon that "there is nothing within reach of this army. . . . The country is swept clear," and "we have but two days' supplies." Or perhaps not even that: for three days at the beginning of February, "his troops beyond Petersburg had been in line of battle . . . in snow, hail *without a mouthful* of meat," and lacked "the physical strength to march and fight." By the end of January, he was reduced to circulating a plea for "arms and equipments" in civilian hands "to arm and equip an additional force of cavalry."[3]

At the beginning of the siege, Lee's soldiers had shrugged off the prospect of long months in the trenches. Grant "thinks that he can dig in to Richmond as he did at Vicksburg," wrote one Virginia artilleryman, "but he has for Mas Robert to contend with. He may dig as he pleases and when he is done he will find out that he will have to go back to Washington city with what few men that he will have left." That optimism soon began to falter. The Army of Northern Virginia was experiencing an ominous uptick in absences, and the absences became epidemic as winter advanced. "There have been more desertions of late than ever before," Charles Blackford wrote. "The hard lives they lead and a certain degree of hopelessness which is stealing over the conviction of the best and bravest will have some effect in inducing demoralization hitherto unknown." In the last ten days of November, sixty men from Powell Hill's corps took off, while a hundred more sat in the guardhouse, charged with the attempt.

By January, desertion had become "alarming" to Lee, something he blamed squarely on "the insufficiency of food and non-payment of the troops." In desperation, he published two general orders as an appeal in the *Richmond Dispatch* on February 15, offering pardons for all who "return to the standards which they once illustrated by their valor, and to the comrades who are welcome to ready them once more to their side." But he told the naval captain Raphael Semmes that "his army was melting away," and by March he was threatening that even jokes about desertion would incur "the presumption of guilt" for which "the penalty . . . is death." The reason was only too plain: from mid-February to mid-March 1865, 3,000 of Lee's men deserted, and if this continued, "I cannot keep the army together." In the 5th Alabama, pickets were told that "if a man sees another deserting to [the] enemy & succeeds in shooting him he will get a 30 day furlough."[4]

One bright star was the return of James Longstreet to command of his corps in October, and although his right arm "was quite paralyzed and useless" from his wound in the Wilderness, so that he was compelled to take "oceans of morphine," Longstreet assumed command of the "troops operating on the north side of the James" and relieved Lee of the burden of watching over that end of the siege lines. Otherwise, Lee set for himself a grim regimen of personal oversight and even grimmer predictions. He rode the lines, "superintending in person the fortifications multiplied everywhere for the defense of the city," his engineer's eye checking on gaps in the emplacements and deterioration due to the winter weather. "I always find something to correct on the lines," he told Jefferson Davis.

All idea of surrendering decision making to his subordinates seems to have disappeared entirely, and he unnerved one brigade commander by standing on the parapet of a battery with his field glasses in full view of Union pickets. Another officer who he had been informed was taking up comfortable quarters in Petersburg was greeted by Lee with biting sarcasm: "Good morning, General Blank. Are you not afraid to trust yourself so far from the city, and to come where all this firing and danger is?" "And," wrote Dabney Maury, "he turned from him with a scorn as withering as his words." But his deepest bitterness was reserved for the politicians. "Well, Mr. Custis," he snarled to his son after a consultation with the Virginia delegation to the Confederate Congress in March, "I have been up to see The Congress and they do not seem to be able to do anything except eat peanuts and chew tobacco, while my army is starving." He returned to a theme he had not articulated since the spring of his decisions in 1861, and that was the folly of secession: "When this war began, I was opposed to it, bitterly opposed to it." And, he added, as it had turned out, he had been right to oppose it, because the secessionists had failed the test of perfect commitment. "I told these people that unless every man should do his whole duty, they would repent it; and now . . . they will repent."[5]

But even repentance would not be enough at this late day as all the hideous miscalculations of secession, states' rights, and slavery now stood in glaring relief. Against those who confidently boasted of the superior virtues of a slave society, nearly 200,000 African Americans now stood in arms, as the U.S. Colored Troops, against them. For those who once imagined that the vast stretches of the Confederacy would swallow up Lincoln's armies like Russia had swallowed Napoleon's, cruel reality showed them that all that now remained of the Confederate States of America were amputated pieces of Virginia, the Carolinas, Mississippi, Alabama, Florida, and Texas. For those who once were sure that aristocratic Britain and imperial France would come to the aid of the cotton kings, not a single gesture of solidarity had been forthcoming that didn't have a convenient profit margin attached to it. The arch-secessionist Edmund Ruffin learned from neighbors who had interviewed Lee's soldiers that

> *provisions were very scarce in the army, & the daily rations often fell short of the allowance—sometimes no meat; the pay was long in arrear, (even in some cases 9 to 12 months,) to many of the troops—clothing much wanting, & the army in the Valley especially destitute & suffering for necessary clothing: there was much discontent, & general beginning*

> *of despondency since the late disasters in Ga & Ten: The desertions from Lee's army were numerous & even to the enemy. Many deserted every night. . . . Under such circumstances, Gen. Lee's army must be melting away, & losing not more in numbers, by desertion & all other cases, than in its spirit & sanguine hopes for the future. I greatly fear—indeed scarcely doubt—that Gen. Lee will soon be unable to continue his defense of R[ichmon]d & P[etersbur]g. & that he must evacuate both cities.*[6]

In mid-November, Sherman contemptuously abandoned Atlanta and stomped across the abdomen of Georgia to Savannah against only the feeblest resistance and then turned north, ripping apart the disintegrating fabric of South Carolina and moving inexorably toward a juncture with Grant sometime in the spring. Just as Sherman designed, his march created "a chilling apprehension of the futility" of resistance. In the west, the hapless John Bell Hood tried to distract Sherman by loosing the Army of Tennessee on its namesake state, only to meet with a bloody defeat at Franklin, Tennessee, in November and near destruction at Nashville in December. All the while, Southerners thought only of their own backyards. As William Hardee sadly informed Jefferson Davis on January 29, "The people of Charleston . . . are so entirely wrapped up in their own State and City as to be unmindful of the wants of other portions of our country," and "they are willing that Lee should give up Richmond . . . so that their selfish ambition might be gratified." "Affairs are gloomy enough," wrote the War Department clerk John Jones. Even "Gen. Lee is despondent."[7]

It was the season of desperation, and in desperation the Confederate Congress demanded that Jefferson Davis surrender his military powers as the Confederate commander in chief and appoint Robert E. Lee general in chief of all the Confederate armies—or what was left of them. On January 9, Davis's legion of critics introduced legislation calling for the creation of a general in chief, whom everyone assumed would have to be Lee. "Some of the Georgia members," reported Jones, "declare that their State will re-enter the Union unless Lee be speedily put at the head of military affairs in the field." The bill was revised and watered down, but it passed the Senate on the fifteenth and the House four days later, and Davis duly appointed Lee to his new command on February 6. This was not the vacuous command rank Davis had extended back in 1862, but actual control of all the Confederate forces—and perhaps even more. "A large number of the croaking inhabitants censure the President for our many misfortunes, and openly declare in favor of Lee as Dictator," wrote John Jones in his diary on Christmas Day. Some "see him as King or Dictator," because Lee "is one of the few great men who ever lived, who could be trusted."

It was not a responsibility Lee particularly wanted, and because Davis provided "no instructions as to my duties, I do not know what he desires me to undertake." Nor did Davis yield gracefully. Lee tried to cushion the blow to the president by assuring Davis this new appointment was seen by Lee as a strategy to "relieve you from a portion of the constant labor and anxiety which now presses upon you." But when Lee began laying plans for an abandonment of Richmond, starting with directives to his headquarters staff "to be in marching order, to lose no time, to begin my preparations to-morrow," Davis at once objected. He learned on February 25 that Lee was planning to move the government archives, books, and papers to Lynchburg for safety, and Davis warned him that this "will produce panic. If you can spare the time I wish you to come" to Richmond. Lee did not have the time and said so, which provoked a touchy declaration from Davis, "Rest assured I will never ask your views" about the archives again. "Your counsels are no longer wanted in this matter."

One thing Lee did insist upon, however, was the authority to remove or reinstate army and department commanders. "I must . . . rely upon the several commanders for the conduct of the military operations with which they are charged," Lee warned Davis, and "in the event of their neglect or failure I must ask for their removal." That would begin as he sorted out the wrecked pieces of the Army of Tennessee and put them once again under Joe Johnston, on the outside chance that Johnston could concentrate them in the Carolinas and do something to slow down Sherman's advance. But Johnston knew that the time for hope had passed. He could glue together barely 13,500 men from the ruins of Hood's mismanagement. "Sherman's course cannot be hindered by the small force I have," he wearily informed Lee on March 23. "I can do no more than annoy him."[8]

It was the season of desperation, and in desperation there were Southern voices prepared to speak now what before they had scarcely dared to think: conscript slaves as soldiers, promise them emancipation if necessary, but put them into gray uniforms and send them to save the Confederacy from doom. Lee began edging in that direction in September 1864, when he proposed to Jefferson Davis "relieving all able bodied white men employed as teamsters, cooks, mechanics and laborers, and supplying their places with negroes." Lee continued to recommend the impressment of slave workers, whether their owners agreed or not, "to labor on the fortifications" of Richmond. But in October, he took the further step of writing to William Porcher Miles, the chair of the Confederate House of Representatives' Military Affairs Committee, to urge a program of African American enlistment, accompanied by emancipation. Anything less than guaranteeing "the freedom of those slaves . . . makes the plan more than useless."[9]

Rumor of Lee's endorsement of slave enlistment was covered with incredulity by Confederate hard-liners. John Jones was taken aback to learn, through the Virginia representative James Lyons, that "Gen. Lee" was "always a thorough emancipationist," and Jones wondered, "If it be really so, and if it were generally known, that Gen. Lee is, and always has been opposed to slavery, how soon would his great popularity vanish like the mist of the morning!" He did not have to wait long. *The Charleston Mercury* at once accused Lee of old-time "Federalism" and "a profound disbelief in the institution of slavery." Any talk about Lee as a dictator, for the moment at least, was forgotten.

> *Gen. Lee, the advocate, if not the author of this scheme of . . . emancipation, is said by those who are acquainted with the families and the family opinions of men in Virginia, to be a hereditary Federalist and a disbeliever in the institution of slavery. It is with these sentiments that he aims to advise us. What else then could his advice be than what it is? But are we in the Cotton States . . . to turn a somersault in all of our political and social views, and to lay down our arms at the feet of Southern Federalism? . . . The whole question is one—John C. Calhoun or . . . Robert E. Lee.*

The Georgia politician-general Howell Cobb denounced the notion of enlisting and emancipating slaves as "the most pernicious idea that has been suggested since the war began," and Cobb found it "a source of deep mortification and regret to see the name of that good and great man and soldier, General R. E. Lee, given as authority for such a policy." Edmund Ruffin predicted that this "cannot fail to lead to general emancipation of our slaves," and Catherine Edmondston decided that she would "have rejoiced" more in "Gen Lee's Commandership . . . had he not sanctioned the suicidal scheme of conscripting & emancipating an indefinite number of negroes & their families." No, exclaimed Edmondston, "freedom for whites, slavery for negroes, God has so ordained it!"[10]

Still, on January 7, 1865, the Virginia state senator Andrew Hunter wrote directly to Lee to ask his views on "the expediency and propriety of bringing to bear against our relentless enemy . . . the element of military strength supposed to be found in our negro population." Lee replied swiftly, sweetening the pill he was about to administer with the admission that "the relation of master and slave, controlled by humane laws and influenced by Christianity," was "the best that can exist between the white and black races." But, he plunged on, the Union armies will "in course of time penetrate our country and get access to a large part of our negro population" and inevitably "recruit them into the Union forces." That left little choice that Lee could see. It was time for Southerners to decide whether "slavery shall be extinguished by our enemies and the slaves used against us, or use them ourselves at the risk of the effects which may be produced upon our social institution."

He did not recommend half measures. Enlistment would require "giving immediate freedom to all who enlist, and freedom at the end of the war to the families of those who discharge their duties faithfully." Nor could it stop merely with those who served in the Confederate forces. Once begun, military emancipation would have to be accompanied by "a well-digested plan of gradual and general emancipation." He would, he hinted to a British journalist, even be in favor of holding "out to them the certainty" not only of emancipation "but of a home when they shall have rendered efficient service."[11]

Within days, Lee's letter "on the subject of negro enlistment" was being copied, circulated, damned, and hailed. The War Department bureau chief Robert Kean confessed himself "astonished" that Lee "favors emancipation per se" and advocates "large enlistments accompanied by the promise of prospective emancipation of the families of the negro soldier." There was enough uncertainty about whether the Army would back its general that on February 11, 1865, the Confederate secretary of state, Judah P. Benjamin, asked Lee to poll his Army about "an expression of its desire to be reinforced by such negroes as for the boon of freedom will volunteer to go to the front." Lee at once initiated the query throughout the Army of Northern Virginia, using Benjamin's "boon of freedom" wording. The results were at best ambivalent, some units endorsing black recruitment "with great spirit and entire unanimity," others hearing the question "with anxiety and apprehension . . . seriously doubting its expediency and practicability." Even James Longstreet was skeptical, because "such a measure will involve the necessity of abolishing slavery entirely in the future, and that, too, without materially aiding us in the present."

Lee ignored the results. One week later, he wrote to the Mississippi congressman Ethelbert Barksdale, who had introduced legislation to recruit slave soldiers (but not require their emancipation), to urge "the employment of negroes as soldiers" as "not only expedient, but necessary." (According to the diarist John Jones, Lee "said the white fighting men were exhausted, and that black men must recruit the army—and it must be done at once.") He insisted, however, that "placing them on the footing of soldiers" should also come "with their freedom assured." Finally, Lee asked Jefferson Davis for direct authorization to "carry" black enlistment "into effect as soon as practicable," and on March 27 he anxiously requested confirmation from John C. Breckinridge (James Seddon's replacement as the Confederate secretary of war) "for raising and organizing the colored troops." Lee thought the extremity of the situation would persuade slave owners to eagerly surrender their slaves for army service. He was wrong, as the poll of his own troops indicated. And anyway, by that point, it was too late—if there *had* ever actually been a time for slaves to fight in defense of their own enslavement.[12]

It was the season of desperation, and in desperation Jefferson Davis responded to a personal plea from old Francis Preston Blair to send commissioners to a meeting at Hampton Roads to talk peace. Back in the prewar days, Davis had been something of a protégé of Blair's, and after Jubal Early's raiders torched Blair's Silver Spring property outside Washington, Blair determined to use a proposal to recover papers stolen from Silver Spring as an excuse for a pass from Lincoln through the lines to Richmond to meet with Davis. Lincoln agreed, but without giving Blair any negotiating authority, and Blair's arrival in Richmond on January 12 set off an uproar of speculation. John Jones was "assured by one of the President's special detectives that Francis P. Blair, Sr. is truly in this city." And it soon raced through the Army. "The air has been filled with rumors . . . that Frank P. Blair [is] now in Richmd & has come to offer terms of peace," wrote one Alabama soldier.

Cagey about overcommitting himself, Davis was nevertheless ready to let Blair believe that he was ready for any sort of negotiation "to secure peace to the two countries." He agreed "to appoint persons to have conferences" with representatives from Lincoln and dispatched the Confederate vice president, Alexander Stephens, the Virginia senator Robert M. T. Hunter, and the former Supreme Court justice John A. Campbell. They passed through the lines at Petersburg on January 31 to meet with Lincoln and Secretary of State Seward at Hampton Roads, far from prying eyes, on board the steamer *River Queen.* But Lincoln would have nothing to do with any negotiations short of an immediate restoration of "our one common country," and that included the disbanding of the Confederate armies, the abolition of slavery, and the restoration of the Union. Hunter incredulously asked Lincoln whether that meant "we of the South have committed treason." "Yes," Lincoln replied. "You have stated the proposition better than I did. That is about the size of it."[13]

When the commissioners returned to Richmond, Jefferson Davis interpreted Lincoln's unwillingness to compromise as a full justification for dismissing any further talk of peace and calling for renewed vigor in waging the war. "The enemy refuse to enter into negotiations with the Confederate States or any one of them separately . . . on any other basis than our unconditional submission," Davis reported gleefully to Congress on February 6. That evening, he addressed a mass meeting in Richmond and announced his "ecstatic joy" at the reborn enthusiasm he was sure Lincoln's rebuke would engender in Southern hearts. Alexander Stephens, listening to Davis, was appalled. Davis's speech, he thought, was "not much short of dementation." Stephens was not alone in that conclusion. Judge Campbell (who was now convinced "that we are arrived at the last days of the Confederacy") pronounced the "embarrassments" the Confederacy was suffering to be "insoluble" and publicly asked "that General Lee be requested to give his opinion upon the condition of the country."

Officially, Lee wanted to be known as being "in accord with his civil chief on that question, and was determined to fight and risk the last defiance of fortune." But that was the opinion of a soldier who had spent a lifetime watching other, greater soldiers get washed out to sea the moment they ventured to put a foot into political currents. Privately, Lee was as convinced as Stephens that Davis was delusional, that he was (as Lee would later say), "of course, one of the extremist politicians." Shortly after the return of the commissioners to Richmond, Lee paid a call on Robert M. T. Hunter, Nicodemus-like by night, and urged Hunter that if "there was a chance for any peace" other than unconditional surrender, it was Hunter's "duty to make the effort." They talked "nearly through the night." Hunter explained that any appeal he might make to reopen the negotiations would be "misrepresented." But if Lee—if *Robert E. Lee*—"were to recommend peace negotiations publicly," Davis would have to listen. "To this he made no reply." Lee could not bring himself to cross the political line. And though Lee never explicitly said that "the chances were over," Hunter remembered that "the tone and tenor of his remarks made that impression on my mind."[14]

Hunter was not the only one to whom Lee confided his certainties that the war was lost, and the Confederacy lost, too, unless some dramatic political gesture was made by Davis to Lincoln. But for such a gesture, "every one looked for some expression from General R. E. Lee to direct public opinion and lead the way to success." At every suggestion, he declined to take action himself. John Brown Gordon recalled another late-night meeting with Lee "during the first week in March" in which Lee laid out the same fatal scenario. Gordon, like Hunter, "frankly" told him to "make terms with the enemy, the best we can get." But Lee replied that "he scarcely felt authorized to suggest to the civil authorities the advisability of making terms . . . that he was a soldier, that it was his province to obey the orders of the Government, and to advise or counsel with the civil authorities only upon questions directly affecting his army and its defence of the capital and the country."

When Lee described his doubts to William Mahone, who was now commanding a division in Longstreet's corps, Mahone urged Lee to take "matters in his own hands," even to use Mahone's division to march on Richmond and force Davis to listen to reason. Lee shook his head. "There was a government in Richmond," and it was Lee's obligation to wait on its decisions. When John

Breckinridge took over as secretary of war, he solicited a statement from Lee about the prospects of further resistance; again Lee pulled back, explaining at great length that there was "no strong prospect of a marked success" but then crossing his wires by adding, "Everything in my opinion has depended and still depends upon the disposition and feelings of the people. Their representatives can best decide how they will bear the difficulties and sufferings of their condition."[15]

What Hunter and Gordon and Mahone did not know was that Lee was already preparing for eventualities. On February 21, Edward O. C. Ord, who had replaced the flabby Benjamin Butler in command of the Union troops at Bermuda Hundred in January, sent a message across the lines under a flag of truce to James Longstreet, an old prewar acquaintance. The subject was militarily negligible—it concerned bartering back and forth between the troops—but it provided an excuse for Ord and Longstreet to confer face-to-face on February 25, and the burden on Ord's mind was not bartering but military negotiation. "The war had gone on long enough," Ord told Longstreet. If the politicians could not agree on peace, perhaps the soldiers could: Would Lee be agreeable to a meeting with Grant on "the possibility of arriving at a satisfactory adjustment of the present unhappy difficulties by means of a military convention"? So on March 2, Lee wrote to Grant in torturously apolitical language to suggest they meet "at such convenient time and place as you may designate, with the hope that upon an interchange of views it may be found practicable to submit the subjects of controversy between the belligerents to a convention." Lee gave the letter personally to Longstreet to hand deliver to Ord and ordered him to make sure it was sealed "before transmitting."[16]

This might, at a distance, have looked only like soldiers talking to soldiers, which explained Lee's willingness to participate, but both Grant and Lee were concealing from themselves that the subject really was politics, and when it came to politics, Grant learned very quickly that neither Lincoln nor Secretary of War Stanton was willing to authorize any such talks. Especially Stanton. Lincoln was on the eve of his second inauguration, and Lee's note appealed to "all the better and kindlier impulses of his nature." But Stanton angrily vetoed the notion, and Lincoln, on reflection, agreed. "The President directs me to say to you that he wishes you to have no conference with Gen Lee unless it be for the capitulation of Lees army, or on solely minor and purely military matters," Stanton wired to Grant the next day. "You are not to decide, discuss, or confer upon any political question: such questions the President holds in his own hands." And he added, ominously, this was exactly the same thing McClellan and his staffer John Key had tried to do in 1862, leaving Grant and Ord to imagine for themselves what the consequences would be. Grant was compelled to tell Lee that there had been some misunderstanding; he would be open to discussing only matters "such as are purely of a military character."

Jefferson Davis was hardly more accommodating. Lee might proceed if he wished and should consider himself "clothed with all the supplemental authority you may need," but only for "a military convention." In the end, even Lee admitted that "I am not sanguine." Davis was obsessive in his belief "of still winning our independence" and "very pertinacious in opinion and purpose." The War Department bureaucrat Robert Kean, ears always pressed to the wall, learned of the conference proposal and "had hopes of a conference between Generals Lee and Grant," but nothing happened, and the Confederacy had, in the words of the Richmond *Dispatch,* "no choice but to continue this contest to a final issue."[17]

Lee had no illusions about what that "final issue" would be. The siege, by "requiring the troops to be always on duty and prepared for any movements of the enemy" and by starving them of food and equipment, was enfeebling the Army of Northern Virginia at the same time as it was allowing Grant's army, with its enormous supply base at City Point on the James and a military railroad to support its every part, to grow in strength. By the end of January, Lee was warning Davis that once the spring thaws set in, Grant would resume slipping his army westward, cutting the last roads into Petersburg, and perhaps even "enveloping Richmond." In that case, Lee added to James Longstreet, "we shall have to abandon our position on the James River as lamentable as it is on every count." He would, he promised Mary, "endeavor to do my duty & fight to the last," but that did not necessarily mean fighting for Richmond or Petersburg. "In the event of the necessity of abandoning our position on the James River," he would not wait for Grant to close the jaws around the Army of Northern Virginia but would bolt westward, "endeavor to unite the corps of the army about Burkeville," and then strike south to link up with Joe Johnston. What Mary would do, immobilized in Richmond with Agnes, the younger Mary, and Mildred, he could not guess. "Should it be necessary to abandon our position to prevent being surrounded, what will you do? Will you remain or leave the city?" There had been rumors, even as early as the beginning of March, that "Gen. L.'s family are preparing to leave the city." But Mary had no plans to go anywhere, and she resolutely refused to tolerate any talk of failure.[18]

Lee had one more card worth playing, and that was to unleash a preemptive strike at Grant with "a select body" of troops while Grant was "marshaling & preparing his troops for some movement." He still had 68,000 men on the rolls at the end of February. So, in the predawn darkness of March 25, Lee launched three divisions under John Brown Gordon at Fort Stedman, a large earthen-work artillery bastion at the eastern end of the Union trenches around Petersburg. Lee hoped that if he could punch a hole wide enough in Grant's line, he "could sweep along his entrenchments to the south" with the breakout divisions, pin the rest of Grant's army into place, and allow Gordon's attack force to "unite with Genl Johnston" and give Johnston a fighting chance to strike "a blow against Sherman before the latter can join Genl Grant." If Sherman could be stopped, then all of the Confederate forces could rejoin Lee at Petersburg and confront Grant.

Exactly how Lee would be able to hold on afterward at Petersburg, minus "a select body" of his own diminishing army, or how that "select body" would find its way to Johnston without transportation or logistical support, or whether they could do anything more than temporarily stop Sherman, Lee could not say. All he could offer as an alternative was desperation, in the season of desperation: "If unsuccessful I should be in no worse condition," because if he did nothing, Grant would surely compel him "to withdraw from [the] James River."[19]

The attack on Fort Stedman failed. "Daylight found the plan only half executed," Porter Alexander recalled, "& the Federal troops & batteries swarmed upon it." For Lee, the last hour at Petersburg had arrived, and he began ordering the destruction of anything the Union forces might find valuable, including "large quantities of tobacco and cotton" in Petersburg warehouses. He planned what he hoped would be "an orderly & decent retreat," and to that end he organized train schedules, supplies, and equipment so that the Army of Northern Virginia would be "taking with them, or sending ahead, stores & supplies & many things in Richmond without which our army could not long keep the field."

What he could not order was extra time to do it all. Five days later, Grant reached around Lee's western flank and proceeded to cut the South Side Railroad at Five Forks. On April 1, Grant ordered "a general assault along the lines," and the next morning, at 4:00, a signal gun sent three federal divisions smashing through the paper-thin Confederate defenses. Lee's men "were brushed away with an emphasis that precluded all ideas of an attempt to reform" and close the breach. Union skirmishers who raced toward the South Side Railroad's track encountered Powell Hill, trying to stem the rout, and shot him dead. Only a tenacious last stand made at Forts Gregg and Whitworth kept the Federals from overrunning Lee's headquarters at the Turnbull farm. "I see no prospect of doing more than holding our position here til night," Lee desperately wired John Breckinridge at 10:40 a.m. "I advise that all preparation be made for leaving Richmond tonight."[20]

—

"During the whole day," remembered Walter Taylor, Lee "was engaged in issuing orders and sending dispatches by couriers and by telegraph," until a federal shell came crashing through Edge Hill and forced him to abandon it. It was a tribute to Lee the engineer and his meticulous planning for the evacuation that he managed to extricate the corps of Hill and Longstreet from Petersburg and beyond and get them to the north side of the Appomattox River, where they joined John Brown Gordon (now commanding Richard Ewell's old corps) and scooped up the various units of the Richmond garrison.

Once again the model of calmness ("self-contained and serene," in Walter Taylor's eyes), Lee issued his orders for the westward retreat of his "sadly reduced army and the relinquishment of the position so long and successfully held against the greatly superior force opposed to him." They would all rendezvous at Amelia Court House, on the Richmond and Danville Railroad, the last rail line linking Richmond itself with the Carolinas, and rumors inflamed an optimism that "Joe Johnston had eluded Sherman and was within a few hours' march of Grant's left flank." Jefferson Davis and the heads of the Confederate government would take the last train from Richmond on the Richmond and Danville, and the Army of Northern Virginia would follow them along the rail line's long arc west and south. Altogether, Lee now had fewer than 60,000 men of all services and descriptions, including his three sons, Custis, Rooney, and young Rob. Mary and his daughters he would have to leave to the mercies of the Union soldiers who occupied Petersburg and Richmond and trust that Grant, as he moved to occupy the Confederate capital, would not harass or exploit them as hostages. "Citizens gathered on the corners discussing the situation and feeling that the star of the Confederacy was about to go down," remembered one soldier. "There was no such thing as sleeping in Petersburg that night."[21]

Despite the planning, disorder plagued every aspect of the operation's execution. The rendezvous at Amelia Court House was supposed to have been met by supply trains from Richmond that would fill his soldiers' haversacks and cartridge boxes for this new campaign. In the welter of confusion, the orders for the supplies from Richmond went undelivered, and Lee was forced to spend a day at Amelia Court House, allowing his men to forage for food, while he camped in the yard of a refugee from Alexandria whom he had known in happier times. It did not help, either, that Richard Ewell and the last of the Richmond garrison were lagging behind, needing to take a wide detour to find a crossing of the Appomattox River. The 15th Alabama's William McClendon "saw General Lee on an old traveler, surrounded by a few of his staff" and looking "very serious, as if he were brooding over the disappointment that we had met in getting no rations." Grant, meanwhile, showed no inclination to stage a lengthy occupation celebration in Richmond. Posting only a garrison to hold the city, he and the Army of the Potomac, with Sheridan and his cavalry in the lead, leaped at once to the pursuit. Lee's survival would thus depend on two things: staying far ahead enough of Grant to find daylight for a turn south to "try and get to" Joe Johnston, and meeting fresh supplies brought eastward from Lynchburg.[22]

He succeeded in neither. On April 6, Grant caught up with the Army of Northern Virginia's rear guard at Sailor's Creek, slicing it off and capturing 7,700 prisoners, among them Richard Ewell and Custis Lee. "My God!" Lee moaned, picking up one of the Army's slashed red battle flags to form a rallying point. "Has this army dissolved!" But he could do no more than disengage the remainder of his Army from those already lost to Union capture. Floating among the officers who had been swept out of Richmond in the retreat was Henry Wise, who had caused so much grief for Lee long before in western Virginia and who now proceeded to make more by haranguing Lee. "These men have already endured more than I believed flesh and blood could stand," Wise orated. "The blood of every man who is killed from this time forth is on your head, General Lee." Lee angrily dismissed him: "General, do not talk so wildly. My burdens are heavy enough!"

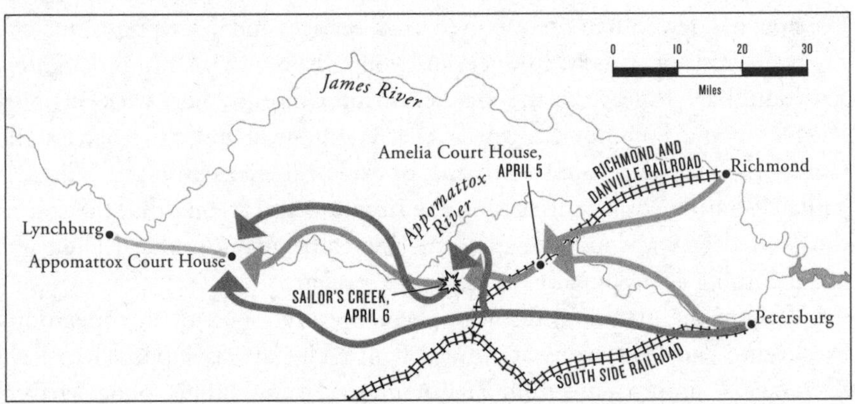

But even as Lee stared "at the throng surging upon the roads and in the fields," he could offer little disagreement. Those who evaded capture simply vanished into the woods, no longer confident that there was anything to hope for. Squads and troops quietly feathered away into the dark, not eager to die for a cause that was palpably lost and just as unwilling to fall into the hands of a Union general whose reputation was built around words like "unconditional surrender." In the eyes of the U.S. government, Lee's men were not the soldiers of an independent nation but an illegal assembly that had raised its hand against the authority of its own flag and government, and for that no other term was fitting except "traitor." Traitors found with weapons in their hands could be punished by any means designated—humiliating Roman-style triumphs through Northern cities, even military trials and drumhead executions. Through much of the war, the federal government had legally winked at "exchanges of prisoners and other acts," as though the rebels were citizens of a sovereign nation. But the end of the war would remove the need for winking; what then would be the status of Confederates who surrendered *unconditionally*?[23]

As the retreat staggered onward, Lee could exercise only the thinnest of control. "There seemed to be no one present exercising any authority," with artillery and wagons "almost inextricably entangled" with cavalry and infantry. Even if they had no conscious intention to desert, thousands of soldiers "were leaving their commands and wandering about the devastated country in quest of food, *and they had no muskets.*" Others struggled to hang together with their regiments. "I saw men apparently fast asleep in ranks, standing up, & waking enough to move on a few yards at a time," wrote Ewell's stepson, Campbell Brown. "During the whole night, our command could not have made over three or four miles." In odd cases, Confederate artillerymen took to burying the gun-tubes of their pieces "rather than for them to fall into the hands of the Yankees"; staff officers littered the roadsides with thrown-away papers and books, and even Walter Taylor ordered "the valuable books and papers" he had kept as "the headquarters archive" burned. From this increasing anarchy, Lee began to draw the conclusion he knew from the beginning, back in 1861, he would probably have to draw: "A few more Sailors' Creeks and it will all be over—ended—just as I have expected it would end from the first."

Grant could not help noticing the wide fan of Confederate desertions, and it did not take much calculating to guess what it meant for Lee's power of resistance. On April 7, Grant sent a note under a flag of truce to Lee, imploring him to recognize "the hopelessness of further resistance on the part of the Army of Northern Virginia." Lee read the note and shook his head: "If I were to say a word to the Federal commander he would regard it as such a confession of weakness as to make it the condition of demanding unconditional surrender," and Lee could not do that to his officers and men. And the phlegmatic Longstreet agreed: "Not yet."

At last, Lee consented to send a reply, asking Grant to state "the terms you will offer," clearly adding, "on condition of its surrender." Grant's reply was disturbingly opaque: "The men and officers surrendered shall be disqualified for taking up arms again." That was not enough to reassure Lee, and in turn he sent Grant an even more opaque letter, declining to surrender the Army of Northern Virginia but returning to the question raised by Ord and Longstreet in February, whether Grant was interested in talking about a general "restoration of peace." Grant was not. No "restoration" of anything, especially if Lee was implying a return of some sort to the prewar status quo, was even thinkable, and in any case Stanton and Lincoln's letter in March had struck away any such larger negotiating power. There was no choice but to keep pushing west.[24]

When the Army of Northern Virginia finally reached Appomattox Station, where Lee expected to find supplies from Lynchburg, Philip Sheridan's cavalry were already there and blocking the stage road that led westward to Lynchburg from the nearby village of Appomattox Court House. Although his available forces had dwindled to fewer than 30,000, Lee would try one more time on the morning of April 9 to break free, sending John Brown Gordon's corps to push Sheridan's cavalry out of the Army of Northern Virginia's path. "I will strike that man a blow in the morning," he promised Longstreet in "loud, almost fierce tones." And though Longstreet was dubious about "the strength and condition of his command," he loyally added, "You have only to give me the order and the attack will be made in the morning."

All the while, Lee tried to keep up appearances of good order: a "young officer" reported to him with one pant leg hanging carelessly out of his boot, which Lee sharply compared to "a huge misshapen bologna sausage." The officer "turned blood-red at the rebuke," but Lee hastened to add that he merely wanted his officers, "especially those who were near the persons of high commanders, to avoid anything on a retreat which might look like demoralization." But appearances were wearing thin. Three of Grant's infantry corps had moved up behind Sheridan's troopers, and Gordon's attack stalled. "I fear I can do nothing unless I am heavily supported by Longstreet's corps," Gordon helplessly reported, while federal cavalry hovered "away beyond musket range on the left . . . as ill-omened birds of prey, awaiting their opportunity." When Charles Venable brought him the news, Lee knew that the end of the tether had been reached. "Then there is nothing left for me but to go and see General Grant," and, he added, "I would rather die a thousand deaths."[25]

Perhaps, in the depths of his despair, Lee *did* contemplate dying a death right there. "How easily I could get rid of all this and be at rest," Lee said drearily. "I have only to ride along the lines and all will be over." When William Nelson Pendleton was delegated to speak for Lee's senior officers and urged him to embrace the idea of surrender, Lee replied, "I have resolved to die first." But he consoled himself with the realization that the way the war was ending was not his design, that this was what he had all along prophesied would be the Confederacy's end if it did not offer the same dedication he had offered. "I have never believed we could, against the gigantic combination for our subjugation, make good in the long run our independence," he said to Pendleton, something he repeated to William Mahone and to anyone who would listen. "He had advised the Confederate authorities at the start that the contest on which we had entered could not be over-estimated and that our chance to win was to be found by throwing the whole military or fighting power of the Confederacy vigorously into the struggle," but this "he manifestly thought had not been done."

But Lee did keep one reservation in the back of his mind: if Grant did indeed behave like Ulysses Grant and demand a graceless and unconditional surrender, Lee would walk away, and they would fight to the finish, right there, right then. There must be some concessions to protect his men and officers, and "if this were not agreed to Gen. Lee would cut his army out with what he could." He sent several messages to Grant, again under a flag of truce, and waited along the Richmond-Lynchburg stage road, under an apple tree, while a cease-fire damped down the last shots. Lee dozed there until noon, when Grant's aide Colonel Orville Babcock arrived in the company of a member of Longstreet's staff with "a note from Gen. Grant" and a request for Lee to select a meeting place.[26]

Lee turned to Charles Marshall and Walter Taylor to accompany him, but Taylor, heartsick at the prospect of the surrender, pleaded exhaustion. Babcock and Lee, accompanied by Marshall and an orderly, Joshua Johns, rode into Appomattox Court House, where "they met one of the residents, named Wilmer McLean," who offered "his own house" as the meeting place. Lee entered, sat, and waited again. Knots of Union officers and some local civilians began to cluster around the McLean house, and inevitably stories blossomed that, according to "a distinguished general officer," Lee was surrendering because "the rebel general is not and has never been a secessionist. He did not believe in secession at the start and does not now." Lee looked "much jaded and worn," but to *The New York Herald*'s correspondent he "nevertheless presented the same magnificent physique for which he has always been noted," and still wearing a uniform "without embroidery or any insignia of rank, except three stars worn on the turned position of his coat collar," although with "an elegant sword, sash and gauntlets." (After all, Lee grimly declared to William Nelson Pendleton, "if I am to be General Grant's prisoner to-day, I intend to make my best appearance.")

> *His cheeks were much bronzed by exposure, but still shone ruddy underneath it all. He is growing quite bald, and wears one of the side locks of his hair thrown across the upper portion of his forehead, which is as white and fair as a woman's. He stands fully six feet one inch in height, and weighs something over two hundred pounds, without being burdened with a pound of superfluous flesh. . . . His demeanor was that of a thoroughly possessed gentleman who had a very disagreeable duty to*

perform, but was determined to get through it as well and as soon as he could.

Grant arrived around 1:30, trailed by his principal staff, dressed only in "a slouched hat without cord; common soldier's blouse, unbuttoned, on which, however, the four stars; high boots, mud-splashed to the top . . . no sword . . . all his faculties gathered into intense thought and mighty calm." Embarrassed to find Lee outfitted in "a full uniform which was entirely new . . . wearing a sword of considerable value, very likely the sword which had been presented by the State of Virginia," Grant stumbled out some apologies. "Gen. Lee, I have no sword; I have been riding all night." Lee merely bowed "with that coldness of manner . . . which, after all, became him wonderfully well." They sat down in the McLean parlor, exchanging some uncomfortable chitchat over old times in Mexico. "I met you once before, General Lee, while we were serving in Mexico, when you came over from General Scott's head-quarters to visit Garland's brigade," and "I have always remembered your appearance." Yes, Lee replied politely, "I know I met you on that occasion . . . and tried to recollect how you looked, but I have never been able to recall a single feature." It was a dignified way of admitting that he had no real remembrance of Grant, who was then only a shavetail lieutenant.[27]

It was time to come to business, and what Grant sketched out took Lee gratefully by surprise. Grant proposed to receive the surrender of the Army of Northern Virginia, but to immediately parole all who surrendered there—no triumphal parades, no trials—and to permit all officers to keep their side-arms (no humiliating turning over of officers' personal weapons as tokens of defeat), and, at a suggestion from Lee, to allow any Confederate soldiers to take home an army horse or mule for "planting a spring crop." (One of Grant's officers, when Grant mentioned "their spring crops," thought the remark worth noting, because it "demonstrated more completely his idea that *the war was over,* and that these warlike men and horses would go at once to work *planting corn.*") Lee was overcome with relief. "This would have a happy effect upon his army," he declared. The terms were written out, and after Charles Marshall drafted a brief acceptance letter, Lee signed it. No unconditional surrender after all.

What Lee did not know was that Grant was in no position to demand unconditional surrenders of any sort. The pell-mell pursuit of the Army of Northern Virginia to Appomattox Court House had stretched his own army far beyond its logistical supports (hence, Grant's unkempt dress; his baggage wagon, with a suitable uniform to match Lee's, was miles behind), and if Lee had balked at a demand for an unconditional surrender, Grant would have been forced to break off the pursuit, and Lee might very well have escaped, at least to Lynchburg. "I was in a position of extreme difficulty," Grant admitted. "I was marching away from my supplies, while Lee was falling back on his supplies. If Lee had continued his flight another day I should have had to abandon the pursuit, fall back to Danville, build the railroad, and feed my army. So far as supplies were concerned, I was almost at my last gasp when the surrender took place." And "if Lee had escaped and joined Johnston in North Carolina, or reached the mountains," Grant admitted, "it would have imposed upon us continued armament and expense." Lincoln had specifically warned him that "the country would break down financially under the terrible strain on its resources." The terms had to be generous to ensure that Lee would take them. They might not have been the ideal, but they were, in Grant's estimate, "the best and only terms."

What Grant did not know was that Lee's officers had come to him with exactly the proposition Grant dreaded: dissolve the Army of Northern Virginia, and allow its men with weapons in their hands to scatter into the mountains in the distance, or "take to the bushes on the first sign of a flag of truce," and carry on a guerrilla war—such a guerrilla war as John Brown had once dreamed of. "Order the army to disperse," urged Porter Alexander, now commanding what was left of Lee's artillery, "and, every man for himself, to take to the woods and make his way either to Johnston's army in Carolina, or to his home, taking his arms, and reporting to the governor of his State. . . . If there is any hope for the Confederacy, it is in delay."[28]

But Lee would have none of it. "The surrender of this army is the end of the Confederacy," and "we have now simply to look the fact in the face that the Confederacy has failed." Whether that meant they were entitled to take the results into their own hands was a very different question, "and, as Christian men, Gen. Alexander . . . we must consider only the effect which our action will have upon the country at large." The effect of his proposal would be nothing less than catastrophic. "Suppose I should take your suggestion & order the army to disperse & make their way to their homes," Lee asked him. It would be the march to Antietam all over again, and worse. "The men would have no rations & they would be under no discipline. . . . They would have to plunder & rob to procure subsistence. The country would be full of lawless bands in every part, & a state of society would ensue from which it would take the country years to recover."

And that said nothing for what the now-masterless slaves might do, the Nat Turners who had been waiting for an opportunity for two hundred years to exact revenge on unprotected Southern whites. That was the kind of war Scott had taken such care to avoid in Mexico, and Lee would have none of it now. He had not wanted war in the first place; he had not wanted it conducted the way it had been carried on; and in his mind, it was now over, and the only proper response was a surrender on appropriate terms. What had been offered to him was more than appropriate. For Lee, the terms meant no retaliation; for Grant, they meant a clean and complete erasure of the only Confederate army worth any worry.[29]

The two men stood up, and "after a little general conversation had been indulged," Marshall and Grant's military secretary, Ely S. Parker, made copies of their letters for the generals to exchange. In a "whispered conversation" with Grant, Lee raised the issue of his men's starving condition, and Grant quietly agreed to make some sort of provision for them from his own thinned stores. Until that moment, only Lee and Marshall, plus Grant and Parker, had occupied the parlor; now the door was opened and a small troop of Grant's staffers entered to be introduced to Lee: Sheridan, Seth Williams (who had been Lee's adjutant in the West Point superintendent years), Orville Babcock, and a newly minted captain, Robert Todd Lincoln, the twenty-one-year-old son of the president. One officer—probably Seth Williams—"trying to relieve the awkwardness of the occasion," ventured to ask Lee, "What became of the white horse you rode in Mexico? He might not be dead yet, he was not so old." Lee could have choked: the horse was Grace Darling, who had been ridden off from White House by some unknown Union officer back in 1862. "I left him at the White House on the Pamunkey river," Lee allowed himself to reply, "and I have not seen him since."

Grant and Lee shook hands, and "after three o'clock" Lee stepped out onto the porch of the McLean house and "signaled to his orderly to bring up his horse" in a "hoarse, half-choked voice." An Illinois cavalry officer, George Forsyth, noticed how every Union officer on the porch "sprang to his feet . . . every hand . . . raised in military salute." Lee appeared to Forsyth as

> *a finely formed man apparently about sixty years of age, well above the average height, with a clear ruddy complexion—just then suffused by a deep crimson flush, that rising from his neck over-spread his face and even slightly tinged his broad forehead . . . abundant gray hair, silky and fine in texture, with a full gray beard and mustache, neatly trimmed and not overlong, but which nevertheless almost completely concealed his mouth. A splendid uniform of Confederate-gray cloth, that had evidently seen but little service, which was closely buttoned about him, and fitted him to perfection. An exquisitely mounted sword, attached to a gold-embroidered Russia-leather belt, trailed loosely on the floor at his side, and in his right hand he carried a broad-brimmed soft gray felt hat, encircled by a golden cord, while in his left he held a pair of buckskin gauntlets . . . a soldier and a gentleman, bearing himself in defeat with an all-unconscious dignity that sat well upon him.*

He looked "sadly" to the east, where the Army of Northern Virginia lay in what would be its last encampment, "thrice smote the palm of his left hand slowly with his right fist," then descended the McLean house steps and mounted Traveller. As he turned to leave, Grant came out to the steps "and saluted him by raising his hat," and Lee reciprocated. Collecting Traveller's reins, Robert E. Lee "rode off at a slow trot to break the sad news to the brave fellows whom he had so long commanded."[30]

They were waiting for him, because word of the surrender had already spread from the McLean house all the way across the valley where the Army of Northern Virginia was encamped. Porter Alexander's artillerymen were the first Lee would encounter himself, and Alexander had drawn them up "in line along the road, with instructions to uncover in silence as he rode by." William Mahone's division had likewise "strung ourselves along both sides of the road." What they saw moved them in ways deeper than Lee's eternal composure had ever moved them. "He lifted his hat and kept it in his usual salute," and men could see that "his eyes were swollen" and "he looked O so aged and sad!"

The men could not contain their own response. "He had hardly reached the line . . . when some one started a cheer, which was taken up by others, and then both infantry and artillery broke their lines and crowded about his horse in the road." One of Longstreet's staff remembered how men "rushed en masse to the road, and so surrounding" Lee's little party that "it was with difficulty they could make their way through the crowd." Lee had never been an orator, and he now spoke briefly and simply, as to a theater company after its last curtain: "I have done for you all that it was in my power to do. You have done all your duty. Leave the result to God. Go to your homes and resume your occupations. Obey the laws and become as good citizens as you were soldiers."

Across the Army of Northern Virginia, the reactions were as varied as the men. "Strong war-worn smoke-begrimed, powder-burnt men" lay "on the ground with tears streaming from their eyes and crying like children." Other "ragged veterans rushed up and shook Gen. Lee's hand," and one "more ragged if possible" than the rest, "crying as if his heart would break," sobbed out, "Genl., I wish every damned Yankee was in the bottom of hell. Don't you?" Another soldier threw down his musket and shouted, "holding his hand aloft," "Blow, Gabriel, blow! My God, let him blow. I am ready to die!" Others were stunned into resignation. "The rank and file of Lee's army are said to be well satisfied to give up the struggle, believing that they have no hope of success," Lorenzo L. Crounse of *The New York Times* discovered when he mingled with the Confederates. But, he added, they "say that if Gen Lee had refused to surrender, they would have stuck to him to the last."[31]

Finally, Lee reached the apple orchard where he had received Grant's message from Orville Babcock that morning, "dismounted . . . and took a seat under one of the trees." To the officers clustering around him, he spoke not of duty but of despair. "I could wish that I were numbered among the fallen in the last battle." He subsided into "one of his savage moods, and when these moods were on him it was safer to keep out of his way." In the distance, federal artillerymen began firing a celebratory salute, until Grant ordered them silenced out of respect. "The war is over, the rebels are our countrymen again," Grant insisted, "and the best sign of rejoicing after the victory will be to abstain from all demonstrations in the field." But people could hear "the far off roar of what we knew were cannon" all the way to Charlottesville, and there was no order to stop Union gunners in Richmond from "the rapid firing of cannon" between nine and ten o'clock that night—a "hundred-gun salute," according to Henri Garidel.

This was not the only noise in Richmond: "The shouts of joy of the Negroes were making Richmond tremble as much as the cannon." "We called to passers-by," wrote Judith McGuire in her diary, " 'What do these guns mean?' " She eventually got a reply, "pertly, wickedly," " 'General Lee has surrendered, thank God!' " Far away in Alabama, Confederate troops were told that Lee had surrendered, but that it was only Fitzhugh Lee and "a small rear guard," that "General R. E. Lee had effected a junction with Johnston, had crushed Sherman, and was turning northward to recover the lost ground." The next courier disabused them with "the dismal truth," and "a sadder night never shut in upon crushed hopes and suffering hearts."[32]

That night, it rained, and

Mixed with the knightly growth that fringed his lips.
So like a shattered column lay the King.

CHAPTER EIGHTEEN

An Indictment for Treason

Through its last week, the Army of Northern Virginia washed away so many deserters that by the time the formal surrender parade of the infantry was held on April 12, only 26,018 men presented themselves for the hastily printed parole slips that overworked relays of Federal soldiers produced on a small portable printing press, set up in the local tavern. The task of paroling the Confederates was not made easier by the uncertainties the retreat had created about who was still serving with whom, who was authorized to sign parole slips, and who was in charge of any surrender ceremonies. "Many of the rebel officers did not clearly understand their own organization," complained their Union captors, and many of Lee's soldiers "animadverted strongly upon their abandonment by their own officers."[1]

Grant, however, was already thinking beyond the technicalities of the surrender. He proposed a second meeting with Lee at ten o'clock the following morning, at the Army of Northern Virginia's picket line just east of Appomattox Court House. Lee agreed, and both were accompanied by a handful of staffers and orderlies under a white flag. It was an awkward conversation, Lee half congratulating Grant in obtaining the surrender of his army, because otherwise "the South was a big country" and Union armies "might have to march over it three or four times before the war entirely ended."

Avoiding a drawn-out consequence like that was exactly what Grant wanted to discuss with Lee. There was still Joe Johnston's army in the Carolinas, and other Confederate commands scattered from Georgia to Texas, and it gave Grant no enthusiasm to think about trying to track them all down one by one and extinguish them. Jefferson Davis (accompanied by Breckinridge and the rest of the Confederate cabinet, along with Smith Lee) was somewhere on the loose near Johnston, and there would certainly be no help from him. Lee had hinted a few days before at the possibility of lending his hand to a general military peace that could end all the fighting. Grant's fingertips had been burned once by suggesting something like this, but if it was beyond the bounds for Grant to negotiate, perhaps Lee would go and meet with Lincoln, whether in Richmond or Washington, and "agree upon terms" that would end the war and bring about "the surrender of all the armies" of the Confederacy?

"There was not a man in the Confederacy whose influence with the soldiery and the whole people was as great as his," and Grant had no doubt "his advice would be followed with alacrity." (This would quickly give rise to the story that Lee "signified very emphatically his desire for a total cessation of hostilities," that Lee would head for Danville to persuade "all other commanders of Southern armies to surrender," or that "he will be present at the convening of the Rebel Virginia Legislature, and urge the immediate passage of a resolution restoring the Old Dominion to the Union.") But it was now Lee's turn to play obdurate. He "said that he could not do that without consulting the President first." For one last time, he would refuse to cross the political line. Not, as it turned out, that it would make much difference. Joe Johnston would surrender to William Sherman two weeks later, Jefferson Davis would be captured on the run in northern Georgia on May 10, and the rest of the Confederate commands would surrender, one after another, by mid-June. The two generals rode away, Grant departing almost immediately for Washington to make a personal report to Lincoln.[2]

Lee's indifference about a general surrender was a product of some other preoccupations, too. He felt the need to issue a final general order, disbanding the Army of Northern Virginia and including some form of military farewell. But he could not concentrate his mind on how to say any of this and, as usual, turned the drafting of what became General Orders No. 9 to Charles Marshall. What Marshall produced was an episode in bitterness. "After four years of arduous service," Marshall began, "marked by unsurpassed courage and fortitude," Lee's army had been forced to surrender to "overwhelming numbers and resources." *Not* to Grant's relentless strategic perception that, after all, Richmond had been the real object of the war, and that Lee's army had dropped into his hands like ripe fruit a week after Richmond fell; *not* to Grant's impeccably timed pursuit from Richmond to Appomattox; *not* to Sherman's extraordinary campaign across Georgia and the Carolinas and the damage done to soldier morale at Petersburg by the thought of their families in Sherman's path; and certainly *not* to the military ineptitude and political halfheartedness of the Confederate leadership that Lee had condemned from almost his first day in command.

Instead, the Army of Northern Virginia was portrayed by Marshall as a dauntless band of heroes whose resistance had simply been ground down by Yankee numbers, Yankee bullets, Yankee capitalism, and Yankee rations. (Or, as Marshall would elaborate in later years, by "a powerful flotilla . . . a profusion of military supplies of all kinds," and "ten men to take the place of every soldier lost," while the Confederates were "very often . . . nearly naked, and nearly always poorly fed.") In Marshall's framing of the surrender, the war had been an unfair fight from the start, and nothing had been proven by Confederate defeat except that unfairness. Slavery, the states' rights braggadocio, secession—all of these ducked out of view. It was the beginning of a mythology of defeat—the "Lost Cause"—that was to have long and destructive innings in the Southern imagination (and that Marshall would embellish over the years as "the cause for which it was a duty to fight and sweet and honorable to die"). It was a myth that would, in the long run, make the possibility of a real reconstruction of the Union almost impossible, so long as people clung to it.[3]

It was not necessarily Lee's myth. Lee read over Marshall's draft and "struck out a paragraph, which he said would tend to keep alive the feeling existing between the North and the South." But he was in too much of a hurry to notice that what was left after editing would still be incendiary. Lee had a longer document of his own to write, his final report to Jefferson Davis, and it carried a significantly different message. The report reviewed the Army of Northern Virginia's movements in the week since abandoning Richmond and Petersburg, and it began with a harsh complaint about the "fatal" oversight that failed to deliver the needed rations to Amelia Court House. On its retreat, the Army of Northern Virginia was plagued not by "overwhelming" Yankee "numbers and resources" but by poor discipline as "the men depressed by fatigue and hunger . . . threw away their arms, while others followed the wagon trains and embarrassed their progress." And the surrender negotiations were not a corner into which a noble handful had been forced by barbarian hordes at a Confederate Roncesvalles; the surrender terms were actually "the best under all the circumstances by which we were surrounded."

The cover letter he composed was full of the same lament: once the Army of Northern Virginia evacuated Richmond, "it began to disintegrate, and straggling from the ranks increased" to the point where, on the day of the surrender, he had fewer than 8,000 infantry ready for action. Even before the retreat, "the troops . . . in the entrenchments . . . were not marked by the boldness and decision which formerly characterized them," and all along the march they appeared to Lee "feeble; and a want of confidence seemed to possess officers and men." It was the last and final declaration by Lee of the fundamental lack of perfection he had faulted Southerners for during all four years of what Marshall decided to characterize as "unsurpassed courage and fortitude." Only through highlighting their imperfections could he deal with the inevitable consequence of admitting imperfection in his own conduct.[4]

Once these documents were finished, the thought uppermost in Lee's mind was not the Lost Cause but his family. On the day Lee bolted west, Richmond was swept by fires, originally set to destroy government property, and he had received no word since then concerning Mary or his daughters. Custis was taken prisoner at Sailor's Creek, and there was no word from him, either. Lee's nephew Fitzhugh Lee galloped off with his cavalry for Lynchburg rather than surrender, and young Rob disappeared early during the retreat. The only one left with him was Rooney. Because Grant was leaving the details of managing the surrender in the hands of a joint commission of Union and Confederate officers, Lee saw no point in staying much longer in Appomattox and prepared urgently to return to whatever remained of his world in Richmond.

That night, an impromptu ensemble of soldiers gathered near his headquarters tent "to offer a moonlight serenade" to Lee. The next morning, April 11, his tent was struck for the last time with the Army of Northern Virginia. Officers stopped by with hurriedly completed final reports to be filed, although this time there was no "savage" mood, only "words of encouragement and advice" that sent "almost every one of the officers . . . away in tears." After a soldiers' breakfast of hardtack, bacon, and black coffee, Lee and a handful of his remaining staff, accompanied by a baggage wagon and a rickety ambulance, along with an escort from the 4th Massachusetts Cavalry, took to the road heading east and north, toward Richmond.

They made it to Buckingham Court House, a hefty twenty miles, the first day. They pushed onward another twenty miles, to Cumberland Court House, the next day, where Lee dismissed his Union escort. "I am in my own country and among friends and do not need an escort, I am giving you unnecessary trouble." By Friday, they had reached Windsor, the Powhatan County plantation of Charles Carter Lee, where he could at last get a generous dinner (even though he refused Carter's urging to sleep indoors, staying the night under his field tent). Rooney, who stayed behind at Appomattox to participate in the surrender of what was left of the cavalry, caught up with his father and uncle there. But all around them, chaos reigned. Civilians "have been appropriating all the public property they could find—wagons, old iron picks, &c &c—distributing the assets of the Confederate States."[5]

On Saturday afternoon, April 15, the little cavalcade crossed a makeshift bridge into the former Confederate capital, through streets still covered with broken glass from the explosions and fires of the week before. The dress uniform and ceremonial sword were packed in the wagon, and Lee scarcely seemed the same man who had left Richmond only two weeks before. "The chieftain looked fatigued, and rode along at a jaded gait," passing twenty blocks gutted and blackened by fire, from the river to Capitol Square. The pastor of the Grace Street Baptist Church, William Eldridge Hatcher, looking out his window, saw "a horseman" pass by, "his steed . . . bespattered with mud, and his head hung down as if worn by long travelling." Hatcher recognized him at once as Lee:

> *The horseman himself sat his horse like a master; his face was ridged with self-respecting griefs; his garments were worn in the service and stained with travel; his hat was slouched and spattered with mud and only another unknown horseman rode with him, as if for company and for love. Even in the fleeting moment of his passing by my gate, I was awed by his incomparable dignity. His majestic composure, his rectitude and his sorrow, were so wrought and blended into his visage and so beautiful and impressive to my eyes that I fell into violent weeping.*[6]

When Lee turned in to Franklin Street, he could breathe easily again. The house had barely been missed by the flames. Through the night of the fire, neighbors were formed into a bucket brigade by "Daughter" Mary to douse sparks, and the Union occupation commandant, Godfrey Weitzel (who had been a cadet at West Point during Lee's superintendency), posted three soldiers as guards and put an ambulance at the ready if Mary needed to flee. The winds shifted, the danger subsided; the next morning, Mary sent breakfast out to the soldiers.

Happily, Custis was there already. While in Union captivity after Sailor's Creek, he heard a rumor that his mother had died in the fire, and he appealed to Grant, on his honor, for a pass. Grant generously agreed, and Custis was now in Richmond to find the same relief his father was finding. (Custis, with typical Lee attention to the niceties of Grant's allowance, presented himself to the Union provost marshal in Richmond to be re-imprisoned, only to be told that Grant's orders were that "General Custis Lee should not be received as a prisoner of war," and so "he never succeeded in getting back into prison or any sort of captivity.") Rob, as it turned out, was safely somewhere in North Carolina, along with his uncle Smith and Jefferson Davis, while Fitzhugh Lee eventually turned back from Lynchburg and enrolled himself under the protection of the Appomattox paroles. The Lees survived.[7]

Lee dismounted from Traveller, while a "motley crowd" of "citizens and Rebel soldiers, Union soldiers and officers" gathered. They called "tumultuously for a speech." But Lee only handed the reins to his wagon driver, raised his hat in acknowledgment, and walked up the steps toward whatever strange future now awaited him.[8]

There are six signatories on Robert E. Lee's Appomattox parole, beginning at the top of the list with Lee himself and including Taylor, Venable, and Marshall, and it was formally countersigned by Grant's assistant provost marshal George H. Sharpe with this comment: "The above-named officers will not be disturbed by United States authorities as long as they observe their parole and the laws in force where they may reside."

That promise of non-disturbance met with general approval for exactly five days, until the night of April 14, when Lincoln was assassinated at Ford's Theatre. Denunciations of Jefferson Davis and Robert E. Lee as traitors, and fit subjects for treason proceedings, afterward ascended with the rapidity of shell bursts. It made no difference that on the morning of his assassination Lincoln had spoken "very kindly of Lee" in his last cabinet meeting. Any such sentiments were forgotten, if they had ever been known. "What has General Robert Lee done to deserve mercy or forbearance from the people and the authorities of the North?" the *Boston Daily Advertiser* shrilly demanded. "If any man in the United States—that is, any rebel or traitor—should suffer the severest punishment, Robert E. Lee should be the man." The *Philadelphia Inquirer* called Lee "a dangerous man" whose only regret was that "he was unable to get men enough to kill and destroy every man who was disposed to stand by the Union. . . . If any man is responsible for this Rebellion, his hands are as deep as anyone." After all, didn't Lincoln himself once describe Lee as one of those "known to be traitors then as now"?[9]

Chief among those eager to levy vengeance was John Curtiss Underwood, who would become Robert E. Lee's particular bête noire. Underwood was born (in 1809) and educated (at Hamilton College) in New York. But he married a Virginian—in fact, Maria Underwood was a first cousin of Stonewall Jackson's—and set up a law practice in Clarke County. His move to Virginia, however, abated none of his Northern criticisms of slavery; those criticisms made him decidedly unpopular, and presently Underwood was "exiled from the State for my opinions in favor of human equality." With Lincoln's election, Underwood was briefly mentioned as a possible cabinet nominee and finally appointed as the district judge for the newly reorganized federal District of Virginia—which in effect meant the strip of Union-occupied Virginia running from Alexandria down to Norfolk—in June 1864.[10]

From his bench, Underwood looked forward to a day of retribution against his tormentors, and the most obvious targets for that wrath after Lincoln's murder were, for Underwood, the former Confederate president and his general in chief. As he explained to Lincoln's newly inaugurated successor, Andrew Johnson, "It is more than folly to talk of clemency and mercy to these worse than Catalines, for clemency and mercy to them is cruelty and murder to the innocent and unborn." But in the path of Underwood's retributive justice stood Lee's Appomattox parole. Or at least it did until Lincoln's death changed the tune of public fury from Lincoln's "malice toward none" into Andrew Johnson's vow that "treason must be made infamous."

On April 26, Johnson's attorney general, James Speed, gave the Appomattox paroles a very different twist than Lee expected. "We must consider in what capacity General Grant was speaking," Speed wrote in reply to a query from Secretary of War Edwin Stanton. "It must be presumed that he had no authority from the President, except such as the commander-in-chief could give to a military officer." Presidents, only, grant pardons; hence, Grant's paroles could not have drawn a blanket of immunity over treason. And as the "highest judicial officer in the Eastern District of Virginia," and the sole functioning federal district judge operating anywhere in Virginia, Underwood had the authority to bring the penalties of treason down on the head of Robert E. Lee.[11]

Underwood would have the full endorsement of President Johnson, too. Although Johnson issued an amnesty proclamation at the end of May, the amnesty "excepted from the benefits of this Proclamation . . . all who shall have been military or naval officers of said pretended confederate government above the rank of colonel in the army or lieutenant in the navy," and especially "all military and naval officers in the rebel service, who were educated by the government in the Military Academy at West Point or the United States Naval Academy," all of which seemed tailored to fit Robert E. Lee. Five days later, a grand jury in Underwood's court in Norfolk returned an indictment of Lee and thirty-six other high-ranking Confederates.[12]

Lee had some whiff of what was afoot "soon after his return to Richmond," when "a gentleman was requested by the Federal commander in the city to communicate to General Lee the fact that he was about to be indicted in the United States courts for treason." Lee might also have had suspicions from the first that Grant's paroles would be challenged, because he was determined to keep as low a political profile as he could and "procure some humble home for my family until I can devise some means of providing it with subsistence." He spent hardly a week in Richmond before he rode off to the Pamunkey River farm of his cousin Thomas Carter, looking for real estate possibilities.

News of the indictment reached Lee when he returned to his family's borrowed quarters in Richmond. He squared off at once to fight back and appealed to Grant on June 13, demanding to know on what grounds he could "be indicted for treason by the grand jury at Norfolk," because "the officers and men of the Army of Northern Virginia were, by the terms of their surrender, protected by the United States government from molestation so long as they conformed to its condition."[13]

Grant, who had just returned from a tumultuous appearance at a "mass meeting" at New York City's Cooper Institute, immediately forwarded Lee's letter to Secretary of War Stanton with his own endorsement, confirming that "in my opinion the officers and men paroled at Appomattox C.H . . . cannot be tried for treason so long as they observe the terms of their parole." For Grant, this was as much a personal as a legal issue. "Good faith as well as true policy dictates that we should observe the conditions of that convention." Neither Stanton nor Johnson was moved, and so Grant confronted Johnson directly in a cabinet meeting. "Mr. Johnson spoke of Lee and wanted to know why any military commander had a right to protect an arch-traitor from the laws." Grant, who "was angry at this," heatedly explained to Johnson that he, as president, "might do as he pleased about civil rights, confiscation of property and so on . . . but a general commanding troops has certain responsibilities and duties and power, which are supreme." That included granting a parole carrying immunity from prosecution. Besides, if he had not given such a parole, "Lee would never have surrendered, and we should have lost many lives in destroying him." And then the stinger: "I should have resigned the command of the army rather than have carried out any order directing me to arrest Lee or any of his commanders who obeyed the laws."[14]

Grant wrote back to Lee on June 20, assuring him that he had put Lee's case before Stanton and Johnson with his recommendation to "quash all indictments found against paroled prisoners of war, and to desist from the further prosecution of them." He added, hopefully, that "this opinion . . . is substantially the same as that entertained by the Government." Still, Grant remembered that the only member of the cabinet who agreed with him was William Henry Seward.

Lee, who was never an instinctive optimist, was not an optimist now. He told Walter Taylor that he had "made up my mind to let the authorities take their course. I have no wish to avoid any trial the government may order." To his brother Carter, he wrote resignedly "all about the indictments" on June 21. "The papers are arguing the Subject pro & Con, & I presume the Gov't will decide in favour of the stronger party. I am here to answer any accusations against me & Cannot flee." Nevertheless, Lee would not allow the politicians an entirely free hand. "I have rec'd offers of professional Services from several Gentn: Reverdy Johnson, Tazewell Taylor, Mr [William H.] Macfarland, &c, in the event of being tried, & shall take advantage of them if necessary."[15]

—

Whether Judge Underwood realized it, there were serious constitutional, legal, and practical obstacles in the path of a conviction—or even a trial—for treason of the Confederacy's most famous soldier. In the first place, the Constitution's definition of treason is a very narrow one—"shall consist only in levying War against them, or in adhering to their Enemies, giving them Aid and Comfort"—which made it nearly impossible to obtain convictions for treason, something that was dramatically exposed in the celebrated trial of Aaron Burr. Congress attempted to give better statutory teeth to the treason clause through the Conspiracies Act (July 31, 1861), the Crimes Act (August 6, 1861), and the Second Confiscation Act. Not enough teeth, though. Lincoln had already muddied the waters of treason litigation with his December 1863 "amnesty and reconstruction" offer, and in any case the fundamental problem in the Civil War was that treason was a crime involving "adherence to a foreign enemy with which the United States are at war . . . and that adherence to a domestic enemy was not an adherence to an enemy within the meaning of the Constitution." The Lincoln administration had all along insisted that the Confederacy was not a *foreign* enemy (because secession was a legal and constitutional impossibility, the Confederacy didn't even have legal existence in Lincoln's eyes). And, as the Kentucky senator Garrett Davis was happy to remind his fellow solons, "adherence to a domestic enemy was not an adherence to an enemy within the meaning of the Constitution." It only confused matters more that the Confederates had been accorded prisoner-of-war rights during the conflict; that concession could imply, in a court of law, that Confederate officers like Lee really had been the servants not of a treasonous domestic conspiracy but of a separate, sovereign nation. In that case, Lee was an *enemy* and a paroled prisoner of war but could not be legally classified as a *traitor*.[16]

Another obstruction emerged from the Constitution's stipulation that "the Trial of all Crimes, except in Cases of Impeachment, shall be by Jury; and such Trial shall be held in the State where the said Crimes shall have been committed." (The Sixth Amendment gets even more specific: such a trial would have to take place in the "district wherein the crime shall have been committed.") That meant, at the least, that a trial of Lee would probably take place in Virginia, arguably in Richmond, where he had accepted Virginia's commission in 1861. While it had not been difficult for John Underwood to create a cooperative grand jury for an indictment in Norfolk, it would be a much more monumental task to find a civilian petit jury in Richmond willing to convict Robert E. Lee. Underwood certainly understood that this would be one of his most formidable obstacles. When he was quizzed, six months later, about finding "it practicable to get a jury of loyal men in your court," he glumly replied, "Not unless it is what might be called a packed jury." Without such packing, Underwood was unsure whether a jury would vote to convict Lee of treason. "It would be perfectly idle to think of such a thing. . . . Ten or eleven out of the twelve on any jury, I think, would say that Lee was almost equal to Washington, and was the noblest man in the State."[17]

An odder complication emerged from an unforeseen dispute with the chief justice of the Supreme Court, Salmon P. Chase. The Supreme Court and the federal judiciary as a whole played a muted role in the conduct of the war. But as soon as the shooting stopped, Chase and the Court once again moved to reassert their prerogatives over against the executive and legislative branches of the government, and for Chase that took the form of a refusal to participate in his auxiliary role as a federal circuit judge so long as rival military tribunals were operating anywhere within a given district. (Chase would later undermine the entire judicial fabric of military tribunals in *Ex parte Milligan* in 1866.) Military tribunals were obviously operating in Virginia as the tide of Union occupation rolled over the Old Dominion, and as long as they did, Chase would refuse to cooperate. But without Chase's participation in a capital case, Judge Underwood would have to try Lee's treason by himself, and that would produce a verdict of something less than unchallenged authority. As it was, Chase did not have a particularly high opinion of Underwood's competence as a judge. "The 'Anxious' man," Chase remarked drily, "can have a trial before Judge Underwood" anytime he wants. But "the Court will be a quasi-military court," and Chase would have nothing to do with it.[18]

And then there was Lee's own legal reasoning, which dangled on whose jurisdiction—Virginia's or the United States'—claimed his original allegiance back in 1861. Nowhere in the Constitution, as it was written in 1787, was the concept of citizenship actually defined. In the five places where the Constitution refers to citizenship, it speaks of citizens of the states and citizens of the United States. But the Constitution made no effort to sort out the relationship between the two, leaving the strange sense that Americans possessed a kind of dual citizenship, in their "native State" (as Lee had called it) and in the Union. Beginning, then, with the premise that "all that the South has ever desired was that the Union, as established by our forefathers, should be preserved; and that the government, as originally organized, should be administered in purity and truth," Lee had no trouble in arguing that Virginia and the other rebel states "were merely using the reserved right" of state sovereignty when they seceded.

This was an argument that, back in 1861, Lee had condemned as revolutionary nonsense, but in 1861 he was not facing a trial for his life. In "my view," Lee now reasoned, that meant that "the action of the State, in withdrawing itself from the government of the United States," required its citizens to act with it. "The act of Virginia, in withdrawing herself from the United States, carried me along as a citizen of Virginia" because "her laws and her acts were binding on me." He was willing to admit that the Civil War had exploded that theory by sheer force. "The war," he explained to his nephew Edward Childe, "originated from a doubtful question of Construction of the Constitution, about which our forefathers differed at the time of framing it," and it had now been settled "by the arbitrament of arms." But neither Lee nor any other individual Confederate could be called a traitor for having followed that line of reasoning back in 1861. Hence, "the State was responsible for the act, not the individual."[19]

Taken together with Grant's threat to resign if the Appomattox paroles were set aside, the indictment began to falter. President Johnson seemed "anxious to conciliate rather than resolved to command" Grant, and on June 11, 1865, Judge Underwood was called to Washington for a full week of consultations with Attorney General Speed that effectively sent the Lee indictment to the back burner until the next term of the circuit court in Norfolk in October. "When Judge Underwood of Virginia was here a few days ago," smirked the *Alexandria Gazette,* "he did not succeed in getting an order for the arrest of Gen. Lee, and that distinguished officer is to be left unmolested."

Underwood and Johnson had a bigger fish to fry in the person of Jefferson Davis, who lay imprisoned in Fort Monroe since his capture in Georgia. Davis had no Appomattox parole to shelter behind, and Johnson and Underwood turned all their attention to indicting and trying the former Confederate president as a larger and easier legal target. On June 23, *The Norfolk Post* announced that "all speculations concerning the trial of General Lee for treason in consequence of his indictment at Norfolk may as well be abandoned at once," and a month later *The Wheeling Daily Intelligencer* quietly announced that "it is understood here that . . . when the treason indictments against Gen. Lee and other noted rebels will be called up . . . the President will direct *nolle pros.* [nolle prosequi: do not prosecute] to be entered, and dispose of each defendant, as he proposes to dispose of other leading rebels who have been active participants in the war, namely, by putting them on long probation, and then as a condition, precedent to pardon, imposing such penalties and restrictions as may be justified by the circumstances."[20]

Even Davis's prosecution went aground repeatedly on legal technicalities, while President Johnson's political attention was increasingly distracted by his impeachment by Radical Republicans in 1868. Johnson barely survived the impeachment, and on Christmas Day 1868, in a gesture of contempt for the Republicans who had nearly destroyed him, Johnson issued "a full pardon and amnesty for the offense of treason" to "all and to every person who directly or indirectly participated in the late insurrection or rebellion." The sword dangling over the heads of Davis, Lee, and the others was finally withdrawn.

Johnson's distraction relieved Lee only of the threat of a trial for treason; he would not see the daylight of the general "pardon and amnesty" until the end of 1868. Until then, Lee still hoped to obtain the restoration of enough civil privileges to allow him to conduct business (he was, at least on paper, the executor of his sister Anne's estate in Baltimore), to own property, and to resolve the still-unfinished tangles of the Custis estate. To that end, he applied for one of the immediate pardons Johnson offered in his May 1865 proclamation, and even sent the pardon petition directly to Grant for his endorsement. (He failed to file the stipulated oath of allegiance but subsequently sent a notarized copy of the oath to the State Department on October 2, 1865.)

At the same time, Lee was also taking no chances about the indictment. He wanted to be out of Richmond as soon as possible and to bury himself somewhere out of sight and hopefully out of mind in the Virginia countryside. Despite his constant anxieties that the war would render him a "pauper," Lee's losses were largely confined to real estate—most obviously, the confiscation of Arlington and Smith Island. Throughout the war, his bankers in Alexandria and Winchester discreetly drew no attention to his personal investments, and the federal confiscation acts did little more than make a handful of threatening gestures. (Arlington's seizure and sale had taken place as a tax delinquency, not under the confiscation legislation.) His surviving assets probably amounted to $60,000, which would still have pegged him close to a millionaire in current terms. Even the family silver had survived "in two large chests" that had been "entrusted to the care of an old and faithful sergeant at the Virginia Military Institute."

But getting out of Richmond was harder for Lee than it might have seemed. A flood of letters and gifts came to him, for which Custis now became the secretary and manager, and he was interrupted constantly by a stream of callers, many of them old soldiers who merely wanted to come and shake their former general's hand. Two "in very dilapidated clothing" announced that they were the spokesmen for a band of sixty old soldiers who wanted to offer him "a good house and farm" in Botetourt County, where they were ready to fight "the entire Federal Army" if it came hunting to try him for treason. Gently, he said "he had to decline."[21]

There were, inevitably, inquiries from Confederate officers, perplexed and bewildered in the strange new world of white ruin and black emancipation; to them all, Lee wrote as if he were sure every word was being read by hostile eyes. "I believe it to be the duty of everyone to unite in the restoration of the country, and the re-establishment of peace and harmony," he replied to a former Confederate naval officer. The war had settled all questions, and there was no practical alternative but to accept that verdict. "The war being at an end, the Southern states having laid down their arms," any raging against the dictates of Providence was pointless. History will eventually judge the rights or wrongs of the Confederacy, and that judgment will come faster if allowed to come on its own time. "It appears to me that the allayment of passion, the dissipation of prejudice, and the restoration of reason, will alone enable the people of the country to acquire a true knowledge and form a correct judgment of the events of the past four years."

Politicians got the same advice. Every Southerner, Lee wrote to the former governor John Letcher, "should unite in honest efforts to obliterate the grievous effects of war, & to restore the blessings of peace . . . promote harmony & good feeling, qualify themselves to work; & the healing of all dissensions." Journalists, likewise, waited on him, and to them he gave the most cautious and placatory sorts of interviews. "I was opposed to the war at the outset," he said, surprising one Ohio interviewer. "I wept when I heard of the bombardment of Fort Sumter . . . but when Virginia, my native State, seceded, there was only one course for me to pursue, namely, to follow her fortunes." Lincoln's murder was "not only a crime against our Christian civilization" but "a terrible blow to the vanquished." And he was careful to praise Grant, whose "treatment of the Army of Southern [*sic*] Virginia is without parallel in the history of the civilized world."[22]

The most unusual caller was the celebrated wartime photographer Mathew Brady, who appeared on the Franklin Street doorstep the day after Lee's return. Brady had met Lee years before, when he photographed General Scott, so the request for a sitting was not entirely that of an intruder. Brady also had a note from Robert Ould, who had been with Lee on the day of John Brown's capture and served as the head of the prisoner-exchange system during the war, and so Lee relented, allowing Brady to set up his camera and tripod on the back porch. There, Brady made six images, four of Lee, and two more with Lee, Custis, and Walter Taylor (who would, like Charles Venable, leave Lee's service in another two weeks for home and marriage to his fiancée). In one pose, Lee stands with his right hand resting on an upholstered chair, his left hand clutching the brim of a roundabout hat, the six-panel porch door and its glass surround framing him; the chair is then set aside and Lee stands for two poses with Brady's floor brace behind him, holding him clearly in position for the camera's twelve-second delay.

At this moment, someone—probably Brady—noticed that an irreverent Union graffitist had chalked the word "devil" onto a brick on the back door's right hand; some determined rubbing made it disappear (and Brady made sure it would hardly be visible in the prints he made afterward). Then came two group poses, Lee sitting with the hat in his lap, Custis to his right and Walter Taylor to his left (in one pose, Taylor's right hand rests behind Lee's back; Custis crushes his hat in his right hand in one shot, then transfers it to his left). Then, one final solo pose for Lee in profile, sitting in the chair and looking to his right.

This time, there were no concessions to defeat. They are all wearing their Confederate uniforms, Lee with his three stars still visible on the coat lapel. Custis's and Taylor's expressions are blank, but Lee's solo standing poses show a face of remarkable determination and defiance, almost as if daring the viewer to challenge him, to charge him, to correct him. It is here, more than in any other Lee photograph, that the physique and appearance that impressed so many of those who met Lee over the years are apparent: a man tall and straight but not stiff, with most of his height in his trunk rather than his legs, dominating but without demonstration. The published prints "all were pronounced admirable pictures" even before Brady headed off to Petersburg "to revel in 'fresh fields and pastures new.'"[23]

The arch-looking reserve in Lee's face belied the self-condemnation lodged deep in his mind, not for treason, but for imperfection. "Praise I never deserve," he sadly rebuked Markie Williams, when she sent him some newspaper clippings lauding his noble bearing after Appomattox, "& the censure of others is so much lighter than what I inflict on myself, that it fails in its object." He was still thinking about how he could remove himself from the spotlight in Richmond. "My purpose is to procure some humble home for my family until I can devise some means of providing it with subsistence," he wrote to William D. Cabell, a former Confederate official from Nelson County, and the old fantasy of a quiet, remote farmstead came bubbling back up again. "I am looking for some little, quiet home in the woods," he told Lindsay Long, "where I can procure shelter and my daily bread, if I am permitted by the victor."

The Stewarts made it clear that they would accept no rental payments from Lee for the months Mary and Custis had lived in the Franklin Street house—unless, they insisted melodramatically, the rent was paid "in Confederate currency"—which made it easy to uproot when an opportunity materialized. That opportunity came in June, in the form of an invitation from Elizabeth Randolph Preston Cocke to spend the summer at Derwent, a farm she owned in Powhatan County with a two-story, three-bay house and a single-story attached "little house." The nearby James River meant that Mary could make a comfortable journey along the water, using the James & Kanawha Canal, and Carter Lee's farm was just twenty miles away. It took only a single night's easy travel by canal for the Lees to reach Powhatan County, debarking at Oakland (the Cocke home on the riverside) and then a week later jolting only six miles overland to reach Derwent.[24]

Rooney and Rob had, by this time, already detached themselves, Rooney to rebuild the ruins of White House, Rob to Romancoke. Their father was still not entirely sure about their title to the properties. "Title can be given" only by "a deed signed by me as Executor of your Grd Father's will," he wrote to Rob in July, and he could not do that until "the courts are in operation & I am restored to civil rights (if I shall be)." For himself, his visit in April to Thomas Carter put into his mind the idea that he should settle on "some grass country, where the natural product of the land will do much for my subsistence"—which was a delicate way of saying, in a rare moment of revealed racial bitterness, that he did not want to find himself forced to rely on free black farm labor, because (as he told Carter) "I have always observed that wherever you find the negro, everything is going down around him, and wherever you find the white man, you see everything around him improving." In August, he made an extended foray into neighboring Fluvanna County and then into Albemarle County.

His mind also began turning in a more curious direction, reminiscent of Light Horse Harry and his failed attempt to recoup his fortunes by writing his military memoirs. "I am desirous," he wrote to Walter Taylor at the end of July, "that the bravery & devotion of the Army of N. Va. shall be correctly transmitted to posterity." His mind had already been gravitating toward imagining the "Army of N. Va." in the gauzy light of the Lost Cause rather than the army he had described in disarray three months before—and who better to do that than Lee himself? What project would better serve to wipe out the imperfections of himself and others during the war? Even more reminiscent of Light Horse Harry, he now began to think about working up a new edition of his father's Revolutionary War memoir. He corresponded with a publisher and then with his brother Carter, who held most of the family correspondence of Light Horse Harry. He was, he admitted, "fully alive to the propriety of making both works if possible a source of profit." After all, "I have to labour for my living & I am ashamed to do nothing that will give me an honest support."[25]

But he was never entirely sure if the treason indictment might somehow bark back into life. "I am considered such a reprobate," he half joked, that "I hesitate to darken the doors of those whom I regard; lest I should bring upon them some disaster." In that valley of self-deprecation, nothing could have come as a greater surprise to Robert E. Lee than to be offered the presidency of Washington College—or come as a greater surprise to others than that he accepted.

CHAPTER NINETEEN

Every Student Must Be a Gentleman

In the months after the surrender, and in spite of the thunderbolt of Underwood's treason indictment, Lee was offered at least two business partnerships—and turned them both down. It took no great discernment to see that what was wanted was a name for a letterhead or an advertisement, or both, and he was disinclined to give himself away for either. Spending his whole life dancing at the end of someone else's string—the Army, the Custises, the Confederacy—he had tolerated the strings only because they promised him security, and security might lead to independence. He no longer believed the promises.

Then, in August, came yet another offer, this time from the trustees of Washington College, in Stonewall Jackson's old home in Lexington, at the upper end of the Shenandoah. This was not nearly so financially attractive a prospect as the businesses. Washington College was not, despite the name, much of a college. It dated its origins to 1749 and a classical academy run by Robert Alexander; it then moved to Lexington in 1776 to become Liberty Hall Academy. A timely donation from George Washington of one hundred shares in the James River Canal Company induced the trustees to rename the institution in his honor, and it began granting baccalaureate degrees in 1813. But its location in remote Lexington did nothing to boost the college's profile. Lexington was "an indifferent town and rather small, with muddy streets" and few easy connections over the mountains; the James & Kanawha Canal brought travelers only as far as Lynchburg, and another eighteen-hour trek was required from there to reach Lexington. Nor did its curriculum offer anything particularly sensational to compensate for these disadvantages, because the college remained resolutely wedded to studies built around the classical languages, without the slightest hint that it was preparing its students for any particular vocation.[1]

By the eve of the Civil War, Washington College's student body—just 93 students in 1859—lagged behind the student population of the University of Virginia (419), Hampden-Sydney College (119), and even its more famous neighbor in Lexington, the Virginia Military Institute (150). The outbreak of the Civil War nearly blotted Washington College from view, first by diverting students to Confederate military service (in the 4th, 25th, 52nd, and 58th Virginia Infantry and 14th Virginia Cavalry), and then by attracting the unwanted attention of marauding Union forces under David Hunter in 1864. "Hunters Army" ensured that "all closed doors were broken down" and "Window Glass & Sash were smashed to pieces," so that the trustees were "compelled to report the buildings in a very dilapidated condition." By that summer's end, Washington College barely had a pulse: there were no seniors or juniors enrolled, and just seven sophomores and ten freshmen. All that remained of the college's endowment was $2,458.29 in worthless Confederate currency, a few minuscule real estate investments, and George Washington's original stock gift. When it prepared to open for classes in 1865, it could count on the services of only four instructors: James J. White, a classics professor; John L. Campbell, a chemist, geologist, and Presbyterian elder; Carter Johns Harris, another classicist; and Alexander L. Nelson, a mathematician.[2]

The outlook could not have been very hopeful when, on August 4, 1865, the trustees met to review the college's woeful situation and fill the office of president, which had been vacant during the war after the resignation in 1861 of the ardent Virginia unionist George Junkin. After "several highly respectable gentlemen and scholars" were discussed, one member of the board, Bolivar Christian, "arose and said, in a somewhat hesitating manner," that he had heard through "a lady friend of his, who was also a friend of Miss Mary Lee, daughter of General Robert E. Lee," that the onetime general was desirous of productive employment "by which he could earn a living for himself and family." Almost at once, "all other names were immediately withdrawn," and the board "unanimously" elected Lee and then stared at themselves in surprised apprehension. How were *they* to recruit the inestimable General Lee? After realizing that merely sending Lee a letter would be risibly inadequate, the board commissioned Judge John White Brockenbrough (its chair and the most politically prominent of the trustees), who had sat in the Confederate Congress, to make a presentation directly to the general. Even so, they had to dig into their own pockets to find enough money to buy Brockenbrough a reasonably respectable suit.[3]

When Brockenbrough arrived at Derwent to plead his case, Lee's first response was not encouraging. He was an engineer by education, with small patience for paperwork, and the vagaries of Latin declensions and Greek participles were only dimly glimpsed in his teenage past in Alexandria. When he took a few days to ask around about the college, Lee was warned that "the institution was one of local interest and comparatively unknown." More days went by after Brockenbrough left, and no response from Lee was forthcoming. Finally, Brockenbrough felt obliged to dispatch a lengthy follow-up letter, still struggling to convince the general that "you alone can fill [the college's] halls, by attracting to them not the youth of Virginia alone, but of all the Southern and some even of the Northern states."

Lee had not actually been ignoring him. Elizabeth Cocke, his host at Derwent, had sent her son Edmund to Washington College, and Edmund had only just returned from a prisoner-of-war camp in June after capture at Sailor's Creek, so Lee had an immediate point of reference. And the college did offer the advantages of providing a roof over his head in the form of the president's house, an income (which the trustees promised to set at $1,500 per annum, plus a percentage of the student fees), and above all as much distance from federal judges as Virginia could afford without violating the terms of the Appomattox parole.[4]

On August 24, Lee at last replied to the trustees, protesting frankly that given the ups and downs of his health during the war the position "requires not only great ability, but, I fear, more strength than I now possess." If he did take the job, he would not, as college presidents then routinely did, teach classes, even the traditional senior class in moral philosophy, which almost every antebellum college reserved for its president. "I do not feel able to undergo the labour of conducting classes in regular courses of instruction," and they would have to take him or leave him on that basis. There was also the matter of the Underwood indictment, which might "cause injury to an institution which it would be my highest desire to advance." But if those considerations formed no obstacle to the trustees, "I will yield to your judgment and accept."

They formed no obstacle at all: the trustees hastily replied that Lee's appointment "will greatly promote [the college's] prosperity, and advance the general interest of education." Lee arrived in Lexington on September 18, alone except for Traveller, with whom "he does not like to part even for a time," and on October 2 was duly inducted into the office of president of Washington College. He was no longer wearing his uniform, only "a military coat divested of all marks of rank; even the military buttons had been removed."[5]

—

In the weeks after Lee's acceptance, congratulations poured in upon the college. "The accession of this distinguished gentleman . . . as its honored chief," cheered *The Charleston Daily News,* "is destined, we trust, to mark the commencement of a new era in its history, and we most cordially do congratulate its numerous friends on this most auspicious event." None of the congratulations was more glowing than the letter one of Lee's former major generals, Isaac R. Trimble, sent to John Brockenbrough on September 7. "I congratulate you on the acceptance of Genl Lee (as announced in the papers) of the Presidency of your College," Trimble gushed. But "you must not give him too much to do—Tis his name we want—Let the course of studies be determined by a board of professors—not by him."

If those were the terms on which Washington College thought they were acquiring the services of Robert E. Lee, they could not have been more mistaken. It would have been West Point all over again. "When he first took charge of Washington College," recalled John William Jones, a local Baptist clergyman and eventually Lee's biographer, "he at once, in his quiet way, gave both professors and students to understand that he was president, and meant to control the affairs of the institution." Lee would take not only an active but almost a solo role in rebuilding—and reconfiguring—Washington College.[6] He would play the Prince of Castaways as the part had never been played before—almost to the point of wondering whether it could be said that he played.

Not making his high place the lawless perch
Of winged ambitions, nor a vantage-ground
For pleasure.

No one had bothered, in the rush to hire him, to inquire after Lee's philosophy of education, or even whether he had one. But he most certainly did, explaining to the Presbyterian minister George W. Leyburn that "I consider the proper education" of the South's "youth one of the most important objects now to be attained." What was absent from that concern was any interest in reviving classical education. "The fundamental principle of the Collegiate System should be to give to the Commercial, Agricultural & mechanical Classes the advantages of an education but adapted to their wants." In notes for a lecture he sent in 1867 to John Barbee Minor of the University of Virginia, Lee defined education "in its broad and comprehensive sense" as anything that "embraces the physical, moral and intellectual instruction of a child from infancy to manhood," and not just the classics. As far as Lee was concerned, "any useful pursuit of life will be sure to secure prosperity & fame," and therefore anything that prepared someone for that goal was worth studying. "Success," he added, "will result from engaging in that business in which the generality of mankind are interested." Edward Southey Joynes, whom Lee hired for the faculty in 1866, found Lee "a strong advocate of practical, even technical education," if for no other reason than that they were "at present the most important interest of the Southern people & must continue for years to come." Studying "the Classics" was "optimal" only for those who needed "an education other than for professional purposes." Aristotle and Cicero could wait.[7]

So, for that matter, could any hint of military education. He staggered one student when he told him, "The great mistake of my life was taking a military education." His first love was the engineers; he had only allowed himself to be dragged into the other worlds of soldiering by what he saw as necessity, and he had no interest in revisiting that world now. While postwar Congresses scrambled to fund military education in varieties of educational legislation passed under Reconstruction, Lee resolutely looked the other way. When he was sent a copy of the British colonel Edward Bruce Hamley's *Operations of War Explained and Illustrated* (1866), Lee set it aside. "The subject is one in which I have had some experience," he coldly observed, "& hope never again to have to need of recurring to, & there fore have never read the book." There are, he would explain in a more patient moment, "but few questions which require the intervention of war," and he recommended instead that "governments ought to try every honorable means for their settlement before resorting to" war. When the Franco-Prussian War broke out in 1870, Lee "regretted that they did not submit their differences to the arbitration of the other Powers. . . . It would have been a grand moral victory over the passions of men, and would have so elevated the contestants in the eyes of the present and future generations as to have produced a beneficial effect." But that, he added despairingly, "might have been expecting too much from the present standard civilization, & I fear we are destined to kill and slaughter each other for ages to come."

At least at Washington College, there would be no military instruction and no military display, and those who yearned after such could be pointed down the street to the Virginia Military Institute. Whenever the students from the college and the cadets from VMI found themselves marching in parades with Lee and their commandant, Francis H. Smith, Lee always deliberately marched out of step.[8]

Within his first month in office, Lee persuaded the trustees to endorse an overhaul of the curriculum to introduce "a more thorough and extended course of scientific instruction embracing more particularly the application of scientific principles to the useful Arts." He did not intend to eliminate "literature and the classics," but they would now have to share space with "Drawing Architecture, mechanism and the nature and profession of building, and their application in the construction of railroads, canals and bridges," along with applied mathematics and modern languages (French, Spanish, German, and Italian).

By the following April, Lee had convinced the board not only that "the present College Curriculum be abolished" but that the college itself be reorganized into a series of nine "independent schools" that would grant their own degrees in classics, mathematics, chemistry, "Moral Philosophy," and "Modern Languages." He incorporated the small law academy run by Judge Brockenbrough as the college's law school, and by 1869 he was even urging the creation of "a Commercial School . . . to give instruction in bookkeeping & the forms of & details of business," along with "the principles of Commercial economy, trade & Mercantile Law," as well as a school of journalism.[9]

None of this would be possible without a greatly expanded faculty, the money to pay for it, and the students who would attend its classes, and so Lee embarked on one of the most unlikely campaigns of his life: fund-raising. Lee began, as other Virginia institutions did, with appeals to the newly reconstituted Virginia state government, asking for financial help in funding additional professorships and pleading that "the moral & intellectual culture of our youth is of greatest importance to the country." But the new free-state government set up by Virginia unionists in the first flush of postwar reconstruction turned out to be both short-lived and short of money. Lee was forced to plan a series of appeals farther north, beginning with prominent sons of Virginia who had scored financial success in the Northern states and might be recalled by nostalgia to the support of a Virginia college.

He wrote first on November 28, 1865, to Cyrus Hall McCormick, a native of the Lexington area and a transplant to Illinois, whose mechanical reaper had made him both wealthy and famous. "To you who are so conversant with the necessities of the country," Lee began, it "will be at once apparent" how useful would be "the benefit of applying scientific knowledge & research, to agriculture, mining, manufacturing, architecture, & the construction of ordinary roads, R. Roads, canals, bridges, etc.," especially if a college would devote its attention to such subjects, "& it is this consideration that has emboldened me, to bring it to your notice." McCormick appreciated boldness. He wrote back with a promise of "a donation of Ten Thousand Dollars reserving the privilege of adding to it hereafter as proposed by you should it be found 'convenient' to do so when it shall become more clear that the full complement of Professorships embraced in your plans will be met by corresponding contributions."[10]

Corresponding contributions were not long in coming from Virginia emigrants like the New York lawyer Warren Newcomb or Northern Democrats like the banker William Wilson Corcoran, whom Lee had known in prewar Washington. Lee's single biggest score was with a Massachusetts philanthropist, George Peabody, who not only donated $60,000 for the college but accepted an invitation from Lee to spend part of the summer with him at the nearby White Sulphur Springs resort. By the spring of 1866, the college had shrunk its deficits to just $1,237.37, "which will be regarded [as] a gratifying result when it is recollected that we commenced the year without a dollar in the Treasury and have met current expenses during the year." A year later, the pendulum swung upward, now showing a total endowment of $234,207.36.

The most sensational donor cultivation event followed a year later, a public meeting held for Washington College at New York City's Cooper Institute—the same Cooper Institute that had launched Lincoln toward the presidential nomination in 1860—and sponsored by the cream of New York City's clergy. The resolutions for the meeting were composed by the brightly beaming abolitionist Henry Ward Beecher, urging a "generous hand for upbuilding in the South of the institutions which are necessary to the full development of its powers." And for anyone who thought it strange that a veteran abolitionist should be passing the hat on behalf of a Confederate general who had been indicted for treason, Beecher unhesitatingly affirmed that "if he had been born in Virginia, brought up amid her institutions [and] educated in a Southern college, he might have been prompted to take a course just as bad or erratic as did Lee." Besides, whatever "had been his error in the war, now he had devoted himself to the sacred cause of education," and for Beecher "every man who gave himself for the recuperation of his country was his brother."[11]

The new funds, in turn, allowed Lee to begin hiring new faculty in 1866, beginning with Richard Sears McCulloh, who left his position at Columbia (where he taught physics) in 1863 to ally himself with the Confederacy as a developer of chemical weapons. Treacly as that experience might seem, Lee had no qualms about installing him as Washington College's professor of experimental philosophy and practical mechanics. William Allan, a former colonel who had served during the war as a staffer for Stonewall Jackson and was working as a bank cashier in Staunton in the months after the war, was tagged by Lee to teach applied mathematics and would go on to publish three books on mechanics. Allan was accompanied by Edward Joynes in the chair of Modern Languages, and John Lycan Kirkpatrick, a Presbyterian clergyman and editor who had until 1866 been president of Davidson College in North Carolina.[12]

These hirings betray at least two patterns in Lee's thinking. The first concerned religion. Washington College was not a denominationally connected college. But Lexington "was largely settled by Scotch-Irish, who seem to be born Presbyterians of the strictest sect" and who considered the college "a Presbyterian institution" in a town where the righteous Stonewall Jackson was the most famous Presbyterian native son. Robert E. Lee was an Episcopalian, and there were some voices in the college not all that discreet in observing that "it went something against the grain that an Episcopalian should become its official head." Lee quietly outflanked sectarian collisions with his usual mixture of piety and blandness. He designed a campus chapel in 1866 and saw it open in 1868 but appointed no chaplain to give it a denominational identity. He was determined that the chair in moral philosophy eventually filled by John Lycan Kirkpatrick should be occupied by "a man of true piety, learning, & science" and "so imbued with the Heavenly principles of the blessed Gospel of Christ; as to make His Holy religion attractive to the young, to impress it on their hearts, & to make them humble Christians." But such a professor should also "not only be free from bigotry, but clear of Sectarianism; having for his whole object the teaching of wisdom & the conversion of all the students to the religion of Christ, of whatever sect or denomination." Inquiries about the religious complexion of the campus were met with soothing disclaimers by Lee about denominational enthusiasms. "On the subject of religion," he explained to a prospective Episcopalian donor, "I do not know that it has ever been sectarian in its character." Located as it is "in a Presbyterian community, it is natural that most of its trustees and faculty should be of that denomination," but the college had never been and "certainly is not so now."[13]

Lee was careful to respect the upper Shenandoah's Presbyterian sensibilities. But he was equally careful to keep any public religious exercises limited to prayer meetings whose supervision he cautiously divided up among Lexington's resident Protestant clergy. And even those prayer meetings had limits imposed by Lee. One particularly zealous clergyman, who waxed too eloquently in praying "for the Jews, the Turks, the heathen, the Chinese, and every body else," tended to "run into the regular hours for our college recitations." So perhaps, Lee suggested, it would be better if he confined "his morning prayers to us poor sinners at the college, and pray for the Turks, the Jews, the Chinese, and the other heathen, some other time." The unsectarian John Kirkpatrick remembered that Lee "was accustomed to inquire of each student, when entering the college, to what religious denomination his parents belonged," and "then introduce the student to the pastor of the same denomination in the town." There would be no denominational proselytization on the Washington College campus if Lee could help it.[14]

Lee's hirings were also flavored (whether or not Henry Ward Beecher was aware) by a preference for Confederate veterans. This was especially true for those who had provided some worthwhile service to Lee's Army of Northern Virginia, like McCulloh, Joynes, and Allan. "The deeper I go," wrote Frank Smyth, a reporter for the New York *Sun* who visited Lexington in 1869, "the more entangling I find the network of Confederate soldiers." The college's "teachers and students, since its organization, have been the soldiers and orphans of the Confederacy." Applicants for faculty positions who were not "soldiers and orphans," or who had not been to Lee's satisfaction, received scant attention. The North Carolinian Alfred Mordecai, who sat out the conflict as an officer of the Mexico & Pacific Railroad, was given the cold shoulder by Lee, even after Mordecai's wife, Sara, appealed to Lee on her husband's behalf for an appointment "for the position of Profr of Practical Mechanics & Experimental Philosophy." Daniel Harvey Hill, who served under Lee on the peninsula and in Maryland in 1862 (and briefly taught at Washington College before the war), appealed to John Brockenbrough for appointment to a chair in "Military Science . . . should a Chair corresponding to it be established." But Hill had long been rumored to be the man who had dropped the Lost Orders before Antietam; after the battle, Lee had exiled him to commands in North Carolina for most of the war, and after the war he did nothing to bring Hill closer to him again.[15]

The new influx of money also made student scholarships more abundant, and that—together with Lee's prestige, the new faculty, and the new programs—sent student enrollment at Washington College soaring. After less than a year in office, Lee was able to report to the trustees that "the whole number of students" now stood at 146. All but 8 hailed from the former Confederacy, and even those 8 came from West Virginia and Maryland. But more dramatic shifts were under way in the student population, and in June 1867, Lee could announce that the student body now stood at 399, this time with 37 from beyond the old Confederate boundaries, including Pennsylvania, Massachusetts, and New Jersey. The growth peaked in 1868 at 411 and then dropped back in Lee's final report for 1869 to 348 students. But by then, Washington College was drawing new applicants from Ohio, California, Illinois, New York, and even Mexico. Lee, declared the *Richmond Times,* had become the college's "second founder":

> *The radical changes which have taken place in this college have given it prodigious popularity. The course of studies has been enlarged, the corps of professors increased, and General Lee now presides over the destinies of a well endowed and most prosperous college. . . . Washington College is no longer the purely sectarian institution which it was for nearly*

three-quarters of a century, and this is a change which has increased its popularity.

This growth stood in striking contrast to the stagnant enrollment numbers in other Virginia colleges. The College of William & Mary could boast only 42 students in 1870; the University of Virginia recruited 258 students for its first postwar class and boosted that number the next year to 490, only to see it gradually fall away to 317 students in 1870–71 (it still managed to recruit just 532 even in the 1890s). Roanoke College had only 151 students in 1871, and as late as the eve of World War I, Hampden-Sydney College would enroll even fewer.

Lee, in effect, had, as the most unlikely of innovators, built an educational powerhouse out of the most unlikely of institutions and in the most unlikely of places. "This place is made up of big bugs," boasted one student to his brother in the winter of 1868, "for we have Gen Lee of course, and . . . it is the home of Gov Letcher, and we now have Gen [John C.] Breckinridge . . . on a visit to the place, besides many other too numerous to mention." If his brother "wishes to see some fine stock, just . . . come over here. . . . We have some six or seven hundred young men at this place (all students) so you may imagine it looks something like New York when we all get on the streets at once."[16]

It is difficult to believe that Washington College would have survived the war without Lee. It is equally difficult to believe that Lee would have survived without the college, because Washington College finally granted him the independence of action he had always sought, along with a security of standing he had never before known. At last, for the first time in his life, he could be what he always wanted to be, "one & alone in the World." Or almost.

Lee's dramatic success in scaling up the student population of Washington College was also a source of mounting stress for the aging general, who turned sixty in 1867. Much of that stress was self-imposed: Lee was not taking any more chances with unreliable subordinates. The new chapel he proposed to the trustees in 1866 was probably drawn up by Thomas Williamson, but Lee could not resist tinkering with the engineering. He dickered with Edwards, Lee & Co. of Baltimore for "one of your No. 4 church organs for the Chapel of Washington College," along with "the dimensions, price &c & the time at which you could have it in place," and proposed to redesign the chapel's heating system by drawing his own plans and a description of how "the smoke pipes must pass through the brick partition walls into the flues in the outer walls of the chapel. Apertures have been left in the outer walls, but will have to be made in the partition walls, & proper collars must be inserted in them that the pipes can be removed & cleaned when necessary." Lee, wrote Edward Joynes, "had an eye for the supervision of every detail. The buildings, the repairs, the college walks and grounds, the wood-yard, the mess-hall, all received his attention, and a large portion of his time was given to the purely business affairs of the College."[17]

Lee shouldered the same burden in student affairs. He personally wrote letters to prospective students that accompanied the college's "prospectus of the Course of studies . . . which I hope will furnish you with all the information you desire." When they arrived in Lexington, Lee interviewed them and surprised them with the announcement: "We have no printed rules. We have but one rule here, and it is that every student must be a gentleman"—which sounded delightfully gracious until it was realized that by substituting his own rule of gentility for a student code, Robert E. Lee made himself the sole court of conduct in the college and acquired the means to impose the full measure of perfection he had been unable to demand of so many others over the years. When they sat for examinations, Lee wrote out the grade reports, along with "Remarks" (which varied from "Distinguished" downward), and when it became evident that a student was failing, Lee wrote the inevitable letter to his parents or guardian:

> *I fear your son John has not been as attentive to his studies as he might have been. But, however that may be, he certainly has not progressed as I desired him, or as you might wish him. . . . I have, in a friendly way, called his attention to his apparent neglect of his studies . . . and, unless he should show some marked improvement before the end of the session, I would recommend you to withdraw him from the college.*[18]

Unlike the old days under Joseph Totten at West Point, Lee could be sure that such decisions would be final, and appeals from disappointed parents were met with the reply that their plea had been "read to such of the Faculty as I could assemble," and invariably "the Opinion expressed was that they could not reverse their former decision unless good ground could be shown for so doing." When, as unavoidably happened, a student died on campus, it was Lee who wrote the notification letter. "It grieves me to address you on a subject which has already been announced to you in all its woe, & which has brought to your heart such heavy affliction," Lee wrote to the mother of a student drowned in a boating accident in the spring of 1868. "It may be some consolation in your bereavement to know, that your son was highly appreciated by the officers & students, & that this whole community unite in sorrow at his untimely death."[19]

Part of Lee's determination to be in control of student behavior was connected to the volatile situation created by the new racial alignments Reconstruction brought to Lexington and across the South. Never far from Lee's mind was the ease with which a single racial outrage, committed by arrogant white students who were perceived as "Lee's Boys," might mushroom into the closure of the college by federal military authorities, or even into some fresh legal pursuit of Lee himself. Despite the well-wishing of Beecher and other Northerners, Lee remained an object of suspicion to both Radical Republicans and embittered Southern unionists who frantically asked Andrew Johnson, "Aren't you ashamed to give Lee the privilege of being a President of a college? Satan wouldn't have him to open the door for fresh arrivals, and you have pardoned him and allowed him to take a position of the greatest responsibility." John Bright, the British parliamentarian who had faithfully supported the Northern cause all through the war, was also puzzled by Lee as a college president. "Treason was the greatest crime of all crimes, and must be punished as such," Bright wrote to Charles Sumner. But "now nobody is punished. Lee is allowed to become Principal of a College to teach loyalty to your young men, and I suppose bye and bye [Jefferson] Davis will be free, and may again make his appearance in the Senate at Washington." Walking across eggshells of such brittleness, Lee understood that any missteps—especially involving the freed people—would trigger demands that officials see that "the College was closed."[20]

And Lexington did not see much peace in Reconstruction. The town's population numbered about two thousand, one-third of it African Americans who were trying to create new lives for themselves, often with the assistance of federal agencies like the Freedmen's Bureau or private educational charities like the American Missionary Association. No similar assistance was extended by the college, and hostility between Lexington's blacks and the college's students was almost palpable. The New York *Sun*'s Frank Smyth interviewed one of Lee's new professors, William Preston Johnston, the son of the Confederate general Albert Sidney Johnston and a wartime officer and aide to Jefferson Davis, and found that Johnston's "contempt for the blacks was undisguisedly expressed. Every tenth word was a contemptuous allusion to the black man. He thought slavery good for them. . . . They were his servants, he said, and he would not have his children associate with them in the public schools."

The same attitude prevailed among the students. Harry McDonald, who worked as an agricultural hand to pay for his tuition, resented having to labor "for the same wages, and by the side of negroes." They resented still more the Northern teachers who came to Lexington under the aegis of the American Missionary Association to open black schools. A female teacher, Julia Shearman, complained that Washington College students would "stare and laugh at us & make rude remarks as they dare," and when the AMA's William Coan arrived in Lexington in November 1865, he was warned that "General Lee's boys" would make it "a hard place" for him.[21]

Quickly, racial incidents festered. On March 19, 1866, the AMA school in Lexington had its windows broken by stone throwing; in July "a freed boy named Eli King" was attacked by "a white boy, Joseph Ayers, with a stone"; in the fall of 1866, one of John Brockenbrough's law students, John J. Johnston, shot and killed a black man, Patrick Thompson, in a dispute on Lexington's Main Street; and on March 22, 1867, Washington College students led another attack on the AMA school in Lexington. Less than a year later, one of Judge Brockenbrough's sons, Francis Henry Brockenbrough, was "walking home, in Lexington, with his mother and another lady, when they were met by a negro man and some negro women, who refused to give them any way on the pavement. . . . After he had escorted his companions home," Brockenbrough tracked down the "negro man," Caesar Griffin, "having in his hand a small stick or switch." Griffin, however, was carrying "a small pistol" and "shot Mr. Brockenbrough in the breast, inflicting a dangerous if not fatal wound." Brockenbrough would eventually recover, but Griffin was arrested and nearly lynched. (Griffin was eventually tried and sentenced to two years in jail for "unlawful shooting" in September.)[22]

No incident earned the college more unwanted notoriety than an attack on a white man, Erastus C. Johnston, who had originally arrived in Lexington as an AMA teacher but who also opened a store in Lexington and attempted to organize a chapter of the Loyal League. On February 4, 1868, Johnston went skating on the frozen-over North River, only to be surrounded by a gang of Washington College students who threatened to "calathump" him if he did not leave town. Johnston drew a revolver and managed to get off with little worse than insults, but he took his case at once to the federal commandant under the new Reconstruction regime, Orlando B. Willcox, and from there to the pages of the New York *Independent* (a weekly Congregationalist newspaper under the editorship of the Radical Republican Theodore Tilton), to *The Yale Courant,* and to the *Chicago Tribune.* Johnston's lurid accounts of the miseries of life in Reconstruction Lexington concentrated on the college's students, none of whom "can remain in the college who is not a rebel," and whom he accused of finding their "chief amusement" in the seduction of "young colored girls." This "outrage . . . reflects injuriously upon Gen. Lee's conduct in connection therewith," and not the least because it occurred almost simultaneously with the college's great Cooper Institute fund-raising event. It was chilling to have *The Independent* inform its readers that "we should think that every Northern man who has given a cent to General Lee's college would see and feel that he has been imposed upon and that his money has been worse than thrown away."[23]

Lee's responses were swift and unsparing. The March 1867 attack on the AMA school prompted Lee to identify five students as the culprits and to bring the ringleader, J. A. McNeill, before the faculty to be "dismissed from the College." He acted to suppress any outburst on the campus over the Brockenbrough shooting, on the one hand assuring the local Freedmen's Bureau commissioner, Jacob Wagner, "I can find no foundation for your apprehension that the students of Washington College contemplate any attack upon the man confined in jail," and on the other directing the student president of the Young Men's Christian Association to warn "the students to abstain from any violation of the law, and to unite in preserving quiet and order on this and every occasion." He denounced Erastus Johnston's "slanderous article . . . against Washington College" and waved away the Johnston incident as "a difficulty wherein . . . Johnston, a recent resident of this place, allowed himself to be drawn into with some little boys of Lexington." He assured the New York banker George King Sistare that "so far as the students were concerned . . . the only two found implicated (the eldest of whom was 16) were dismissed." When, in November 1868, restless students planned a counterdemonstration to a "contemplated assembly . . . of the coloured people of Lexington," Lee promised the Freedmen's Bureau that "everything . . . in our power will be done by the Faculty as well as myself, to prevent any of the students attending," and he admonished the students to "abstain from attending this & all similar meetings" because "should any disturbance occur, efforts will be made to put the blame on Washington College."[24]

That last sentence captures Lee's principal concern, because neither emancipation nor Reconstruction had converted Robert E. Lee into any form of a racial egalitarian. But the thuggery of the newly nascent Ku Klux Klan and the White Leagues was equally repellant to his prickly sense of the genteel. Hence, he was only too happy to conceal racial incidents involving students from the public eye if he could, even as he dealt sharply with them internally as a violation of his definition of the behavior of a "gentleman." In January 1869, he wrote to the mother of Henry Neel that her son "had been engaged on the streets of the town in a difficulty which resulted in the shooting and wounding of a negro man." The "faculty felt constrained . . . to pass a resolution dismissing him," but happily for the school Neel "left the College without permission, or indeed without making any application to do so, and has not since reported in any way to the authorities of the College"—thus conveniently absolving the college of any further responsibility.[25]

Privately, Lee preferred to think of the postwar racial geography as composing separate spheres, in which black and white went their own politically unequal ways. He opposed "any system of laws which would place the political power of the country in the hands of the negro race" because "the negroes have neither the intelligence nor the qualifications which are necessary to make them safe depositaries of political power," and he dreaded the prospect of "the South" being "placed under the dominion of the negroes." He was so contemptuous of the "farce" of Reconstruction that he expected "all decent white people would be forced to retire" from Washington. (Mary was, if anything, even more disdainful of African Americans; she could not forget the sight, in occupied Richmond, of Lincoln's being greeted by "blacks whooping & cheering like so many demons.") Yet, at the same time, Lee conceded that any plan that completely excluded blacks from voting would surely fail. He favored instead a scheme of "impartial suffrage"—setting conditions on voting rights so high that some blacks would indeed qualify, but not enough to command any real political power. His plan "would have excluded ten negroes and one white man," and thus tossed a tub to the Reconstruction whale.

"You will never prosper with the blacks," he warned his youngest son in 1868. "I wish them no evil in the world—on the contrary, will do them every good in my power." But it remained "abhorrent to a reflecting mind to be supporting and cherishing those" whom Lee would always suspect of "plotting and working for your injury, and all of whose sympathies and associations are antagonistic to yours." Of all the innovations in college education Lee sponsored, a racially integrated Washington College was not one of them, and when Edward Payson Walton, one of the college's fund-raising agents, suggested "that possibly [black students] might be admitted" in order to open more Northern donor pocketbooks, he was soundly rebuked.[26]

CHAPTER TWENTY

From the Great Deep to the Great Deep He Goes

For most of his life, Lee had been a mild unionist Whig, always cautiously shunning any overt politics. And publicly, that remained his stance until Andrew Johnson finally lifted the threat of the treason indictment with his amnesty proclamation on Christmas Day 1868. Until then, he soothingly urged reconciliation and submission and encouraged "all our young men to adhere to their states & friends, & aid both in restoration of the country." A "humbly-clad man" who stopped at Lee's gate to chat was pointed out afterward by Lee as "one of our old soldiers who is in necessitous circumstances." When an inquirer asked what part of the Confederate army he had served in, Lee replied, "He fought on the other side, but we must not remember that against him now." When the unrepentant Jubal Early wrote to Lee from Mexico, urging him to join a group of Confederate military exiles there, Lee discreetly refused. "Mexico is a beautiful country, fertile, of vast resources," but his hope was "that peace will be restored to the country, and that the South may enjoy some measure of prosperity." In the meantime, "all controversy, I think, will only serve to prolong bitter feeling, and postpone the period when reason and charity may resume their sway." And he warned Varina Davis, whose husband was still awaiting trial in Fort Monroe, that "controversy of all kinds will, in my opinion, only serve to continue excitement and passion." A proposal to erect a monument to the Confederate war dead was smoothly rebuffed by Lee. "However gratified it would be to the feelings of the South, the attempt in the present Condition of the Country would have the effect of retarding, instead of accelerating," the recovery of the South "& of continuing, if not adding to, the difficulties under which the Southern people labour."[1]

But his argument was a pragmatic one: Lee never hinted that such a monument might not be *deserved.* And his advice to Jubal Early was to wait until the attitude of the public had wearied of Reconstruction, and then, perhaps, some new political opportunity would develop for white Southerners. Until then, Lee proposed to be as wise as the serpent while remaining as harmless as a dove. In February 1866, he was alarmed by a summons to Washington to testify before the congressional Joint Committee on Reconstruction. Surprisingly, the questioning was polite, lasting two and a half hours, and Lee's answers were politely disarming. When queried about "the state of feeling among what we call secessionists," Lee glibly answered, "I have been living very retired, and have had but little communication with politicians." His best estimate of the "feeling of loyalty towards the government of the United States" was that there was "no single person who either feels or contemplates any resistance to the government of the United States." He blandly announced that "he knew nothing of the policy of the [Confederate] government. I had no hand or part in it."

He insisted particularly that he bore no ill will toward the freed people: "I . . . have always been in favor of emancipation—gradual emancipation." Nor did other Virginians. "Every one with whom I associate expresses kind feelings towards the freedmen," Lee declared. "They wish to see them get on in the world, and particularly to take up some occupation for a living and to turn their hands to some work." He said nothing about black voting or office holding. Ultimately, "I think it would be better for Virginia if she could get rid of them" by deporting "the colored population" to "Alabama, Louisiana, and the other southern States." When he finished, "quite a crowd collected about the door of the committee room, awaiting his exit," and "a large number of his old Washington acquaintances . . . called upon him."[2]

What he would not give the committee was an admission that he had been "rather wheedled or cheated into" joining the Confederacy "by politicians." That would have been tantamount to admitting that his decisions in 1861 had not been entirely his own, an admission that would have been uncomfortably close to the truth in 1861 but that Lee would not admit in 1866. It might have been, he told the committee, "that the great masses of the people . . . would have avoided" the war but for "the politicians of the country." But it was not true, he maintained, "that I had been individually wheedled by the politicians." All the same, Lee was undergoing a political wheedling that reshaped his prewar Whiggism, with all of its reverence for Union and nation. The transformation started quietly enough as he criticized "with great severity" the execution of Mary Surratt in July 1865 as one of the four Booth conspirators condemned by military tribunal and hanged in Washington. Whatever assurances he gave to the Reconstruction Committee, he nursed the conviction that "the Southern people" were "acting under compulsion, not of their free choice," in Reconstruction. It grew as he began to embrace Charles Marshall's Lost Cause as his own (Edward Pollard gave the ideology a name when he published his *Lost Cause: A New Southern History of the War of the Confederates* in 1866), insisting that "it will be difficult to get the world to understand the odds against which we fought."[3]

Throughout 1866, Lee vented an increasing bitterness at the outcome of the war and the direction of Reconstruction. "All that the South has ever desired," he wrote to the Northern Democrat Chauncey Burr, the editor of the rabidly anti-Republican and white supremacist newspaper *The Old Guard,* "was that the Union, as established by our forefathers, should be preserved, and that the government as originally organized should be administered in purity and truth." In the "justice of that cause" he was unashamedly confident. He complained to Reverdy Johnson that the Radical Republicans were intent on "a policy which will continue the prostration of one-half the country, alienate the affections of its inhabitants from the government, and which must eventually result in injury to the country and the American people." His summons to Washington did not improve his state of mind, he explained to Markie Williams, especially when the train "which leads to the city" chugged slowly past Arlington to deposit him at the Metropolitan Hotel in the District. "The changed times & circumstances did recall sad thoughts." Herman Melville, almost preternaturally, caught Lee's frame of mind:

Demurring not, promptly he comes
By ways which show the blackened homes,
And—last—the seat no more his own,
But Honor's; patriot grave-yards fill
The forfeit slopes of that patrician hill,
And fling a shroud on Arlington.
The oaks ancestral all are low;
No more from the porch his glance shall go
Ranging the varied landscape o'er,
Far as the looming Dome—no more.
One look he gives, then turns aside,
Solace he summons from his pride:
"So be it! They await me now
Who wrought this stinging overthrow;
They wait me; not as on the day
Of Pope's impelled retreat in disarray—

By me impelled—when toward yon Dome
The clouds of war came rolling home."
The burst, the bitterness was spent,
The heart-burst bitterly turbulent,
And on he fared.

That night "a gentleman" caught a glimpse of Lee at Arlington "standing in the street that passes through the middle of his old estate . . . with folded arms" and a "sorrowful attitude."[4]

Lee began corresponding with his French-raised nephew, Edward Lee Childe, after a long hiatus during the war, and to Childe he poured out torrents of political anguish. "The papers inform you of our political condition," he wrote in January 1867. "I wish I could give you a cheering account of things," but he could not, especially in Virginia. Congress was about to enact the first of a series of Reconstruction Acts that would convert the former Confederacy into a series of military occupation districts, and a new state constitutional convention was scheduled for the fall, a convention dominated by John Curtiss Underwood. "Judge Underwood," Lee wrote irritably, "would be well pleased, I presume, if the business were left to them and the negroes." But Lee's concern spilled over the boundaries of Virginia. Everywhere, "the Conservatives are too weak to resist successfully the radicals, who have every thing their own way." Lee feared that a federal government directed by the Radical Republicans, overconfident of success and righteousness, would aim at creating "one vast Government, sure to become aggressive abroad & despotic at home; & I fear will follow that road, which history tell us, all such Republics have trod, Might is believed to be right, & the popular Clamor, the voice of God."

This was an odd juxtaposition: accusations that Republicans (and before them, Whigs) wanted to create "one vast Government" had long been a page in the Jacksonian, and later Confederate, political script, but distaste for the *vox populi, vox dei* was still a nod in the direction of Whiggism. A few weeks later, he was even sharper. "The greatest danger," Lee wrote, is "the subversion of the old form of Government & the substitution in its place of a great Consolidated central power, which wielded by the will of the majority party, will soon disregard every constitutional check, trample upon the reserved rights of the states, & in time annihilate the Constitution." He found it ironic that Andrew Johnson "is threatened with impeachment & deposition" for carrying out what were, at least in 1861, "the avowed objects of the war, the restoration 'of the Union with all the dignity, equality & rights of the states unimpaired.'"[5]

In time, he began to doubt the very possibility of democratic self-government. "Notwithstanding all our boastful assertions to the world for nearly a century, that our government was based on the consent of the people," the war and Reconstruction had only demonstrated that "it rests upon force as much as any government that ever existed." In January 1868, he concluded that if "the South is to be placed under the dominion of the negroes," the newly enfranchised blacks in the South would swamp "the Conservative votes of the whites at the north" and elect a Radical Republican president to succeed Andrew Johnson. This showed to a onetime Whig only what a bruised reed democracy was. The genius of the American founding, Lee insisted to a British sympathizer, John Edward Dalberg-Acton (soon to become Lord Acton), was "the maintenance of the rights and authority reserved to the States and to the people." But that was not what "the radical party" wanted. Reconstruction was a device for concentrating power in the hands of the central government, and in the party controlling it. Thus centralized "into one vast republic," the United States was "sure to be aggressive abroad and despotic at home." He had no objection to the Thirteenth Amendment's abolition of slavery as national policy, since "that is an event that has been long sought, though in a different way, and by none has it been more earnestly desired than by citizens of Virginia." But he wanted nothing more than that, and certainly not what was being proposed by Radical Republicans as a fourteenth and fifteenth amendment, establishing black citizenship and voting rights. This kind of "centralization of power," he told Annette Carter, would produce "the annihilation of the Constitution, the liberty of the people and of the country," spell "an end of Republic[anism] on this continent," and allow "our trusted self government" to become "the jeer and laughing stock of the world."

He would still, as he told Edward Lee Childe, favor "Republican forms of Govt." But much of the reason why the American republic had sidled too far toward centralization was its accommodation of democratic norms that promoted levelling and gave no discouragement to ignorance. A republic "requires a virtuous people . . . & the world has not yet I fear reached the proper standard of morality & integrity to live under the rule of religion & reason." He added, "Spain I think showed her wisdom in adopting a constitutional monarchy." When the Republicans nominated Ulysses Grant for the presidency that summer, Lee dismissed him as a mere tool in the hands of the Radicals; when young Cazenove Gardner Lee quizzed his famous cousin on whom he thought the greatest of the Union generals, "he replied at once, with great emphasis, McClellan, by all odds."[6]

This was paying a higher tribute to the conspiratorial skills of the Republicans and the infirmities of democracy than they deserved, or than Reconstruction bore out. But it occurred to some Virginians, beginning with

Robert Ould, that Lee, instead of complaining about Reconstruction, would be better advised to do something directly about it. In 1866, the soon-to-be-dissolved unionist legislature proposed inviting Lee to run for governor, "which met with the applause of the House, as well as the gallery." But Lee refused. "I duly appreciate the spirit that has led them to name me for that high position," he replied to Ould, but "I candidly confess . . . that my feelings induce me to prefer private life, which I think more suitable to my condition and age, and where I believe I can better advance the interests of my State than in that you propose."[7]

But two years later, as federal Reconstruction authorities shrank gradually into noninterference in Virginia affairs, he reversed himself far enough to sign a public letter created for the former Union general William Starke Rosecrans, urging Northern and Southern Democrats to unite in opposing Grant's election. Rosecrans and Lee had once opposed each other in the early days of the war in West Virginia. But there had been little love lost between Rosecrans and Grant after Grant dropped him from command in the west following Rosecrans's humiliating defeat at Chickamauga. That Rosecrans was also an Ohio Democrat only endeared him to Northern Democratic opinion in general and to Andrew Johnson in particular and convinced both that Rosecrans had been a victim as much of Republican politics as of Confederate strategy. After the war, Johnson picked Rosecrans for the diplomatic mission to Mexico, and on his way he stopped at White Sulphur Springs, where Lee was vacationing, and hatched the idea of enlisting Lee and a bevy of former Confederates behind a letter that would pledge Southerners to decent treatment of the freed people, and thus remove a major talking point for Grant and the Republicans.[8]

Lee agreed to sponsor a meeting of thirty-one other prominent Southerners at the Springs, and that in turn produced a letter which Lee and the others signed for Rosecrans on August 26. Typical of Lee's insistence that "the arbitrament of arms" had settled all questions about slavery, the letter promised that "whatever opinions may have prevailed in the past in regard to African slavery, or the right of a State to secede from the Union . . . the Southern people . . . consider that those questions were decided by the war, and that it is their intention in good faith to abide by that decision." Just as Lee had insisted to the Joint Committee on Reconstruction, "the people of the South entertain no unfriendly feeling towards the government of the United States," and "the idea that the Southern people are hostile to the negroes, and would oppress them if it were in their power to do so, is entirely unfounded." Lee's name headed the list of signatories, which included Pierre Beauregard, Alexander Stephens, and John Letcher. And it seems to have persuaded no one. The *New York Sun* sneered at the meeting as "the great Democratic Love-

Feast"; the *Tribune* announced that "Gen. Rosecrans has been fooled by the defeated worthies of the Rebellion, and his offer to go surety for their loyalty is regarded as a little Quixotic." Grant won in November in a landslide, a sizable portion of it built from the votes of newly enfranchised Southern blacks.[9]

Grant's victory did nothing to impress Lee. In January, Lee rebuffed a suggestion that the president-elect be invited to visit Washington College. "If I were to invite him to do so, it might not be agreeable to him, and I fear my motives might be misunderstood at this time . . . and that evil would result instead of good." Grant nevertheless invited Lee to Washington in May, hoping to recruit Lee's support for a new Virginia state constitution that would enfranchise blacks but also make the disenfranchisement of former Confederates a separate ballot issue, and thus have a better chance of success. Lee was unenthusiastic and "very brief." The meeting lasted for "about fifteen minutes," and neither managed "a word on political matters."[10]

Lee might have been more explicit about the politics of the war and the Southern cause if he had pushed forward with the project to create his history of the Army of Northern Virginia's campaigns. As early as July 1865, he began writing to former staffers and colleagues to see what surviving records and documents they had on hand, beginning with Walter Taylor. He had little himself to go on. As he explained, "All my records, reports, returns, etc., etc., with the headquarters of the army, were needlessly destroyed by the clerks having them in charge on the retreat from Petersburg." But many of them had little more on hand than Lee did, and by June 1866 he was having to explain, half apologetically, "I am merely collecting information for such a history, nor can I say that it will be written." Six months later, he had to admit to John Dalberg-Acton that "as to my being engaged in preparing a narrative of the campaigns in Virginia, I regret to state that I progress slowly in the collection of the necessary documents."

Not that he would have lacked for an audience. His mail thickened with clamors for a book on the entire war, and not just Virginia, especially after newspapers began leaking news "that the General desires to write a history of the war." Publishers leaped to offer a contract, led by Joseph L. Topham, who boasted that he owned "the largest book-publishing house in America" and could offer Lee a $50,000 advance. Lee deflated them all. "I cannot, at present, undertake such a work," Lee told Topham (and had to tell him twice again when Topham kept pestering him). "I cannot now undertake the work you propose," he replied to Scranton & Burr, a subscription publisher in Connecticut, "nor can I enter into an engagement to do what I may not be able to accomplish." When Markie Williams inquired about the rumored history, Lee merely replied that she "had been led into errour by the newspaper statements. I am not writing a history of the war." A book that extended its gaze beyond the campaigns in Virginia would inevitably have forced him into judgments about the western campaigns, which for Joe Johnston's sake he was loath to do, and into judgments about Davis, the Confederate Congress, and the Confederate governors, which he struggled to avoid. "Lee holds himself utterly aloof from the disputes and passions of the hour," wrote an admiring Northern reporter. "No man more courteous than he, none more high-bred, none more generous, none more kindly in his intercourse with his neighbors," gushed the reporter, and Lee wanted it to stay that way.[11]

As the presidency of Washington College ate up more and more of his time, even the idea of writing a history of the Army of Northern Virginia gradually dissipated. He did, however, persevere with the task of preparing a fresh edition of his father's Revolutionary memoirs, and it is no small marker of how much the Lexington years allowed Robert E. Lee to finally achieve some harmony with the shadows of his youth that he could return to the memory of his father with more enthusiasm than he had shown in younger adulthood.

He had gradually been coming to terms with Light Horse Harry ever since coming into his own as a soldier and commander in 1861, when he paid his first visit to Harry Lee's grave. Now he was ready to offer a long-denied tribute to his father's life in the form of the longest written composition he would ever put to paper, a seventy-nine-page introduction to a reprinting of Harry Lee's narrative of his exploits in the Revolution's Carolina campaigns, *Memoirs of the War in the Southern Department of the United States.* Even as his interest in the Army of Northern Virginia history was evaporating, he began a second letter-writing broadcast in the summer of 1866 to locate letters of Harry Lee beyond those held by his brother Carter. For a publisher, he turned to a popular purveyor of wartime histories, Charles B. Richardson of New York, who had "called on me in Richmond & made to me . . . proposals" for publishing the army history and who now signed on to Lee's newest venture.[12]

Lee's introduction was tuned invariably to Light Horse Harry's praise as the apex of the Lee family's history in early Virginia. Light Horse Harry would become "one of the first fellows" among students at Princeton, the hero of Valley Forge, Stony Point, and Paulus Hook, the confidant of Washington and Lafayette's chief intelligence gatherer, and the innovative commander of a mixed-arms legion in Nathanael Greene's southern army. All mention of Light Horse Harry's cocky abrasiveness disappeared; his impulsive execution of deserters was limited to a single bland paragraph; and his abrupt departure from the army shortly after Yorktown was due entirely to "broken health produced by his long and arduous services." Likewise, one paragraph sufficed to marry him to Matilda Lee and make him master of Stratford.

It was more difficult for Lee to deal with Light Horse Harry's Federalism, and with it his "devotion to the Federal Government." Nevertheless, the son found a chink in his father's unionist ardor by insisting that Harry Lee had "recognized a distinction between his 'native country' "—in other words, Virginia—"and that which he had labored to associate with . . . in the strictest bonds of union." This happened to be exactly the position Lee himself claimed to occupy, and he tried to drive the distinction home by treating Light Horse Harry's role in suppressing the Whiskey Rebellion as two-tiered, because "the insurgents resisted by force of arms not only the authority of the United States but that of Pennsylvania, their 'native country.' " (Robert had to explain this to Carter: "I see no similarity in the cause or course of the Whiskey Insurrection, with the secession of the South; & am unwilling to recognize a parallel.") Matilda vanished from the narrative in a cloud of vagueness ("She is mentioned no more in their correspondence"), while Ann Carter Lee materializes as Light Horse Harry's second wife almost without introduction.

Lee was more interested in Light Horse Harry's political career as governor and member of the Virginia legislature, which allowed him to demonstrate that "the State of Virginia was his country, whose will he would obey, however lamentable the fate to which it might subject him." Not a single word hints at Harry Lee's disastrous investments, and Light Horse Harry departs Stratford for Alexandria "for the purpose of educating his children." The letters Robert borrowed from Carter (for the years of Light Horse Harry's self-imposed exile in the West Indies) were full of noble exhortations to "the practice of virtue" and the reading of classical authors, even though Harry was no telling example of the first, and Robert no practitioner in Lexington of the second. But it could only have given Lee pleasure to read his father's plea to Carter to "tell me about my dear Smith and Robert" and to learn that Harry believed that "Robert was always good, and will be confirmed in his happy turn of mind by his ever-watchful mother."[13]

Robert called these "letters of love and wisdom." They might have been better characterized as Harry Lee's pious wishes, of more or less the same seriousness as his land speculations, and the overall tone of the introduction had something of the see-no-evil attitude that marked Robert's wartime official reports. The work Robert and Carter expended on the new edition seems to have generated the worst possible reaction in Carter, who at once began dreaming again of reinvesting in the old western Virginia properties of the Lees. Robert had to talk his brother out of it: "I think when you see the ruined financial condition of the White Sulphur, Sweet Red Hot & Warm Springs, it ought to make you very cautious how you invest your means. . . . The springs I have named with all the advantages, periodically roll up a heavy debt & pass into new hands, which seem to fare as their predecessors." It was enough that the new edition of Light Horse Harry's *Memoirs* could reintroduce a fresh generation of Americans to a Revolutionary hero; it was enough that Robert could at last pay tribute, even a glowingly unrealistic tribute, to the father who had left so large a hole in his young life.

Even then, he moved cautiously. He had the manuscript of his introduction ready for Richardson in October 1867, but he was suspicious that Richardson was not "prepared to publish" and was holding out for something more interesting from Lee's pen. As late as January 1869, Lee was still dickering about the *Memoirs* with Richardson, who "promises they will be out in March." But in July, he had to tell Carter that although "I heard from Richardson that the Memoirs are in the hands of the printers, from what I hear I fear he is embarrassed"—a polite term for "bankrupt." Still, Richardson was nimble: the publisher reorganized his enterprise as the University Publishing Company (with Jefferson Davis, Joe Johnston, and Custis Lee among its three thousand stockholders), and the book would at last appear under the University Publishing imprint in the spring of 1870—when, ironically, Lee was about to pay his final visit to his father's grave.[14]

If Robert E. Lee grew at peace with himself and his past in Lexington, his family—Mary, the three daughters, and Custis, who now had a teaching post at the nearby Virginia Military Institute—did not. At the time her husband decided to accept the presidency, Mary did "not think that he is very fond of teaching," but was merely "willing to do anything that will give him honorable support." She underestimated the gusto with which he undertook the complete overhaul of the college.

He made the first journey to Lexington alone in the fall of 1865; Mary followed by canal boat from Derwent in November. The president's house had only just been vacated by a previous tenant, and much of the decorating had to be done with used curtains and carpets salvaged from Arlington at the beginning of the war. In another year, though, Lee would supervise the construction of a new president's house, under his own engineer's eye, fitted with rolling ramps for Mary's ease, which they occupied in 1869. It also had, as one observer wryly noted, a "covered way to the stable" so that Lee could "know that his horse—his favorite Traveller—was under the same roof as himself."

Lexington was a vastly different environment than Mary had ever experienced—Scots-Irish psalm singers from the valley and the surrounding mountains—and Mary admitted that while "people up here are very kind, well educated and excellent," she could never find them to be "as the friends of my earlier and happier days." Lexingtonians coolly returned the favor: Mary Lee and her three daughters "don't seem to like Lexington much, think the people stiff and formal, which is very much the case." The women of Lexington began a "reading club" in 1866, and the Lee daughters tried to join in with as much grace as they could summon. But Agnes admitted that "the reading is usually a small matter," and Agnes herself was gossiped about as having "a little haughty way about her that seems to give offense here."

There was one small Episcopal congregation in town, Grace Church, whose pastor was Lee's onetime artillery chief William Nelson Pendleton, and Lee rented a pew there, fourth row from the front. Robert himself made no remarkable devotional gestures, while Mary Lee lavished increasing amounts of her social energies on tasks and events that would build up its modest dimensions, because, as Robert wryly noticed, "the Episcopalians are few in numbers and light in purse, and must be resigned to small return." But Mary's energies were cramped by the unforgiving grip of her rheumatoid arthritis and her memories. Young Rob remembered, even during the summer at Derwent, that Mary "was a great invalid from rheumatism, and had to be lifted wherever she moved." In a cushioned wheelchair, "she could propel herself on a level floor" and with crutches could "move about her room very slowly and with great difficulty." She had the help of "the servants"—African Americans who flitted almost invisibly through references in her correspondence, like Sam, Louisa, and Esther—but she resented the difficulty she had in keeping them, because "the girls are all crowded in the cities, which they are unwilling to leave."[15]

Lee's redesign of the president's house was intended to accommodate Mary more than himself (his office was in the basement of the new college chapel). But nothing in Lexington could efface for Mary what the war had cost her. Unlike her husband, she began writing a caustic "My Reminiscences of the War, Waged Against the South by the United States Abolition Faction Immediately After the Election of Lincoln." Almost all of its seven pages were devoted to the desecration of Arlington and her denunciations of "the new code of morals that designated the defense of our rights & liberties a crime, but theft, murder, & arson military virtues." She was "entirely cut off from all that I have ever known and loved in my youth" and devoutly wished that somehow "we get rid of the Freedman's Bureau," for if we "can take the law in our hands we may perhaps do better." It infuriated her still more that in the waning days of Andrew Johnson's administration the president ordered the return to the Lees of china and furniture confiscated from Arlington, only to have to countermand the order when a congressional resolution denounced the release of the property "to the custody of any one person, much less a rebel like General Lee."

Only the coming of summer brought Mary any measure of relief, and most of those summers were spent just over the mountains at the Rockbridge Alum Springs, the White Sulphur Springs, and the Greenbrier Springs. "I think your cousin M[ary] received some benefit from her visit to the baths," Lee wrote optimistically to Annette Carter at the end of the summer of 1866. "The swelling of her feet, ankles, hands &c. with which she was troubled, was removed, and although she can walk no better, she is less sensitive to motion and pain and can ride with comfort." But, Mary admitted, "my heart yearns for the home & scenes of my past life." So did her daughters. "None ever seemed so fair to me" as Arlington, "this Kingdom of my childhood," mourned Mildred, and when she thought of Arlington, "everywhere, as far as my aching eyes could see, graves, graves, graves, in memory of the men who had robbed me of my beautiful home."[16]

For all of his public role in the life of Lexington and the college, Lee's personal circle seemed to shrink. His address book contained only eighteen entries—his brothers, Carter and Smith, his nephew Fitz Lee, Stonewall Jackson's widow, the daughter of the long-lost John Washington, and several important donors. He made a regular practice of inviting "new students to an entertainment in his home, where he would talk with them personally and learn their names," and he was frequently seen "in the stores and shops of the town," so that everyone who met him could "hand it down as an event in their history that they had a visit from General Lee!" But he made no effort to bring his old staff and generals to Lexington (the way Grant did, as president, to Washington). Although a popular lithograph was titled *Lee Kneeling at the Grave of Jackson* in Lexington, there is no evidence that any such visit ever took place. He corresponded infrequently with Longstreet, Beauregard, William Mahone, Charles Marshall, and Walter Taylor, but with hardly anyone beyond those few. In 1869, he pointedly refused an invitation from David McConaughy of Gettysburg to "a Re-Union" of all the major officers of both the Army of the Potomac and the Army of Northern Virginia "to confer together" at the Katalysine Springs Hotel (newly constructed on the site of the first day's fighting at Gettysburg) "and determine the positions and important points" of the armies during the battle. Not only did his "engagements" preclude a return visit to Gettysburg, but he thought it better "not to keep open the Sores of War, but to follow the examples of those nations who endeavour to obliterate the marks of Civil Strife & to Commit to oblivion the feelings it engendered."[17]

He was as sparing with incoming as outgoing invitations. Students who manifested romantic interests in the Lee daughters were given only the chilliest of encouragements. Gentleman callers could visit in the president's parlor, but only while the president read aloud to his wife in the dining room, and at ten o'clock Lee would begin closing the shutters, the sign that it was time for visitors to go. Frankly, Lee did not want his daughters to marry, although he had no similar objection to Rooney's remarriage to Mary Tabb Bolling in November 1867. He hoped that Agnes "had made up her mind to eschew weddings and stick to her papa," and he warned Mildred that "notwithstanding all appearances to the contrary, you will never receive such a love as is felt for you by your mother and father."

He was a man with friends and no friend, except for Traveller, and it was with Traveller that he took long and often lonely rides over the green-felted mountains above Lexington. Occasionally, one of his daughters might accompany him; occasionally it was Helen White, the daughter of one of the college's professors (who remembered that Lee "never talked of the war to us, nor said anything to make you think he was an awe-inspiring general"). "My only pleasure now is a solitary ride over the mountains," he told Annette Carter. "Traveller is my only companion; I may say my only pleasure. He and I, whenever practicable, wander out in the mountains and enjoy sweet confidence."[18]

Lee's family could not afford to complain too much about their narrowed life in Lexington, if only because Lee's health was becoming a much more looming worry. The man whom Brady had captured on photographic plates in 1865 showed no signs of the two heart attacks he had suffered. When he was summoned to Washington in February 1866 to be grilled by the Reconstruction Committee, Alexander Gardner lured him into his Seventh and D Street studio to take four sitting poses, and they show a thickly bearded but clear-eyed college president in a sober suit of black.

These proved to be very popular images, especially in the fashionable *carte de visite* format, and Lee was forced to order a hundred extra *cartes de visite* from Gardner to keep up with the demand for autographed pictures. Brady, willing to lose nothing to Gardner, also persuaded Lee to come around to his Pennsylvania Avenue studio for four more sittings, and a sitting Lee gave to Charles Rees in Richmond in the fall of 1867 made him look so relaxed and assured that Lee thought his image in the photographs "looked more like a prosperous Southern gentleman than a defeated warrior." By 1869, however, photographs of Lee taken by Michael Miley in Lexington show a face slack with signs of enfeeblement, and a group photograph taken at White

Sulphur Springs at the time of his political letter for Rosecrans clearly shows an aging man. In his last photograph, once more taken by Miley, Lee appears near dozing.[19]

The appearances were not deceiving. As early as the summer of 1867, Lee was complaining of weariness and fatigue, to the point where he wondered to Rooney whether by the following year, having "done all the good I can for the college," he "should . . . retire to some quiet spot, east of the mountains." There, contemplating his own mortality, "I might prepare a home for your mother and sisters after my death." His visit to White Sulphur Springs that summer was marred by vaguely defined illnesses: he was, he explained to Carter Lee, "detained in the mountains three weeks by sickness," and he warned the college faculty that he was "so feeble that the Dr is reluctant for me to make the journey" back to Lexington in time for the commencement of the new academic year. He rushed to reassure Carter, "I am improving slowly," but it is entirely possible that he had suffered a third heart attack.

Once again, he tried to dismiss the problem as a severe cold, but he admitted to Markie Williams that "it seems to me if all the sickness I ever had in all my life was put together, it would not equal the attack I experienced." By the end of October, he could tell Carter that he was finally "able to attend to my duties" at the college; even so, "I am not yet well." But he wanted no one to be alarmed. At his age, he reminded Edward Lee Childe, "I have probably reached that stage of life when I can no longer expect to be exempt from disease."[20]

Just how little these cavalier dismissals really meant became apparent in the summer of 1868, when the family set off for their usual warm-weather pilgrimage to the mountains. This time he left Traveller behind. He was no longer well enough to make the cross-mountain journey on horseback. "I think I am better than when I came here," he told Edward Gordon, his college secretary, at the beginning of September 1868, and "hope I shall continue to improve." And for a while he did. He was reminded of mortality yet again when his brother Smith Lee "died suddenly" on July 22, 1869, "a grievous affliction to me which I must bear as well as I can." He had been with Smith only seven weeks before in Alexandria. But he was cheered by the pending appearance of Light Horse Harry's *Memoirs,* and he felt enough return of strength to allow himself to be drafted as president of the local Rockbridge County Bible Society, made a life member of the Lynchburg Agricultural & Mechanical Society, an honorary member of Lexington's Franklin Society & Library Company, and a delegate to the annual convention of the Episcopal Diocese of Virginia.[21]

He began to discover, after years dreading the stigma of treason, that he was a celebrity across the white South, and even some parts of the North.

Buoyed up on the popularity of the Lost Cause, Lee became the symbol of the South's nobility in the face of ignoble defeat. "One name has magic power in the South," declared the *Richmond Dispatch.* "What tribute can we pay to him, whom no words of praise can reach?" A Richmond journalist, James McCabe, published a worshipful 717-page biography, *Life and Campaigns of General Robert E. Lee,* wishing him a "peaceful and modest retirement" in Lexington, "surrounded by the love and respect of his countrymen, and the admiration of those in all lands that honor the Christian soldier, who, having been charged with the fate of a nation, never failed in his duty, but was faithful to the end." Parents sent him notice that sons had been named for him (he dutifully advised Marquis Lafayette Karr of Carrollton, Kentucky, to raise Robert E. Lee Karr so that "truthfulness, integrity, & piety, & . . . virtue & usefulness may be his constant aim"), and after the Episcopal diocesan convention adjourned in Fredericksburg in May 1869, he was so beset by admirers and well-wishers that "I soon took refuge in Alexandria" with Cassius Francis Lee—where "my old friends and neighbors" besieged him all over again. "So large a number of friends called upon the General," according to the Baltimore newspapers, "that it was arranged for him to have a reception at the Mansion House, where for three hours a constant stream of visitors poured into the reception room." In August, when he went to Richmond for the baptism of Rooney's newborn son (and yet another namesake), "great numbers came to call on him" again, "so that he was compelled to hold an informal reception in the large parlours" of the Exchange Hotel. A steamer bearing his name plied the Mississippi; the Louisiana Base Ball Park Association named one of its clubs for "R. E. Lee."[22]

But in October, he suffered another "attack of cold" that proved "very severe," to the point where "rapid exercise on horseback or on foot produced pain and difficulty in breathing." This was, in all likelihood, his fourth heart attack, and it was, if not the most severe, certainly the longest lasting in its effects. He was still suffering from his "wretched cold" when he wrote to Rooney at the beginning of December, and although he forced himself back to his regimen of riding, he admitted that "Traveller's trot is harder to me than it used to be and fatigues me." He remained so ill in January that he could not attend the funeral of George Peabody, embarrassing as that appeared for a Northern donor who had been so generous to the college, and Lee was sensitive enough to the look of his absence that he explained to another major donor that as much as "it would be some relief to witness the respect paid to [Peabody's] remains & participate in commemorating his virtues . . . I have been sick all the winter and am still under medical treatment."

He returned to his rides on Traveller "when the weather permits." But the winter of 1870 was particularly harsh, with snow on the ground in Lexington until March, and he admitted to Mildred that although "I am getting better, I hope . . . I cannot walk much farther than to the college." He was even more candid, and more clinical, with Edward Lee Childe. "I have been unable to do more than to attend to my ordinary business & writing is more irksome than it was, nor is confinement advantageous," he wrote to his nephew in Paris. "The affection in my chest under which I labour, adhesion of the lungs & pleura or whatever it is, incapacitates me from exertion & as yet I cannot walk farther than from my house to the College without pain, & I have to proceed carefully at that." Even in March, he was complaining to Childe, "I still feel the effects of . . . pains through my body & chest."[23]

Lee's failure to throw off his "cold" now attracted the alarmed attention of the faculty, trustees, and even students of the college. "I don't think I ever saw a man break down more rapidly than he has in the last year," one student wrote. On March 17, a faculty committee, noticing that Lee "was evidently labouring under great depression of spirits," presented him with a series of faculty resolutions, urging him "to take at once a journey and a couple of months' relaxation" and allow "a professor to attend to his duties during his absence." The realization that he had not been able to conceal his failing health evidently depressed him still more. But he admitted that "he was old" and "felt he might at any moment die," and finally he agreed. The trustees ratified the faculty proposal, and within a week he had laid out an itinerary for a restorative journey southward (with Agnes as his "kind and uncomplaining nurse") to Richmond, to Warrenton, North Carolina, "to visit my dear Annie's grave before I die," and thence to Savannah.[24]

The trip did Lee more good than he might have imagined. The first leg, to Richmond, proved "a more comfortable journey than I had expected," and the doctors he consulted in Richmond "examined me for two hours" and left him feeling "better than when I left Lexington, certainly stronger." But the real tonic was the rapturous reception he received at every point. The Virginia Senate unanimously adopted a resolution to offer Lee "the privileges of the floor" (he declined, pleading "the condition of my health"), and when his train passed through Raleigh, crowds chanted, "Lee! Lee!" There were no crowds waiting at Warrenton, which allowed him to visit Annie's grave in peace on March 29, and though he found "my visit . . . mournful," it was somehow "soothing to my feelings." But in Charlotte "a large number of citizens went to the depot to get a sight of the distinguished gentleman," and when Lee tried to avoid them, the city's mayor beseeched him to come out and "show himself on the platform." At Columbia, "several hundred citizens" assembled at the depot to greet Lee, and a delegation of his old officers, headed by Porter Alexander, elbowed their way up to the rear platform of Lee's train to shake hands with their old commander.

When they arrived in Augusta, Lee had to submit to being driven through the city in a carriage so that "all eyes" could "catch a view of the features of the noble patriot and Christian gentleman whose presence had awakened such universal interest." Savannah outdid itself, with crowds and bands and, as the apex, "the Messrs. Mackay got down from Etowah . . . all of my former acquaintances and many new ones," including no one less than Joe Johnston, with whom he sat for three photographs at Ryan's Gallery. Savannah gave him the excuse for a further side trip; he and Agnes took a coastal steamer down to Florida's St. Johns River, but en route they stopped at Cumberland Island, and there he paid his last visit to the man whose shadow had cast, by its vacancy, so vast an influence. "We visited Cumberland Island," he wrote to Mary, "and Agnes decorated my father's grave with beautiful fresh flowers. I presume it is the last time I shall be able to pay to it my tribute of respect."[25]

Lee spent more time with doctors in Savannah, who "examined me for about an hour" and concluded that "my trouble arises from some adhesion of the parts, not from any injury of the lungs and heart." That optimistic judgment sat ill beside "the pain along the breast bone," which "ever returns on my making any exertion." But he was already chafing to return home, and on April 25 he left Savannah on the return journey, once more wading through crowds and bands in Charleston, Wilmington, and Norfolk. In Charleston, Lee was greeted by "Dixie" and "The Bonnie Blue Flag" and "three-times-three cheers" from "not less than two thousand persons . . . all of whom united in paying their respect to their loved chieftain"; in Wilmington, "he was received with patriotic enthusiasm by all, and the corps of cadets paid him military respect"; in Norfolk, the crowds were led by Walter Taylor, and "the air, during his passage through the assemblage, was vocal with shouts of welcome to the old chieftain . . . not of the measured 'hip-hip-hurrah' kind now in vogue, but . . . the genuine, old-fashioned Confederate yells."

From Norfolk, he turned inland to visit Shirley Plantation, another nod in the direction of both his mother and his father, where he was received with almost the awe of a classical deity. "How lovely he was to all of us girls," wrote one of the Carter daughters, and they returned the kindness with near worship. "We regarded him with the greatest veneration. We had heard of God, but here was General Lee!" He moved on to Rooney's rebuilt home at White House, where he rendezvoused with Mary (who had come down by canal boat), and to young Rob at Romancoke, and finally to Richmond for more doctor's consultations, before at last returning to Lexington on May 28.[26]

Lee wanted to believe that the journey had done its work in restoring his health. "I feel benefited by my visit to the South; am stronger & have less rheumatic pains," he wrote to the college faculty, although it was true that "the pain in my chest is ever present when I make any exertion & I still have a cough though it is not troublesome." He presided at the college's commencement, wrote letters of commendation, joined a meeting of the stockholders of the Valley Railroad Company to promote railroad construction to link the Shenandoah with eastern Virginia, and, surprisingly, visited Cassius Francis Lee at his country farm, Menokin, to discuss a legal strategy for the recovery of Arlington. He had no desire actually to reoccupy Arlington: the grounds were now a cemetery, and any "prospect" of literally repossessing the property "is not promising." But so long as G.W.P.'s estate remained unresolved, there was always the chance that some form of cash settlement could be extracted from the federal government that would allow Lee to pay off all the requirements G.W.P. had imposed more than a decade before.[27]

At the opening faculty meeting in September, his energies seemed so restored that William Preston Johnston sensed "an unusual elation . . . at the increased prospect that long years of usefulness and honor would yet be added to his glorious life." In the valley, the summer weather had been unusually dry since July, but on September 17 the "blessed rain has come at last," and then, on September 28, there came "a tremendous rain-storm . . . pouring in torrents" so that "all modes of travel have been interrupted." That morning, Lee waded through the usual academic paperwork in his office, dashing off a note to Samuel H. Tagart, a Baltimore lawyer, assuring him that "in time I may improve still more." He went home for a late lunch and then sat through an extended meeting of the little Episcopal church's vestry. He walked back through the rain and the litter of leaves and tree branches to his house at seven thirty, shrugged off his streaming "military cape," and stood at the dinner table to say a brief grace.[28]

What came out was only a mumble, and then nothing.

Mildred remembered that he was "looking very strange—& speaking incoherently." He sat down. Mary thought he was simply tired and tried to pour him a cup of tea, but the look on his face "alarmed me." He still could not speak. Two doctors who were members of the vestry were still in easy hailing distance, and they were brought into the house to examine Lee, where they had the ailing general laid out on a cot by the dining room fireplace. He had had a stroke, although the actual severity of it was not clear. He quickly recovered some speech facility, but he continued to lie "straight & motionless," responding to frantic questions with little more than a nod of the head, and occasionally a short phrase: "I am so weary."

Outside, the weather whipped itself into a torrent that overflowed creeks and rivers and submerged roads, with the wind lacing the downward rods of rain against the windows. In Staunton, bridges were swept away; in Lynchburg, the gasworks were flooded, "and the city was left in total darkness." Inside the president's house, Lee "slept almost continuously" for two days and two nights; thereafter, he lay conscious but inert, sometimes speaking but only in short bursts.[29]

The news that filtered through the churning storm mentioned Lee's illness for the first time only on October 4, and only then to announce that "Gen. Lee is very decidedly better to-day, and his friends and his physicians pronounce him out of danger." He was only suffering from what the *Staunton Spectator* called "unusual fatigue," and *The Norfolk Virginian* even claimed that he was "quite cheerful and communicative." He was neither. When one of his doctors, Robert L. Madison, tried to rouse him with expectations by saying, "You must haste and get well; Traveller has been standing so long in the stable that he needs exercise," Lee merely "shook his head and closed his eyes." He would sometimes relent and accept medications but at other times would helplessly whisper, "It is of no use." By October 7, the newspaper reports were turning dark "in anticipation of the death of General Lee." Mary, in her wheelchair, stayed with him, "always greeted . . . with an outstretched hand & kindly pressure."

Then, on Monday the tenth, "during the afternoon," his pulse became irregular "and his breathing hurried." What the stroke had not done, his weakened heart would finish. He sank into a coma, his mind wandering, giving orders to armies only he could see. "Tell Hill he *must* come up!" Rooney and young Rob were on their way to Lexington; "Daughter" Mary was in the Midwest and had no chance of reaching them; Custis, Agnes, and Mildred had joined the death watch, Agnes "kneeling by his side—moistening his lips—fanning him—he lying on his right side—drawing long hard breaths." Mary "sat with his hand in mine all moist with heavy perspiration," until the morning of Wednesday, October 12, when his breathing became labored and he seemed gasping for air. "These became more frequent and intense & after 2 very severe ones, his breath seemed to pass away gently." At the end, somewhere in the darkening recesses of his mind, he knew the last battle was over. "Strike the tent," Lee gasped. And he was gone, finally escaping as he had always striven to escape in this life the imperfections and the insecurities that had always shadowed his days.[30]

An old man's wit may wander ere he die.
Rain, rain, and sun! a rainbow on the lea! . . .
Rain, sun, and rain! and the free blossom blows:
Sun, rain, and sun! and where is he who knows?
From the great deep to the great deep he goes.

Epilogue: The Crime and the Glory of Robert E. Lee

General Lee—Death of the Great Southern Chief," ran the headline the next day in *The New York Herald,* and its coverage wept unaccustomed Northern tears. "Here in the North, forgetting that the time was when the sword of Robert Edmund [*sic*] Lee was drawn against us—forgetting and forgiving all the years of bloodshed and agony—we have long since ceased to look upon him as the Confederate leader, but have claimed him as one of ourselves." Even Horace Greeley's *New-York Tribune,* the most resolutely antislavery newspaper in America for decades, conceded that "Lee was not absolutely without honor and even affection in the North," and "while hot tears flow for him" in the South, "a sympathy, not unallied to pity, will be felt for him here." In Philadelphia, *The Evening Telegraph* promised that "the passionate feelings engendered by the conflict have so far died away that there is a general disposition to dwell upon his personal virtues rather than to follow him to the grave with denunciations." Lee had come to the surrender at Appomattox as though it were a stage, without any notice of catcalls that might have greeted him, and walked wordlessly away into the wings of the postwar years without flinging a single gesture of public rage at his condemners and with such dignity as to turn the catcalls into thunderous applause.[1]

Below the Potomac, even the slightest reservations fell away in an upwelling of grief and honorifics. In Richmond, church bells tolled from sunrise to sunset, and the news "brought sorrow to the heart of every man, woman, and child in the city, and ere an hour had passed, the whole community was shrouded in gloom." Stores along the main streets closed and photographs of Lee, hung in crepe, appeared in windows. The legislature and city council proclaimed days of mourning, and formal resolutions were adopted requesting that "General Lee may be buried in the State section at Hollywood," the cemetery already filled with Virginia's Civil War dead. In Alexandria, where he had grown up, all the town offices and stores on King Street "are draped in mourning . . . the flags of the steamers and shipping in port are flying at half mast"—where they could be seen conspicuously across the river in Washington—"and the bells of the city are tolled at intervals." Alexandria, too, hoped "that his remains would be brought here for interment." *The New-Orleans Times* suspended the publication of its evening edition "as a mark of respect to the memory of General Lee." Even in Britain, *The Pall Mall Gazette* ranked him "among the great men of the present time" and predicted that "when political animosity has calmed down, and when Americans can look back on those years of war with feelings unbiased by party strife, then will General Lee's character be appreciated by all his countrymen as it is now by a part, and his name will be honored as that of one of the noblest soldiers who have ever drawn a sword in a cause which they believed just."[2]

The regrets were not, however, uniform. Frederick Douglass complained, after wading through the obituaries for Lee, that "we can scarcely take up a newspaper . . . that is not filled with *nauseating* flatteries of the late Robert E. Lee" and his "bad cause." Douglass was not surprised that many of these tributes came "from the South," but he was amazed that "many Northern journals also join in these undeserved tributes to his name." Douglass wanted to remind readers that "if Lee has gone to heaven we are sincerely glad of it," but he did so in spite of "the liberation of four millions of slaves and their elevation to manhood." When a motion was made to adjourn the Court of Common Pleas of New York in Lee's honor, the presiding judge refused, because "he was not sufficiently known as a member of the bar to entitle him to the honor." The unionist Reconstruction mayor of New Orleans, Benjamin Flanders, was so irked at the displays he saw from an uptown streetcar that he burst out, "Where's the use in all this nonsense?" Lee was "a very ordinary, commonplace man," argued Flanders, and the mayor refused to hang crepe on city hall. "I think it safe to say," declared Vermont's U.S. senator George F. Edmunds, that no one "has committed the crime of treason against more light, against better opportunities of knowing he was committing it," than Lee.

Nor did the denunciations end there. The Soldiers' and Sailors' Union League (a forerunner of the Grand Army of the Republic) angrily lamented, "in the name of the defenceless heroes who perished at Andersonville, Belle Isle, and Libby," that Lee had been placed "beyond the jurisdiction of the military tribunals of the land, before which he could have been summoned to answer to the charge of treason, and received the reward of a traitor." In

Savannah, the collector of the Customs House, T. R. Robb, was incensed to discover that his deputy had put the U.S. flag at half-mast, and ordered it hoisted to the top. In Atlanta, James Fitzpatrick—"a degenerate son of the 'Emerald Isle' "—stood up in the middle of a mass meeting honoring Lee and read a "protest" against memorializing "a man who, more than all the others, attempted to destroy the best government under the sun."[3]

But these voices were drowned in the chorus of Lee hallelujahs. In Lexington, bells tolled, both Washington College and the Virginia Military Institute suspended classes until after the funeral, and "even the colored barbers" prudently "shut up their shops." Despite Richmond's plea to have Lee buried in the onetime Confederate capital, neither Lexington nor Mary Lee had any intention of allowing Lee's burial to occur anywhere far afield, and Custis Lee gracefully but firmly informed the legislature that "the remains have been committed to the authorities of Washington College."

Lee's body was dressed in a "simple suit of black," and because the furious rains of the weeks before had made shipment of a coffin from Richmond impossible, a slightly undersized one had to be retrieved from the banks of the James River, where it had washed up during the storms. Lee was then carried to the college chapel by an "escort of honor, consisting of officers and soldiers of the late Confederate army," by Traveller ("the old gray war horse . . . with saddle and bridle covered with crepe"), and by the trustees, faculty, and students of both Washington College and VMI. There, in the chapel Lee had designed, the body was watched over by "a students' guard of honor," with the coffin "open, allowing mourners to gaze upon the face of their friend, general, and president one last time."

> *All pressed forward, men, women and children, to take one last, long look at the face—that face which had been to them a pillar of fire by night, and a cloud by day, during the long, weary days of the rebellion—and then retired, fearing to stay longer, lest their self-possession should give way.*

An Episcopal service was conducted by William Nelson Pendleton, who preached from verses of Psalm 37: "The steps of a good man are ordered by the Lord: and he delighteth in his way. Though he fall, he shall not be utterly cast down: for the Lord upholdeth him with his hand." And Pendleton pressed them for all they were worth. "Of him may it reverently be said . . . the Lord delighted in his way." It was true, Pendleton had to acknowledge, that Lee had not always been "in the full communion of the Church," but he was quick to add that "the law of God was, I doubt not . . . 'in his heart.' "[4]

Lee was buried "in a brick vault" in the basement of the college chapel on

Saturday the fifteenth, after a public procession that wound from the chapel through the streets of Lexington and then finally back to the chapel, while artillery from VMI fired salutes every three minutes, "the sudden thunder" of the guns awaking echoes from the mountains. "Every class, young and old, rich and poor, white and black, turned out to do him honor, for he was the friend of all." The break in the weather allowed Walter Taylor and Charles Venable to reach Lexington for the ceremonies, and all through the town "the buildings were all appropriately draped, and crowds gathered on corners and in the balconies to see the procession pass." In a quiet nod to the political realities of Reconstruction, no Confederate flags were in view—VMI instead flew "the flags of all of the States of the late Southern Confederacy"—and "the old soldiers" in the procession "wore their ordinary citizens' dress, with a simple black ribbon in the lapel of their coats." At the chapel, Pendleton read the Episcopal burial office, but "no sermon was preached, it having been the desire of General Lee that there should be none," and as a hymn was sung, the coffin, "literally strewed with flowers, which had to be removed separately," was lowered into the chapel's basement, to lie under a marble slab that bore only the inscription:[5]

Gen. Robert Edward Lee,
Born Jan 11, 1807
Died Oct 12, 1870.

It represented one final departure from perfection: as the *Richmond Dispatch* ruefully admitted on October 20, "there seems also to be some discrepancy as to the date of his birth."

The trustees were aware of how much the college stood to lose by Lee's death, and in order to keep Lee's association with the college as prominent as possible, they met on the day of Lee's funeral to propose a "suitable monument" in the college chapel for Lee's remains and an amendment of the college charter to rename it Washington and Lee. Even before Lee was buried, the Lee Memorial Association had been called into being in Lexington to supervise the monument, and within days Mary Lee had given her approval to a plan to rebuild the apse of the college chapel (which would also be renamed the Lee Chapel) as a mausoleum for her husband's coffin, with a new crypt on the basement level and an honorific space for the monument on the level above, opening out into the chapel itself. (All of the members of Lee's immediate family, including Light Horse Harry, would eventually be buried there, too.)

The upper level of the new apse would feature the monument, a recumbent statue not unlike the tomb effigies of European monarchs. The model for Lee's face would be a bust of Lee made by a Richmond sculptor, Edward Virginius Valentine, back in the spring of 1870, and Valentine himself was summoned to Lexington as the most logical sculptor for the tomb effigy. Valentine met with the Memorial Association in November 1870, armed with a variety of photographs and drawings of historic European funeral statuary. Of them all, Mary Lee's preference ran to the recumbent sculpture that adorns the tomb of the nineteenth-century king of Prussia, Friedrich Wilhelm III, in Charlottenburg Castle. (This posed no problem for Valentine, because the Charlottenburg tomb effigy had been sculpted by Christian Daniel Rauch, and Valentine had studied under Rauch's star pupil, August Kiss, in Berlin.) Like Lee, Friedrich Wilhelm had resisted a powerful invader; hence, the king's tomb sculpture shows him in battle dress, dozing under a light blanket, as if ready at any moment for the trumpet's blast. Valentine would follow this model, down to the exposed boots of both king and general, so that Lee would appear (like the Prussian monarch) as if "lying asleep on his field cot during the campaigns of the war," in full Confederate uniform, resting his left hand on a half-hidden sword. The Memorial Association wanted no mere obelisks or tablets; they wanted an Arthurian figure, ready to awake and lead his people to renewed warfare, and Valentine gave it to them.[6]

However, the Reconstruction South was not flowing with cash, and it took another four and a half years before Valentine completed the commission, in marble. It took eight years more for sufficient funds to be raised by the association to have Baltimore architect J. Crawford Neilson make the alterations needed in the chapel. Not until 1883 could Lee be reburied in the new crypt, and Valentine's memorial be appropriately installed on the level above, flanked by portraits (of Lee, Washington, Jefferson, and other Southern worthies) rescued from Arlington. Despite Lee's refusal, in the postwar years, to encourage displays of Southern military nostalgia, Valentine's recumbent Lee is very much the general (and in 1930 twelve Confederate battle flags, reminiscent of the flags displayed at Napoleon's tomb in Les Invalides, were ranged around Valentine's sculpture).[7]

The dedication ceremonies, in June 1883, were yet another occasion for choruses of praise for Lee. While the "President and Congress of the United States made conditions of pardon and absolution" that rendered Reconstruction intolerable, orated John Warwick Daniel (a Confederate veteran who was positioning himself as one of the Lost Cause's chief remembrancers), Lee benignly and "thoroughly understood and accepted the situation." Lee "realized fully that the war had settled . . . the peculiar issues which had embroiled it," but he was determined to share the South's "humiliation," and even though he was "indicted for treason . . . never word of bitterness escaped him; but, on the contrary, only counsels of forbearance, patience and diligent attention to works of restoration." He had become a kind of Southern redeemer, bearing the South's cross (for whose "issues" he had done nothing himself to acquire guilt) and urging nothing afterward but forgiveness for the madmen who had inflicted his, and the South's, pain.[8]

Other ex-Confederates with ambitions to speak for the postwar South also pinned their reputation onto the tails of Lee's coat. Hardly had the Lee Memorial Association surged into action than the rival Lee Monument Association, headed by Jubal Early, burst onto the scene to demand that a bigger and better monument to Lee be erected in Richmond. The two associations alternately offered cooperation and denunciation of each other, with the most dramatic moment occurring in 1872, when the Lee Memorial Association unwisely invited Early to speak in Lexington in honor of Lee's birthday. Early had no intention of surrendering to Lexington his own project for a Lee monument in Richmond, and he justified that project by claiming the mantle of protector of Lee's military reputation. "Very few, comparatively, have formed a really correct estimate of his marvellous ability and boldness as a military commander," Early announced, and from that point Early declared war on any potential rivals for Southern admiration—not Jefferson Davis, not Stonewall Jackson, not Pierre Beauregard, not James Longstreet, not Joe Johnston nor Albert Sidney Johnston, but Lee and Lee only was the mastermind of the Confederacy. Far from being a rival, "General Jackson had always appreciated, and sympathized with the bold conceptions of the commanding General, and entered upon their execution with the most cheerful alacrity and zeal." And far from being reliable, James Longstreet had cost Lee victory at Gettysburg for not executing Lee's "plans with that confidence and faith necessary to success" and thus guaranteeing that victory "was not achieved." Echoing Lee himself, Early claimed that "had General Lee's orders been promptly and rigidly carried out by his subordinates," the Peninsula Campaign would have ended in "a crushing defeat" for the Union. Notwithstanding the Lost Orders, Antietam was "one of the most remarkable battles of the war" and the overall Maryland campaign "had been a grand success."

Even at Appomattox, Early insisted, "the vast superiority of the Confederate Commander over his antagonist, in all the qualities of a great Captain, and of the Confederate soldier over the Northern, were made most manifest to the dullest comprehension, and none were made more sensible of it than our adversaries. General Lee had not been conquered in battle, but surrendered because he had no longer an army with which to give battle."

No, my friends, it is a vain work for us to seek anywhere for a parallel to the great character which has won our admiration and love. Our beloved

Chief stands, like some lofty column which rears its head among the highest, in grandeur, simple, pure and sublime, needing no borrowed lustre; and he is all our own.

To the suffering servant had been added the image of the perfect miracle worker, and in at least one Lee legend "a riding switch" that he stuck into the ground at Appomattox took root, and "now a tree stands as a living testimony."[9]

Early's address positioned him—and his association—as Lee's chief lionizers. Although the Lee Memorial Association hoped that the Lee Chapel would remake Lexington into a "Mecca, visited by caravans of Summer wanderers, who come to do honor" to Lee, the authority of Lexington's Lee was usurped by Early, and in 1900 the Lee Monument Association erected its far more dramatic equestrian Lee statue in Richmond. Another twelve Lee statues would be erected by 2003 (including in New Orleans in 1884, at Gettysburg in 1917, at Charlottesville and on the face of Stone Mountain, Georgia, in 1924, at the University of Texas in Austin in 1933, in Baltimore in 1948, and most recently on private property adjacent to the Antietam National Battlefield—all of them clothing him in the Confederate military uniform that in his last years he deliberately eschewed).

Mary Custis Lee did not live to see any of these monuments unveiled. She mourned her husband, but she mourned Arlington even more. She "did not think I can die in peace till I have seen it once more," and in 1872, while visiting Ravensworth, she got her wish. She was not prepared for it to make her happy, and it didn't. "I could not have realized that it was Arlington but for the few old oaks they had spared & the trees planted on the lawn by the Genl & myself." She grimly petitioned Congress for the return of her father's Washington artifacts that had been removed and stored during the war in the U.S. Patent Office and in 1872 made a bid for compensation for Arlington from the federal government, all to no avail. In the fall of 1873, Agnes fell ill, probably of dysentery, and died on October 15, holding the New Testament Orton Williams had given her a decade earlier. The death of Agnes crushed Mary; three weeks later, she was dead, too, and was buried in the vault beside her husband.[10]

It was Custis, the titular heir of Arlington, who managed to retrieve compensation from the federal government for the loss of his grandfather's estate. In 1874, rising on the tide of decisions from the U.S. Supreme Court that began with *Bennett v. Hunter,* Custis filed a test suit in *Lee v. Chase* for the recovery of the mill at Arlington and won a judgment that declared that the tax commissioners had exceeded their statutory authority in 1864 when they refused payment of the Arlington taxes by "agents and friends of absent owners." In 1877, Custis initiated a new action for the recovery of the entire Arlington property, dodging the U.S. government's sovereign immunity from civil action and instead suing the Army officers and the residents of the Freedmen's Village who had occupied the estate, and in 1882 the U.S. Supreme Court handed down a 5–4 decision that invalidated the tax sale of Arlington.

Custis had no more intention than his father of actually repossessing Arlington and uprooting the federal dead who had been buried on the grounds there since 1864; he asked instead for $200,000 in compensation and finally settled for $150,000 the following February. It was, sadly, the high point of his life. Eager to keep the Lee name in front of their donors, the trustees of the newly renamed Washington and Lee University appointed Custis to succeed his father as president. It was a job he disliked and one from which he frequently attempted to resign, frankly describing himself as "utterly useless here, with but little probability of ever being more useful to the university." Enrollments and donations plummeted, and in 1897 the trustees grudgingly accepted yet another attempt at resignation. He lived out his final years in seclusion (especially after fracturing his hip in a fall in 1911) at Ravensworth until his death on February 18, 1913.[11]

Custis's brothers, Rooney and Rob, enjoyed more fulfilling careers. Rooney never made it to his father's bedside in Lexington, but he did succeed in rebuilding White House and fathered two sons, George Bolling Lee and Robert E. Lee III, to carry on the Lee name. When old Anna Maria Fitzhugh died in April 1874, Rooney inherited Ravensworth and moved there. The following year, he was elected to the Virginia legislature, and in 1886 was elected to Congress from Virginia's Eighth Congressional District (although as a former Confederate officer, enabling legislation under the terms of the Fourteenth Amendment had to be passed to permit him to serve). Like his father, Rooney "was a born gentleman . . . a strikingly handsome man, tall, erect, and in height several inches over six feet." He died on October 15, 1891, again like his father, of heart failure. Ravensworth was inherited by his son George Bolling Lee but burned to the ground in 1926, taking with it many of Rooney's papers and allowing numerous Lee artifacts to appear mysteriously in Alexandria antiques shops. (George Bolling Lee would live to receive an honorary degree in 1934 from Gettysburg College, on the grounds his grandfather had fought for in 1863, along with Ulysses S. Grant III.)

Rob married Mildred's friend Charlotte Haxall in 1871, only to lose her to tuberculosis less than a year later. He did not remarry until twenty-two years later, to Juliet Carter. He was the only member of the general's immediate family to write a memoir of him, *Recollections and Letters of General*

Robert E. Lee, published in 1904, but it was a major contribution to the growing biographical pile, and a surprisingly unstiff and affectionate view from within an otherwise tightly buttoned family circle. Rob and Juliet Lee had two daughters, yet another Anne Carter Lee and yet another Mary Custis Lee, the latter of whom followed in her father's footsteps by editing Agnes Lee's journal of her girlhood at West Point and Arlington, *Growing Up in the 1850s* (1984), which also included two brief recollections from 1884 and 1890 by Mildred Lee.

Mildred, who divided time between Romancoke and Lexington when she was not traveling, died in 1905 in New Orleans, followed by Rob in January 1916. The last of the Lee siblings, Mary, was also the most adventurous, making four round-the-world trips (including a venture north of the Arctic Circle with Mildred in 1879) and horrifying white Virginia society by occupying "the portion reserved for colored people" on a Washington, Alexandria, & Mount Vernon streetcar. She had "a reputation for extreme haughtiness" and "was as unrestrained in her speech as she was unconventional in her conduct." Mary died on November 22, 1918, and, charting her own course to the end, was the only Lee to be cremated.[12]

By that time, the shelf of Lee biographies to which Rob had contributed was groaning under the weight of adoration. The McCabe biography was already in circulation before Lee's death (although Lee declined to read it and was irked at McCabe's claim to have been "a member of my staff" during the war). John Esten Cooke, who had been a member of J. E. B. Stuart's staff and published a "Life" of Stonewall Jackson "from official papers" in 1866, produced a Lee biography within five months of Lee's death that hailed him as a "military genius," but even more as "a genuinely honest man, incapable of duplicity in thought or deed, wholly good and sincere." In a narrative of 501 pages, Cooke devoted only 22 to Lee's life before 1861; virtually everything else positioned Lee not only "among the greatest soldiers of history" but as the "noblest illustration of . . . dignity and moderation."

Cooke claimed to have been working on the project for four years with Lee's "consent and approval," but he was almost at once overshadowed by the publication, less than a year later, of Emily Virginia Mason's *Popular Life of Gen. Robert Edward Lee,* whose title page proclaimed that it was "dedicated by permission to Mrs. Lee." Mason certainly had the inside track: she was a cousin of Smith Lee's wife and had earned a reputation during the war as the Florence Nightingale of the Confederate nursing service. And she was determined that "a cold history of his campaigns was not wanted." Mason, instead, provided "the story of his inner life, of his domestic virtues." For Mason, Lee was the model "of self-restraint and self-denial." But the "most distinguishing trait of his character" was "his unaffected sweetness" and "generous kindness," which Mason illustrated by family letters and Lee's own papers, borrowed from Mary and from Custis.

Not even Mason, though, could speak with the authority of Lee's nephew Edward Lee Childe, writing from Paris in 1875, in *The Life and Campaigns of General Lee.* Of course, Childe had known Lee personally only in the general's last years, and even then intermittently, when Childe visited from Europe, and so the book devoted only eleven pages to Lee's life before 1861. After that, Childe's *Life and Campaigns* is almost entirely a history of the campaigns rather than the life. There were fewer than a dozen of Lee's letters in the book, and Childe's principal aim remained to offer "further and greater proof of his superiority" as a "model of military skilfulness." But Childe, inevitably, took up Mason's declaration that Lee's life was characterized by "a paternal sweetness," which his soldiers recognized "amid the tiresomeness of the march and in the tumult of battle" by crying aloud, "*There is Uncle Robert.*" Ironically, the last five years of Lee's life, when Childe was in frequent correspondence with his uncle, received only eleven pages.[13]

The Lee Memorial Association in Lexington hoped to stake its claim to Lee biography by publishing a volume of memorial essays by Lee associates, but the project broke down when Charles Marshall, who was designated the lead contributor, backed out. Into the vacuum created by Marshall stepped the Lexington Baptist pastor John William Jones, who had served as a Confederate chaplain during the war. He belonged to the circle of local clergy whom Lee invited to deliver public prayers in the Washington College chapel for the students, and when the memorial volume project fell apart, Jones eagerly proffered his services and guided into publication *Personal Reminiscences of General Robert E. Lee* in August 1874. The book was a mishmash of reminiscences, letters, addresses, and essays, but it was valuable for bringing between two covers a wide sampling of Lee letters that Jones had been able to borrow from Mary Lee before her death (the book is dedicated to her for "her kind encouragement" and "valuable aid"). And until the publication of Rob Lee's *Recollections and Letters,* it was a principal source for a wave of reminiscences from Lee's staff: first, Walter Taylor's *Four Years with General Lee* (1877), which was intent on "establishing the fact of the great numerical odds against which the army under General Lee had to contend," and *General Lee: His Campaigns in Virginia, 1861–1865* (1906), which offered a more "comprehensive account" of the war in Virginia; then Lindsay Long's *Memoirs of Robert E. Lee* (1886); and then yet another military biography in August 1894, in D. Appleton's "Great Commanders" series, by Smith Lee's son Fitzhugh simply titled *General Lee.*

Fitzhugh Lee's biography was the most sophisticated military study of Lee yet to appear, but it nevertheless still arrived at the same judgment as the others, that Robert E. Lee "stands in the front rank of the warriors of the world" and was only denied complete success by the "behavior of a corps commander"—Longstreet—who "defeated the well-devised designs of Lee at Gettysburg."[14] Not to be outdone, the determined John William Jones returned to eulogizing Lee, this time in a narrative biography, *Life and Letters of Robert Edward Lee, Soldier and Man,* in 1906. In the intervening years, Jones had emerged as a major promoter of the Lost Cause, using his post as editor of the Southern Historical Society's *Papers* to paint the Confederacy as a righteous endeavor to preserve liberty, independence, and states' rights from a ravenous, all-powerful centralized federal government.

By then, Lee had ceased to be the property merely of Confederate adorers. In 1908, Thomas Nelson Page, who was best known for sentimental fiction glorifying the Old South, wrote a rambling, top-lofty Lee biography titled *Robert E. Lee, The Southerner* and located his "successes" in "a poise unaffected by conditions which might startle or seduce," a "poise" that Lee somehow inherited from the "character" of "the Southern people." Just as quickly, Gamaliel Bradford replied with *Lee the American* in 1912, claiming Lee instead as a pattern of behavior for the entire nation and in the process questioning whether Lee had ever been a true convert to the Confederate cause. Bradford deplored "the growth of a Lee legend," and especially one that attached him to the Lost Cause. Lee's attempt "toward the very end of the war, to have negroes enlisted as soldiers," together with his seeming "indifference" toward "the future of the Confederacy" in its final months, suggested that he had never brimmed with expectations for Confederate success. And once the war was over, "he instantly adapted himself to new circumstances and began to work as a loyal and devoted citizen, even when the United States still refused him the rights and privileges of citizenship." Thus, Lee died "a loyal, a confident, a hopeful American, and one of the very greatest" and a model "that future Americans may study with profit as long as there is an America."

It remained for Douglas Southall Freeman, the editor of *The Richmond News Leader* and the son of a veteran of the Army of Northern Virginia, to twine these threads together in a four-volume apotheosis of Lee, *R. E. Lee,* based (by Freeman's estimate) on 1,200 unpublished Lee letters and reports. The biography, which cost him twenty years of labor, garnered him the Pulitzer Prize for biography in 1935. It also pedestaled Lee as simultaneously the champion of the Lost Cause *and* the noblest American. Lee was the apex of "five generations of clean living" in Virginia (although one supposes this did not include either Light Horse or Black Horse Harry), as well as the pattern for the first wave at Normandy, inspiring young soldiers to remember "in that hour that you come from America." Lee's "correspondence does not contain" even "the echo of a liaison, the shadow of an oath, or the stain of a single obscene suggestion." He disliked both slavery and secession, yet never hesitated to stand with Virginia after secession, and at the close "accepted fame without vanity and defeat without repining." In the end, Lee transcended even America. He was, like Valentine's recumbent memorial, "the Southern Arthur."[15]

For all that Freeman, Bradford, Page, and Jones had established about the nobility of Lee's character, it was less clear what Lee's standing as a soldier was. In the earliest biographies, the fact that Lee had held off the vast resources of the Army of the Potomac for four years was, on its face, evidence of military genius of the first order. Grant's "plan of destroying Lee's army" by breaking "down the wonderful *morale*" and depleting "the ranks of that army . . . by incessant attack" was a cynical, almost underhanded route to Union victory and "lamentably deficient in strategic science," argued the editor of *The Southern Bivouac* in 1885. But given the genius of Lee, "it was the only plan which could have won." Those moments where Lee's genius seemed to falter, as at Gettysburg, were swiftly excused by Early, Jones, and the Southern Historical Society *Papers* as the fault of Longstreet or Stuart, and the final triumph of Grant at Appomattox could be explained, in echoes of General Orders No. 9, by the simple attrition Grant's superior numbers afforded him. Even as late as John Joseph Bowen's *Strategy of Robert E. Lee* in 1914, it was still possible to rank Lee's military prowess as "well-nigh miraculous."[16]

The weaponry, the administrative expansion, and above all the carnage of World War I produced some very different, and much more hesitant, views of Lee's battles, beginning with the British general Sir Frederick Maurice's *Robert E. Lee, the Soldier* in 1925. Maurice paid due homage to Lee for his management of the peninsula as "supreme in conception" and of the Overland Campaign for being "fifty years ahead of the time." But Maurice also rated Lee poorly in his staff management and found him tempted too often to "rashness" and guilty of serious overreach at Gettysburg. Another British general, the eccentric J. F. C. Fuller, was even more critical in his 1933 *Grant and Lee,* dismissing Lee outright as "one of the most incapable Generals-in-Chief in history." Fuller's acolyte, Basil Henry Liddell Hart, in his *Strategy,* not only gave Lee short shrift in his analysis of the American Civil War but announced that "Lee and Jackson" were responsible for "a disproportionate attention" being paid to "the eastern theatre of the war," whereas (according to Liddell Hart) "it was in the west that the decisive blows were struck."[17]

Fuller and Liddell Hart set the stage for a large-scale reevaluation not only of the place of the Civil War in modern warfare but of Lee himself. In 1977, Thomas L. Connelly launched a frontal assault on Lee's reputation, first as a strategist and then, even more significantly, as the knightly model. Connelly had emerged in the 1960s as the premier historian of the Confederacy's western army, the Army of Tennessee, and he bitterly resented the flippancy with which Civil War historians dismissed both the Army of Tennessee and the Confederate west. Too many Southerners "saw things through Lee's eyes only and considered the hills around Gettysburg more important than those at Perryville or Chickamauga." In 1969, Connelly aimed an attack at Lee in the scholarly quarterly *Civil War History,* questioning "whether Lee possessed a sufficiently broad military mind to deal with overall Confederate matters" and wondering whether "the South may not have fared better had it possessed no Robert E. Lee." Eight years later, he published *The Marble Man: Robert E. Lee and His Image in American Society,* a full-fledged attack not only on "the Lee image" but on what Connelly called the "Virginia Pattern" (or "Virginia Syndrome"), which used Lee to promote "the ultimate proof of the superiority of Southern life and Anglo-Saxon supremacy."

Connelly's Lee was no Southern Arthur. Connelly reminded the Lee cultists that Lee had been a professional soldier for thirty years before the Civil War without doing much of any great significance; that his marriage to Mary Custis was socially brilliant but emotionally unfulfilling for Lee; and that Lee was ridden by a dread of failure, in the shadow of Light Horse Harry, and by a guilt fed by Calvinist evangelicalism. The war provided him with emotional release—hence, his reckless offensive strategy—and an opportunity to rise above failure. But the outcome of the war left him increasingly marked by self-pity and depression, and by the time of his death Lee was anything but serene and self-controlled. It is not difficult to find many of Connelly's accusations contrived: Lee could scarcely be construed as a Calvinist, or even much of an evangelical, and he did not fear failure nearly as much as he demanded of himself and others an almost unscalable level of perfection. But Connelly's real offense was to question Lee at all. "Many Southerners," observed Emory Thomas in his review of *The Marble Man,* "will accuse Connelly at least of apostasy, at most of treason, against his native Southland." He was right: Connelly's "ill-starred adventure in revisionism" was charged by reviewer after reviewer with having "mishandled" evidence, with having merely presented "too exactly a reverse image of Freeman," and with having dabbled "in the realm of psychiatry, a field in which the historian is quite inadequately trained." Thomas himself joined the accusations, describing *The Marble Man* as "a flawed book" and tagging Connelly with "inverse snobbery."[18]

These objections were not necessarily defenses of the Lost Cause. Emory Thomas would go on, two years later, to publish a comprehensive history of the Confederacy, *The Confederate Nation, 1861–1865,* which treated the Confederacy with scrupulous evenhandedness as a failed effort in the construction of nineteenth-century nationalism. When Thomas turned to publishing a Lee biography in 1995, he labored to lighten Connelly's bleak interpretation of Lee and insist that Lee was in many ways a "tragic hero" who longed to escape the restraints imposed on him by his father, by his profession, and even by his "children who seemed incapable of stepping beyond Lee's shadow and becoming themselves." This was also a Lee who possessed "a comic vision of life," who "lived for women," and who chose to plunge himself into the Civil War "in order to escape conflict."

Thomas's *Robert E. Lee: A Biography* remains the best and most balanced of any single-volume Lee biography. But Connelly had introduced a rupture in the dike of historical adulation of Lee that not even Thomas could repair. In 1991, Alan Nolan, an Indianapolis lawyer and keen amateur historian, published *Lee Considered: General Robert E. Lee and Civil War History,* which picked up where Connelly left off. Nolan was a civil rights activist, and *Lee Considered* took as a particular target any notion that Lee harbored enlightened, or even sympathetic, views on race. Lee's distaste for slavery was purely an abstraction, Nolan argued, and Lee's views on race fit easily "in the mainstream of the attitudes of the Southern political leadership." Michael Fellman, in *The Making of Robert E. Lee* (2000), was even more caustic. Lee would, in the event of a Confederate victory, have done nothing to prevent "the reinstitution of slavery." Lee never wavered in "his belief in the inferiority of blacks as a race." But just as reprehensible, Lee also entertained a "negative view of the white lower classes . . . more pronounced than Southern gentlemen could allow themselves to express in public." That, Fellman claimed, more than any concern about the future of a reunited country, fueled Lee's resistance to the idea of a prolonged guerrilla war rather than surrender.[19]

The greatest blow to Lee's reputation would come not through a book but through a riot. On August 12, 2017, fanatical factions of Ku Klux Klan and neo-Nazi goons clashed in the streets of Charlottesville with black-clad partisans of the "Antifa" left, leaving one woman dead and the entire nation stunned into silence. Much of the violence swirled around a twenty-six-foot-high equestrian statue of Lee in one of the city's parks, and almost as if he had caught a racist virus merely through his statue's location, Lee became a symbol in many apprehensive minds of a reenergized white supremacy movement. "The Lee sculpture honors a dishonorable man," claimed Jamil Smith in a *Los Angeles Times* op-ed on August 14, "while encouraging his ideological descendants and expressing to black people that America is not ours, too."

In a swift arc, Lee statues in Dallas, in Baltimore, and at the University of Texas and Duke University were removed or defaced. Schools and parks contracted the same unease. The North East Independent School District in Texas was pressured to drop "Robert E. Lee" from the name of its high school but blanched at the $1.3 million cost of changing signage and ordering new team uniforms and settled for renaming the school the Legacy of Educational Excellence High School—Lee High School—and just removing the "Robert E." Oklahoma City kept the name Lee for an elementary school, explaining that it was now named for a local philanthropist, Adelaide Lee. The Washington & Lee High School, a few miles from Stratford Hall, was renamed Washington-Liberty High School to avoid changing its W-L seal. Grace Episcopal Church in Lexington, whose vestry meeting had been Lee's last outing before his stroke, changed its name after his death to R. E. Lee Memorial; in September 2017, the vestry voted to return the church to its original name. In Brooklyn, St. John's Church removed a plaque remembering Lee's service on the vestry when he was stationed at Fort Hamilton. Calls went up for removal of the Charlottesville statue as well, and for several months thereafter the statue was shrouded in a black plastic tarp. It, too, would probably have been taken down by the city, except for a restraining order issued in February 2018 in Virginia Commonwealth court, based on the Commonwealth's ownership of the statue.[20]

No place agonized more over the Lee identity than the institution that he rescued from collapse. Once Washington and Lee University began to be integrated in the 1960s, the abundant Lee imagery on the campus increasingly grated on African American sensibilities. In August 2014, students successfully pressed the university to remove the displays of Confederate battle flags from the chapel. Three years later, the echoes of the Charlottesville riot had hardly died away before Washington and Lee's president, William C. Dudley, announced that because of the university's "complex history" it would be necessary to review how Confederate symbols were displayed there. A yearlong self-study made it clear that "Lee, our former president and one of our namesakes, has become a particularly polarizing figure," and although the recommendations of a twelve-member commission pulled shy of erasing Lee's name from the institution entirely, they did propose moving official functions away from the chapel and converting it into a museum, changing all references to Lee from "General" to "President," and replacing portraits of Lee in uniform with portraits in civilian dress, or else replacing Lee portraits entirely with others "who represent the university's complete history." But only two years later, in the wake of the George Floyd killing and the nationwide protests over it, a renewed surge of calls from the faculty demanded the removal of Lee's name from the university, and a special faculty meeting in July 2020 voted by a resounding 79 percent in favor of the Lee removal motion.[21]

It is unclear at this moment what the future of the Lee name will be at the university, because the final decision lies with the trustees and, ultimately, the Virginia state legislature (which is responsible for the university's charter). The likelihood of its retention, however, is dim. What this, in turn, will mean for the Lee Chapel and for Valentine's Lee monument is even more unpredictable.[22] Although antiracist protests have involved numerous incidents of statue toppling and statue defacement, protest gestures have not, at least to this point, involved the removal of tomb statuary or grave desecration. Yet it will be difficult to see how the Lee Chapel and the Valentine memorial can remain as nagging reminders of the Lee presence at the university, or even whether the Lee family in the crypt may not be the object of removal.

The controversy over the Charlottesville statue stands as something of a marker for Lee's ambiguous place in American history. Because the Charlottesville statue went up in 1924, at the apex of white supremacy in the South, it was easy to suppose that it was put there to teach black people to mind their place in a Virginia that took white supremacy for granted. But the dedication ceremonies in 1924 featured high school bands, the cadets of the Virginia Military Institute, the university faculty, and the American Legion—not the Ku Klux Klan. And the dedication speeches were about the Lee whose decision to surrender at Appomattox averted "scattered guerrilla warfare for many years," who "in the shadows of the defeat of war" pointed Southerners to "the star of hope with its radiant promise and prophecy of the triumphs of peace." These words came from M. Ashby Jones, the son of John William Jones and himself a Baptist pastor who had denounced segregation and antiblack violence and had been likewise targeted by the Klan. The pedestal read only ROBERT EDWARD LEE, and the statue itself was completed by an Italian-born sculptor, Leo Lentelli, and cast in Brooklyn. If the statue had criminal intent, there was little historical evidence for it.[23]

An even larger irony of the rash of de-namings, renamings, and statue removals is that Lee would likely have been the first to have condemned the rioters, having punished lesser outrages by students at Washington College during his presidency. That does not necessarily absolve him from the taint of white supremacist thinking, because Lee's attitudes and ideas on race were clearly on the side of white hierarchy, and cannot even be massaged into mere acquiescence with the post–Civil War Southern order. There were certainly many Southern whites in those years who recognized the evils of both slavery and race and who bravely linked themselves with the freedmen's cause—and Lee was not one of them. But there were also substantially many more Southern whites, teeming with sneering and subversive hatred of the black people they had used and abused in bondage, whose ideas and behavior were infinitely more malevolent and destructive (and that does not begin to account for many Northern whites who were no improvement). If there is at least one favorable way to speak of Robert E. Lee, it is that his garments were cleaner in the postwar years than many of his contemporaries'.

On the other hand, comparative harmlessness is not much of a historically significant quality. Apart from the statues, there are few abiding monuments to Lee. The dikes Lee built to protect the St. Louis waterfront were washed away by subsequent flooding; not until 1867 was Bloody Island finally and firmly attached to the Illinois shore, where it is today part of East St. Louis. The mansion at Arlington that still stands at the center of what is now the nation's most honored cemetery is known as the Robert E. Lee Memorial, but Lee neither designed nor built it, and never actually owned it, either. (And in the wake of Charlottesville, the National Park Service quietly rewrote its rationale for retaining the Lee name, saying it was based on Lee's "role in promoting peace and reunion after the Civil War" and was intended to promote "study and contemplation of the meaning of some of the most difficult aspects of American History: military service; sacrifice; citizenship; duty; loyalty; slavery and freedom.")[24] Fort Pulaski and Fort Monroe still survive, but Lee's contribution to them was one of many hands; Fort Hamilton also survives, but less because of Lee's engineering skills and more because it serves as the U.S. Army's last administrative outpost in New York City; Fort Carroll remains in Baltimore harbor, unfinished as Lee left it and hardly noticed by motorists driving over it on the Francis Scott Key Bridge.

If there are grounds to speak of glory, they have to be found in his surprising career as a Confederate general—*surprising,* because most of his career in the Army had been served as an engineer rather than in command of any significant body of soldiers in battle. There, the task is not nearly as difficult as Thomas Connelly portrayed it. One has only to compare Lee's management of the campaigns in the eastern theater with those of his predecessors, Joe Johnston and Pierre Beauregard, to understand that neither of them would have been able to hold off George McClellan's inexorable advance on Richmond in 1862, and with Richmond gone, the Confederacy would not have long survived. Lee's stature as a commander stands still higher when compared with his talentless counterparts in the west—Braxton Bragg, John Bell Hood, and Joe Johnston again. The same might be said when comparing Lee with many of his federal counterparts. Ambrose Burnside, Joseph Hooker, and George Meade shrink into various curls of timidity when compared with Lee, and Meade's victory at Gettysburg had more to do with Lee's miscalculations than any tactical genius displayed by Meade—something Meade demonstrated all too well by his mindless hesitation at Williamsport, when he might have crushed the Army of Northern Virginia, and by his dithering campaign at Bristoe Station and Mine Run afterward.

Only Grant emerged in the war with military gifts on a par with Lee, and even then it took Grant almost a year to force Lee's Confederates to their knees at Appomattox. There is glory for Lee in that achievement. But it is a glory in technique, to be acknowledged with a decent reluctance, as Winston Churchill did when he spoke in 1942 of the genius of Erwin Rommel: "We have a very daring and skillful opponent against us, and, may I say across the havoc of war, a great general." More to the point is the question of what made Lee so effective on active campaign. Thomas Connelly's principal complaint against Lee was that whatever tactical skill he showed on the battlefield, he was defective in his overall strategic vision, by over-privileging the defense of Virginia. But the truth lies in exactly the opposite direction: Lee's glory as a strategist lay precisely in his perception that the South could not sustain a drawn-out war with the North, that it must strike aggressively and score victories early, not so much in expectation of conquering or destroying the Northern armies as in spreading enough political discouragement through the Northern public that Northerners would themselves demand an end to the war. Those blows could only be struck in the east, in Maryland and Pennsylvania, where the failure of public support for the Lincoln administration would certainly doom Lincoln's prosecution of the war. Lee showed how clearly he understood this as early as April 1862, if not earlier; his disappointment that more Southerners did *not* see this fueled his frequent predictions of Southern defeat. As Charles Marshall wrote in retrospect, "Lee was conscious that if the war were to continue much longer on a scale of such magnitude, the South must fail from exhaustion. . . . It therefore became important to consider how to accomplish quickly the greatest possible results with the smallest loss."[25]

That Lee came chillingly close to accomplishing such "results," and on two occasions, is remarkable in itself; that it took until Lincoln's reelection in November 1864 before that possibility finally evaporated is more remarkable still. In that same year, less than six months were required for Prussian and Austrian forces to overrun Denmark's fabled fortification lines of Dybbøl and pry loose the provinces of Schleswig and Holstein. Two years later, the Prussians and Italians needed only six weeks to force the Austrian Empire to negotiations, and four years later Prussia and the German states took less than a year to humble the French Second Empire (including a five-month siege of Paris) and annex the provinces of Alsace and Lorraine. When stood beside the witless French generals Bazaine and MacMahon, or beside the fumbling but well-intentioned Austrian von Benedek, Lee rises to Napoleonic proportions.

It is less easy to assess Lee's tactical and managerial skills. "He is indeed a very great soldier," marveled an awed Northern observer. "As a tactician, on the field of battle, he has no equals in this war. . . . The ease with which he seems to handle his troops, and the judgment he shows in throwing them in, is admirable." And Sir Garnet Wolseley, years afterward, believed that not only were "Lee's combinations to secure victory . . . the conceptions of a truly great strategist," but "when they had been effected, his tactics were then almost everything that could be desired up to the moment of victory."[26] Even so, it is possible to raise an eyebrow about Lee as a tactical overseer. Much of what Lee practiced in Virginia, Maryland, and Pennsylvania in 1862 through 1865 was learned from Winfield Scott in Mexico, and that remained more strategic than tactical. Lee was not exaggerating when he told Justus Scheibert that he preferred to leave tactical details on the battlefield to his subordinates, trying to steer a middle path between total Napoleonic control on the one hand, and deferring to useless councils of war on the other. That worked well when he had subordinates equal to such responsibilities, especially Stonewall Jackson. Too often, however, Lee was forced to reach for tactical control himself, and his distaste for doing so showed in the management of Gettysburg and the Wilderness. Lee at Fredericksburg might have seemed to Francis Charles Lawley to be the epitome of battlefield dignity. But he could afford dignity at Fredericksburg because he had Longstreet and Jackson to carry out his overall plans; all of that would change a year and a half later, when both Jackson and Longstreet were gone. At the Wilderness and Spotsylvania, he had to abandon dignity to take immediate tactical charge.

If Lee had a tactical trademark at all, it was a weakness for repetition. If a particular maneuver worked once (as with Longstreet's crushing flank attack at Second Bull Run), he would try it again and again (as at Chancellorsville, the second day at Gettysburg, and the first day of the Wilderness; even Pickett's Charge was, technically, a repetition of Longstreet's flank attack the day before) until it was apparent it had outlived its usefulness. The last two offensive operations he supervised—at Fort Stedman and at Appomattox—abandoned any effort at turning flanks in favor of head-on assaults. That weakness was complicated by another weakness: too often he protected pets, like Powell Hill and William Pendleton and his bland chief of staff, Robert Chilton. The same Lee whom Beauregard complained would lop off the heads of commanders he disliked went miles out of his way to overlook the faults of those he favored. Even Walter Taylor agreed that "he was too careful of the personal feelings of his subordinate commanders" and continued "in command those of whose fitness for their position he was not convinced."[27]

There are lesser marks to be given, too, for Lee's grasp of logistics and his abhorrence of intrusions in politics and by politicians. The fatal under-resourcing of the Army of Northern Virginia was a source of incessant lamentation from Lee during the war, and the cramped dimensions of his staff, as dictated by the parsimony of the Confederate Congress, repeatedly handicapped his oversight of the Army of Northern Virginia and produced its most disastrous mishap, the Lost Orders of the Maryland campaign. What is surprising is how little Lee tried to force on Jefferson Davis the administrative changes necessary to correct many of these shortfalls, starting with the Army of Northern Virginia's supply deficiencies. Taylor, again, thought Lee "too subordinate to his superiors in civil authority" when he should "have been supreme in all matters touching the movements and discipline of his army."[28]

Unhappily, the other major lesson Lee had learned from Scott (and earlier from Gratiot) was precisely that overabundance of caution in dealing with politics, a caution that made him passive where passivity was fatal. (It should be said that Grant was equally shy of putting his foot into the political sphere, but Grant was not dealing with political failures on the order manifested by the Richmond government.) And hidden within these lamentations was a fatal habit of shifting blame. The impulse to assure subordinates that "this is all my fault" tended to dissipate in the weeks and months after a failure, and he never qualified or regretted the blame he spewed over the Confederate leadership and even the Confederate public for sacrificing less than he thought they ought to sacrifice. If there is glory to be found in Lee as a general, it is to be found in Lee the strategist more than the tactician, and certainly more than Lee the manager.

Always balancing any acknowledgment of Lee's glory, however, is the overriding fact of Lee's crime, which is not a word used idly. Curiously, in the post-Charlottesville rush to unhorse Lee from his numerous monuments, Lee's principal offense seemed to lie in his backward-facing notions of white supremacy, and while Lee was not the racist monster that the White League, Josephus Daniels, or "Pitchfork Ben" Tillman became, those notions are still problematic enough to render impossible much of the unadulterated hero worship that Lee enjoyed for a century after his death. Indifference to slavery is not quite the same thing as its active embrace and promotion, but not by much. His refusal to challenge the breakdown in the prisoner-exchange system over black soldiers could be cloaked behind his reluctance to confront political authority, but international law in the twentieth century has been less and less willing to give credence to such excuses, however much they might have been the rule in the nineteenth century.

Likewise, there is no evidence that Lee had any personal hand in the massacres of black soldiers, on the scale of Fort Pillow or Olustee or even at the Crater. But that merely represents an absence, and is neither a plus nor a minus on the moral scale. Unhappily, absence represents a great deal of what is often said in Lee's defense. He urged postwar Southerners to submit to federal authority and admit that they had lost, but he took no positive steps to cooperate with Reconstruction. As the president of Washington College, he discouraged rancid glorifications of white ruthlessness, but he *only* discouraged them. His greatest gift to the life of the Republic was the decision to surrender his army intact at Appomattox and ensure that the Civil War did not pour over into a more hellish and protracted phase of full-tilt guerrilla warfare. But the South still got outbreaks of violence and quasi-insurgency anyway, all through Reconstruction. What often seems to disappear from view in modern condemnations of Lee was a defect that unsympathetic contemporaries complained was a far greater offense, and that was treason. Even with all the caveats in play that kept Lee from being put on trial for treason, no one seems to conform more plainly to the constitutional definition of treason against the United States—"levying war against them, or in adhering to their enemies, giving them aid and comfort"—than Robert E. Lee. Yet less was heard after Charlottesville about Lee and treason than about Lee and white supremacy.[29]

Perhaps this is because in the cosmopolitan atmosphere of globalism, the notion of treason has acquired an antique feel, like blasphemy or transportation to the antipodes, as if modern individuals should no longer be held to the standard of absolute loyalty to a single political entity. Membership in a nation-state, writes the legal philosopher A. John Simmons, "does not free a man from the burdens of moral reasoning." The task of the citizen, argues Simmons, is not to absorb an obligation to the nation-state and "blithely discharge it in his haste to avoid the responsibility of weighing it against competing moral claims on his action. For surely a nation composed of such 'dutiful citizens' would be the cruellest sort of trap for the poor, the oppressed, and the alienated." Moreover, the assertion of the existence of international standards of human rights runs in direct conflict with how states regard, and are allowed to regard, the disloyal behavior of their nationals. Nor is this merely an exercise of left-internationalism; for many libertarians, too, the charge of treason loses the taint of moral betrayal and becomes a mechanism by which an all-powerful state prevents "dangers to its *own* contentment." Hence, the one inarguable *crime* of Robert E. Lee—the one that caused measurable death and destruction and not just interpretive discomfort—is the one that it has become less and less possible to understand *as* a crime.[30]

And yet the chief difficulty with that reasoning is that denying the reality of treason, or that citizens should be held culpable for it, is to deny that communities can suffer betrayal to the point where their very existence is jeopardized. Whatever the faults of the nation-state, it has proven since the eighteenth century, and perhaps even since the Peace of Westphalia, to be a frail but workable insurance against the kinds of incessant dynastic, ethnic, and religious warfare that used to be the common lot of the human race, and the most stable platform for the emergence and cultivation of democracy. To wave away treason as a crime is to put in jeopardy many of the benefits the nation-state has conferred in the last three centuries.[31]

But perhaps the reluctance to pin on Robert E. Lee the crime of treason has a different root. Perhaps it is a token of an instinct, running back to the Constitutional Convention, to err on the side of absorbing society's defaulters rather than marching them to the scaffold. Even in Lee's lifetime, Walt Whitman thought that passing by the treason of the Confederates was something laudable in the soul of the American Republic, something that "has been paralleled nowhere in the world," because "in any other country on the globe the whole batch of the Confederate leaders would have had their heads cut off." Even Wendell Phillips, the prince of no-compromise abolitionism and an ardent advocate for postwar racial egalitarianism, acknowledged that "we cannot hang men in regiments" or "cover the continent with gibbets. We cannot sicken the nineteenth century with such a sight." The best that Phillips could hope for was to "banish Lee with the rest," even if that banishment meant only dismissing him from cultural attention. In that way, Herman Melville wrote, Lee was not so much punished for a crime as simply rendered harmless.

The captain who fierce armies led
Becomes a quiet seminary's head—
Poor as his privates, earns his bread.

There can be no true compassion without will, but there can be no true will without compassion, for without compassion no one can summon the will to live a true life or fashion a true art. Self-pity played a far larger role than compassion in Lee's character, and his pursuit of perfection froze compassion into obligation. But that need not be the case in us. Mercy—or at least a nolle prosequi—may, perhaps, be the most appropriate conclusion to the crime—and the glory—of Robert E. Lee after all.[32]

Acknowledgments

If the complexities of Robert Edward Lee make the attempt of a biography formidable, the mechanics of creating that biography also prove daunting. Lee ardently disliked formal paperwork, but personal letter writing was another matter: by my unscientific reckoning, between three and four thousand of Lee's letters survive today, and that does not include official reports, orders, sketches, notebooks, and designs. Despite this wealth of material, unlike the other major figures of the Civil War—Abraham Lincoln, Ulysses Grant, Jefferson Davis, even Andrew Johnson—there is no comprehensive edition of Lee's writings. So, at the beginning of this project I had to create a "calendar" of Lee letters, giving each a single entry that identified the recipient, a brief subject, and its source; today, that "calendar" runs to 103 closely printed pages, dating from February 28, 1824, to September 28, 1870.

This task was made all the more tedious because Lee's surviving letters are scattered in groups of varying size in scholarly collections across the North American continent—the Wilson Library at the University of North Carolina, the David Rubenstein Library at Duke University, the Morgan Library in New York City, the Missouri History Museum Archives, the Georgia Historical Society, the Southern Historical Society Collection, the New York Public Library, the Henry E. Huntington Library in San Marino, the Museum of the Confederacy, the U.S. Military Academy at West Point, the Virginia Military Institute (for the maps Lee drew during the Mexican War), the Lee-Fendall House in Alexandria, and the Gilder Lehrman Institute of American History. In fact, until 2002, a substantial collection of Lee family papers remained locked in a bank vault in Alexandria.* Even more maddening, Lee letters also frequently pop up from private collections on a variety of online auction websites. This book is particularly indebted to five collections and the wonderful people who manage them: Judy Hynson of Stratford Hall, whose knowledge of the terrain of Lee materials is unmatched; Michelle Krowl of the Library of Congress, for whom no request for a copy of a document, no matter how obscure the collection, went unfulfilled; John McClure, director of Research and Publications at the Virginia Museum of History and Culture in Richmond; Thomas L. Camden, head of the James G. Leyburn Library's Special Collections at Washington and Lee University; and Regina D. Rush and the staff of the Albert and Shirley Small Special Collections Library at the University of Virginia.

Mercifully, five published (or transcribed) portions of Lee's vast output of letter writing were available: Francis Raymond Adams's 1955 PhD dissertation from the University of Maryland, "An Annotated Edition of the Personal Letters of Robert E. Lee, April 1855–April 1861"; *Lee's Dispatches: Unpublished Letters of General Robert E. Lee, C.S.A., to Jefferson Davis and the War Department of the Confederate States of America, 1862–65,* originally produced by Douglas Southall Freeman in 1915 and updated with additional material by Grady McWhiney in 1957; the compilation *The Wartime Papers of Robert E. Lee,* created by Clifford Dowdey and Louis H. Manarin for the Civil War centennial; *The Daily Correspondence of Brevet Colonel Robert E. Lee, Superintendent, United States Military Academy,* edited by Charles Bowery and Brian Hankinson in 2003; and Frank Screven's "Letters of R. E. Lee to the Mackay Family of Savannah," in Georgia Southern University's Armstrong Campus Library in Savannah. Smaller collections of Lee letters have also been published in *The Virginia Magazine of History and Biography* (most notably Robert E. L. deButts's "Lee in Love: Courtship and Correspondence in Antebellum Virginia"), *The Journal of Southern History* (William Hoyt's "Some Personal Letters of Robert E. Lee, 1850–1858"), and *The Huntington Library Quarterly* (Norma Cuthbert's "To Molly: Five Early Letters from Robert E. Lee to His Wife, 1832–1835"). Probably the richest resource of easily accessible Lee letters is the Lee Family Digital Archive, maintained by Stratford Hall, which includes letters, articles, and other papers pertaining to the entire Lee family. Although Dowdey and Manarin's *Wartime Papers of Robert E. Lee* contains more than a thousand Lee letters, documents, and reports, even that anthology leaves unreproduced a staggeringly large body of Lee correspondence and papers contained in *The War of the Rebellion: A Compila-*

* Linda Wheeler, "In a Dusty Vault, an Abundance of Lee Family Relics," *Washington Post,* Nov. 27, 2002; Glenn W. LaFantasie, "The Confederate We Still Don't Know," *Salon,* July 31, 2011.

tion of the Official Records of the Union and Confederate Armies (127 volumes, 1881–1901).

In the long gestation of this book, I have been supported by two institutions of higher learning, Gettysburg College and, since 2019, Princeton University. At Gettysburg, I have been aided by staffers who would have made me the envy of Robert E. Lee, beginning in 2014 with Brian Matthew Jordan, and then followed by Megan Blount, and finally by the indefatigable Diane Brennan, whose ability to anticipate my requests and fulfill them almost before I had finished making them defines the word "remarkable." (Jonathan W. White of Christopher Newport University, who has a penchant for collecting odds and ends of Civil War memorabilia, joined with Diane in keeping an eye for me on a variety of online auction sites for new Lee materials.) I was also assisted at Gettysburg by a platoon of note-card transcribers—Brandon Hokanson, Elizabeth Hobbs, and Julia Wall—who transferred my reading notes to the four-by-six cards that have become my favorite means for assembling and deploying research materials. At Princeton, as I brought this project to completion, I have enjoyed the fellowship of Sean Wilentz and my chair in the Council of the Humanities, Eric Gregory; and the indulgence and support of the James Madison Program in American Ideals and Institutions through its staff—Debby Parker, Ch'nel Duke, and Evy Behling—and its extraordinary leadership, Robert P. George, Executive Director Bradford P. Wilson, and Matt Franck. An unanticipated gift of this project has been the opportunity to know and work with two Lee descendants, Carter Refo (a great-grandson of Charles Carter Lee) and Robert E. Lee deButts Jr. (the great-great-grandson of the subject of this book). In addition, I want to acknowledge Ryan Cole, who graciously permitted me an advance look at his new biography of Light Horse Harry Lee. In no wise do any of these generous and vital people bear any responsibility for the opinions of the author of this book. Evan Rothera also deserves thanks for his photographing of the *pedregal.*

Portions of this work have already appeared as lectures and interviews, principally with the dean of Southern Civil War historians, Gary W. Gallagher, at the University of Virginia in September 2017; at Washington and Lee University, at the invitation of the esteemed Lucas Morel, in March 2018, and again at Washington and Lee with Lynn Rainville in October 2020; and in the "Reading Lee" lecture series at the Fredericksburg Public Library, as organized in January 2020, by the multitalented Jon Bachman of Stratford Hall, who also sponsored my lecture "The Mexican War and Robert E. Lee," in the November 2017 Lee Symposium at Stratford Hall. I was greatly assisted by John M. Rudy's intimate knowledge of the Harpers Ferry uprising and by Hannah Reynolds with materials on Arlington. Other helpful commentary was provided by Steven E. Woodworth of Texas Christian University, by Gary W. Gallagher, and by Jon White.

Several pieces also were featured as freestanding articles: " 'War Is a Great Evil': Robert E. Lee in the War with Mexico," *Southwestern Historical Quarterly* (July 2018); "Robert E. Lee as a College President: The Washington College Years, 1865–1870," *Journal of the Shenandoah Valley During the Civil War* (2019); "The Trial That Didn't Happen," *The Weekly Standard,* April 13, 2018; "Did Robert E. Lee Commit Treason?," *Athenaeum Review* (Spring/Summer 2019); "The Decision: Why Did Robert E. Lee Turn Down Command of the Union Army and Join the Confederacy in 1861?" and "The Unexpected Robert E. Lee," *Civil War Monitor* (2018 and 2019); "A Yankee in Charlottesville Finds General Lee Under Cover," *The Wall Street Journal,* September 30, 2017; "Honor, Compromise, and Getting History Right," *The American Interest,* November 6, 2017; in collaboration with John M. Rudy, "Of Monuments and Men: How Do We Responsibly Remember Robert E. Lee and the Confederacy?," *Civil War Monitor* (2017); "Robert E. Lee and Slavery," online *Encyclopedia of Virginia* (2017); "An Army on the Move: Robert E. Lee and His Confederates in June 1863," *Civil War News* (2016); and "Uneasy Lies the Head: Lee in Lexington," *The New Criterion,* January 2021.

Nothing that has preceded these words would have been possible without my agent, John Rudolph, of Dystel, Goderich & Bourret, and Andrew Miller, my editor at Knopf. Both were unstinting in their encouragement of this project from its inception; both were models of patience when the angst of professional transitions and a deadly attack of meningitis caused the missing of deadlines. The time and effort lavished in polishing and tightening the manuscript goes far beyond my poor power to add or detract, and I can no other answer make but thanks, and thanks, and ever thanks. Assembling the images for this book required the patience of Job from Maris Dyer at Knopf, and the welcome cooperation of Lynn Rainville, William Rasmussen (at the Virginia Museum of History and Culture), Kimberly Robinson at Arlington, and Bryn Cooley at Tudor Place.

Several of the chapter titles are taken from Tennyson's *Idylls of the King,* that Victorian hymn of praise to the virtues of Prince Albert, who struck Tennyson as being the most genteel and noble of aristocrats, and one best fitted to the spirit of an England less and less patient with its aristocrats. In the summer of 2016, I took up the rereading of the *Idylls* for the first time since having encountered them under the tutelage of my beloved high school English teacher, Miss Janet Hirt, and was intrigued by how closely Tennyson's portrayal of King Arthur (and Prince Albert) paralleled Robert E. Lee. As it turned out, I would not be the only one for whom Lee conjured up associations with the Arthurian legends. Hence, the titles.

Tennyson, however, only intrigued me. The real love behind this book comes from neither Tennyson nor Lee but Debra, who has accompanied research journeys, suffered through endless re-visionings of the Lee materials, and sympathized with the burdens Lee placed on her husband. For her and to her goes all my love in return.

Paoli, Pennsylvania
December 2020

Notes

Abbreviations

ACL—Anne Carter Lee ("Annie")
CCL—Charles Carter Lee
EAL—Eleanor Agnes Lee
GWCL—George Washington Custis Lee
GWPC—George Washington Parke Custis
MChL—Mildred Childe Lee ("Precious Life")
MCL—Mary Anna Randolph Custis Lee
MCL Jr.—Mary Custis Lee ("Daughter")
REL—Robert Edward Lee
SSL—Sidney Smith Lee
TJJ—Thomas Jonathan "Stonewall" Jackson
WHFL—William Henry Fitzhugh Lee ("Rooney")

AQRM—American Quarterly Register and Magazine
LFDA—Lee Family Digital Archive (leefamilyarchive.org)
OR—War of the Rebellion: A Compilation of the Official Records of the Union and Confederate Armies (Washington, D.C.: Government Printing Office, 1881–1901)
PLREL—Francis Raymond Adams, "An Annotated Edition of the Personal Letters of Robert E. Lee, April 1855–April 1861" (PhD diss., University of Maryland, 1955)
SHSP—Southern Historical Society Papers
VMHB—Virginia Magazine of History and Biography
VMHC—Virginia Museum of History and Culture
WMQ—William and Mary Quarterly
WPREL—Wartime Papers of Robert E. Lee, ed. Clifford Dowdey and L. H. Manarin (Boston: Little, Brown, 1961)

Prologue: The Mystery of Robert E. Lee

1. Elizabeth Keckley, *Behind the Scenes; or, Thirty Years a Slave, and Four Years in the White House* (1868; Salem, N.H.: Ayer, 1985), 137; "Address of General Gordon," in *Army of Northern Virginia Memorial Volume,* ed. J. W. Jones (Richmond: J. W. Randolph & English, 1880), 25; Ulysses S. Grant, *Personal Memoirs* (New York: C. L. Webster, 1886), 2:490.
2. Douglas Southall Freeman, *R. E. Lee* (New York: Charles Scribner's, 1935), 4:505; Burton Hendrick, *The Lees of Virginia: Biography of a Family* (Boston: Little, Brown, 1935), 429; Clifford Dowdey, *Lee: A Biography* (1965; New York: Skyhorse, 2015), 493; Armistead Lindsay Long, *Memoirs of Robert E. Lee: His Military and Personal History,* ed. Marcus Wright (New York: J. M. Stoddart, 1886), 433.
3. "Will of Robert E. Lee, 1846 August 31 (Including Indorsement of 1870 November 7)," LFDA/Jessie Ball duPont Library, Stratford Hall, Stratford, Va.; Emory M. Thomas, *Robert E. Lee: A Biography* (New York: W. W. Norton, 1995), 421.
4. To Alan Nolan in 1991, Lee was "a typical Southern partisan," with all the "Southern aristocrat's feeling about the inferiority of Northern people"; to Michael Fellman in 2000, Lee was really an exemplar of "the dark side of the white supremacist road"; to Roy Blount (probably the most unlikely of all Lee biographers) in 2003, Lee was mentally, and pathologically, "disturbed." See Alan Nolan, *Lee Considered: General Robert E. Lee and Civil War History* (Chapel Hill: University of North Carolina Press, 1991), 150; Michael Fellman, *The Making of Robert E. Lee* (New York: Random House, 2000), 306; and Roy Blount, *Robert E. Lee: A Life* (New York: Penguin, 2003), 183–84.
5. Adams to Richard Bland Lee, Aug. 11, 1819, in *The Works of John Adams, Second President of the United States* (Boston: Little, Brown, 1856), 10:389. There were actually *six* Lee brothers (and two sisters), but two of them, Philip Ludwell Lee and Thomas Ludwell Lee, did not outlive the Revolution.
6. Milton Lomask, *The Biographer's Craft* (New York: HarperCollins, 1987), 98.
7. Joseph Harsh, *Confederate Tide Rising: Robert E. Lee and the Making of Southern Strategy, 1861–1862* (Kent, Ohio: Kent State University Press, 1998), 56–59.

Chapter One: The Garden Spot of Virginia

1. "Ancient Buildings of Virginia," *Weekly National Intelligencer,* Dec. 16, 1848; Robert E. Lee, "Life of General Henry Lee," in Henry Lee, *Memoirs of the War in the Southern Department of the United States* (New York: University Publishing, 1870), 41; Myron Magnet, *The Founders at Home: The Building of America, 1735–1817* (New York: W. W. Norton, 2014), 53–55; Charles Carter Lee, *The Maid of the Doe: A Lay of the Revolution* (Washington, D.C.: Robert Farnham, 1842), 153.
2. Connie H. Wyrick, "Stratford and the Lees," *Journal of the Society of Architectural Historians* 30 (March 1971): 70–76; Walter Briscoe Norris Jr., *Westmoreland County, Virginia* (Marceline, Mo.: Walsworth, 1983), 233–35; Cazenove Gardner Lee Jr., *Lee Chronicle: Studies of the Early Generations of the Lees of Virginia* (New York: New York University Press, 1957), 249.
3. See Broadway's *Trinity—Elvis and Jesus and Robert E. Lee,* Ogden Museum of Southern Art, New Orleans, ogdenmuseum.org.
4. Alden T. Vaughan, *American Genesis: Captain John Smith and the Founding of Virginia* (Boston: Little, Brown, 1975), 167; Carville V. Earle, "Environment, Disease, and Mortality in

Early Virginia," in *The Chesapeake in the Seventeenth Century: Essays on Anglo-American Society,* ed. Thad W. Tate and David L. Ammerman (New York: W. W. Norton, 1979), 119.

5. Frederick Warren Alexander, *Stratford Hall and the Lees Connected with Its History, Biographical, Genealogical, and Historical* (privately published, 1912), 27; "James Clayton, of James City, Afterwards of Crofton, Yorkshire," *WMQ,* 2nd ser., 1 (1921): 114; Stephen Adams, *The Best and Worst Country in the World: Perspectives on the Early Virginia Landscape* (Charlottesville: University of Virginia Press, 2001), 151; "Papers from the Records of Surry County—Restoration of Charles II," *WMQ,* 1st ser., 3 (Oct. 1894): 122.
6. Hendrick, *Lees of Virginia,* 7, 12, 14–15, 22; C. G. Lee, *Lee Chronicle,* 19–20, 22, 24–25, 26; Thomas A. Wolf, *Historic Sites in Virginia's Northern Neck and Essex County* (Warsaw, Va.: Preservation Northern Neck and Middle Peninsula, 2011), 147–48; "Representation of Edward Randolph as to Virginia," Aug. 31, 1696, in *Calendar of State Papers, Colonial Series, America and West Indies, 15 May 1696–31 October 1697,* ed. J. W. Fortescue (London: HM Stationery Office, 1904), 89.
7. "The Northern Neck of Virginia," *WMQ* 6 (April 1898): 222–26; Stanley Phillips Smith, "The Northern Neck's Role in American Legal History," *VMHB,* July 1969, 277–78; Fairfax Harrison, "The Proprietors of the Northern Neck: Chapters of Culpeper Genealogy," *Virginia Historical Magazine,* Jan. 1926, 24.
8. W. Stitt Robinson, *Mother Earth: Land Grants in Virginia, 1607–1699* (Williamsburg, Va.: Virginia 350th Anniversary Celebration Corporation, 1957), 66–72; Edmund S. Morgan, *American Slavery, American Freedom: The Ordeal of Colonial Virginia* (New York: W. W. Norton, 1975), 244–45; William Fitzhugh to Phillip Ludwell, Dec. 14, 1695, in "William Fitzhugh and the Northern Neck Proprietary," *VMHB,* Jan. 1981, 42.
9. Charles O. Paullin, "Early Landmarks Between Great Hunting Creek and the Falls of the Potomac," *Records of the Columbia Historical Society* 31/32 (1930): 62–63; Laurie Ossman and Debra A. McClane, "Stratford," in *The Gentleman's Farm: Elegant Country House Living* (New York: Rizzoli, 2016), 94.
10. Paul C. Nagel, *The Lees of Virginia: Seven Generations of an American Family* (New York: Oxford University Press, 1990), 35–36, 43; C. G. Lee, *Lee Chronicle,* 262–63; Hendrick, *Lees of Virginia,* 44–45, 58–59, 60–61; Alice Proctor James, *The Ohio Company: Its Inner History* (Pittsburgh: University of Pittsburgh Press, 1959), 5, 30; Norris, *Westmoreland County,* 233; Robert E. Lee, "Life of General Henry Lee," 41.
11. Edmund Jennings Lee, *Lee of Virginia, 1642–1892: Biographical and Genealogical Sketches of the Descendants of Colonel Richard Lee* (Westminster, Md.: Heritage Books, 2008), 131–32; Hendrick, *Lees of Virginia,* 57; C. G. Lee, *Lee Chronicle,* 62, 64, 66; Norris, *Westmoreland County,* 237; Edward C. Mead, *Genealogical History of the Lee Family of Virginia and Maryland from A.D. 1300 to A.D. 1866* (New York: University Publishing, 1871), 76.
12. James Boswell, *Life of Johnson,* ed. R. W. Chapman (1904; New York: Oxford University Press, 1998), 767; Adams, diary entry for Sept. 2, 1774, in *The Adams Papers: Diary and Autobiography of John Adams,* ed. L. H. Butterfield (Cambridge, Mass.: Harvard University Press, 1961), 2:120.
13. George Fitzhugh, "The Northern Neck of Virginia," *DeBow's Review,* Sept. 1859, 281; Albert H. Tillson, *Accommodating Revolutions: Virginia's Northern Neck in an Era of Transformations, 1760–1810* (Charlottesville: University of Virginia Press, 2010), 13–15, 102; Fithian to Enoch Green, Nov. 2, 1773, in *Journal and Letters of Philip Vickers Fithian, 1773–1774: A Plantation Tutor of the Old Dominion,* ed. H. D. Farish (Williamsburg, Va.: Colonial Williamsburg, 1965), 21, 242.
14. Tillson, *Accommodating Revolutions,* 36, 159, 186; Jackson Turner Main, "The One Hundred," *WMQ* 11 (July 1954): 354–84; Donald M. Sweig, "The Importation of African Slaves

to the Potomac River, 1732–1772," *WMQ* 42 (Oct. 1985): 512–17; Ryan L. Cole, *Light Horse Harry Lee* (Washington, D.C.: Regnery, 2018), 158.

15. Nagel, *Lees of Virginia,* 43; T. H. Breen, *Tobacco Culture: The Mentality of the Great Tidewater Planters on the Eve of Revolution* (Princeton, N.J.: Princeton University Press, 1985), 40; Richard S. Dunn, *A Tale of Two Plantations: Slave Life and Labor in Jamaica and Virginia* (Cambridge, Mass.: Harvard University Press, 2014), 70–71; Emory G. Evans, *A "Topping People": The Rise and Decline of Virginia's Old Political Elite* (Charlottesville: University of Virginia Press, 2009), 114; Paullin, "Early Landmarks Between Great Hunting Creek and the Falls of the Potomac," 67–68.
16. Laura Croghan Kamoie, *Irons in the Fire: The Business History of the Tayloe Family and Virginia's Gentry, 1700–1860* (Charlottesville: University of Virginia Press, 2007), 18–19, 38–39, 40; Lauren F. Winner, *A Cheerful and Comfortable Faith: Anglican Religious Practice in the Elite Households of Eighteenth-Century Virginia* (New Haven, Conn.: Yale University Press, 2010), 15, 36–37; Dunn, *Tale of Two Plantations,* 50, 53, 181; "Narrative of George Fisher," *WMQ* 17 (Oct. 1908): 135–37.
17. Keith Thomas, *In Pursuit of Civility: Manners and Civilization in Early Modern England* (New Haven, Conn.: Yale University Press, 2018), 111; Bertram Wyatt-Brown, *Southern Honor: Ethics and Behavior in the Old South* (New York: Oxford University Press, 2007), 126–27, 129, 164–65; John K. Nelson, *A Blessed Company: Parishes, Parsons, and Parishioners in Anglican Virginia, 1690–1776* (Chapel Hill: University of North Carolina Press, 2001), 135; Jonathan Boucher, *Reminiscences of an American Loyalist, 1738–1789, Being the Autobiography of the Revd. Jonathan Boucher, Rector of Annapolis in Maryland and Afterwards Vicar of Epsom, Surrey, England* (1925; Port Washington, N.Y.: Kennikat Press, 1967), 31; Fithian, journal entry for Aug. 12, 1774, in *Journal and Letters of Philip Vickers Fithian,* 161.
18. James Blair, "Hypocrisy in Our Prayers to Be Avoided," in *Our Saviour's Divine Sermon on the Mount* (London: J. Brotherton, 1740), 3:52–53; "The Virginia Chronicle," in *The Writings of the Late Elder John Leland, Including Some Events in His Life, Written by Himself, with Additional Sketches, &c.* (New York: G. W. Wood, 1845), 108; Robert Baylor Semple, *A History of the Rise and Progress of the Baptists in Virginia* (Richmond: John O'Lynch, 1810), 35, 37; Andrew Levy, *The First Emancipator: Slavery, Religion, and the Quiet Revolution of Robert Carter* (New York: Random House, 2005), 136–38; Fithian, journal entry for March 6, 1774, in *Journal and Letters of Philip Vickers Fithian,* 72; Rhys Isaac, *The Transformation of Virginia, 1740–1790* (Chapel Hill: University of North Carolina Press, 1982), 168; Robert Carter to Thomas Jefferson, July 27, 1778, in *Papers of Thomas Jefferson,* ed. Julian P. Boyd (Princeton, N.J.: Princeton University Press, 1950), 2:206–7; Shomer S. Zwelling, "Robert Carter's Journey: From Colonial Patriarch to New Nation Mystic," *American Quarterly* 38 (Autumn 1986): 622–24, 628–31.
19. Carter to Washington, May 2, 1776, in *American Archives: Fourth Series, Containing a Documentary History of the English Colonies in North America,* ed. Peter Force (Washington, D.C.: M. S. Clarke & Peter Force, 1846), 6:39.
20. R. H. Lee to George Mason, June 9, 1779, in *The Letters of Richard Henry Lee, 1779–1794,* ed. J. C. Ballagh (New York: Macmillan, 1914), 2:65.
21. Henry Lee to William Lee, March 1, 1775, in Edmund Jennings Lee, *Lee of Virginia,* 293; C. G. Lee, *Lee Chronicle,* 243.
22. Norris, *Westmoreland County, Virginia,* 181; Nagel, *Lees of Virginia,* 66–67; Hendrick, *Lees of Virginia,* 87; "Narrative of George Fisher," 136.
23. Noel B. Gerson, *Light-Horse Harry: A Biography of Washington's Great Cavalryman, General Henry Lee* (Garden City, N.Y.: Doubleday, 1966), 1; C. G. Lee, *Lee Chronicle,* 85–87, 316–17; "Henry Lee Jr.," in *Princetonians, 1769–1775: A Biographical Dictionary* (Princeton, N.J.: Princeton University Press, 1980), 301–3; Willard Thorp, *The Lives of Eighteen from Princeton*

(Princeton, N.J.: Princeton University Press, 1946), 112–14; Charles Boyd, *Light-Horse Harry Lee* (New York: Charles Scribner's Sons, 1931), 2, 5; Cole, *Light Horse Harry Lee,* 31.

24. Robert E. Lee, "Life of General Henry Lee," 16–17; Charles Royster, *Light-Horse Harry Lee and the Legacy of the American Revolution* (Baton Rouge: Louisiana State University Press, 1981), 26; Cecil B. Hartley, *Life of Major General Henry Lee: Commander of Lee's Legion in the Revolutionary War* (New York: Derby & Jackson, 1859), 33; Hendrick, *Lees of Virginia,* 337–38; Lee to Washington, March 31, 1778, and Washington to Lee, April 1, 1778, in *The Papers of George Washington, Revolutionary War Series,* ed. David R. Hoth (Charlottesville: University of Virginia Press, 2004), 14:368–69.
25. Lee to Greene, May 2, 1781, in George F. Scheer, "Henry Lee on the Southern Campaign," *VMHB,* April 1943, 145; Greene to George Weedon, Sept. 6, 1779, in *The Papers of General Nathanael Greene,* ed. R. K. Showman et al. (Chapel Hill: University of North Carolina Press, 1986), 4:364; Charles Royster, *A Revolutionary People at War: The Continental Army and American Character, 1775–1783* (Chapel Hill: University of North Carolina Press, 1979), 80–81, 312; Harry M. Ward, *George Washington's Enforcers: Policing the Continental Army* (Carbondale: Southern Illinois University Press, 2006), 196; Richard M. Ketchum, *Victory at Yorktown: The Campaign That Won the Revolution* (New York: Henry Holt, 2004), 74–77; Washington to Lee, July 10, 1779, in *Papers of George Washington,* 21:422; Washington to James Duane, June 5, 1780, in *The Writings of George Washington,* ed. J. C. Fitzpatrick (Washington, D.C.: U.S. Government Printing Office, 1937), 18:479.
26. Albert Louis Zambone, *Daniel Morgan: A Revolutionary Life* (Yardley, Pa.: Westholme, 2018), 212; "Henry Lee," in *American Military Biography: Containing the Lives, Characters, and Anecdotes of the Officers of the Revolution* (Norberts & Burr, 1827), 127; William Johnson, *Sketches of the Life and Correspondence of Nathanael Greene* (Charleston, S.C.: A. E. Miller, 1822), 2:461; Lee, *Memoirs of the War in the Southern Department of the United States,* 278; John Buchanan, *The Road to Guilford Courthouse* (New York: John Wiley, 1997), 396; Royster, *Light-Horse Harry Lee,* 35. My particular thanks to Ryan Cole for sharing the Revolutionary War pension application of David Williams (Pension Application of David Williams S3578, State of Tennessee, Rutherford County: Court of Pleas & Quarter Sessions August Term 1832), which describes Light Horse Harry's "rage" for battle at Guilford Court House.
27. Greene to Jean-Baptiste Donatien de Vimeur, comte de Rochambeau, Feb. 18, 1782, duPont Library; Gerson, *Light-Horse Harry,* 146–48; Royster, *Light-Horse Harry Lee,* 48, 57; REL, "Life of General Henry Lee," 41, 66; Greene to Lee, May 22, 1781, in "Notes and Queries," *Rhode Island Historical Magazine,* Oct. 1882, 134.
28. *Journals of the Continental Congress, 1774–1789,* ed. J. C. Fitzpatrick (Washington, D.C.: Government Printing Office, 1934), 30:125, 149, 197, 408, 338, and 31:494–98, 965.
29. Washington to John Posey, June 24, 1767, in *Papers of George Washington,* 8:1–4.
30. Jon Kukla, "A Spectrum of Sentiments: Virginia's Federalists, Antifederalists, and 'Federalists Who Are for Amendments,' 1787–1788," *VMHB,* July 1988, 279; *Debates and Other Proceedings of the Convention of Virginia,* ed. David Robertson (Richmond: Ritchie & Worsley, 1805), 41, 71, 73, 76, 419; Richard Labunski, *James Madison and the Struggle for the Bill of Rights* (New York: Oxford University Press, 2006), 106; Royster, *Light-Horse Harry Lee,* 96; Hendrick, *Lees of Virginia,* 361–63. The Northern Neck was strongly supportive of the new Constitution, even to the point of threatening to secede from Virginia if the Commonwealth failed to ratify. See Michael J. Klarman, *The Framers' Coup: The Making of the United States Constitution* (New York: Oxford University Press, 2016), 465, 478.
31. Kevin T. Barksdale, "Our Rebellious Neighbors: Virginia's Border Counties During Pennsylvania's Whiskey Rebellion," *VMHB* 111, no. 1 (2003): 16–22; Washington to Lee, Oct. 20, 1794, duPont Library; "Notes of a Conversation with George Washington," Feb. 7, 1793, in *Papers of Thomas Jefferson,* 25:154; Lee to Alexander Hamilton, Jan. 5, 1795, in *The Papers*

of Alexander Hamilton, ed. Harold C. Syrett (New York: Columbia University Press, 1973), 18:11–12.

32. Nagel, *Lees of Virginia,* 167; C. G. Lee, *Lee Chronicle,* 320–22; Wyrick, "Stratford and the Lees," 78; Edmund Jennings Lee, *Lee of Virginia,* 167; Hendrick, *Lees of Virginia*, 371.
33. Washington to James Madison, Nov. 28, 1784, and to Lafayette, Feb. 15, 1785, and Lee to Washington, Sept. 8, 1786, in *Papers of George Washington, Confederation Series,* 2:155–57, 366, 4:241; Joel Achenbach, *The Grand Idea: George Washington's Potomac and the Race to the West* (New York: Simon & Schuster, 2004), 130, 175; Royster, *Light-Horse Harry Lee,* 75; Douglas R. Littlefield, "The Potomac Company: A Misadventure in Financing an Early American Internal Improvement Project," *Business History Review* 58 (Winter 1984): 572–73.
34. Gerson, *Light-Horse Harry,* 202; Royster, *Light-Horse Harry Lee,* 75; Magnet, *Founders at Home,* 84–85; Richard Henry Lee to William Shippen, May 8, 1775, in *Letters of Richard Henry Lee,* 2:356; Franklin Sawvel, ed., *The Complete Anas of Thomas Jefferson* (New York: Roundtable Press, 1903), 61; Hartley, *Life of Major General Henry Lee,* 269; Paullin, "Early Landmarks Between Great Hunting Creek and the Falls of the Potomac," 70–71.
35. Gerson, *Light-Horse Harry,* 167; "'Light-Horse Harry' (1756–1818)," *Frank Leslie's Popular Monthly,* March 1896, 265; Nagel, *Lees of Virginia,* 165; Hendrick, *Lees of Virginia,* 371–72; Robert Kirk Headley, *Genealogical Abstracts from 18th-Century Virginia Newspapers* (Baltimore: Clearfield, 2007), 203; Washington to Lee, Aug. 27, 1790, duPont Library.
36. Washington to Lee, May 6, 1793, in Fitzpatrick, *Writings of George Washington,* 32:449–50; Gerson, *Light-Horse Harry,* 178.
37. Hendrick, *Lees of Virginia,* 377–78; Hartley, *Life of Major General Henry Lee,* 273–75; Washington to Lee, July 21, 1793, in Fitzpatrick, *Writings of George Washington,* 33:24; Theodore R. Reinhart and Judith A. Habicht, "Shirley Plantation in the Eighteenth Century: A Historical, Architectural, and Archaeological Study," *VMHB,* Jan. 1984, 37; Laurie Ossman, *Great Houses of the South* (New York: Rizzoli, 2010), 20; Margaret Sanborn, *Robert E. Lee: A Portrait, 1807–1861* (Philadelphia: J. B. Lippincott, 1966), 12–13.
38. Washington to Lee, April 2, 1797, in "Three Interesting Letters," *Pennsylvania Magazine of History and Biography* 35 (1911): 109; Hendrick, *Lees of Virginia,* 381, 389; Charles Royster, *The Fabulous History of the Dismal Swamp Company: A Story of George Washington's Times* (New York: Knopf, 1999), 385; Royster, *Light-Horse Harry Lee,* 175, 177.
39. Gerson, *Light-Horse Harry,* 217–18; Royster, *Light-Horse Harry Lee,* 179, 184–85; Timothy Pickering to Hamilton, Nov. 17, 1795, in *Papers of Alexander Hamilton,* 19:437; Edward L. Ryan, "Imprisonment for Debt: Its Origin and Repeal," *VMHB,* Jan. 1934, 58; C. G. Lee, *Lee Chronicle,* 88–89; Norman K. Risjord, "The Virginia Federalists," *Journal of Southern History* 33 (Nov. 1967): 498–99; Bertram Wyatt-Brown, "Robert E. Lee and the Concept of Honor," in *Virginia's Civil War,* ed. Peter Wallenstein and Bertram Wyatt-Brown (Charlottesville: University of Virginia Press, 2005), 30–31.
40. Royster, *Light-Horse Harry Lee,* 82–83; Ann Carter Lee, Jan. 11, 1807, LFDA/duPont Library; Nagel, *Lees of Virginia,* 196.
41. Sanborn, *Robert E. Lee: A Portrait,* 26; Magnet, *Founders at Home,* 86. The story, originally confected by Ethel Armes, that Robert had wandered off and, after some frantic searching, was found in front of the central hall's fireplace, forlornly bidding farewell to the cherubs embossed on the fireback, is almost certainly apocryphal.

Chapter Two: The Making of an Engineer

1. George William Van Cleve, *We Have Not a Government: The Articles of Confederation and the Road to the Constitution* (Chicago: University of Chicago Press, 2017), 41–42; Isaac, *Trans-*

formation of Virginia, 312–13; Dunn, *Tale of Two Plantations,* 182, 187; Drew A. Swanson, *A Golden Weed: Tobacco and Environment in the Piedmont South* (New Haven, Conn.: Yale University Press, 2014), 20; Jeremiah Bell Jeter, *The Recollections of a Long Life* (Richmond: Religious Herald, 1891), 145–46; Cole, *Light Horse Harry Lee,* 157; Gerson, *Light-Horse Harry,* 150. On the emerging consensus that "something 'truly disastrous' happened to the American economy between the Revolution and 1790," see Dael A. Norwood, "The Constitutional Consequences of Commercial Crisis: The Role of Trade Reconsidered in the 'Critical Period,'" *Early American Studies* 18 (Fall 2020): 502–3.

2. Hendrick, *Lees of Virginia,* 404; Main, "One Hundred," 366; Winner, *Cheerful and Comfortable Faith,* 179, 180–81; William Meade, *Old Churches, Ministers, and Families of Virginia* (Philadelphia: J. B. Lippincott, 1900), 1:369.
3. Gay Montague Moore, *Seaport in Virginia: George Washington's Alexandria* (Charlottesville: University Press of Virginia, 1949), 3–4, 5, 7–8; George G. Kundahl, *Alexandria Goes to War* (Knoxville: University of Tennessee Press, 2004), 2–4; *The Charter and Laws of the City of Alexandria, Va.: And an Historical Sketch of Its Government* (Alexandria: Gazette Book & Job Office, 1874), 9–10, 13; J. P. Brissot de Warville, *New Travels in the United States of America Performed in 1788* (Dublin: W. Corset, 1792), 426–27; Eugene Beauharnais Jackson, *The Romance of Historic Alexandria: A Guide to the Old City* (Atlanta: A. B. Caldwell, 1921), 42; Washington to Sally Fairfax, May 16, 1798, in Fitzpatrick, *Writings of George Washington,* 36:264–65; Robert H. Gudmestad, "The Troubled Legacy of Isaac Franklin: The Enterprise of Slave Trading," *Tennessee Historical Quarterly* 62 (Fall 2003): 193–217.
4. Anne Ritson, *A Poetical Picture of America: Being Observations Made During a Residence of Several Years, at Alexandria, and Norfolk, in Virginia* (London: Vernor, Hood & Sharpe, 1809), 44–45; Lee to T.H.M., March 10, 1811, *Historical Magazine,* July 1858, 197; Royster, *Light-Horse Harry Lee,* 189, 196; Cole, *Light-Horse Harry Lee,* 319.
5. Gerson, *Light-Horse Harry,* 153; "Account of the Late Riots," *Niles' Weekly Register,* Aug. 8, 1812, 373–80; Royster, *Light-Horse Harry Lee,* 164–67, 227; Frank A. Cassell, "The Great Baltimore Riot of 1812," *Maryland Historical Magazine* 70 (Fall 1975): 256–58; Bertram Wyatt-Brown, *A Warring Nation: Honor, Race, and Humiliation in America and Abroad* (Charlottesville: University Press of Virginia, 2014), 73–74; Cole, *Light-Horse Harry Lee,* 302–15.
6. "Antebellum Reminiscences of Alexandria, Virginia, Extracted from the Memoirs of Mary Louisa Slacum Benham," trans. Anna Modigliani Lynch and Kelsey Ryan, Barrett Library, Alexandria, Va.
7. Nagel, *Lees of Virginia,* 198; Royster, *Light-Horse Harry Lee,* 179, 182–85, 232–33, 241; Juan Christian Pellicer, "'I Hear Such Strange Things of the Union's Fate': Charles Carter Lee's Virginia Georgics," *Early American Literature* 42 (2007): 131; Cole, *Light-Horse Harry Lee,* 326.
8. Michal Jan Rozbicki, "Between Private and Public Spheres: Liberty as Cultural Property in Eighteenth-Century British America," in *Cultures and Identities in Colonial British America,* ed. Robert Olwell and Alan Tully (Baltimore: Johns Hopkins University Press, 2004), 310; Gordon Wood, *The Radicalism of the American Revolution: How a Revolution Transformed a Monarchical Society into a Democratic One Unlike Any That Had Ever Existed* (New York: Knopf, 1991), 90–91, 135–36, 190, 195; Crèvecoeur, *Letters from an American Farmer and Sketches of Eighteenth-Century America,* ed. Albert Stone (New York: Penguin Books, 1981), 70; Paul A. Gilje, "The Baltimore Riots of 1812 and the Breakdown of the Anglo-American Mob Tradition," *Journal of Social History* 13 (Summer 1980): 554.
9. Thomas, *Pursuit of Civility,* 16, 19, 31, 33, 36; Breen, *Tobacco Culture,* 160; Cary Carson, *Face Value: The Consumer Revolution and the Colonization of America* (Charlottesville: University of Virginia Press, 2017), 17; John Adams to Mercy Otis Warren, Jan. 8, 1776, in *Warren-Adams Letters: Being Chiefly a Correspondence Among John Adams, Samuel Adams, and James*

Warren (Boston: Massachusetts Historical Society, 1917), 1:201; Catharine Maria Sedgwick, *Home* (Boston: James Monroe, 1850), 39.

10. Thomas West, *The Political Theory of the American Founding: Natural Rights, Public Policy, and the Moral Conditions of Freedom* (New York: Cambridge University Press, 2017), 262; John F. Kasson, *Rudeness and Civility: Manners in Nineteenth-Century Urban America* (New York: Hill and Wang, 1990), 170; Richard L. Bushman, *The Refinement of America: Persons, Houses, Cities* (New York: Knopf, 1992), 216, 217, 258, 282, 285, 287, 321–23; Richard L. Bushman, "The Genteel Republic," *Wilson Quarterly* (Autumn 1996): 13–23.
11. Ann Hill Lee to CCL, July 17, 1816, in Ethel Armes, *Stratford Hall: The Great House of the Lees* (Richmond: Garrett & Massie, 1936), 356–57; Light Horse Harry Lee to CCL, Feb. 9, 1817, in REL, "Life of General Henry Lee," 63; R. David Cox, *The Religious Life of Robert E. Lee* (Grand Rapids: Wm. B. Eerdmans, 2017), 30–31; Ann Lee to SSL, April 10, 1827, in Douglas Southall Freeman, *R. E. Lee: A Biography* (New York: Charles Scribner's, 1934), 1:90.
12. Emily V. Mason, *Popular Life of Gen. Robert Edward Lee* (Baltimore: John Murphy, 1874), 22; "Personal Recollections of General Robert E. Lee by His Cousin, Marietta Fauntleroy Powell," in Mariette Minnegerode Andrews, *Scraps of Paper* (New York: E. P. Dutton, 1929), 198; REL to MCL, June 15, 1857, in PLREL, 1:365.
13. U.S. Federal Census 1810, Westmoreland County, Va., 12; Thomas, *Robert E. Lee,* 35; Robert R. Brown, *The Spiritual Pilgrimage of Robert E. Lee* (Shippensburg, Pa.: White Mane, 1998), 7–8; Joseph Packard, *Recollections of a Long Life* (Washington, D.C.: Byron S. Adams, 1902), 160; Ethel Armes, *Stratford on the Potomac* (Greenwich, Conn.: William Alexander Jr. Chapter, United Daughters of the Confederacy, 1928), 10–11; Mason, *Popular Life of Gen. Robert Edward Lee,* 23; William C. Davis, *Crucible of Command: Ulysses S. Grant and Robert E. Lee—the War They Fought, the Peace They Forged* (Boston: Da Capo Press, 2014), 502.
14. J. Patten Abshire, "The History of the Boyhood Home of Robert E. Lee," *Alexandria Chronicle* 3 (Winter 1995/96): 1–4; Dabney Herndon Maury, *Recollections of a Virginian in the Mexican, Indian, and Civil Wars* (New York: Charles Scribner's Sons, 1894), 3; Hendrick, *Lees of Virginia,* 404–5; Moore, *Seaport in Virginia,* 202–8, 226–27; C. G. Lee, *Lee Chronicle,* 287–88, 289.
15. John Morgan Dederer, "The Origins of Robert E. Lee's Bold Generalship: A Reinterpretation," *Military Affairs* 49 (July 1985): 120; Jackson, *Romance of Historic Alexandria,* 25–26, 44; Norris, *Westmoreland County, Virginia,* 353–57; C. G. Lee, *Lee Chronicle,* 265; Moore, *Seaport in Virginia,* 239–42; *Autobiography of Benjamin Hallowell* (Philadelphia: Friends Book Association, 1883), 100–101; Kundahl, *Alexandria Goes to War,* 21–23; Beauharnais, *Romance of Historic Alexandria,* 39; Davis, *Crucible of Command,* 5–6, 500–501; Freeman, *R. E. Lee,* 1:40; Mason, *Popular Life of Gen. Robert Edward Lee,* 261.
16. *Autobiography of Benjamin Hallowell,* 103; Moore, *Seaport in Virginia,* 247–48; Bruce R. Smith, "Benjamin Hallowell of Alexandria," *VMHB,* July 1977, 346–47; REL to Mary Anna Custis, May 13, 1831, in Robert E. Lee deButts Jr., "Lee in Love: Courtship and Correspondence in Antebellum Virginia," *VMHB* 115 (2007): 541.
17. "A Letter Written by General Lee," *Alexandria Gazette,* March 8, 1886; Elizabeth Brown Pryor, "Rediscovered: Robert E. Lee's Earliest-Known Letter," *VMHB,* Jan. 2007, 110.
18. Freeman, *R. E. Lee,* 1:42; Thomas, *Robert E. Lee,* 42; Long, *Memoirs of Robert E. Lee,* 28; Robert Elder, *Calhoun: American Heretic* (New York: Basic Books, 2021), 162.
19. REL to Calhoun, April 1, 1824, LFDA/duPont Library.
20. "Of the Troops in Service of the United States," Oct. 2, 1788, in *Journals of the American Congress: From 1774 to 1788* (Washington, D.C.: Way & Gideon, 1823), 4:874; Russell F. Weigley, *History of the United States Army* (New York: Macmillan, 1967), 81; Paul A. C. Koistinen, *Beating Plowshares into Swords: The Political Economy of American Warfare, 1606–1865* (Lawrence: University Press of Kansas, 1996), 47.

21. William H. Gaines, "The Forgotten Army: Recruiting for a National Emergency (1799–1800)," *VMHB,* July 1948, 279; Sidney Forman, "Why the United States Military Academy Was Established in 1802," *Military Affairs* 29 (Spring 1965): 22; Alexis de Tocqueville, "Of Discipline in Democratic Armies," in *Democracy in America,* trans. Henry Reeve (New York: Colonial Press, 1899), 2:293–94.
22. Barton C. Hacker, "Engineering a New Order: Military Institutions, Technical Education, and the Rise of the Industrial State," *Technology and Culture* 34 (Jan. 1993): 12; Stephen E. Ambrose, *Duty, Honor, Country: A History of West Point* (Baltimore: Johns Hopkins University Press, 1966), 12; "Military Academy, and Reorganization of the Army," Jan. 14, 1800, in *American State Papers: Documents, Legislative and Executive, of the Congress of the United States* (Washington, D.C.: Gales and Seaton, 1832), 133–34.
23. Edward Carlisle Boynton, *History of West Point: And Its Military Importance During the American Revolution and the Origin and Progress of the United States Military Academy* (New York: D. Van Nostrand, 1871), 217; Ambrose, *Duty, Honor, Country,* 19, 40–41, 67, 74, 90; Review of "Military Laws of the United States" and "Documents from the Department of War," *North American Review* 53 (Oct. 1826): 271; Koistinen, *Beating Plowshares into Swords,* 21–22, 62, 81–82, 84–85, 92; J. P. Clark, *Preparing for War: The Emergence of the Modern U.S. Army, 1815–1917* (Cambridge, Mass.: Harvard University Press, 2017), 32; John H. B. Latrobe, *Reminiscences of West Point from September, 1818 to Mar., 1882* (East Saginaw, Mich.: Evening News, 1887), 19.
24. Review of "Military Laws of the United States" and "Documents from the Department of War," 271; "Memorial of Certain Non-commissioned Officers of the Army," Jan. 16, 1837, in *American State Papers: Documents, Legislative and Executive, of the Congress of the United States* (Washington, D.C.: Gales and Seaton, 1861), 6:988.
25. Albert E. Church, *Personal Reminiscences of the Military Academy from 1824 to 1831: A Paper Read to the U.S. Military Service Institute, West Point, March 28, 1878* (West Point, N.Y.: USMA Press, 1879), 9, 40, 43, 46, 47–48, 51–52; "Synopsis of the Course of Studies at the Military Academy" (1825), in *American State Papers: Documents, Legislative and Executive, of the Congress of the United States* (Washington, D.C.: Gales and Seaton, 1860), 3:150; Ian C. Hope, *A Scientific Way of War: Antebellum Military Science, West Point, and the Origins of American Military Thought* (Lincoln: University of Nebraska Press, 2015), 40–43, 86, 92–98; Andrei N. Kolmogorov and Adolf P. Yushkevich, eds., *Mathematics of the 19th Century: Geometry, Analytic Function, Theory* (Berlin: Birkhauser, 1996), 3; William Enfield, *Institutes of Natural Philosophy, Theoretical and Experimental* (London: J. Johnson, 1785), vii; Michael Bonura, *Under the Shadow of Napoleon: French Influence on the American Way of Warfare from the War of 1812 to the Outbreak of WWII* (New York: New York University Press, 2012), 76; Frederic H. Smith, *West Point Fifty Years Ago: An Address Delivered Before the Association of Graduates of the U.S. Military Academy, West Point* (New York: D. Van Nostrand, 1879), 5; Charles F. O'Connell, "The Corps of Engineers and Modern Management, 1827–1856," in *Military Enterprise and Technological Change: Perspectives on the American Experience,* ed. M. R. Smith (Cambridge, Mass.: MIT Press, 1985), 93; Edgar S. Dudley, "Was 'Secession' Taught at West Point?," *Century Magazine,* May 1909, 635.
26. King to C. Gore, June 22, 1821, in *The Life and Correspondence of Rufus King, Comprising His Letters, Private and Official, His Public Documents, and His Speeches,* ed. Charles R. King (New York: G. P. Putnam, 1900), 6:394; Erasmus D. Keyes, *Fifty Years' Observations of Men and Events, Civil and Military* (New York: C. Scribner's Sons, 1884), 190; Richard Weingardt, *Engineering Legends* (Reston, Va.: American Society of Civil Engineers, 2005), 1–2, 4–5; Robert J. Kapsch, *Historic Canals and Waterways of South Carolina* (Columbia: University of South Carolina Press, 2010), 7.
27. Boynton, *History of West Point,* 240–41; Hope, *Scientific Way of War,* 111–14; Weingardt, *Engineering Legends,* 122–23; Jon Scott Logel, *Designing Gotham: West Point Engineers and the Rise*

of Modern New York, 1817–1898 (Baton Rouge: Louisiana State University Press, 2016), 30–31, 52–53; "Report of the Minority of the Board of Visitors at West Point, June 25, 1840," in *Message from the President of the United States to the Two Houses of Congress, at the Commencement of the Second Session of the Twenty-Sixth Congress* (Washington, D.C.: Blair & Rives, 1840), 150–51.

28. King to C. Gore, June 22, 1821, in *Life and Correspondence of Rufus King,* 6:394.
29. *The Life and Speeches of the Hon. Henry Clay,* ed. Daniel Mallery (New York: A. S. Barnes, 1857), 1:88; Peter B. Porter, "Report of the Secretary of War," Nov. 24, 1828, in *The National Calendar: And Annals of the United States* (Washington, D.C.: Peter Force, 1829), 7:273; William B. Skelton, *An American Profession of Arms: The Army Officer Corps, 1784–1861* (Lawrence: University Press of Kansas, 1992), 295–97.
30. Latrobe, *Reminiscences of West Point,* 2, 5; Augusta Blanche Berard, *Reminiscences of West Point in the Olden Time* (East Saginaw, Mich.: Evening News Printing, 1886), 24, 29, 32; Samuel E. Tillman, "The Academic History of the Military Academy, 1802–1902," in *The Centennial of the United States Military Academy at West Point, New York* (Washington, D.C.: Government Printing Office, 1904), 1:258; Freeman, *R. E. Lee,* 1:51.
31. George Washington Cullum, *Biographical Register of the Officers and Graduates of the U.S. Military Academy at West Point, N.Y.* (Boston: Houghton, Mifflin, 1891), 1:421–47.
32. *American State Papers: Documents, Legislative and Executive, of the Congress of the United States,* 3:575, 674; Ann Lee to SSL, April 10, 1829, duPont Library.
33. William Nelson Pendleton, "Personal Recollections of General Lee," *Southern Magazine,* Dec. 1874, 604; Johnston, in Long, *Memoirs of Robert E. Lee,* 71; Lasalle Pickett, "The Wartime Story of General Pickett," *Cosmopolitan,* Jan. 1914, 184.
34. "Address of President Davis," in Jones, *Army of Northern Virginia Memorial Volume,* 14; Jones, *Personal Reminiscences,* 340.
35. Freeman, *R. E. Lee,* 1:72–73; Benjamin Hallowell, *Geometrical Analysis, or the Construction and Solution of Various Geometrical Problems* (Philadelphia: J. B. Lippincott, 1872), 10; Felix Gilbert, "Machiavelli: The Renaissance of the Art of War," in *Makers of Modern Strategy from Machiavelli to the Nuclear Age,* ed. Peter Paret (Oxford: Clarendon Press, 1986), 27; Charles de Warnery, *Thoughts and Anecdotes Military and Historical, Written About the Year 1774* (London: T. Egerton, 1811), 86; "Warnery's Thoughts and Anecdotes," *Anti-Jacobin Review and True Churchman's Magazine,* May 1911, 41.

Chapter Three: Marriage and the Third System

1. Boynton, *History of West Point,* 223; Cazenove G. Lee, "Ann Hill Carter," *WMQ* 16 (July 1936): 419; Edmund Jennings Lee, *Lee of Virginia,* 404; Thomas, *Robert E. Lee,* 38–39; Louise Pecquet du Bellet, *Some Prominent Virginia Families* (Lynchburg, Va.: J. P. Bell, 1907), 1:264; Pellicer, "'I Hear Such Strange Things of the Union's Fate,'" 132; REL to CCL, Oct. 12, 1830, Robert E. Lee Papers, Albert and Shirley Small Special Collections Library, University of Virginia; Ann Carter Lee to SSL, May 17, 1822, duPont Library.
2. Nagel, *Lees of Virginia,* 204–7, 226–27; C. G. Lee, *Lee Chronicle,* 91; Henry Lee to William Berkeley Lewis, July 26, 1833, Lee Family Papers, VMHC.
3. "Personal Recollections of General Robert E. Lee by His Cousin, Marietta Fauntleroy Powell," 198–99.
4. Jennifer Hanna, *Arlington House: The Robert E. Lee Memorial* (Washington, D.C.: U.S. Department of the Interior, 2001), 31; Benton J. Lossing, "Arlington House: The Seat of G. W. P. Custis," *Harper's New Monthly Magazine,* Sept. 1853, 436; William George Rudy, "Interpreting America's First Grecian Style House: The Architectural Legacy of George

Washington Parke Custis and George Hadfield" (master's thesis, University of Maryland, College Park, 2010), 10.

5. Clayton Torrence, ed., "Arlington and Mount Vernon 1856 as Described in a Letter of Augusta Blanche Berard," *VMHB,* April 1949, 150; Hanna, *Arlington House,* 20, 39; Kundahl, *Alexandria Goes to War,* 77; Godfrey T. Vigne, *Six Months in America* (Philadelphia: Thomas T. Ash, 1833), 55; Jonathan Horn, *The Man Who Would Not Be Washington: Robert E. Lee's Civil War and His Decision That Changed American History* (New York: Scribner, 2015), 37; Packard, *Recollections of a Long Life,* 156; Rudy, "Interpreting America's First Grecian Style House," 33, 36.
6. Davis, *Crucible of Command,* 26; Henry S. Foote, *Casket of Reminiscences* (Washington, D.C.: Chronicle, 1874), 16–17; Sanborn, *Robert E. Lee: A Portrait,* 75.
7. Freeman, *R. E. Lee,* 1:69, 72; Nagel, *Lees of Virginia,* 231, 233–34; Ann Lee to SSL, April 10, 1829, duPont Library.
8. Freeman, *R. E. Lee,* 1:81–82; Eben Swift, "The Military Education of Robert E. Lee," *VMHB,* April 1927, 101–4; "Cadets Arranged in Order of Merit, in Their Respective Classes, as Determined at the General Examination, in June, 1829," in *Official Register of the Officers and Cadets of the U.S. Military Academy, June, 1829* (West Point, N.Y.: USMA, 1884), 6; Edward M. Coffman, "The Army Officer and the Constitution," *Parameters: The U.S. Army War College Quarterly* 17 (Sept. 1987): 4.
9. Long, *Memoirs of Robert E. Lee,* 26; Ann Lee to SSL, April 10, 1829, duPont Library; Edmund Jennings Lee, "General Robert E. Lee," in Robert A. Brock, *Gen. Robert Edward Lee: Soldier, Citizen, and Christian Patriot* (Richmond: Royal, 1897), 368; "Personal Recollections of General Robert E. Lee by His Cousin, Marietta Fauntleroy Powell," 198.
10. Ann Carter Lee Will, July 24, 1829, Fairfax County Court House, Will Book, P-1, 1827–1830, 277–28; Sanborn, *Robert E. Lee,* 66–67.
11. "Mr. Adams' Oration," *Niles' Weekly Register,* July 21, 1821, 331; Henry Wager Halleck, "Report on the Means of National Defence," Oct. 20, 1843, in *Senate Executive Documents Printed by Order of the Senate of the United States, Second Session of the Twenty-Eighth Congress* (Washington, D.C.: Gales & Seaton, 1845), 3:85/9.
12. Hope, *Scientific Way of War,* 55–59; Emmanuel Raymond Lewis, *Seacoast Fortifications of the United States: An Introductory History* (Washington, D.C.: Smithsonian Institution Press, 1970), 37–45; John R. Weaver, *A Legacy in Brick and Stone: American Coastal Defense Forts of the Third System, 1816–1867* (Missoula, Mont.: Pictorial Histories/Redoubt Press, 2001), 2–12; Angus Konstam, *American Civil War Fortifications (1): Coastal Brick and Stone Forts* (Osceloa, Wis.: Osprey, 2003), 7–19.
13. Mark A. Smith, "A Crucial Leavening of Expertise: Engineer Soldiers and the Transmission of Military Proficiency in the American Civil War," *Civil War History* 66 (March 2020): 11; J. E. and H. W. Kaufmann, *Fortress America: The Forts That Defended America, 1600 to the Present* (Boston: Da Capo Press, 2005), 207; Konstam, *American Civil War Fortifications,* 19; J. William Kamphuis, *Introduction to Coastal Engineering and Management* (Hackensack, N.J.: World Scientific, 2010), 9, 27, 29–30, 162–64, 171.
14. Robert E. Lee Jr., *Recollections and Letters of General Robert E. Lee* (New York: Doubleday, Page, 1904), 443–44; Rogers W. Young, *Robert E. Lee and Fort Pulaski* (Washington, D.C.: National Park Service, 1941), 4; REL to CCL, May 8 and Nov. 16, 1830, Robert E. Lee Papers, Small Special Collections Library; REL to Mary Custis, Nov. 11, 1830, in deButts, "Lee in Love," 520.
15. DeButts, "Lee in Love," 491, 494, 495, 515–17; REL to CCL, Sept. 22 and 30, 1830, Robert E. Lee Papers, Small Special Collections Library.
16. REL to Mary Custis, Nov. 11, 1830, in deButts, "Lee in Love," 520; REL to CCL, Nov. 16, 1830, Robert E. Lee Papers, Small Special Collections Library; REL to Eliza Ann Mackay,

April 13, 1831, in Frank Screven, ed., "The Letters of R. E. Lee to the Mackay Family of Savannah" (typescript, Georgia Southern University, Armstrong Campus Library, 1952), 5; Young, *Robert E. Lee and Fort Pulaski,* 14.

17. REL to Mary Custis, Oct. 30 and Dec. 1, 1830, April 3, 1831, in deButts, "Lee in Love," 517, 523, 536; REL to CCL, Jan. 4 and Feb. 27, 1831, Robert E. Lee Papers, Small Special Collections Library.
18. REL to John Mackay, Nov. 3, 1831, in Screven, "Letters of R. E. Lee to the Mackay Family," 8; REL to Mary Ann Mackay Stiles, May 24, 1856, in Adams, PLREL, 1:124–25; Sanborn, *Robert E. Lee: A Portrait,* 79–82.
19. REL to Mary Custis, Nov. 11 and 19, Dec. 1 and 28, 1830, April 3, 1831, in deButts, "Lee in Love," 520, 521, 522, 523, 525, 535; R. M. E. MacDonald, *Mrs. Robert E. Lee* (New York: Ginn, 1939), 261; Edward M. Coffman, *The Old Army: A Portrait of the American Army in Peacetime, 1784–1898* (New York: Oxford University Press, 1986), 78.
20. REL to CCL, May 20 and June 15, 1831, Robert E. Lee Papers, Small Special Collections Library; REL to Mary Custis, May 24, 1831, Lee Family Papers, VMHC; REL to Mary Custis, May 13, 1831, in deButts, "Lee in Love," 540.
21. William Sparrow, in *Annals of the American Pulpit,* ed. W. B. Sprague (New York: Robert Carter & Bros., 1859), 5:628; REL to Mary Custis, June 12, 1831, in deButts, "Lee in Love," 546; REL to Mary Custis, May 24, 1831, and to Talcott, July 13, 1831, Lee Family Papers, VMHC; Packard, *Recollections of a Long Life,* 156.
22. "The Confessions of Nat Turner," in *Slave Narratives,* ed. William L. Andrews and Henry Louis Gates (New York: Library of America, 2000), 252–53.
23. John V. Quarstein and Dennis P. Mroczkowski, *Fort Monroe: The Key to the South* (Charleston, S.C.: Arcadia, 2000), 26; Scot French, *The Rebellious Slave: Nat Turner in American Memory* (Boston: Houghton Mifflin, 2004), 34–35; Fitzhugh Lee, *General Lee* (New York: D. Appleton, 1895), 27–28; REL to Mary Fitzhugh Custis, Sept. 4, 1831, Lee Family Papers, VMHC.
24. U.S. Federal Census 1810, Westmoreland County, Va., 12; REL to CCL, Jan. 4, 1831, and Feb. 24, 1835, Robert E. Lee Papers, Small Special Collections Library; Mason, *Popular Life of General Robert Edward Lee,* 23.
25. REL to CCL, Sept. 28, 1832, Robert E. Lee Papers, Small Special Collections Library; "Views of a Virginia Slaveholder in 1827," *Sacramento Daily Union,* Jan. 6, 1865; Custis, in *The Ninth Annual Report of the American Society for Colonizing the Free People of Color of the United States* (Washington, D.C.: Way & Gideon, 1826), 12; Edward Carter Turner, in Sanborn, *Robert E. Lee: A Portrait,* 1:129; Hanna, *Arlington House,* 45.
26. Mary Fitzhugh Custis and MCL to REL, June 11, 1831, in deButts, "Lee in Love," 544–45; REL to MCL, June 2, 1832, and REL to Andrew Talcott, April 10, 1834, Lee Family Papers, VMHC; MacDonald, *Mrs. Robert E. Lee,* 40–41.
27. REL to Talcott, Aug. 2, Nov. 22, and Dec. 1, 4, and 16, 1833, Feb. 15, 21, and 27, 1834; REL to Captain J. Monroe, May 3, 1833, Literary and Historical Manuscripts, Pierpont Morgan Library, New York.
28. REL to MCL, April 17, 1832, in Norma B. Cuthbert, "To Molly: Five Early Letters from Robert E. Lee to His Wife, 1832–1835," *Huntington Library Quarterly* 15 (May 1952): 262–63; REL to Captain J. Monroe, May 3, 1833, Pierpont Morgan Library; W. G. Bean, "Memoranda of Conversations Between General Robert E. Lee and William Preston Johnston: May 7, 1868, and March 18, 1870," *VMHB,* Oct. 1965, 477; REL to CCL, Sept. 28, 1832, Robert E. Lee Papers, Small Special Collections Library.
29. MacDonald, *Mrs. Robert E. Lee,* 42; REL to Lloyd, March 6, 1833, www.maxrambod.com/_images/catalog/Civil%20War/Lee10600.jpg.
30. "Will of Robert E. Lee, 1846 August 31 (Including Indorsement of 1870 November 7),"

LFDA/duPont Library; Martha Gilkeson, "The Story of Howard's Lick," West Virginia Department of Arts, History, and Culture, www.wvculture.org; Thomas D. Perry, *The Dear Old Hills of Patrick: J. E. B. Stuart and Patrick County, Virginia* (CreateSpace Independent Publishing Platform, 2015), freestateofpatrick.blogspot.com; Thomas, *Robert E. Lee,* 108–9.

31. Coffman, *Old Army,* 49; REL to CCL, Oct. 12, 1831, and Aug. 17, 1832, Robert E. Lee Papers, Small Special Collections Library.
32. REL to CCL, April 6 and Sept. 28, 1832, Robert E. Lee Papers, Small Special Collections Library.
33. Coffman, *Old Army,* 52.
34. REL to CCL, Sept. 1, 1831, April 6, 1832, and July 24, 1843, Robert E. Lee Papers, Small Special Collections Library; Skelton, *American Profession of Arms,* 25, 202; Logel, *Designing Gotham,* 12–13; Coffman, *Old Army,* 50; Pellicer, " 'I Hear Such Strange Things of the Union's Fate,' " 133, 150.
35. REL to MCL, April 17, 1832, and Nov. 27, 1833, in Cuthbert, "To Molly," 260–61, 266, 268–69; REL to Mackay, Jan. 23 and Feb. 18, 1833, in Screven, "Letters of R. E. Lee to the Mackay Family," 17–18; REL to Talcott, June 6, 1834, Lee Family Papers, VMHC; Thomas, *Robert E. Lee,* 76; Mary Fitzhugh Custis to MCL, Oct. 6, 1831, Lee Family Papers, VMHC; Freeman, *R. E. Lee,* 1:127–28.

Chapter Four: Mission to the Mississippi

1. *Register of All Officers and Agents, Civil, Military, and Naval, in the Service of the United States,* ed. William A. Weaver (Washington, D.C.: Francis Preston Blair, 1833), 96; REL to Talcott, Nov. 1, 1834, Talcott Papers, VMHC.
2. Harry L. Watson, *Liberty and Power: The Politics of Jacksonian America* (New York: Hill and Wang, 1990), 157–58; Robert V. Remini, *Andrew Jackson and the Course of American Democracy, 1833–1845* (New York: Harper & Row, 1984), 114.
3. REL to Mackay, June 26, 1834, in Screven, "Letters of R. E. Lee to the Mackay Family," 22; Henry Vernon Somerville to CCL, April 22, 1835, duPont Library; "Political—Presidential," *Niles' Political Register,* Oct. 24, 1844.
4. MCL to Eliza Stiles, Jan. 23, 1836, duPont Library; *The American Almanac and Repository of Useful Knowledge for the Year 1838* (Boston: Charles Bowen, 1837), 147; REL to Cullum, May 18, 1837, Special Collections, James G. Leyburn Library, Washington and Lee University, Lexington, Va.; REL to Mackay, June 22, 1836, in Screven, "Letters of R. E. Lee to the Mackay Family," 27–28.
5. P.J.K., "The Gratiot Portraits by Thomas Sully," *Record of the Art Museum, Princeton University* 20 (1961): 55; James Neal Primm, *Lion of the Valley: St. Louis, Missouri, 1764–1980* (St. Louis: Missouri Historical Society Press, 1998), 73; "United States Army," *Niles' Weekly Register,* June 15, 1816, 353; Frederic Louis Billon, *Annals of St. Louis in Its Territorial Days, from 1804 to 1821* (St. Louis: Frederic Billon, 1888), 19, 172–73; John Fletcher Darby, *Personal Recollections of Many Prominent People Whom I Have Known* (St. Louis: G. I. Jones, 1880), 226; REL to Talcott, Feb. 13, 1836, Talcott Papers, VMHC; Thomas, *Robert E. Lee,* 83–84.
6. REL to CCL, Feb. 24 and May 17, 1835, Robert E. Lee Papers, Small Special Collections Library; MacDonald, *Mrs. Robert E. Lee,* 56.
7. REL to Talcott, May 5, 1836, Talcott Papers, VMHC; Mary P. Coulling, *The Lee Girls* (Winston-Salem, N.C.: John F. Blair, 1987), 9; MacDonald, *Mrs. Robert E. Lee,* 57; Robert E. Lee Jr., *Recollections and Letters,* 19.
8. REL to CCL, May 2, 1836, Robert E. Lee Papers, Small Special Collections Library; Aloysius I. Mudd, "The Theatres of Washington from 1835 to 1850," *Records of the Columbia Historical*

Society 6 (1903): 230; Murray H. Nelligan, "American Nationalism on the Stage: The Plays of George Washington Parke Custis (1781–1857)," *VMHB,* July 1950, 322.

9. Cong. Globe, June 13, 1834, 23rd Cong., 1st Sess., 444; REL to Talcott, Dec. 8, 1834, Brock Collection, Huntington Library, San Marino, Calif.; Sanborn, *Robert E. Lee: A Portrait,* 106; Thomas, *Robert E. Lee,* 82–83.
10. REL to George Cullum, July 31, 1835, Lee Family Papers, VMHC; REL to MCL, Aug. 21, 1835, in Cuthbert, "To Molly," 271–72. See also John L. Gignilliat, "A Historian's Dilemma: A Posthumous Footnote for Freeman's *R. E. Lee,*" *Journal of Southern History* 43 (May 1977): 221–23.
11. REL to Talcott, Feb. 2, 1837, Talcott Papers, VMHC.
12. Richard Edwards, *Edwards's Great West and Her Commercial Metropolis: Embracing a General View of the West and a Complete History of St. Louis, from the Landing of Ligueste, in 1764, to the Present Time* (New York: C. V. Alvord, 1860), 270, 328; Thomas Allen, "The Commerce and Navigation of the Mississippi and Its Tributaries," *Western Journal of Agriculture, Manufactures, Mechanic Arts, Internal Improvement, Commerce, and General Literature* 1 (March 1848): 160; Charles Dahlinger, "The *New Orleans,* Being a Critical Account of the Beginning of Steamboat Navigation on the Western Rivers of the United States," *Pittsburgh Legal Journal* 59 (Oct. 1911): 580; Zadok Cramer, *The Navigator: Containing Directions for Navigating the Monongahela, Allegheny, Ohio, and Mississippi Rivers* (Pittsburgh: Cramer & Spear, 1821), 21, 142; "Chronicle," *Niles' Weekly Register,* July 1, 1815, 320; Dan Elbert Clark, *The Middle West in American History* (New York: Thomas Crowell, 1937), 107.
13. *St. Louis Business Directory, for 1847: Containing the History of St. Louis* (St. Louis, 1847), 77; Adam B. Chambers, *Proceedings of the St. Louis Chamber of Commerce, in Relation to the Improvement of the Navigation of the Mississippi River and Its Principal Tributaries and the St. Louis Harbor* (St. Louis: Chambers & Knapp, 1842), 8; Emerson W. Gould, *Fifty Years on the Mississippi; or, Gould's History of River Navigation* (St. Louis: Nixon-Jones, 1889), 216; Louis C. Hunter, *Steamboats on the Western Rivers: An Economic and Technological History* (Cambridge, Mass.: Harvard University Press, 1949), 16; Elihu Hotchkiss Shepard, *The Early History of St. Louis and Missouri: From Its First Exploration* (St. Louis: Southwestern Book and Publishing, 1870), 119–20.
14. William L. Burton, "The Life and Death of Bloody Island: A Ferry Tale," *Western Illinois Regional Studies* 11 (Spring 1988): 7–10; Stella Drum, "Robert E. Lee and the Improvement of the Mississippi River," *Missouri Historical Society Collections* 6 (Feb. 1929): 158–59.
15. Florence L. Dorsey, *Master of the Mississippi: Henry Shreve and the Conquest of the Mississippi* (Boston: Houghton Mifflin, 1941), 189–90; Kamphuis, *Introduction to Coastal Engineering and Management,* 171; J. E. Griffith, "The Des Moines Rapids of the Mississippi River, and Its Improvements," *Annals of Iowa* 8 (April 1870): 149–50; Hunter, *Steamboats on the Western Rivers,* 13–17; Giacomo Costantino Beltrami, *A Pilgrimage in Europe and America, Leading to the Discovery of the Sources of the Mississippi and Bloody River* (London: Hunt & Clark, 1828), 2:149.
16. Gratiot, "Report from the Engineer Department," Nov. 30, 1836, and Shreve, "Annual Report of Work Done for the Improvement of the Navigation of the Mississippi River Above the Mouth of the Ohio," Sept. 30, 1836, in *American State Papers: Documents, Legislative and Executive, of the Congress of the United States for the First and Second Sessions of the Twenty-Fourth Congress—Military Affairs* (Washington, D.C.: Gales & Seaton, 1861), 6:855, 892–94; "Rivers and Harbors—Again," June 29, 1836, Cong. Globe, 24th Cong., 1st Sess., 576–77; Darby, *Recollections,* 226–27; REL to Jack Mackay, Oct. 22, 1837, in Screven, "Letters of R. E. Lee to the Mackay Family," 31–32; Freeman, *R. E. Lee,* 1:139; REL to Talcott, June 29, 1837, Talcott Papers, VMHC.
17. Russell F. Weigley, *Quartermaster General of the Union Army: A Biography of M. C. Meigs*

(New York: Columbia University Press, 1959), 32–33; Robert O'Harrow Jr., *The Quartermaster: Montgomery Meigs, Lincoln's General, Master Builder of the Union Army* (New York: Simon & Schuster, 2016), 7–8.

18. REL to Lloyd, Aug. 15, 1837, Lloyd Family Papers, Library of Congress; REL to MCL, Aug. 5, 1837, Lee Family Papers, VMHC; Sanborn, *Robert E. Lee: A Portrait,* 111–13; Freeman, *R. E. Lee,* 1:140.
19. REL to CCL, Aug. 15, 1837, Robert E. Lee Papers, Small Special Collections Library; REL to MCL, Sept. 10, 1837, MSS 1L51c20, Lee Family Papers; REL to Talcott, Oct. 11, 1837, Talcott Papers, VMHC.
20. REL to CCL, Oct. 8, 1837, Robert E. Lee Papers, Small Special Collections Library; REL to MCL, Sept. 10, 1837, Lee Family Papers, VMHC; Sanborn, *Robert E. Lee: A Portrait,* 114–15; REL to Mackay, Oct. 22, 1837, in Screven, "Letters of R. E. Lee to the Mackay Family," 32.
21. Darby, *Personal Recollections,* 228; REL, in "Report from the Secretary of War, in Compliance with a Resolution of the Senate of the 25th Instant, in Relation to the Rock River and Des Moines Rapids of the Mississippi River," Dec. 6, 1837, in *Public Documents Printed by Order of the Senate of the United States, Second Session of the Twenty-Fifth Congress* (Washington, D.C.: Blair & Rives, 1838), 3:7–13; Drum, "Robert E. Lee and the Improvement of the Mississippi River," 163–64; "Harbour of St. Louis," *Daily Commercial Bulletin and Missouri Literary Register,* April 25, 1838.
22. "Harbor of St. Louis," March 21 and July 6, 1838, Cong. Globe, 25th Cong., 2nd Sess., 248, 500; MacDonald, *Mrs. Robert E. Lee,* 66; REL to Mary Fitzhugh Custis, May 24, 1838, Lee Family Papers, VMHC.
23. REL to Kayser, Feb. 1 and March 9, 1838, Robert E. Lee Collection, Missouri Historical Society Archives, St. Louis; Ruth Musser and John C. Krantz, "The Friendship of General Robert E. Lee and Dr. Wm. Beaumont," *Bulletin of the Institute of the History of Medicine* 6 (May 1938): 470–72; REL to Harriet Talcott, May 29, 1838, Talcott Papers, VMHC; Reginald Horsman, *Frontier Doctor: William Beaumont, America's First Great Medical Scientist* (Columbia: University of Missouri Press, 1996), 254–55.
24. REL to Mackay, June 27 and Oct. 19, 1838, in Screven, "Letters of R. E. Lee to the Mackay Family," 35, 37; Freeman, *R. E. Lee,* 1:150–55; "Proceedings," *Daily Commercial Bulletin,* July 31 and Oct. 2, 1838; REL, "The Erection of a Pier in the Mississippi River, near Saint Louis," Oct. 24, 1838, in *The Executive Documents Printed by Order of the Senate of the United States for the Second Session of the Forty-Sixth Congress, 1879–'80* (Washington, D.C.: Government Printing Office, 1880), 1:45; Drum, "Robert E. Lee and the Improvement of the Mississippi River," 167; Sanborn, *Robert E. Lee: A Portrait,* 120.
25. REL to Mary Fitzhugh Custis, Nov. 7, 1839, Lee Family Papers, and REL to Talcott, Feb. 2, 1827, Talcott Papers, VMHC.
26. REL to Mrs. Richard S. Hackly, Aug. 7, 1838, and to Colonel A. P. Christian, May 7, 1839, R. E. Lee Letterbook 1, Section 39, Lee Family Papers, VMHC; REL to CCL, Jan. 7, 1839, Robert E. Lee Papers, Small Special Collections Library; Thomas, *Robert E. Lee,* 93–94; MacDonald, *Mrs. Robert E. Lee,* 75–79; REL to Mackay, June 27, 1838, in Screven, "Letters of R. E. Lee to the Mackay Family," 34. Lee wrote a supplementary report on the clearance of snags in the Mississippi and Ohio in November: "Ohio and Mississippi Rivers from Louisville to New Orleans," Nov. 20, 1839, in *Public Documents Printed by Order of the Senate of the United States During the Second Session of the Twenty-Sixth Congress* (Washington, D.C.: Blair & Rives, 1841), 1:22–24.
27. REL to Kayser, Feb. 1, 1838; "Charles Gratiot, Plaintiff in Error, v. The United States, Defendants in Error," in Richard Peters, *Reports of Cases Argued and Adjudged in the Supreme Court of the United States, January Term, 1841* (Philadelphia: Thomas, Cowperthwait, 1841), 15:338; REL to Charles Gratiot, Dec. 23, 1838, and to Mrs. Anne Gratiot, April 19, 1839, R. E. Lee

Letterbook 1, Lee Family Papers, VMHC; REL to CCL, Dec. 24, 1838, Robert E. Lee Papers, Small Special Collections Library.

28. REL to Bliss, March 27, 1839, R. E. Lee Letterbook 1, Lee Family Papers, VMHC; REL to Mackay, June 27, 1838, in Screven, "Letters of R. E. Lee to the Mackay Family," 34.
29. Thomas, *Robert E. Lee,* 97; Sanborn, *Robert E. Lee: A Portrait,* 129–31; "Proceedings," *Daily Commercial Bulletin and Missouri Literary Register,* Nov. 5, 1838; REL, "The Erection of a Pier in the Mississippi River near Saint Louis," Oct. 21, 1839, in *Executive Documents of the Forty-Sixth Congress,* 1:45–46; REL to Kayser, Jan. 7, 1840, Robert E. Lee Collection, Missouri Historical Society Archives; REL to Hill Carter, Jan. 25, 1840, LFDA/duPont Library.
30. REL to Kayser, Jan. 7, 1840, Robert E. Lee Collection, Missouri Historical Society Archives; REL to Wm. L. Marshall, Stuart, and CCL, Jan. 20, 25, and 30, 1840, Lee Letterbook 1, Lee Family Papers, VMHC; REL to CCL, Aug. 22, 1840, Robert E. Lee Papers, Small Special Collections Library; C. G. Lee, *Lee Chronicle,* 91.
31. REL to Mackay, July 23, 1840, in Screven, "Letters of R. E. Lee to the Mackay Family," 44; REL to Bliss, March 31, 1840, R. E. Lee Letterbook 1, Lee Family Papers, VMHC; REL to Kayser, June 16, 1840, Robert E. Lee Collection, Missouri Historical Society Archives; REL, "Mississippi River Above the Ohio, and Pier in the Harbor of St. Louis," Oct. 6, 1840, in *Public Documents Printed by Order of the Senate of the United States During the Second Session of the Twenty-Sixth Congress,* 5:135–36.
32. REL to Obed Waite, Feb. 4, 1839, and Jan. 6, 1840, to Thomas Williamson, March 25, 1839, and Jan. 18, 1840, to Dr. L. Riley, April 6, 1840, to Thomas Biddle, June 29, 1840, to James H. Lynch, Jan. 4, 1841, and to Lloyd, March 22, 1839, Lee Letterbook 1, Section 39, Lee Family Papers, VMHC; REL to Kayser, May 13 and Nov. 23, 1841, Oct. 15, 1845, Robert E. Lee Collection, Missouri Historical Society Archives.
33. REL to Mrs. Richard Shippey Hackley, Aug. 7, 1838, R. E. Lee Letterbook 1, Section 39, Lee Family Papers, VMHC; REL to Hill Carter, Jan. 25, 1840, LFDA/duPont Library; REL to CCL, March 18 and 23, 1848, Robert E. Lee Papers, Small Special Collections Library.
34. REL to Mackay, March 18, 1841, in Screven, "Letters of R. E. Lee to the Mackay Family," 47; REL to Totten, July 9, 1839, and to Fred A. Smith, Aug. 12, 1839, R. E. Lee Letterbook 1, Lee Family Papers, VMHC; J. G. Barnard, "Memoir of Joseph Gilbert Totten, 1788–1864," in *National Academy of Sciences: Biographical Memoirs* (Philadelphia: Collins, 1877), 1:39, 58; Joseph Totten, *Essays on Hydraulic and Common Mortars and on Limeburning* (New York: Wiley & Putnam, 1842), 227–53; Joseph Totten, *Report Addressed to the Hon. Jefferson Davis, Secretary of War, on the Effects of Firing with Heavy Ordnance from Casemate Embrasures* (Washington, D.C.: Taylor & Maury, 1857), 32; "Joseph Gilbert Totten," in *Collections of the State Historical Society of North Dakota,* ed. O. G. Libby (Bismarck, N.D.: Tribune, State Printers, 1910), 3:208–9; "Joseph Gilbert Totten," in *Professional Memoirs, Corps of Engineers, United States Army and Engineer Department at Large* (Washington, D.C.: Press of the Engineer School, 1911), 3:313–14.
35. REL to Totten, Aug. 10, 1842, deButts-Ely Collection of Lee Family Papers, Library of Congress.
36. Hunt, in Long, *Memoirs of Robert E. Lee,* 66–67; REL Engineering Notebook, 1841–1842, MSS Col 1719, Manuscripts and Archives Division, New York Public Library; REL to Adam Thoman, April 30, 1842, duPont Library; REL to John P. Austin, May 3, 1842, to A. and C. S. Brainerd, May 21, 1842, to Lieutenant Duncan, May 24, 1842, to Totten, July 18, 1842, Aug. 23, 1843, Aug. 5 and Sept. 25, 1845, to William S. Steen, July 24, 1842, to Warren Gates, July 21, 1845, deButts-Ely Collection; "Report of the Chief Engineer," Nov. 1, 1845, in *Message from the President of the United States to the Two Houses of Congress at the Commencement of the First Session of the Twenty-Ninth Congress* (Washington, D.C.: Ritchie & Heiss, 1845), 247.
37. REL to Sarah Beaumont, March 11, 1843, Ethel Armes Collection of Lee Family Papers,

Library of Congress; REL to Anna Maria Fitzhugh, March 5, 1842, Robert E. Lee Papers, 1749–1975, David M. Rubenstein Rare Book and Manuscript Library, Duke University; REL to John Carroll Brent, April 2, 1843, duPont Library.

38. REL to MCL, April 14, 1841, Robert E. Lee Papers, Small Special Collections Library; REL to Mackay, March 18, 1841, in Screven, "Letters of R. E. Lee to the Mackay Family," 46; Sanborn, *Robert E. Lee: A Portrait,* 141–42; MacDonald, *Mrs. Robert E. Lee,* 84.

39. Leigh Kirkland, "'A Human Life: Being the Autobiography of Elizabeth Oakes Smith': A Critical Edition and Introduction" (PhD diss., Georgia State University, 1994), 135–36; "Arrival of the President in New York," *Brooklyn Daily Eagle,* June 27, 1844; MacDonald, *Mrs. Robert E. Lee,* 86; REL to Martha Custis Williams, Dec. 14, 1844, in *"To Markie": The Letters of Robert E. Lee to Martha Custis Williams,* ed. Avery Craven (Cambridge, Mass.: Harvard University Press, 1933), 9; Coffman, *Old Army,* 131; REL to Kayser, Dec. 19, 1845, Robert E. Lee Collection, Missouri Historical Society Archives; Mary Bandy Daughtry, *Gray Cavalier: The Life and Wars of General W. H. F. "Rooney" Lee* (Cambridge, Mass.: Da Capo Press, 2002), 6–7; Sanborn, *Robert E. Lee,* 150–51; Coulling, *Lee Girls,* 13, 17; Thomas, *Robert E. Lee,* 105; REL to MCL, Nov. 7, 1839, in Lee Family Papers, VMHC; REL to GWCL, Nov. 30 and Dec. 1845, in Lee Family Papers, VMHC, and Robert E. Lee Papers, Small Special Collections Library; J. William Jones, *Life and Letters of Robert Edward Lee, Soldier and Man* (New York, 1906), 37–39; Cox, *Religious Life of Robert E. Lee,* 100–101.

40. REL to Mary Fitzhugh Custis, Nov. 7, 1839, R. E. Lee Letterbook 1, Lee Family Papers, VMHC; Robert Bruce Mullin, *Episcopal Vision/American Reality: High Church Theology and Social Thought in Evangelical America* (New Haven, Conn.: Yale University Press, 1986), 149–52, 159–66; E. Clowes Chorley, *Men and Movements in the American Episcopal Church* (New York: Charles Scribner's Sons, 1950), 31–50; Richard Rankin, *Ambivalent Churchmen and Evangelical Churchwomen: The Religion of the Episcopal Elite in North Carolina, 1800–1860* (Columbia: University of South Carolina Press, 1993), 67; Alvin W. Skardon, *Church Leader in the Cities: William Augustus Muhlenberg* (Philadelphia: University of Pennsylvania Press, 1971), 179–88.

41. Cox, *Religious Life of Robert E. Lee,* 83–85; *Journal of the Proceedings of the Fifty-Ninth Convention of the Protestant Episcopal Church in the Diocese of New York* (New York: Church Depository, 1843), 89, 107, 183; Long, *Memoirs of Robert E. Lee,* 67–68.

42. REL to Alexander Kayser, Nov. 25, 1843, Robert E. Lee Collection, Missouri Historical Society Archives; REL to Mackay, March 18, 1845, in Screven, "Letters of R. E. Lee to the Mackay Family," 49; REL to CCL, July 24, 1843, and July 13, 1846, in Robert E. Lee Papers, Small Special Collections Library; REL to Totten, June 17, 1845, deButts-Ely Collection; Thomas, *Robert E. Lee,* 101, 108.

Chapter Five: Ruling the Aztec Sky

1. "What Means This War?," *New-York Tribune,* May 13, 1846.
2. Freeman, *R. E. Lee,* 1:117; "Debates in the Federal Convention of 1787 as Reported by James Madison," in *Documents Illustrative of the Formation of the Union of the American States,* ed. Charles C. Tansill (Washington, D.C.: Government Printing Office, 1927), 589, 590.
3. "Speech of Mr. Talmadge," Feb. 15, 1819, in *Papers Relative to the Restriction of Slavery: Speeches of Mr. King, in the Senate, and of Messrs. Taylor and Talmadge in the House of Representatives of the United States* (Philadelphia: Hall & Atkinson, 1819), 22.
4. "Gen. Harrison an Abolitionist," *Staunton Spectator and General Advertiser,* June 25, 1840; David A. Clary, *Eagles and Empire: The United States, Mexico, and the Struggle for a Continent* (New York: Bantam Books, 2009), 60, 66, 100; Amy S. Greenberg, *A Wicked War: Polk, Clay,*

Lincoln, and the 1846 U.S. Invasion of Mexico (New York: Knopf, 2012), 101; diary entry for March 26, 1846, in *Fifty Years in Camp and Field: Diary of Major-General Ethan Allen Hitchcock,* ed. W. A. Croffut (New York: G. P. Putnam's Sons, 1909), 213.

5. Polk, diary entry for May 11, 1846, in *The Diary of James K. Polk During His Presidency, 1845 to 1849,* ed. M. M. Quaife (Chicago: A. C. McClurg, 1910), 1:390; K. Jack Bauer, *The Mexican War, 1846–1848* (New York: Macmillan, 1974), 69–70; Clary, *Eagles and Empire,* 99–100; James E. Lewis, *John Quincy Adams: Policymaker for the Union* (Wilmington, Del.: Scholarly Resources, 2001), 135; Wilmot, "Message—Foreign Intercourse," Aug. 8, 1846, and Davis, "Negotiation with Mexico," Aug. 10, 1846, Cong. Globe, 29th Cong., 1st Sess., 1217, 1221.
6. REL to Martha Williams, June 7, 1846, in *"To Markie,"* 17–18; REL to John Mackay, June 21, 1846, Special Collections, University of Texas at Arlington; REL to CCL, Sept. 1, 1844, Robert E. Lee Papers, Small Special Collections Library; REL to Henry Kayser, July 4, 1846, Robert E. Lee Collection, Missouri Historical Society Archives. See also REL to CCL, July 13, 1846, Robert E. Lee Papers, Special Collections, University of Virginia.
7. REL to Henry Kayser and Thomas Biddle, Sept. 1, 1846, and to George W. Townsend, Sept. 9, 1846, deButts-Ely Collection; REL to CCL, Sept. 1, 1846, Robert E. Lee Papers, Small Special Collections Library.
8. REL to MCL, Dec. 25, 1846, deButts-Ely Collection; William M. S. Rasmussen and Robert S. Tilton, *Lee and Grant* (London: Giles, 2007), 127; Francis Baylies, *A Narrative of Major General Wool's Campaign in Mexico in the Years 1846, 1847, and 1848* (Albany: Little, 1851), 12; George W. Hughes, *Memoir Descriptive of the March of a Division of the United States Army, Under the Command of Brigadier General John E. Wool, from San Antonio de Bexar, in Texas, to Saltillo, in Mexico,* in *Executive Documents Printed by Order of the Senate of the United States, 31st Cong., 1st Sess.* (Washington, D.C., 1849), 5, 9, 15, 16, 18.
9. REL to MCL, Oct. 11, 1846, in Jones, *Life and Letters,* 50.
10. John R. Kenly, *Memoirs of a Maryland Volunteer: War with Mexico, in the Years 1846–7–8* (Philadelphia, 1873), 62–63; William S. Henry, *Campaign Sketches of the War with Mexico* (New York, 1847), 260.
11. William B. Campbell to David Campbell, Nov. 2 and 9, 1845, in "Mexican War Letters of William Bowen Campbell, of Tennessee, Written to Governor David Campbell, of Virginia, 1846–1847," ed. St. George L. Sioussat, *Tennessee Historical Magazine,* June 1915, 146–47; R. B. Winders, *Mr. Polk's Army: The American Military Experience in the Mexican War* (College Station: Texas A&M University Press, 1997), 8, 33; Polk, diary entries for May 22, 1846, and Jan. 14, 1847, in *Diary of James K. Polk,* 1:417–18, 2:328; Timothy D. Johnson, *A Gallant Little Army: The Mexico City Campaign* (Lawrence: University Press of Kansas, 2007), 15.
12. *Memoirs of Lieut.-General Scott, LL.D., Written by Himself* (New York: Sheldon, 1864), 2:423; REL to Mary Fitzhugh Custis, Feb. 22, 1847, Lee Family Papers, VMHC; *To Mexico with Scott: Letters of Captain E. Kirby Smith to His Wife,* ed. E. J. Blackwood (Cambridge, Mass.: Harvard University Press, 1917), 114; George C. Furber, *The Twelve Months Volunteer; or, Journal of a Private, in the Tennessee Regiment of Cavalry* (Cincinnati: J. A. & U. P. James, 1850), 521.
13. J. Jacob Oswandel, *Notes of the Mexican War, 1846–47–48: Comprising Incidents, Adventures, and Everyday Proceedings and Letters While with the United States Army in the Mexican War* (Philadelphia, 1885), 83.
14. Hitchcock, *Fifty Years in Camp and Field,* 245; W. G. Temple, "Memoir of the Landing of the United States Troops at Vera Cruz in 1847," in P. S. P. Connor, *The Home Squadron Under Commodore Conner, 1846–1847* (Philadelphia, 1896), 67; REL to SSL, March 27, 1847, Lee Family Papers, Huntington Library; Maury, *Recollections of a Virginian,* 34–35; *Autobiography of the Late Col. Geo. T. M. Davis, Captain and Aid-de-Camp, Scott's Army of Invasion (Mexico) from Posthumous Papers* (New York: Jenkins & McCowan, 1891), 138.
15. Henry Hunt, in Long, *Memoirs of Robert E. Lee,* 69–70.

16. Cadmus Marcellus Wilcox, *History of the Mexican War* (Washington, D.C.: Church News, 1892), 278; John S. D. Eisenhower, *Agent of Destiny: The Life and Times of General Winfield Scott* (New York: Free Press, 1997), 251–52; REL to MCL, April 25, 1847, in Jones, *Life and Letters,* 51.
17. John S. Jenkins, *History of the War Between the United States and Mexico, from the Commencement of Hostilities to the Ratification of the Treaty of Peace* (Auburn, N.Y.: Derby, Miller, 1848), 273–74, 277, 279–80, 284; John Frost, *Life of Major General Zachary Taylor: With Notices of the War in New Mexico, California, and in South Mexico and Biographical Sketches of Officers Who Have Distinguished Themselves in the War with Mexico* (New York: D. Appleton, 1847), 250–51; "From the Army—Despatches from General Scott," *Weekly National Intelligencer,* May 22, 1847; Richard McSherry, *El Puchero; or, A Mixed Dish from Mexico: Embracing General Scott's Campaign, with Sketches of Military Life, in Field and Camp, of the Character of the Country, Manner and Ways of the People, etc.* (Philadelphia: Lippincott, Grambo, 1850), 189, 219, 220–21; George Ballentine, *Autobiography of an English Soldier in the United States Army, Comprising Observations and Adventures in the States and Mexico* (New York: Stringer & Townsend, 1853), 189.
18. Thomas Claiborne, "Reminiscences of the Mexican War," Thomas Claiborne Papers, Southern Historical Collection, Louis Round Wilson Library, University of North Carolina; McSherry, *El Puchero,* 218; Scott to William L. Marcy, April 23, 1847, in *Memoirs of Lieut.-General Scott,* 2:450; REL to Matilda, March 28, 1847, GLC07815, Gilder Lehrman Institute of American History Collection, New-York Historical Society; REL to GWCL and to MCL, April 25, 1847, in Jones, *Life and Letters,* 51; Freeman, *R. E. Lee,* 1:247.
19. *An Artillery Officer in the Mexican War, 1846–7: Letters of Robert Anderson,* ed. Eba Anderson Lawton (New York: G. P. Putnam's Sons, 1911), 211; McSherry, *El Puchero,* 100.
20. Raphael Semmes, *Service Afloat and Ashore During the Mexican War* (Cincinnati: Wm. H. Moore, 1851), 380.
21. REL to Catlyna Pearson Totten, Aug. 22, 1847, in "Proceedings of Two Courts of Inquiry in the Case of Major General Pillow," in *Executive Documents Printed by Order of the Senate of the United States, During the First Session of the Thirtieth Congress* (Washington, D.C.: Wendell & Van Benthuysen, 1847), 8:461–62. REL's memorandum on the Chalco route is in Roswell S. Ripley, *The War with Mexico* (New York: Harper & Bros., 1849), 2:647.
22. REL to Catlyna Pearson Totten, Aug. 22, 1847, in *Executive Documents,* 462; John Bonnet, "Scott's Battles in Mexico," *Harper's New Monthly Magazine,* Aug. 1855, 316; Jenkins, *History of the War,* 354–55; "Official Despatches," *Washington Daily Union,* Nov. 13, 1847; John Frost, *The Mexican War and Its Warriors: Comprising a Complete History of All the Operations of the American Armies in Mexico* (New Haven, Conn.: H. Mansfield, 1848), 160; George H. Gordon, "The Battles of Contreras and Churubusco," March 12, 1883, in *Civil and Mexican Wars, 1861, 1846* (Boston: Military Historical Society of Massachusetts, 1913), 574–75.
23. REL to Major J. L. Smith, Aug. 21, 1847, deButts-Ely Collection; REL to Catlyna Pearson Totten, Aug. 22, 1847, in *Executive Documents,* 463–64; Jenkins, *History of the War,* 355–56; Frost, *Mexican War and Its Warriors,* 165; Gustavus Woodson Smith, *Company A, Corps of Engineers, U.S.A., 1846–1848, in the Mexican War,* ed. Leone M. Hudson (Kent, Ohio: Kent State University Press, 2001), 39; Gordon, "Battles of Contreras and Churubusco," 581–82.
24. REL to Major J. L. Smith, Aug. 21, 1847, deButts-Ely Collection; REL testimony, March 31, 1848, in "Proceedings of Two Courts of Inquiry in the Case of Major General Pillow," in *Executive Documents,* 75–76, 79; "Battles of Contreras and Churubusco—Report of Major-General Scott," Aug. 19, 1847, *AQRM* 2 (Sept. 1848): 575–76; H. Judge Moore, *Scott's Campaign in Mexico from the Rendezvous on the Island of Lobos to the Taking of the City* (Charleston: J. R. Nixon, 1849), 132, 135; Nathan Covington Brooks, *A Complete History of the Mexican War: Its Causes, Conduct, and Consequences* (Philadelphia: Grigg, Elliot, 1849), 372.

25. REL to Catlyna Pearson Totten, Aug. 22, 1847, in *Executive Documents,* 465; *With Beauregard in Mexico: The Mexican War Reminiscences of P. G. T. Beauregard,* ed. T. Harry Williams (Baton Rouge: Louisiana State University Press, 1956), 56; Jenkins, *History of the War Between the United States and Mexico,* 365–66; Kenly, *Memoirs of a Maryland Volunteer,* 346.
26. "Army Intelligence," Aug. 28, 1847, *Washington Daily Union,* Sept. 16, 1847; Scott, "Battles of Contreras and Churubusco—Report of Major-General Scott," Aug. 19 and 28, 1847, 577, 579, 584; Testimony of Winfield Scott, March 31, 1848, in "Proceedings of Two Courts of Inquiry in the Case of Major General Pillow," in *Executive Documents,* 73; Johnson, in John William Jones, *Personal Reminiscences, Anecdotes, and Letters of Gen. Robert E. Lee* (New York: D. Appleton, 1875), 59; *The Mexican War and Its Heroes* (Philadelphia: Grigg, Elliot, 1849), 120, 127.
27. REL to Major J. L. Smith, Aug. 21, 1847, deButts-Ely Collection; REL to Catlyna Pearson Totten, Aug. 22, 1847, and REL Testimony, March 31, 1848, in *Executive Documents,* 76, 464–65; Johnson, *Gallant Little Army,* 186–87; "Official Despatches," *Washington Daily Union,* Nov. 13, 1847, and *Weekly National Intelligencer,* Nov. 20, 1847.
28. REL Testimony, March 31, 1848, in *Executive Documents,* 77; Scott to Wm. L. Marcy, Sept. 18, 1847, in *Memoirs of Lieut.-General Scott,* 2:508; Jenkins, *History of the War,* 394; Edward D. Mansfield, *The Mexican War: A History of Its Origin, and a Detailed Account of the Victories Which Terminated in the Surrender of the Capital* (New York: A. S. Barnes, 1849), 290; "Report of Molino del Rey—Report of Major-General Scott," Sept. 11, 1847, *AQRM 1* (May 1848): 586, 592.
29. REL to Mackay, Oct. 2, 1847, in " 'We Are Our Own Trumpeters': Robert E. Lee Describes Winfield Scott's Campaign to Mexico City," ed. Gary W. Gallagher, *VMHB,* July 1987, 370–71; REL Testimony, March 31 and April 8, 1848, in *Executive Documents,* 78, 144; "Battle of Mexico—Capture of the City—Report of Major-General Scott," Sept. 18, 1847, *AQRM,* 1 (May 1848): 592, 593–94, 600; Jenkins, *History of the War,* 384, 400–401, 405; REL to Major J. L. Smith, Sept. 13, 1847, deButts-Ely Collection; Hitchcock, *Fifty Years in Camp and Field,* 293, 301; George H. Gordon, "The Battles of Molino del Rey and Chapultepec," Dec. 10, 1883, in *Civil and Mexican Wars, 1861, 1846,* 619–20; Kenly, *Memoirs of a Maryland Volunteer,* 353.
30. REL to Major J. L. Smith, Sept. 13, 1847, deButts-Ely Collection; REL to Mackay, Oct. 2, 1847, in Gallagher, " 'We Are Our Own Trumpeters,' " 371; the Santa Anna complaint was recorded in an "Anecdote of Santa Anna," note by John W. Geary, John White Geary Mexican War Papers, Western Americana Collection, Beinecke Rare Book and Manuscript Library, Yale University; Johnson, *Gallant Little Army,* 215, 227, 232–33, 237–39; Bauer, *Mexican War,* 322; Clary, *Eagles and Empire,* 372–75; Thomas, *Robert E. Lee,* 136.
31. Lew Wallace, *An Autobiography* (New York: Harper & Bros., 1906), 2:896.
32. Gordon, "Battles of Molino del Rey and Chapultepec," 637–38; McSherry, *El Puchero,* 114, 128, 131; Paul D. Casdorph, *Confederate General R. S. Ewell: Robert E. Lee's Hesitant Commander* (Lexington: University Press of Kentucky, 2004), 50–51; *Autobiography of the Late Col. Geo. T. M. Davis,* 132–33.
33. Charles G. Sellers, *James K. Polk* (Princeton, N.J.: Princeton University Press, 1966), 2:213; "Manifest Destiny Doctrines," *Niles' National Register,* Jan. 22, 1848, 334–36; Bauer, *Mexican War,* 369.
34. John L. O'Sullivan, "Annexation," *United States Magazine and Democratic Review,* July/Aug. 1845, 5–10; Michael Paul Rogin, *Fathers and Children: Andrew Jackson and the Subjugation of the American Indian* (New York: Knopf, 1975), 308; Sean Wilentz, *The Rise of American Democracy: Jefferson to Lincoln* (New York: W. W. Norton, 2005), 562; Reginald Horsman, *Race and Manifest Destiny: The Origins of American Racial Anglo-Saxonism* (Cambridge, Mass.: Harvard University Press, 1981), 228–48; Paul Foos, *A Short, Offhand, Killing Affair:*

Soldiers and Social Conflict During the Mexican-American War (Chapel Hill: University of North Carolina Press, 2002), 113–54; Henry T. Cheever, *Life in the Sandwich Islands; or, The Heart of the Pacific, as It Was and Is* (New York: A. S. Barnes, 1856), 340; William Henry Hurlbert, *Gan-Eden; or, Pictures of Cuba* (New York: J. P. Jewett, 1854), 225–27; Thomas L. Clingman, "Conclusion of the Slavery Discussion," in *Selections from the Speeches and Writings of Hon. Thomas L. Clingman, of North Carolina, with Additions and Explanatory Notes* (Raleigh, N.C.: John Nichols, 1877), 569; Daniel Walker Howe, *What Hath God Wrought: The Transformation of America, 1815–1848* (New York: Oxford University Press, 2007), 702–6; Nicholas Guyatt, *Providence and the Invention of the United States, 1607–1876* (New York: Cambridge University Press, 2007), 219–30.

35. Winthrop, "Arbitration of the Oregon Question," Jan. 3, 1846, in *Addresses and Speeches on Various Occasions* (Boston: Little, Brown, 1852), 490; Watson, *Liberty and Power,* 245; Lee Benson, *The Concept of Jacksonian Democracy: New York as a Test Case* (Princeton, N.J.: Princeton University Press, 1961), 240; Frederick Merk, *Manifest Destiny and Mission in American History: A Reinterpretation* (New York: Knopf, 1963), 170; "The Destiny of the Country," *American Whig Review,* March 1847, 233, 234, 239.
36. REL to John Lloyd, March 22, 1839, John Lloyd Papers, Library of Congress; REL to CCL, Oct. 8, 1837, Lee Papers, University of Virginia; REL to "Dear Major," Feb. 28, 1847, LFDA/duPont Library; REL to Mackay, Oct. 2, 1847, in Gallagher, "'We Are Our Own Trumpeters,'" 371–72; REL to Matilda Mason, Sept. 20, 1847, GLC08894, Gilder Lehrman Institute of American History.
37. Clary, *Eagles and Empire,* 403–6; Bauer, *Mexican War,* 380–88.
38. Packard, *Recollections of a Long Life,* 158; MCL to Eliza Anne Mackay Stiles, Nov. 1, 1847, duPont Library; REL to Matilda Mason, Sept. 20, 1847, GLC08894, Gilder Lehrman Institute of American History; REL to Joseph G. Totten, Jan. 1 and April 21, 1848, to MCL, Feb. 8, 1848, and to EAL, Feb. 12, 1848, deButts-Ely Collection. "Charlollita," whom Lee described as the daughter of "an Englishman" and a "French lady" in Mexico City, might have been the child of "Mr. Drusini . . . a wealthy English merchant, about 45 or 50 years of age," who gave a dinner in honor of Scott for Persifor Smith, Lee, the English chargé d'affaires, and several others on February 19, 1848 (Hitchcock, *Fifty Years in Camp and Field,* 320).
39. REL to Matilda Mason, Nov. 1, 1847, at Live Auctioneers, new.liveauctioneers.com/item/39925478_robert-e-lee-autograph-letter-mexican-war-date; REL to MCL, Feb. 8 and 13, 1848, deButts-Ely Collection; REL to Matilda Mason, Sept. 20, 1847, GLC08894, Gilder Lehrman Institute of American History Collection.
40. CCL to Nat Burwell Jr., Feb. 1, 1848, Special Collections, Leyburn Library; "Army General Order" (General Orders No. 47, Aug. 24, 1848), *Washington Daily Union,* Aug. 31, 1848; *Official Army Register for 1850* (Washington, D.C.: Adjutant General's Office, 1850), 38; George Washington Cullum, *Biographical Register of the Officers and Graduates of the U.S. Military Academy* (New York: James Miller, 1879), 2:3–4; REL to GWPC, April 8, 1848, deButts-Ely Collection; Cassandra Good, "Washington Family Fortune: Lineage and Capital in Nineteenth-Century America," *Early American Studies* 18 (Winter 2020): 117.
41. REL to GWPC, April 8, 1848, duPont Library; Anderson, April 1, 1847, in *Artillery Officer in the Mexican War,* 107–8.
42. "Great Battle of Mexico," *New Orleans Daily Delta,* Sept. 10, 1847; "Proceedings of Two Courts of Inquiry in the Case of Major General Pillow," in *Executive Documents,* 8:320–22, 455; Allan Peskin, *Winfield Scott and the Profession of Arms* (Kent, Ohio: Kent State University Press, 2003), 148; Timothy D. Johnson, *Winfield Scott: The Quest for Military Glory* (Lawrence: University Press of Kansas, 1998), 210–11.
43. Eisenhower, *Agent of Destiny,* 310–13; Nathaniel Cheairs Hughes and Roy P. Stonesifer, *The Life and Wars of Gideon J. Pillow* (Chapel Hill: University of North Carolina Press, 1993), 112.

44. REL to SSL, March 4, 1848, duPont Library.
45. REL Testimony, March 28, 1848, in "Proceedings of Two Courts of Inquiry in the Case of Major General Pillow," in *Executive Documents,* 8:55; "Defence of Maj. Gen. Pillow," *Washington Daily Union,* July 27, 1848; "From the Army—a Very Interesting Letter from a Distinguished Officer to His Correspondent in Washington," *Washington Daily Union,* Sept. 20, 1847.
46. REL to Anna Maria Fitzhugh, April 12, 1848, deButts-Ely Collection. George Welker, who appears in the inquiry proceedings as "Welcher," might have been more liable to questioning than Lee, but Welker had died on May 24, 1848, in Savannah (see Cullum's *Biographical Register,* 1:629).
47. Bauer, *Mexican War,* 373–74; REL to GWPC, April 8, 1848, to CCL, March 18 and May 15, 1848, Lee Family Papers, Small Special Collections Library.
48. REL to GWPC, April 8, 1848, and to Captain Fred[eric A.] Smith, Dec. 13, 1851, Breckinridge Long Papers, 1486–1948, Library of Congress; REL to CCL, March 18 and May 15, 1848, Lee Family Papers, Small Special Collections Library; REL to SSL, May 21, 1848, GLC00215, Gilder Lehrman Institute of American History Collection; REL to Martha "Markie" Custis Williams, May 21, 1848, Lee Family Papers, Huntington Library; REL to Lieutenant Gustavus W. Smith, May 22, 1848, GLC02641, Gilder Lehrman Institute of American History Collection; REL to McClellan, June 6, 1848, George B. McClellan Papers, Library of Congress; REL to MCL, June 14, 1848, deButts-Ely Collection.
49. REL to Jerome Napoleon Bonaparte, Feb. 25, 1855, in "Some Personal Letters of Robert E. Lee, 1850–1858," ed. William D. Hoyt, *Journal of Southern History* 12 (Nov. 1946): 469; REL to Brantz Mayer, Sept. 6, 1857, and to Isaac Ingalls Stevens, Aug. 15, 1851, deButts-Ely Collection.
50. REL to Mackay, June 21, 1846, Miscellaneous Mexican War File, box GA-43, folder 9, Special Collections, University of Texas at Austin.
51. Robert Anderson to Eliza Bayard Anderson, May 29, 1847, in *Artillery Officer in the Mexican War,* 191; Cabell to CCL, March 1859, LFDA/duPont Library.

Chapter Six: To Serve as a Model for the Mighty World

1. REL to Mary Custis, May 24, 1831, Lee Family Papers, VMHC; "Personal Recollections of General Robert E. Lee by His Cousin, Marietta Fauntleroy Powell," 203; Hugh Mercer, in Sanborn, *Robert E. Lee: A Portrait,* 201–2; Mason, *Popular Life of Gen. Robert Edward Lee,* 35–36.
2. Screven, "Letters of R. E. Lee to the Mackay Family," 56; REL to Martha Williams, May 21, 1848, in *"To Markie,"* 20–21; J. G. Wilson and J. Fiske, eds., *Appleton's Cyclopedia of American Biography* (New York: D. Appleton, 1889), 24; REL to SSL, June 30, 1848, in Robert E. Lee Jr., *Recollections and Letters,* 4–5.
3. Polk, "Special Message," July 6, 1848, in *Supplement to the Statesman's Manual, Brought Down to President Taylor's Inaugural Address, March, 1849* (New York: Edward Walker, 1849), 1743; Napoleon Jackson Tecumseh Dana to Susan Sandford Dana, March 28, 1847, in *Monterrey Is Ours! The Mexican War Letters of Lieutenant Dana, 1845–1847,* ed. Robert H. Ferrell (Lexington: University Press of Kentucky, 1990), 103.
4. *The American Almanac and Repository of Useful Knowledge for the Year 1851* (Boston: Little & Brown, 1851), 101; MCL to Cora C. Peters, Oct. 26, 1848, Special Collections, Leyburn Library; *The American Almanac and Repository of Useful Knowledge for the Year 1852* (Boston: Little & Brown, 1852), 187.
5. MCL to Cora C. Peters, Oct. 26, 1848, Special Collections, Leyburn Library.

6. "Lee in Baltimore," *Baltimore Sun,* Jan. 19, 1953; "When Robert E. Lee Lived in Baltimore," *Baltimore Sun,* Jan. 17, 1954; "Municipal Visit to the U.S. Steamer Mississippi," *Baltimore Sun,* May 31, 1852; "Damage from the Storm . . . Arrival of Lt. Lee," *Baltimore Sun,* Sept. 4, 1852; Robert E. Lee Jr., *Recollections and Letters,* 11; 1850 U.S. Federal Census, Baltimore Ward 20, Baltimore, 565–66, www.ancestry.com. Rob remembered the school as belonging to "a Mr. Rollins on Mulberry Street," but no entry for a Rollins, either on Mulberry Street or as a schoolmaster, appears in the Baltimore City directories for the 1850s. Mary Lee had evidently inquired about bringing Arlington slaves to Baltimore, because slavery was legal in Maryland, but Maryland imposed registration and fees on slaves imported into the state, and Robert advised against it. See REL to MCL, Sept. 25, 1849, Lee Family Papers, VMHC.
7. "The Defence of Baltimore—Fort Carroll," *Baltimore Sun,* Aug. 2, 1852; "Fort Carroll," Department of Planning, Maryland Historical Trust, mht.maryland.gov; John Thomas Scharf, *History of Baltimore City and County, from the Earliest Period to the Present Day* (Philadelphia: Louis H. Everts, 1881), 23, 291–92; "Report of the Chief Engineer," in *Message from the President of the United States to the Two Houses of Congress at the Commencement of the Second Session of the Thirty-First Congress* (Washington, D.C.: House of Representatives, 1850), 2:355; REL to Martha Williams, May 10, 1851, in *"To Markie,"* 26.
8. Packard, *Recollections of a Long Life,* 158; Richard S. Ewell to Rebecca Ewell, Feb. 25, 1850, in *The Letters of General Richard S. Ewell: Stonewall's Successor,* ed. Donald Pfanz (Knoxville: University of Tennessee Press, 2012), 100; Ross J. Kelbaugh, "The Swedish Nightingale and the Baltimore Daguerreians," *Daguerreian Annual* (1991): 155–59; Robert E. Lee Jr., *Recollections and Letters,* 10–11.
9. Sanborn, *Robert E. Lee: A Portrait,* 203–4; REL to Scott, Feb. 5, 1850, deButts-Ely Collection; "Cadets," *Baltimore Sun,* March 13, 1850; REL to Mrs. E. P. Lewis, July 29, 1850, deButts-Ely Collection.
10. REL to SSL, June 30, 1848, and to GWCL, May 4, 1851, in Jones, *Life and Letters,* 58, 72; REL to Mary Fitzhugh Custis, June 22, 1850, Tudor Place Historic House and Garden Archives, Washington, D.C.; REL to Mary Fitzhugh Custis, March 17, 1852, Lee Family Papers, VMHC.
11. "Defence of Baltimore—Fort Carroll"; REL to GWCL, Aug. 3, 1851, in Freeman, *R. E. Lee,* 1:311; REL to Martha Williams, May 10, 1851, in *"To Markie,"* 26; Sanborn, *Robert E. Lee,* 202–3; Mary Fitzhugh Custis to GWCL, Oct. 1851, in MacDonald, *Mrs. Robert E. Lee,* 105.
12. REL to GWCL, June 22, 1851, deButts-Ely Collection.
13. Jefferson Davis, "Remarks of President Davis," Nov. 3, 1870, in *Organization of the Lee Monument Association, and the Association of the Army of Northern Virginia* (Richmond: J. W. Randolph & English, 1871), 14; Robert Granville Caldwell, *The Lopez Expeditions to Cuba, 1848–1851* (Princeton, N.J.: Princeton University Press, 1915), 47–49; Robert E. May, *Manifest Destiny's Underworld: Filibustering in Antebellum America* (Chapel Hill: University of North Carolina Press, 2002), 16, 25–32; Tom Chaffin, *Fatal Glory: Narciso López and the First Clandestine U.S. War Against Cuba* (Baton Rouge: Louisiana State University Press, 2003), 47–48; "The Late General Lopez," *Washington Daily American Telegraph,* Sept. 8, 1851.
14. Lincoln, "Speech at Peoria, Illinois," Oct. 16, 1854, in *Collected Works of Abraham Lincoln,* ed. R. P. Basler (New Brunswick, N.J.: Rutgers University Press, 1953), 2:252; "Wilmot Proviso," in *Cyclopædia of Political Science, Political Economy, and of the Political History of the United States,* ed. John J. Lalor (New York: Maynard, Merrill, 1899), 3:1115–16; Grover, Cong. Globe, Jan. 7, 1847, 29th Cong., 2nd Sess., 136; Eric Foner, "The Wilmot Proviso Revisited," *Journal of American History* 56 (Sept. 1969): 276–77.
15. Calhoun, "The Slavery Question," Feb. 19, 1847, Cong. Globe, 29th Cong., 2nd Sess., 455; Cass to A. O. P. Nicholson, Dec. 24, 1847, in William T. Young, *Sketch of the Life and Public Services of General Lewis Cass* (Detroit: Markham & Elwood, 1852), 323; Taylor to Jefferson

Davis, July 27, 1847, in Holman Hamilton, *Zachary Taylor: Soldier in the White House* (Indianapolis: Bobbs-Merrill, 1951), 45.

16. Calhoun, "The Compromise," March 5, 1850, Cong. Globe, 31st Cong., 1st Sess., 463; Thurlow Weed Barnes, *Memoir of Thurlow Weed* (Boston: Houghton, Mifflin, 1884), 2:177; "The Fourth of July," *Weekly National Intelligencer,* July 6, 1850; K. Jack Bauer, *Zachary Taylor: Soldier, Planter, Statesman of the Old Southwest* (Baton Rouge: Louisiana State University Press, 1985), 314–15.
17. Holman Hamilton, *Prologue to Conflict: The Crisis and Compromise of 1850* (1964; Lexington: University of Kentucky Press, 2005), 156–61; Michael S. Green, *Politics and America in Crisis: The Coming of the Civil War* (Santa Barbara, Calif.: ABC/CLIO, 2010), 19; Z. Collins Lee to George W. Lewis, Feb. 17, 1851, LFDA/duPont Library; "The Latest from the Capitol," *New York Herald,* Sept. 8, 1850.
18. Fergus M. Bordewich, *America's Great Debate: Henry Clay, Stephen A. Douglas, and the Compromise That Preserved the Union* (New York: Simon & Schuster, 2012), 345; Martin H. Quitt, *Stephen A. Douglas and Antebellum Democracy* (New York: Cambridge University Press, 2012), 123; Michael E. Woods, "The Compromise of 1850 and the Search for a Usable Past," *Journal of the Civil War Era* 9 (Sept. 2019): 438–56.
19. Lincoln, "Speech at Peoria, Illinois," Oct. 16, 1854, in *Collected Works,* 2:282; Robert J. Cook, *Civil War Senator: William Pitt Fessenden and the Fight to Save the American Republic* (Baton Rouge: Louisiana State University Press, 2011), 86; Thomas H. Gladstone, *The Englishman in Kansas; or, Squatter Life and Border Warfare* (New York: Miller, 1857), 69; Elizabeth R. Varon, *Disunion! The Coming of the American Civil War, 1789–1859* (Chapel Hill: University of North Carolina Press, 2008), 251–68.
20. REL to GWCL, Dec. 28, 1851, in Jones, *Life and Letters,* 76–77; Kevin E. Kearney, "Autobiography of William Marvin," *Florida Historical Quarterly* 36 (Jan. 1958): 195; REL to Nat Burwell, Jan. 5, 1852, LFDA/duPont Library; REL to Jerome Napoleon Bonaparte, Feb. 6, 1852, in Hoyt, "Some Personal Letters of Robert E. Lee, 1850–1858," 560.
21. WHFL and MCL to GWCL, Feb. 15, 1852, Special Collections, Leyburn Library; REL to GWCL, March 28, 1852, Lee Family Papers, VMHC; REL to GWCL, Feb. 1, 1852, in Bernice-Marie Yates, *The Perfect Gentleman: The Life and Letters of George Washington Custis Lee* (Xulon Press, 2003), 1:115; Sanborn, *Robert E. Lee: A Portrait,* 212; REL to Mary Fitzhugh Custis, March 17, 1852, deButts-Ely Collection; MCL to "My dear Abbey," Aug. 22, 1851, Special Collections, Leyburn Library.
22. REL to Totten, July 9, 1839, and May 28 and July 25, 1852, R. E. Lee Letterbook 1, Lee Family Papers, VMHC; Thomas, *Robert E. Lee: A Biography,* 152; REL to Eveleth, Aug. 1, 1852, duPont Library; REL to Beauregard, June 25, 1852, in "A Robert E. Letter to P. G. T. Beauregard," *Maryland Historical Magazine,* Sept. 1956, 250; Sanborn, *Robert E. Lee: A Portrait,* 213; Freeman, *R. E. Lee,* 1:317.
23. James E. Morrison, *"The Best School": West Point, 1833–1866* (Kent, Ohio: Kent State University Press, 1986), 71; Boynton, *History of West Point,* 225–26, 245, 247; Freeman, *R. E. Lee,* 1:319; "An Act for the Organization of Sappers, Miners, and Pontoniers," May 15, 1846, in *Message from the President of the United States to the Two Houses of Congress at the Commencement of the First Session of the Twenty-Ninth Congress,* 289; Anderson, Aug. 6, 1847, in *Artillery Officer in the Mexican War,* 276; William S. Henry, *Campaign Sketches of the War with Mexico* (New York: Harper & Bros., 1847), 112.
24. Church, in *Annual Report of the Superintendent of the United States Military Academy* (Washington, D.C.: Government Printing Office, 1896), 60; Church, *Personal Reminiscences,* 46, 48–49; Logel, *Designing Gotham,* 7–8.
25. Morrison, *"Best School,"* 47–53; Ambrose, *Duty, Honor, Country,* 132–34; Boynton, *History of West Point,* 246; *Register of All Officers and Agents, Civil, Military, and Naval, in the Service*

of the United States (Washington, D.C.: J. & G. S. Gideon, 1843), 178; EAL, journal entry for June 18, 1854, in *Growing Up in the 1850s: The Journal of Agnes Lee,* ed. M. C. L. deButts (Chapel Hill: University of North Carolina Press, 1984), 38–39. See the list of signatories to the "Report of the Board of Visiters, on the United States Military Academy, at West Point, for 1826," at digital-library.usma.edu.

26. *Reports on the Course of Instruction in Yale College, by a Committee of the Corporation and the Academical Faculty* (New Haven, Conn.: Hezekiah Howe, 1828), 36; "Annual Report of the Board of Visitors of the United States Military Academy," *North American Review* 52 (Jan. 1841): 29; "Report of the Board of Visitors of the United States' Military Academy," *Quarterly Christian Spectator* 6 (Sept. 1834): 355; Morrison, *"Best School,"* 105; Skelton, *American Profession of Arms,* 169; Hope, *Scientific Way of War,* 141–45.
27. Davis, "Military Academy Bill," March 14, 1860, Cong. Globe, 36th Cong., 1st Sess., 1145; Clark, *Preparing for War,* 58–59; Hope, *Scientific Way of War,* 159–60.
28. Peter Michie, "Reminiscences of Cadet and Army Service," Oct. 4, 1893, in *Personal Recollections of the War of the Rebellion: Addresses Delivered Before the Commandery of the State of New York, Military Order of the Loyal Legion of the United States,* ed. A. N. Blakeman (New York: G. P. Putnam's Sons, 1897), 186; REL to Totten, Sept. 2 and 6 and Oct. 6, 7, 9, and 11, 1852, in *The Daily Correspondence of Brevet Colonel Robert E. Lee, Superintendent, United States Military Academy, September 1, 1852, to March 24, 1855,* ed. C. R. Bowery and B. D. Hankinson (West Point, N.Y.: U.S. Military Academy Library Occasional Papers no. 5, 2003), 1, 2, 16; "Rodman McCamley Price," in G. W. Sullivan, *Early Days in California: The Growth of the Commonwealth Under American Rule* (San Francisco: Enterprise, 1888), 1:207.
29. REL to Totten, Sept. 16, Oct. 15, Nov. 30, and Dec. 9, 1852, in *Daily Correspondence,* 5, 17, 25–26, 27–28; Freeman, *R. E. Lee,* 1:324–25; Cullum, *Biographical Register of the Officers and Graduates of the U.S. Military Academy at West Point, N.Y.,* 2:521–22.
30. REL to Totten, Jan. 6, 1853, in *Daily Correspondence,* 39; Cullum, *Biographical Register of the Officers and Graduates of the U.S. Military Academy at West Point, N.Y.,* 2:104; REL to Totten, Jan. 24, Feb. 8, and March 14, 1853, in *Daily Correspondence,* 45, 50, 65; REL to Totten, Dec. 11 and 15, 1852, in *Daily Correspondence,* 29–30; REL to Totten, Dec. 29, 1852, in *Daily Correspondence,* 37; Freeman, *R. E. Lee,* 1:324; REL to Totten, March 15 and 21, April 1 and 20, 1853, in *Daily Correspondence,* 67, 72, 76, 83–84; Thomas, *Robert E. Lee: A Biography,* 154; REL to Totten, Feb. 25, 1853, in *Daily Correspondence,* 59; Walter Creigh Preston, *Lee: West Point and Lexington* (Yellow Springs, Ohio: Antioch Press, 1934), 40–41.
31. REL to Bonaparte, July 31, 1852, March 12 and May 11, 1853, in Hoyt, "Some Personal Letters of Robert E. Lee, 1850–1858," 560–61, 564; REL to Martha Williams, Sept. 9, 1853, Jan. 2 and May 25, 1854, in *"To Markie,"* 34, 40, 45; Sanborn, *Robert E. Lee: A Portrait,* 225; REL to Thomas Fisher, Oct. 20, 1854, in *Daily Correspondence,* 232.
32. REL to Price, Feb. 22, 1855, and to Conrad and Totten, Feb. 10, 1853, in *Daily Correspondence,* 51–52, 281; "Army List," in David W. Camp, *The American Year-Book and National Register for 1869* (Hartford: O. D. Case, 1869), 111; Preston, *Lee: West Point and Lexington,* 20–23; Freeman, *R. E. Lee,* 1:326.
33. REL to Alpheus Frank, June 29, 1853, in *Daily Correspondence,* 103; George Thomas Little, *Genealogical and Family History of the State of Maine* (New York: Lewis Historical Publishing, 1905), 2:555; REL to Lewis S. Coryell, Aug. 5, 1854, in *Daily Correspondence,* 211–12; William W. H. Davis, *History of Bucks County, Pennsylvania: From the Discovery of the Delaware to the Present Time* (New York: Lewis, 1905), 2:189–90; REL to Totten, June 23, 1854, in *Daily Correspondence,* 194.
34. "West Point Cadets," *Alexandria Gazette,* Aug. 22, 1853; Yates, *Perfect Gentleman,* 1:124; Cullum, *Biographical Register of the Officers and Graduates of the U.S. Military Academy at West Point, N.Y.,* 2:572; EAL, journal entry for June 18, 1854, in *Growing Up in the 1850s,* 38.

35. REL to Totten, Dec. 19, 1853, in *Daily Correspondence,* 155; Edward G. Longacre, *Fitz Lee: A Military Biography of Major General Fitzhugh Lee, C.S.A.* (Cambridge, Mass.: Da Capo Press, 2005), 11, 31–32; Freeman, *R. E. Lee,* 1:333–34; REL to Totten, July 24, 1854, in *Daily Correspondence,* 216; Sanborn, *Robert E. Lee: A Portrait,* 220–21; Jefferson Davis, "Robert E. Lee," in *Battles and Leaders of the Civil War,* ed. Peter J. Cozzens (Urbana: University of Illinois Press, 2004), 6:92; Wyatt-Brown, *Southern Honor,* 108–9; REL to MCL, April 12, 1856, deButts-Ely Collection; Robert E. Lee Jr., *Recollections and Letters,* 19; Freeman, *R. E. Lee,* 1:332–34, 339.
36. MacDonald, *Mrs. Robert E. Lee,* 110; REL to Major John Symington, March 8, 1853, at Bidsquare Auctions, www.bidsquare.com/online-auctions/brunk/robert-e-lee-letter-lithograph-53010; Robert E. Lee Jr., *Recollections and Letters,* 11; Laura Lemon, "The Foundation of American Horsemanship Lies in Fort Riley," *Chronicle of the Horse,* Feb. 10 and 17, 2020, 39–43; Gordon Wright, *The Cavalry Manual of Horsemanship and Horsemastership* (Garden City, N.Y.: Doubleday, 1962), 23–36; EAL, journal entry for Oct. 20, 1853, in *Growing Up in the 1850s,* 26; Kundahl, *Alexandria Goes to War,* 80.
37. EAL, journal entries for Nov. 8, 1853, Feb. 2, March 11, and June 18, 1854, in *Growing Up in the 1850s,* 27–28, 31–32, 38–39, 45–46; Peter Guardino, *The Dead March: A History of the Mexican-American War* (Cambridge, Mass.: Harvard University Press, 2017), 194; "Present State of Mexico," in *Executive Documents Printed by Order of the Third Session of the Thirty-Seventh Congress, 1862–'63* (Washington, D.C.: Government Printing Office, 1863), 6:320; *Ten Years in the Saddle: The Memoir of William Woods Averell,* ed. Edward K. Eckert and Nicholas J. Amato (San Rafael, Calif.: Presidio Press, 1978), 42; "Original Pencil Drawing by Mary Custis Lee Presented to Stuart at the United States Military Academy at West Point, Circa 1854," Heritage Auctions Lot 52187, historical.ha.com/itm/military-and-patriotic/civil-war/-jeb-stuart-original-pencil-drawing-by-mary-custis-lee-presented-to-stuart-at-the-united-states-military-academy-at-west-p/a/6034-52187.s; Edward S. Holden, *Biographical Memoir of William H. C. Bartlett, 1804–1893* (Washington, D.C.: National Academy of Sciences, 1911), 187; Mark Nesbitt, *Saber and Scapegoat: J. E. B. Stuart and the Gettysburg Controversy* (Mechanicsburg, Pa.: Stackpole Books, 1994), 7; REL to Martha Williams, May 27 and June 29, 1854, in *"To Markie,"* 46, 48.
38. Charles deKay, "Captain Theophile Marie D'Oremieulx," and Laura D'Oremieulx, "Recollections of West Point in 1853," *Association of Graduates of the United States Military Academy* 3 (May 1903): 39–40, 44; Keyes, *Fifty Years' Observations,* 185; John M. Schofield, *Forty-Six Years in the Army* (New York: Century, 1897), 15; Elizabeth Lindsay Lomax, diary entry for Dec. 20, 1854, in *Leaves from an Old Washington Diary, 1854–1863,* ed. L. L. Wood (New York: E. P. Dutton, 1943), 29; William Whitman Bailey, "The Lees at West Point," Special Collections, Leyburn Library.
39. EAL, journal entries for May 4 and Aug. 26, 1853, in *Growing Up in the 1850s,* 13, 21–22; Obituaries in *Washington Daily Union,* April 24, 1853, *Washington Republic,* April 28, 1853, *Weekly National Intelligencer,* April 20, 1853, and *Alexandria Gazette,* April 26 and May 16, 1853; MCL, in "Funeral of Mrs. G. W. P. Custis and Death of General R. E. Lee," *VMHB,* Jan. 1927, 23; William Meade, "Bishop Meade's Recollections," *Protestant Episcopal Quarterly Review and Church Register* 3 (Jan. 1856): 97; REL to Bonaparte, May 11, 1853, in Hoyt, "Some Personal Letters of Robert E. Lee, 1850–1858," 564; REL to Martha Williams, June 23 and Sept. 9, 1853, in *"To Markie,"* 31, 34; Sanborn, *Robert E. Lee: A Portrait,* 226.
40. EAL, journal entry for June 1, 1853, in *Growing Up in the 1850s,* 14; John Esten Cooke, *A Life of Gen. Robert E. Lee* (New York: D. Appleton, 1871), 47; Robert Cornwall, "The Rite of Confirmation in Anglican Thought During the Eighteenth Century," *Church History* 68 (June 1999): 361–62, 366; John A. Clark, *The Pastor's Testimony* (Philadelphia: W. Marshall, 1835), 46; Stephen H. Tyng, *Guide to Confirmation* (Philadelphia: George, Latimer, 1833), 7, 16; Rankin, *Ambivalent Churchmen and Evangelical Churchwomen,* 58–59; Cox, *Religious Life*

of Robert E. Lee, 109–12; Freeman, *R. E. Lee,* 1:330; MCL to Mary Meade, Oct. 12, 1870, in "Funeral of Mrs. G. W. P. Custis and Death of General R. E. Lee," 25.

41. REL to Totten, Jan. 20 and July 8, 1854, in *Daily Correspondence,* 164; *Memoir of Joseph Gilbert Totten,* 71, 76; Totten, *Report Addressed to the Hon. Jefferson Davis, Secretary of War, on the Effects of Firing with Heavy Ordnance from Casement Embrasures,* 37, 65, 161.
42. Davis to Totten, Aug. 19, 1854, in *The Papers of Jefferson Davis,* ed. L. L. Crist and M. S. Dix (Baton Rouge: Louisiana State University Press, 1985), 5:82–83; Pryor, "Robert E. Lee's Earliest-Known Letter," 116; Boynton, *History of West Point,* 248–49; REL to Totten, Aug. 28, 1854, in *Daily Correspondence,* 214–15; Morrison, *"Best School,"* 114–16; Preston, *Lee: West Point and Lexington,* 42–45; REL to Totten, Dec. 29, 1854, in *Daily Correspondence,* 258; Brett Bowden, *The Strange Persistence of Universal History in Political Thought* (Cham, Switzerland: Palgrave Macmillan, 2017), 10; REL to Totten, Sept. 8, 1854, in *Daily Correspondence,* 219–20.
43. REL to Edward Lee Childe, Oct. 31, 1853, duPont Library; REL to Livingston, Oct. 20, 1854, in *Daily Correspondence,* 231; EAL, journal entry for Nov. 8, 1853, in *Growing Up in the 1850s,* 27–28; Robert E. Lee Jr., *Recollections and Letters,* 12–13.
44. REL to Martha Williams, Sept. 16, 1853, in *"To Markie,"* 37; REL to Bonaparte, Feb. 28, 1855, in Hoyt, "Some Personal Letters of Robert E. Lee, 1850–1858," 569; Daughtry, *Gray Cavalier,* 16–17; EAL, journal entry for March 9, 1854, in *Growing Up in the 1850s,* 33–34.

Chapter Seven: The Unpleasant Legacy

1. EAL, journal entry for March 11, 1855, in *Growing Up in the 1850s,* 47–48; "Appointments Confirmed," *New York Herald,* March 5, 1855.
2. Sam Houston, "Army Appropriation Bill," Jan. 29, 1855, Cong. Globe, 33rd Cong., 2nd Sess., 441; Clayton Newell, *The Regular Army Before the Civil War, 1845–1860* (Washington, D.C.: Center of Military History, 2014), 31–32; Davis to Franklin Pierce, Dec. 16, 1854, in *Papers of Jefferson Davis,* 5:94; Richard W. Johnson, *A Soldier's Reminiscences in Peace and War* (Philadelphia: J. B. Lippincott, 1886), 88–90; James R. Arnold, *Jeff Davis's Own: Cavalry, Comanches, and the Battle for the Texas Frontier* (New York: John Wiley & Sons, 2000), 16–22; "Military Appointments," *Washington Sentinel,* March 6, 1855; "The Field Officers of the New Regiments," *Washington Daily Union,* March 15, 1855.
3. William Preston Johnston, *The Life of Gen. Albert Sidney Johnston: Embracing His Services in the Armies of the United States, the Republic of Texas, and the Confederate States* (New York: D. Appleton, 1878), 185; Davis, "Speech at Richmond," Nov. 3, 1870, in *Papers of Jefferson Davis,* 12:502–6; "The New Regiments—Capacity and Qualifications to Lead Troops," *Washington Daily Union,* March 13, 1855; William Preston, "Speech of General Preston," in *Robert E. Lee: In Memoriam, a Tribute of Respect Offered by the Citizens of Louisville* (Louisville: John P. Morton, 1870), 16.
4. William C. Davis, *Jefferson Davis: The Man and His Hour* (New York: HarperCollins, 1991), 231; REL to Cullum, March 13, 1855, Swann Auction Galleries, catalogue.swanngalleries.com/asp/fullCatalogue.asp?salelot=2333++++++14+&refno=++662213&saletype=; Coffman, *Old Army,* 49.
5. Frederick Law Olmsted, *A Journey Through Texas; or, A Saddle-Trip on the Southwestern Frontier* (New York: Dix, Edwards, 1857), 98, 117, 124, 130; EAL, journal entry for March 11, 1855, in *Growing Up in the 1850s,* 48; REL to Martha Williams, in *"To Markie,"* 53.
6. EAL, journal entries for April 16, 17, 20, and 23, 1855, in *Growing Up in the 1850s,* 52, 57, 61, 62, 63; REL to Cooper, March 15, 1855, and to Totten, March 15 and 22, 1855, in *Daily Correspondence,* 287–89.
7. Cullum, *Biographical Register,* 1:717–18, 2:33, 150; *A Soldier's Honor: With Reminiscences of*

Major-General Earl Van Dorn (New York: Abbey Press, 1902), 21; Nathaniel Cheairs Hughes and Thomas Clayton Ware, *Theodore O'Hara: Poet-Soldier of the Old South* (Knoxville: University of Tennessee Press, 1998), 43–54, 85–86.

8. REL to CCL, May 10, 1855, and to MCL, July 1 and 9, Aug. 5, 1855, in PLREL, 1:14, 31, 41; REL to Samuel Cooper, May 18, 1855, Special Collections, Leyburn Library; Sanborn, *Robert E. Lee: A Portrait,* 239.

9. REL to MCL, May 10, July 1 and 9, Aug. 7 and 26, Sept. 3, 1855, in PLREL, 1:14, 21, 22, 30, 46, 57, 63; Daughtry, *Gray Cavalier,* 19; Coulling, *Lee Girls,* 54–60; Jennifer Harrison, "Nineteenth-Century Virginia Female Institutes, 1850–1890: An Analysis of the Effect of Education on Social Life" (master's thesis, University of Richmond, 2000), 32; EAL, journal entry for March 16, 1856, in *Growing Up in the 1850s,* 77; S. A. Wallis, "Rev. Dr. Edward Russell Lippitt," in *History of the Theological Seminary in Virginia and Its Historical Background,* ed. W. A. R. Goodwin (Rochester, N.Y.: Du Bois Press, 1923), 558. "Rev. Prof. Lippitt's Select School" was originally opened (at 481 West Tenth Street in the District) for "Young Ladies," according to an advertisement in the Washington *Evening Star,* Sept. 13, 1854; he opened a "Family School for Boys" in September 1856 near the Virginia Theological Seminary, the neighbors of Arlington; see *Alexandria Gazette,* July 31, 1856.

10. James Hildreth, *Dragoon Campaigns to the Rocky Mountains, Being a History of the Enlistment, Organization, and First Campaigns of the Regiment of United States Dragoons* (New York: Wiley & Long, 1836), 46; REL to MCL, July 1, Aug. 5, Sept. 3 and 9, Nov. 1, 1855, in PLREL, 23, 40, 41, 63, 69, 72; Averell, *Ten Years in the Saddle,* 69–70; Eliza Johnston, diary entry for Oct. 29, 1855, in "The Diary of Eliza (Mrs. Albert Sidney) Johnston: The Second Cavalry Comes to Texas," *Southwestern Historical Quarterly* 60 (April 1957): 467; Harold B. Simpson, *Cry Comanche: The 2nd U.S. Cavalry in Texas, 1855–1861* (Hillsboro, Tex.: Hill College Press, 1988), 30, 39, 46; Arnold, *Jeff Davis's Own,* 38, 39; Albert G. Brackett, *History of the United States Cavalry: From the Formation of the Federal Government to the 1st of June, 1863* (New York: Harper & Bros., 1865), 169.

11. REL to Wickham, Jan. 2, Feb. 15 and 18, March 1, 1856, in PLREL, 1:80, 84, 86, 88; Freeman, *R. E. Lee,* 1:363.

12. Johnston, *Life of Gen. Albert Sidney Johnston,* 188; Arnold, *Jeff Davis's Own,* 42; Simpson, *Cry Comanche,* 47–49; Carl Coke, *Robert E. Lee in Texas* (Norman: University of Oklahoma Press, 1946), 16–17; Brackett, *History of the United States Cavalry,* 172.

13. REL to MCL, April 12, 1856, in PLREL, 1:111; "Report of Capt. R. B. Marcy," in *Reports of the Secretary of War, with Reconnaissances of Routes from San Antonio to El Paso* (Washington, D.C.: Union Office, 1850), 185; Simpson, *Cry Comanche,* 58; Gary Clayton Anderson, *The Conquest of Texas: Ethnic Cleansing in the Promised Land, 1820–1875* (Norman: University of Oklahoma Press, 2005), 172–73; Brian Delay, "The Wider World of the Handsome Man: Southern Plains Indians Invade Mexico, 1830–1848," *Journal of the Early Republic* 27 (Spring 2007): 87, 96.

14. Simpson, *Cry Comanche,* 62; Arnold, *Jeff Davis's Own,* 54, 61, 122, 131; J. M. Morphis, *History of Texas, from Its Discovery and Settlement, with a Description of Its Principal Cities and Counties, and the Agricultural, Mineral, and Material Resources of the State* (New York: United States Publishing, 1875), 385; Colonel George Croghan to Captain James H. Ralston, March 6, 1847, in "Colonel George Croghan and the Indian Situation in Texas in 1847," ed. Martin L. Crimmins, *Southwestern Historical Quarterly* 56 (Jan. 1953): 457; "'I Am Already Quite a Texan': Albert J. Myer's Letters from Texas, 1854–1856," ed. David A. Clary, *Southwestern Historical Quarterly* 82 (July 1978): 41–42; Baylor, Sept. 12, 1856, in "Report of the Secretary of the Interior," in *Message of the President of the United States to the Two Houses of Congress, at the Commencement of the Third Session of the Thirty-Fourth Congress* (Washington, D.C.: Cornelius Wendell, 1856), 728.

15. William B. Parker, *Notes Taken During the Expedition Commanded by Capt. R. B. Marcy, U.S.A., Through Unexplored Texas in the Summer and Fall of 1854* (Philadelphia: Hayes & Zell, 1856), 180; Arnold, *Jeff Davis's Own,* 84, 118; REL to MCL, April 12, 1856, and to Mary Mackay Stiles, May 24, 1856, in PLREL, 1:114, 122–23; Frances Mayhugh Holden, *Lambshead Before Interwoven: A Texas Range Chronicle, 1848–1878* (College Station: Texas A&M University Press, 1982), 51–52; Francis R. Adams, "Robert E. Lee and the Concept of Democracy," *American Quarterly* 12 (Autumn 1960): 367–68; Freeman, *R. E. Lee,* 364.
16. Rister, *Robert E. Lee in Texas,* 38–39; REL to Mary Mackay Stiles, May 24, 1856, in PLREL, 1:124; "Colonel J. F. K. Mansfield's Report of the Inspection of the Department of Texas in 1856," ed. M. L. Crimmins, *Southwestern Historical Quarterly* 42 (April 1939): 369–73; Simpson, *Cry Comanche,* 78; REL to MChL, April 28, 1856, Lee Family Papers, VMHC.
17. Johnston, *Life of Gen. Albert Sidney Johnston,* 171; Simpson, *Cry Comanche,* 68–69, 74; Arnold, *Jeff Davis's Own,* 85; Rister, *Robert E. Lee in Texas,* 40–52; REL to MCL, July 28 and Aug. 4, 1856, in PLREL, 1:134, 141.
18. REL to Martha Williams, Feb. 12, 1855, in *"To Markie,"* 51; Freeman, *R. E. Lee,* 1:356–57; Rister, *Robert E. Lee in Texas,* 19.
19. Michael Todd Landis, *Northern Men with Southern Loyalties: The Democratic Party and the Sectional Crisis* (Ithaca, N.Y.: Cornell University Press, 2014), 140; William E. Gienapp, *The Origins of the Republican Party, 1852–1856* (New York: Oxford University Press, 1987), 305; Foote, *Casket of Reminiscences,* 111; Michael F. Holt, *The Rise and Fall of the American Whig Party: Jacksonian Politics and the Onset of the Civil War* (New York: Oxford University Press, 1999), 756, 763, 766, 768, 771.
20. REL to MCL, Nov. 19, Dec. 13 and 27, 1856, in PLREL, 1:214, 234, 244; Averell, *Ten Years in the Saddle,* 71; Coffman, *Old Army,* 93; Pierce, "Fourth Annual Message," Dec. 2, 1856, in *A Compilation of the Messages and Papers of the Presidents, 1789–1897,* ed. James D. Richardson (Washington, D.C.: Government Printing Office, 1897), 5:398.
21. REL to MCL, Dec. 27, 1856, in PLREL, 1:245; Allan Nevins, *Ordeal of the Union: Fruits of Manifest Destiny, 1847–1852* (New York: Scribner, 1947), 283.
22. John Leyburn, "An Interview with General Robert E. Lee," *Century Magazine,* May 1885, 167; REL to MCL, Dec. 27, 1856, in PLREL, 1:245; Henry Lee, *Memoirs of the War in the Southern Department of the United States* (Washington, D.C.: Peter Force, 1827), 121; Sanborn, *Robert E. Lee: A Portrait,* 255; Freeman, *R. E. Lee,* 1:372–73; William H. Freehling, *The Road to Disunion: Secessionists at Bay, 1776–1854* (New York: Oxford University Press, 1990), 24.
23. William Rasmussen and Robert S. Tilton, *Lee and Grant* (London: Giles, 2007), 161; Marie Tyler-McGraw, *An African Republic: Black and White Virginians in the Making of Liberia* (Chapel Hill: University of North Carolina Press, 2007), 120–22; MCL to REL, in John Perry, *Lady of Arlington: The Life of Mrs. Robert E. Lee* (Sisters, Ore.: Multnomah Press, 2001), 212; REL to Phineas Gurley, Dec. 24, 1835, and to W. McLain, Feb. 8, 1855, American Colonization Society Papers, Library of Congress; Leyburn, "Interview with General Robert E. Lee," 167; "Arlington and Mount Vernon 1856 as Described in a Letter of Augusta Blanche Berard," 161. For the reports of one of Arlington's Liberia colonists to Robert and Mary Lee, see William Burke to REL, Aug. 20 and 21, 1854, Feb. 20, 1859, in *Slave Testimony: Two Centuries of Letters, Speeches, Interviews, and Autobiographies,* ed. J. W. Blassingame (Baton Rouge: Louisiana State University Press, 1977), 100–107.
24. REL to MCL, Dec. 27, 1856, in PLREL, 1:245–46. This was the argument satirized by John Quincy Adams in his appeal on behalf of the *Amistad* slave mutineers in 1841: "As for slavery, every one knows it an evil, but it was entailed upon us by our ancestors; it was provided for by the constitution granted by the Lords Proprietors; it was encouraged from motives of policy by the Royal Government, and what right has any one to question our practice of it now! It was once lawful—who shall say it shall not be lawful forever!" Adams mocked the

contradiction of conjoining "vituperation of the slave trade in words, with a broad shield of protection carefully extended over it in deeds. Slavery acknowledged an evil, and the inveteracy of its abuse urged as an unanswerable argument for its perpetuity: the best of actions imputed to the worst of motives, and a bluster of mental energy to shelter a national crime behind a barrier of national independence." *Argument of John Quincy Adams, Before the Supreme Court of the United States in the Case of the United States, Appellants, vs. Cinque, and Others, Africans Captured in the Schooner* Amistad, *by Lieut. Gedney* (New York: S. W. Benedict, 1841), 110.

25. "Management of Negroes upon Southern Estates," *DeBow's Review,* June 1851, 621; Lacy K. Ford, *Deliver Us from Evil: The Slavery Question in the Old South* (New York: Oxford University Press, 2009), 526.
26. Rister, *Robert E. Lee in Texas,* 70, 76, 78–79, 92; Arnold, *Jeff Davis's Own,* 100–101, 161; Charles P. Roland, *Albert Sidney Johnston, Soldier of Three Republics* (Lexington: University Press of Kentucky, 2001), 185; Johnston, *Life of Gen. Albert Sidney Johnston,* 205, 209; REL to MCL, May 18 and July 27, 1857, and to ACL, Aug. 8, 1857, in PLREL, 1:344, 2:381, 391; Kenneth M. Stampp, *America in 1857: A Nation on the Brink* (New York: Oxford University Press, 1990), 196–308.
27. REL to MCL, Aug. 4 and 18, Sept. 13, Nov. 1, Dec. 5, 1856, May 18 and Aug. 12, 1857, to MChL, Jan. 9, 1857, and to WHFL, Nov. 1, 1856, in PLREL, 1:140, 156–57, 170, 196, 219, 343, 2:378, 397; Sanborn, *Robert E. Lee: A Portrait,* 263; Coulling, *Lee Girls,* 62; Richard Henry Dana, *Two Years Before the Mast* (New York: Random House/Modern Library, 1945), 3; *The Education of Henry Adams* (Boston: Houghton Mifflin, 1918), 57; Daughtry, *Gray Cavalier,* 24, 33; Elisha E. Meredith and Samuel Pasco, in *Memorial Addresses on the Life and Character of William H. F. Lee* (Washington, D.C.: Government Printing Office, 1891), 7, 76–78.
28. Rasmussen and Tilton, *Grant and Lee,* 160; REL to MCL, July 28, Aug. 4, 11, and 18, Sept. 13, Oct. 3, 1856, Jan. 31, May 25, July 27, Sept. 9, 1857, in PLREL, 1:133, 139, 145, 154, 171, 173, 281, 2:382, 418; J. S. Gibbons, "The Panic of 1857," *Moody's Magazine,* June 1907, 372–77; Ben Wilson, *Heyday: The 1850s and the Dawn of the Global Age* (New York: Basic Books, 2016), 332–34.
29. REL to Winston, July 24, 1856, Robert E. Lee Papers, Small Special Collections Library; REL to MCL, July 28 and Oct. 31, 1856, Aug. 12, 1857, in PLREL, 1:133, 190, 2:399.
30. REL to Mary Mackay Stiles, May 24, 1856, in Screven, "Letters of R. E. Lee to the Mackay Family," 60–61; REL to MCL, Oct. 24, 1856, and March 7, 1857, and to ACL, Aug. 8, 1857, in PLREL, 1:186, 296–97, 2:393; Long, *Memoirs of Robert E. Lee,* 439; Robert E. Lee Jr., *Recollections and Letters,* 20; "Our Army Votes," *New York Times,* Sept. 15, 1856.
31. Tammi L. Shlotzhauer, *Living with Rheumatoid Arthritis* (Baltimore: Johns Hopkins University Press, 2014), 4–6, 14, 28; Ray Fitzpatrick et al., *Understanding Rheumatoid Arthritis* (New York: Routledge, 1996), 3, 8–11, 16–18, 111; W. S. C. Copeman, *A Short History of the Gout* (Berkeley: University of California Press, 1964), 153, 165, 169; Andrea Avery, "I Was Going to Be a Concert Pianist. And Then Rheumatoid Arthritis Appeared," *Washington Post,* June 20, 2017.
32. REL to MCL, July 28, Aug. 11 and 28, Sept. 1 and 13, Oct. 31, 1856, Jan. 7 and 31, 1857, and to Mary Mackay Stiles, Aug. 14, 1856, in PLREL, 1:132, 144, 148, 160, 163, 170, 189, 257, 284; MCL to REL, Sept. 2, 1856, deButts-Ely Collection; MCL to Harriot Talcott Hackley, Feb. 19, 1857, Talcott Family Papers, VMHC; Coulling, *Lee Girls,* 60–61; REL to Edward Vernon Childe, Jan. 9, 1857, duPont Library; MacDonald, *Mrs. Robert E. Lee,* 116, 125–26; Margaret Vance, *The Lees of Arlington: The Story of Mary and Robert E. Lee* (New York: E. P. Dutton, 1949), 135.
33. REL to MCL, Aug. 11, 1856, June 9 and 22, 1857, PLREL, 1:144, 360, 370; REL to Edward Vernon Childe, Nov. 1 and 9, 1856, and Jan. 9, 1857, duPont Library; Matthew J. Mancini,

Alexis de Tocqueville and American Intellectuals: From His Times to Ours (Lanham, Md.: Rowman & Littlefield, 2009), 55–56; Tocqueville to Edward Vernon Childe, June 1856, and to Edward Lee Childe, June 1856, in *Tocqueville on America After 1840: Letters and Other Writings,* ed. Aurelian Criatu and Jeremy Jennings (New York: Cambridge University Press, 2009), 176–77.

34. "Death of Mr. Custis," *Weekly National Intelligencer,* Oct. 17, 1857.
35. MCL, "Memoir," in *Recollections and Private Memoirs of Washington, by His Adopted Son, George Washington Parke Custis, with a Memoir of the Author* (New York: Derby & Jackson, 1860), 68; "National Agricultural Fair," *Washington Union,* Aug. 26, 1857; EAL, journal entry for Oct. 13, 1857, in *Growing Up in the 1850s,* 99–100; Coulling, *Lee Girls,* 67; "Funeral of G. W. P. Custis," *Washington Evening Star,* Oct. 13, 1857; Daughtry, *Gray Cavalier,* 43.
36. REL to Johnston, Oct. 25, 1857, in Marilyn McAdams Sibley, "Robert E. Lee to Albert Sidney Johnston, 1857," *Journal of Southern History* 29 (Feb. 1963): 103–4; "Last Hours of Mr. Custis," *Richmond Dispatch,* Oct. 15, 1857; REL to Anna Maria Fitzhugh, Nov. 22, 1857, to GWCL, Jan. 17 and Feb. 15, 1858, in PLREL, 2:443, 456; Karl Decker and Angus McSween, "The Will of George Washington Parke Custis," in *Historic Arlington: A History of the National Cemetery from Its Establishment to the Present Time* (Washington, D.C.: Gibson Bros., 1892), 80–81; Lomax, diary entry for Sept. 22, 1857, in *Leaves from an Old Washington Diary,* 76.
37. REL to GWCL, March 17, 1858, and to Anna Maria Fitzhugh, Nov. 22, 1857, in PLREL, 2:443, 468–69; Sanborn, *Robert E. Lee: A Portrait,* 274.
38. REL to Anna Maria Fitzhugh, Nov. 22 and 26, 1857, to Turner, Feb. 12, 1858, to Custis Lee, Feb. 15, 1858, in PLREL, 2:443, 447, 460, 461–63; REL to Martha Williams, Dec. 3, 1857, in *"To Markie,"* 54; "The Weather," *Alexandria Gazette,* Feb. 20, 1858; "Cold Weather," *Alexandria Gazette,* March 6, 1858; Diary of Mrs. Sydney Smith Lee, box 1, Fitzhugh Lee Papers, Small Special Collections Library; Lomax, diary entries for Dec. 25, 1857, and March 8, 1858, in *Leaves from an Old Washington Diary,* 79, 82.
39. REL to Turner, Feb. 12, 1858, to GWCL, Jan. 17, March 17, and May 17, 1858, Jan. 5 and May 30, 1859, to Anna Maria Fitzhugh, Sept. 13 and Nov. 20, 1858, and Jan. 30, 1859, in PLREL, 2:455, 460, 469, 482, 500, 506, 516, 518, 529, 530; Hanna, *Arlington House,* 61; Robert E. Lee Jr., *Recollections and Letters,* 20; Joseph C. Robert, "Lee the Farmer," *Journal of Southern History* 3 (Nov. 1937): 433; "The Steuben Monument Festival," *Washington Union,* July 23 and 25, 1858; "The Steuben Festival," *Washington Union,* July 27, 1858; "Ryland Chapel Excursion," *Washington Evening Star,* Aug. 26, 1858; REL to MCL, March 20, 1839, deButts-Ely Collection.
40. REL to GWCL, May 17, 1858, May 30 and July 2, 1859, in PLREL, 2:479, 529, 539, 541; MacDonald, *Mrs. Robert E. Lee,* 128; Daughtry, *Gray Cavalier,* 41, 48; John Walter Wayland, *A History of Shenandoah County, Virginia* (Strasburg, Va.: Shenandoah Publishing, 1927), 240; William Burke, *The Mineral Springs of Western Virginia: With Remarks on Their Use, and the Diseases to Which They Are Applicable* (New York: Wiley & Putnam, 1842), 65–67.
41. MacDonald, *Mrs. Robert E. Lee,* 126; Freeman, *R. E. Lee,* 1:381; MChL, "Recollections by Mildred Lee," July 20, 1890, in *Growing Up in the 1850s,* 120; REL to Irvin McDowell, Oct. 22, 1858, in PLREL, 2:504; "The Slaves of Mr. Custis," *New York Times,* Dec. 30, 1857; "Mr. Custis's Slaves," *Alexandria Gazette,* Jan. 5, 1858.
42. REL to GWCL, Jan. 17, 1858, Jan. 2, 1859, and to A. E. S. Keese, April 28, 1858, in PLREL, 2:456–57, 472, 515; REL to WHFL, May 30, 1858, George Bolling Lee Papers, VMHC; Davis, *Crucible of Command,* 82–83; Thomas, *Robert E. Lee,* 177; Elizabeth Brown Pryor, *Reading the Man: A Portrait of Robert E. Lee Through His Private Letters* (New York: Viking, 2007), 266. John William Jones, in *Life and Letters,* 93–94, excised the description of the rebellion of "Reuben, Parks & Edward."

43. Tyler-McGraw, *African Republic,* 122; "Lee and His Slaves," *New-York Tribune,* March 26, 1866; see similar accounts in "A Christian Soldier," *New-York Tribune,* May 9, 1865, "Robert E. Lee—His Brutality to His Slaves," *National Anti-slavery Standard,* April 14, 1866, and "Notes on the United States Since the War," *British Quarterly Review* 42 (Oct. 2, 1865): 469; Coulling, *Lee Girls,* 73. Seven years later, Lee would declare the "statement" to be "not true" (Robert E. Lee Jr., *Recollections and Letters,* 224–25). Norris would, quite literally, have the last laugh; he enjoyed a post–Civil War career as "the Prince of Colored Comedians" (see *Bangor Daily Whig and Courier,* July 22, 1886).
44. "Some Facts That Should Come to Light," *New-York Tribune,* June 24, 1859; REL to GWCL, July 2, 1859, in PLREL, 2:541–42; Freeman, *R. E. Lee,* 1:390–92.

Chapter Eight: I Will Cling to It to the Last

1. REL to WHFL, Aug. 7, 1858, to GWCL, Jan. 2, 1859, to Anna Maria Fitzhugh, Jan. 30, 1859, and to Lorenzo Dow Thomas, June 16, 1859, in PLREL, 2:494, 515, 518, 534–35.
2. Daughtry, *Gray Cavalier,* 46–48; REL to WHFL, Jan. 1 and May 30, 1859, and to GWCL, Aug. 17, 1859, in PLREL, 2:512, 528–29, 544–45.
3. Grace H. Sharp, "Colored Servant of Adopted Son of George Washington," *Christian Science Monitor,* Sept. 24, 1924. The Harpers Ferry armory was one of three federally operated weapons facilities there: the armory, which sat along the Potomac River side of the town and was protected by a brick wall around its perimeter; the arsenal, which was directly across the street and acted as the storage facility for the weapons produced or altered by the armory; and a rifle factory on the Shenandoah River side of the town that the federal government had bought from John Hall.
4. "The Insurrection at Harper's Ferry," *Richmond Dispatch,* Oct. 19, 1859; Evan Carton, *Patriotic Treason: John Brown and the Soul of America* (New York: Free Press, 2006), 302; Tony Horwitz, *Midnight Rising: John Brown and the Raid That Sparked the Civil War* (New York: Henry Holt, 2011), 142; Kathleen Waters Sander, *John W. Garrett and the Baltimore and Ohio Railroad* (Baltimore: Johns Hopkins University Press, 2017), 101; David S. Reynolds, *John Brown, Abolitionist: The Man Who Killed Slavery, Sparked the Civil War, and Seeded Civil Rights* (New York: Vintage, 2005), 317.
5. Emory Thomas, *Bold Dragoon: The Life of J. E. B. Stuart* (1986; Norman: University of Oklahoma Press, 1999), 46, 53–54; " 'The Greatest Service I Rendered the State': J. E. B. Stuart's Account of the Capture of John Brown," ed. Emory Thomas, *VMHB,* July 1986, 352; REL to GWCL, Aug. 17, 1859, in PLREL, 2:547; "Arrival of the Baltimore Military," *Washington Evening Star,* Oct. 19, 1859.
6. "The Insurrection at Harpers Ferry," *Alexandria Gazette,* Oct. 19, 1859; " 'Greatest Service I Rendered the State,' " 352; Thomas, *Bold Dragoon,* 56–58; Sanborn, *Robert E. Lee: A Portrait,* 285.
7. *The Life, Trial, and Execution of Captain John Brown Known as "Old Brown of Ossawatomie," with a Full Account of the Attempted Insurrection at Harper's Ferry* (New York: Robert De Witt, 1859), 32, 81; Stuart, in Jones, *Life and Letters,* 106; Carton, *Patriotic Treason,* 309; "Harper's Ferry—Great Excitement," *Virginia Free Press and Farmers' Repository,* Oct. 20, 1859.
8. "Colonel Lee to the Adjutant General," Oct. 19, 1859, in *Report of the Select Committee of the Senate Appointed to Inquire into the Late Invasion and Seizure of the Public Property at Harper's Ferry* (Washington, D.C., 1860), 41, 43–44; Oswald Garrison Villard, *John Brown, 1800–1859: A Biography Fifty Years After* (Boston: Houghton Mifflin, 1910), 452; "The Riot at Harper's Ferry," *Wheeling Daily Intelligencer,* Oct. 19, 1859; "Colonel Baylor's Report," *Alexandria Gazette,* Oct. 31, 1859.

9. Alexander R. Boteler, "Recollections of the John Brown Raid," *Century Magazine,* May 1883, 409; Israel Green, "The Capture of John Brown," *North American Review* 141 (Dec. 1885): 565–67. In later years, one of Brown's hostages, Jesse W. Graham, would claim that he saw a Brown raider, Edwin Coppoc, draw "a deadly bead on Lee." As Graham told the story, he sprang forward, pushed Coppoc's Sharps rifle aside, and "during the struggle Lee stepped out of range." See Benjamin G. Gue, *History of Iowa from the Earliest Times to the Beginning of the 20th Century* (Chicago: Century, 1903), 2:9. Although no hostage named Jesse W. Graham appears in the Mason Committee's listing of Brown's ten hostages (p. 41), Graham's name does appear among a much longer listing of hostages that appeared in "Daring Abolition Foray!," *Charles Town Independent Democrat,* Oct. 25, 1859. Graham is identified as a workman at the arsenal and is quoted extensively in Richard J. Hinton, *John Brown and His Men with Some Account of the Roads They Travelled to Reach Harper's Ferry* (New York: Funk & Wagnalls, 1894), 305.
10. "The Insurrection at Harpers Ferry," *Alexandria Gazette,* Oct. 20, 1859; "Insurrection at Harper's Ferry," *Richmond Enquirer,* Oct. 21, 1859; REL to Floyd, Oct. 18, 1859, in *Report,* 45, and app., 8–9; Freeman, *R. E. Lee,* 1:401; Villard, *John Brown, 1800–1859,* 456; James Vallandigham, *A Life of Clement L. Vallandigham* (Baltimore: Turnbull Bros., 1872), 113; "Speech of Governor Wise," *Richmond Enquirer,* Oct. 25, 1859; Craig Simpson, *A Good Southerner: The Life of Henry A. Wise of Virginia* (Chapel Hill: University of North Carolina Press, 1985), 209; "The Harper's Ferry Insurrections," *Baltimore Daily Exchange,* Oct. 21, 1859; "Our Despatch from Washington," *New York Herald,* Oct. 21, 1859; "Returned," *Washington Evening Star,* Oct. 20, 1859.
11. "The Harper's Ferry Riot—Its Moral and Consequences," *Richmond Enquirer,* Oct. 21, 1859; "The Latest Despatches," *New York Herald,* Oct. 21, 1859; William Marvel, *A Place Called Appomattox* (Chapel Hill: University of North Carolina Press, 2000), 69.
12. "The League of Treason—Practical Organization of Seward's Irrepressible Conflict," *New York Herald,* Oct. 22, 1859; Seward, "The State of the Country," Feb. 29, 1860, in *The Works of William H. Seward,* ed. George E. Baker (Boston: Houghton, Mifflin, 1884), 4:637; William A. Blair, *With Malice Toward Some: Treason and Loyalty in the Civil War Era* (Chapel Hill: University of North Carolina Press, 2014), 32; Wendell Phillips, "Harper's Ferry," Nov. 1, 1859, in *Speeches, Lectures, and Letters* (Boston: James Redpath, 1863), 274; James Freeman Clarke, "John Albion Andrew," in *Memorial and Biographical Sketches* (Boston: Houghton, Osgood, 1878), 20; "The Sympathy Meeting in Boston," *New York Herald,* Nov. 23, 1859; "Brown Sentenced," *Virginia Free Press and Farmers' Repository,* Nov. 3, 1859; "Brown of Ossawatomie," in *The Complete Poetical Works of John Greenleaf Whittier* (Boston: Houghton Mifflin, 1895), 201.
13. "Affairs at Charlestown," *Richmond Daily Dispatch,* Dec. 1, 1859; "News of the Day," *Alexandria Gazette,* Dec. 1, 1859; *Alexandria Gazette,* Dec. 14, 1859; REL to MCL, Dec. 1, 1859, in PLREL, 2:550, 552; Stephen B. Oates, *To Purge This Land with Blood: A Biography of John Brown* (New York: Harper & Row, 1970), 336; REL to Henry Carter Lee, Dec. 6, 1859, Lee Family Papers, VMHC.
14. "Meeting at Charlestown, Va.," *Alexandria Gazette,* Jan. 26, 1860; *Report,* 29, 46–47; REL to T[homas] P. August, Dec. 20, 1859, in PLREL, 2:554; "Legislature of Virginia," *Richmond Enquirer,* Dec. 13, 1859; *Wheeling Daily Intelligencer,* Oct. 22, 1859; "General Assembly of Virginia," *Richmond Dispatch,* Jan. 25, 1860; "Two Worthy Sons of Virginia," *Richmond Enquirer,* Jan. 24, 1860; "Legislature of Virginia," *Richmond Enquirer,* Jan. 27, 1860; George Green Shackelford, *George Wythe Randolph and the Confederate Elite* (Athens: University of Georgia Press, 1988), 49.
15. Martin L. Crimmins, "An Episode in the Texas Career of General David E. Twiggs," *Southwestern Historical Quarterly* 41 (Oct. 1937): 172; *Alexandria Gazette,* Dec. 7, 1859; REL to

R. Jacquelin Ambler, Feb. 4, 1860, and to Anna Maria Fitzhugh, Feb. 9, 1860, in PLREL, 2:563, 565–66; Yates, *Perfect Gentleman,* 1:185–86; REL to Ella Carter, Jan. 29, 1860, in William Franklin Chaney, *Duty Most Sublime: The Life of Robert E. Lee as Told Through the "Carter Letters"* (Baltimore: Gateway Press, 1996), 55.

16. REL to Annette Carter, Feb. 10, 1860, in Chaney, *Duty Most Sublime,* 56; REL to GWCL, Feb. 14, 1860, in Jones, *Life and Letters,* 109; Mason, *Popular Life of General Robert Edward Lee,* 68; Arnold, *Jeff Davis's Own,* 177, 251–55, 286–91; Rister, *Robert E. Lee in Texas,* 139–40; Simpson, *Cry Comanche,* 130, 132–33; Longacre, *Fitz Lee,* 21–24; Freeman Cleaves, *Rock of Chickamauga: The Life of General George H. Thomas* (Norman: University of Oklahoma Press, 1948), 58–59; Thomas T. Smith, "U.S. Combat Operations in the Indian Wars of Texas, 1849–1881," *Southwestern Historical Quarterly* 99 (April 1996): 506–7.

17. Jerry Thompson, *Cortina: Defending the Mexican Name in Texas* (College Station: Texas A&M University Press, 2007), 37–63; Armando C. Alonzo, *Tejano Legacy: Rancheros and Settlers in South Texas, 1734–1900* (Albuquerque: University of New Mexico Press, 1997), 194–96; "Captain Thompson's Report," Oct. 25, 1859, and Cortina, "Proclamation," Sept. 30 and Nov. 23, 1859, in *Executive Documents Printed by Order of the House of Representatives During the First Session of the Thirty-Sixth Congress, 1859–'60* (Washington, D.C.: Thomas B. Ford, 1860), 69, 71, 80; Arnold, *Jeff Davis's Own,* 268–69; Rister, *Robert E. Lee in Texas,* 110–11; "Late from Brownsville," *Dallas Herald,* Dec. 7, 1859, and Jan. 18, 1860; "Another Fight on the Rio Grande," *Texas Republican,* April 14, 1860.

18. "Major Heintzelman to General Twiggs," Dec. 16, 1859, and "S. Hart to the President," Jan. 21, 1860, in *Executive Documents,* 87–88; Arnold, *Jeff Davis's Own,* 268–69; Thompson, *Cortina,* 61.

19. "Frontier Matters," *Dallas Herald,* March 7, 1860; "Col. R. E. Lee," *Dallas Herald,* March 21, 1860; REL to ACL, Feb. 22, 1860, and to GWCL, Feb. 28 and March 13, 1860, in PLREL, 2:571, 575, 585; Governor Houston to Mr. Floyd, Feb. 20, 1860, Major Thomas to Colonel Seawell, Feb. 22, 1860, Adjutant General to Colonel Lee, Feb. 24, 1860, Colonel Lee to General Scott, March 6, 1860, and Colonel Lee to the Adjutant General, March 12, 1860, in *Executive Documents,* 131, 132, 133, 135–36, 145; Rister, *Robert E. Lee in Texas,* 102, 104.

20. "Latest News from the Rio Grande," *Dallas Herald,* Jan. 4, 1860; REL to MCL, March 24, April 1 and 17, 1860, and to GWCL, April 12, 1860, in PLREL, 2:589, 597, 612, 616; REL to Andrés L. Treviño, April 2, 1860, and to Guadalupe Garcia, April 12, 1860, in Jones, *Life and Letters,* 111–12; Thompson, *Cortina,* 87, 91; Michael L. Collins, *Texas Devils: Rangers and Regulars on the Lower Rio Grande, 1846–1861* (Norman: University of Oklahoma Press, 2008), 199.

21. REL, "Special Orders, Head Quarters, Department of Texas," April 30, 1860, in Samuel Peter Heintzelman Papers (Military Papers, 1822–1869, box 10), Library of Congress; REL to George H. Thomas, Feb. 21, 1860, at viaLibri (Reisse & Son Auctioneers), www.vialibri.net/552display_i/year_1892_0_0.html; REL to GWCL, April 16, 1860, to EAL, June 8, 1860, and to Earl Van Dorn, June 27, 1860, in PLREL, 2:612–13, 644, 662; Jones, *Life and Letters,* 114; Stephen Bonsal, *Edward Fitzgerald Beale, a Pioneer in the Path of Empire, 1822–1903* (New York: G. P. Putnam's Sons, 1912), 201–7; *Texas Republican,* June 30, 1860; REL to Houston, April 20, 1860, in Robert E. Lee Papers, Dolph Briscoe Center for American History, University of Texas at Austin; Davis, *Crucible of Command,* 111–12.

22. Stephen B. Oates, ed., *Rip Ford's Texas* (Austin: University of Texas Press, 1963), 302; Rister, *Robert E. Lee in Texas,* 157–58; Kate Merritt Clarkson, "Belle of the Sixties Recalls Dramatic Incidents," in *Women Tell the Story of the Southwest,* ed. Mattie L. I. Wooten (San Antonio: Naylor, 1940), 11.

23. REL to ACL, Feb. 22 and March 25, 1860, to MCL, March 3 and April 25, 1860, and to Anna Maria Fitzhugh, June 6, 1860, in PLREL, 2:571, 578, 591, 622, 638; EAL, journal entry for

Dec. 13, 1857, in *Growing Up in the 1850s,* 101; MCL, "Memoir of George Washington Parke Custis," 11; Sanborn, *Robert E. Lee: A Portrait,* 291.

24. REL to MCL, March 3, 1860, and to ACL, June 16 and Aug. 27, 1860, in PLREL, 2:578, 646, 686; Sanborn, *Robert E. Lee: A Portrait,* 295.

25. REL to GWCL, Feb. 28, 1860, to WHFL, Aug. 22, 1860, and to MCL, April 4 and June 18, 1860, in PLREL, 2:575, 602, 653–54, 682; REL to EAL, April 14, 1860, Lehigh University Digital Archive, digital.lib.lehigh.edu.

26. Daughtry, *Gray Cavalier,* 49–50; REL to MCL, Nov. 8, 1856, April 1 and 17, May 2, June 3, 1860, to WHFL, April 2, 1860, to ACL, Aug. 27, 1860, and to EAL, June 8, 1860, in PLREL, 1:202, 2:595, 600, 617, 626, 630, 642, 684.

27. J. P. Benjamin, *Defence of the National Democracy Against the Attack of Judge Douglas* (Washington, D.C.: L. Towers, 1860), 11, 16.

28. Robert W. Johannsen, *Stephen A. Douglas* (1973; Urbana: University of Illinois Press, 1997), 756, 771–72; Michael F. Holt, *The Election of 1860: "A Campaign Fraught with Consequences"* (Lawrence: University Press of Kansas, 2017), 129; "The Presidential Battle Made Up—the Two Democratic Tickets," *New York Herald,* June 25, 1860; "The Baltimore Convention—the Democratic Candidates" and "Presidential—Proceedings of the Disunited Democracy," *New York Times,* June 25, 1860.

29. REL to Van Dorn, July 3, 1860, in PLREL, 2:671; "Mary Custis Lee's 'Reminiscences of the War,'" ed. R. E. L. deButts, *VMHB* 109 (2001): 312.

30. REL to GWCL, Nov. 24, 1860, in PLREL, 2:697; "To the Reading Public" and "Our Ticket," *Alamo Express,* Aug. 18, 1860; "Banner Presentation," *Alamo Express,* Nov. 5, 1860; Dale Baum, *The Shattering of Texas Unionism: Politics in the Lone Star State During the Civil War Era* (Baton Rouge: Louisiana State University Press, 1998), 40; James M. Smallwood, "The Impending Crisis: A Texas Perspective on the Causes of the Civil War," in *The Seventh Star of the Confederacy: Texas During the Civil War,* ed. Kenneth Wayne Howell (Denton: University of North Texas Press, 2009), 47; Randolph B. Campbell, *Sam Houston and the American Southwest* (New York: HarperCollins, 1993), 187.

31. REL to GWCL, Dec. 5, 1860, in PLREL, 2:702; Adams, "Letter from Washington," Jan. 1, 1861, in *Henry Adams in the Secession Crisis: Dispatches to the Boston "Daily Advertiser," December 1860–March 1861,* ed. M. J. Stegmaier (Baton Rouge: Louisiana State University Press, 2012), 65; "Message of Gov. Letcher to the Legislature of Virginia," *Richmond Enquirer,* Jan. 8, 1861; Scott, "Views," Oct. 29, 1860, in *Works of James Buchanan,* ed. J. B. Moore (Philadelphia: J. B. Lippincott, 1910), 11:301–3; Peskin, *Winfield Scott and the Profession of Arms,* 234–35; Eisenhower, *Agent of Destiny,* 346, 357; Johnson, *Winfield Scott,* 222–23.

32. REL to GWCL, Dec. 14, 1860, in PLREL, 2:710; REL to Annette Carter, Jan. 16, 1861, in Chaney, *Duty Most Sublime,* 61.

33. REL to Martha Williams, Jan. 22, 1861, in *"To Markie,"* 58; REL to GWCL, Jan. 23, 1861, in PLREL, 2:721; REL to WHFL, Jan. 29, 1861, in "'Secession Is Nothing but Revolution': A Letter of R. E. Lee to His Son 'Rooney,'" ed. W. M. E. Rachal, *VMHB,* Jan. 1961, 6; Davis, *Crucible of Command,* 113–14. Lee might have been referring to a letter Jefferson wrote to Thomas Lehre in November 1808 characterizing "the opposition to the late laws of embargo" as tantamount to "rebellion and treason." See Arthur Scherr, *Thomas Jefferson's Image of New England: Nationalism Versus Sectionalism in the Young Republic* (Jefferson, N.C.: McFarland, 2016), 146.

34. Caroline Baldwin Darrow, "Recollections of the Twiggs Surrender," in *Battles and Leaders of the Civil War,* ed. C. C. Buel and R. U. Johnson (New York: Century, 1884), 1:33–35; Jeanne T. Heidler, "'Embarrassing Situation': David E. Twiggs and the Surrender of United States Forces in Texas, 1861," in *Lone Star Blue and Gray: Essays on Texas and the Civil War,* ed. R. A. Wooster and Robt. Wooster (Austin: Texas State Historical Association, 1995), 65–80; J. J.

Bowden, *The Exodus of Federal Forces from Texas* (Austin, Tex.: Eakin Press, 1986), 61–62; Russell K. Brown, "'An Old Woman with a Broomstick': General David E. Twiggs and the U.S. Surrender in Texas, 1861," *Military Affairs* 48 (April 1984): 58–59; "The Treason of Gen. Twiggs," *New York Times*, Feb. 27, 1861.

35. Johnson, *Soldier's Reminiscences in Peace and War*, 132–33; Heintzelman, diary entry for March 25, 1861, Heintzelman Papers; "Special Orders No. 16," Feb. 4, 1861, in *OR*, ser. 1, 1:586; *General Orders of the War Department, Embracing the Years 1861, 1862, and 1863, Adapted Especially for the Use of the Army and Navy of the United States*, ed. Thomas M. O'Brien and Oliver Diefendorf (New York: Derby & Miller, 1864), 1:23; Arnold, *Jeff Davis's Own*, 304; Simpson, *Cry Comanche*, 158–59. Elizabeth Brown Pryor speculates that Lincoln might have orchestrated Lee's recall with a view to giving Lee command of a contemplated rescue mission that would secure the position of Texas's anti-secessionist governor, Sam Houston, and pull Texas back out of the arms of secession. See Elizabeth Brown Pryor, *Six Encounters with Lincoln: A President Confronts Democracy and Its Demons* (New York: Viking, 2017), 44–45.
36. Darrow, "Recollections of the Twiggs Surrender," 36; Johnson, *Soldier's Reminiscences*, 133; Charles Anderson, *Texas, Before, and on the Eve of the Rebellion* (Cincinnati: Peter G. Thompson, 1884), 24; Rister, *Robert E. Lee in Texas*, 160; Arnold, *Jeff Davis's Own*, 301–2; "Seizure of Contraband Articles," *Baltimore Daily Exchange*, May 23, 1861.

Chapter Nine: The Decisions

1. Pryor, *Six Encounters*, 43; Horn, *Man Who Would Not Be Washington*, 105–6; Julia Ward Howe, *Reminiscences, 1819–1899* (Boston: Houghton Mifflin, 1900), 272; D. H. Hill, "Military Spirit and Genius of the South," *Alexandria Gazette*, March 30, 1861.
2. William Allan, "Memoranda of Conversations with General Robert E. Lee," Feb. 25 and March 10, 1868, in *Lee the Soldier*, ed. Gary W. Gallagher (Lincoln: University of Nebraska Press, 1996), 9–10, 12; MCL to Elizabeth Stiles, Feb. 9, 1861, and to MChL, Feb. 24, 1861, duPont Library, and Lee Family Papers, VMHC.
3. John Minor Botts testimony, Feb. 15, 1866, in *Report of the Joint Committee on Reconstruction at the First Session of the Thirty-Ninth Congress* (Washington, D.C.: Government Printing Office, 1866), 114–15; Russell McClintock, *Lincoln and the Decision for War: The Northern Response to Secession* (Chapel Hill: University of North Carolina Press, 2008), 242–44; Lincoln, "Proclamation Calling Militia and Convening Congress," April 15, 1861, in *Collected Works*, 4:332–33.
4. William W. Freehling and Craig M. Simpson, *Showdown in Virginia: The 1861 Convention and the Fate of the Union* (Charlottesville: University of Virginia Press, 2010), 157–58, 162, 176; Simpson, *Good Southerner*, 248–52; William W. Freehling, *The Road to Disunion: Secessionists Triumphant, 1854–1861* (New York: Oxford University Press, 2007), 524–26; Daniel W. Crofts, *Reluctant Confederates: Upper South Unionists in the Secession Crisis* (Chapel Hill: University of North Carolina Press, 1989), 335.
5. Daniel W. Crofts, *A Secession Crisis Enigma: William Henry Hurlbert and "The Diary of a Public Man"* (Baton Rouge: Louisiana State University Press, 2010), diary entry for Feb. 25, 1861, 234; F. P. Blair to Montgomery Blair, March 5, 1861, box 3, reel 2, Francis Preston Blair, 1840–1867, Blair Family Papers, Library of Congress.
6. "Letter from Montgomery Blair," *New York Evening Post*, Aug. 8, 1866; "Letter from Hon. Montgomery Blair," *Daily National Intelligencer*, Aug. 9, 1866.
7. "Senator from Maryland," Feb. 19, 1868, Cong. Globe, 40th Cong., 2nd Sess., 1270. In 1887, Cameron returned to the subject in an interview, although in this second version he substantially walked back his accusation of Lee as a deserter. "It is true that Gen. Robert E. Lee was

tendered the command of the Union Army," Cameron now agreed, and at "the wish of Mr. Lincoln's Administration." Blair, and not Lee, initiated the "tender of the command of our forces" because Blair believed "that General Lee could be held to our cause by the offer of the chief command of our forces." Cameron was therefore surprised when Lee's "resignation was received . . . and General Lee went South," and on reflection Cameron was unsure "whether General Lee ever seriously considered the matter." Cameron had been carried along by Blair's confidence in Lee, and "from what Senator Blair said to me I never had any doubt at the time but that he did." See "Just Before the War—Simon Cameron Recalls His Experiences When a Member of Lincoln's Cabinet," *Dubuque Daily Herald,* March 17, 1887; Jones, *Life and Letters,* 130.

8. "Virginia Convention," *Alexandria Gazette,* April 18, 1861; William Allan, "Memoranda of Conversations with General Robert E. Lee," Feb. 25, 1868, in Gallagher, *Lee the Soldier,* 9–10; Jones, *Personal Reminiscences,* 141–42; "Memoranda of Conversations Between General Robert E. Lee and William Preston Johnston: May 7, 1868, and March 16, 1870," ed. Bean, 483.
9. Blair's account of the interview, made on April 14, 1871, surfaced in a peculiarly roundabout way; it originated as a "Statement" made by Captain James May, one of Lee's "oldest and most cherished friends," two weeks later to Chief Justice Salmon P. Chase and not published until 1895 as a long footnote in the third volume of James Ford Rhodes's history of the Civil War era. See James Ford Rhodes, *History of the United States from the Compromise of 1850* (New York: Harper & Bros., 1895), 3:365. Later that same year, Mary Custis Lee, in a letter written for use by Wade Hampton in a memorial address, added one further detail, that Blair urged Lee to "go to see Mr. Lincoln." But Lee demurred: "That would be useless, but I must go and take leave of Gen. Scott." See MCL, in Wade Hampton, *Address on the Life and Character of Gen. Robert E. Lee, Delivered on the 12th of October, 1871, Before the Society of Confederate Soldiers and Sailors, in Maryland* (Baltimore: John Murphy, 1871), 16. On the news from Richmond as it was known in Washington, see "Virginia Convention," *Washington National Republican,* April 18, 1861.
10. *Memoirs of Lieut.-Gen. Scott,* 423, 432, 444, 446, 450, 471, 475, 479–80, 484–86, 500, 508, 512, 533.
11. REL to Scott, April 20, 1861, duPont Library. See also Jones, *Life and Letters,* 132–33; Freeman, *R. E. Lee,* 1:441–42; and *WPREL,* 8–9. In his 1868 letter to Reverdy Johnson, Lee alludes briefly to going "from the interview with Mr. Blair to the office of General Scott," where he "told him of the proposition that had been made to me, and my decision."
12. Keyes, *Fifty Years' Observations,* 206–7. Freeman, to the contrary, believes the meeting Keyes describes to have occurred in March (*R. E. Lee,* 1:433–34).
13. Edward D. Townsend, *Anecdotes of the Civil War in the United States* (New York: D. Appleton, 1884), 30–31. Freeman, in *R. E. Lee,* 1:437–38, dismisses the reliability of Townsend, but it is evident that Freeman was more disturbed by Townsend's introduction of "the property" as a factor in Lee's decision, because this would compromise the shining integrity in which Freeman wanted to clothe Lee. This, Freeman objected, "does not sound like Lee," although Lee's concern with property and finance runs through all of his correspondence from the 1830s onward.
14. "Virginia News," *Alexandria Gazette,* April 30, 1861; "General Lee and General Scott," *Household Journal of Popular Information, Amusement, and Domestic Economy,* Aug. 10, 1861, 295.
15. Coulling, *Lee Girls,* 13, 37, 51–52, 62, 66; MacDonald, *Mrs. Robert E. Lee,* 25, 35, 40, 127; Wyatt-Brown, *Southern Honor,* 110.
16. Ruffin, diary entry for April 21, 1861, in *The Diary of Edmund Ruffin,* ed. W. K. Scarborough (Baton Rouge: Louisiana State University Press, 1972–89), 1:609; "Views of Current Events—the Town of Alexandria and Its Present Condition," *New York Times,* June 3, 1861.
17. "The Rebel Gen. Lee," *New York Times,* Aug. 6, 1861; Kundahl, *Alexandria Goes to War,* 82;

Anthony J. Gaughan, *The Last Battle of the Civil War: United States Versus Lee, 1861–1883* (Baton Rouge: Louisiana State University Press, 2011), 54. Just how serious Confederate sequestrations and confiscations were to become is evident from Brian Dirck, "Posterity's Blush: Civil Liberties, Property Rights, and Property Confiscation in the Confederacy," *Civil War History* 48 (Sept. 2002): 237–56.

18. "The Climactic Wise-Baldwin Debate," April 17, 1861, in *Showdown in Virginia: The 1861 Convention and the Fate of the Union,* ed. William W. Freehling and Craig M. Simpson (Charlottesville: University of Virginia Press, 2010), 200; "Letter from Loudoun," *Alexandria Gazette,* April 19, 1861; FitzGerald Ross, *Cities and Camps of the Confederate States,* ed. Richard B. Harwell (Urbana: University of Illinois Press, 1958), 178.
19. "Local Items," *Alexandria Gazette,* April 19, 1861; Sanborn, *Robert E. Lee: A Portrait,* 1:312; *The Memoirs of Colonel John S. Mosby,* ed. Charles Wells Russell (Boston: Little, Brown, 1917), 379.
20. Jones, *Life and Letters,* 132; MCL, in Wade Hampton, *Address on the Life and Character of Gen. Robert E. Lee,* 16. Both the Jones account and the Hampton letter are linked to a document MCL began in September 1865, speaking briefly of how REL was "summoned to Washington where every motive & argument was used to induce him to accept the command of the army destined to *invade* the South. He was enabled to resist them all, even the sad parting words of his old Commander. Then came the severest struggle of his life to resign a commission he had held for more than 30 years." See "Mary Custis Lee's 'Reminiscences of the War,'" 314. George Lyttleton Upshur, a Lee cousin, in a memoir published as *As I Recall Them: Memories of Crowded Years* (New York: Wilson-Erickson, 1936), endorsed the "struggle" scenario, and even recalled seeing Lee "pacing up and down among the trees" on the Arlington grounds:

> *He came in and went up to his room—that room in which stood the bed upon which Washington had died, and which was brought to Arlington after Mrs. Washington's death in 1802. After an hour of thought and prayer, Lee wrote his resignation from the United States Army, and, descending the long stair-way with it in his hand, said to his wife: "Mary, your husband is no longer an officer of the United States Army." The resignation was handed to an orderly and taken to General Winfield Scott. . . . Lee and his family left Arlington the next day for Richmond and never returned to live there again.* (pp. 16–17)

But Upshur was only five years old at the time, and though it is credible that he was present at Arlington—his aunt was Markie Williams—and might have absorbed pieces of family lore about the decision, his recollection not only is too precise to be relied upon but contains errors (the "orderly" and the immediate departure of the entire family from Arlington) and variations that appear built on a subsequent acquaintance with Jones's account in *Life and Letters.*

21. Allan, "Memoranda of Conversation with General Robert E. Lee," Feb. 25, 1868, 10; MCL Jr., in Elizabeth Brown Pryor, "'Thou Knowest Not the Time of Thy Visitation': A Newly Discovered Letter Reveals Robert E. Lee's Lonely Struggle with Disunion," *VMHB,* Sept. 2011, 290. One person who certainly experienced pangs of agony over Lee's resignation was Winfield Scott. Markie Williams's brother, Orton, who was a member of Scott's staff, came over to Arlington in the afternoon of the twentieth and related "how heavily the blow had fallen upon the 'poor old General,' as he called him, how very unwell, & lying upon a sofa, he had refused to see every one, & mourned as for the loss of a son. To some one, Gen. [George W.] Cullum, I think, who rather lightly alluded to the fact, he said, with great emotion, 'dont mention Robert Lee's name to me again, I cannot bear it.'"

See Elizabeth Brown Pryor, "The General in His Study," *New York Times,* April 19, 2011;

Harold W. Hurst, *Alexandria on the Potomac: The Portrait of an Antebellum Community* (Lanham, Md.: University Press of America, 1991), 18; Mason, *Popular Life of Gen. Robert Edward Lee,* 405; and Horn, *Man Who Would Not Be Washington,* 110–11. Reverdy Johnson, who later claimed to have been with Scott when the resignation letter was delivered, "saw what pain the fact caused him"; see Johnson's comment in his eulogy of Lee, "Tributes to General Lee," *Southern Magazine,* Jan. 1871, 32. Cullum had only just been appointed an aide-de-camp on Scott's staff; see "Washington Items," *Alexandria Gazette,* April 19, 1861, and "The City," *Washington National Republican,* April 19, 1861.

22. REL to Scott, April 20, 1861, in PLREL, 2:750–51.
23. *Proceedings of the First Three Republican National Conventions of 1856, 1860, and 1864* (Minneapolis: Charles W. Johnson, 1893), 172; REL to Anne Kinloch Lee Marshall, April 20, 1861, duPont Library. Robert E. Lee Jr. and J. William Jones (in *Recollections and Letters* and *Life and Letters*) silently edit out Lee's protestations about abhorring himself and loving his sister "till death." Curiously, William Louis Marshall visited Arlington "several times" before May 6, but there is no indication that Lee consulted with him personally over the decision. See EAL to ACL, May 6, 1861, Lee Family Papers, VMHC.
24. REL to SSL, April 20, 1861. See the text offered for sale by Sotheby's in 2011 in Steve Szkotak, "Civil War Trove Set for Sotheby's Auction," *New York Daily News,* June 16, 2011, and in www.sothebys.com/en/auctions/ecatalogue/2011/fine-books-and-manuscripts-n08755/lot.161.html. Robert E. Lee Jr. and J. William Jones once again silently emend Lee's letter, this time to change the damning "ordinance of revolution" to "ordinance of secession." See *Recollections and Letters,* 26, and *Life and Letters,* 134. Curiously, no similar letter was addressed to Lee's other brother, Charles Carter Lee, or at least none that survives. Carter was "not a secessionist per se—but an ardent Southern sympathizer," and as a civilian was facing no crisis over resignation from federal appointments, so perhaps Robert felt no letter was needed. See J. F. Lay, "Reminiscences of the Powhatan Troop of Cavalry in 1861," *SHSP* 8 (Aug./Sept. 1880): 419, and Charles Carter Lee's speech, "Soldiers!," May 1861, Mary Custis Lee Papers, VMHC.
25. "Rebel Gen. Lee," *New York Times,* Aug. 6, 1861.
26. Wayne Wei-Siang Hsieh, *West Pointers and the Civil War: The Old Army in War and Peace* (Chapel Hill: University of North Carolina Press, 2009), 102, 109–10; Wayne Wei-Siang Hsieh, "'I Owe Virginia Little, My Country Much': Robert E. Lee, the United States Regular Army, and Unconditional Unionism," in *Crucible of the Civil War: Virginia from Secession to Commemoration,* ed. E. L. Ayers, G. W. Gallagher, and A. J. Torget (Charlottesville: University of Virginia Press, 2006), 45–46; Kundahl, *Alexandria Goes to War,* 26–27; C. G. Lee, "Reminiscences," Lee-Fendall House Archives, Alexandria, Va. On Alfred Mordecai, see Stanley L. Falk, "Alfred Mordecai, American Jew," *American Jewish Archives* 10 (Oct. 1958): 130–31, and Stanley L. Falk, "Divided Loyalties in 1861: The Decision of Major Alfred Mordecai," in *Jews and the Civil War: A Reader,* ed. Jonathan D. Sarna and Adam D. Mendelsohn (New York: New York University Press, 2010), 207, 213.
27. Coulling, *Lee Girls,* 82–83; Sarah L. Lee, "War Time in Alexandria, Virginia," *South Atlantic Quarterly* 4 (July 1905): 235; Constance Cary Harrison, *Recollections Grave and Gay* (New York: Charles Scribner's, 1916), 25; Moore, *Seaport in Virginia,* 227–29.
28. "From Washington," *Alexandria Gazette,* April 20, 1861; "General Scott," *Washington Evening Star,* April 22, 1861; "Oath of Allegiance," *Washington National Republican,* April 23, 1861; *OR,* ser. 1, vol. 51, pt. 2, 21; Eisenhower, *Agent of Destiny,* 372; Townsend, *Anecdotes of the Civil War,* 4–5; Douglas Southall Freeman, *Lee's Lieutenants: A Study in Command* (New York: Charles Scribner's Sons, 1942), 1:712; Kundahl, *Alexandria Goes to War,* 130.
29. *Journal of the Acts and Proceedings of a General Convention of the State of Virginia,* April 20, 1861, 169; Allan, "Memoranda of Conversation with General Robert E. Lee," Feb. 25,

1868, 10. Letcher had dispatched an earlier messenger, David Funsten, who failed to reach Alexandria due to disruptions in train schedules. See Thomas, *Robert E. Lee,* 188–89; Nolan, *Lee Considered,* 40; F. N. Boney, *John Letcher of Virginia: The Story of Virginia's Civil War Governor* (Tuscaloosa: University of Alabama Press, 1966), 119; and Freeman, *R. E. Lee,* 1:637.

30. C. G. Lee, "Reminiscences," Lee-Fendall House Archives; "Alexandria," *Alexandria Gazette,* April 20 and 22, 1861; Edward L. Ayers, *The Thin Light of Freedom: Civil War and Emancipation in the Heart of America* (New York: W. W. Norton, 2017), 364. The Washington *Evening Star* carried an announcement of Lee's resignation under "Army Officers Resigned" on April 23, 1861.
31. Lincoln to Reverdy Johnson, April 24, 1861, in *Collected Works,* 4:343; "Rebel Gen. Lee," *New York Times,* Aug. 6, 1861. Lincoln repeated his comments to a delegation from the Baltimore Young Men's Christian Association chapters ("Interview with the President," *Richmond Dispatch,* April 26, 1861).
32. Cassius F. Lee to REL, April 23, 1861, LFDA/duPont Library; W. W. Scott, "Some Personal Memories of General Robert E. Lee," *WMQ* 6 (Oct. 1926): 280.
33. "Local Matters," "The Virginia People Demand Union with the Confederate States," and "Arrival of Ex-Gov. Floyd," *Richmond Dispatch,* April 23, 1861; "The Solid Men of Richmond," *Richmond Enquirer,* April 23, 1861; *Richmond During the War: Four Years of Personal Observation, by a Richmond Lady* (New York: G. W. Carleton, 1867), 20; Ernest B. Furgurson, *Ashes of Glory: Richmond at War* (New York: Knopf, 1996), 37–39.
34. "Serenade to Vice President Stephens," *Richmond Dispatch,* April 23, 1861; "News Items," *Washington National Republican,* April 25, 1861.
35. *Journals and Papers of the Virginia State Convention of 1861,* ed. R. W. Church and G. H. Reese (Richmond: Virginia State Library, 1966), 1:185–88; "Reception of Major General Robert E. Lee," *Richmond Enquirer,* April 25, 1861. Lee's acceptance speech grew by embellishments in the years after the war. See "Address of General Preston," in Jones, *Army of Northern Virginia Memorial Volume,* 22. That evening, Stephens politely sounded out Lee's support for a "practical alliance . . . between the Confederate States and the Commonwealth of Virginia." Stephens had apprised Jefferson Davis of Lee's arrival in Richmond, predicting that Lee would be "looked to as the commander" of Virginia's forces, and he was sure now that even "a look, or an intonation of voice . . . would have defeated the measure." Lee, however, had no intention of imbruing his hands in politics. Two days later, the secession convention ratified the Confederate Constitution without any recorded comment from Lee. Alexander H. Stephens, *A Constitutional View of the Late War Between the States: Its Causes, Character, Conduct, and Results* (Philadelphia: National, 1870), 2:383–84, 386; Stephens to Davis, April 22, 1861, in *OR,* ser. 1, vol. 51, pt. 2, 24.
36. Critcher, in Mosby, "Personal Recollections of General Lee," *Munsey's Magazine,* April 1911, 68; "Movements of the Hour," *Buffalo Commercial Advertiser,* April 25, 1861.

Chapter Ten: This Is Not the Way to Accomplish Our Independence

1. Chesnut, diary entry for April 27, 1861, in *Mary Chesnut's Civil War,* ed. C. Vann Woodward (New Haven, Conn.: Yale University Press, 1981), 54–55; "War Items," *Pittsfield Sun,* April 25, 1861; "Latest from Washington and Annapolis," *New York Herald,* April 25, 1861; G. Moxley Sorrel, *Recollections of a Confederate Staff Officer,* ed. Bell Irvin Wiley (Wilmington, N.C.: Broadfoot, 1995), 14–15; Jones, diary entry for April 24, 1861, in *A Rebel War Clerk's Diary: At the Confederate States Capital,* ed. James I. Robertson (Lawrence: University Press of Kansas, 2015), 1:15; William P. Snow, *Lee and His Generals* (New York: Richardson, 1867), 20.

2. "General Orders, No. 1," in *WPREL,* 11; Kundahl, *Alexandria Goes to War,* 309; Jones, diary entry for May 31, 1861, in *Rebel War Clerk's Diary,* 1:32; "Munitions of War," *Richmond Enquirer,* April 30, 1861; "Adjournment of the Convention," *Richmond Enquirer,* May 3, 1861; Furgurson, *Ashes of Glory,* 43–44, 60; Walter Taylor, *General Lee: His Campaigns in Virginia, 1861–1865, with Personal Reminiscences* (Norfolk, Va.: Nusbaum Book & News, 1906), 21.
3. John V. Quarstein, *C.S.S.* Virginia: *Mistress of Hampton Roads* (Lynchburg, Va.: H. E. Howard, 2000), 23; "Military Notices," "Virginia State Convention," "The March to Sewall's Point," "General Headquarters," and "True Southern Patriotism," *Richmond Enquirer,* April 30, May 10, May 24, May 28, June 13, and July 2, 1861; "The Capture at Old Point," *Richmond Dispatch,* April 29, 1861; "From Norfolk," *Richmond Dispatch,* May 18, 1861; Taylor, *General Lee,* 25; George S. Bernard, "Reminiscences of Norfolk, May–June 1861," in *Civil War Talks: Further Reminiscences of George S. Bernard and His Fellow Veterans,* ed. Hampton Newsome et al. (Charlottesville: University of Virginia Press, 2012), 17; Henry Alexander Wise, *Seven Decades of the Union: The Humanities and Materialism* (Philadelphia: J. B. Lippincott, 1876), 281–82.
4. REL to Cassius F. Lee, April 25, 1861, duPont Library; REL to Cocke, April 23, 1861, in Pryor, *Reading the Man,* 572; REL to Ruggles, April 24, 1861, and to Jackson, April 27 and May 12, 1861, in *WPREL,* 11–12, 13, 27; REL to Lyons, April 25, 1861, Brock Collection; Dennis E. Frye, *2nd Virginia Infantry* (Lynchburg, Va.: H. E. Howard, 1984), 8.
5. Bledsoe to Davis, May 10, 1861, in *Papers of Jefferson Davis,* 7:160–61; D. G. Duncan to Walker, April 26, 1861, in *OR,* ser. 1, vol. 51, pt. 2, 39; Chesnut, diary entry for June 10, 1861, in *Mary Chesnut's Civil War,* 70–71; Maury, *Recollections of a Virginian,* 143; Walter Taylor, *Four Years with General Lee: Being a Summary of the More Important Events Touching the Career of General Robert E. Lee* (New York: D. Appleton, 1878), 11–12; John D. Imboden, "Reminiscences of Lee and Jackson," *Galaxy,* Nov. 1871, 628; J. William Jones, "The Friendship Between Lee and Scott," *SHSP* 11 (Aug./Sept. 1883): 426.
6. Mary Livermore, "War Excitement in Chicago," in *Reminiscences of Chicago During the Civil War,* ed. Mabel McIlvaine (Chicago: Lakeside Press, 1914), 69; John Austin Stevens, *The Union Defence Committee of the City of New York: Minutes, Reports, and Correspondence* (New York: Union Defence Committee, 1885), 5–6; "The Union Forever!," *New York Times,* April 21, 1861; REL to MCL, April 26 and April 30, 1861, in *WPREL,* 15, and Lee Family Papers, VMHC; Mary V. Thompson, "'A Sacred Duty': Mount Vernon During the Years of the Civil War," *Alexandria Chronicle* (2003/2004): 4.
7. MCL, in Perry, *Lady of Arlington,* 222; MacDonald, *Mrs. Robert E. Lee,* 148–49; Kundahl, *Alexandria Goes to War,* 169; "Mary Custis Lee's 'Reminiscences of the War,'" 315–17; REL to MCL, May 2 and 11, 1861, in *WPREL,* 18, 26; REL to MCL, in Robert E. Lee Jr., *Recollections and Letters,* 30; MCL to Scott, May 5, 1861, in Jones, *Life and Letters,* 140.
8. Kundahl, *Alexandria Goes to War,* 82; "Mary Custis Lee's 'Reminiscences of the War,'" 305, 318–20; "University Military School," *Richmond Dispatch,* July 10, 1861; MCL to MChL, May 9, 1861; Perry, *Lady of Arlington,* 228; Pryor, *Reading the Man,* 302.
9. "Local Items," *Alexandria Gazette,* May 25, 1861; Hanna, *Arlington House,* 72–74; "The War for the Union" and "The Latest War News," *New-York Tribune,* May 27, 1861.
10. Brian Holden Reid, *The Scourge of War: The Life of William Tecumseh Sherman* (New York: Oxford University Press, 2020), 88; EAL to MChL, May 23, 1861, Lee Family Papers, VMHC; MCL to Sandford, May 30, 1861, in Coulling, *Lee Girls,* 88–89; Kim A. O'Connell, "Arlington's Enslaved Savior," *Civil War Times* 54 (Feb. 2015): 33–37; McDowell to MCL, May 30, 1861, in *OR,* ser. 1, 2:655; "Affairs at the National Capital," *New York Times,* June 13, 1861; "Mrs. Lincoln in Danger," *New York Times,* June 22, 1861; Winthrop, "Washington as a Camp," *Atlantic Monthly,* July 1861, 117; Averell, *Ten Years in the Saddle,* 282.
11. "The Secession Forces in Virginia" and "The Rebel Congress," *Philadelphia Inquirer,* May 8,

1861; "Virginia Joins the Confederacy," *Vicksburg Whig,* May 8, 1861; Emory M. Thomas, *The Confederate Nation, 1861–1865* (New York: Harper & Row, 1979), 99, 102.

12. Daniel W. Crofts, *Reluctant Confederates: Upper South Unionists in the Secession Crisis* (Chapel Hill: University of North Carolina Press, 1993), 341; REL to MCL, May 25, June 9, and July 12, 1861, to Leroy Pope Walker, May 25, 1861, REL to Jefferson Davis, May 7, 1861, and to Letcher, June 15, 1861, in *WPREL,* 21, 35, 36, 46, 50–52; REL to MCL, May 28, 1861, Lee Family Papers, VMHC; Charles Lee Lewis, *Matthew Fontaine Maury, the Pathfinder of the Seas* (Annapolis: U.S. Naval Institute, 1927), 146; "Letter from St. Louis—More of General Lee," *San Francisco Daily Bulletin,* July 15, 1861.
13. Davis, *Jefferson Davis,* 356; Taylor, *General Lee,* 24; Kundahl, *Alexandria Goes to War,* 34–35; "Generals in the Confederate States Service," *Richmond Dispatch,* July 11, 1861; Edward D. C. Campbell, "The Fabric of Command: R. E. Lee, Confederate Insignia, and the Perception of Rank," *VMHB,* April 1990, 289–90.
14. Jones, diary entry for June 12, 1861, in *Rebel War Clerk's Diary,* 1:37; REL to MCL, June 24, 1861, in *WPREL,* 54; REL to Thomas A. Dodamead, July 5, 1861, Brock Collection; REL to Letcher, June 14, 1861, in *OR,* ser. 1, 2:926; Edward G. Longacre, *The Early Morning of War: Bull Run, 1861* (Norman: University of Oklahoma Press, 2014), 75; William Howard Russell, in *The Rebellion Record: A Diary of American Events, with Documents, Narratives, Illustrative Incidents, Poetry, Etc.,* ed. Frank Moore (New York: G. P. Putnam, 1862), 2:55; Chestnut to Beauregard, July 16, 1861, in *OR,* ser. 1, 2:506–7; William C. Davis, *Battle at Bull Run: A History of the First Major Campaign of the Civil War* (Garden City, N.Y.: Doubleday, 1977), 67, 143; Steven E. Woodworth, *Davis and Lee at War* (Lawrence: University Press of Kansas, 1995), 24.
15. Beauregard, "The First Battle of Bull Run," and Johnston, "Responsibilities of the First Bull Run," in Buel and Johnson, *Battles and Leaders of the Civil War,* 1:225, 259; MCL to ACL, July 30, 1861, Lee Family Papers, VMHC.
16. Lincoln, "Memoranda of Military Policy Suggested by the Bull Run Defeat," July 23, 1861, in *Collected Works,* 4:457; Davis, *Battle at Bull Run,* 245, 253.
17. Freehling and Simpson, *Showdown in Virginia,* 203; James Morton Callahan, *Semi-centennial History of West Virginia* (Semi-centennial Commission of West Virginia, 1913), 449; "A Declaration of the People of Virginia, Represented in Convention, at the City of Wheeling, Thursday, June 13th, 1861," in *Ordinances of the Convention, Assembled at Wheeling, on the 11th of June, 1861* (Wheeling, Va., 1861), 40; "Address to the Soldiers of the Expedition," May 26, 1861, in *OR,* ser. 1, 2:49.
18. Stephen W. Sears, *George B. McClellan: The Young Napoleon* (New York: Ticknor & Fields, 1988), 3, 6, 7–8; Keyes, *Fifty Years' Observations,* 197; *Forgotten Valor: The Memoirs, Journals, and Civil War Letters of Orlando B. Willcox,* ed. R. G. Scott (Kent, Ohio: Kent State University Press, 1999), 55; Russell H. Beatie, *The Army of the Potomac: Birth of Command, November 1860–September 1861* (Cambridge, Mass.: Da Capo Press, 2002), 389; Ethan S. Rafuse, *McClellan's War: The Failure of Moderation in the Struggle for the Union* (Bloomington: Indiana University Press, 2005), 35.
19. Stephen Sears, "Little Mac and the Historians," in *Controversies and Commanders: Dispatches from the Army of the Potomac* (New York: Houghton Mifflin, 1999), 14; McClellan, diary entry for Dec. 6, 1846, in *The Mexican War Diary of George B. McClellan,* ed. William Starr Myers (Princeton, N.J.: Princeton University Press, 1917), 16; Rafuse, *McClellan's War,* 68–69, 93, 103; William Starr Myers, *A Study in Personality: General George Brinton McClellan* (New York: D. Appleton–Century, 1934), 107.
20. REL to Porterfield, May 24 and June 13, 1861, in *WPREL,* 34, 49; Porterfield to Garnett, May 16, 1861, in Granville Davisson Hall, *Lee's Invasion of Northwest Virginia in 1861* (Chicago: Mayer & Miller, 1911), 38, 49, 63, 64; Clayton R. Newell, *Lee vs. McClellan: The First*

Campaign (Washington, D.C.: Regnery, 1996), 112–13; REL to Joseph E. Johnston, June 7, 1861, in *WPREL,* 43.

21. Newell, *Lee vs. McClellan,* 119, 121, 138–39; Hall, *Lee's Invasion,* 66, 106; Davis to Floyd, May 14, 1861, in *OR,* ser. 1, 2:838; Wise to Davis, May 15, 1861, in *Papers of Jefferson Davis,* 7:168; Simpson, *Good Southerner,* 254; Taylor, *General Lee,* 23; "General Lee on Sewall Mountain," *Southern Bivouac,* March 1883, 183.
22. McClellan to E. D. Townsend, July 14, 1861, in *The Civil War Papers of George B. McClellan: Selected Correspondence, 1860–1865,* ed. Stephen W. Sears (New York: Ticknor & Fields, 1989), 56; Woodworth, *Davis and Lee at War,* 45; Davis to Joseph E. Johnston, Aug. 1, 1861, in *Papers of Jefferson Davis,* 7:271; REL to MCL, July 27, 1861, Lee Family Papers, VMHC; "Come Forth Virginians!," *Richmond Enquirer,* July 30, 1861; Thomas Goree to Sarah Goree, Aug. 19, 1861, in *Longstreet's Aide: The Civil War Letters of Major Thomas J. Goree,* ed. Thomas W. Cutrer (Charlottesville: University of Virginia Press, 1995), 35.
23. REL to MCL, Aug. 4, 1861, Lee Family Papers, VMHC.
24. Daughtry, *Gray Cavalier,* 55; Sam R. Watkins, *"Co. Aytch": Maury Grays, First Tennessee Regiment; or, A Side Show of the Big Show* (Chattanooga: Times, 1900), 19; Jacob van Meter et al. to Jefferson Davis, Sept. 10, 1861, and REL, "Special Orders No. 239," Aug. 5, 1861, in *OR,* ser. 1, 5:770, 845; REL to MCL, Aug. 4 and 9, 1861, REL to EAL and ACL, Aug. 29, 1861, and REL to Wise, Aug. 8, 21, and 27, 1861, in *WPREL,* 61, 63, 64, 66, 67; REL to Alfred Beckley, Aug. 8 and 24, 1861, duPont Library; Taylor, *Four Years with General Lee,* 18; Woodworth, *Davis and Lee at War,* 59.
25. A. L. Long, "Lee's West Virginia Campaign," in *The Annals of the War, Written by Leading Participants North and South,* ed. A. K. McClure (Philadelphia: Times, 1878), 88–89.
26. REL, "Special Order No. 28," in John Levering, "Lee's Advance and Retreat in the Cheat Mountain Campaign of 1861," in *Military Essays and Recollections: Essays and Papers Read Before the Illinois Commandery, Military Order of the Loyal Legion of the United States* (Chicago: Cozzens & Beaton, 1907), 4:16–18, 30–35; Newell, *Lee vs. McClellan,* 177, 231; REL to MCL, Sept. 17, 1861, in *WPREL,* 73; REL to John Letcher, Sept. 17, 1861, in Taylor, *Four Years with General Lee,* 30; REL to Louisa Washington, Sept. 16, 1861, LFDA/duPont Library.
27. REL to Wise, Sept. 9, 1861, Samuel Cooper to REL, Sept. 12, 1861, and "General Orders No. 15," Oct. 22, 1861, in *OR,* ser. 1, 5:842, 848, 913; "Gen. Lee's Army," *Richmond Enquirer,* Sept. 20, 1861; "The New Programme for Western Virginia," *Richmond Dispatch,* Oct. 7, 1861; Long, *Memoirs of Robert E. Lee,* 494; C. H. Ambler, "General R. E. Lee's Northwest Virginia Campaign," *West Virginia History* 5 (Jan. 1944): 101; John William Thomason, *Jeb Stuart* (1929; Lincoln: University of Nebraska Press, 1994), 131; REL to MCL, Oct. 7, 1861, Lee Family Papers, VMHC; Taylor, *Four Years with General Lee,* 32–33; Jones, diary entry for Dec. 2, 1861, in *Rebel War Clerk's Diary,* 1:81.
28. REL, "Special Orders," Sept. 9 and 14, 1861, and C. Q. Tompkins to REL, Sept. 9, 1861, in *OR,* ser. 1, 5:192–93, 841; REL to Wise, Sept. 21 and 25, 1861, and REL to MCL, Aug. 4 and Sept. 17, 1861, in *WPREL,* 61, 74, 76, 77; REL to Louisa Washington, Sept. 16, 1861, in Freeman, *R. E. Lee,* 1:570.
29. "Remarks of President Davis," in *Organization of the Lee Monument Association,* 14; "Gen. Lee in Richmond," *Richmond Enquirer,* Nov. 1, 1861; Jefferson Davis, *The Rise and Fall of the Confederate Government* (New York: D. Appleton, 1881), 1:309; "Special Orders No. 206," Nov. 5, 1861, "Reports of Brig. Gen. Thomas W. Sherman," Nov. 8, 1861, and "Report of Brigadier General Thomas F. Drayton," Nov. 24, 1861, in *OR,* ser. 1, 6:3, 8, 309; REL to MCL, Nov. 5, 1861, in *WPREL,* 83.
30. "Arrival of General Lee," *Richmond Dispatch,* Nov. 8, 1861; REL to Benjamin, Nov. 9, 1861, "Special Orders No. 1," Nov. 16, 1861, and Brown to Benjamin, Nov. 7 and 21, 1861, in *OR,* ser. 1, 6:310, 312, 322; REL to MCL, Nov. 18, 1861, in *WPREL,* 87; "Autobiography of Hubert W.

Mealing, 1843–1917," New York State Military Museum and Veterans Research Center, dmna .ny.gov; "General News Items," *Edgefield Advertiser,* Nov. 14, 1861; "Brisk Trade in Trunks," *Edgefield Advertiser,* Nov. 20, 1861; "From Beaufort," *Yorkville Enquirer,* Nov. 28, 1861; "From Gen. Floyd's Command," *Edgefield Advertiser,* Dec. 4, 1861; "Camp Notes," *Yorkville Enquirer,* Dec. 5, 1861; William Harden, *A History of Savannah and South Georgia* (Chicago: Lewis, 1913), 2:738; Taylor, *Four Years with General Lee,* 37.

31. Brown to Benjamin, Nov. 11, 1861, A. R. Lawton to REL, Nov. 10, 1861, REL to Samuel Cooper, Nov. 21, 1861, in *OR,* ser. 1, 6:314, 315, 327; Johnson to Davis, Nov. 11, 1861, in *Papers of Jefferson Davis,* 7:409; Chesnut, diary entries for Nov. 8 and 14, 1861, in *Mary Chesnut's Civil War,* 230, 237; Ruffin, diary entry for Nov. 30, 1861, in *Diary of Edmund Ruffin,* 2:177.
32. REL to GWCL, Dec. 29, 1861, Robert E. Lee Papers, 1749–1975, Rubenstein Rare Book and Manuscript Library; REL to ACL, Dec. 8, 1861 and March 2, 1862, to Magrath, Dec. 24, 1861, to MCL, Feb. 8, 1862, in *WPREL,* 91, 93; REL to MChL, Nov. 15, 1861, Lee Family Papers, VMHC.
33. REL to Benjamin, Dec. 20, 1861, in *Official Records of the Union and Confederate Navies in the War of the Rebellion,* ed. E. K. Rawson et al. (Washington, D.C.: Government Printing Office, 1901), ser. 1, 12:423; REL to MCL Jr., Dec. 25, 1861, Mary Custis Lee Papers, and REL to MCL, Dec. 25, 1861, Lee Family Papers, VMHC; REL to GWCL, Jan. 19, 1862, in *WPREL,* 105.
34. REL to EAL and ACL, Nov. 22, 1861, duPont Library; REL to MCL, Dec. 25, 1861, Lee Family Papers, VMHC.
35. REL to William Allan, March 10, 1868, in "Memoranda of Conversations with General Robert E. Lee," 12; REL to MCL, Jan. 18, 1862, Lee Family Papers, VMHC; REL to GWCL, Jan. 4, 1862, Robert E. Lee Papers, 1749–1975, Rubenstein Rare Book and Manuscript Library; Long, *Memoirs of Robert E. Lee,* 23. See also the debate on whether Lee might have visited Light Horse Harry's grave in 1830, during his assignment to Cockspur Island, in John Martin Dederer, "Robert E. Lee's First Visit to His Father's Grave," *VMHB,* Jan. 1994, 73–88; J. A. Thomson and C. M. Santos, "The Mystery in the Coffin: Another View of Lee's Visit to His Father's Grave," *VMHB,* Jan. 1995, 75–94; and Dederer in reply, "In Search of the Unknown Soldier: A Critique of 'The Mystery in the Coffin,'" *VMHB,* Jan. 1995, 95–112.
36. Davis, *Crucible of Command,* 160–63; REL to ACL, March 2, 1862, Lee Family Papers, VMHC; Benjamin to Lee, Feb. 24, 1862, and Davis to REL, March 2, 1862, in *OR,* ser. 1, 6:398, 400, and 53:221.

Chapter Eleven: To Dash Against Mine Enemy and to Win

1. "Inaugural Ceremonies," *Richmond Dispatch,* Feb. 24, 1862; Jones, diary entry for Feb. 22, 1862, in *Rebel War Clerk's Diary,* 1:96; Davis to Johnston, Feb. 28, 1862, in *OR,* ser. 1, 5:1085.
2. Jones, diary entry for March 30, 1862, in *Rebel War Clerk's Diary,* 1:102; "An Act Supplementary to an Act to Establish the War Department," Feb. 27, 1862, "An Act to Create the Office of Commanding General of the Armies of the Confederate States," March 6, 1862, and "An Act to Provide a Staff and Clerical Force for Any General Who May Be Assigned by the President to Duty at the Seat of Government," March 25, 1862, in *OR,* ser. 1, 5:688, and ser. 4, vol. 1, pt. 2, 954, 997–98, 1021; "From Tennessee Congressmen," March 8, 1862, in *Papers of Jefferson Davis,* 8:88; Taylor, *General Lee,* 42; Woodworth, *Davis and Lee at War,* 102.
3. "Gen. Lee," *Richmond Dispatch,* March 17, 1862; Perry, *Lady of Arlington,* 247; "From Richmond—Correspondence of the Charleston Mercury," *New York Times,* April 20, 1862; REL to MCL, March 14 and 15, 1862, Lee Family Papers, VMHC; MCL to Stiles, March 8, 1862, and REL to CCL, March 14, 1862, LFDA/duPont Library.

4. Taylor, *General Lee,* 26–27, 55, 56–57; Venable, "Personal Reminiscences of the Confederate War," box 5, McDowell-Miller-Warner Papers, Small Special Collections Library; John Majewski, *Modernizing a Slave Economy: The Economic Vision of the Confederate Nation* (Chapel Hill: University of North Carolina Press, 2006), 81–84; Koistinen, *Beating Plowshares into Swords,* 220–21, 224, 226–28, 232–33; William R. Plum, *The Military Telegraph During the Civil War in the United States* (Chicago: Jansen, McClurg, 1882), 1:135.
5. Charles Marshall, *An Aide-de-Camp of Lee, Being the Papers of Colonel Charles Marshall,* ed. Frederick Maurice (Boston: Little, Brown, 1927), 18, 20–21; George Fitzhugh, "The Conduct of the War," *DeBow's Review,* Jan./Feb. 1862, 140; Taylor, *General Lee,* 46; Robert Kean, diary entry for Aug. 23, 1863, in *Inside the Confederate Government: The Diary of Robert Garlick Hill Kean,* ed. Edward Younger (New York: Oxford University Press, 1957), 101; *Campbell Brown's Civil War: With Ewell and the Army of Northern Virginia,* ed. Terry L. Jones (Baton Rouge: Louisiana State University Press, 2001), 142–43.
6. "General Orders No. 16," March 24, 1862, in *OR,* ser. 4, vol. 1, pt. 2, 1020; REL to Edward Johnson, March 21, 1862, in *WPREL,* 133; Marshall, *Aide-de-Camp of Lee,* 30–31; Davis, "To the Senate and House of Representatives of the Confederate States," March 28, 1862, in *Journal of the Congress of the Confederate States of America, 1861–1865* (Washington, D.C.: Government Printing Office, 1904), 2:106; "Confederate Congress," *Richmond Dispatch,* March 31, 1862; "The Conscription Bill," *Richmond Dispatch,* April 17, 1862; "An Act to Further Provide for the Public Defense," in *OR,* ser. 4, 1:1095–97; Thomas, *Confederate Nation,* 152–53; George C. Rable, *The Confederate Republic: A Revolution Against Politics* (Chapel Hill: University of North Carolina Press, 1994), 138–43.
7. Craig L. Symonds, *Joseph E. Johnston: A Civil War Biography* (New York: W. W. Norton, 1992), 145; Johnston, *Narrative of Military Operations, Directed, During the Late War Between the States* (New York: D. Appleton, 1874), 96, 102; Steven H. Newton, *Joseph E. Johnston and the Defense of Richmond* (Lawrence: University Press of Kansas, 1990), 47–58; Davis to Johnston, March 13, 1862, in *OR,* ser. 1, 5:527; REL to Holmes, March 16, 1862, in *WPREL,* 130; "The Fall of New Orleans," *Richmond Enquirer,* April 28, 1862; Woodworth, *Davis and Lee at War,* 133.
8. Jones, diary entries for April 25 and 26, 1862, in *Rebel War Clerk's Diary,* 1:106; Robert McAllister to Ellen McAllister, Nov. 20, 1861, in *The Civil War Letters of General Robert McAllister,* ed. J. I. Robertson (New Brunswick, N.J.: Rutgers University Press, 1965), 96–97; John Nicolay to Therena Bates, Nov. 20, 1861, in *With Lincoln in the White House: Letters, Memoranda, and Other Writings of John G. Nicolay, 1860–1865,* ed. Michael Burlingame (Carbondale: Southern Illinois University Press, 2000), 62–63.
9. McClellan, "General Report" and "President's Special War Order No. 1," Jan. 31, 1862, in *OR,* ser. 1, 5:7, vol. 12, pt. 1, 222.
10. John Tucker, in McClellan, "General Report," in *OR,* ser. 1, 5:46; Stephen W. Sears, *To the Gates of Richmond: The Peninsula Campaign* (New York: Ticknor & Field, 1992), 24; Rafuse, *McClellan's War,* 196; Russell H. Beatie, *The Army of the Potomac: McClellan's First Campaign, March 1862–May 1862* (New York: Savas Beatie, 2007), 3:274–75; McClellan to Mary Ellen McClellan, April 1, 1862, in *Civil War Papers of George B. McClellan,* 223.
11. McClellan to Lorenzo Dow Thomas, April 1, 1862, in *Civil War Papers of George B. McClellan,* 222–23; Rafuse, *McClellan's War,* 203; REL to Joseph E. Johnston, March 25 and 28, 1862, and to J. B. Magruder, March 26, 1862, in *WPREL,* 135, 138; REL to Magruder, March 15, 1862, in *OR,* ser. 1, 11:68; John V. Quarstein and J. M. Moore, *Yorktown's Civil War Siege: Drums Along the Warwick* (Charleston, S.C.: History Press, 2012), 82–83; Glenn David Brashear, *The Peninsula Campaign and the Necessity of Emancipation: African Americans and the Fight for Freedom* (Chapel Hill: University of North Carolina Press, 2012), 108; Thomas, *Robert E. Lee,* 220; Pender to Fanny Pender, April 14, 1862, in *One of Lee's Best Men: The Civil*

War Letters of General William Dorsey Pender, ed. W. W. Hassler (Chapel Hill: University of North Carolina Press, 1999), 134; Taylor, *Four Years with General Lee,* 38.

12. McClellan to Edwin M. Stanton, April 7, 1862, and to Lincoln, April 7 and 20, 1862, in *Civil War Papers of George B. McClellan,* 232, 233, 246; Quarstein and Moore, *Yorktown's Civil War Siege,* 97, 102; Symonds, *Johnston,* 152; Johnston to REL, April 29, 1862, in *OR,* ser. 1, vol. 12, pt. 3, 473; Sears, *To the Gates of Richmond,* 43; Harsh, *Confederate Tide Rising,* 35–36; Ethan S. Rafuse, *Robert E. Lee and the Fall of the Confederacy, 1863–1865* (Lanham, Md.: Rowman & Littlefield, 2008), 12.
13. Clifford Dowdey, *The Seven Days: The Emergence of Lee* (Boston: Little, Brown, 1964), 69; Thomas C. De Leon, *Four Years in Rebel Capitals: An Inside View of Life in the Southern Confederacy* (Mobile, Ala.: Gossip, 1892), 194; Joseph Davis to Jefferson Davis, April 20, 1862, to William M. Brown, May 8, 1862, to Varina Howell Davis, May 13, 1862, in *Papers of Jefferson Davis,* 147, 167, 174; REL to MCL, May 13, 1862, Lee Family Papers, VMHC; "Organization of the Army of Northern Virginia, Commanded by General Joseph E. Johnston, on the Peninsula, About April 30, 1862," in *OR,* ser. 1, vol. 11, pt. 3, 479–84; Jones, diary entry for May 19, 1862, in *Rebel War Clerk's Diary,* 1:111; Marshall, *Aide-de-Camp of Lee,* 50; Judith W. McGuire, diary entry for May 14, 1862, in *Diary of a Southern Refugee During the War* (New York: E. J. Hale & Son, 1867), 112–13; "Public Meeting at City Hall," *Richmond Enquirer,* May 16, 1862.
14. REL to MCL, April 4, 1862, in *WPREL,* 142; Richard E. Killblane, "White House Landing: Sustaining the Army of the Potomac During the Peninsula Campaign," Army Transportation Corps History, 10–11, www.transportation.army.mil; Sally Nelson Robins, "Mrs. Lee During the War," in Brock, *Gen. Robert Edward Lee,* 326; Perry, *Lady of Arlington,* 248–49; MacDonald, *Mrs. Robert E. Lee,* 161–64; George H. Lyman, "Some Aspects of the Medical Service in the Armies of the United States During the War of the Rebellion," in *Civil and Mexican Wars, 1861, 1846,* 13:193; Furgurson, *Ashes of Glory,* 142–43; Brasher, *Peninsula Campaign,* 157–58, 165; Ruffin, diary entry for June 11, 1862, in *Diary of Edmund Ruffin,* 1:337; Journal of Mrs. Henry Grafton Dulany, June 9, 1862, in Andrews, *Scraps of Paper,* 18; "Release of Mrs. Gen. Lee," *Richmond Enquirer,* June 20, 1862; "Occupation of the 'White House' in Virginia," House Executive Document 145, in *Executive Documents Printed by Order of the House of Representatives During the Second Session of the Thirty-Seventh Congress, 1861–'62* (Washington, D.C.: Government Printing Office, 1862).
15. Steven H. Newton, *The Battle of Seven Pines, May 31–June 1, 1862* (Lynchburg, Va.: H. E. Howard, 1993), 5, 17, 83; Dowdey, *Seven Days,* 84–92; Johnston, *Narrative,* 131–32, 138, 142; John H. Reagan, *Memoirs, with Special Reference to Secession and the Civil War,* ed. W. F. McCaleb (New York: Neale, 1906), 139; Maury, *Recollections of a Virginian,* 150–51; Jones, diary entry for March 31, 1862, in *Rebel War Clerk's Diary,* 1:102; Harsh, *Confederate Tide Rising,* 45; Davis to Lee, June 1, 1862, in *OR,* ser. 1, vol. 11, pt. 3, 568–69; Furgurson, *Ashes of Glory,* 137–38.
16. William Miller Owen, *In Camp and Battle with the Washington Artillery of New Orleans: A Narrative of Events During the Late Civil War from Bull Run to Appomattox and Spanish Fort* (Boston: Ticknor, 1885), 382; George Cary Eggleston, *A Rebel's Recollections* (New York: G. P. Putnam's, 1905), 142; Sorrel, *Recollections of a Confederate Staff Officer,* 67–68; Campbell, "Fabric of Command," 286; Jones, *Personal Reminiscences,* 148; Evander McIver Law, "The Fight for Richmond in 1862," *Southern Bivouac,* April 1887, 652; REL to Charlotte Wickham Lee, June 22, 1862, in *WPREL,* 197; McGuire, diary entry for May 18, 1863, in *Diary of a Southern Refugee,* 214–15.
17. Dowdey, *Lee,* 210–13; "Special Orders No. 22," in *WPREL,* 181; Marshall, *Aide-de-Camp of Lee,* 71, 80–81, 183; Harsh, *Confederate Tide Rising,* 64–65, 225; Joseph T. Glatthaar, *General Lee's Army: From Victory to Collapse* (New York: Free Press, 2008), 128.

18. Long, *Memoirs of Robert E. Lee,* 162–64; Davis, "Robert E. Lee," *North American Review* 150 (Jan. 1890): 62; Thomas Goree to Sarah Goree, April 26, 1862, in *Longstreet's Aide,* 123; George Wilson Booth, *A Maryland Boy in Lee's Army: Personal Reminiscences of a Maryland Soldier in the War Between the States, 1861–1865,* ed. E. J. Mink (Lincoln: University of Nebraska Press, 2000), 108; REL to Stevens, June 3, 1862, to Stuart, June 11, 1862, and to Charlotte Wickham Lee, June 22, 1862, in *WPREL,* 182, 192; Sears, *To the Gates of Richmond,* 156; Longacre, *Fitz Lee,* 60; Daughtry, *Gray Cavalier,* 68–77; "The Exploit of General Stuart," *Richmond Dispatch,* June 16, 1862; Taylor, *General Lee,* 95.
19. *Fighting for the Confederacy: The Personal Recollections of General Edward Porter Alexander,* ed. G. W. Gallagher (Chapel Hill: University of North Carolina Press, 1989), 89; Susan Leigh Blackford and Charles Minor Blackford, *Letters from Lee's Army; or, Memoirs of Life in and out of the Army in Virginia During the War Between the States* (1947; Lincoln: University of Nebraska Press, 1998), 96; Rafuse, *Robert E. Lee and the Fall of the Confederacy,* 16–17; Long, *Memoirs of Robert E. Lee,* 164, 169–70; James I. Robertson, *Stonewall Jackson: The Man, the Soldier, the Legend* (New York: Macmillan, 1997), 7, 85, 108; Casdorph, *Confederate General R. S. Ewell,* 142; Taylor, *General Lee,* 60.
20. Robert G. Tanner, *Stonewall in the Valley: Thomas J. "Stonewall" Jackson's Shenandoah Valley Campaign, Spring 1862* (Garden City, N.Y.: Doubleday, 1976), 68–82, 327; REL to TJJ, April 21 and 25, 1862, in *WPREL,* 151, 156; REL to TJJ, April 29, 1862, in Taylor, *Four Years with General Lee,* 38–39; John D. Imboden, "Stonewall Jackson in the Shenandoah," in Buel and Johnson, *Battles and Leaders of the Civil War,* 2:297; Peter Cozzens, *Shenandoah 1862: Stonewall Jackson's Valley Campaign* (Chapel Hill: University of North Carolina Press, 2008), 512–13.
21. Alexander Boteler, "Stonewall Jackson in Campaign of 1862," *SHSP* 11 (Sept. 1915): 165; Robertson, *Stonewall Jackson,* 269, 416; Sears, *To the Gates of Richmond,* 152; REL to T. E. Chambliss, May 22, 1862, in "Impressments," *Richmond Enquirer,* June 10, 1862; REL to Davis, June 5, 1862, in *WPREL,* 183–84; Harsh, *Confederate Tide Rising,* 62; Christian B. Keller, *The Great Partnership: Robert E. Lee, Stonewall Jackson, and the Fate of the Confederacy* (New York: Pegasus, 2019), 13.
22. Taylor, *Four Years with General Lee,* 39; Robert L. Dabney, *Life and Campaigns of Lieut.-Gen. Thomas J. Jackson* (1865; Harrisonburg, Va.: Sprinkle, 1976), 431; Furgurson, *Ashes of Glory,* 139; REL to Davis, June 5, 1862, in *WPREL,* 184; Marshall, *Aide-de-Camp of Lee,* 79; Long, *Memoirs of Robert E. Lee,* 165–66.
23. Catherine Edmondston, diary entry for June 8, 1862, in *Journal of a Secesh Lady: The Diary of Catherine Ann Devereux Edmondston, 1860–1866,* ed. Beth G. Crabtree and James W. Patton (Raleigh, N.C.: Division of Archives and History, 1979), 189; Jones, diary entry for June 24, 1862, in *Rebel War Clerk's Diary,* 1:119; McClellan to Lincoln, April 20, 1862, in Sears, *Civil War Papers of George B. McClellan,* 244–45; Alexander, *Fighting for the Confederacy,* 91; Glatthaar, *General Lee's Army,* 133–34; Taylor, *General Lee,* 59–60; Sorrel, *Recollections,* 73, 120; Woodworth, *Davis and Lee at War,* 152; Keller, *Great Partnership,* 1–16.

Chapter Twelve: The Savior of Richmond

1. Taylor, *Four Years with General Lee,* 53–55.
2. Marshall, *Aide-de-Camp to Lee,* 89, 90; D. H. Hill, "Lee's Attacks North of the Chickahominy," in Buel and Johnson, *Battles and Leaders of the Civil War,* 2:347, 361; Taylor, *General Lee,* 66; Taylor, *Four Years with General Lee,* 49; "General Orders No. 75," June 24, 1862, in *WPREL,* 198–99; Justus Scheibert, *Seven Months in the Rebel States During the North American War, 1863,* trans. J. C. Hayes (Tuscaloosa: University of Alabama Press, 2009),

75; Thomas, *Robert E. Lee,* 232–33; Geoffrey Wawro, *The Austro-Prussian War: Austria's War with Prussia and Italy in 1866* (New York: Cambridge University Press, 1996), 17–18; Cathal J. Nolan, *The Allure of Battle: A History of How Wars Have Been Won and Lost* (New York: Oxford University Press, 2017), 275.

3. REL to Benjamin Huger, June 26, 1862, in *WPREL,* 201; Dowdey, *Seven Days,* 159, 168, 183, 187; Marshall, *Aide-de-Camp of Lee,* 94; Sears, *To the Gates of Richmond,* 201; Joseph L. Brent, *Memoirs of the War Between the States* (New Orleans: Fontana, 1940), 161.
4. McClellan to E. M. Stanton, June 27 and 28, 1862, in *Civil War Papers of George B. McClellan,* 317, 322; Robertson, *Stonewall Jackson,* 475–76; Keller, *Great Partnership,* 24–25.
5. REL to MCL, June 25, 1862, Lee Family Papers, VMHC; John Esten Cooke, *Hammer and Rapier* (New York: Geo. W. Carleton, 1870), 79.
6. MCL to daughters, June 29, 1862, Lee Family Papers, VMHC; REL to Davis and to Huger, June 27, 1862, in *WPREL,* 202; "Despatch from General Lee to President Davis," *Richmond Enquirer,* July 1, 1862; Elizabeth R. Varon, *Armies of Deliverance: A New History of the Civil War* (New York: Oxford University Press, 2019), 99.
7. REL to Davis, June 29, 1862, in *WPREL,* 206; REL to Magruder, June 29, 1862, and "Reports of General Robert E. Lee, C.S. Army, Commanding Army of Northern Virginia, of the Battles of Mechanicsville, Gaines' Mill, and Savage Station, Engagement at White Oak Swamp Bridge, and Battles of Frazier's Farm and Malvern Hill," March 6, 1863, in *OR,* ser. 1, vol. 11, pt. 2, 495, 687; John B. Goode, *Recollections of a Lifetime* (New York: Neale, 1906), 58.
8. Sears, *To the Gates of Richmond,* 308–12; Dowdey, *Seven Days,* 338; Fitz John Porter, "The Battle of Malvern Hill," in Buel and Johnson, *Battles and Leaders of the Civil War,* 2:417, 419; "Report of Maj. Robert M. Sands, Third Alabama Infantry," July 17, 1862, and "Report of Col. Bradley T. Johnson," July 7, 1862, in *OR,* ser. 1, vol. 11, pt. 2, 622, 637; Brian K. Burton, *Extraordinary Circumstances: The Seven Days Battles* (Bloomington: Indiana University Press, 2001), 330, 333.
9. Sallie Brock Putnam, *Richmond During the War: Four Years of Personal Observation* (New York: G. W. Carleton, 1867), 151; "Gen. Lee's Address to His Soldiers," *Richmond Dispatch,* July 11, 1862; "List of Casualties in the Army of Northern Virginia in the Fights Before Richmond," April 11, 1863, and "Report of Maj. Gen. Daniel H. Hill," July 3, 1862, in *OR,* ser. 1, vol. 11, pt. 2, 506, 629; McClellan to Lincoln, July 4, 1862, in *Civil War Papers of George B. McClellan,* 337; Philip Kearney to Cortlandt Parker, July 24, 1862, in *Letters from the Peninsula: The Civil War Letters of General Philip Kearny,* ed. W. B. Styple (Kearny, N.J.: Belle Grove, 1988), 138; Sears, *George B. McClellan,* 116.
10. Furgurson, *Ashes of Glory,* 150, 156–57; Harrison, *Recollections Grave and Gay,* 89; "The Battles and the Localities," *Richmond Dispatch,* July 2, 1862; "Gen. Lee," *Richmond Dispatch,* July 4, 1862; Jones, diary entry for July 9, 1862, in *Rebel War Clerk's Diary,* 1:126; Tally Simpson to Caroline Virginia Taliaferro Miller, July 14, 1862, in *Far, Far from Home: The Wartime Letters of Dick and Tally Simpson, 3rd South Carolina Volunteers,* ed. Guy R. Everson and Edward W. Simpson Jr. (New York: Oxford University Press, 1994), 136.
11. Chesnut, diary entry for July 24, 1862, in *Mary Chesnut's Civil War,* 116.
12. Venable, "Personal Reminiscences of the Confederate War," Small Special Collections Library; Harsh, *Confederate Tide Rising,* 105; REL to Jefferson Davis, July 4 and 6, 1862, in *WPREL,* 208, 209; Marshall, *Aide-de-Camp to Lee,* 117–18; Snow, *Lee and His Generals,* 103; Rafuse, *Robert E. Lee and the Fall of the Confederacy,* 18.
13. "Rumors of a Change in the Cabinet and in the Command of the Army," *Washington Evening Star,* June 26, 1862; "Gen. Pope's New Command," *Washington Evening Star,* June 27, 1862; Pope, "To the Officers and Soldiers of the Army of Virginia," July 14, 1862, in *OR,* ser. 1, vol. 12, pt. 3, 474; "General Orders No. 5," "General Orders No. 7," and "General Orders

No. 11," July 18, 1862, in *OR,* ser. 1, vol. 12, pt. 2, 50–52; John Hennessy, *Return to Bull Run: The Campaign and Battle of Second Manassas* (New York: Simon & Schuster, 1993), 12, 14–15; Samuel Fessenden to William Pitt Fessenden, June 15, 1862, in Fergus M. Bordewich, *Congress at War: How Republican Reformers Fought the Civil War, Defied Lincoln, Ended Slavery, and Remade America* (New York: Knopf, 2020), 163.

14. REL to MCL, Jan. 19 and Aug. 3, 1862, to TJJ, July 27, 1862, and to MChL, July 28, 1862, in *WPREL,* 106, 239, 240, 243; "Pope's Army—Virginia to Be Laid Waste," *Richmond Dispatch,* July 24, 1862; Daughtry, *Gray Cavalier,* 83; Thomas L. Broun, "General R. E. Lee's War-Horse: A Sketch of Traveller by the Man Who Formerly Owned Him," *SHSP* 35 (1907): 99–100; Scott Patchan, *Second Manassas: Longstreet's Attack and the Struggle for Chinn Ridge* (Washington, D.C.: Potomac Books, 2011), 4; REL to Halleck, Aug. 2, 1862, in *OR,* ser. 2, 4:330. On Traveller's pedigree, see www.allbreedpedigree.com/traveller6. On Traveller's sire, Grey Eagle, as a competitive racer, see Henry William Herbert, *Frank Forester's Horse and Horsemanship of the United States and British Provinces of North America* (New York: Geo. E. Woodward, 1871), 1:267–68.

15. REL to Lafayette McLaws, July 25, 1862, in *OR,* ser. 1, vol. 11, pt. 3, 653; Harsh, *Confederate Tide Rising,* 102–4; Taylor, *Four Years with General Lee,* 59; J. Boone Bartholomees, *Buff Facings and Gilt Buttons: Staff and Headquarters Operations in the Army of Northern Virginia, 1861–1865* (Columbia: University of South Carolina Press, 1998), 83; Venable, "Personal Reminiscences of the Confederate War," Small Special Collections Library; Boteler, "Stonewall Jackson in Campaign of 1862," 181; Woodworth, *Davis and Lee at War,* 178. George Booth, in his memoirs, also mentions this first "lost order," in *Maryland Boy in Lee's Army,* 47–48.

16. REL to TJJ, Aug. 7, 1862, in *OR,* ser. 1, vol. 12, pt. 3, 926; "Engagement with Louisiana Cavalry," *Richmond Dispatch,* July 19, 1862; Robert K. Krick, *Stonewall Jackson at Cedar Mountain* (Chapel Hill: University of North Carolina Press, 1990), 7–8, 21, 299, 319; REL to TJJ, Aug. 12, 1862, in *WPREL,* 251; Taylor, *General Lee,* 87–88; Woodworth, *Davis and Lee at War,* 176; Keller, *Great Partnership,* 41.

17. Halleck to McClellan, Aug. 3, 1862, and "Report of Maj. Gen. George B. McClellan, U.S. Army, Commanding Army of the Potomac," Aug. 4, 1863, in *OR,* ser. 1, vol. 11, pt. 1, 80–81, 90, 94; Long, *Memoirs of Robert E. Lee,* 185; Rafuse, *McClellan's War,* 245, 248; *McClellan's Own Story: The War for the Union, the Soldiers Who Fought It, the Civilians Who Directed It, and His Relations to It and to Them* (New York: Charles L. Webster, 1887), 509; Edmondston, diary entry for Aug. 20, 1862, in *Journal of a Secesh Lady,* 239.

18. REL to D. H. Hill, Aug. 13, 1862, in *OR,* ser. 1, vol. 11, pt. 3, 674; Jones, diary entry for Aug. 14, 1862, in *Rebel War Clerk's Diary,* 1:132; Marshall, *Aide-de-Camp of Lee,* 124; Matt Spruill, *Decisions at Second Manassas: The Fourteen Critical Decisions That Defined the Battle* (Knoxville: University of Tennessee Press, 2018), 19; Pope to Halleck, Aug. 18, 1862, in *OR,* ser. 1, vol. 12, pt. 3, 591; Hennessy, *Return to Bull Run,* 42–43, 49; James Longstreet, *From Manassas to Appomattox: Memoirs of the Civil War in America* (Philadelphia: J. B. Lippincott, 1896), 161–62; Long, *Memoirs of Robert E. Lee,* 187; Woodworth, *Davis and Lee at War,* 179.

19. REL to Stuart, Aug. 7, 1862, in *OR,* ser. 1, vol. 12, pt. 3, 925; Harsh, *Confederate Tide Rising,* 134, 137; Daughtry, *Gray Cavalier,* 91; Marshall, *Aide-de-Camp of Lee,* 127; Long, *Memoirs of Robert E. Lee,* 190; W. A. McClendon, *Recollection of War Times* (Montgomery, Ala.: Paragon Press, 1909), 104–5; Greenlee Davidson to J. D. Davidson, Aug. 28, 1862, in *Captain Greenlee Davidson, C.S.A., Diary and Letters, 1851–1863,* ed. C. W. Turner (Verone, Va.: McClure Press, 1975), 44–45.

20. John E. Divine, *8th Virginia Infantry* (Lynchburg, Va.: H. E. Howard, 1983), 13; Hennessy, *Return to Bull Run,* 196, 225, 39; Longstreet, *From Manassas to Appomattox,* 183; Patchan, *Second Manassas,* 124; James Longstreet, "The Mistakes of Gettysburg," in McClure, *Annals of the War,* 629–30. In the midst of pounding Pope's retreat, Lee was told by his adjutant,

A. P. Mason, that a gunner in a nearby battery wished to speak to him. "Well, my man, what can I do for you?" Lee asked. "Why, General, don't you know me?" the soldier said, grinning. Lee looked again: it was his son Rob, "face and hands . . . blackened with powder-sweat" from service in the Rockbridge Artillery. Robert E. Lee Jr., *Recollections and Letters,* 76.

21. Hennessy, *Return to Bull Run,* 437, 449; Long, *Memoirs of Robert E. Lee,* 199.
22. Pender to Fanny Pender, Sept. 7, 1862, in *One of Lee's Best Men,* 173; Venable, "Personal Reminiscences of the Confederate War," Small Special Collections Library; "List of Casualties," in *Reports of the Operations of the Army of Northern Virginia: From June 1862 to and Including the Battle of Fredericksburg, Dec. 13, 1862* (Richmond: R. M. Smith, 1864), 52; D. Scott Hartwig, *To Antietam Creek: The Maryland Campaign of September 1862* (Baltimore: Johns Hopkins University Press, 2012), 55–56; McLaws to Emily McLaws, Sept. 4, 1862, in *A Soldier's General: The Civil War Letters of Major General Lafayette McLaws,* ed. John C. Oeffinger (Chapel Hill: University of North Carolina Press, 2002), 154–55; "Four Days Among the Rebels," *Philadelphia Inquirer,* Sept. 13, 1862; Keith S. Bohannon, "Dirty, Ragged, and Ill-Provided For: Confederate Logistical Problems in the 1862 Maryland Campaign and Their Solutions," in *The Antietam Campaign,* ed. Gary W. Gallagher (Chapel Hill: University of North Carolina Press, 1999), 110; Frye, *2nd Virginia Infantry,* 37.
23. REL to Davis, Sept. 3 and 4, 1862, in *OR,* ser. 1, vol. 19, pt. 2, 590–92; REL interview with William Allan, Feb. 15, 1868, in Gallagher, *Lee the Soldier,* 7; Bradley T. Johnson, "Address on the First Maryland Campaign," *SHSP* 12 (Oct./Nov./Dec. 1884): 506; Davis, *Crucible of Command,* 240–41; Keller, *Great Partnership,* 70–71.
24. Davis, "To the Army of Eastern Virginia," July 5, 1862, in *OR,* ser. 1, vol. 11, pt. 3, 690; Taylor, *Four Years with General Lee,* 66; Longstreet, *Manassas to Appomattox,* 285; Woodworth, *Davis and Lee at War,* 186–87; Richard Slotkin, *The Long Road to Antietam: How the Civil War Became a Revolution* (New York: Liveright, 2012), 142–43, 157; Greenlee Davidson to James D. Davidson, Sept. 17, 1862, in *Diary and Letters, 1851–1863,* 48; Pender to Fanny Pender, Sept. 7, 1862, in *One of Lee's Best Men,* 173; Mason, *Popular Life of General Robert Edward Lee,* 137; Long, *Memoirs of Robert E. Lee,* 207; REL to Davis, Sept. 7, 9, and 13, 1862, and "To the People of Maryland," Sept. 8, 1862, in *WPREL,* 298, 299, 303, 306; Hay, diary entry for Sept. 1, 1862, in *Inside Lincoln's White House: The Complete Civil War Diary of John Hay,* ed. Michael Burlingame and J. R. T. Ettlinger (Carbondale: Southern Illinois University Press, 1997), 37–38.
25. John Scott, "The Black Horse Cavalry," in *Annals of the War,* 600; Sorrel, *Recollections of a Confederate Staff Officer,* 96–97; Taylor, *General Lee,* 115; Long, *Memoirs of Robert E. Lee,* 206; "Wounds of Gen. Lee," *Philadelphia Inquirer,* Sept. 13, 1862; Harsh, *Confederate Tide Rising,* 166, 206; Slotkin, *Long Road to Antietam,* 160; Longstreet, *From Manassas to Appomattox,* 220; John G. Walker, "Jackson's Capture of Harper's Ferry," in Buel and Johnson, *Battles and Leaders of the Civil War,* 2:606; REL to Davis, Sept. 8 and 12, 1862, "Special Orders No. 191," Sept. 9, 1862, in *WPREL,* 300, 301, 302, 304.
26. REL interview with E. C. Gordon, Feb. 15, 1868, in Gallagher, *Lee the Soldier,* 26; McClellan to Lincoln, Sept. 13, 1862, in *OR,* ser. 1, vol. 19, pt. 2, 281; Ezra A. Carman, *The Maryland Campaign of September 1862,* vol. 1, *South Mountain,* ed. T. G. Clemens (El Dorado, Calif.: Savas Beatie, 2010), 279–80; James V. Murfin, *The Gleam of Bayonets: The Battle of Antietam and Robert E. Lee's Maryland Campaign, September 1862* (New York: Bonanza Books, 1965), 133; Hartwig, *To Antietam Creek,* 284.
27. REL interview with E. C. Gordon, Feb. 15, 1868, in Gallagher, *Lee the Soldier,* 26; Brian Matthew Jordan, *Unholy Sabbath: The Battle of South Mountain in History and Memory, September 14, 1862* (El Dorado, Calif.: Savas Beatie, 2012), 112; Longstreet, *Manassas to Appomattox,* 227; Marshall, *Aide-de-Camp of Lee,* 160–61; Taylor, *General Lee,* 124–25; Long, *Memoirs of Robert E. Lee,* 213; Slotkin, *Long Road to Antietam,* 206–7; Joseph Harsh, *Sounding the Shal-*

lows: A Confederate Companion for the Maryland Campaign of 1862 (Kent, Ohio: Kent State University Press, 2000), 170–74; Stephen W. Sears, "The Curious Case of the Lost Order," *Civil War Monitor* 6 (Winter 2016): 32–40, 73.

28. TJJ to REL, Sept. 14 and 15, 1862, in *OR,* ser. 1, vol. 12, pt. 1, 951; Robertson, *Stonewall Jackson,* 603; Carman, *Maryland Campaign,* 1:253, 139; Slotkin, *Long Road to Antietam,* 271; William Henry Morgan, *Personal Reminiscences of the War of 1861–5: In Camp—en Bivouac—on the March—on Picket—on the Skirmish Line—on the Battlefield—and in Prison* (Lynchburg, Va.: J. P. Bell, 1911), 141; Owen, *In Camp and Battle with the Washington Artillery of New Orleans,* 139; REL to Davis, Sept. 16, 1862, in *WPREL,* 310; Murfin, *Gleam of Bayonets,* 203; John G. Walker, "Sharpsburg," in Buel and Johnson, *Battles and Leaders of the Civil War,* 2:675; Alexander, *Fighting for the Confederacy,* 145–46; Taylor, *General Lee,* 129; Taylor, *Four Years with General Lee,* 68; Harsh, *Sounding the Shallows,* 193.

29. Stephen W. Sears, *Landscape Turned Red: The Battle of Antietam* (New York: Ticknor & Fields, 1983), 195, 234, 265; Murfin, *Gleam of Bayonets,* 235–36, 241; Jedediah Hotchkiss, "Virginia," in *Confederate Military History,* ed. C. C. Evans (Atlanta: Confederate, 1899), 352; John Brown Gordon, *Reminiscences of the Civil War* (New York: Charles Scribner's Sons, 1904), 84; James Longstreet, "The Invasion of Maryland," in Buel and Johnson, *Battles and Leaders of the Civil War,* 2:671; Robert E. Lee Jr., *Recollections and Letters,* 78; Mason, *Popular Life of General Robert E. Lee,* 152; Robert E. L. Krick, "Defending Lee's Flank: J. E. B. Stuart, John Pelham, and Confederate Artillery on Nicodemus Heights," in Gallagher, *Antietam Campaign,* 220. William Poague, who commanded Rob Lee's battery, thought this incident took place earlier, at eleven o'clock, and near the Dunker church. See *Gunner with Stonewall: Reminiscences of William Thomas Poague, Lieutenant, Captain, Major, and Lieutenant Colonel of Artillery, Army of Northern Virginia, CSA, 1861–1865,* ed. M. F. Cockrell (1957; Lincoln: University of Nebraska Press, 1998), 48.

30. Sears, *Landscape Turned Red,* 276–77, 285; James I. Robertson, *General A. P. Hill: The Story of a Confederate Warrior* (New York: Random House, 1987), 143; Stephen D. Pool, "Tenth Regiment," in *Histories of the Several Regiments and Battalions from North Carolina in the Great War, 1861–'65,* ed. Walter Clark (Raleigh, N.C.: H. M. Uzzell), 1:575; Lesley J. Gordon, *A Broken Regiment: The 16th Connecticut's Civil War* (Baton Rouge: Louisiana State University Press, 2014), 39; Alexander, *Fighting for the Confederacy,* 153.

Chapter Thirteen: It Is Well This Is So Terrible!

1. "The Very Latest from Our Army," *New-York Tribune,* Sept. 18, 1862; Freeman, *Lee's Lieutenants,* 2:253; Sears, *Landscape Turned Red,* 298; Darrell L. Collins, *The Army of Northern Virginia: Organization, Strength, Casualties, 1861–65* (Jefferson, N.C.: McFarland, 2015), 280; Ethan S. Rafuse, *Antietam, South Mountain, and Harpers Ferry: A Battlefield Guide* (Lincoln: University of Nebraska Press, 2008), 116; Longstreet, "Invasion of Maryland," 672; "New Lights on Sharpsburg," *Richmond Dispatch,* Dec. 20, 1896; Sorrel, *Recollections,* 108; Harsh, *Sounding the Shallows,* 207–9.

2. "New Lights on Sharpsburg," *Richmond Dispatch,* Dec. 20, 1896; Murfin, *Gleam of Bayonets,* 291, 294–95; REL to Davis, Sept. 18, 1862, in *WPREL,* 311; E. C. Gordon to William Allan, Nov. 18, 1866, Special Collections, Leyburn Library.

3. Rafuse, *McClellan's War,* 328–29; McClellan to Mary Ellen McClellan, Sept. 18, 1862, in *Civil War Papers of George B. McClellan,* 469; William H. Monroe, "The Battle of Antietam: A Military Study," *Journal of the Military Service Institution of the United States* 49 (Sept./Oct. 1911): 277–78; "A Queer McClellan Story," *Baltimore News,* Jan. 12, 1904, in *The Good Fight That Didn't End: Henry P. Goddard's Accounts of Civil War and Peace,* ed. Calvin Goddard

Zon (Columbia: University of South Carolina Press, 2008), 310–11; Tally Simpson to Mary Simpson, April 24, 1862, in *Far, Far from Home,* 117; Edwin M. Stanton to McClellan, June 21, 1862, in *OR,* ser. 1, vol. 11, pt. 1, 1056; William B. Styple, *McClellan's Other Story: The Political Intrigue of Colonel Thomas M. Key, Confidential Aide to General George B. McClellan* (Kearny, N.J.: Belle Grove, 2012), 131, 252–53; John Hay, diary entry for Sept. 26, 1862, in Hay, *Inside Lincoln's White House,* 41, 295; Slotkin, *Long Road to Antietam,* 178–79.

4. "Reports of Maj. Gen. George B. McClellan, U.S. Army, Commanding the Army of the Potomac, of Operations August 14–November 9," Oct. 15, 1862, REL to Samuel Cooper, Aug. 19, 1862, and "Report of Lieut. Gen. James Longstreet, C.S. Army, Commanding Army Corps, of Operations September 2–18," Oct. 10, 1862, in *OR,* ser. 1, vol. 19, pt. 1, 32, 151, 841; Sears, *Landscape Turned Red,* 307; McClendon, *Recollection of War Times,* 152; Walker, "Sharpsburg," 682.
5. Sears, *Landscape Turned Red,* 307–8; REL to Myers, Sept. 21, 1862, to Longstreet and TJJ, Sept. 22, 1862, and to Davis, Sept. 25, 1862, in *OR,* ser. 1, vol. 19, pt. 2, 614, 618–19, 626–27; Jedediah Hotchkiss, diary entry for Oct. 7, 1862, in *Make Me a Map of the Valley: The Civil War Journal of Stonewall Jackson's Topographer,* ed. Archie P. McDonald (Dallas: Southern Methodist University Press, 1973), 87; Glatthaar, *General Lee's Army,* 181–82; Benjamin Franklin Cooling, *Counter-thrust: From the Peninsula to the Antietam* (Lincoln: University of Nebraska Press, 2007), 255; Gary W. Gallagher, *Lee and His Army in Confederate History* (Chapel Hill: University of North Carolina Press, 2001), 11, 23, 29–30, 37; *Richmond Enquirer,* Feb. 13, 1865. Davis sent Custis Lee to Martinsburg to report on the condition of his father's army, and Custis unsparingly noted that "our troops were shaky from the day they went into Maryland," partly from the lackluster welcome they received there but also from the "long marches and hard fighting," plus being "poorly clad, with many of them without shoes." He had found the road "from Harrisonburg to Martinsburg, full of stragglers . . . the majority without apparently anything the matter with them." GWCL to Davis, Sept. 25, 1862, in *Papers of Jefferson Davis,* 8:405–6; Yates, *Perfect Gentleman,* 1:252–53.
6. REL to Stuart, Oct. 13, 1862, Samuel Smith Family Papers, Library of Congress; "Gen. Stuart's Last Expedition," *Richmond Dispatch,* Oct. 15, 1862; Taylor, *General Lee,* 139–40; REL to Davis, Oct. 2, 1862, in *Papers of Jefferson Davis,* 8:422.
7. "The Hon. Mr. Nincompoop for Governor," *New York Herald,* Sept. 11, 1862; Strong, diary entry for Nov. 5, 1862, in *Diary of the Civil War, 1860–1865,* ed. Allan Nevins (New York: Macmillan, 1962), 271; Louis P. Masur, *Lincoln's Hundred Days: The Emancipation Proclamation and the War for the Union* (Cambridge, Mass.: Harvard University Press, 2012), 151–55; Mark E. Neely, *Lincoln and the Democrats: The Politics of Opposition in the Civil War* (New York: Cambridge University Press, 2017), 54–55; Stephen D. Engle, *Gathering to Save a Nation: Lincoln and the Union's War Governors* (Chapel Hill: University of North Carolina Press, 2016), 242–48.
8. Chase to Charles Sumner, Nov. 9, 1862, in *The Salmon P. Chase Papers: Correspondence, 1858–March 1863,* ed. John Niven (Kent, Ohio: Kent State University Press, 1996), 314; McClellan to Henry Wager Halleck, Sept. 22, 1862, and "General Orders No. 182," Nov. 5, 1862, in *OR,* ser. 1, vol. 19, pt. 2, 341, 545; Carman, *Maryland Campaign of September 1862,* 1:420, 422; "Conversation with Hon. O. M. Hatch, Springfield, June, 1875," in *An Oral History of Abraham Lincoln: John G. Nicolay's Interviews and Essays,* ed. Michael Burlingame (Carbondale: Southern Illinois University Press, 1996), 16.
9. James Longstreet, "The Battle of Fredericksburg," in Buel and Johnson, *Battles and Leaders of the Civil War,* 3:70; Edmondston, diary entry for Oct. 4, 1862, in *Journal of a Secesh Lady,* 268; Frye, *2nd Virginia Infantry,* 39, 44; Randolph to REL, Oct. 8, 1862, in *OR,* ser. 1, vol. 19, pt. 2, 656–57; REL to Louis T. Wigfall, Sept. 21, 1862, Robert E. Lee Papers, Briscoe Center

for American History; John B. Jones, diary entry for Feb. 23, 1863, in *Rebel War Clerk's Diary,* 1:233.

10. Philip Katcher, *The Army of Robert E. Lee* (London: Arms & Armour, 1994), 74; Edward Hewett, in Jay Luvaas, *The Military Legacy of the Civil War* (Lawrence: University Press of Kansas, 1988), 27–28; "The Contrabands of Harper's Ferry," *New-York Tribune,* Sept. 18, 1862.
11. Gary W. Gallagher, *The Confederate War* (Cambridge, Mass.: Harvard University Press, 1997), 96, 122; Keller, *Great Partnership,* 86; Joseph T. Glatthaar, "A Tale of Two Armies: The Confederate Army of Northern Virginia and the Union Army of the Potomac and Their Cultures," *Journal of the Civil War Era* 6 (Sept. 2016): 318, 321, 327; James I. Robertson, *Soldiers Blue and Gray* (Columbia: University of South Carolina Press, 1988), 124; Colin E. Woodward, *Marching Masters: Slavery, Race, and the Confederate Army During the Civil War* (Charlottesville: University of Virginia Press, 2014), 38; Jones, diary entry for Sept. 26–27, 1862, in *Rebel War Clerk's Diary,* 1:140; Scheibert, *Seven Months in the Rebel States,* 75.
12. Long, *Memoirs of Robert E. Lee,* 264; REL to Davis, Oct. 2, 1862, in *Papers of Jefferson Davis,* 421; REL to George W. Randolph, Oct. 27, 1862, in *OR,* ser. 1, vol. 19, pt. 2, 683; Freeman, *Lee's Lieutenants,* 2:243, Sorrel, *Recollections of a Confederate Staff Officer,* 31–32, 48; Francis Dawson, *Reminiscences of Confederate Service, 1861–1865,* ed. B. I. Wiley (Baton Rouge: Louisiana State University Press, 1980), 128; Edmondston, diary entry for Jan. 3, 1863, in *Journal of a Secesh Lady,* 332.
13. Andrews, *Scraps of Paper,* 122; Pender, letter fragment from Sept. 19, 1862, in *One of Lee's Best Men,* 175; REL to George W. Randolph, with pencil note by Beauregard, Oct. 24, 1862, in P. G. T. Beauregard Papers, Library of Congress; Robertson, *Stonewall Jackson,* 627–28; Robertson, *General A. P. Hill,* 131–35, 153, 249; Freeman, *Lee's Lieutenants,* 2:244; Greenlee Davidson to John Letcher, Feb. 22, 1863, in *Captain Greenlee Davidson, C.S.A., Diary and Letters,* 69; Alexander, *Fighting for the Confederacy,* 336; Maury, *Recollections of a Virginian,* 72; Sorrel, *Recollections of a Confederate Staff Officer,* 114.
14. Tally Simpson to Mary Simpson, Dec. 2, 1862, in *Far, Far from Home,* 163; Charles Venable, "General Lee in the Wilderness Campaign," in Buel and Johnson, *Battles and Leaders of the Civil War,* 4:240; REL to Randolph, Oct. 8 and Nov. 7, 1862, in *OR,* ser. 1, vol. 19, pt. 2, 659, 699, 702; Jones, diary entry for Oct. 14, 1863, in *Rebel War Clerk's Diary,* 2:62; Kean, diary entry for Feb. 15, 1863, in *Inside the Confederate Government,* 39; Jones, diary entry for Dec. 3, 1862, in *Rebel War Clerk's Diary,* 1:179.
15. Sorrel, *Recollections of a Confederate Staff Officer,* 68–69, 75; Bartholomees, *Buff Facings and Gilt Buttons,* 4, 177–78; Long, *Memoirs of Robert E. Lee,* 161, 262; Taylor, *General Lee,* 155–56; Taylor, *Four Years with General Lee,* 7, 77; Maury, *Recollections of a Virginian,* 238–39; Taylor to Elizabeth Saunders, Aug. 8 and Dec. 27, 1863, in *Lee's Adjutant: The Wartime Letters of Colonel Walter Herron Taylor, 1862–1865,* ed. R. Lockwood Tower (Columbia: University of South Carolina Press, 1995), 68, 182; Marshall, *Aide-de-Camp of Lee,* 179, 181.
16. Pender to Fanny Pender, Sept. 2, 1862, in *One of Lee's Best Men,* 171; Sorrel, *Recollections of a Confederate Staff Officer,* 120; Varon, *Armies of Deliverance,* 241; James A. Walker, "Life in the Army—the Private Soldier's Spirit," May 25, 1894, in *Civil War Talks: Further Reminiscences of George S. Bernard and His Fellow Veterans,* ed. Hampton Newsome, John Horn, and John G. Selby (Charlottesville: University of Virginia Press, 2012), 175; "Salmagundi," *Southern Bivouac,* July 1885, 127.
17. REL to CCL, March 14, 1862, Robert E. Lee Papers, Small Special Collections Library; REL to MCL, Dec. 2, 1861, Jan. 28 and Dec. 7, 1862, REL to GWCL, Jan. 19 and Nov. 28, 1862, in *WPREL,* 90, 105, 108, 354; Joseph P. Reidy, "'Coming from the Shadow of the Past': The Transition from Slavery to Freedom at Freedmen's Village, 1863–1900," *VMHB,* Oct. 1987,

405–6; Kali Holloway, "Unpaid Debts," *Nation,* April 6, 2020, 20; Kenneth J. Winkle, *Lincoln's Citadel: The Civil War in Washington, DC* (New York: W. W. Norton, 2013), 278; Perry, *Lady of Arlington,* 254–55; REL to WHFL, Feb. 16, 1862, in Fellman, *Making of Robert E. Lee,* 196.

18. REL to GWCL, Jan. 11, 1863, in Jones, *Life and Letters,* 286; REL to MCL, Nov. 11, 1863, and Jan. 24, 1864, in *WPREL,* 622, 661; Thomas, *Robert E. Lee,* 273–74.
19. "Gov. Pierpont," *Wheeling Daily Intelligencer,* June 13, 1865; Edmondston, diary entry for Feb. 10, 1864, in *Journal of a Secesh Lady,* 524. This might have been what John B. Jones, the Confederate War Department clerk, heard and translated in December into musings that "it might be well for the South if 500,000 of the slaves were suddenly emancipated. The loss would not be felt—and the North would soon be conscious of having gained nothing." See Jones, diary entry for Dec. 3, 1862, in *Rebel War Clerk's Diary,* 1:179–80.
20. Rafuse, *Robert E. Lee and the Fall of the Confederacy,* 23; Lincoln to McClellan, Sept. 13, 1862, in *Collected Works,* 5:460–61; Bernard Holland, *The Life of Spencer Compton, Eighth Duke of Devonshire* (London: Longmans, Green, 1911), 1:47; *Reminiscences of General Herman Haupt* (Milwaukee: Wright and Joys, 1901), 160; William Marvel, *Burnside* (Chapel Hill: University of North Carolina Press, 1991), 163; "Reports of Maj. Gen. Ambrose E. Burnside, U.S. Army, Commanding Army of the Potomac, of Operations November 9, 1862–January 25, 1863," in *OR,* ser. 1, 21:84.
21. Taylor, *Four Years with General Lee,* 79; George C. Rable, *Fredericksburg! Fredericksburg!* (Chapel Hill: University of North Carolina Press, 2002), 67, 80, 88; REL to Stuart, Nov. 7, 1862, and to TJJ, Nov. 9, 1862, in *OR,* ser. 1, vol. 19, pt. 2, 703, 706; Taylor, *General Lee,* 140–41; REL to GWCL, Nov. 10, 1862, in *WPREL;* Yates, *Perfect Gentleman,* 1:259; REL to George W. Randolph, Nov. 17, 1862, in *OR,* ser. 1, 21:1015.
22. Woodworth, *Davis and Lee at War,* 207; REL to Davis, Nov. 20, 1862, in *Lee's Dispatches: Unpublished Letters of General Robert E. Lee, C.S.A., to Jefferson Davis and the War Department of the Confederate States of America, 1862–65,* ed. D. S. Freeman (New York: G. P. Putnam's Sons, 1915), 66; REL to MCL, Nov. 22, 1862, in *WPREL,* 343; Cooke, *Life of General Robert E. Lee,* 177.
23. REL to Davis, Nov. 27, 1862, and to TJJ, Dec. 2, 1862, in *WPREL,* 348, 351; Frank A. O'Reilly, *The Fredericksburg Campaign: Winter War on the Rappahannock* (Baton Rouge: Louisiana State University Press, 2003), 51, 75, 81; "Report of Lieut. Michael H. McGrath, Fiftieth New York Engineers," Dec. 13, 1862, in *OR,* ser. 1, 21:179.
24. Stephen Minot Weld to William Gordon Weld, Dec. 11, 1862, in *War Diary and Letters of Stephen Minot Weld, 1861–1865* (Boston: Massachusetts Historical Society, 1979), 152; George Kimball, *A Corporal's Story: Civil War Recollections of the Twelfth Massachusetts,* ed. Alan Gaff and D. H. Gaff (Norman: University of Oklahoma Press, 2014), 191; Cooke, *Life of General Robert E. Lee,* 177; O'Reilly, *Winter War on the Rappahannock,* 107, 117–18, 125; Frank A. O'Reilly, *The Fredericksburg Campaign: "Stonewall" Jackson at Fredericksburg, the Battle of Prospect Hill, December 13, 1862* (Lynchburg, Va.: H. E. Howard, 1993), 24.
25. A. Wilson Greene, "Opportunity to the South: Meade Versus Jackson at Fredericksburg," in *Whatever You Resolve to Be: Essays on Stonewall Jackson* (Baltimore: Butternut & Blue, 1992), 130–38; William Henry Powell, *The Fifth Army Corps (Army of the Potomac): A Record of Operations During the Civil War in the United States of America, 1861–1865* (New York: G. P. Putnam's Sons, 1896), 388; Rable, *Fredericksburg!,* 262, 288; Benjamin Borton, *On the Parallels; or, Chapters of Inner History: A Story of the Rappahannock* (Woodstown, N.J.: Monitor-Register Print, 1903), 231; Max Wycoff, *A History of the Second South Carolina Infantry, 1861–65* (Wilmington, N.C.: Broadfoot, 2011), 145.
26. Longstreet, *From Manassas to Appomattox,* 312; Cooke, *Life of General Robert E. Lee,* 181, 183,

184; "The Civil War in America," *Reynolds's Newspaper,* Jan. 18, 1863; Mason, *Popular Life of Gen. Robert Edward Lee,* 160–61; Longstreet, "Battle of Fredericksburg," 81; REL to James A. Seddon, Dec. 13, 1862, in *OR,* ser. 1, 21:546; Peter Beckford, *Thoughts on Hunting: In a Series of Familiar Letters to a Friend* (London: Debretts, 1777), 162. On the variations of Lee's comment on being too fond of war, see Gallagher, *Lee and His Army in Confederate History,* 80.

27. Longstreet, "Battle of Fredericksburg," 82; O'Reilly, *Winter Warfare on the Rappahannock,* 436, 450.
28. "From Fredericksburg," *Richmond Enquirer,* Dec. 19 and 27, 1862; McGuire, diary entry for Dec. 14, 1862, in *Diary of a Southern Refugee,* 175; "The Great Battle of Fredericksburg," *Richmond Dispatch,* Dec. 16, 1862; Varon, *Armies of Deliverance,* 178; Whitman to Thomas Jefferson Whitman, Jan. 8, 1863, in *Civil War Letters of George Washington Whitman,* ed. Jerome M. Loving (Durham, N.C.: Duke University Press, 1976), 80.
29. REL to Samuel Cooper, April 10, 1863, in *OR,* ser. 1, 21:556; Long, *Memoirs of Robert E. Lee,* 569; REL to MCL, Dec. 25, 1862, and to MChL, Dec. 25, 1862, in *WPREL,* 379–80, 381; "Letter from Major-General Henry Heth, of A. P. Hill's Corps, A.N.V.," *SHSP* 4 (Oct. 1877): 153.
30. REL to CCL, March 14, 1862, LFDA/duPont Library; REL to MCL, March 14, 1862, and March 9, 1863, and to Charlotte Wickham Lee, Dec. 10, 1862, in *WPREL,* 128, 357, 413; Cooke, *Life of General Robert E. Lee,* 47; Coulling, *Lee Girls,* 110–11; REL to MCL, Oct. 26, 1862, in Jones, *Life and Letters,* 199, 200; Taylor, *General Lee,* 76; Taylor, *Four Years with General Lee,* 76; Robert E. Lee Jr., *Recollections and Letters,* 80; Daughtry, *Gray Cavalier,* 106.
31. Jones, diary entry for Dec. 19, 1862, in *Rebel War Clerk's Diary,* 1:193; Shackelford, *George Wythe Randolph,* 89; Glatthaar, *General Lee's Army,* 212; Koistinen, *Beating Plowshares into Swords,* 229, 234, 235–36; George Washington Whitman to Louisa Whitman, Nov. 10, 1862, in *Civil War Letters,* 73; Robert McAllister to his family, Nov. 28, 1862, in *Civil War Letters of General Robert McAllister,* 228; Long, *Memoirs of Robert E. Lee,* 245–46.
32. Long, *Memoirs of Robert E. Lee,* 247–48; Taylor, *General Lee,* 154; REL to Seddon, Dec. 16, 1862, and Jan. 10, 1863, in *WPREL,* 363, 388; Woodworth, *Davis and Lee at War,* 213; Longstreet, *From Manassas to Appomattox,* 323; Jedediah Hotchkiss and William Allan, *The Battle-Fields of Virginia: Chancellorsville* (New York: Van Nostrand, 1867), 15–16; REL to Seddon, April 10, 1863, in *OR,* ser. 1, 21:556; Glatthaar, *General Lee's Army,* 215; REL to TJJ, Feb. 7, 1863, in *OR,* ser. 1, vol. 51, pt. 2, 678–79.
33. Lucy Rebecca Buck, diary entry for July 22, 1863, in *In Shadows on My Heart: The Civil War Diary of Lucy Rebecca Buck of Virginia,* ed. E. R. Baer (Athens: University of Georgia Press, 1997), 236–37; Garnet Joseph Wolseley, "A Month's Visit to the Confederate Headquarters," *Blackwood's Edinburgh Magazine,* Jan. 1863, 18; "The Battle of Fredericksburg," *London Times,* Jan. 13, 1863; "The Commanders in the Confederate Armies," *Reynolds's Newspaper,* Jan. 4, 1863; Peter Alexander, "Robert E. Lee," *Southern Literary Messenger* 37 (Jan. 1863): 34. He charmed another Virginia belle in Staunton when visiting her home in 1863. Lee was "a grand and beautiful man with gray hair, gray uniform and wonderful dark eyes," she wrote. "There was no crown upon his forehead or golden scepter in his hand, yet he was the realization of all that I had read in story books." See Margaret Briscoe Stuart Robertson, *My Childhood Recollections of the War: Life in the Confederate Stronghold of Staunton, Virginia* (Staunton, Va.: Charles Culbertson, 2013).
34. Venable, "General Lee in the Wilderness Campaign," 420; Susan P. Lee, *Memoirs of William Nelson Pendleton, D.D.: Rector of Latimer Parish* (Philadelphia: J. B. Lippincott, 1893), 295; REL to GWCL, Feb. 12, 1863, in Thomas, *Robert E. Lee,* 277.
35. Hotchkiss, diary entry for March 13, 1862, in *Make Me a Map of the Valley,* 120; MacDonald, *Mrs. Robert E. Lee,* 166; Perry, *Lady of Arlington,* 251, 264; REL to MCL, March 27 and

April 5, 1863, in *WPREL,* 419, 428; William Preston Johnston, in Jones, *Personal Reminiscences,* 444; Hotchkiss, diary entry for March 29, 1863, in *Make Me a Map of the Valley,* 124.

36. REL to MCL, April 3 and 5, 1863, in *WPREL,* 427–28; John J. Hennessy, "Belvoir: The Thomas Yerby Place, Spotsylvania County," 3, 8–9, npsfrsp.files.wordpress.com; D. S. Freeman, "Lee and the Ladies: Unpublished Letters of Robert E. Lee," *Scribner's Magazine,* Oct. 1925, 462; REL to GWCL, March 31, 1863, in Yates, *Perfect Gentleman,* 1:273; Richard A. Reinhart, "Robert E. Lee's Right Ear and the Relation of Earlobe Crease to Coronary Artery Disease," *American Journal of Cardiology* 120, no. 2 (2017): 327–30; Richard A. Reinhart, "Historical Implications of a Failing Heart: Robert E. Lee's Medical History in Context of Heart Disease, Medical Education, and the Practice of Medicine in the Nineteenth Century," National Museum of Civil War Medicine, www.civilwarmed.org; REL to EAL, April 11, 1863, Lee Family Papers, VMHC.

Chapter Fourteen: In This Heathen War the Fire of God Fills Him

1. Davis to REL, Dec. 8, 1862, and to Seddon, Dec. 15, 1862, in *Papers of Jefferson Davis,* 8:533, 551; Davis, *Jefferson Davis,* 482; Thomas L. Connelly, *The Marble Man: Robert E. Lee and His Image in American Society* (New York: Knopf, 1977), 40–41, 104–5.
2. REL to Seddon, April 9, 1863, to Cooper, April 16, 1863, and to Davis, April 16, 1863, in *OR,* ser. 1, vol. 25, pt. 2, 713–14; Woodworth, *Davis and Lee at War,* 220–21; Archer Jones, *Civil War Command and Strategy: The Process of Victory and Defeat* (New York: Free Press, 1992), 123–24; Thomas L. Connelly, *Autumn of Glory: The Army of Tennessee, 1862–1865* (Baton Rouge: Louisiana State University Press, 1971), 104–5.
3. REL to Cooper, April 16, 1863, and to Davis, April 16, 1863, in *OR,* ser. 1, vol. 25, pt. 2, 724–26; REL to MCL, April 19, 1863, Lee Family Papers, VMHC.
4. Jones, diary entry for Feb. 6, 1863, in *Rebel War Clerk's Diary,* 1:226; Ernest B. Furgurson, *Chancellorsville, 1863: The Souls of the Brave* (New York: Knopf, 1992), 30; Stephen W. Sears, *Chancellorsville* (New York: Houghton Mifflin, 1996), 18.
5. Furgurson, *Chancellorsville,* 30; Sears, *Chancellorsville,* 80; John Bigelow, *The Campaign of Chancellorsville: A Strategic and Tactical Study* (New Haven, Conn.: Yale University Press, 1910), 108; H. Seymour Hall, "Fredericksburg and Chancellorsville," April 4, 1894, in *War Talks in Kansas: A Series of Papers Read Before the Kansas Commandery of the Military Order of the Loyal Legion of the United States* (Kansas City, Mo.: Franklin Hudson, 1906), 194.
6. Hooker to Lincoln, April 11, 1863, in *OR,* ser. 1, vol. 25, pt. 2, 199; Lincoln, "Memorandum on Joseph Hooker's Plan of Campaign Against Richmond," April 6–10, 1863, in *Collected Works,* 6:164.
7. Hotchkiss, diary entry for April 29, 1863, in *Make Me a Map of the Valley,* 136; REL to Longstreet, April 27, 1863, Samuel Cooper to Longstreet, April 29, 1863, and REL to R. H. Anderson, April 29, 1863, in *OR,* ser. 1, 18:1024, and vol. 25, pt. 2, 758; Richard Meade Bache, *Life of General George Gordon Meade: Commander of the Army of the Potomac* (Philadelphia: Henry T. Coates, 1897), 260.
8. REL, telegram, April 30, 1863, in *Lee's Dispatches,* 86; "General Orders No. 47," April 30, 1863, in *OR,* ser. 1, vol. 25, pt. 1, 171; Long, *Memoirs of Robert E. Lee,* 251; Bigelow, *Chancellorsville,* 258–59; Sears, *Chancellorsville,* 192; Gallagher, *Lee and His Army in Confederate History,* 224–25; *Colonel Alexander K. McClure's Recollections of Half a Century* (Salem, Mass.: Salem Press, 1902), 348.
9. Alexander, *Fighting for the Confederacy,* 200; Marshall, *Aide-de-Camp of Lee,* 167–70; R. T. Bennett, "An Address Before the Ladies Memorial Association," May 10, 1906, *SHSP* 34 (1906): 55; "Address of General Fitzhugh Lee," Oct. 29, 1879, in Jones, *Army of Northern*

Virginia Memorial Volume, 317; G. F. R. Henderson, *Stonewall Jackson and the American Civil War* (London: Longmans, Green, 1913), 2:432; Long, *Memoirs of Robert E. Lee,* 252; Robertson, *Stonewall Jackson,* 714; Keller, *Great Partnership,* 150–56.

10. T. M. Cook, "Operations on Saturday," *New York Herald,* May 7, 1863; Sears, *Chancellorsville,* 365; Charles Marshall, "Tributes to General Lee," *Southern Magazine,* Jan. 1871, 29; Marshall, *Aide-de-Camp of Lee,* 173; Tally Simpson to Richard Franklin Simpson, May 7, 1863, and to Caroline Virginia Miller, May 10, 1863, in *Far, Far from Home,* 225–26, 230.
11. Hotchkiss, diary entry for May 2, 1863, in *Make Me a Map of the Valley,* 138; Dabney, *Life and Campaigns of Lieut.-Gen. Thomas J. Jackson,* 701–2, 716; Robertson, *Stonewall Jackson,* 729; Robert K. Krick, *The Smoothbore Volley That Doomed the Confederacy: The Death of Stonewall Jackson and Other Chapters on the Army of Northern Virginia* (Baton Rouge: Louisiana State University Press, 2002), 31–32; Keller, *Great Partnership,* 170; Jones, *Personal Reminiscences,* 155–56.
12. Alexander, *Fighting for the Confederacy,* 213; Jedediah Hotchkiss, "The Chancellorsville Campaign and the Death of Jackson," in *Confederate Military History: Virginia,* ed. Clement A. Evans (Atlanta: Confederate, 1899), 3:392; Woodworth, *Davis and Lee at War,* 224; Sears, *Chancellorsville,* 492, 501; "Letter from Major-General Henry Heth, of A. P. Hill's Corps, A.N.V.," *SHSP* 4 (Oct. 1877): 154; Longstreet to Lafayette McLaws, July 25, 1873, in Cory M. Pfarr, *Longstreet at Gettysburg: A Critical Reassessment* (Jefferson, N.C.: McFarland, 2019), 22.
13. "Fernando Wood's Peace Meeting," *New-York Tribune,* May 19, 1863; Michael Burlingame, *Abraham Lincoln: A Life* (Baltimore: Johns Hopkins University Press, 2008), 2:446, 498; Horace Greeley, *The American Conflict: A History of the Great Rebellion in the United States of America* (Hartford: O. D. Case, 1866), 2:484.
14. Hotchkiss, diary entry for Feb. 23, 1863, in *Make Me a Map of the Valley,* 116; Dorsey Pender to Fanny Pender, April 8, 1863, in *One of Lee's Best Men,* 221; William Swallow, "From Fredericksburg to Gettysburg," *Southern Bivouac,* Nov. 1885, 352; Keller, *Great Partnership,* 120.
15. James Longstreet, "Lee in Pennsylvania," in McClure, *Annals of the War,* 415–17; REL to Seddon, May 10 and June 10, 1863, in *OR,* ser. 1, vol. 25, pt. 2, 790, and vol. 27, pt. 3, 868; Long, *Memoirs of Robert E. Lee,* 269; Marshall, *Aide-de-Camp of Lee,* 250–51; R. L. DiNardo and Albert A. Nofi, *James Longstreet: The Man, the Soldier, the Controversy* (Boston: Da Capo Press, 1998), 79–80.
16. Jones, diary entries for May 15–16, 1863, in *Rebel War Clerk's Diary,* 1:288–89; Reagan, *Memoirs,* 150–51; Woodworth, *Davis and Lee at War,* 230–31; REL to Davis, June 10, 1863, in *OR,* ser. 1, vol. 27, pt. 3, 881–82.
17. Pender to Fanny Pender, March 26 and May 14, 1863, in *One of Lee's Best Men,* 211, 237; Robertson, *General A. P. Hill,* 193; REL to Davis, May 20, 1863, in *OR,* ser. 1, vol. 25, pt. 2, 810; REL to Davis, May 25, 1863, in *Lee's Dispatches,* 91–92.
18. REL to Hood, May 21, 1863, in *WPREL,* 490.
19. Charles Minor Blackford to Susan Blackford, June 12 and 16, 1863, in *Letters from Lee's Army,* 175, 177; "The News from the Potomac," *Richmond Dispatch,* June 20, 1863; Kean, diary entry for June 21, 1863, in *Inside the Confederate Government,* 76; Taylor, *General Lee,* 181–83; George Boutwell, in A. T. Rice, ed., *Reminiscences of Abraham Lincoln by Distinguished Men of His Time* (New York: North American Publishing, 1886), 128.
20. Isaac R. Trimble, "The Battle and Campaign of Gettysburg," *SHSP* 26 (1898): 121; Long, *Memoirs of Robert E. Lee,* 268; Hotchkiss, diary entry for June 26, 1863, in *Make Me a Map of the Valley,* 155; Taylor, *General Lee,* 180, 183–84; Kean, diary entry for June 21, 1863, in *Inside the Confederate Government,* 75; Ross, *Cities and Camps of the Confederate States,* 25–26.
21. *Reminiscences of a Louisiana Tiger: The Civil War Memoirs of Captain William J. Seymour,* ed. Terry L. Jones (Baton Rouge: Louisiana State University Press, 1991), 58; L. M. Blackford, in Ayers, *Thin Light of Freedom,* 31, 50–51; Tally Simpson to Mary Simpson, June 26, 1863, in

Far, Far from Home, 248–49; Rafuse, *Robert E. Lee and the Fall of the Confederacy,* 54–55, 56; "General Orders No. 73," June 27, 1863, in *OR,* ser. 1, vol. 27, pt. 3, 942.

22. Walter Taylor, "The Campaign in Pennsylvania," in McClure, *Annals of the War,* 306–7; *Campbell Brown's Civil War,* 204–5; James Power Smith, "General Lee at Gettysburg: A Paper Read Before the Military Historical Society of Massachusetts, on the Fourth of April, 1905," *SHSP* 33 (1905): 139; Sorrel, *Recollections of a Confederate Staff Officer,* 147–48; Marshall, *Aide-de-Camp of Lee,* 218–19; Thomas J. Ryan, "The Art of Command and Intelligence: Jeb Stuart in the Gettysburg Campaign," *Gettysburg Magazine,* Jan. 2021, 30–33. Lee is supposed to have remarked on Meade's appointment with unusually well-informed respect, "General Meade will commit no mistakes on my front, and should I make one, will be quick to seize upon it" (or alternately, "General Meade will not blunder in my front, and if I make one will seize upon it"), but there is no contemporary source for this comment. See David L. Shultz and Scott L. Mingus, *The Second Day at Gettysburg: The Attack and Defense of the Union Center on Cemetery Ridge, July 2, 1863* (El Dorado, Calif.: Savas Beatie, 2015), 15n35.
23. Longstreet, "Lee in Pennsylvania," 420; Long, *Memoirs of Robert E. Lee,* 275; J. D. S. Cullen, in Scott Bowden and Bill Ward, *Last Chance for Victory: Robert E. Lee and the Gettysburg Campaign* (Cambridge, Mass.: Da Capo Press, 2001), 146, 160–68; "The Memoirs of Henry Heth," ed. James L. Morrison, *Civil War History* 8 (Sept. 1962): 305; Taylor, *Four Years with General Lee,* 93; Leslie J. Perry, "General Lee and the Battle of Gettysburg," *SHSP* 23 (1895): 253–59.
24. Ross, *Cities and Camps of the Confederate States,* 76; J. Coleman Alderson, "Lee and Longstreet at Gettysburg," *Confederate Veteran,* Oct. 1904, 488; REL to Samuel Cooper, Jan. 20, 1864, and "Report of Lieut. Gen. Ambrose P. Hill, C.S. Army, Commanding Third Army Corps," Nov. 1863, in *OR,* ser. 1, vol. 27, pt. 2, 318, 607; A. N. Gambone, *Lee at Gettysburg: A Commentary on Defeat* (Baltimore: Butternut & Blue, 2002), 117, 122, 124; "Address of Major Daniel," Oct. 29, 1875, in Jones, *Army of Northern Virginia Memorial Volume,* 103; Taylor, "Campaign in Pennsylvania," 308–9; Taylor, *General Lee,* 190; Taylor, *Four Years with General Lee,* 95; *Campbell Brown's Civil War,* 325–27; George Gordon Meade, "The Battle of Gettysburg—What Gen. Ewell Wished to Do," *National Tribune,* Jan. 7, 1882; Casdorph, *Confederate General R. S. Ewell,* 256–57.
25. Longstreet, "Lee in Pennsylvania," 421; Longstreet, *From Manassas to Appomattox,* 358.
26. John Bell Hood, "Leading Confederates on the Battle of Gettysburg," *SHSP* 4 (Oct. 1877): 147; Hood to Longstreet, June 28, 1875, in *Advance and Retreat: Personal Experiences in the United States and Confederate States Armies* (1880; Lincoln: University of Nebraska Press, 1996), 56–57; Gary W. Gallagher, "'If the Enemy Is There, We Must Attack Him': R. E. Lee and the Second Day at Gettysburg," in *Three Days at Gettysburg: Essays on Confederate and Union Leadership,* ed. Gary W. Gallagher (Kent, Ohio: Kent State University Press, 1999), 124, 125; Troy Harman, *Lee's Real Plan at Gettysburg* (Mechanicsburg, Pa.: Stackpole Books, 2003), 19.
27. "Colonel Hilary A. Herbert's 'History of the Eighth Alabama Volunteer Regiment, C.S.A.,'" ed. M. S. Fortin, *Alabama Historical Quarterly* 39 (1977): 117; James Risque Hunter to John W. Daniel, n.d., John Warwick Daniel Papers, Small Special Collections Library; "Report of Col. Henry A. Morrow, Twenty-Fourth Michigan Infantry," Feb. 22, 1864, in *OR,* ser. 1, vol. 27, pt. 1, 272; *Campbell Brown's Civil War,* 222.
28. Longstreet, "Lee in Pennsylvania," 429; Longstreet, *From Manassas to Appomattox,* 385; James Longstreet, "Lee's Right Wing at Gettysburg," in Buel and Johnson, *Battles and Leaders of the Civil War,* 3:343; Sorrel, *Recollections of a Confederate Staff Officer,* 166–67; "Charge of Pickett's Division," *Southern Bivouac,* July 1884, 522; A. H. Moore, "Heth's Division at Gettysburg," *Southern Bivouac,* May 1885, 389; William Swallow, "The Third Day at Gettysburg," *Southern Bivouac,* Feb. 1886, 565.

29. "Artillery Heard at Gettysburg," *Washington Daily National Republican,* July 3, 1863; John S. D. Cook, "Personal Reminiscences of Gettysburg," Dec. 17, 1903, in *War Talks in Kansas,* 334; "Address by Col. Andrew Cowan," in *In Memoriam, Alexander Stewart Webb, 1835–1911* (Albany, N.Y.: J. B. Lyon, 1916), 66; William Mitchell to J. B. Bachelder, Jan. 10, 1866, in *The Bachelder Papers: Gettysburg in Their Own Words,* ed. David Lang and Audrey Lang (Dayton: Morningside Bookshop, 1994), 1:231; Richard S. Thompson, "A Scrap of Gettysburg," Feb. 11, 1897, in *Military Essays and Recollections: Papers Read Before the Commandery of the State of Illinois, Military Order of the Loyal Legion of the United States* (Chicago: Dial Press, 1899), 3:106.
30. Taylor, *Four Years with General Lee,* 104; J. H. McNeilly, "War's Fascination," *Confederate Veteran,* Feb. 1916, 92; Charles T. Loehr, *War History of the Old First Virginia Infantry Regiment, Army of Northern Virginia* (Richmond: William Ellis Jones, 1884), 36; Robert A. Bright, "Pickett's Charge," *SHSP* 31 (1903): 234; Moore, "Heth's Division at Gettysburg," 392.
31. Dana to Charles Francis Adams, March 3, 1865, in Charles Francis Adams, *Richard Henry Dana: A Biography* (Boston: Houghton Mifflin, 1891), 2:274–75; Augustus Buell, "Story of a Cannoneer," *National Tribune,* Oct. 24, 1889; "Camp Gettysburg," *Philadelphia Inquirer,* Aug. 5, 1884.
32. REL to Davis, July 7, 1863, and "The Gettysburg Campaign," in *OR,* ser. 1, vol. 27, pt. 2, 299, 346; Samuel Penniman Bates, *The Battle of Gettysburg* (Philadelphia: T. H. Davis, 1875), 199; William Allan, "General Lee's Strength and Losses at Gettysburg," *SHSP* 1 (July 1877): 34; John D. Vautier, "The Loss at Gettysburg," *Southern Bivouac,* March 1886, 639. Joseph Glatthaar, in *General Lee's Army,* 283, puts Lee's total casualties at 23,500—with 4,700 killed, 13,000 wounded, and 5,800 missing.

Chapter Fifteen: I Consider My Presence Here Always Necessary

1. Samuel Pickens, diary entry for July 5, 1863, in *Voices from Company D: Diaries by the Greensboro Guards, Fifth Alabama Infantry Regiment, Army of Northern Virginia,* ed. G. Ward Hubbs (Athens: University of Georgia Press, 2003), 185; William Ralston Balch, *The Battle of Gettysburg: An Historical Account* (Harrisburg, Pa.: Lane S. Hart, 1885), 92; R. K. Beecham, "Adventures of an Iron Brigade Man," *National Tribune,* Oct. 16, 1902, 3; John W. Daniels, in Andrews, *Scraps of Paper,* 242; Rod Gragg, *Covered with Glory: The 26th North Carolina Infantry at the Battle of Gettysburg* (New York: HarperCollins, 2000), 222; REL to Davis, July 7, 1863, in *OR,* ser. 1, vol. 27, pt. 2, 299; *Campbell Brown's Civil War,* 388; "The Situation on the Potomac—the Battle Delayed by the Rains," *New York Herald,* July 14, 1863.
2. Aaron Levy, "Meade's Opportunity: It Came at Williamsport and He Let It Slip," *National Tribune,* Aug. 11, 1904, 3; Ranald Mackenzie to G. K. Warren, July 12, 1863, in *OR,* ser. 1, vol. 27, pt. 3, 669; Louis Leon, diary entries for July 14 and 20, 1863, in *Diary of a Tar Heel Confederate Soldier* (Charlotte, N.C.: Stone, 1913), 41–42; Scheibert, *Seven Months in the Rebel States,* 78; REL to Davis, July 14, 1863, in *Lee's Dispatches,* 106; Taylor, *General Lee,* 213, 218; Thomas J. Ryan and Richard R. Schaus, " 'Gen. Meade Showed No Disposition to Attack Us': Lee's Uncontested Escape Across the Potomac, July 14, 1863," *Gettysburg Magazine,* July 2020, 27–37.
3. "The Escape of Lee," *New York Times,* July 16, 1863; Meade to Margaretta Meade, June 9, 1864, in George G. Meade Jr., *Life and Letters of George Gordon Meade: Major-General United States Army* (New York: Charles Scribner's, 1913), 2:168; Rable, *Confederate Republic,* 199; J. R. Davis to Jefferson Davis, July 22, 1863, in *Papers of Jefferson Davis,* 9:296; "Aggressive War," *Charleston Mercury,* July 30, 1863; "Editor's Table," *Southern Literary Messenger* 37 (Sept. 1863): 572; Kean, diary entry for July 26, 1863, in *Inside the Confederate Government,*

85; REL to Jefferson Davis, July 4, 7, and 29, 1863, in *OR,* ser. 1, vol. 27, pt. 2, 298, 299, and pt. 3, 1049; "Letter from Major-General Henry Heth," 155.

4. REL to Davis, July 31, 1863, in *Lee's Dispatches,* 110; REL to Davis, Jan. 4, 1864, in *OR,* ser. 1, vol. 27, pt. 2, 321; *Campbell Brown's Civil War,* 248; Donald C. Pfanz, *Richard S. Ewell: A Soldier's Life* (Chapel Hill: University of North Carolina Press, 1998), 326; Glenn Tucker, *Lee and Longstreet at Gettysburg* (1968; Dayton: Press of Morningside Bookshop, 1982), 208–9. Lee's criticism of Stuart would have been harsher if Lee had allowed the version originally drafted by Charles Marshall to stand; Marshall claimed in 1887 that he had even urged Lee to have Stuart court-martialed. See Warren C. Robinson, *Jeb Stuart and the Confederate Defeat at Gettysburg* (Lincoln: University of Nebraska Press, 2007), 113–14; Eric Wittenberg and J. David Petruzzi, *Plenty of Blame to Go Around: Jeb Stuart's Controversial Ride to Gettysburg* (New York: Savas Beatie, 2006), 183.

5. REL to MCL and Margaret Stuart, July 26, 1863, in *WPREL,* 560, 561. (Lee was related to Margaret Stuart by one of those interminable skeins of cousinage that linked him back to his half brother, Black Horse Harry Lee, and Stratford; Lee's oldest daughter, Mary, lived with the Stuarts at Cedar Grove in King George County.) Frye, *2nd Virginia Infantry,* 55–56; Samuel Pickens, diary entry for Aug. 14, 1863, in *Voices from Company D,* 194; REL to Davis, July 27, 1863, in *OR,* ser. 1, vol. 27, pt. 3, 1041; Jones, diary entry for Aug. 1, 1863, in *Rebel War Clerk's Diary,* 2:1–2; Mark A. Weitz, *More Damning Than Slaughter: Desertion in the Confederate Army* (Lincoln: University of Nebraska Press, 2005), 155–56; Davis, "Proclamation," in *OR,* ser. 4, 2:687–88.

6. Davis to REL, July 28 and Aug. 11, 1863, in *Papers of Jefferson Davis,* 9:308–9, 337–38; REL to Davis, Aug. 8, 1863, in *OR,* ser. 1, vol. 51, pt. 2, 752–53; Margaret Sanborn, *Robert E. Lee: The Complete Man, 1861–1870* (Philadelphia: J. B. Lippincott, 1967), 143–44; Woodworth, *Davis and Lee at War,* 250–51; Gallagher, *Lee and His Army in Confederate History,* 114.

7. Glenn Tucker, *Chickamauga: Bloody Battle in the West* (1961; Dayton: Press of Morningside Bookshop, 1976), 87–88, 92; William Glenn Robertson, *River of Death: The Chickamauga Campaign,* vol. 1, *The Fall of Chattanooga* (Chapel Hill: University of North Carolina Press, 2018), 328, 356–57, 449; Longstreet to REL, Sept. 2 and 5, 1863, Seddon to W. H. C. Whiting, Sept. 8, 1863, and REL to Davis, Sept. 9, 1863, in *OR,* ser. 1, vol. 29, pt. 2, 693, 699, 703, 706; Connelly, *Autumn of Glory,* 152; Kean, diary entry for Sept. 5, 1863, in *Inside the Confederate Government,* 103; Furgurson, *Ashes of Glory,* 231–32; Longstreet, *From Manassas to Appomattox,* 436–37.

8. REL to EAL, Dec. 26, 1862, in *WPREL,* 382; Varon, *Armies of Deliverance,* 206.

9. "Proclamation of Jeff Davis," Dec. 23, 1862, in Frank Moore, *The Rebellion Record: A Diary of American Events* (New York: G. P. Putnam, 1863), 6:293; Seddon to Davis, Aug. 23, 1863, in *OR,* ser. 2, vol. 6, 194; Lincoln, "Order of Retaliation," July 30, 1863, in *Collected Works,* 6:357.

10. Glatthaar, *General Lee's Army,* 358; REL to McClellan, July 21, 1862, to MCL, April 26, 1863, and to MChL, July 27, 1863, in *WPREL,* 234, 440, 562; REL to "Dear Madam," Sept. 23, 1862, Special Collections, Leyburn Library; REL to James Seddon, Jan. 10, 1863, and to Henry W. Halleck, Jan. 10, 1863, in *OR,* ser. 1, 21:1085–86, and ser. 3, 3:11; Gallagher, *Lee and His Army in Confederate History,* 187; Varon, *Armies of Deliverance,* 206; Guild to S. P. Moore, May 22, 1863, in H. H. Cunningham, "The Confederate Medical Officer in the Field," *U.S. Armed Forces Medical Journal* 9 (Nov. 1958): 1588; A. G. Olmsted, "Joint Resolution," March 23, 1865, in *OR,* ser. 2, 8:426; Kent Masterson Brown, *Retreat from Gettysburg: Lee, Logistics, and the Pennsylvania Campaign* (Chapel Hill: University of North Carolina Press, 2005), 383.

11. "An Act for the Collection of Direct Taxes in Insurrectionary Districts Within the United States," June 7, 1862, in *The Statutes at Large, Treaties, and Proclamations of the United States of America from December 5, 1859, to March 3, 1863,* ed. G. P. Sanger (Boston: Little, Brown,

1863), 12:422; "Collection of Taxes in Insurrectionary States," *New York Times,* July 3, 1862; Horn, *Man Who Would Not Be Washington,* 205–6, 211; "Sales of Land for Unpaid Taxes in Insurrectionary Districts," *Philadelphia Legal Intelligencer,* Jan. 15, 1864, 24; Hanna, *Arlington House,* 81–87; Reidy, "'Coming from the Shadow of the Past,'" 409–11; Varon, *Armies of Deliverance,* 202–3; O'Harrow, *Quartermaster,* 207; Weigley, *Quartermaster General of the Union Army,* 296; Walter Stahr, *Stanton: Lincoln's War Secretary* (New York: Simon & Schuster, 2017), 351; Isabel Worrell Hall, "Sacred Arlington," *National Tribune,* May 21, 1903, 6.

12. REL to MCL, June 14, 1863, Lee Family Papers, VMHC; Coulling, *Lee Girls,* 114–15; Perry, *Lady of Arlington,* 225, 260–61; William Gilmore Breymer, "Williams, C.S.A.," *Harper's Monthly Magazine,* Sept. 1909, 508; Charles Bracelen Flood, *Lee: The Last Years* (Boston: Houghton Mifflin, 1981), 75; Sanborn, *Robert E. Lee: The Complete Man,* 140–41; *Campbell Brown's Civil War,* 184–85.

13. Eric Wittenberg and D. T. Davis, *Out Flew the Sabres: The Battle of Brandy Station, June 9, 1863* (El Dorado, Calif.: Savas Beatie, 2016), 71; Daughtry, *Gray Cavalier,* 141–44; Jones, diary entry for June 27, 1863, in *Rebel War Clerk's Diary,* 1:321; REL to MCL, June 11, 1863, and to Charlotte Wickham Lee, June 11, 1863, in *WPREL,* 511, 512; "Fitzhugh Lee's Capture," *National Tribune,* June 4, 1896, 3.

14. REL to MCL, July 7, 1863, in *WPREL,* 542; A. J. L. Fremantle, *Three Months in the Southern States: April–June, 1863* (London: William Blackwood, 1863), 294; "The Yankee Raid Near Richmond," *Richmond Dispatch,* June 27, 1863; "Capture of Gen. W. F. Lee, a Colonel, and Other Officers," *New-York Tribune,* June 29, 1863; "From Sandusky, Ohio—the Execution of Spies on Johnson's Island," *Cincinnati Inquirer,* May 16, 1863; "The Rebel Threats of Retaliation," *New York Times,* July 26, 1863; Carlos Emmor Godfrey, *Sketch of Major Henry Washington Sawyer: First Regiment, Cavalry, New Jersey* (Trenton: Adjutant-General's Office, 1907), 4–5; "General Orders No. 114," May 4, 1863, and Henry W. Halleck to William H. Ludlow, July 15, 1863, in *OR,* ser. 2, 5:566 and 6:118; Eric Wittenberg, *The Battle of Brandy Station: North America's Largest Cavalry Battle* (Charleston, S.C.: History Press, 2010), 203–4.

15. REL to GWCL, Aug. 7, 1863, LFDA/duPont Library; Daughtry, *Gray Cavalier,* 150, 158, 162; REL to Charlotte Wickham Lee, July 26, 1863, in Jones, *Life and Letters,* 277; Yates, *Perfect Gentleman,* 1:286; Chesnut, diary entry for March 18, 1864, in *Mary Chesnut's Civil War,* 589; REL to MCL, Dec. 27, 1863, in Robert E. Lee Jr., *Recollections and Letters,* 118.

16. Donald A. Hopkins, *Robert E. Lee in War and Peace: The Photographic History of a Confederate and American Icon* (El Dorado, Calif.: Savas Beatie, 2013), 32–35; REL to MCL, April 24, 1863, in *WPREL,* 440; Davis, *Crucible of Command,* 293. The Minnis and Cowell standing pose resembles a woodcut of Lee that appeared in the February 1863 issue of *The Illustrated London News,* drawn by Frank Vizetelly, and might have been modeled by Minnis and Cowell on that drawing.

17. REL to MCL, Feb. 23, March 2, Dec. 16 and 25, 1862, in *WPREL,* 118, 121, 364, 379; Moore, "Memorial Discourse on the Death of General Robert E. Lee," *Christian Advocate,* Nov. 5, 1870.

18. REL to MCL, Dec. 25, 1862, to MChL, Dec. 25, 1862, in *WPREL,* 380, 381; REL to WHFL, April 24, 1864, in Jones, *Life and Letters,* 298–99; REL to WHFL, April 28, 1864, in Daughtry, *Gray Cavalier,* 166–67; Cox, *Religious Life of Robert E. Lee,* 179–92; Stephen F. Cameron to REL, Feb. 15, 1864, Robert E. Lee Headquarters Papers, folder 29, VMHC. The reason for the unusually jeremiad-like language may be that Marshall drafted it. The original order, signed by Lee, is in the Jessie Ball duPont Library.

19. REL to MCL, Sept. 4, 1863, in *WPREL,* 595; Sanborn, *Robert E. Lee: The Complete Man,* 147–48; R. Ransom to Samuel Jones, Oct. 9, 1863, in *OR,* ser. 1, vol. 29, pt. 2, 781; REL to MCL, Nov. 5, 1863, in Robert E. Lee Jr., *Recollections and Letters,* 114.

20. Meade to Henry W. Halleck, July 28, 1863, Lincoln to Halleck, July 29, 1863, and Halleck to

Meade, July 31, 1863, in *OR,* ser. 1, vol. 27, pt. 1, 103, 105, 107–8; Rafuse, *Robert E. Lee and the Fall of the Confederacy,* 100–101, 105.

21. Seymour, *Reminiscences of a Louisiana Tiger,* 86, 89, 96; "Sketch of the 27th Regiment," in *Brief Sketches of the North Carolina State Troops in the War Between the States,* ed. James S. Birdsong (Raleigh, N.C.: Josephus Daniels, 1894), 80; REL to MCL, Oct. 19, 1863, in *WPREL,* 610; Edmondston, diary entry for Oct. 24, 1863, in *Journal of a Secesh Lady,* 481; A. P. Hill to Henry Heth, Jan. 13, 1864, in *OR,* ser. 1, vol. 51, pt. 2, 811; Gallagher, *Lee and His Army in Confederate History,* 196; Jeffrey Hunt, *Meade and Lee at Bristoe Station: The Problems of Command and Strategy After Gettysburg, from Brandy Station to the Buckland Races, August 1 to October 21, 1863* (El Dorado, Calif.: Savas Beatie, 2019), 375; Long, *Memoirs of Robert E. Lee,* 311; REL to MCL, Dec. 4, 1863, in *WPREL,* 631; Robertson, *General A. P. Hill,* 272.

22. Meade to Margaretta Meade, Dec. 2, 1863, in *Life and Letters of George Gordon Meade,* 2:156; Charles Minor Blackford, Oct. 11, 1863, in *Letters from Lee's Army,* 219; REL to Leonidas Polk, Oct. 26, 1863, and Jefferson Davis to REL, Dec. 5, 1863, in *OR,* ser. 1, vol. 30, pt. 2, 69, and vol. 31, pt. 3, 785; REL to MCL, Dec. 4, 1863, and to Stuart, Dec. 9, 1863, in *WPREL,* 632, 642; Sanborn, *Robert E. Lee: The Complete Man,* 156; Rafuse, *Robert E. Lee and the Fall of the Confederacy,* 128; Davis, *Jefferson Davis,* 528–30; Rable, *Confederate Republic,* 237–38; Furgurson, *Ashes of Glory,* 235; Woodworth, *Davis and Lee at War,* 262–63.

23. Symonds, *Joseph E. Johnston,* 250–56; Richard M. McMurry, *Atlanta 1864: Last Chance for the Confederacy* (Lincoln: University of Nebraska Press, 2000), 37–38; Johnston, *Narrative of Military Operations,* 272; Larry J. Daniel, *Soldiering in the Army of Tennessee: A Portrait of Life in a Confederate Army* (Chapel Hill: University of North Carolina Press, 1991), 141; Larry J. Daniel, *Conquered: Why the Army of Tennessee Failed* (Chapel Hill: University of North Carolina Press, 2019), 250; Stanley F. Horn, *The Army of Tennessee* (Norman: University of Oklahoma Press, 1953), 312; John Witherspoon Du Bose, *General Joseph Wheeler and the Army of Tennessee* (New York: Neale, 1912), 274; Frye, *2nd Virginia Infantry,* 60; Collins, *Army of Northern Virginia,* 171; Alfred C. Young, *Lee's Army During the Overland Campaign: A Numerical Study* (Baton Rouge: Louisiana State University Press, 2013), 229–30; Charles Minor Blackford, Jan. 7, 1864, in *Letters from Lee's Army,* 231; Robert Tutwiler, in J. Tracy Power, *Lee's Miserables: Life in the Army of Northern Virginia from the Wilderness to Appomattox* (Chapel Hill: University of North Carolina Press, 1998), 2, 11–12; Mac Wyckoff, *A History of the 3rd South Carolina Regiment: Lee's Reliables* (Wilmington, N.C.: Broadfoot, 2008), 236; Glatthaar, *General Lee's Army,* 363.

24. REL to Cary Robinson, Dec. 8, 1863, Robinson Family Papers, VMHC; REL to Taylor, Dec. 12, 1863, duPont Library; REL to Northrop, Jan. 5, 1864, to Seddon, Jan. 22, 1864, to Davis, Jan. 20 and 27, 1864, in *WPREL,* 647, 656, 659, 662; REL to CCL, Feb. 20, 1864, Special Collections, Leyburn Library; REL to Robert E. Lee Jr., Jan. 17, 1864, in Jones, *Life and Letters,* 300; J. F. J. Caldwell, *The History of a Brigade of South Carolinians: Known First as "Gregg's"* (Philadelphia: King & Baird, 1866), 113; William Wallace Bennett, *A Narrative of the Great Revival Which Prevailed in the Southern Armies During the Late Civil War Between the States of the Federal Union* (Philadelphia: Claxton, Remsen & Haffelfinger, 1877), 362; Taylor to Elizabeth Saunders, Dec. 5, 1863, in *Lee's Adjutant,* 94; Taylor, *Four Years with General Lee,* 121.

25. Bruce M. Venter, *Kill Jeff Davis: The Union Raid on Richmond, 1864* (Norman: University of Oklahoma Press, 2013), 92, 231, 241–42; Fitzhugh Lee to Samuel Cooper, March 4, 1864, in *OR,* ser. 1, 3:217.

26. "The Late Raid," *Richmond Enquirer,* March 8, 1864; "Dahlgren," *Richmond Dispatch,* March 11, 1864; "The Dahlgren Raid," *Southern Confederacy,* March 10, 1864; Furgurson, *Ashes of Glory,* 254–55; Ruffin, diary entry for March 3, 1864, in *Diary of Edmund Ruffin,* 3:355; Jones, diary entry for Feb. 29, 1864, in *Rebel War Clerk's Diary,* 2:143; Taylor, *General*

Lee, 228–29; Taylor, *Four Years with General Lee,* 122–23; Seddon to REL, March 5, 1864, in *OR,* ser. 1, 33:218; REL to Seddon, March 6, 1864, in *WPREL,* 678; Stephen Sears, "Raid on Richmond," in *Controversies and Commanders,* 243–46; REL to Meade, April 1, 1864, Kilpatrick to Seth Williams, April 16, 1864, and Meade to REL, April 17, 1864, in *OR,* ser. 1, 33:178, 180; REL to WHFL, April 24, 1864, in Jones, *Life and Letters,* 299.

27. Yates, *Perfect Gentleman,* 1:227–28, 232; Robins, "Mrs. Lee During the War," 328; Perry, *Lady of Arlington,* 271–72; Chesnut, diary entry for Feb. 26, 1864, in *Mary Chesnut's Civil War,* 573; MacDonald, *Mrs. Robert E. Lee,* 181; Jones, diary entries for Feb. 26 and March 14, 1863, in *Rebel War Clerk's Diary,* 2:142, 152; Coulling, *Lee Girls,* 134–36; REL to MCL, Jan. 15 and 24, Feb. 6, and March 24, 1864, in *WPREL,* 652, 661, 668, 680; Taylor to Sister, Nov. 14, 1863, in *Lee's Adjutant,* 83; REL to EAL, May 4, 1864, Lee Family Papers, VMHC; REL to Margaret Stuart, Dec. 25, 1863, in Jones, *Life and Letters,* 296.

Chapter Sixteen: We Must Destroy This Army of Grant's

1. REL to Davis, Feb. 3 and April 15, 1864, in *OR,* ser. 1, vol. 32, pt. 2, 687, and 33:1283; Davis, *Jefferson Davis,* 550; REL to Davis, Feb. 18, 1864, in *WPREL,* 675; Rafuse, *Robert E. Lee and the Fall of the Confederacy,* 131.
2. Lincoln to James C. Conkling, Aug. 26, 1863, and "Proclamation of Amnesty and Reconstruction," Dec. 8, 1863, in *Collected Works,* 6:410 and 7:53–56; "The Next Presidency," *New York Times,* Jan. 15, 1864; Strong, diary entry for March 18, 1864, in *Diary of the Civil War, 1860–1865,* 416.
3. REL to Davis, March 25, 1864, and to Longstreet, March 28, 1864, in *WPREL,* 682–83, 684; Grant to E. M. Stanton, July 22, 1865, Lincoln to H. W. Halleck, Sept. 19, 1863, and Grant to Meade, April 9, 1864, in *OR,* ser. 1, vol. 29, pt. 2, 208, 33:828, and 36:22; Mark Grimsley, *And Keep Moving On: The Virginia Campaign, May–June 1864* (Lincoln: University of Nebraska Press, 2002), 4.
4. REL to Davis, April 5, 1864, and to Bragg, April 7, 1864, in *WPREL,* 690, 692; REL to Longstreet, April 20, 1864, Special Collections, Leyburn Library; Venable, "General Lee in the Wilderness Campaign," 240–41; Long, *Memoirs of Robert E. Lee,* 327; William Lawrence Royall, *Some Reminiscences* (New York: Neale, 1909), 28.
5. Morris Schaff, *The Battle of the Wilderness* (Boston: Houghton Mifflin, 1910), 249; Gallagher, *Lee and His Army in Confederate History,* 196; Noah Andre Trudeau, *Bloody Roads South: The Wilderness to Cold Harbor, May–June 1864* (Boston: Little, Brown, 1989), 76, 89; Clifford Dowdey, *Lee's Last Campaign: The Story of Lee and His Men Against Grant* (New York: Bonanza Books, 1960), 128, 153–54; Taylor, *General Lee,* 235; Taylor, *Four Years with General Lee,* 128; Long, *Memoirs of Robert E. Lee,* 330–31; "Address of Private Leigh Robinson," Nov. 1, 1877, in Jones, *Army of Northern Virginia Memorial Volume,* 229–30; Robert K. Krick, "'Lee to the Rear,' the Texans Cried," in *The Wilderness Campaign,* ed. Gary W. Gallagher (Chapel Hill: University of North Carolina Press, 2007), 173–79; Grimsley, *And Keep Moving On,* 49; Power, *Lee's Miserables,* 44; Gordon C. Rhea, *The Battle of the Wilderness, May 5–6, 1864* (Baton Rouge: Louisiana State University Press, 1994), 304.
6. Casdorph, *Confederate General R. S. Ewell,* 290; Rhea, *Battle of the Wilderness,* 428–29; Taylor, *General Lee,* 236; Elihu Washburne, diary entry for May 6, 1864, in Elihu Washburne Diaries, Manuscripts and Archives, Sterling Library, Yale University; Sorrel, *Recollections of a Confederate Staff Officer,* 233; Grimsley, *And Keep Moving On,* 53.
7. Stuart to Walter Taylor, May 7, 1864, in *OR,* ser. 1, vol. 36, pt. 2, 970; REL to Seddon, May 8, 1864, in *WPREL,* 724; Sorrel, *Recollections of a Confederate Staff Officer,* 238–39; George S. Bernard, diary entry for May 10, 1864, in *Civil War Talks,* 221; Gordon C. Rhea, *The Battles*

for Spotsylvania Court House and the Road to Yellow Tavern, May 7–12, 1864 (Baton Rouge: Louisiana State University Press, 1997), 28, 43, 77–78.

8. Venable, "General Lee in the Wilderness Campaign," 242; "Address of Colonel C. S. Venable," Oct. 30, 1873, in Jones, *Army of Northern Virginia Memorial Volume,* 52–53, 56–58; Morrison, "Memoirs of Henry Heth," 313; *Campbell Brown's Civil War,* 253; WHFL to REL, May 11, 1864, in *OR,* ser. 1, vol. 51, pt. 2, 916–17; Earl J. Hess, *Trench Warfare Under Grant and Lee* (Chapel Hill: University of North Carolina Press, 2007), 58–59; Rafuse, *Robert E. Lee and the Fall of the Confederacy,* 151; William W. Old, "Trees Whittled Down at Horseshoe," *SHSP* 33 (1905): 24; William W. Old, "General Funkhouser's Letter," July 6, 1906, *SHSP* 34 (1906): 220–21; Seymour, *Reminiscences of a Louisiana Tiger,* 124–25; Rhea, *Battles for Spotsylvania Court House,* 171, 226, 249–50, 255–56, 269–70, 311, 406; Taylor, *General Lee,* 240, 242; Grimsley, *And Keep Moving On,* 86–87; Dowdey, *Lee's Last Campaign,* 199–216; Trudeau, *Bloody Roads South,* 176–77.
9. Cooke, *Life of Gen. Lee,* 66; Robert E. Lee Jr., *Recollections and Letters,* 125; B. B. Vaughan, "A Trooper's Reminiscences: Wilderness to Yellow Tavern," in *Civil War Talks,* 203; "Special Orders No. 126," May 14, 1864, in *OR,* ser. 1, vol. 36, pt. 2, 1001; George Taylor Lee, "Reminiscences of General Robert E. Lee, 1865–68," *South Atlantic Quarterly* 26 (July 1927): 249–50.
10. Grant, *Memoirs,* 2:234; William W. Hassler, *A. P. Hill: Lee's Forgotten General* (1957; Chapel Hill: University of North Carolina Press, 1962), 199; Casdorph, *Confederate General R. S. Ewell,* 307, 310; Gallagher, *Lee and His Army in Confederate History,* 206–7; Rhea, *Battles for Spotsylvania Court House,* 11, 76; REL to Davis, June 15, 1864, in *Lee's Dispatches,* 243.
11. Venable, "General Lee in the Wilderness Campaign," 244; "Address of Colonel C. S. Venable," Oct. 30, 1873, in Jones, *Army of Northern Virginia Memorial Volume,* 61; Gordon C. Rhea, *To the North Anna River: Grant and Lee, May 13–25, 1864* (Baton Rouge: Louisiana State University Press, 2000), 27–28, 156–57, 265, 319; Taylor to Elizabeth Saunders, May 30, 1864, in *Lee's Adjutant,* 164; Robertson, *General A. P. Hill,* 276; Jones, diary entry for May 30, 1864, in *Rebel War Clerk's Diary,* 2:199; Taylor, *General Lee,* 249; Ruffin, diary entry for June 2, 1864, in *Diary of Edmund Ruffin,* 3:448; Booth, *Maryland Boy in Lee's Army,* 109–10; REL to A. P. Hill, June 1864, in *OR,* ser. 1, vol. 40, pt. 2, 702–3.
12. Glatthaar, *General Lee's Army,* 359; Charles H. Porter, "The Battle of Cold Harbor," Dec. 12, 1881, and John Codman Ropes, "Grant's Campaign in Virginia in 1864," May 19, 1884, in *The Wilderness Campaign, May–June 1864; Papers of the Military Historical Society of Massachusetts* (1905; Wilmington, N.C.: Broadfoot, 1989), 4:372, 373; Rhea, *To the North Anna River,* 21, 322–23, 344–45, 353; Sanborn, *Robert E. Lee: The Complete Man,* 184; Collins, *Army of Northern Virginia,* 199, 340–41; Grant to H. W. Halleck, May 26, 1864, in *OR,* ser. 1, vol. 36, pt. 3, 206; Horace Porter, *Campaigning with Grant* (New York: Century, 1897), 172.
13. St. Clair Mulholland, *The Story of the 116th Regiment, Pennsylvania Volunteers in the War of the Rebellion* (Philadelphia: F. McManus, 1903), 255; Porter, *Campaigning with Grant,* 173; Asa W. Bartlett, *History of the Twelfth Regiment, New Hampshire Volunteers in the War of the Rebellion* (Concord, N.H.: Ira C. Evans, 1897), 203; Gordon C. Rhea, *Cold Harbor: Grant and Lee, May 26–June 3, 1864* (Baton Rouge: Louisiana State University Press, 2002), 320–23.
14. E. M. Law, "From the Wilderness to Cold Harbor," in Buel and Johnson, *Battles and Leaders of the Civil War,* 4:141; William C. Oates, *The War Between the Union and the Confederacy, and Its Lost Opportunities* (New York: Neale, 1905), 366–67; "Report of Maj. Gen. George G. Meade, U.S. Army," Nov. 1, 1864, and "Reports of Maj. Gen. Winfield S. Hancock, U.S. Army," Sept. 21, 1865, in *OR,* ser. 1, vol. 36, pt. 1, 195, 345; Rhea, *Cold Harbor,* 358–62.
15. Ruffin, diary entry for June 5, 1864, in *Diary of Edmund Ruffin,* 3:452–53; Blackford to Susan Blackford, May 30, 1864, in *Letters from Lee's Army,* 249; Porter, *Campaigning with Grant,* 179; "Gen. Lee and the Army," *Richmond Dispatch,* June 1, 1864; Varon, *Armies of Deliverance,* 336.

16. Charles A. Dana, *Recollections of the Civil War: With the Leaders at Washington and in the Sixties* (New York: D. Appleton, 1913), 214–15; Robertson, *General A. P. Hill,* 289; Grant, *Memoirs,* 2:570; Gordon C. Rhea, *On to Petersburg: Grant and Lee, June 4–15, 1864* (Baton Rouge: Louisiana State University Press, 2017), 4–5, 62–63.
17. REL to Richard Heron Anderson, June 4, 1864, and to Braxton Bragg, June 9, 1864, in *WPREL,* 765, 770; REL to Davis, June 6, 1864, in *Lee's Dispatches,* 218, 222; Trudeau, *Bloody Roads South,* 301; Rhea, *On to Petersburg,* 150; Ayers, *Thin Light of Freedom,* 157–68; *Richmond Enquirer,* June 17, 1864; REL to Davis, June 11, 1864, in *OR,* ser. 1, vol. 51, pt. 2, 1003; Rhea, *On to Petersburg,* 52, 80–81, 187.
18. Rhea, *On to Petersburg,* 172, 202, 208–9, 237–41, 253; Thomas J. Howe, *The Petersburg Campaign: Wasted Valor, June 15–16, 1864* (Lynchburg, Va.: H. E. Howard, 1988), 16; A. Wilson Greene, *A Campaign of Giants: The Battle for Petersburg* (Chapel Hill: University of North Carolina Press, 2018), 1:64; REL to Davis, June 14, 1864, in *WPREL,* 777; P. G. T. Beauregard, "The Battle of Petersburg," in Cozzens, *Battles and Leaders of the Civil War,* 6:416; Roman, *Military Operations of General Pierre Beauregard,* 2:477.
19. Earl J. Hess, *In the Trenches at Petersburg: Field Fortifications and Confederate Defeat* (Chapel Hill: University of North Carolina Press, 2009), 9–11; Rhea, *On to Petersburg,* 146.
20. Howe, *Petersburg Campaign: Wasted Valor,* 27; REL to Davis, June 18, 1864, in *Lee's Dispatches,* 249; Caldwell, *History of a Brigade of South Carolinians,* 162; Henri Garidel, diary entry for Sept. 30, 1864, in *Exile in Richmond: The Confederate Journal of Henri Garidel,* ed. M. B. Chesson and L. J. Roberts (Charlottesville: University of Virginia Press, 2001), 221; James Morris Morgan, *Recollections of a Rebel Reefer* (Boston: Houghton Mifflin, 1917), 210–11; Furgurson, *Ashes of Glory,* 279–80; Jones, diary entry for Oct. 1, 1864, in *Rebel War Clerk's Diary,* 2:270; "Address of Captain W. Gordon McCabe," Nov. 2, 1876, in Jones, *Army of Northern Virginia Memorial Volume,* 141.
21. "The Future," *Richmond Enquirer,* Feb. 9, 1864; Long, *Memoirs of Robert E. Lee,* 383; Michael A. Cavanaugh and William Marvel, *The Petersburg Campaign: The Battle of the Crater, "The Horrid Pit," June 25–August 6, 1864* (Lynchburg, Va.: H. E. Howard, 1989), 12; Joseph W. Eggleston, "Artillery Experiences at Petersburg and Elsewhere," Jan. 3, 1895, in *Civil War Talks,* 357–58; Grant to H. W. Halleck, Aug. 1, 1864, in *OR,* ser. 1, vol. 40, pt. 1, 17–18; Rhea, *On to Petersburg,* 185–88; "Address of Captain W. Gordon McCabe," 150, 158–59; Richard Slotkin, *No Quarter: The Battle of the Crater, 1864* (New York: Random House, 2009), 213–14, 318; Earl J. Hess, *Into the Crater: The Mine Attack at Petersburg* (Columbia: University of South Carolina Press, 2010), 114–15, 196, 200.
22. Thomas J. Ward, "Enemy Combatants: Black Soldiers in Confederate Prisons," *Army History* (Winter 2011): 37; "Circular," Oct. 15, 1864, Grant to REL, Oct. 2, 1864, and REL to Grant, Oct. 3, 1864, in *OR,* ser. 2, 7:909, 914, 8:27; Jefferson Davis, "Andersonville and Other War-Prisons," *Belford's Magazine,* Feb. 1890, 344–45. Davis would have preferred that any free blacks in blue uniforms simply be executed outright, but Lincoln's promise of tit-for-tat retaliation cooled that threat. That still left large numbers of black prisoners in a risky and unpleasant limbo. The Confederate government refused to exchange them under the terms of the usual prisoner-of-war exchanges that had prevailed up to this point. That would have been to concede that they were indeed soldiers, and worse still, exchanging them for Confederate prisoners would have implied precisely the sort of equality, man for man, that the Confederacy was dedicated to denying. The Lincoln administration responded by suspending prisoner-of-war exchanges, only to have transit stockades like Camp Sumter at Andersonville, Georgia, and Camp Rathbun at Elmira, New York, silted up with prisoners that the camps had no way of supporting.
23. Raymond, in Burlingame, *Abraham Lincoln: A Life,* 2:669; Schuyler Hamilton, Aug. 11, 1864, in *Recollected Words of Abraham Lincoln,* ed. Don Fehrenbacher and Virginia Fehrenbacher

(Stanford, Calif.: Stanford University Press, 1996), 196–97; Francis A. Walker, *General Hancock* (New York: D. Appleton, 1895), 228–29.

24. "To the Democratic Nomination Committee," Sept. 4, 1864, in *Civil War Papers of George B. McClellan,* 590; Stephen W. Sears, "McClellan and the Peace Plank of 1864: A Reappraisal," *Civil War History* 36 (March 1990): 63–64; "Democratic National Platform, 1864," in *The Political History of the United States of America During the Period of Reconstruction,* ed. Edward McPherson (Washington, D.C.: Solomons & Chapman, 1875), 118; Longstreet to A. R. Lawton, March 5, 1864, in *OR,* ser. 1, vol. 32, pt. 3, 588; Taylor, *General Lee,* 262–63; Taylor to Elizabeth Saunders, Aug. 28, 1864, in *Lee's Adjutant,* 186; Jones, diary entry for Aug. 21, 1864, in *Rebel War Clerk's Diary,* 2:243–44.
25. Davis, *Jefferson Davis,* 561; Rable, *Confederate Republic,* 264; REL to Davis, July 12, 1864, in *WPREL,* 821; REL to MCL, Nov. 12, 1864, Lee Family Papers, VMHC.

Chapter Seventeen: Just as I Have Expected It Would End from the First

1. Morgan, *Recollections of a Rebel Reefer,* 215; Ruffin, diary entry for Dec. 10, 1864, in *Diary of Edmund Ruffin,* 3:674; "Fresh in the River," *Richmond Dispatch,* Jan. 11, 1865; Jones, diary entry for Dec. 24, 1864, and Feb. 15/16, 1865, in *Rebel War Clerk's Diary,* 2:326, 382–83; "Lee and Longstreet," *Liverpool Mercury,* Nov. 17, 1864.
2. REL to MCL, Nov. 12, 16, and 25, 1864, Lee Family Papers, VMHC; Thomas, *Robert E. Lee,* 338; Taylor, *General Lee,* 253, 257, 261, 383; Taylor, *Four Years with General Lee,* 141; Robertson, *General A. P. Hill,* 291–92; Edmund Jennings Lee, *Lee of Virginia,* 126; Perry, *Lady of Arlington,* 277; Hopkins, *Robert E. Lee in War and Peace,* 55–59. On Lee's relations to the Shippens, see REL to Martha Williams, Dec. 1, 1866, in *"To Markie,"* 72.
3. Thomas, *Confederate Nation,* 284; Jones, diary entries for Jan. 13, 14, 18, and 22, 1865, in *Rebel War Clerk's Diary,* 2:348, 354, 357; Kean, diary entry for Feb. 10, 1865, in *Inside the Confederate Government,* 200; REL to Davis, Dec. 14, 1864, in *Lee's Dispatches,* 307–8; REL to Seddon, Jan. 11, 1865, and Circular, Jan. 25, 1865, in *OR,* ser. 1, vol. 46, pt. 2, 1035, 1134.
4. Taylor, *General Lee,* 265; Joseph F. Shaner, in Hess, *Trench Warfare Under Grant and Lee,* 200; Hess, *In the Trenches at Petersburg,* 227; Marvel, *Place Called Appomattox,* 192–93; Blackford to Susan Blackford, July 17, 1864, in *Letters from Lee's Army,* 267; REL to Seddon, Jan. 27, 1865, General Orders No. 8, March 27, 1865, and to Samuel Cooper, Feb. 25, 1865, in *OR,* ser. 1, vol. 46, pt. 2, 1143, 1258, and vol. 46, pt. 3, 1357; Power, *Lee's Miserables,* 260; "General Lee's Last Appeal," *Richmond Dispatch,* Feb. 15, 1865; Raphael Semmes, *Memoirs of Service Afloat: During the War Between the States* (Baltimore: Kelly, Piet, 1869), 801; Samuel Pickens, diary entry for Jan. 9, 1865, in *Voices from Company D,* 342; Glatthaar, *General Lee's Army,* 408–20.
5. Sorrel, *Recollections of a Confederate Staff Officer,* 262; "Lee and Longstreet," *Liverpool Mercury,* Nov. 17, 1864; Hess, *In the Trenches at Petersburg,* 211, 237; Jones, diary entry for Oct. 27, 1864, in *Rebel War Clerk's Diary,* 288; REL to Davis, Nov. 2, 1864, in *Lee's Dispatches,* 306; Maury, *Recollections of a Virginian,* 237–38; George Taylor Lee, "Reminiscences of General Robert E. Lee, 1865–68," 237; Yates, *Perfect Gentleman,* 1:325; Sanborn, *Robert E. Lee: The Complete Man,* 209.
6. Ruffin, diary entry for Jan. 15, 1865, in *Diary of Edmund Ruffin,* 3:718–19.
7. Andrew Magrath to Davis, Dec. 23, 1864, in *OR,* ser. 1, 44:986; Hardee to Davis, Jan. 29, 1865, in *Papers of Jefferson Davis,* 11:359; Jones, diary entry for Jan. 2, 1865, in *Rebel War Clerk's Diary,* 2:338.
8. Jones, diary entries for Dec. 25, 1864, and Jan. 8 and 19, 1865, in *Rebel War Clerk's Diary,* 2:331, 344, 354–55; Taylor, *Four Years with General Lee,* 143; Davis, *Jefferson Davis,* 582–83;

Woodworth, *Davis and Lee at War,* 310–11; REL to Samuel Cooper, Feb. 4, 1865, to Davis, Feb. 9, 1865, and Johnston to REL, March 23, 1865, in *OR,* ser. 1, vol. 46, pt. 2, 1199, vol. 51, pt. 2, 1083, and vol. 47, pt. 3, 1055; Rable, *Confederate Republic,* 286; Gallagher, *Confederate War,* 87–89; Charles Venable to Walter Taylor, March 29, 1878, in Walter Herron Taylor Papers, box 8, M2009.425, Stratford Hall; William C. Davis, "The Confederate Peacemakers of 1865," in *Petersburg to Appomattox: The End of the War in Virginia,* ed. Caroline Janney (Chapel Hill: University of North Carolina Press, 2018), 148.

9. REL to Davis, Sept. 2, 1864, in *OR,* ser. 1, vol. 52, pt. 2, 1228; Bruce Levine, *Confederate Emancipation: Southern Plans to Free and Arm Slaves During the Civil War* (New York: Oxford University Press, 2005), 183; "Letter from General Lee on the Negro Enlistment," *Richmond Enquirer,* Feb. 24, 1865; Philip D. Dillard, *Jefferson Davis's Final Campaign: Confederate Nationalism and the Fight to Arm the Slaves* (Macon, Ga.: Mercer University Press, 2017), 192–96.

10. Jones, diary entries for Sept. 23, 1864, and Jan. 25, 1865, in *Rebel War Clerk's Diary,* 2:264, 360; "General Robert E. Lee—Federalism," *Charleston Mercury,* Feb. 3, 1865; "Latest Northern News," *Charleston Mercury,* March 27, 1865; Cobb to James A. Seddon, Jan. 8, 1865, in *OR,* ser. 4, 3:1009; Nolan, *Lee Considered,* 20–21; Ruffin, diary entry for Dec. 27, 1864, in *Diary of Edmund Ruffin,* 3:692; Edmondston, diary entries for Dec. 20, 1864, and Jan. 29, 1865, in *Journal of a Secesh Lady,* 650–51, 660.

11. REL to Hunter, Jan. 11, 1865, in "General Lee's Views on Enlisting the Negroes," *Century Magazine,* Aug. 1888, 599–601; Robert F. Durden, *The Gray and the Black: The Confederate Debate on Emancipation* (Baton Rouge: Louisiana State University Press, 1972), 207; Snow, *Lee and His Generals,* 149.

12. Kean, diary entry for Jan. 24, 1865, in *Inside the Confederate Government,* 492; Benjamin to REL, Feb. 11, 1865, and O. Latrobe to James Kershaw, Feb. 16, 1865, in *OR,* ser. 1, vol. 46, pt. 2, 1229, 1236; Durden, *The Gray and the Black,* 217, 223; Eli N. Evans, *Judah P. Benjamin: The Jewish Confederate* (New York: Free Press, 1988), 286; *Richmond Enquirer,* Feb. 21, 1865; REL to Barksdale, Feb. 18, 1865, in James Dabney McCabe, *Life and Campaigns of General Robert E. Lee* (Philadelphia: National, 1866), 574; Levine, *Confederate Emancipation,* 114–15, 122; Jones, diary entry for Feb. 10, 1865, in *Rebel War Clerk's Diary,* 2:372; REL to Davis, March 10, 1865, in *WPREL,* 914; REL to Davis, March 24, 1865, in *OR,* ser. 1, vol. 46, pt. 3, 1339; REL to Breckinridge, March 27, 1865, in Jones, *Life and Letters,* 362; Casdorph, *Confederate General R. S. Ewell,* 327; Rable, *Confederate Republic,* 295; Thomas, *Confederate Nation,* 290–96; Edward Spencer, "Confederate Negro Enlistments," in McClure, *Annals of the War,* 551–552.

13. Jones, diary entry for Jan. 12, 1865, in *Rebel War Clerk's Diary,* 2:347–48; Samuel Pickens, diary entry for Jan. 18, 1865, in *Voices from Company D,* 346; "Conversation with Francis Preston Blair," Jan. 12, 1865, in *Papers of Jefferson Davis,* 11:319; James B. Conroy, *Our One Common Country: Abraham Lincoln and the Hampton Roads Peace Conference of 1865* (Guilford, Conn.: Lyons Press, 2014), 89, 130–32, 195.

14. Davis, "Message to Congress" and "African Church Speech," Feb. 6, 1865, in *Papers of Jefferson Davis,* 11:377–78, 383; Conroy, *Our One Common Country,* 216–19, 233–34; Stephens, diary entry for June 21, 1865, in *Recollections of Alexander H. Stephens: His Diary Kept When a Prisoner at Fort Warren,* ed. M. L. Avary (1910; Baton Rouge: Louisiana State University Press, 1998), 241; Jones, diary entry for March 15, 1865, in *Rebel War Clerk's Diary,* 2:407; Campbell to Breckinridge, March 5, 1865, in *Reminiscences and Documents Relating to the Civil War During the Year 1865* (Baltimore: John Murphy, 1887), 29, 31; Fitzhugh Lee, "The Failure of the Hampton Conference," in Cozzens, *Battles and Leaders,* 6:503; "The Peace Commission—Hon. R. M. T. Hunter's Reply to President Davis' Letter," *SHSP* 4 (Dec. 1877): 308–9; William C. Davis, "Lee and Jefferson Davis," in *Lee the Soldier,* 302.

15. St. John Liddell, "Liddell's Record of the Civil War," *Southern Bivouac,* Dec. 1885, 413; Gordon, *Reminiscences of the Civil War,* 386–90; William Mahone, "What I Saw and Heard During the Closing Days of the Army of Northern Virginia," July 25, 1895, in Newsome, *Civil War Talks,* 438; Jones, *Personal Reminiscences,* 223–24; Mark Grimsley, "Learning to Say 'Enough,'" in *The Collapse of the Confederacy,* ed. Mark Grimsley and Brooks D. Simpson (Lincoln: University of Nebraska Press, 2001), 5–51; Furgurson, *Ashes of Glory,* 300; Davis, *Crucible of Command,* 442–47; REL to Breckinridge, March 9, 1865, in *WPREL,* 912–13.
16. Longstreet, *From Manassas to Appomattox,* 583–87, 647–49; Perry D. Jamieson, *Spring 1865: The Closing Campaigns of the Civil War* (Lincoln: University of Nebraska Press, 2015), 290–91; Brooks D. Simpson, *Let Us Have Peace: Ulysses S. Grant and the Politics of War and Reconstruction, 1861–1868* (Chapel Hill: University of North Carolina Press, 1991), 75–76; Bernarr Cresap, *Appomattox Commander: The Story of General E. O. C. Ord* (San Diego: A. S. Barnes, 1981), 164–66; "Correspondence of Gens. Lee and Grant, on a Military Convention," in *The Political History of the United States of America During the Great Rebellion,* ed. Edward McPherson (Washington, D.C.: James J. Chapman, 1882), 597–98; Woodworth, *Davis and Lee at War,* 314–15.
17. Davis to REL, Feb. 28, 1865, in *Papers of Jefferson Davis,* 11:427–28; REL to Davis, in *Lee's Dispatches,* 371–72; Kean, diary entry for March 23, 1865, in *Inside the Confederate Government,* 203; "The Peace Conference—Military Convention—Interview Between Generals Longstreet and Ord," *Richmond Dispatch,* March 15, 1865; Davis, *Jefferson Davis,* 592; Furgurson, *Ashes of Glory,* 305.
18. REL to Seddon, Dec. 11, 1864, and to Breckinridge, Feb. 21, 1865, in *OR,* ser. 1, vol. 52, pt. 3, 1267, and vol. 56, pt. 2, 1244; Steven E. Sodergren, *The Army of the Potomac in the Overland and Petersburg Campaigns: Union Soldiers and Trench Warfare, 1864–1865* (Baton Rouge: Louisiana State University Press, 2017), 152–57, 163–65; Marvel, *Place Called Appomattox,* 192–93; REL to Davis, Jan. 29, 1865, in *Lee's Dispatches,* 330; A. Wilson Greene, *The Final Battles of the Petersburg Campaign: Breaking the Backbone of the Rebellion* (Knoxville: University of Tennessee Press, 2008), 106; REL to MCL, Feb. 21, 1865, in *WPREL,* 907; Jones, diary entry for March 4, 1865, in *Rebel War Clerk's Diary,* 2:397–98; Coulling, *Lee Girls,* 141–42.
19. REL to Davis, Feb. 23, 1865, in *Papers of Jefferson Davis,* 11:421; REL to EAL, March 28, 1865, in *WPREL,* 919; REL to Davis, March 26, 1865, in *Lee's Dispatches,* 343–44; Hess, *In the Trenches at Petersburg,* 246; William Marvel, *Lee's Last Retreat: The Flight to Appomattox* (Chapel Hill: University of North Carolina Press, 2002), 7.
20. REL to Breckinridge, April 2, 1865, in *WPREL,* 924–25; Jones, diary entry for April 1, 1865, in *Rebel War Clerk's Diary,* 2:421; Robertson, *General A. P. Hill,* 314–15, 318; Alexander, *Fighting for the Confederacy,* 507, 511; Greene, *Final Battles of the Petersburg Campaign,* 188, 196, 225, 261, 278; J. P. Williamson, "Cockade City's Surrender, Delivered to the Federals," May 22, 1894, in Newsome, *Civil War Talks,* 408–9; Taylor, *General Lee,* 272–73; Kean, diary entry for June 1, 1865, in *Inside the Confederate Government,* 39; Chris M. Calkins, *The Appomattox Campaign, March 29–April 9, 1865* (Lynchburg, Va.: Schroeder, 2008), 47–48.
21. Taylor, *General Lee,* 275; Taylor, *Four Years with General Lee,* 150; McHenry Howard, "Closing Scenes of the War About Richmond," *SHSP* 31 (1903): 129–30; Marvel, *Place Called Appomattox,* 196, 202–4; Mahone, "What I Saw and Heard During the Closing Days of the Army of Northern Virginia," 418; G. W. Camp, "Interesting Facts Connected with the Occupation of the City by the Federals Following Evacuation in April 1865," in Newsome, *Civil War Talks,* 425–26; Woodworth, *Davis and Lee at War,* 318–19.
22. Williamson, "Cockade City's Surrender, Delivered to the Federals," 409; Chris M. Calkins, *Lee's Retreat: A History and Field Guide* (Richmond: Page One Historical Pubs., 2000), 41; McClendon, *Recollection of War Times,* 228–29; Charles W. Field, "Campaign of 1864 and

1865," *SHSP* 14 (1886): 560–61; Rafuse, *Robert E. Lee and the Fall of the Confederacy,* 230; Marvel, *Lee's Last Retreat,* 49–51, 207–10.

23. Greg Eanes, *Black Day of the Army, April 6, 1865: The Battles of Sailor's Creek* (Burkeville, Va.: E&H, 2001), 135, 166; Mahone, "What I Saw and Heard During the Closing Days of the Army of Northern Virginia," 429–30; John Sergeant Wise, *The End of an Era* (Boston: Houghton Mifflin, 1902), 429, 434.

24. Frank P. Cauble, *The Surrender Proceedings: April 9, 1865, Appomattox Court House* (Lynchburg, Va.: H. E. Howard, 1987), 2–4, 7, 12–14; W. S. White, "Stray Leaves from a Soldiers' Journal," *SHSP* 11 (Dec. 1883): 558; Brown to Charles Venable, Jan. 13, 1888, in *Campbell Brown's Civil War,* 279; McClendon, *Recollection of War Times,* 230–31; Marvel, *Place Called Appomattox,* 213, 215; Taylor, *General Lee,* 280–81; Jones, *Personal Reminiscences,* 297; Marshall, *Aide-de-Camp of Lee,* 258–59; Howard, "Closing Scenes of the War About Richmond," 138; Elizabeth R. Varon, *Appomattox: Victory, Defeat, and Freedom at the End of the Civil War* (New York: Oxford University Press, 2014), 23–50.

25. Eanes, *Black Day of the Army,* 160; Chris M. Calkins, *The Battle of Appomattox Station and Appomattox Court House, April 8–9, 1865* (Lynchburg, Va.: H. E. Howard, 1987), 79–101; A. H. R. Ranson, "General Lee as I Knew Him," *Harper's Monthly Magazine,* Feb. 1911, 335; Thomas G. Jones, "Last Days of the Army of Northern Virginia," *SHSP* 17 (1893): 71, 97; John Herbert Claiborne, "Personal Reminiscences of the Last Days of Lee and His Paladins," *SHSP* 28 (1900): 38–39; Marvel, *Place Called Appomattox,* 222–23, 231; Long, *Memoirs of Robert E. Lee,* 421–22; Jones, *Personal Reminiscences,* 143–44.

26. Mahone, "What I Saw and Heard During the Closing Days of the Army of Northern Virginia," 432, 436, 438; Pendleton, in Jones, *Personal Reminiscences,* 149–50, 297; Mason, *Popular Life of Gen. Robert Edward Lee,* 300–301, 314; Taylor, *General Lee,* 282–83; Taylor, *Four Years with General Lee,* 152–53; Giles Cooke, "A Brief Account of the Surrender on the 9th of April 1865, at Appomattox Court House," Giles Buckner Cooke Papers, VMHC; Cauble, *Surrender Proceedings,* 27–29, 31, 44–46, 114–15; Davis, *Crucible of Command,* 440–41.

27. Marvel, *Place Called Appomattox,* 352; Joshua Lawrence Chamberlain, "Appomattox," Oct. 7, 1903, in *Personal Recollections of the War of the Rebellion: Addresses Delivered Before the Commandery of the State of New York, Military Order of the Loyal Legion of the United States,* ed. A. N. Blakeman (New York: G. P. Putnam's Sons, 1907), 271; "Mr. S. T. Bulkely's Despatches," "John Brady's Despatches," and Sylvanus Cadwallader, "Grant—Interesting Details of the Surrender of Lee and His Army," *New York Herald,* April 14, 1865; Jones, *Personal Reminiscences,* 147; Marshall, *Aide-de-Camp of Lee,* 262.

28. Cauble, *Surrender Proceedings,* 52; Calkins, *Battle of Appomattox Station and Appomattox Court House,* 179; Calkins, *Appomattox Campaign,* 175; Grant in John Russell Young, *Around the World with General Grant* (New York: American News, 1879), 2:301, 456, 460, 627. In a reminiscence published in *The National Tribune* in 1913, a veteran of the 1st Maine Cavalry admitted that they had begun the pursuit to Appomattox with "but three days' rations" on hand and "had stretched and spun out that 'three days' short rations'" until it "would have outclassed in fineness the greatest triumph of the silk spinner's art." B. A. Osborn, "Got Lee's Dinner," *National Tribune,* Jan. 30, 1913, 7.

29. E. P. Alexander, "Lee at Appomattox: Personal Recollections of the Break-Up of the Confederacy," and John Gibbon, "Personal Recollections of Appomattox," *Century Magazine,* April 1902, 925–27, 940; Alexander, *Fighting for the Confederacy,* 532.

30. George H. Sharpe, "The Last Day of the Lost Cause," *National Tribune,* Oct. 1, 1879, 78; George Forsyth, "The Closing Scene at Appomattox Court House," *Harper's New Monthly Magazine,* April 1898, 708; Cauble, *Surrender Proceedings,* 53, 59; Wesley Merritt, "Note on the Surrender of Lee," *Century Magazine,* April 1902, 944; L. L. Crounse, "The Sur-

render," *New York Times,* April 14, 1865. Horace Porter recorded a remarkable story about this moment in *Campaigning with Grant* (p. 481) and "The Surrender at Appomattox Court House," in Buel and Johnson, *Battles and Leaders of the Civil War,* 4:741. As Grant was introducing his officers, Lee "did not exhibit the slightest change of features . . . until Colonel Parker"—Grant's military secretary—"was presented to him." Parker was a Tonawanda Seneca who had been educated at Cayuga Academy and studied engineering at Rensselaer Polytechnic Institute, and had joined Grant's staff in 1863. According to Porter, "when Lee saw his swarthy features he looked at him with evident surprise" and "the natural surmise was that he at first mistook Parker for a negro, and was struck with astonishment." Parker himself, recounting the incident, claimed that Lee recognized his identity at once, and "extended his hand and said, 'I am glad to see one real American here.'" Parker replied in one of the golden sentences of the Civil War: "I shook his hand and said, 'We are all Americans.'" Porter mentions only Lee's surprise and insists that Lee "did not utter a word while the introductions were going on" except to Seth Williams; no other officer in the McLean parlor, including Grant, recorded this exchange. Yet, Parker related the story "several times" and insisted on its veracity. See Arthur Caswell Parker, *The Life of General Ely S. Parker: Last Grand Sachem of the Iroquois and General Grant's Military Secretary* (Buffalo, N.Y.: Buffalo Historical Society, 1919), 133; Joy Porter, *To be Indian: The Life of Iroquois-Seneca Arthur Caswell Parker* (Norman, Okla.: University of Oklahoma Press, 2001), 42; William H. Armstrong, *Warrior in Two Camps: Ely S. Parker, Union General and Seneca Chief* (Syracuse, N.Y.: Syracuse University Press, 1978), 109–110.

31. Bryan Grimes, "The Surrender at Appomattox," *SHSP* 27 (1899): 96; Charles W. Field, "Campaign of 1864 and 1865," *SHSP* 14 (1886): 562; Alexander, "Lee at Appomattox," 929; H. A. Minor, "Surrender of Mahone's Division," *Confederate Veteran,* July 1914, 313; Taylor, *General Lee,* 289; Jones, *Personal Reminiscences,* 346; George C. Rable, *God's Almost Chosen Peoples* (Chapel Hill: University of North Carolina Press, 2010), 389; Thomas Goree to E. P. Alexander, Dec. 6, 1887, in *Longstreet's Aide,* 67; Walter N. Jones, "Some Recollections of Service by One Who Claims to Have Been the Youngest Confederate Who Surrendered at Appomattox," April 5, 1894, in Newsome, *Civil War Talks,* 447; Marvel, *Place Called Appomattox,* 240–41; Crounse, "Surrender."
32. Sanborn, *Robert E. Lee: The Complete Man,* 233; "Recollections of Judge R. T. W. Duke Jr.," ed. Helen R. Duke, *Papers of the Albemarle County Historical Society* 3 (1942–43): 47; Garidel, diary entry for April 9, 1865, in *Exile in Richmond,* 375; McGuire, diary entry for April 10, 1865, in *Diary of a Southern Refugee,* 351–52; "An Incident," *Southern Bivouac,* March 1884, 311; Porter, "The Surrender at Appomattox Court House," in Buel and Johnson, *Battles and Leaders of the Civil War,* 4:741; Nelson Lankford, *Richmond Burning: The Last Days of the Confederate Capital* (New York: Viking, 2002), 209–10.

Chapter Eighteen: An Indictment for Treason

1. Glatthaar, *General Lee's Army,* 470; Marvel, *Place Called Appomattox,* 222–23; Chris M. Calkins, *The Final Bivouac: The Surrender Parade at Appomattox and the Disbanding of the Armies, April 10–May 20, 1865* (Lynchburg, Va.: H. E. Howard, 1988), 204–8; Peter G. Tsouras, *Major General George H. Sharpe and the Creation of American Military Intelligence in the Civil War* (Philadelphia: Casemate, 2018), 363.
2. Grant, *Memoirs,* 2:634; Marshall, *Aide-de-Camp of Lee,* 275; Marvel, *Place Called Appomattox,* 249; Gibbon, "Personal Recollections of Appomattox," 940; John Gibbon, *Personal Recollections of the Civil War* (1928; Dayton: Press of Morningside Bookshop, 1988), 326–27;

Crounse, "Surrender"; L. L. Crounse, "Gen. Lee," *New York Times,* April 14, 1865; "Visit of Lee to Danville," *New York Herald,* April 14, 1865.

3. Marshall, *Aide-de-Camp of Lee,* 278; "General Orders No. 9," April 10, 1865, in *OR,* ser. 1, vol. 46, pt. 1, 1267; Marvel, *Place Called Appomattox,* 253; Fellman, *Making of Robert E. Lee,* 191–92; Marshall, *Address Delivered Before the Lee Monument Association, at Richmond, Virginia, October 27, 1887* (Baltimore: John Murphy, 1888), 44, 48.
4. REL to Davis, April 12, 1865, in *Papers of Jefferson Davis,* 11:533, 534; REL to Davis, April 20, 1865, in *WPREL,* 939, and *OR,* ser. 1, vol. 46, pt. 1, 1265–67; Marvel, *Lee's Last Retreat,* 189– 90; Thomas, *Confederate Nation,* 303. Edmund Ruffin also remarked on the collapse of discipline in the Army of Northern Virginia on the retreat to Appomattox "& consequent misconduct of portions of them," but Ruffin, who had never entirely trusted Lee's dedication to the Confederacy, believed "Gen. Lee greatly, if not principally to blame." See Ruffin, diary entry for April 8, 1865, in *Diary of Edmund Ruffin,* 3:840–41.
5. Robert E. Lee Jr., *Recollections and Letters,* 155–56; William B. Arnold, in *The Fourth Massachusetts Cavalry in the Closing Scenes of the War for the Maintenance of the Union, from Richmond to Appomattox* (Boston, 1911), 31–32; Calkins, *Final Bivouac,* 42; Taylor, *General Lee,* 296; Taylor, *Four Years with General Lee,* 154; Marvel, *Place Called Appomattox,* 356; Daughtry, *Gray Cavalier,* 274; Ayers, *Thin Light of Freedom,* 333.
6. Glatthaar, *General Lee's Army,* 471; Taylor, *General Lee,* 297; McGuire, diary entry for April 3, 1865, in *Diary of a Southern Refugee,* 345; William Eldridge Hatcher, *Along the Trail of the Friendly Years* (New York: Fleming H. Revell, 1910), 118–19; Marshall Fishwick, *Lee After the War* (New York: Dodd, Mead, 1963), 1–2, 18–19.
7. Lankford, *Richmond Burning,* 144; Furgurson, *Ashes of Glory,* 356–57; Perry, *Lady of Arlington,* 284–85; Yates, *Perfect Gentleman,* 1:351; Robert Stiles, *Four Years Under Marse Robert* (New York: Neale, 1910), 239; Longacre, *Fitz Lee,* 188–89.
8. "The Latest from Richmond—Lee's Arrival," *Philadelphia Inquirer,* April 18, 1865.
9. "Parole of Honor—Gen. Lee," RG 94, file E501R&P 520058, National Archives and Records Administration, Washington, D.C.; Adam Badeau, *Grant in Peace: From Appomattox to Mount McGregor, a Personal Memoir* (Hartford: S. S. Scranton, 1887), 19; Stahr, *Stanton,* 414; Keckley, *Behind the Scenes,* 137; "General Lee," *Boston Daily Advertiser,* June 15, 1865; "The News in Richmond," *Philadelphia Inquirer,* April 19, 1865; Flood, *Lee: The Last Years,* 58; Lincoln to Erastus Corning and others, June 12, 1863, in *Collected Works,* 6:265; Thomas H. Reese, "An Officer's Oath," *Military Law Review* 25 (July 1964): 27.
10. Patricia Hickin, "John C. Underwood and the Antislavery Movement in Virginia, 1847–60," *VMHB,* April 1965, 159, 161–62, 164; Underwood to Henry Carey, Nov. 6, 1860, Edward Carey Gardiner Collection, Historical Society of Pennsylvania; Underwood to William Henry Seward, March 24, 1856, and Feb. 2, 1858, John C. Underwood Correspondence, Rare Books and Special Collections, Rush Rees Library, University of Rochester; "Proscription in Virginia: Letter from John C. Underwood," *New York Times,* Jan. 6, 1857.
11. *Speech of John C. Underwood at Alexandria, July 4, 1863* (Washington, D.C.: McGill & Witherow, 1863), 6, 10; Underwood, in Savage, *Life and Public Services of Andrew Johnson,* 267; Howard B. Means, *The Avenger Takes His Place: Andrew Johnson and the 45 Days That Changed the Nation* (New York: Harcourt, 2006), 117; James Speed, "Surrender of the Rebel Army of Northern Virginia," April 22, 1865, in *Official Opinions of the Attorneys General of the United States,* ed. J. Hubley Ashton (Washington, D.C.: W. H. & O. H. Morrison, 1869), 206; "Judge Underwood and General Lee," *Norfolk Post,* June 22, 1865; Underwood to William D. Kelley, Jan. 24, 1866, Dreer Collection of American Lawyers, Historical Society of Pennsylvania; Blair, *With Malice Toward Some,* 236–37.
12. Underwood to George C. Wedderburn, April 28, 1865, John C. Underwood Papers, 1865–

1870, Huntington Library; "By the President of the United States of America: A Proclamation," May 29, 1865, in *Statutes at Large,* 13:758–59; "Opinion of Attorney General Speed," *Washington Daily National Republican,* May 30, 1865; Grant to Henry W. Halleck, May 6, 1865, in *OR,* ser. 2, 8:535–36; "Case No. 3621a. Case of Davis," in *The Federal Cases: Comprising Cases Argued and Determined in the Circuit and District Courts of the United States* (St. Paul: West, 1894), 7:64–65; "Names of Those Indicted for Treason at Norfolk," *New York Times,* June 19, 1865; "Indictment of Gen. Lee and Others," *Alexandria Gazette,* June 19, 1865.

13. Cooke, *Life of Gen. Robert E. Lee,* 489; REL to William Cabell, May 24, 1865, Special Collections, Leyburn Library; "Indictments for Treason," *Alexandria Gazette,* June 10, 1865; Freeman, *R. E. Lee,* 4:198–201; REL to Grant, June 13, 1865, in Jones, *Personal Reminiscences,* 179–80.
14. "Our President. A Meeting Last Night at Cooper Institute," *New York Herald,* June 8, 1865; REL to Grant, June 20, 1865, and "Interview," July 6, 1878, in *The Papers of Ulysses S. Grant,* ed. John Y. Simon (Carbondale: Southern Illinois University Press, 1988), 15:210–11 and 28:421; Young, *Around the World with General Grant,* 2:460–61.
15. Grant to REL, June 20, 1865, in *OR,* ser. 1, vol. 46, pt. 3, 1287; REL to Taylor, June 17, 1865, in Taylor, *General Lee,* 298; REL to CCL, July 21, 1865, duPont Library. Grant would continue to insist that "the paroles given to the surrendered armies lately in rebellion against the Government should be held inviolate, unless in cases where all rules of civilized warfare have been violated." See Grant to Johnson, Dec. 21, 1865, in *OR,* ser. 2, 8:815.
16. "An Act to Define and Punish Certain Conspiracies," July 31, 1861, and "An Act to Punish Certain Crimes Against the United States," Aug. 6, 1861, in *Statutes at Large,* 12:284, 317; William Blair, "Friend or Foe: Treason and the Second Confiscation Act," in *Wars Within a War: Controversy and Conflict over the American Civil War,* ed. Joan Waugh and Gary W. Gallagher (Chapel Hill: University of North Carolina Press, 2009), 48.
17. Examination of Judge John C. Underwood, Jan. 31, 1866, in *Report of the Joint Committee on Reconstruction,* 7; J. M. Humphries to Underwood, May 15, 1866, Underwood Papers, Library of Congress.
18. "Judge Underwood's Decision," *New York Times,* April 16, 1866; Chase to Horace Greeley, June 1 and 5, 1866, Chase to Underwood, Nov. 19, 1868, and Jan. 14, 1869, and Chase to Thomas Conway, Sept. 19, 1870, in *The Salmon P. Chase Papers: Correspondence, 1865–1873,* ed. John Niven (Kent, Ohio: Kent State University Press, 1998), 100–101, 106–7, 183, 285–86, 292.
19. REL to Martha Williams, June 20, 1865, in *"To Markie,"* 62–63; REL to Chauncey Burr, Jan. 5, 1866, in Jones, *Personal Reminiscences,* 189; Examination of Robert E. Lee, Feb. 17, 1866, in *Report of the Joint Committee on Reconstruction,* 133; REL to Edward Lee Childe, Jan. 16, 1866, LFDA/duPont Library.
20. Simpson, *Let Us Have Peace,* 101; *Alexandria Gazette,* July 18, 1865; "Extra Session of the Virginia Legislature—Circular from the Attorney General," *Daily Cleveland Herald,* June 13, 1865; "The Indictments Against General Lee and Others," *Baltimore Sun,* June 19, 1865; "The Indictment Against Gen. Lee," *Boston Post,* June 19, 1865. See also *Alexandria Gazette,* June 12 and 21, 1865, and *Norfolk Post,* June 23, 1865.
21. Gambone, *Lee at Gettysburg,* 38–39; Freeman, *R. E. Lee,* 4:389–94; REL to Johnson, June 13, 1865, and Grant to REL, June 20, 1865, in Jones, *Life and Letters,* 384; "From Washington: Gen. Lee Takes the Amnesty Oath," *New York Times,* Oct. 16, 1865; Clement Sulivane, "Last Meeting with Gen. R. E. Lee," *Confederate Veteran,* Dec. 1920, 459–60; Elmer Oris Parker, "Why Was Lee Not Pardoned?," *Prologue* 2 (Winter 1970): 181; John Reeves, *The Lost Indictment of Robert E. Lee: The Forgotten Case Against an American Icon* (Lanham, Md.: Rowman & Littlefield, 2018), 2–4; REL to Dr. S. B. Anderson, May 17, 1865, duPont Library; REL to George M. Brockett, May 27, 1865, LFDA/duPont Library; Robert E. Lee Jr., *Recollections*

and Letters, 160, 204; Jones, *Personal Reminiscences,* 320; Mason, *Popular Life of Gen. Robert Edward Lee,* 319–20.

22. REL to Letcher, Aug. 28, 1865, LFDA/duPont Library; REL to Josiah Tatnall, Sept. 7, 1865, in Jones, *Life and Letters,* 388; "A Talk with Gen. R. E. Lee," *New York Times,* Aug. 12, 1879.
23. "General Lee and Staff," *Richmond Whig,* April 21, 1865; "Brady, the Grand Old Man of American Photography," *Photographic Times: An Illustrated Monthly Magazine,* June 1891, 303; Robert Wilson, *Mathew Brady: A Biography* (New York: Bloomsbury, 2013), 190–92; "The Photographic Corps," *Richmond Whig,* April 27, 1865; Hopkins, *Robert E. Lee in War and Peace,* 71–81; Michael D. Gorman, "Lee the 'Devil' Discovered," *Battlefield Photographer* 3 (Feb. 2006): 1, 3–5.
24. REL to Martha Williams, June 24, 1865, in *"To Markie,"* 64; REL to Cabell, May 24, 1865, Special Collections, Leyburn Library; Long, *Memoirs of Robert E. Lee,* 170; Yates, *Perfect Gentleman,* 2:30; Byrd Pendleton Jervey, "Derwent in Powhatan County and General Robert E. Lee's Sojourn There in the Summer of 1865," *VMHB,* Jan. 1950, 85; Robert E. Lee Jr., *Recollections and Letters,* 174, 178.
25. REL to Robert E. Lee Jr., July 10, 1865, Lee Family Papers, VMHC; REL to WHFL, July 29, 1865, and to CCL, Aug. 18, 1865, Special Collections, Leyburn Library; Robert E. Lee Jr., *Recollections and Letters,* 168, 176, 178; REL to Taylor, July 31, 1865, and to Mrs. Julie G. Chouteau, March 21, 1866, duPont Library.

Chapter Nineteen: Every Student Must Be a Gentleman

1. Oren F. Morton, *A History of Rockbridge County, Virginia* (Baltimore: Regional, 1980), 188–93; Jared Sparks, *The Life of George Washington* (Boston: Ferdinand Andrews, 1839), 384; Archibald Alexander, *Address Delivered Before the Alumni Association of Washington College, Virginia, on Commencement Day, June 29, 1843* (Lexington, Va.: R. H. Glass, 1843), 11–12.
2. *The American Almanac and Repository of Useful Knowledge for the Year 1859,* 201–2; Washington College Records of Board of Trustees, Feb. 21, 1845–Sept. 1873, 104, 118, 123, 140–41, Special Collections, Leyburn Library; Scott, "Some Personal Memories of General Robert E. Lee," 283; Morton, *History of Rockbridge County,* 126–27; Charles A. Bodie, *Remarkable Rockbridge: The Story of Rockbridge County, Virginia* (Lexington, Va.: Rockbridge County Historical Society, 2011), 181; Committee on Finance to the Board of Trustees, July 1, 1865, Special Collections, Leyburn Library; Fishwick, *Lee After the War,* 142–43; "James Jones White and Carter Johns Harris," *Alumni Bulletin of the University of Virginia* 1 (Nov. 1894): 83–84; "Professor John L. Campbell," *Journal of Education for Home and School* 8 (March 1886): 9. The University of Virginia's highest prewar enrollment occurred in 1856, when it counted 645 students. See Virginius Dabney, *Mr. Jefferson's University: A History* (Charlottesville: University of Virginia Press, 1981), 24.
3. Washington College Trustee Minute Book, Aug. 4, 1865, Special Collections, Leyburn Library; Alexander L. Nelson, "How Lee Became a College President," in *General Robert E. Lee After Appomattox,* ed. F. L. Riley (New York: Macmillan, 1922), 1–3; Ollinger Crenshaw, *General Lee's College: The Rise and Growth of Washington and Lee University* (New York: Random House, 1969), 146; Preston, *Lee: West Point and Lexington,* 50–51.
4. Brockenbrough to REL, Aug. 10, 1865, in Allen W. Moger, "Letters to General Lee After the War," *VMHB* 64 (1956): 45; "Capt. Edmund Randolph Cocke," *Confederate Veteran,* June 1922, 226.
5. REL to the Trustees of Washington College, Aug. 24, 1865, in Robert E. Lee Jr., *Recollections and Letters,* 181–82; Washington College Trustee Minute Book, Aug. 4, 1865, 149, and Washington College Records of Board of Trustees, Feb. 21, 1845–Sept. 1873, Sept. 20 and Oct. 2,

1865, 152, 153–54, 165–66, Special Collections, Leyburn Library; Jones, *Personal Reminiscences,* 86; MCL to Emily Mason, in MacDonald, *Mrs. Robert E. Lee,* 204.

6. "Gen. Lee Accepts the College Presidency," *Charleston Daily News,* Sept. 12, 1865; "Robert E. Lee in a New Role," *New-York Tribune,* Oct. 3, 1865; "Gen. Lee and Washington College," *Alexandria Gazette,* Sept. 5, 1865; Trimble to Brockenbrough, Sept. 7, 1865, Washington College Trustee Minute Book, Special Collections, Leyburn Library; Jones, *Personal Reminiscences,* 284–85.
7. REL to Leyburn, in Jones, *Personal Reminiscences,* 214; Lee to Minor, Jan. 17, 1867, Lee Letterbook 1 and Memorandum Book (Oct. 1865), Special Collections, Leyburn Library; E. S. Joynes, "General Robert E. Lee as College President," in Riley, *General Robert E. Lee After Appomattox,* 20; Thomas, *Robert E. Lee,* 399.
8. M. W. Humphreys, "Reminiscences of General Lee as President of Washington College," in Riley, *General Robert E. Lee After Appomattox,* 38; Michael David Cohen, *Reconstructing the Campus: Higher Education and the American Civil War* (Charlottesville: University of Virginia Press, 2012), 61–65; REL to Edward Lee Childe, Jan. 22, 1867, and July 10, 1868, duPont Library; REL to W. W. Corcoran, Aug. 23 and Sept. 23, 1870, W. W. Corcoran Papers, Library of Congress; REL, "Letters of Gen. R. E. Lee," *SHSP* 7 (March 1879): 154; Flood, *Lee: The Last Years,* 156; Fishwick, *Lee After the War,* 179; Preston, *Lee: West Point and Lexington,* 78–79.
9. Washington College Records of Board of Trustees, Feb. 21, 1845–Sept. 1873, Oct. 24, 1865, and April 26, 1866, 167–68, 177, and REL to the Washington College Board of Trustees, Jan. 9, 1869, Special Collections, Leyburn Library; Goode, *Recollections of a Lifetime,* 27; Preston, *Lee: West Point and Lexington,* 61–62; Flood, *Lee: The Last Years,* 111, 133.
10. REL to J. B. Baldwin and M. S. Harmon, Nov. 22, 1865, to S. G. Cabell and A. A. Graham, Dec. 15, 1865, and to James J. Wall, Oct. 1865, Lee Letterbook 1, and McCormick to Brockenbrough, Jan. 1, 1865, Washington College Trustee Minute Book, Special Collections, Leyburn Library; Sean M. Heuvel and Lisa L. Heuvel, *The College of William and Mary in the Civil War* (Jefferson, N.C.: McFarland, 2013), 135, 138, 153, 159; REL to McCormick, Nov. 28, 1865, LFDA/duPont Library; Crenshaw, *General Lee's College,* 170.
11. REL to Newcomb, March 22, 1866, in Jones, *Personal Reminiscences,* 245; Franklin Parker, "Robert E. Lee, George Peabody, and Sectional Reunion," *Peabody Journal of Education* 78 (2003): 91–97; "To the Hon. John W. Brockenbrough," April 26, 1866, and June 19, 1867, Washington College Trustee Minute Book, Special Collections, Leyburn Library; Catharine Roach, "Robert E. Lee's Financial Impact on Washington College," *Washington and Lee Spectator* (Fall 2014): 9; "Education in the South," *New York Times,* March 3, 1868.
12. M. H. Thomas, "Professor McCulloh of Princeton, Columbia, and Points South," *Princeton University Library Chronicle* 9 (Nov. 1947): 17–29; Jane Singer, *The Confederate Dirty War: Arson, Bombings, Assassination, and Plots for Chemical and Germ Attacks on the Union* (Jefferson, N.C.: McFarland, 2005), 100–116; Donald W. Gunter, "William Allan," *Dictionary of Virginia Biography,* ed. J. T. Kneebone et al. (Richmond: Library of Virginia, 2006), 1:70–71; "Rev. John Lycan Kirkpatrick," in *Encyclopaedia of the Presbyterian Church in the United States of America,* ed. Alfred Nevin (Philadelphia: Presbyterian Encyclopedia, 1884), 1172–73.
13. Scott, "Some Personal Memories of General Robert E. Lee," 283; REL to Churchill S. Gibson, Jan. 24, 1866, Special Collections, Leyburn Library; Cox, *Religious Life of Robert E. Lee,* 215; REL to Ann Upshur Jones, June 24, 1867, Robert E. Lee Letterbook 1, Special Collections, Leyburn Library.
14. REL to the Ministers of the Baptist, Episcopal, Methodist, and Presbyterian Churches in Lexington, Va., Sept. 11, 1869, and Sept. 12, 1870, Robert E. Lee Letterbook 1, Special Collections, Leyburn Library; Kirkpatrick, in Jones, *Personal Reminiscences,* 112, 424.
15. "General Lee's College: The University of Southern Principles," *New York Sun,* Oct. 26,

1869; Sara Mordecai to Lee, April 18, 1866, and Hill to Brockenbrough, Feb. 8, 1866, Special Collections, Leyburn Library; Hal Bridges, *Lee's Maverick General: Daniel Harvey Hill* (New York: McGraw-Hill, 1961), 23; see also Hal Bridges, ed., "A Lee Letter on the 'Lost Dispatch' and the Maryland Campaign of 1862," *VMHB,* April 1958, 164–66.

16. REL, Report to the Board of Trustees, June 1866, June 19, 1867, June 16, 1868, June 22, 1869, Washington College Trustee Minute Book, Special Collections, Leyburn Library; *Richmond Times,* Aug. 31, 1866; Heuvel and Heuvel, *College of William and Mary,* 147; *Report of the Commissioner of Education for the Year 1871* (Washington, D.C.: U.S. Government Printing Office, 1871), 16, 648–49; *The World Almanac and Book of Facts 1892* (New York: Press Publishing), 175; *The World Almanac and Encyclopedia* (New York: Press Publishing, 1914), 588; Dabney, *Mr. Jefferson's University,* 28; J. Rainey to brother, Feb. 27, 1868, in J. Rainey Correspondence, Library of Congress. Two of Breckinridge's sons, Clifton and Owen, were attending Washington College. See REL to Breckinridge, June 26, 1869, in Breckinridge Family Papers, Library of Congress.
17. REL to Messrs. Edwards Lee & Co., Sept. 25, 1868, and to J. Weatherby & Sons, July 8, 1868, Special Collections, Leyburn Library; Edward Joynes, "General Lee, as a College President," *University Monthly: A Journal of School and Home Education* 1 (March 1871): 5.
18. John B. Collyar, "A College Boy's Observation of General Lee," in Riley, *Robert E. Lee After Appomattox,* 66; S. H. Chester memoir, in Henry Boley, *Lexington in Old Virginia* (Richmond: Garrett & Massie, 1936), 121; REL to Wesley E. Gatewood, June 2, 1866, at Bruce Gimelson Autographs, www.brucegimelson.com/content.asp?c=1; grade report for W. S. Graves, Feb. 8, 1868, Robert E. Lee Letterbook 2, Special Collections, Leyburn Library; REL to Colonel J. W. Lapsley, June 5, 1866, in Jones, *Personal Reminiscences,* 253.
19. REL to H. S. Moss, Jan. 31, 1867, and Lee to Mrs. E. H. Bierly, April 6, 1868, Robert E. Lee Letterbook 2, Special Collections, Leyburn Library; John William Jones, *Christ in the Camp; or, Religion in Lee's Army* (Richmond: B. F. Johnson, 1887), 66.
20. M. Le B—— to Johnson, Oct. 1, 1865, in *Documentary History of Reconstruction: Political, Military, Social, Religious, Educational, and Industrial, 1865 to the Present Time,* ed. W. L. Fleming (Cleveland: Arthur H. Clarke, 1906), 1:36; Bright to Sumner, Oct. 20, 1865, in "The Bright-Sumner Letters, 1862–1872," ed. J. F. Rhodes, *Proceedings of the Massachusetts Historical Society* (Boston: Massachusetts Historical Society, 1913), 12:145; Hugh Moran to Mrs. N. M. Moran, Feb. 26, 1868, Hugh A. Moran Papers, Special Collections, Leyburn Library.
21. "General Lee's College: The University of Southern Principles"; David W. Coffey, "Reconstruction and Redemption in Lexington," *Proceedings of the Rockbridge Historical Society* 12 (1995–2002): 275, 279; John M. McClure, "The Freedmen's Bureau School in Lexington Versus 'General Lee's Boys,'" in Wallenstein and Wyatt-Brown, *Virginia's Civil War,* 189; Freeman, *R. E. Lee,* 4:354–55.
22. "Records Relating to Murders and Outrages," Bureau of Refugees, Freedmen, and Abandoned Lands, 1865–1869, National Archives Microfilm Publication No. 1048, roll 59; Bodie, *Remarkable Rockbridge,* 191, 193; McClure, "Freedmen's Bureau School," 193–94; "The Lexington Outrage," *Staunton Spectator,* May 19, 1868; "Letter from Lexington," *Richmond Dispatch,* Sept. 18, 1868; Flood, *Lee: The Last Years,* 183–84.
23. "General Lee's College," *New York Independent,* April 2, 1868; *College Courant,* April 8, 1868; *Chicago Tribune,* April 6, 1868; "Alleged Outrage at Lynchburg, Va.," *New-York Tribune,* April 20, 1868; Freeman, *R. E. Lee,* 4:345–48; McClure, "Freedmen's Bureau School," 194–95; Bodie, *Remarkable Rockbridge,* 195; David W. Coffey, "Reconstruction and Redemption in Lexington," in *After the Backcountry: Rural Life in the Great Valley of Virginia, 1800–1900,* ed. Kenneth E. Koons and Warren R. Hofstra (Knoxville: University of Tennessee Press, 2000), 218; Preston, *Lee: West Point and Lexington,* 76, 78–79, 84–86; Crenshaw, *General Lee's College,* 154.

24. REL to Sistare, April 10, 1868, to Captain J. W. Sharp, April 13, 1867, to Wagner, May 4 and 11, 1868, to G. B. Strickler, May 10, 1868, to F. B. Lewis, May 18, 1868, to Colonel John W. Jordan, Nov. 20, 1868, in Robert E. Lee Jr., *Recollections and Letters,* 299–300; Jones, *Life and Letters,* 429; Jones, *Personal Reminiscences,* 99; Robert E. Lee Letterbook 2, Special Collections, Leyburn Library.
25. REL to Mrs. E. Neel, Jan. 29, 1869, Robert E. Lee Letterbook 2, Special Collections, Leyburn Library; MCL, in Pryor, *Six Encounters with Lincoln,* 278.
26. REL to William S. Rosecrans, Aug. 26, 1868, *Staunton Valley Spirit,* Sept. 16, 1868; REL to Edward Lee Childe, Jan. 16, 1868, duPont Library; REL to Cousin Ellen, Feb. 22, 1867, Robert E. Lee Collection, Missouri Historical Society Archives; William Preston Johnston, "Memoranda of Conversations with General R. E. Lee," in Gallagher, *Lee the Soldier,* 30; REL to Robert E. Lee Jr., March 12, 1868, in Robert E. Lee Jr., *Recollections and Letters,* 306; Crenshaw, *General Lee's College,* 167. Forty years after Appomattox, "Col. T. L. Broun, of Charleston, W. Va.," told the *Richmond Times-Dispatch* that "two months after the evacuation of Richmond," he had been present in St. Paul's Episcopal Church for Sunday services when, at the invitation to the Eucharist, the white congregation was shocked to see "a tall, well dressed negro man; very black . . . with an air of military authority," come forward to the altar rail ("Negro Communed at St. Paul's Church," April 16, 1905). This was interpreted by the congregation as a deliberate provocation by "the Federal authorities, to offensively humiliate them." But Robert E. Lee saved the day by going forward to the rail himself "and reverently knelt down to partake of the communion, and not far from where the negro was." This was interpreted by the *Times-Dispatch* as a token of genteel defiance, "a grand exhibition of superiority shown by a true Christian and great soldier under the most trying offensive circumstances." The story was repeated several months later in the August issue of *Confederate Veteran* (p. 360), although the date now became a question. In the *Times-Dispatch* article, Broun placed the timing of the event as "two months after the evacuation of Richmond," which would have been June 1865, but he instead identified that moment as "June 1866." The *Confederate Veteran* version presents the date firmly as "June, 1865." Thomas Broun was a lawyer and Confederate veteran—in fact, it was Broun who sold Traveller to Lee in 1862—but his story would eventually be taken up as evidence that Lee was attempting to promote racial reconciliation in Virginia by this gesture. That was certainly not Broun's intention, but it became the point of how the story was told in Flood, *Lee: The Last Years,* 65–66, and Thomas, *Robert E. Lee,* 19, and in a more muted fashion by David Cox in *Religious Life of Robert E. Lee,* 253.

    The reliability of Broun's story cannot be rated very highly. The reminiscence was separated by four decades from the event it purported to describe; no subsequent witness ever stepped forward to corroborate it; there is no clue to the identity of the black communicant; and the original dating in the *Times-Dispatch* article (as June 1866) would have made it unlikely that either Broun or Lee would have been in Richmond. The officiating clergyman, Charles Minnigerode, left no memoir that might have described this event, nor is there any reference to it in the lengthy memorial essay written after his death in the *Southern Churchman,* "The Late Rev. Dr. Minnigerode," Oct. 27, 1894, 523–24, or in a biographical feature that appeared in the *Times-Dispatch:* "Immigrant Boy to St. Paul's Rector," Nov. 11, 1934. There is also no mention of it in the Richmond newspapers for either June 1865 or June 1866.

Chapter Twenty: From the Great Deep to the Great Deep He Goes

1. REL to Philip Slaughter, Aug. 31, 1865, LFDA/duPont Library; REL to Early, March 16, 1866, and to Varina Davis, Feb. 23, 1866, and Edmund Randolph Cocke to Robert E. Lee Jr.,

in Robert E. Lee Jr., *Recollections and Letters,* 221–23; REL to Richard L. Maury, July 31, 1865, to Matthew F. Maury, Sept. 3, 1865, and to Cadmus Wilcox, Dec. 23, 1865, in Jones, *Personal Reminiscences,* 196–97; REL to Thomas L. Rosser, Dec. 13, 1866, Robert E. Lee Papers, Small Special Collections Library.

2. REL to Early, March 15, 1866, in Jubal Anderson Early Papers, Library of Congress; Testimony of Robert E. Lee, Feb. 17, 1866, in *Report of the Joint Committee on Reconstruction at the First Session, Thirty-Ninth Congress* (Washington, D.C.: Government Printing Office, 1866), 2:130; "Robert E. Lee Before the Reconstruction Committee," *New York Daily Herald,* Feb. 18, 1866; Thomas, *Robert E. Lee,* 381.
3. Edmund Randolph Cocke, in Robert E. Lee Jr., *Recollections and Letters,* 172; REL to Dabney Maury, May 23, 1867, in Jones, *Personal Reminiscences,* 227.
4. REL to Martha Williams, April 7, 1866, in *"To Markie,"* 69; "Gen. Lee," *New-York Tribune,* Feb. 17, 1866; Herman Melville, "Lee in the Capitol," April 1866, in *The Writings of Herman Melville: Published Poems* (Evanston, Ill.: Northwestern University Press, 2009), 163–64; "Pen, Pencil, and Scissors," *Washington National Republican,* Feb. 22, 1866.
5. REL to Edward Lee Childe, Jan. 5 and 22, 1867, duPont Library; REL to "Cousin Ellen," Feb. 22, 1867, Robert E. Lee Collection, Missouri Historical Society Archives; REL to Dabney H. Maury, May 23, 1867, Lee Family Papers, VMHC.
6. REL to Edward G. W. Butler, Oct. 11, 1867, in "Unpublished Letters of Gen. Lee," *Missouri Republican,* Oct. 3, 1885; David D. Plater, *The Butlers of Iberville Parish, Louisiana: Dunboyne Plantation in the 1800s* (Baton Rouge: Louisiana State University Press, 2015), 185; REL to Edward Lee Childe, Jan. 16, 1868, duPont Library; REL to Annette Carter, March 28, 1868, in Chaney, *Duty Most Sublime,* 146; Flood, *Lee: The Last Years,* 221; Fishwick, *Lee After the War,* 134–35; Franklin L. Riley, "What General Lee Read After the War," in Riley, *General Robert E. Lee After Appomattox,* 168–69.
7. "Hon. John Minor Botts on Reconstruction," *Washington National Republican,* Feb. 24, 1866; REL to Ould, Feb. 4, 1867, in Jones, *Life and Letters,* 395.
8. "Gen. Rosecrans and Gen. R. E. Lee," *Staunton Spectator,* Sept. 8, 1868; David G. Moore, *William S. Rosecrans and the Union Victory: A Civil War Biography* (Jefferson, N.C.: McFarland, 2014), 189–90.
9. "The Great Democratic Love-Feast," *New York Sun,* Aug. 26, 1868; "Washington," *New-York Tribune,* Aug. 31, 1868; Michael Fellman, "Robert E. Lee: Myth and Man," in Wallenstein and Wyatt-Brown, *Virginia's Civil War,* 20; Marvel, *Place Called Appomattox,* 289–90.
10. REL, Jan. 8, 1869, in Robert E. Lee Jr., *Recollections and Letters,* 334, 349; Badeau, *Grant in Peace,* 26–27; Marvel, *Place Called Appomattox,* 302–3; "Letter from Washington," *Baltimore Sun,* May 3, 1869; Kundahl, *Alexandria Goes to War,* 27.
11. Allen W. Moger, "General Lee's Unwritten 'History of the Army of Northern Virginia,'" *VMHB,* July 1963, 342–46, 352, 355; REL to Walter Taylor, July 31, 1865, and to Jonathan R. Thompson, June 9, 1866, Special Collections, Leyburn Library; REL to Topham, Aug. 26, 1865, and to W. B. Reed, in Robert E. Lee Jr., *Recollections and Letters,* 219, 221; Noah Andre Trudeau, "Unwritten History: The War Memoirs Robert E. Lee Chose Not to Write," *Civil War Times* 49 (Aug. 2010): 54–59; REL to Scranton & Burr, Oct. 23, 1865, in Jones, *Personal Reminiscences,* 245; REL to Martha Williams, Dec. 20, 1865, in *"To Markie,"* 66; REL to W. P. Moore, March 2, 1866, Robert E. Lee Collection, Missouri State Historical Archives; "News of the Day," *Alexandria Gazette,* June 28, 1866; "A Northern Correspondent's Account of General Lee," *Alexandria Gazette,* Sept. 18, 1866.
12. REL to Topham, Oct. 6, 1865, Special Collections, Leyburn Library; REL to William B. Reed, Aug. 30, 1866, in Jones, *Personal Reminiscences,* 254–55; Moger, "General Lee's Unwritten 'History of the Army of Northern Virginia,'" 347–49; Nagel, *Lees of Virginia,* 294. Richardson had already published a laudatory biographical sketch of Lee in William Parker

Snow's *Southern Generals: Who They Are, and What They Have Done* in 1865, and contributed an engraving of Lee to a "Sketch of General Robert E. Lee" in *The Old Guard,* Jan. 1866, 58, which declared that "when every Democratic editor will speak out his real thought, and say boldly and defiantly that he believes men like Gen. Robert B. Lee to be patriots, and men like Stanton and Seward to be seditionists and traitors, there will be more honest men in the land than there are now, and there will be a better hope for liberty—for our country's lasting peace and honor!"

13. REL, "Life of General Henry Lee," 15, 16, 22–23, 38–39, 43, 46–47, 49, 50, 57, 60, 61, 65; REL to CCL, March 19, 1867, Special Collections, Leyburn Library.
14. REL, "Life of General Henry Lee," 78; REL to CCL, Oct. 24, 1867, and Jan. 15, 1869, Special Collections, Leyburn Library; REL to Edward Lee Childe, March 8, 1870, duPont Library; Robert I. Curtis, "Confederate Classical Textbooks: A Lost Cause?," *International Journal of the Classical Tradition* 3 (Spring 1997): 447.
15. MacDonald, *Mrs. Robert E. Lee,* 209–10, 216, 219, 256, 283; Fishwick, *Lee After the War,* 156, 173, 181, 212–13; Scott, "Some Personal Memories of General Robert E. Lee," 283; REL to MChL, Dec. 21, 1866, in Robert E. Lee Jr., *Recollections and Letters,* 248.
16. Robert E. Lee Jr., *Recollections and Letters,* 196; MacDonald, *Mrs. Robert E. Lee,* 274; Perry, *Lady of Arlington,* 290, 299; "Mary Custis Lee's 'Reminiscences of the War,'" 318; Fishwick, *Lee After the War,* 129–30, 170–71; "Congressional," *Washington Evening Star,* March 4, 1869; REL to Annette Carter, Aug. 30, 1866, LFDA/duPont Library; MChL, "Recollections by Mildred Lee," *Growing Up in the 1850s,* 116, 120.
17. R. E. Lee Memorandum Book, Oct. 1865, Special Collections, Leyburn Library; Perry, *Lady of Arlington,* 304; Fishwick, *Lee After the War,* 181; S. H. Chester memoir, in Boley, *Lexington in Old Virginia,* 122; Jones, *Personal Reminiscences,* 99–100, 235–36; REL to McConaughy, Aug. 5, 1869, and WHFL to McConaughy, Aug. 14, 1869, David McConaughy Papers, Special Collections, Musselman Library, Gettysburg College; "The Gettysburg Identification—Confederate Generals Not Likely to Be Present," *Richmond Dispatch,* Aug. 23, 1869. When Lee passed through Richmond in March 1870, John S. Mosby, who had commanded partisan rangers in northern Virginia during the war, paid a call at Lee's hotel. He wrote that Lee was "pale and haggard, and did not look like the Apollo I had known in the army." Worse, Mosby brought George Pickett to visit Lee, and remarked that "the interview was cold and formal," partly because Lee wanted to avoid discussing the war, and partly because Pickett blamed Lee—"that old man"—for sending his division to its destruction at Gettysburg. "He had my division massacred," Pickett complained to Mosby afterward. See Mosby, "Personal Recollections of General Lee," 68–69, and "Picture Pickett as Enemy of Lee," *Richmond Times-Dispatch,* March 21, 1911.
18. Helen White Bruce, box 13—Reminiscences, Association Items, Funeral Obituaries, Robert E. Lee Papers, Special Collections, Leyburn Library; REL to MCL, Nov. 21 and Dec. 21, 1865, in Robert E. Lee Jr., *Recollections and Letters,* 199, 247, 264, 271; REL to Annette Carter, May 18, 1866, in Chaney, *Duty Most Sublime,* 161; Gamaliel Bradford, "The Social and Domestic Life of Robert E. Lee," *South Atlantic Quarterly* 10 (April 1911): 117; REL to Edward Lee Childe, Oct. 25, 1868, duPont Library.
19. Hopkins, *Robert E. Lee in War and Peace,* 84–91, 93–96, 100–110, 130, 134–35, 142; Donald A. Hopkins, "A Portrait of Lee We Were Not Supposed to See," *Military Images* 32 (Winter 2014): 26–29; REL to Gardner, April 25, 1866, LFDA/duPont Library.
20. REL to Robert E. Lee Jr., June 8, 1867, in Robert E. Lee Jr., *Recollections and Letters,* 260; REL to CCL, Sept. 16, 1867, and to Edward Lee Childe, Jan. 16, 1868, duPont Library; REL to Martha Williams, Oct. 4, 1867, in *"To Markie,"* 76; REL to J. L. Campbell, Sept. 9, 1867, and to CCL, Sept. 16, 1867, Special Collections, Leyburn Library.
21. Moger, "Letters to General Lee After the War," 43, 59, 65; "Our Honored Dead," *Richmond*

Dispatch, May 11, 1866; Flood, *Lee: The Last Years,* 194; REL to Gordon, Sept. 2, 1868, and to Samuel H. Tagart, May 18, 1869, LFDA/duPont Library; REL to Edward Lee Childe, Sept. 9, 1869, duPont Library; REL to William Nelson Pendleton et al., Jan. 11, 1869, Robert E. Lee Letterbook 2, Special Collections, Leyburn Library; REL to Alexander McDonald, Oct. 11, 1869, Penn Letterbook, Special Collections, Leyburn Library; Kundahl, *Alexandria Goes to War,* 28.

22. REL to M. L. Karr, Feb. 16, 1869, www.liveauctioneers.com/item/27468042_49008-robert-e-lee-autograph-letter-signed; "General Lee in Alexandria," *Baltimore Sun,* May 7, 1869; Robert E. Lee Jr., *Recollections and Letters,* 365; "Base Ball," *New Orleans Times-Picayune,* March 31, 1870; McCabe, *Life and Campaigns of Robert E. Lee,* 637.
23. REL to WHFL, Dec. 2, 1869, to MChL, Feb. 2, 1870, and to WHFL, Feb. 14, 1870, in Robert E. Lee Jr., *Recollections and Letters,* 373–74, 379–80, 383, 384; REL to Nahum Capen and Sidney Root, Jan. 21, 1870, Special Collections, Leyburn Library; REL to W. W. Corcoran, Jan. 26, 1870, in "Letters of Gen. R. E. Lee," *SHSP* 7 (March 1879): 154; REL to Edward Lee Childe, Feb. 19 and March 8, 1870, duPont Library; Flood, *Lee: The Last Years,* 223.
24. J. Rainey to brother, March 1870, in J. Rainey Correspondence; Johnston, "Memoranda of Conversations with General R. E. Lee," March 18, 1870, 32; Trustee Minutes, April 19, 1870, Washington College Records of Board of Trustees, Feb. 21, 1845–Sept. 1873, 269, Special Collections, Leyburn Library; REL to MChL, March 21, 1870, and to WHFL, March 22, 1870, in Robert E. Lee Jr., *Recollections and Letters,* 384–87.
25. REL to MCL, March 29, April 17 and 18, 1870, and EAL to MCL, April 3, 1870, in Robert E. Lee Jr., *Recollections and Letters,* 388–89, 392, 395, 398; "General Assembly of Virginia," *Richmond Dispatch,* March 29, 1870; "Gen. R. E. Lee Passes Through Our Town," *Wilmington Daily Journal,* March 31, 1870; Flood, *Lee: The Last Years,* 232–33; Sanborn, *Robert E. Lee: The Complete Man,* 354–55; "Arrival of General Lee," *Charleston Daily News,* March 31, 1870; "General Lee," *Charlotte Democrat,* April 5, 1870; "General Lee at Augusta, Ga.," *Wilmington Morning Star,* April 6, 1870; Hopkins, *Robert E. Lee in War and Peace,* 137–38; Karl A. Bickel, "Robert E. Lee in Florida," *Florida Historical Quarterly* 27 (July 1948): 62–64; Fishwick, *Lee After the War,* 195–97.
26. REL to MCL, April 18, 1870, in Robert E. Lee Jr., *Recollections and Letters,* 399, 405; Flood, *Lee: The Last Years,* 245; "Gen. Lee," *Charleston Daily Courier,* April 30, 1870; "The Old Hero," *Charleston Daily News,* April 28, 1870; "Arrival of Gen. Robert E. Lee—His Reception," *Wilmington Daily Journal,* April 29, 1870; Harrison W. Burton, *The History of Norfolk, Virginia* (Norfolk: Norfolk Virginian Job Print, 1877), 134; Daughtry, *Gray Cavalier,* 290.
27. REL to William Preston Johnston, April 21, 1870, Special Collections, Leyburn Library; REL to Annette Carter, May 20, 1870, in Chaney, *Duty Most Sublime,* 121; REL to Cassius Francis Lee, June 6, 1870, duPont Library; REL to William W. Corcoran, Aug. 23, 1870, Corcoran Papers; "Tax Sales" and "Tax Sale Case," *Alexandria Gazette,* Feb. 17 and 19 and March 21, 1870; "Bennett v. Hunter," in *Cases Argued and Adjudged in the Supreme Court of the United States, December Term, 1869,* ed. J. W. Wallace (Washington, D.C.: William H. Morris, 1870), 9:326–38; REL to MCL, July 15, 1870, in Robert E. Lee Jr., *Recollections and Letters,* 414.
28. REL to Miss Maggie Smith, Sept. 9, 1870, Special Collections, Leyburn Library; REL to W. W. Corcoran, Aug. 23, 1870, in "Letters of Gen. R. E. Lee," *SHSP* 7 (March 1879): 155; William Preston Johnston, "Death and Funeral of General Lee," in Riley, *General Robert E. Lee After Appomattox,* 207; "The Next Agricultural Fair," *Richmond Dispatch,* Sept. 2, 1870; "The Rain," *Alexandria Gazette,* Sept. 17, 1870; "Heavy Flood in Virginia," *Richmond Dispatch,* Sept. 30, 1870.
29. Marvin P. Rozear et al., "R. E. Lee's Stroke," *VMHB,* April 1990, 292; MChL, "My Recollections of My Father's Death," Aug. 21, 1888, Lee Family Papers, VMHC; MCL to Mary Meade, Oct. 12, 1870, in "Funeral of Mrs. G. W. P. Custis and Death of General R. E.

Lee," 24; "The Great Virginia Flood" and "From Lynchburg," *Richmond Dispatch,* Oct. 4, 1870.

30. "The Great Flood," *Richmond Dispatch,* Oct. 4, 1870; "Gen. R. E. Lee's Health," *Alexandria Gazette,* Oct. 4, 1870; "Heavy Rain," *Staunton Spectator,* Oct. 4, 1870; Richard D. Mainwaring and Harris D. Riley, "The Lexington Physicians of General Robert E. Lee," *Southern Medical Journal* 98 (Aug. 2005): 803–4; Harris D. Riley, "Robert E. Lee's Battle with Disease," *Civil War Times Illustrated* 18 (Dec. 1979): 22; Harris D. Riley, "General Robert E. Lee: His Medical Profile," *Virginia Medical Monthly,* July 1978, 495–500; Richard D. Mainwaring and Curtis G. Trible, "The Cardiac Illness of General Robert E. Lee," *Journal of Surgery, Gynecology, and Obstetrics* 174 (March 1992): 237–44; Johnston, "Death and Funeral of General Lee," 210, 211; "General Lee," *Norfolk Virginian,* Oct. 7, 1870; MCL to Mary Meade, Oct. 12, 1870, in "Funeral of Mrs. G. W. P. Custis and Death of General R. E. Lee," 25; Robert E. Lee Jr., *Recollections and Letters,* 433; Sanborn, *Robert E. Lee: The Complete Man,* 376–77. On Lee's deathbed utterances, see Pryor, *Reading the Man,* 465.

Epilogue: The Crime and the Glory of Robert E. Lee

1. "General Lee—Death of the Great Southern Chief," *New York Herald,* Oct. 13, 1870; "Death of Gen. Lee," *New York Times,* Oct. 13, 1870; "Robert E. Lee," *New-York Tribune,* Oct. 13, 1870; "Robert E. Lee," *Philadelphia Evening Telegraph,* Oct. 13, 1870.
2. "The News of the Death of General Lee," *Richmond Dispatch,* Oct. 13, 1870; "The Death of Gen'l Lee," *Richmond Dispatch,* Oct. 14, 1870; "Death of Gen. Lee," *Alexandria Gazette,* Oct. 14, 1870; "Death of Gen. Robert E. Lee," *Vicksburg Times and Republican,* Oct. 14, 1870; "General Robert E. Lee," *Pall Mall Gazette,* Oct. 14, 1870.
3. "Bombast," *New National Era,* Nov. 10, 1870; David W. Blight, *Frederick Douglass' Civil War: Keeping Faith in Jubilee* (Baton Rouge: Louisiana State University Press, 1989), 229; Edmunds, in "Mrs. R. E. Lee," Dec. 13, 1870, Cong. Globe, 41st Cong., 3rd Sess., 74; "The Traitor, Lee," *Lehigh Register,* March 20, 1866; "The Death of General Lee," *Chicago Tribune,* Oct. 14, 1870; "General Lee and the Bar of New York," *Richmond Dispatch,* Oct. 17, 1870; "The Grief at Lee's Death," *Atlanta Constitution,* Oct. 15, 1870; Michael A. Ross, "The Commemoration of Robert E. Lee's Death and the Obstruction of Reconstruction in New Orleans," *Civil War History* 51 (June 2005): 135, 148.
4. "Our Great Loss," *Charleston Daily News,* Oct. 14, 1870; "Latest from Lexington," *Richmond Dispatch,* Oct. 15, 1870; Fishwick, *Lee After the War,* 219–20; Scott, "Some Personal Memories of General Robert E. Lee," 286.
5. Johnston, "Death and Funeral of General Lee," 215–21; "The Funeral of Gen. Lee," *Richmond Dispatch,* Oct. 17, 1870; Cooke, *Life of Gen. Robert E. Lee,* 501–5; "The Funeral Services of General Robert Edward Lee, at Lexington, Va.," *Frank Leslie's Illustrated Magazine,* Nov. 5, 1870. Johnston describes the singing of "the 124th hymn of the Episcopal collection" at the burial, which, in the 1859 edition of the Episcopal hymnal, was "Lift Your Glad Voices in Triumph on High." Johnston then adds that after the interment "the congregation sang the grand old hymn, 'How firm a foundation, ye saints of the Lord,'" which Johnston claimed "was always a favorite hymn of General Lee's." Oddly, "How Firm a Foundation" nowhere appears in that hymnal, or in the supplement published in 1870, nor did Lee in his letters ever refer to any particular preference in hymns.
6. Christopher R. Lawton, "Constructing the Cause, Bridging the Divide: Lee's Tomb at Washington College," *Southern Cultures* 15 (Summer 2009): 12, 20–22.
7. Douglas W. Bostick, *Memorializing Robert E. Lee: The Story of Lee Chapel* (Charleston, S.C.:

Joggling Board Press, 2005), 43, 51; "The History of the Flags in Lee Chapel and Museum," my.wlu.edu.

8. John Warwick Daniel, "Oration," in *Ceremonies Connected with the Inauguration of the Mausoleum and the Unveiling of the Recumbent Figure of General Robert Edward Lee at Washington and Lee University, June 28, 1883* (Richmond: West Johnston, 1883); John Warwick Daniel, "Lee," *Southern Bivouac,* Sept. 1883, 1–10; "A Salute to the Day," *Richmond Dispatch,* June 28, 1883.
9. Jubal Anderson Early, *The Campaigns of General Robert E. Lee: An Address* (Baltimore: John Murphy, 1872), 4, 10, 36, 45, 51; Benjamin Franklin Cooling, *Jubal Early: Robert E. Lee's Bad Old Man* (Lanham, Md.: Rowman & Littlefield, 2014), 140–42; Connelly, *Marble Man,* 55–56; "The Surrender Grounds at Appomattox," *Confederate Veteran,* April 1926, 129.
10. MacDonald, *Mrs. Robert E. Lee,* 294–95, 299; Coulling, *Lee Girls,* 179–80; *Alexandria Gazette and Virginia Advertiser,* Nov. 8, 1873; "Items," *Richmond Daily State Journal,* Nov. 8, 1873.
11. Trustee Minutes, Oct. 15, 1870, Washington College Trustee Minute Book, 346–52, Washington College Records of Board of Trustees, Feb. 21, 1845–Sept. 1873, Special Collections, Leyburn Library; Gaughan, *Last Battle of the Civil War,* 65–66, 74, 93, 166–67, 181; Enoch Aquila Chase, "The Arlington Case: George Washington Custis Lee Against the United States of America," *Virginia Law Review* 15 (Jan. 1929): 214–33; "The Arlington Estate Case," *New Orleans Times-Democrat,* Dec. 5, 1882; "The Arlington Estate Case," *Washington National Republican,* Dec. 5, 1882; "They May Rest in Peace," *Washington National Republican,* Dec. 6, 1882; "Justice for the Lees," *Richmond Dispatch,* Dec. 5, 1882; Yates, *Perfect Gentleman,* 2:227; "General Custis Lee and Lexington," *Alexandria Gazette,* April 22, 1897.
12. David S. Turk, *A Family's Path in America: The Lees and Their Continuing Legacy* (Westminster, Md.: Heritage Books, 2007), xi, 1–3, 16, 21–23, 29, 38, 60–62, 74, 77–79, 124; Daughtry, *Gray Cavalier,* 292–93, 297; on Robert E. Lee Jr., see Frederick S. Daniel, "A Visit to a Colonial Estate," *Harper's New Monthly Magazine,* March 1888, 517–24, and "Married," *Staunton Spectator,* Nov. 28, 1871; Coulling, *Lee Girls,* 182–89; "Gen. Lee's Daughter's Case," *New York Times,* June 15, 1902; "Attend Miss Lee's Funeral," *Alexandria Gazette,* Nov. 26, 1918.
13. REL to W. W. Austin, Sept. 30, 1867, LFDA/duPont Library; "James D. McCabe," *Southern Planter* 69 (Nov. 1908): 999; Cooke, *Life of Gen. Robert E. Lee,* 1–2, 468–69; "Esten Cooke's Life of Lee," *New Orleans Times-Picayune,* Jan. 28, 1871; "Robert E. Lee," *New Orleans Times-Picayune,* Jan. 21, 1872; Mason, *Popular Life of Gen. Robert Edward Lee,* iii, 344, 346; Edward Lee Childe, *The Life and Campaigns of General Lee,* trans. George Litting (London: Chatto and Windus, 1875), 164, 262.
14. Connelly, *Marble Man,* 40–41; Fitzhugh Lee, *General Lee,* 423; Taylor, *General Lee,* v; "Publications of the Past Week," *New York Times,* Sept. 28, 1894.
15. Freeman, *R. E. Lee,* 1:330, 4:502, 505; Thomas Nelson Page, *Robert E. Lee, the Southerner* (New York: Charles Scribner's Sons, 1909), 288; Gamaliel Bradford, *Lee the American* (Boston: Houghton Mifflin, 1912), 25, 82, 91, 97, 99, 266; David E. Johnson, *Douglas Southall Freeman* (Gretna, La.: Pelican, 2002), 15, 159; Gignilliat, "Historian's Dilemma," 218–19; Connelly, *Marble Man,* 143, 145. One aspiring Southern biographer of Lee, Allen Tate, eventually abandoned his project in 1931, convinced that "the egoism of self-righteousness" had prevented Lee from taking dictatorial control of the Confederacy into his hands and thus saving the South from defeat. See Glenn C. Arbery, "General Lee and the Siren: Allen Tate's Failed Biography," *Mississippi Quarterly* 64 (Winter/Spring 2011): 204.
16. Jones, *Life and Letters,* 381; "The Editor's Table," *Southern Bivouac,* June 1885, 60; John Joseph Bowen, *The Strategy of Robert E. Lee* (New York: Neale, 1914), 46, 60.
17. Frederick Maurice, *Robert E. Lee, the Soldier* (Boston: Houghton Mifflin, 1925), 84, 278, 291; Luvaas, *Military Legacy of the Civil War,* 210; J. F. C. Fuller, *Grant and Lee: A Study in*

Personality and Generalship (1933; Bloomington: Indiana University Press, 1967), 8; Liddell Hart, *Strategy* (1954; New York: Praeger, 1967), 154; Brian Holden Reid, *Robert E. Lee: Icon for a Nation* (Amherst, N.Y.: Prometheus Books, 2007), 43.

18. Connelly, *Autumn of Glory,* 535; Thomas L. Connelly, "Robert E. Lee and the Western Confederacy: A Criticism of Lee's Strategic Ability," *Civil War History* 15 (June 1969): 130, 132; Connelly, *Marble Man,* xiii, 165–76, 191, 201, 212; Emory Thomas, review of *The Marble Man, VMHB,* Jan. 1978, 120–21; Ludwell H. Johnson, review of *The Marble Man, Historical Magazine of the Protestant Episcopal Church,* March 1979, 122; Steve Davis, review of *The Marble Man, Georgia Historical Quarterly* 62 (Spring 1978): 101; John L. Gignilliat, review of *The Marble Man, Journal of Southern History* 44 (Feb. 1978): 128. Connelly's Lee was part of what Matthew Stanley calls a "victimhood narrative" of the war in which "now-neglected western soldiers" were presented as the real protagonists of the Civil War. Matthew Stanley, "The Original 'Forgotten Americans': A New Category of Civil War Memory?," *Civil War History* 65 (Dec. 2019): 391.
19. Thomas, *Robert E. Lee,* 413–14; Nolan, *Lee Considered,* 15; Fellman, *Making of Robert E. Lee,* 63, 218–23, 265–66.
20. Wynton Marsalis, "Why New Orleans Should Take Down Robert E. Lee's Statue," *New Orleans Times-Picayune,* May 17, 2017; Jamil Smith, "Why Would Charlottesville Racists Do So Much to Protect a Robert E. Lee Statue?," *Los Angeles Times,* Aug. 14, 2017; Nick Roll, "Robert E. Lee Statue Vandalized at Duke," *Inside Higher Ed,* Aug. 18, 2017, www.insidehighered.com; Ralph M. K. Haurwitz, "UT Removes Confederate Statues from South Mall," *Austin American-Statesman,* Aug. 22, 2017; Kristin Lam, "Confederate Statue That Prompted Charlottesville Rally Must Stay, Judge Rules," *USA Today,* Sept. 15, 2019; Matthew Haag, "Dallas Can Remove Robert E. Lee Statue, Judge Rules," *New York Times,* Sept. 7, 2017; Nicholas Fandos, "Baltimore Mayor Had Statues Removed in 'Best Interest of My City,'" *New York Times,* Aug. 16, 2017; Tawnell D. Hobbs, "Schools Keep Lee, Dump Robert E.," *Wall Street Journal,* June 25, 2019; Peter J. Boyer, "The Complicated History of Washington & Lee University," *Weekly Standard,* Nov. 19, 2018; Tea Kvetenadze and Lia Eustachewich, "Robert E. Lee Plaque Removed from Brooklyn Church," *New York Post,* Aug. 16, 2017; Robert Sullivan, "A Confederate General in Brooklyn," *New Yorker,* June 19, 2017.
21. Scott Jaschik, "Race, History, and Robert E. Lee," *Inside Higher Ed,* May 29, 2018; Andrew Adkins, "Report Calls for Major Changes in How W&L Teaches and Presents Its History," *Roanoke Times,* May 18, 2018; Boyer, "Complicated History of Washington & Lee University"; Toni Locy, "Letting Go of Robert E. Lee at Washington and Lee University," *Nation,* June 25, 2020; Brandon Hasbrouck, "Both Namesakes of Washington and Lee University Perpetrated Racial Terror. The School Should Be Renamed," *Washington Post,* July 4, 2020; Elizabeth Bell, "Washington and Lee Faculty Vote to Change the University's Name," *Richmond Times-Dispatch,* July 6, 2020.
22. List of National Historic Landmarks by State, www.nps.gov/subjects/nationalhistoriclandmarks/list-of-nhls-by-state.htm.
23. "Robert Edward Lee Sculpture, Albemarle County, Virginia," National Register of Historic Places Registration Form, www.dhr.virginia.gov/registers/Cities/Charlottesville/104-0264_Robert_Edward_Lee_Sculpture_1997_Final_Nomination.pdf; M. Ashby Jones, "Robert E. Lee Day," May 21, 1924, in *Proceedings of the 37th Annual Reunion of the Virginia Grand Camp Confederate Veterans, and of the 29th Reunion of the Sons of Confederate Veterans* (Chattanooga, 1924), 63–64; Paul Harvey, *Redeeming the South: Religious Cultures and Racial Identities Among Southern Baptists, 1865–1925* (Chapel Hill: University of North Carolina Press, 1997), 201.
24. Burton, "Life and Death of Bloody Island," 75; Russell Berman, "The Nation's Official Memorial to Robert E. Lee Gets a Rewrite," *Atlantic,* Aug. 18, 2017.

25. Marshall, *Aide-de-Camp of Lee,* 188.
26. John Codman Ropes to John Chipman Gray, May 11, 1864, in *War Letters, 1862–1865, of John Chipman Gray and John Codman Ropes* (New York: Houghton Mifflin, 1927), 332; "A British General's View," *New York Sun,* March 13, 1887.
27. Thomas, *Robert E. Lee,* 246; Harsh, *Confederate Tide Rising,* 69; Taylor, *Four Years with General Lee,* 146; Reid, *Robert E. Lee: Icon for a Nation,* 42–43, 191, 246.
28. Taylor, *Four Years with General Lee,* 147.
29. Michael Levenson, "Who Are 'Antifa' Activists and How Do They Operate?," *Boston Globe,* Aug. 16, 2017; Gail Russell Chaddock, "Safe Protests and Uncomfortable Conversations," *Christian Science Monitor,* Aug. 22, 2017.
30. A. John Simmons, *Moral Principles and Political Obligations* (Princeton, N.J.: Princeton University Press, 1979), 200; Murray Rothbard, *The Anatomy of the State* (Auburn, Ala.: Ludwig von Mises Institute, 2009), 45–46.
31. Michael Walzer, "Does Betrayal Matter?," review of *On Betrayal,* by Avi Margarlit, *New York Review of Books,* May 11, 2017.
32. Wendell Phillips, "Abraham Lincoln," April 23, 1865, in *Speeches, Lectures, and Letters* (Boston: Lee & Shepard, 1891), 450–51; *Walt Whitman's Civil War,* ed. Walter Lowenfels (New York: Knopf, 1961), 251; Herman Melville, "Lee in the Capitol," April 1866, in *The Writings of Herman Melville: Published Poems,* 163; John Gardner, *On Writers and Writing* (Reading, Mass.: Addison-Wesley, 1994), 139.

Bibliography

Writings of the Lee Family

Adams, Francis Raymond. "An Annotated Edition of the Personal Letters of Robert E. Lee, April 1855–April 1861." PhD diss., University of Maryland, 1955.

Ballagh, J. C., ed. *The Letters of Richard Henry Lee, 1779–1794.* 2 vols. New York: Macmillan, 1914.

Chaney, William Franklin. *Duty Most Sublime: The Life of Robert E. Lee as Told Through the "Carter Letters."* Baltimore: Gateway Press, 1996.

Childe, Edward Lee. *The Life and Campaigns of General Lee.* Translated by George Litting. London: Chatto and Windus, 1875.

Crimmins, Martin L., ed. "Colonel Robert E. Lee's Report on Indian Combats in Texas." *Southwestern Historical Quarterly* 39 (July 1935).

Cuthbert, Norma B. "To Molly: Five Early Letters from Robert E. Lee to His Wife, 1832–1835." *Huntington Library Quarterly* 15 (May 1952).

deButts, Mary Custis Lee, ed. *Growing Up in the 1850s: The Journal of Agnes Lee.* Chapel Hill: University of North Carolina Press, 1984.

deButts, R. E. L., Jr., ed. "Lee in Love: Courtship and Correspondence in Antebellum Virginia." *VMHB* 115 (2007).

———. "Mary Custis Lee's 'Reminiscences of the War.' " *VMHB* 109 (2001).

Dowdey, Clifford, and L. H. Manarin, eds. *Wartime Papers of Robert E. Lee.* Boston: Little, Brown, 1961.

Freeman, Douglas Southall. "Lee and the Ladies: Unpublished Letters of Robert E. Lee." *Scribner's Magazine,* Oct.–Nov. 1925.

Gallagher, Gary W., ed. " 'We Are Our Own Trumpeters': Robert E. Lee Describes Winfield Scott's Campaign to Mexico City." *VMHB,* July 1987.

Hoyt, William D., ed. "Some Personal Letters of Robert E. Lee, 1850–1858." *Journal of Southern History* 12 (Nov. 1946).

Lee, Cazenove Gardner, Jr. "Ann Hill Carter." *WMQ* 16 (July 1936).

———. *Lee Chronicle: Studies of the Early Generations of the Lees of Virginia.* New York: New York University Press, 1957.

Lee, Charles Carter. *The Maid of the Doe: A Lay of the Revolution.* Washington, D.C.: Robert Farnham, 1842.

———. *Virginia Georgics, Written for the Hole and Corner Club of Powhatan.* Richmond: James Woodhouse, 1858.

Lee, Edmund Jennings. *Lee of Virginia, 1642–1892: Biographical and Genealogical Sketches of the Descendants of Colonel Richard Lee.* Westminster, Md.: Heritage Books, 2008.

Lee, Fitzhugh. *General Lee.* New York: D. Appleton, 1894.

Lee, George Taylor. "Reminiscences of General Robert E. Lee, 1865–68." *South Atlantic Quarterly* 26 (July 1927).

Lee, Henry. *Memoirs of the War in the Southern Department of the United States.* 2 vols. Philadelphia: Bradford & Inskeep, 1812.

Lee, Henry, IV. *Observations on the Writings of Thomas Jefferson, with Particular Reference to the Attack They Contain on the Memory of the Late Gen. Henry Lee.* Edited by Charles Carter Lee. Philadelphia: J. Dobson, 1839.

Lee, Mary Custis. "Memoir." In *Recollections and Private Memoirs of Washington, by His Adopted Son, George Washington Parke Custis, with a Memoir of the Author.* New York: Derby & Jackson, 1860.

Lee, Robert E. *The Daily Correspondence of Brevet Colonel Robert E. Lee, Superintendent, United States Military Academy, September 1, 1852, to March 24, 1855.* Edited by C. R. Bowery and B. D. Hankinson. West Point, N.Y.: U.S. Military Academy Library Occasional Papers 5, 2003.

———. *Lee's Dispatches: Unpublished Letters of General Robert E. Lee, C.S.A., to Jefferson Davis and the War Department of the Confederate States of America, 1862–65.* Edited by D. S. Freeman. New York: G. P. Putnam's Sons, 1915.

———. "Life of General Henry Lee." In Henry Lee, *Memoirs of the War in the Southern Department of the United States.* New York: University Publishing, 1870.

———. "Mississippi River Above the Ohio, and Pier in the Harbor of St. Louis" (Oct. 6, 1840) and "Ohio and Mississippi Rivers from Louisville to New Orleans" (Nov. 20, 1839). In *Public Documents Printed by Order of the Senate of the United States During the Second Session of the Twenty-Sixth Congress.* Washington, D.C.: Blair & Rives, 1841.

———. *"To Markie": The Letters of Robert E. Lee to Martha Custis Williams.* Edited by Avery Craven. Cambridge, Mass.: Harvard University Press, 1933.

Lee, Robert E., Jr. *Recollections and Letters of General Robert E. Lee.* New York: Doubleday, Page, 1904.

"Letters of Gen. R. E. Lee." *SHSP* 7 (March 1879).

Rachal, W. M. E., ed. "'Secession Is Nothing but Revolution': A Letter of R. E. Lee to His Son 'Rooney.'" *VMHB,* Jan. 1961.

"A Robert E. Lee Letter to P. G. T. Beauregard." *Maryland Historical Magazine,* Sept. 1956.

Screven, Frank, ed. "The Letters of R. E. Lee to the Mackay Family of Savannah." Typescript, Georgia Southern University, Armstrong Campus Library, 1952.

Shackelford, George Green, ed. "Lieutenant Lee Reports to Captain Talcott on Fort Calhoun's Construction on the Rip Raps." *VMHB,* July 1952.

Sibley, Marilyn McAdams. "Robert E. Lee to Albert Sidney Johnston, 1857." *Journal of Southern History* 29 (Feb. 1963).

Archival Collections

Gilder Lehrman Institute of American History Collection, New-York Historical Society
Historical Society of Pennsylvania, Philadelphia
    Dreer Collection of American Lawyers
    Edward Carey Gardiner Collection
Huntington Library, San Marino, Calif.
    Lee Family Papers, R. A. Brock Collection and Papers
    John C. Underwood Papers, 1865–1870
Robert E. Lee Collection, 1834–1967, Missouri Historical Society Archives, Missouri History Museum, St. Louis
Robert E. Lee Engineering Notebook, 1841–1842 (MSS Col 1719), Manuscripts and Archives Division, New York Public Library
Robert E. Lee Memorial Collection, Arlington House (NPS), Arlington, Va.
Lee-Fendall House Archives, Alexandria, Va.
Library of Congress, Washington, D.C.
    American Colonization Society Papers
    Ethel Armes Collection of Lee Family Papers
    P. G. T. Beauregard Papers
    Blair Family Papers, Series 2 and 5
    Breckinridge Family Papers
    Breckinridge Long Papers, 1486–1948
    deButts-Ely Collection of Lee Family Papers
    Richard Stoddert Ewell Papers, 1838–1896
    Samuel Peter Heintzelman Papers (Military Papers, 1822–1869)
    John Lloyd Family Papers
    George B. McClellan Papers
Literary and Historical Manuscripts, Pierpont Morgan Library, New York
Mackay Family Letters, 1828–1854, Georgia Historical Society, Savannah
David McConaughy Papers, Special Collections, Musselman Library, Gettysburg College, Gettysburg, Pa.
David M. Rubenstein Rare Book and Manuscript Library, Duke University
    William Watts Ball Papers, 1778–1952
    Robert E. Lee Papers, 1749–1975
    Edmund Jennings Lee II Papers, 1797–1877
Albert and Shirley Small Special Collections Library, University of Virginia, Charlottesville
    John Warwick Daniel Papers
    Lee Family Papers
    Fitzhugh Lee Papers
    Robert E. Lee Papers
    McDowell-Miller-Warner Papers
Southern Historical Collection, Louis Round Wilson Library, University of North Carolina
    Thomas Claiborne Papers
    Robert E. Lee Papers, 1847–1869
    Lee and Marshall Family Letters, 1811–1870
    James Longstreet Papers, 1875–1904
    Mackay and Stiles Family Papers, 1743–1975
    William Nelson Pendleton Papers, 1798–1889

Special Collections, James G. Leyburn Library, Washington and Lee University, Lexington, Va.
Lee Letterbooks 1 and 2 and Memorandum Book (Oct. 1865)
Robert E. Lee Penn Letterbook
Washington College Records of Board of Trustees
Washington College Trustee Minute Book
Stratford Hall, Stratford, Va.
Lee Family Digital Archive/Jessie Ball duPont Library
Walter Herron Taylor Papers
Tudor Place Historic House and Garden Archives, Washington, D.C.
John C. Underwood Correspondence, Rare Books and Special Collections, Rush Rees Library, University of Rochester, Rochester, N.Y.
University of Texas at Austin
Robert E. Lee Papers, Dolph Briscoe Center for American History
Miscellaneous Mexican War File, box GA-43, folder 9, Special Collections
Virginia Museum of History and Culture, Richmond
Bryan Family Papers, 1774–1942
Giles Buckner Cooke Papers
Custis-Lee Family Papers
Lee Family Papers, 1638–1867
George Bolling Lee Papers
George Bolling Lee Papers, 1841–1868
Robert E. Lee Headquarters Papers*
Robert E. Lee Letterbook 1
Robinson Family Papers, 1836–1899
Military Papers of J. E. B. Stuart, 1855–1864
Talcott Family Papers, 1816–1915
Yale University, New Haven, Conn.
John White Geary Mexican War Papers, Western Americana Collection, Beinecke Rare Book and Manuscript Library
Elihu Washburne Diaries, Manuscripts and Archives, Sterling Library

Newspapers, Periodicals, Directories, and Almanacs

Alamo Express
Alexandria Gazette
American Almanac and Repository of Useful Knowledge for the Year 1838
American Almanac and Repository of Useful Knowledge for the Year 1851
American Almanac and Repository of Useful Knowledge for the Year 1852
American Almanac and Repository of Useful Knowledge for the Year 1859
American Quarterly Church Review and Ecclesiastical Register
American Quarterly Register and Magazine
American Whig Review
American Year-Book and National Register for 1869
Atlanta Constitution

* Also available in microfilm format on forty-two reels as *Confederate Military Manuscripts: Series A,* ed. Joseph T. Glatthaar and Martin Schipper (Bethesda, Md.: University Publications of America, 1997).

Atlantic Monthly
Austin American-Statesman
Baltimore Daily Exchange
Baltimore News
Baltimore Sun
Bangor Daily Whig and Courier
Boston Daily Advertiser
Boston Globe
British Quarterly Review
Brooklyn Daily Eagle
Charleston Daily Courier
Charleston Daily News
Charleston Mercury
Charles Town Independent Democrat
Charlotte Democrat
Chicago Tribune
Christian Advocate
Christian Science Monitor
Cincinnati Inquirer
Confederate Veteran
Congressional Globe
Daily Cleveland Herald
Daily Commercial Bulletin and Missouri Literary Register
Daily National Intelligencer
Dallas Herald
DeBow's Review
Dubuque Daily Herald
Edgefield Advertiser
Harper's Monthly Magazine
Household Journal of Popular Information, Amusement, and Domestic Economy
Lehigh Register
Liverpool Mercury
London *Times*
Los Angeles Times
Missouri Republican
National Anti-slavery Standard
National Tribune
New National Era
New Orleans Daily Delta
New Orleans Times-Democrat
New Orleans Times-Picayune
New York Evening Post
New York Herald
New York Independent
New York Sun
New York Times
New-York Tribune
Niles' Political Register
Niles' Weekly Register
Norfolk Post

Norfolk Virginian
North American Review
Pall Mall Gazette
Philadelphia Evening Telegraph
Philadelphia Inquirer
Philadelphia Legal Intelligencer
Pittsfield Sun
Quarterly Christian Spectator
Richmond Daily State Journal
Richmond Dispatch
Richmond Enquirer
Richmond Times-Dispatch
Richmond Whig
Sacramento Daily Union
San Francisco Daily Bulletin
Southern Bivouac
Southern Churchman
Southern Magazine
Staunton Spectator
St. Louis Business Directory for 1847: Containing the History of St. Louis
Texas Republican
United States Magazine and Democratic Review
Vicksburg Times and Republican
Vicksburg Whig
Virginia Free Press and Farmers' Repository
Washington Daily American Telegraph
Washington Daily Union
Washington Evening Star
Washington National Republican
Washington Post
Washington Republic
Washington Sentinel
Weekly National Intelligencer
Wheeling Daily Intelligencer
Wilmington Daily Journal
Wilmington Morning Star
World Almanac and Book of Facts 1892
Yorkville Enquirer

General Editions

Baker, George E., ed. *The Works of William H. Seward.* 5 vols. Boston: Houghton, Mifflin, 1884.

Basler, Roy P., ed. *The Collected Works of Abraham Lincoln.* 8 vols., 2 supplements. New Brunswick, N.J.: Rutgers University Press, 1953.

Chase, P. D., et al., eds. *The Papers of George Washington, Revolutionary War Series.* 26 vols. Charlottesville: University of Virginia Press, 1985–2018.

Crist, Lynda Lasswell, ed. *The Papers of Jefferson Davis.* 14 vols. Baton Rouge: Louisiana State University Press, 1991–2015.

Fitzpatrick, John C., ed. *The Writings of George Washington.* 39 vols. Washington, D.C.: U.S. Government Printing Office, 1931–44.

Greeley, Horace. *Proceedings of the First Three Republican National Conventions of 1856, 1860, and 1864.* Minneapolis: Charles W. Johnson, 1893.

Ladd, David, and Audrey Ladd, eds. *The Bachelder Papers: Gettysburg in Their Own Words.* 3 vols. Dayton: Morningside Bookshop, 1994.

Moore, Frank, ed. *The Rebellion Record: A Diary of American Events, with Documents, Narratives, Illustrative Incidents, Poetry Etc.* 11 vols. New York: G. P. Putnam, 1861–68.

Moore, John Bassett, ed. *The Works of James Buchanan: Comprising His Speeches, State Papers, and Private Correspondence.* 12 vols. Philadelphia: J. B. Lippincott, 1910.

Niven, John, ed. *The Salmon P. Chase Papers: Correspondence, 1858–March 1863.* Kent, Ohio: Kent State University Press, 1996.

Quaife, Milo Milton, ed. *The Diary of James K. Polk During His Presidency, 1845 to 1849.* 4 vols. Chicago: A. C. McClurg, 1910.

Richardson, James D., ed. *A Compilation of the Messages and Papers of the Presidents, 1789–1897.* 10 vols. Washington, D.C.: Government Printing Office, 1897.

Scarborough, William Kauffman, ed. *The Diary of Edmund Ruffin.* 3 vols. Baton Rouge: Louisiana State University Press, 1972–89.

Showman, Richard K., et al., eds. *The Papers of General Nathanael Greene.* 13 vols. Chapel Hill: University of North Carolina Press, 1976–2005.

Simon, John Y., and John F. Marszalek, eds. *The Papers of Ulysses S. Grant.* 32 vols. Carbondale: Southern Illinois University Press, 1967–2012.

Syrett, Harold C., ed. *The Papers of Alexander Hamilton.* 27 vols. New York: Columbia University Press, 1961–87.

Government Documents

Cases Argued and Adjudged in the Supreme Court of the United States, December Term, 1869. Edited by John William Wallace. Vol. 9. Washington, D.C.: William H. Morris, 1870.

Church, R. W., and G. H. Reese, eds. *Journals and Papers of the Virginia State Convention of 1861.* 3 vols. Richmond: Virginia State Library, 1966.

The Federal Cases: Comprising Cases Argued and Determined in the Circuit and District Courts of the United States. St. Paul: West, 1894.

General Orders of the War Department, Embracing the Years 1861, 1862, and 1863, Adapted Especially for the Use of the Army and Navy of the United States. Edited by Thomas M. O'Brien and Oliver Diefendorf. 2 vols. New York: Derby & Miller, 1864.

Journal of the Congress of the Confederate States of America, 1861–1865. 7 vols. Washington, D.C.: Government Printing Office, 1904–5.

Official Opinions of the Attorneys General of the United States. Edited by J. Hubley Ashton. Washington, D.C.: W. H. & O. H. Morrison, 1869.

Ordinances of the Convention, Assembled at Wheeling, on the 11th of June, 1861. Wheeling, Va., 1861.

Rawson, E. K., et al., eds. *Official Records of the Union and Confederate Navies in the War of the Rebellion.* 30 vols. Washington, D.C.: Government Printing Office, 1894–1922.

Report of the Joint Committee on Reconstruction at the First Session of the Thirty-Ninth Congress. Washington, D.C.: Government Printing Office, 1866.

Reports of the Operations of the Army of Northern Virginia: From June 1862 to and Including the Battle of Fredericksburg, Dec. 13, 1862. Richmond: R. M. Smith, 1864.

Scott, Robert M., et al., eds. *The War of the Rebellion: A Compilation of the Official Records of the*

Union and Confederate Armies. 127 vols. Washington, D.C.: Government Printing Office, 1881–1901.

The Statutes at Large, Treaties, and Proclamations of the United States of America from December 5, 1859, to March 3, 1863. Edited by G. P. Sanger. Vols. 12–13. Boston: Little, Brown, 1863.

Weaver, William A., ed. *Register of All Officers and Agents, Civil, Military, and Naval, in the Service of the United States.* Washington, D.C.: Francis Preston Blair, 1833.

Primary Materials—Articles and Books

Alderson, J. Coleman. "Lee and Longstreet at Gettysburg." *Confederate Veteran* 10 (Oct. 1904).

Alexander, Edward Porter. *Fighting for the Confederacy: The Personal Recollections of General Edward Porter Alexander.* Edited by Gary W. Gallagher. Chapel Hill: University of North Carolina Press, 1989.

———. "Lee at Appomattox: Personal Recollections of the Break-up of the Confederacy." *Century Magazine,* April 1902.

Allan, William. "General Lee's Strength and Losses at Gettysburg." *SHSP* 1 (July 1877).

———. "Memoranda of Conversations with General Robert E. Lee" (Feb. 25 and March 10, 1868). In Gallagher, *Lee the Soldier.*

Allen, Thomas. "The Commerce and Navigation of the Mississippi and Its Tributaries." *Western Journal of Agriculture, Manufactures, Mechanic Arts, Internal Improvement, Commerce, and General Literature* 1 (March 1848).

Anderson, Robert. *An Artillery Officer in the Mexican War, 1846–7: Letters of Robert Anderson.* Edited by Eba Anderson Lawton. New York: G. P. Putnam's Sons, 1911.

Andrews, Mariette Minnegerode. *Scraps of Paper.* New York: E. P. Dutton, 1929.

Averell, William Woods. *Ten Years in the Saddle: The Memoir of William Woods Averell.* Edited by Edward K. Eckert and Nicholas J. Amato. San Rafael, Calif.: Presidio Press, 1978.

Badeau, Adam. *Grant in Peace: From Appomattox to Mount McGregor, a Personal Memoir.* Hartford: S. S. Scranton, 1887.

Ballentine, George. *Autobiography of an English Soldier in the United States Army, Comprising Observations and Adventures in the States and Mexico.* New York: Stringer & Townsend, 1853.

Barnard, John G. "Memoir of Joseph Gilbert Totten, 1788–1864." In *National Academy of Sciences: Biographical Memoirs.* Philadelphia: Collins, 1877.

Bartlett, Asa W. *History of the Twelfth Regiment, New Hampshire Volunteers in the War of the Rebellion.* Concord, N.H.: Ira C. Evans, 1897.

Baylies, Francis. *A Narrative of Major General Wool's Campaign in Mexico in the Years 1846, 1847, and 1848.* Albany: Little, 1851.

Bean, W. G. "Memoranda of Conversations Between General Robert E. Lee and William Preston Johnston: May 7, 1868, and March 18, 1870." *VMHB,* Oct. 1965.

Beauregard, P. G. T. "The Battle of Petersburg." In Cozzens, *Battles and Leaders of the Civil War,* 6:407–23.

———. "The First Battle of Bull Run." In Buel and Johnson, *Battles and Leaders of the Civil War.* 1:196–228.

Bennett, William Wallace. *A Narrative of the Great Revival Which Prevailed in the Southern Armies During the Late Civil War Between the States of the Federal Union.* Philadelphia: Claxton, Remsen & Haffelfinger, 1877.

Berard, Augusta Blanche. *Reminiscences of West Point in the Olden Time.* East Saginaw, Mich.: Evening News Printing, 1886.

Bernard, George S. "Reminiscences of Norfolk, May–June 1861." In Newsome, *Civil War Talks.*

Blackford, Susan Leigh, and Charles Minor Blackford. *Letters from Lee's Army; or, Memoirs of Life in and out of the Army in Virginia During the War Between the States.* 1947; Lincoln: University of Nebraska Press, 1998.

Bonnet, John. "Scott's Battles in Mexico." *Harper's New Monthly Magazine,* Aug. 1855.

Booth, George Wilson. *A Maryland Boy in Lee's Army: Personal Reminiscences of a Maryland Soldier in the War Between the States, 1861–1865.* Edited by E. J. Mink. Lincoln: University of Nebraska Press, 2000.

Boteler, Alexander R. "Recollections of the John Brown Raid." *Century Magazine,* May 1883.

Boynton, Edward Carlisle. *History of West Point: And Its Military Importance During the American Revolution and the Origin and Progress of the United States Military Academy.* New York: D. Van Nostrand, 1871.

Brackett, Albert G. *History of the United States Cavalry: From the Formation of the Federal Government to the 1st of June, 1863.* New York: Harper & Bros., 1865.

Brent, Joseph L. *Memoirs of the War Between the States.* New Orleans: Fontana Printing, 1940.

Bright, Robert A. "Pickett's Charge." *SHSP* 31 (1903).

Brock, Robert A., ed. *Gen. Robert Edward Lee: Soldier, Citizen, and Christian Patriot.* Richmond: Royal, 1897.

Brooks, Nathan Covington. *A Complete History of the Mexican War: Its Causes, Conduct, and Consequences.* Philadelphia: Grigg, Elliot, 1849.

Brown, Campbell. *Campbell Brown's Civil War: With Ewell and the Army of Northern Virginia.* Edited by Terry L. Jones. Baton Rouge: Louisiana State University Press, 2001.

Buck, Lucy Rebecca. *In Shadows on My Heart: The Civil War Diary of Lucy Rebecca Buck of Virginia.* Edited by E. R. Baer. Athens: University of Georgia Press, 1997.

Buel, C. C., and R. U. Johnson, eds. *Battles and Leaders of the Civil War.* 4 vols. New York: Century, 1884.

Burke, William. *The Mineral Springs of Western Virginia: With Remarks on Their Use, and the Diseases to Which They Are Applicable.* New York: Wiley & Putnam, 1842.

Caldwell, J. F. J. *The History of a Brigade of South Carolinians: Known First as "Gregg's."* Philadelphia: King & Baird, 1866.

Camp, G. W. "Interesting Facts Connected with the Occupation of the City by the Federals Following Evacuation in April 1865." In Newsome, *Civil War Talks.*

Campbell, John Archibald. *Reminiscences and Documents Relating to the Civil War During the Year 1865.* Baltimore: John Murphy, 1887.

Carman, Ezra A. *The Maryland Campaign of September 1862.* Vol. 1, *South Mountain.* Edited by T. G. Clemens. El Dorado, Calif.: Savas Beatie, 2010.

Chamberlain, Joshua Lawrence. "Appomattox" (Oct. 7, 1903). In *Personal Recollections of the War of the Rebellion: Addresses Delivered Before the Commandery of the State of New York, Military Order of the Loyal Legion of the United States,* edited by A. N. Blakeman. New York: G. P. Putnam's Sons, 1907.

Chambers, Adam B. *Proceedings of the St. Louis Chamber of Commerce, in Relation to the Improvement of the Navigation of the Mississippi River and Its Principal Tributaries and the St. Louis Harbor.* St. Louis: Chambers & Knapp, 1842.

Chesnut, Mary. *Mary Chesnut's Civil War.* Edited by C. Vann Woodward. New Haven, Conn.: Yale University Press, 1981.

Church, Albert E. *Personal Reminiscences of the Military Academy from 1824 to 1831: A Paper Read to the U.S. Military Service Institute, West Point, March 28, 1878.* West Point, N.Y.: USMA Press, 1879.

Claiborne, John Herbert. "Personal Reminiscences of the Last Days of Lee and His Paladins." *SHSP* 28 (1900).

Collyar, John B. "A College Boy's Observation of General Lee." In Riley, *General Robert E. Lee After Appomattox.*

Cooke, John Esten. *Hammer and Rapier.* New York: Geo. W. Carleton, 1870.

Cozzens, Peter, ed. *Battles and Leaders of the Civil War.* 6 vols. Urbana: University of Illinois Press, 2004.

Cullum, George Washington. *Biographical Register of the Officers and Graduates of the U.S. Military Academy at West Point, N.Y.* 11 vols. Boston: Houghton, Mifflin, 1891.

Dabney, Robert L. *Life and Campaigns of Lieut.-Gen. Thomas J. Jackson.* 1865; Harrisonburg, Va.: Sprinkle, 1976.

Dana, Charles A. *Recollections of the Civil War: With the Leaders at Washington and in the Sixties.* New York: D. Appleton, 1913.

Daniel, John Warwick. "Oration." In *Ceremonies Connected with the Inauguration of the Mausoleum and the Unveiling of the Recumbent Figure of General Robert Edward Lee at Washington and Lee University, June 28, 1883.* Richmond: West Johnston, 1883.

Darrow, Caroline Baldwin. "Recollections of the Twiggs Surrender." In Buel and Johnson, *Battles and Leaders of the Civil War,* 1:33–39.

Davidson, Greenlee. *Captain Greenlee Davidson, C.S.A., Diary and Letters, 1851–1863.* Edited by C. W. Turner. Verone, Va.: McClure Press, 1975.

Davis, George T. M. *Autobiography of the Late Col. Geo. T. M. Davis, Captain and Aid-de-Camp Scott's Army of Invasion (Mexico) from Posthumous Papers.* New York: Jenkins & McCowan, 1891.

Davis, Jefferson. "Remarks of President Davis" (Nov. 3, 1870). In *Organization of the Lee Monument Association, and the Association of the Army of Northern Virginia.* Richmond: J. W. Randolph & English, 1871.

———. *The Rise and Fall of the Confederate Government.* 2 vols. New York: D. Appleton, 1881.

———. "Robert E. Lee." In Cozzens, *Battles and Leaders of the Civil War,* 6:91–99.

Dawson, Francis. *Reminiscences of Confederate Service, 1861–1865.* Edited by B. I. Wiley. Baton Rouge: Louisiana State University Press, 1980.

De Leon, Thomas C. *Four Years in Rebel Capitals: An Inside View of Life in the Southern Confederacy.* Mobile, Ala.: Gossip, 1892.

D'Oremieulx, Laura. "Recollections of West Point in 1853." *Association of Graduates of the United States Military Academy* 3 (May 1903).

Duke, Helen R., ed. "Recollections of Judge R. T. W. Duke Jr." *Papers of the Albemarle County Historical Society* 3 (1942–43).

Eanes, Greg. *Black Day of the Army, April 6, 1865: The Battles of Sailor's Creek.* Burkeville, Va.: E&H, 2001.

Early, Jubal Anderson. *The Campaigns of General Robert E. Lee: An Address.* Baltimore: John Murphy, 1872.

Edmondston, Catherine Devereux. *Journal of a Secesh Lady: The Diary of Catherine Ann Devereux Edmondston, 1860–1866.* Edited by Beth G. Crabtree and James W. Patton. Raleigh, N.C.: Division of Archives and History, 1979.

Eggleston, George Cary. *A Rebel's Recollections.* New York: G. P. Putnam's, 1905.

Eggleston, Joseph W. "Artillery Experiences at Petersburg and Elsewhere." In Newsome, *Civil War Talks.*

Ewell, Richard S. *The Letters of General Richard S. Ewell: Stonewall's Successor.* Edited by Donald Pfanz. Knoxville: University of Tennessee Press, 2012.

Fehrenbacher, Don, and Virginia Fehrenbacher, eds. *Recollected Words of Abraham Lincoln.* Stanford, Calif.: Stanford University Press, 1996.

Ferrell, Robert H., ed. *Monterrey Is Ours! The Mexican War Letters of Lieutenant Dana, 1845–1847.* Lexington: University Press of Kentucky, 1990.

Field, Charles W. "Campaign of 1864 and 1865." *SHSP* 14 (1886).

Fitzhugh, George. "The Northern Neck of Virginia." *DeBow's Review,* Sept. 1859.

Fleming, Walter Lynwood, ed. *Documentary History of Reconstruction: Political, Military, Social, Religious, Educational, and Industrial, 1865 to the Present Time.* Cleveland: Arthur H. Clarke, 1906.

Foote, Henry S. *Casket of Reminiscences.* Washington, D.C.: Chronicle, 1874.

Forsyth, George. "The Closing Scene at Appomattox Court House." *Harper's New Monthly Magazine,* April 1898.

Freehling, William W., and Craig M. Simpson, eds. *Showdown in Virginia: The 1861 Convention and the Fate of the Union.* Charlottesville: University of Virginia Press, 2010.

Fremantle, Arthur James Lyon. *Three Months in the Southern States: April–June, 1863.* London: William Blackwood, 1863.

Frost, John. *Life of Major General Zachary Taylor: With Notices of the War in New Mexico, California, and in South Mexico and Biographical Sketches of Officers Who Have Distinguished Themselves in the War with Mexico.* New York: D. Appleton, 1847.

———. *The Mexican War and Its Warriors: Comprising a Complete History of All the Operations of the American Armies in Mexico.* New Haven, Conn.: H. Mansfield, 1848.

Furber, George C. *The Twelve Months Volunteer; or, Journal of a Private, in the Tennessee Regiment of Cavalry.* Cincinnati: J. A. & U. P. James, 1850.

Garidel, Henri. *Exile in Richmond: The Confederate Journal of Henri Garidel.* Edited by M. B. Chesson and L. J. Roberts. Charlottesville: University of Virginia Press, 2001.

Gibbon, John. "Personal Recollections of Appomattox." *Century Magazine,* April 1902.

———. *Personal Recollections of the Civil War.* 1928; Dayton: Press of Morningside Bookshop, 1988.

Goddard, Henry P. *The Good Fight That Didn't End: Henry P. Goddard's Accounts of Civil War and Peace.* Edited by Calvin Goddard Zon. Columbia: University of South Carolina Press, 2008.

Goode, John B. *Recollections of a Lifetime.* New York: Neale, 1906.

Gordon, George H. "The Battles of Contreras and Churubusco" (March 12, 1883) and "The Battles of Molino del Rey and Chapultepec" (Dec. 10, 1883). In *Civil and Mexican Wars, 1861, 1846.* Boston: Military Historical Society of Massachusetts, 1913.

Gordon, John Brown. *Reminiscences of the Civil War.* New York: Charles Scribner's Sons, 1904.

Goree, Thomas J. *Longstreet's Aide: The Civil War Letters of Major Thomas J. Goree.* Edited by Thomas W. Cutrer. Charlottesville: University of Virginia Press, 1995.

Grant, Ulysses S. *Personal Memoirs.* 2 vols. New York: C. L. Webster, 1886.

Greeley, Horace. *The American Conflict: A History of the Great Rebellion in the United States of America.* 2 vols. Hartford: O. D. Case, 1866.

Green, Israel. "The Capture of John Brown." *North American Review* 141 (Dec. 1885).

Griffith, J. E. "The Des Moines Rapids of the Mississippi River, and Its Improvements." *Annals of Iowa* 8 (April 1870).

Grimes, Bryan. "The Surrender at Appomattox." *SHSP* 27 (1899).

Hall, H. Seymour. "Fredericksburg and Chancellorsville" (April 4, 1894). In *War Talks in Kansas: A Series of Papers Read Before the Kansas Commandery of the Military Order of the Loyal Legion of the United States.* Kansas City, Mo.: Franklin Hudson, 1906.

Hallowell, Benjamin. *Autobiography of Benjamin Hallowell.* Philadelphia: Friends Book Association, 1883.

———. *Geometrical Analysis; or, the Construction and Solution of Various Geometrical Problems.* Philadelphia: J. B. Lippincott, 1872.

Hampton, Wade. *Address on the Life and Character of Gen. Robert E. Lee, Delivered on the 12th of October, 1871, Before the Society of Confederate Soldiers and Sailors, in Maryland.* Baltimore: John Murphy, 1871.

Harrison, Constance Cary. *Recollections Grave and Gay.* New York: Charles Scribner's, 1916.

Hatcher, William Eldridge. *Along the Trail of the Friendly Years.* New York: Fleming H. Revell, 1910.

Hay, John. *Inside Lincoln's White House: The Complete Civil War Diary of John Hay.* Edited by Michael Burlingame and J. R. T. Ettlinger. Carbondale: Southern Illinois University Press, 1997.

Henry, William S. *Campaign Sketches of the War with Mexico.* New York, 1847.

Herbert, Hilary A. "Colonel Hilary A. Herbert's 'History of the Eighth Alabama Volunteer Regiment, C.S.A.'" Edited by M. S. Fortin. *Alabama Historical Quarterly* 39 (1977).

Heth, Henry. "Letter from Major-General Henry Heth, of A. P. Hill's Corps, A.N.V." *SHSP* 4 (Oct. 1877).

Hildreth, James. *Dragoon Campaigns to the Rocky Mountains, Being a History of the Enlistment, Organization, and First Campaigns of the Regiment of United States Dragoons.* New York: Wiley & Long, 1836.

Hitchcock, Ethan Allen. *Fifty Years in Camp and Field: Diary of Major-General Ethan Allen Hitchcock.* Edited by W. A. Croffut. New York: G. P. Putnam's Sons, 1909.

Holden, Frances Mayhugh. *Lambshead Before Interwoven: A Texas Range Chronicle, 1848–1878.* College Station: Texas A&M University Press, 1982.

Hood, John Bell. *Advance and Retreat: Personal Experiences in the United States and Confederate States Armies.* 1880; Lincoln: University of Nebraska Press, 1996.

———. "Leading Confederates on the Battle of Gettysburg." *SHSP* 4 (Oct. 1877).

Hotchkiss, Jedidiah. "The Chancellorsville Campaign and the Death of Jackson." In *Confederate Military History: Virginia,* edited by Clement A. Evans. Atlanta: Confederate, 1899.

———. *Make Me a Map of the Valley: The Civil War Journal of Stonewall Jackson's Topographer.* Edited by Archie P. McDonald. Dallas: Southern Methodist University Press, 1973.

Hotchkiss, Jedidiah, and William Allan. *The Battle-Fields of Virginia: Chancellorsville.* New York: Van Nostrand, 1867.

Howard, McHenry. "Closing Scenes of the War About Richmond." *SHSP* 31 (1903).

Howard, Oliver Otis. "The Character and Campaigns of General Lee." In Brock, *Gen. Robert Edward Lee.*

Hubbs, G. Ward, ed. *Voices from Company D: Diaries by the Greensboro Guards, Fifth Alabama Infantry Regiment, Army of Northern Virginia.* Athens: University of Georgia Press, 2003.

Hughes, George W. *Memoir Descriptive of the March of a Division of the United States Army, Under the Command of Brigadier General John E. Wool, from San Antonio de Bexar, in Texas, to Saltillo, in Mexico.* Washington, D.C., 1849.

Humphreys, M. W. "Reminiscences of General Lee as President of Washington College." In Riley, *General Robert E. Lee After Appomattox.*

Imboden, John D. "Reminiscences of Lee and Jackson." *Galaxy,* Nov. 1871.

———. "Stonewall Jackson in the Shenandoah." In Buel and Johnson, *Battles and Leaders of the Civil War,* 2:282–97.

Jenkins, John S. *History of the War Between the United States and Mexico, from the Commencement of Hostilities to the Ratification of the Treaty of Peace.* Auburn, N.Y.: Derby, Miller, 1848.

Johnson, Richard W. *A Soldier's Reminiscences in Peace and War.* Philadelphia: J. B. Lippincott, 1886.

Johnston, Joseph E. *Narrative of Military Operations, Directed, During the Late War Between the States.* New York: D. Appleton, 1874.

———. "Responsibilities of the First Bull Run." In Buel and Johnson, *Battles and Leaders of the Civil War,* 1:240–58.

Johnston, William Preston. "Death and Funeral of General Lee." In Riley, *General Robert E. Lee After Appomattox.*

Jones, John Beauchamp. *A Rebel War Clerk's Diary: At the Confederate States Capital.* Edited by James I. Robertson. 2 vols. Lawrence: University Press of Kansas, 2015.

Jones, John William. ed. *Army of Northern Virginia Memorial Volume.* Richmond: J. W. Randolph & English, 1880.

———. "The Friendship Between Lee and Scott." *SHSP* 11 (Aug.-Sept. 1883).

———, *Christ in the Camp; or, Religion in Lee's Army.* Richmond: B. F. Johnson, 1887.

Jones, Thomas G. "Last Days of the Army of Northern Virginia." *SHSP* 17 (1893).

Jones, Walter N. "Some Recollections of Service by One Who Claims to Have Been the Youngest Confederate Who Surrendered at Appomattox." In Newsome, *Civil War Talks.*

Joynes, E. S. "General Lee, as a College President." *University Monthly: A Journal of School and Home Education,* March 1871.

———. "General Robert E. Lee as College President." In Riley, *General Robert E. Lee After Appomattox.*

Kean, Robert Garlick Hill. *Inside the Confederate Government: The Diary of Robert Garlick Hill Kean.* Edited by Edward Younger. New York: Oxford University Press, 1957.

Kearny, Philip. *Letters from the Peninsula: The Civil War Letters of General Philip Kearny.* Edited by William B. Styple. Kearny, N.J.: Belle Grove, 1988.

Keckley, Elizabeth. *Behind the Scenes; or, Thirty Years a Slave, and Four Years in the White House.* 1868; Salem, N.H.: Ayer, 1985.

Kenly, John R. *Memoirs of a Maryland Volunteer: War with Mexico, in the Years 1846–7–8.* Philadelphia, 1873.

Keyes, Erasmus D. *Fifty Years' Observations of Men and Events, Civil and Military.* New York: C. Scribner's Sons, 1884.

Kimball, George. *A Corporal's Story: Civil War Recollections of the Twelfth Massachusetts.* Edited by Alan D. Gaff and Donald H. Gaff. Norman: University of Oklahoma Press, 2014.

Kirkland, Leigh, ed. "'A Human Life: Being the Autobiography of Elizabeth Oakes Smith': A Critical Edition and Introduction." PhD diss., Georgia State University, 1994.

Lacy, J. Horace. "Lee at Fredericksburg." In Cozzens, *Battles and Leaders of the Civil War,* 5:211–16.

Latrobe, John H. B. *Reminiscences of West Point from September, 1818 to Mar., 1882.* East Saginaw, Mich.: Evening News, 1887.

Law, Evander McIver. "The Fight for Richmond in 1862." *Southern Bivouac,* April 1887.

———. "From the Wilderness to Cold Harbor." In Buel and Johnson, *Battles and Leaders of the Civil War,* 4:118–44.

Lay, Col. J. F. "Reminiscences of the Powhatan Troop of Cavalry in 1861." *SHSP* 8 (Aug./Sept. 1880).

Lee, Fitzhugh. "The Failure of the Hampton Conference." In Cozzens, *Battles and Leaders of the Civil War,* 6:500–505.

Levering, John. "Lee's Advance and Retreat in the Cheat Mountain Campaign of 1861." In *Military Essays and Recollections: Essays and Papers Read Before the Illinois Commandery, Military Order of the Loyal Legion of the United States.* Vol. 4. Chicago: Cozzens & Beaton, 1907.

Leyburn, John. "An Interview with General Robert E. Lee." *Century Magazine,* May 1885.

Liddell, St. John. "Liddell's Record of the Civil War." *Southern Bivouac,* Dec. 1885.

Livermore, William R. "Lee's Response to Grant's Overland Campaign of 1864." In Cozzens, *Battles and Leaders of the Civil War,* 5:493–502.

Loehr, Charles T. *War History of the Old First Virginia Infantry Regiment, Army of Northern Virginia.* Richmond: William Ellis Jones, 1884.

Lomax, Elizabeth Lindsay. *Leaves from an Old Washington Diary, 1854–1863.* Edited by L. L. Wood. New York: E. P. Dutton, 1943.

Long, Armistead Lindsay. "Lee's West Virginia Campaign." In McClure, *Annals of the War.*

———. *Memoirs of Robert E. Lee: His Military and Personal History.* Edited by Marcus Wright. New York: J. M. Stoddart, 1886.

Longstreet, James. "The Battle of Fredericksburg." In Buel and Johnson, *Battles and Leaders of the Civil War,* 3:70–85.

———. *From Manassas to Appomattox: Memoirs of the Civil War in America.* Philadelphia: J. B. Lippincott, 1896.

———. "The Invasion of Maryland." In Buel and Johnson, *Battles and Leaders of the Civil War,* 2:663–74.

———. "Lee in Pennsylvania." In McClure, *Annals of the War.*

———. "Lee's Right Wing at Gettysburg." In Buel and Johnson, *Battles and Leaders of the Civil War,* 3:339–53.

———. "The Mistakes of Gettysburg." In McClure, *Annals of the War.*

Mahone, William. "What I Saw and Heard During the Closing Days of the Army of Northern Virginia." In Newsome, *Civil War Talks.*

Mansfield, Edward D. *The Mexican War: A History of Its Origin, and a Detailed Account of the Victories Which Terminated in the Surrender of the Capital.* New York: A. S. Barnes, 1849.

Marshall, Charles. *Address Delivered Before the Lee Monument Association, at Richmond, Virginia, October 27, 1887.* Baltimore: John Murphy, 1888.

———. *An Aide-de-Camp of Lee, Being the Papers of Colonel Charles Marshall.* Edited by Frederick Maurice. Boston: Little, Brown, 1927.

———. "The Last Days of Lee's Army." In Cozzens, *Battles and Leaders of the Civil War,* 6:535–43.

Maury, Dabney Herndon. *Recollections of a Virginian in the Mexican, Indian, and Civil Wars.* New York: Charles Scribner's Sons, 1894.

McAllister, Robert. *The Civil War Letters of General Robert McAllister.* Edited by James I. Robertson. New Brunswick, N.J.: Rutgers University Press, 1965.

McCabe, W. Gordon. "Address of Captain W. Gordon McCabe." In Jones, *Army of Northern Virginia Memorial Volume.*

McClellan, George B. *The Civil War Papers of George B. McClellan: Selected Correspondence, 1860–1865.* Edited by Stephen W. Sears. New York: Ticknor & Fields, 1989.

———. *McClellan's Own Story: The War for the Union, the Soldiers Who Fought It, the Civilians Who Directed It, and His Relations to It and to Them.* New York: Charles L. Webster, 1887.

———. *The Mexican War Diary of George B. McClellan.* Edited by William Starr Myers. Princeton, N.J.: Princeton University Press, 1917.

McClendon, W. A. *Recollection of War Times.* Montgomery, Ala.: Paragon Press, 1909.

McClure, Alexander K. ed. *The Annals of the War, Written by Leading Participants North and South.* Philadelphia: Times, 1878.

———, *Colonel Alexander K. McClure's Recollections of Half a Century.* Salem, Mass.: Salem Press, 1902.

McGuire, Judith W. *Diary of a Southern Refugee During the War.* New York: E. J. Hale & Son, 1867.

McLaws, Lafayette. *A Soldier's General: The Civil War Letters of Major General Lafayette McLaws.* Edited by John C. Oeffinger. Chapel Hill: University of North Carolina Press, 2002.

McPherson, Edward, ed. *The Political History of the United States of America During the Great Rebellion.* Washington, D.C.: James J. Chapman, 1882.

———. *The Political History of the United States of America During the Period of Reconstruction.* Washington, D.C.: Solomons & Chapman, 1875.

McSherry, Richard. *El Puchero; or, A Mixed Dish from Mexico Embracing General Scott's Campaign with Sketches of Military Life, in Field and Camp, of the Character of the Country, Manner and Ways of the People, Etc.* Philadelphia: Lippincott, Grambo, 1850.

Meade, William. "Bishop Meade's Recollections." *Protestant Episcopal Quarterly Review and Church Register* 3 (Jan. 1856).

———. *Old Churches, Ministers, and Families of Virginia.* Philadelphia: J. B. Lippincott, 1900.

Melville, Herman. "Lee in the Capitol." In *Battle-Pieces and Aspects of the War: Civil War Poems,* edited by L. R. Rust. New York: Da Capo Press, 1995.

Merritt, Wesley. "Note on the Surrender of Lee." *Century Magazine,* April 1902.

Michie, Peter. "Reminiscences of Cadet and Army Service" (Oct. 4, 1893). In *Personal Recollections of the War of the Rebellion: Addresses Delivered Before the Commandery of the State of New York, Military Order of the Loyal Legion of the United States,* edited by A. N. Blakeman. New York: G. P. Putnam's Sons, 1897.

Moore, H. Judge. *Scott's Campaign in Mexico from the Rendezvous on the Island of Lobos to the Taking of the City.* Charleston: J. B. Nixon, 1849.

Morgan, James Morris. *Recollections of a Rebel Reefer.* Boston: Houghton Mifflin, 1917.

Morgan, William Henry. *Personal Reminiscences of the War of 1861–5: In Camp—en Bivouac—on the March—on Picket—on the Skirmish Line—on the Battlefield—and in Prison.* Lynchburg, Va.: J. P. Bell, 1911.

Morrison, James L., ed. "The Memoirs of Henry Heth." *Civil War History* 8 (Sept. 1962).

Mosby, John S. *The Memoirs of Colonel John S. Mosby.* Edited by Charles Wells Russell. Boston: Little, Brown, 1917.

———. "Personal Recollections of General Lee." *Munsey's Magazine,* April 1911.

Mulholland, St. Clair. *The Story of the 116th Regiment, Pennsylvania Volunteers in the War of the Rebellion.* Philadelphia: F. McManus, 1903.

Nelson, Alexander L. "How Lee Became a College President." In Riley, *General Robert E. Lee After Appomattox.*

Newsome, Hampton, et al., eds. *Civil War Talks: Further Reminiscences of George S. Bernard and His Fellow Veterans.* Charlottesville: University of Virginia Press, 2012.

Nicolay, John G. *An Oral History of Abraham Lincoln: John G. Nicolay's Interviews and Essays.* Edited by Michael Burlingame. Carbondale: Southern Illinois University Press, 1996.

———. *With Lincoln in the White House: Letters, Memoranda, and Other Writings of John G. Nicolay, 1860–1865.* Edited by Michael Burlingame. Carbondale: Southern Illinois University Press, 2000.

Oates, Stephen B., ed. *Rip Ford's Texas.* Austin: University of Texas Press, 1963.

Oates, William C. *The War Between the Union and the Confederacy, and Its Lost Opportunities.* New York: Neale, 1905.

Olmsted, Frederick Law. *A Journey Through Texas; or, A Saddle-Trip on the Southwestern Frontier.* New York: Dix, Edwards, 1857.

Oswandel, J. Jacob. *Notes of the Mexican War, 1846–47–48: Comprising Incidents, Adventures, and Everyday Proceedings and Letters While with the United States Army in the Mexican War.* Philadelphia, 1885.

Owen, William Miller. *In Camp and Battle with the Washington Artillery of New Orleans: A Narrative of Events During the Late Civil War from Bull Run to Appomattox and Spanish Fort.* Boston: Ticknor, 1885.

Packard, Joseph. *Recollections of a Long Life.* Washington, D.C.: Byron S. Adams, 1902.

Parker, William B. *Notes Taken During the Expedition Commanded by Capt. R. B. Marcy, U.S.A., Through Unexplored Texas in the Summer and Fall of 1854.* Philadelphia: Hayes & Zell, 1856.

Pecquet du Bellet, Louise. *Some Prominent Virginia Families.* Lynchburg, Va.: J. P. Bell, 1907.

Pender, William Dorsey. *One of Lee's Best Men: The Civil War Letters of General William Dorsey Pender.* Edited by William W. Hassler. Chapel Hill: University of North Carolina Press, 1999.

Pendleton, William Nelson. "Personal Recollections of General Lee." *Southern Magazine,* Dec. 1874.

Perry, Leslie J. "General Lee and the Battle of Gettysburg." *SHSP* 23 (1895).

Phillips, Wendell. *Speeches, Lectures, and Letters.* Boston: James Redpath, 1863.

———. *Speeches, Lectures, and Letters.* Boston: Lee & Shepard, 1891.

Poague, William Thomas. *Gunner with Stonewall: Reminiscences of William Thomas Poague, Lieutenant, Captain, Major, and Lieutenant Colonel of Artillery, Army of Northern Virginia, CSA, 1861–1865.* Edited by M. F. Cockrell. 1957; Lincoln: University of Nebraska Press, 1998.

Porter, Charles H. "The Battle of Cold Harbor." In *The Wilderness Campaign, May–June 1864.* Papers of the Military Historical Society of Massachusetts. 1905; Wilmington, N.C.: Broadfoot, 1989.

Porter, Horace. *Campaigning with Grant.* New York: Century, 1897.

———. "The Surrender at Appomattox Court House." In Buel and Johnson, *Battles and Leaders of the Civil War,* 4:729–46.

Powell, William Henry. *The Fifth Army Corps (Army of the Potomac): A Record of Operations During the Civil War in the United States of America, 1861–1865.* New York: G. P. Putnam's Sons, 1896.

[Putnam, Sallie Ann Brock]. *Richmond During the War: Four Years of Personal Observation.* New York: G. W. Carleton, 1867.

Ranson, A. H. R. "General Lee as I Knew Him." *Harper's Monthly Magazine,* Feb. 1911.

Reagan, John H. *Memoirs, with Special Reference to Secession and the Civil War.* Edited by W. F. McCaleb. New York: Neale, 1906.

Riley, Franklin L. ed. *General Robert E. Lee After Appomattox.* New York: Macmillan, 1922.

———, "What General Lee Read After the War." In Riley, *General Robert E. Lee After Appomattox.*

Ripley, Roswell S. *The War with Mexico.* New York: Harper & Bros., 1849.

Robertson, Margaret Briscoe Stuart. *My Childhood Recollections of the War: Life in the Confederate Stronghold of Staunton, Virginia.* Staunton, Va.: Charles Culbertson, 2013.

Robins, Sally Nelson. "Mrs. Lee During the War." In Brock, *Gen. Robert Edward Lee.*

Robinson, Leigh. "Address of Private Leigh Robinson." In Jones, *Army of Northern Virginia Memorial Volume.*

Ross, FitzGerald. *Cities and Camps of the Confederate States.* Edited by Richard B. Harwell. Urbana: University of Illinois Press, 1958.

Rosser, Thomas L. "Personal Traits of General Lee." In Brock, *Gen. Robert Edward Lee.*

Royall, William Lawrence. *Some Reminiscences.* New York: Neale, 1909.

Scheibert, Justus. *Seven Months in the Rebel States During the North American War.* 1863. Translated by J. C. Hayes. Tuscaloosa: University of Alabama Press, 2009.

Scott, John. "The Black Horse Cavalry." In McClure, *Annals of the War.*

Scott, W. W. "Some Personal Memories of General Robert E. Lee." *WMQ* 6 (Oct. 1926).

Scott, Winfield. *Memoirs of Lieut.-General Scott, LL.D., Written by Himself.* New York: Sheldon, 1864.

Semmes, Raphael. *Memoirs of Service Afloat: During the War Between the States.* Baltimore: Kelly, Piet, 1869.

———. *Service Afloat and Ashore During the Mexican War.* Cincinnati: Wm. H. Moore, 1851.

Seymour, William J. *Reminiscences of a Louisiana Tiger: The Civil War Memoirs of Captain William J. Seymour.* Edited by Terry L. Jones. Baton Rouge: Louisiana State University Press, 1991.

Sharpe, George H. "The Last Day of the Lost Cause." *National Tribune,* Oct. 1, 1879.

Simpson, R. W., and Taliaferro N. Simpson. *Far, Far from Home: The Wartime Letters of Dick and Tally Simpson, 3rd South Carolina Volunteers.* Edited by Guy R. Everson and Edward W. Simpson Jr. New York: Oxford University Press, 1994.

Sioussat, St. George L., ed. "Mexican War Letters of William Bowen Campbell, of Tennessee,

Written to Governor David Campbell, of Virginia, 1846–1847." *Tennessee Historical Magazine,* June 1915.

Smith, E. Kirby. *To Mexico with Scott: Letters of Captain E. Kirby Smith to His Wife.* Edited by E. J. Blackwood. Cambridge, Mass.: Harvard University Press, 1917.

Smith, Frederic H. *West Point Fifty Years Ago: An Address Delivered Before the Association of Graduates of the U.S. Military Academy, West Point.* New York: D. Van Nostrand, 1879.

Smith, Gustavus Woodson. *Company A, Corps of Engineers, U.S.A., 1846–1848, in the Mexican War.* Edited by Leone M. Hudson. Kent, Ohio: Kent State University Press, 2001.

Smith, James Power. "General Lee at Gettysburg: A Paper Read Before the Military Historical Society of Massachusetts, on the Fourth of April, 1905." *SHSP* 33 (1905).

Sorrel, G. Moxley. *Recollections of a Confederate Staff Officer.* Edited by Bell Irvin Wiley. Wilmington, N.C.: Broadfoot, 1995.

Spencer, Edward. "Confederate Negro Enlistments." In McClure, *Annals of the War.*

Stegmaier, M. J., ed. *Henry Adams in the Secession Crisis: Dispatches to the Boston "Daily Advertiser," December 1860–March 1861.* Baton Rouge: Louisiana State University Press, 2012.

Stephens, Alexander H. *A Constitutional View of the Late War Between the States: Its Causes, Character, Conduct, and Results.* Philadelphia: National, 1870.

———. *Recollections of Alexander H. Stephens: His Diary Kept When a Prisoner at Fort Warren.* Edited by M. L. Avary. 1910; Baton Rouge: Louisiana State University Press, 1998.

Stiles, Robert. *Four Years Under Marse Robert.* New York: Neale, 1910.

Strong, George Templeton. *Diary of the Civil War, 1860–1865.* Edited by Allan Nevins. New York: Macmillan, 1962.

Swallow, William. "From Fredericksburg to Gettysburg." *Southern Bivouac,* Nov. 1885.

Taylor, Walter Herron. "The Campaign in Pennsylvania." In McClure, *Annals of the War.*

———. *Four Years with General Lee: Being a Summary of the More Important Events Touching the Career of General Robert E. Lee.* New York: D. Appleton, 1878.

———. *General Lee: His Campaigns in Virginia, 1861–1865, with Personal Reminiscences.* Norfolk, Va.: Nusbaum Book & News, 1906.

———. *Lee's Adjutant: The Wartime Letters of Colonel Walter Herron Taylor, 1862–1865.* Edited by R. Lockwood Tower. Columbia: University of South Carolina Press, 1995.

Thompson, Richard S. "A Scrap of Gettysburg" (Feb. 11, 1897). In *Military Essays and Recollections: Papers Read Before the Commandery of the State of Illinois, Military Order of the Loyal Legion of the United States.* Vol. 3. Chicago: Dial Press, 1899.

Torrence, Clayton, ed. "Arlington and Mount Vernon 1856 as Described in a Letter of Augusta Blanche Berard." *VMHB,* April 1949.

Totten, Joseph. *Essays on Hydraulic and Common Mortars and on Limeburning.* New York: Wiley & Putnam, 1842.

———. *Report Addressed to the Hon. Jefferson Davis, Secretary of War, on the Effects of Firing with Heavy Ordnance from Casemate Embrasures.* Washington, D.C.: Taylor & Maury, 1857.

Townsend, Edward D. *Anecdotes of the Civil War in the United States.* New York: D. Appleton, 1884.

Trimble, Isaac R. "The Battle and Campaign of Gettysburg." *SHSP* 26 (1898).

Upshur, George Lyttleton. *As I Recall Them: Memories of Crowded Years.* New York: Wilson-Erickson, 1936.

Vaughan, B. B. "A Trooper's Reminiscences: Wilderness to Yellow Tavern." In Newsome, *Civil War Talks.*

Vautier, John D. "The Loss at Gettysburg." *Southern Bivouac,* March 1886.

Venable, C. S. "Address of Colonel C. S. Venable." In Jones, *Army of Northern Virginia Memorial Volume.*

Venable, Charles. "General Lee in the Wilderness Campaign." In Buel and Johnson, *Battles and Leaders of the Civil War,* 4:240–45.

Vigne, Godfrey T. *Six Months in America.* Philadelphia: Thomas T. Ash, 1833.

Walker, James A. "Life in the Army—the Private Soldier's Spirit." In Newsome, *Civil War Talks.*

Walker, John G. "Jackson's Capture of Harper's Ferry." In Buel and Johnson, *Battles and Leaders of the Civil War,* 2:604–11.

———. "Sharpsburg." In Buel and Johnson, *Battles and Leaders of the Civil War,* 2:675–81.

Warnery, Charles de. *Thoughts and Anecdotes Military and Historical, Written About the Year 1774.* London: T. Egerton, 1811.

Watkins, Sam R. *"Co. Aytch": Maury Grays, First Tennessee Regiment; or, A Side Show of the Big Show.* Chattanooga: Times, 1900.

Weld, Stephen Minot. *War Diary and Letters of Stephen Minot Weld, 1861–1865.* Boston: Massachusetts Historical Society, 1979.

White, W. S. "Stray Leaves from a Soldiers' Journal." *SHSP* 11 (Dec. 1883).

Whitman, George Washington. *Civil War Letters of George Washington Whitman.* Edited by Jerome M. Loving. Durham, N.C.: Duke University Press, 1976.

Wilcox, Cadmus Marcellus. *History of the Mexican War.* Washington, D.C.: Church News, 1892.

Willcox, Orlando B. *Forgotten Valor: The Memoirs, Journals, and Civil War Letters of Orlando B. Willcox.* Edited by R. G. Scott. Kent, Ohio: Kent State University Press, 1999.

Williams, T. Harry, ed. *With Beauregard in Mexico: The Mexican War Reminiscences of P. G. T. Beauregard.* Baton Rouge: Louisiana State University Press, 1956.

Williamson, J. P. "Cockade City's Surrender, Delivered to the Federals." In Newsome, *Civil War Talks.*

Winthrop, Robert C. *Addresses and Speeches on Various Occasions.* Boston: Little, Brown, 1852.

Wise, Henry Alexander. *Seven Decades of the Union: The Humanities and Materialism.* Philadelphia: J. B. Lippincott, 1876.

Wolseley, Garnet Joseph. "A Month's Visit to the Confederate Headquarters." *Blackwood's Edinburgh Magazine,* Jan. 1863.

Young, William T. *Sketch of the Life and Public Services of General Lewis Cass.* Detroit: Markham & Elwood, 1852.

Secondary Materials—Books

Achenbach, Joel. *The Grand Idea: George Washington's Potomac and the Race to the West.* New York: Simon & Schuster, 2004.

Adams, Stephen. *The Best and Worst Country in the World: Perspectives on the Early Virginia Landscape.* Charlottesville: University of Virginia Press, 2001.

Alexander, Bevin. *Robert E. Lee's Civil War.* Holbrook, Mass.: Adams Media Cooperative, 1998.

Alexander, Frederick Warren. *Stratford Hall and the Lees Connected with Its History, Biographical, Genealogical, and Historical.* Privately published, 1912.

Alonzo, Armando C. *Tejano Legacy: Rancheros and Settlers in South Texas, 1734–1900.* Albuquerque: University of New Mexico Press, 1997.

Ambrose, Stephen E. *Duty, Honor, Country: A History of West Point.* Baltimore: Johns Hopkins University Press, 1966.

Anderson, Gary Clayton. *The Conquest of Texas: Ethnic Cleansing in the Promised Land, 1820–1875.* Norman: University of Oklahoma Press, 2005.

Armes, Ethel. *Stratford Hall: The Great House of the Lees.* Richmond: Garrett & Massie, 1936.

———. *Stratford on the Potomac.* Greenwich, Conn.: William Alexander Jr. Chapter, United Daughters of the Confederacy, 1928.

Arnold, James R. *Jeff Davis's Own: Cavalry, Comanches, and the Battle for the Texas Frontier.* New York: John Wiley & Sons, 2000.

Ayers, Edward L. *The Thin Light of Freedom: Civil War and Emancipation in the Heart of America.* New York: W. W. Norton, 2017.

Bache, Richard Meade. *Life of General George Gordon Meade: Commander of the Army of the Potomac.* Philadelphia: Henry T. Coates, 1897.

Bartholomees, J. Boone. *Buff Facings and Gilt Buttons: Staff and Headquarters Operations in the Army of Northern Virginia, 1861–1865.* Columbia: University of South Carolina Press, 1998.

Bates, Samuel Penniman. *The Battle of Gettysburg.* Philadelphia: T. H. Davis, 1875.

Bauer, K. Jack. *The Mexican War, 1846–1848.* New York: Macmillan, 1974.

———. *Zachary Taylor: Soldier, Planter, Statesman of the Old Southwest.* Baton Rouge: Louisiana State University Press, 1985.

Baum, Dale. *The Shattering of Texas Unionism: Politics in the Lone Star State During the Civil War Era.* Baton Rouge: Louisiana State University Press, 1998.

Beatie, Russell H. *The Army of the Potomac: Birth of Command, November 1860–September 1861.* Cambridge, Mass.: Da Capo Press, 2002.

———. *The Army of the Potomac: McClellan's First Campaign, March 1862–May 1862.* New York: Savas Beatie, 2007.

Bigelow, John. *The Campaign of Chancellorsville: A Strategic and Tactical Study.* New Haven, Conn.: Yale University Press, 1910.

Billon, Frederic Louis. *Annals of St. Louis in Its Territorial Days, from 1804 to 1821.* St. Louis: Frederic Billon, 1888.

Birdsong, James S., ed. *Brief Sketches of the North Carolina State Troops in the War Between the States.* Raleigh, N.C.: Josephus Daniels, 1894.

Blair, William A. *With Malice Toward Some: Treason and Loyalty in the Civil War Era.* Chapel Hill: University of North Carolina Press, 2014.

Blight, David W. *Frederick Douglass' Civil War: Keeping Faith in Jubilee.* Baton Rouge: Louisiana State University Press, 1989.

Blount, Roy. *Robert E. Lee: A Life.* New York: Penguin, 2003.

Bodie, Charles A. *Remarkable Rockbridge: The Story of Rockbridge County, Virginia.* Lexington, Va.: Rockbridge County Historical Society, 2011.

Boley, Henry. *Lexington in Old Virginia.* Richmond: Garrett & Massie, 1936.

Bond, Christiana. *Memories of General Robert E. Lee.* Baltimore: Norman, Remington, 1926.

Boney, F. N. *John Letcher of Virginia: The Story of Virginia's Civil War Governor.* Tuscaloosa: University of Alabama Press, 1966.

Bonura, Michael. *Under the Shadow of Napoleon: French Influence on the American Way of Warfare from the War of 1812 to the Outbreak of WWII.* New York: New York University Press, 2012.

Bordewich, Fergus M. *America's Great Debate: Henry Clay, Stephen A. Douglas, and the Compromise That Preserved the Union.* New York: Simon & Schuster, 2012.

———. *Congress at War: How Republican Reformers Fought the Civil War, Defied Lincoln, Ended Slavery, and Remade America.* New York: Knopf, 2020.

Bowden, J. J. *The Exodus of Federal Forces from Texas.* Austin, Tex.: Eakin Press, 1986.

Bowden, Scott, and Bill Ward. *Last Chance for Victory: Robert E. Lee and the Gettysburg Campaign.* Cambridge, Mass.: Da Capo Press, 2001.

Bowen, John Joseph. *The Strategy of Robert E. Lee.* New York: Neale, 1914.

Bradford, Gamaliel. *Lee the American.* Boston: Houghton Mifflin, 1912.

Brashear, Glenn David. *The Peninsula Campaign and the Necessity of Emancipation: African Americans and the Fight for Freedom.* Chapel Hill: University of North Carolina Press, 2012.

Breen, Timothy H. *Tobacco Culture: The Mentality of the Great Tidewater Planters on the Eve of Revolution.* Princeton, N.J.: Princeton University Press, 1985.

Bridges, Hal. *Lee's Maverick General: Daniel Harvey Hill.* New York: McGraw-Hill, 1961.
Brown, Kent Masterson. *Retreat from Gettysburg: Lee, Logistics, and the Pennsylvania Campaign.* Chapel Hill: University of North Carolina Press, 2005.
Brown, Robert R. *The Spiritual Pilgrimage of Robert E. Lee.* Shippensburg, Pa.: White Mane, 1998.
Buchanan, John. *The Road to Guilford Courthouse.* New York: John Wiley, 1997.
Burlingame, Michael. *Abraham Lincoln: A Life.* 2 vols. Baltimore: Johns Hopkins University Press, 2008.
Burton, Brian K. *Extraordinary Circumstances: The Seven Days Battles.* Bloomington: Indiana University Press, 2001.
Burton, Harrison W. *The History of Norfolk, Virginia.* Norfolk: Norfolk Virginian Job Print, 1877.
Bushman, Richard L. *The Refinement of America: Persons, Houses, Cities.* New York: Knopf, 1992.
Caldwell, Robert Granville. *The Lopez Expeditions to Cuba, 1848–1851.* Princeton, N.J.: Princeton University Press, 1915.
Calkins, Chris M. *The Appomattox Campaign, March 29–April 9, 1865.* Lynchburg, Va.: Schroeder, 2008.
———. *The Battle of Appomattox Station and Appomattox Court House, April 8–9, 1865.* Lynchburg, Va.: H. E. Howard, 1987.
———. *The Final Bivouac: The Surrender Parade at Appomattox and the Disbanding of the Armies, April 10–May 20, 1865.* Lynchburg, Va.: H. E. Howard, 1988.
———. *Lee's Retreat: A History and Field Guide.* Richmond: Page One Historical Pubs., 2000.
Callahan, James Morton. *Semi-centennial History of West Virginia.* Semi-centennial Commission of West Virginia, 1913.
Campbell, Randolph B. *Sam Houston and the American Southwest.* New York: HarperCollins, 1993.
Carson, Cary. *Face Value: The Consumer Revolution and the Colonization of America.* Charlottesville: University of Virginia Press, 2017.
Carton, Evan. *Patriotic Treason: John Brown and the Soul of America.* New York: Free Press, 2006.
Casdorph, Paul D. *Confederate General R. S. Ewell: Robert E. Lee's Hesitant Commander.* Lexington: University Press of Kentucky, 2004.
———. *Lee and Jackson: Confederate Chieftains.* New York: Paragon House, 1992.
Cauble, Frank P. *The Surrender Proceedings: April 9, 1865, Appomattox Court House.* Lynchburg, Va.: H. E. Howard, 1987.
Cavanaugh, Michael A., and William Marvel. *The Petersburg Campaign: The Battle of the Crater, "The Horrid Pit," June 25–August 6, 1864.* Lynchburg, Va.: H. E. Howard, 1989.
Chaffin, Tom. *Fatal Glory: Narciso López and the First Clandestine U.S. War Against Cuba.* Baton Rouge: Louisiana State University Press, 2003.
Chorley, E. Clowes. *Men and Movements in the American Episcopal Church.* New York: Charles Scribner's Sons, 1950.
Clark, Dan Elbert. *The Middle West in American History.* New York: Thomas Crowell, 1937.
Clark, J. P. *Preparing for War: The Emergence of the Modern U.S. Army, 1815–1917.* Cambridge, Mass.: Harvard University Press, 2017.
Clary, David A. *Eagles and Empire: The United States, Mexico, and the Struggle for a Continent.* New York: Bantam Books, 2009.
Cleaves, Freeman. *Rock of Chickamauga: The Life of General George H. Thomas.* Norman: University of Oklahoma Press, 1948.
Coffman, Edward M. *The Old Army: A Portrait of the American Army in Peacetime, 1784–1898.* New York: Oxford University Press, 1986.
Cohen, Michael David. *Reconstructing the Campus: Higher Education and the American Civil War.* Charlottesville: University of Virginia Press, 2012.
Cole, Ryan L. *Light Horse Harry Lee.* Washington, D.C.: Regnery, 2018.

Collins, Darrell L. *The Army of Northern Virginia: Organization, Strength, Casualties, 1861–65.* Jefferson, N.C.: McFarland, 2015.

Collins, Michael L. *Texas Devils: Rangers and Regulars on the Lower Rio Grande, 1846–1861.* Norman: University of Oklahoma Press, 2008.

Connolly, Thomas L. *Autumn of Glory: The Army of Tennessee, 1862–1865.* Baton Rouge: Louisiana State University Press, 1971.

———. *The Marble Man: Robert E. Lee and His Image in American Society.* New York: Knopf, 1977.

Conroy, James B. *Our One Common Country: Abraham Lincoln and the Hampton Roads Peace Conference of 1865.* Guilford, Conn.: Lyons Press, 2014.

Cook, Robert J. *Civil War Senator: William Pitt Fessenden and the Fight to Save the American Republic.* Baton Rouge: Louisiana State University Press, 2011.

Cooke, John Esten. *A Life of Gen. Robert E. Lee.* New York: D. Appleton, 1871.

Cooling, Benjamin Franklin. *Counter-thrust: From the Peninsula to the Antietam.* Lincoln: University of Nebraska Press, 2007.

———. *Jubal Early: Robert E. Lee's Bad Old Man.* Lanham, Md.: Rowman & Littlefield, 2014.

Coulling, Mary P. *The Lee Girls.* Winston-Salem, N.C.: John F. Blair, 1987.

Cox, R. David. *The Religious Life of Robert E. Lee.* Grand Rapids: Wm. B. Eerdmans, 2017.

Cozzens, Peter. *Shenandoah 1862: Stonewall Jackson's Valley Campaign.* Chapel Hill: University of North Carolina Press, 2008.

Cramer, Zadok. *The Navigator: Containing Directions for Navigating the Monongahela, Allegheny, Ohio, and Mississippi Rivers.* Pittsburgh: Cramer & Spear, 1821.

Crenshaw, Ollinger. *General Lee's College: The Rise and Growth of Washington and Lee University.* New York: Random House, 1969.

Cresap, Bernarr. *Appomattox Commander: The Story of General E. O. C. Ord.* San Diego: A. S. Barnes, 1981.

Daniel, Larry J. *Conquered: Why the Army of Tennessee Failed.* Chapel Hill: University of North Carolina Press, 2019.

———. *Soldiering in the Army of Tennessee: A Portrait of Life in a Confederate Army.* Chapel Hill: University of North Carolina Press, 1991.

Darby, John Fletcher. *Personal Recollections of Many Prominent People Whom I Have Known.* St. Louis: G. I. Jones, 1880.

Daughtry, Mary Bandy. *Gray Cavalier: The Life and Wars of General W. H. F. "Rooney" Lee.* Cambridge, Mass.: Da Capo Press, 2002.

Davis, Burke. *Gray Fox: Robert E. Lee and the Civil War.* New York: Rinehart, 1956.

Davis, William C. *Battle at Bull Run: A History of the First Major Campaign of the Civil War.* Garden City, N.Y.: Doubleday, 1977.

———. *Crucible of Command: Ulysses S. Grant and Robert E. Lee—the War They Fought, the Peace They Forged.* Boston: Da Capo Press, 2014.

———. *Jefferson Davis: The Man and His Hour.* New York: HarperCollins, 1991.

Dillard, Philip D. *Jefferson Davis's Final Campaign: Confederate Nationalism and the Fight to Arm the Slaves.* Macon, Ga.: Mercer University Press, 2017.

DiNardo, R. L., and Albert A. Nofi. *James Longstreet: The Man, the Soldier, the Controversy.* Boston: Da Capo Press, 1998.

Divine, John E. *8th Virginia Infantry.* Lynchburg, Va.: H. E. Howard, 1983.

Dorsey, Florence L. *Master of the Mississippi: Henry Shreve and the Conquest of the Mississippi.* Boston: Houghton Mifflin, 1941.

Dowdey, Clifford. *Lee: A Biography.* 1965; New York: Skyhorse, 2015.

———. *Lee's Last Campaign: The Story of Lee and His Men Against Grant.* New York: Bonanza Books, 1960.

———. *The Seven Days: The Emergence of Lee.* Boston: Little, Brown, 1964.

Du Bose, John Witherspoon. *General Joseph Wheeler and the Army of Tennessee.* New York: Neale, 1912.

Dunn, Richard S. *A Tale of Two Plantations: Slave Life and Labor in Jamaica and Virginia.* Cambridge, Mass.: Harvard University Press, 2014.

Durden, Robert F. *The Gray and the Black: The Confederate Debate on Emancipation.* Baton Rouge: Louisiana State University Press, 1972.

Edwards, Richard. *Edwards's Great West and Her Commercial Metropolis: Embracing a General View of the West and a Complete History of St. Louis, from the Landing of Ligueste, in 1764, to the Present Time.* New York: C. V. Alvord, 1860.

Eisenhower, John S. D. *Agent of Destiny: The Life and Times of General Winfield Scott.* New York: Free Press, 1997.

Engle, Stephen D. *Gathering to Save a Nation: Lincoln and the Union's War Governors.* Chapel Hill: University of North Carolina Press, 2016.

Evans, Eli N. *Judah P. Benjamin: The Jewish Confederate.* New York: Free Press, 1988.

Evans, Emory G. *A "Topping People": The Rise and Decline of Virginia's Old Political Elite.* Charlottesville: University of Virginia Press, 2009.

Farish, H. D., ed. *Journal and Letters of Philip Vickers Fithian, 1773–1774: A Plantation Tutor of the Old Dominion.* Williamsburg, Va.: Colonial Williamsburg, 1965.

Fellman, Michael. *The Making of Robert E. Lee.* New York: Random House, 2000.

Fishwick, Marshall. *Lee After the War.* New York: Dodd, Mead, 1963.

Flood, Charles Bracelen. *Lee: The Last Years.* Boston: Houghton Mifflin, 1981.

Fogel, Robert William. *Without Consent or Contract: The Rise and Fall of American Slavery.* New York: W. W. Norton, 1985.

Foos, Paul. *A Short, Offhand, Killing Affair: Soldiers and Social Conflict During the Mexican-American War.* Chapel Hill: University of North Carolina Press, 2002.

Ford, Lacy K. *Deliver Us from Evil: The Slavery Question in the Old South.* New York: Oxford University Press, 2009.

Freehling, William H. *The Road to Disunion: Secessionists at Bay, 1776–1854.* New York: Oxford University Press, 1990.

Freeman, Douglas Southall. *Lee's Lieutenants: A Study in Command.* New York: Charles Scribner's Sons, 1942.

———. *R. E. Lee: A Biography.* 4 vols. New York: Charles Scribner's Sons, 1934–35.

French, Scot. *The Rebellious Slave: Nat Turner in American Memory.* Boston: Houghton Mifflin, 2004.

Frye, Dennis E. *2nd Virginia Infantry.* Lynchburg, Va.: H. E. Howard, 1984.

Fuller, J. F. C. *Grant and Lee: A Study in Personality and Generalship.* 1933; Bloomington: Indiana University Press, 1967.

Furgurson, Ernest B. *Ashes of Glory: Richmond at War.* New York: Knopf, 1996.

———. *Chancellorsville, 1863: The Souls of the Brave.* New York: Knopf, 1992.

———. *Not War but Murder: Cold Harbor, 1864.* New York: Knopf, 2000.

Gallagher, Gary W. ed. *The Antietam Campaign.* Chapel Hill: University of North Carolina Press, 1999.

———. *The Confederate War.* Cambridge, Mass.: Harvard University Press, 1997.

———. *Lee and His Army in Confederate History.* Chapel Hill: University of North Carolina Press, 2001.

———. *Lee the Soldier.* Lincoln: University of Nebraska Press, 1996.

———. *The Spotsylvania Campaign.* Chapel Hill: University of North Carolina Press, 1998.

———. *Three Days at Gettysburg: Essays on Confederate and Union Leadership.* Kent, Ohio: Kent State University Press, 1999.

———. *The Wilderness Campaign*. Chapel Hill: University of North Carolina Press, 2007.

Gallagher, Gary W., and Joseph T. Glatthaar, eds. *Leaders of the Lost Cause: New Perspectives on the Confederate High Command*. Mechanicsburg, Pa.: Stackpole Books, 2004.

Gambone, A. N. *Lee at Gettysburg: A Commentary on Defeat*. Baltimore: Butternut & Blue, 2002.

Gaughan, Anthony J. *The Last Battle of the Civil War: United States Versus Lee, 1861–1883*. Baton Rouge: Louisiana State University Press, 2011.

Gerson, Noel B. *Light-Horse Harry: A Biography of Washington's Great Cavalryman, General Henry Lee*. Garden City, N.Y.: Doubleday, 1966.

Glatthaar, Joseph T. *General Lee's Army: From Victory to Collapse*. New York: Free Press, 2008.

———. *Soldiering in the Army of Northern Virginia: A Statistical Portrait of the Troops Who Served Under Robert E. Lee*. Chapel Hill: University of North Carolina Press, 2011.

Godfrey, Carlos Emmor. *Sketch of Major Henry Washington Sawyer: First Regiment, Cavalry, New Jersey*. Trenton: Adjutant-General's Office, 1907.

Goodwin, W. A. R., ed. *History of the Theological Seminary in Virginia and Its Historical Background*. Rochester, N.Y.: Du Bois Press, 1923.

Gordon, Lesley J. *A Broken Regiment: The 16th Connecticut's Civil War*. Baton Rouge: Louisiana State University Press, 2014.

Gould, Emerson W. *Fifty Years on the Mississippi; or, Gould's History of River Navigation*. St. Louis: Nixon-Jones, 1889.

Green, Michael S. *Politics and America in Crisis: The Coming of the Civil War*. Santa Barbara, Calif.: ABC/CLIO, 2010.

Greenberg, Amy S. *A Wicked War: Polk, Clay, Lincoln, and the 1846 U.S. Invasion of Mexico*. New York: Knopf, 2012.

Greene, A. Wilson. *The Final Battles of the Petersburg Campaign: Breaking the Backbone of the Rebellion*. Knoxville: University of Tennessee Press, 2008.

———. *Whatever You Resolve to Be: Essays on Stonewall Jackson*. Baltimore: Butternut & Blue, 1992.

Grimsley, Mark. *And Keep Moving On: The Virginia Campaign, May–June 1864*. Lincoln: University of Nebraska Press, 2002.

Grimsley, Mark, and Brooks D. Simpson, eds. *The Collapse of the Confederacy*. Lincoln: University of Nebraska Press, 2001.

Guardino, Peter. *The Dead March: A History of the Mexican-American War*. Cambridge, Mass.: Harvard University Press, 2017.

Gue, Benjamin G. *History of Iowa from the Earliest Times to the Beginning of the 20th Century*. Chicago: Century, 1903.

Hagarman, Edward. *The American Civil War and the Origins of Modern Warfare: Ideas, Organization, and Field Command*. Bloomington: Indiana University Press, 1988.

Hall, Granville Davisson. *Lee's Invasion of Northwest Virginia in 1861*. Chicago: Mayer & Miller, 1911.

Hamilton, Holman. *Prologue to Conflict: The Crisis and Compromise of 1850*. 1964; Lexington: University of Kentucky Press, 2005.

———. *Zachary Taylor: Soldier in the White House*. Indianapolis: Bobbs-Merrill, 1951.

Hanna, Jennifer. *Arlington House: The Robert E. Lee Memorial*. Washington, D.C.: U.S. Department of the Interior, 2001.

Harden, William. *A History of Savannah and South Georgia*. Chicago: Lewis, 1913.

Harman, Troy. *Lee's Real Plan at Gettysburg*. Mechanicsburg, Pa.: Stackpole Books, 2003.

Harsh, Joseph. *Confederate Tide Rising: Robert E. Lee and the Making of Southern Strategy, 1861–1862*. Kent, Ohio: Kent State University Press, 1998.

———. *Sounding the Shallows: A Confederate Companion for the Maryland Campaign of 1862*. Kent, Ohio: Kent State University Press, 2000.

Hartley, Cecil B. *Life of Major General Henry Lee: Commander of Lee's Legion in the Revolutionary War*. New York: Derby & Jackson, 1859.

Hartwig, D. Scott. *To Antietam Creek: The Maryland Campaign of September 1862*. Baltimore: Johns Hopkins University Press, 2012.

Hassler, William W. *A. P. Hill: Lee's Forgotten General*. 1957; Chapel Hill: University of North Carolina Press, 1962.

Henderson, G. F. R. *Stonewall Jackson and the American Civil War*. London: Longmans, Green, 1913.

Hendrick, Burton. *The Lees of Virginia: Biography of a Family*. Boston: Little, Brown, 1935.

Hennessy, John. *Return to Bull Run: The Campaign and Battle of Second Manassas*. New York: Simon & Schuster, 1993.

Hess, Earl J. *In the Trenches at Petersburg: Field Fortifications and Confederate Defeat*. Chapel Hill: University of North Carolina Press, 2009.

———. *Into the Crater: The Mine Attack at Petersburg*. Columbia: University of South Carolina Press, 2010.

———. *Trench Warfare Under Grant and Lee*. Chapel Hill: University of North Carolina Press, 2007.

Heuvel, Sean M., and Lisa L. Heuvel. *The College of William and Mary in the Civil War*. Jefferson, N.C.: McFarland, 2013.

Hinton, Richard J. *John Brown and His Men with Some Account of the Roads They Travelled to Reach Harper's Ferry*. New York: Funk & Wagnalls, 1894.

Holt, Michael F. *The Election of 1860: "A Campaign Fraught with Consequences."* Lawrence: University Press of Kansas, 2017.

———. *The Rise and Fall of the American Whig Party: Jacksonian Politics and the Onset of the Civil War*. New York: Oxford University Press, 1999.

Holton, Woody. *Unruly Americans and the Origins of the Constitution*. New York: Hill and Wang, 2007.

Hope, Ian C. *A Scientific Way of War: Antebellum Military Science, West Point, and the Origins of American Military Thought*. Lincoln: University of Nebraska Press, 2015.

Hopkins, Donald A. *Robert E. Lee in War and Peace: The Photographic History of a Confederate and American Icon*. El Dorado, Calif.: Savas Beatie, 2013.

Horn, Jonathan. *The Man Who Would Not Be Washington: Robert E. Lee's Civil War and His Decision That Changed American History*. New York: Scribner, 2015.

Horn, Stanley F. *The Army of Tennessee*. Norman: University of Oklahoma Press, 1953.

Horsman, Reginald. *Frontier Doctor: William Beaumont, America's First Great Medical Scientist*. Columbia: University of Missouri Press, 1996.

———. *Race and Manifest Destiny: The Origins of American Racial Anglo-Saxonism*. Cambridge, Mass.: Harvard University Press, 1981.

Horwitz, Tony. *Midnight Rising: John Brown and the Raid That Sparked the Civil War*. New York: Henry Holt, 2011.

Howe, Daniel Walker. *What Hath God Wrought: The Transformation of America, 1815–1848*. New York: Oxford University Press, 2007.

Howe, Thomas J. *The Petersburg Campaign: Wasted Valor, June 15–16, 1864*. Lynchburg, Va.: H. E. Howard, 1988.

Hsieh, Wayne Wei-Siang. *West Pointers and the Civil War: The Old Army in War and Peace*. Chapel Hill: University of North Carolina Press, 2009.

Hughes, Nathaniel Cheairs, and Roy P. Stonesifer. *The Life and Wars of Gideon J. Pillow*. Chapel Hill: University of North Carolina Press, 1993.

Hunt, Jeffrey. *Meade and Lee at Bristoe Station: The Problems of Command and Strategy After Get-*

tysburg, from Brandy Station to the Buckland Races, August 1 to October 21, 1863. El Dorado, Calif.: Savas Beatie, 2019.

Hunter, Louis C. *Steamboats on the Western Rivers: An Economic and Technological History*. Cambridge, Mass.: Harvard University Press, 1949.

Hurst, Harold W. *Alexandria on the Potomac: The Portrait of an Antebellum Community*. Lanham, Md.: University Press of America, 1991.

Isaac, Rhys. *The Transformation of Virginia, 1740–1790*. Chapel Hill: University of North Carolina Press, 1982.

Jackson, Eugene Beauharnais. *The Romance of Historic Alexandria: A Guide to the Old City*. Atlanta: A. B. Caldwell, 1921.

James, Alice Proctor. *The Ohio Company: Its Inner History*. Pittsburgh: University of Pittsburgh Press, 1959.

Jamieson, Perry D. *Spring 1865: The Closing Campaigns of the Civil War*. Lincoln: University of Nebraska Press, 2015.

Janney, Caroline, ed. *Petersburg to Appomattox: The End of the War in Virginia*. Chapel Hill: University of North Carolina Press, 2018.

Jeter, Jeremiah Bell. *The Recollections of a Long Life*. Richmond: Religious Herald, 1891.

Johnson, Timothy D. *A Gallant Little Army: The Mexico City Campaign*. Lawrence: University Press of Kansas, 2007.

———. *Winfield Scott: The Quest for Military Glory*. Lawrence: University Press of Kansas, 1998.

Johnson, William. *Sketches of the Life and Correspondence of Nathanael Greene*. Charleston, S.C.: A. E. Miller, 1822.

Johnston, William Preston. *The Life of Gen. Albert Sidney Johnston: Embracing His Services in the Armies of the United States, the Republic of Texas, and the Confederate States*. New York: D. Appleton, 1878.

Jones, Archer. *Civil War Command and Strategy: The Process of Victory and Defeat*. New York: Free Press, 1992.

Jones, Charles Colcock. *Reminiscences of the Last Days, Death, and Burial of General Henry Lee*. Albany, N.Y.: J. Munsell, 1870.

Jones, John William. *Life and Letters of Robert Edward Lee, Soldier and Man*. New York: Neale, 1906.

———. *Personal Reminiscences, Anecdotes, and Letters of Gen. Robert E. Lee*. New York: D. Appleton, 1875.

Jordan, Brian Matthew. *Unholy Sabbath: The Battle of South Mountain in History and Memory, September 14, 1862*. El Dorado, Calif.: Savas Beatie, 2012.

Kamoie, Laura Croghan. *Irons in the Fire: The Business History of the Tayloe Family and Virginia's Gentry, 1700–1860*. Charlottesville: University of Virginia Press, 2007.

Kamphuis, J. William. *Introduction to Coastal Engineering and Management*. Hackensack, N.J.: World Scientific, 2010.

Kapsch, Robert J. *Historic Canals and Waterways of South Carolina*. Columbia: University of South Carolina Press, 2010.

Kasson, John F. *Rudeness and Civility: Manners in Nineteenth-Century Urban America*. New York: Hill and Wang, 1990.

Katcher, Philip. *The Army of Robert E. Lee*. London: Arms & Armour, 1994.

Kaufmann, J. E., and H. W. Kaufmann. *Fortress America: The Forts That Defended America, 1600 to the Present*. Boston: Da Capo Press, 2005.

Kavanaugh, Thomas W. *The Comanches: A History, 1706–1875*. Lincoln: University of Nebraska Press, 1996.

Keller, Christian B. *The Great Partnership: Robert E. Lee, Stonewall Jackson, and the Fate of the Confederacy.* New York: Pegasus, 2019.

Koistinen, Paul A. C. *Beating Plowshares into Swords: The Political Economy of American Warfare, 1606–1865.* Lawrence: University Press of Kansas, 1996.

Konstam, Angus. *American Civil War Fortifications (1): Coastal Brick and Stone Forts.* Osceloa, Wis.: Osprey, 2003.

Korda, Michael. *Clouds of Glory: The Life and Legend of Robert E. Lee.* New York: Harper, 2014.

Krick, Robert E. L. *Staff Officers in Gray: A Biographical Register of the Staff Officers in the Army of Northern Virginia.* Chapel Hill: University of North Carolina Press, 2003.

Krick, Robert K. *The Smoothbore Volley That Doomed the Confederacy: The Death of Stonewall Jackson and Other Chapters on the Army of Northern Virginia.* Baton Rouge: Louisiana State University Press, 2002.

———. *Stonewall Jackson at Cedar Mountain.* Chapel Hill: University of North Carolina Press, 1990.

Kundahl, George G. *Alexandria Goes to War.* Knoxville: University of Tennessee Press, 2004.

Lambert, Andrew. *Seapower States: Maritime Culture, Continental Empires, and the Conflict That Made the Modern World.* New Haven, Conn.: Yale University Press, 2018.

Landis, Michael Todd. *Northern Men with Southern Loyalties: The Democratic Party and the Sectional Crisis.* Ithaca, N.Y.: Cornell University Press, 2014.

Lankford, Nelson. *Richmond Burning: The Last Days of the Confederate Capital.* New York: Viking, 2002.

Lee, Susan P. *Memoirs of William Nelson Pendleton, D.D.: Rector of Latimer Parish.* Philadelphia: J. B. Lippincott, 1893.

Levine, Bruce. *Confederate Emancipation: Southern Plans to Free and Arm Slaves During the Civil War.* New York: Oxford University Press, 2005.

Levy, Andrew. *The First Emancipator: Slavery, Religion, and the Quiet Revolution of Robert Carter.* New York: Random House, 2005.

Lewis, Charles Lee. *Matthew Fontaine Maury, the Pathfinder of the Seas.* Annapolis: U.S. Naval Institute, 1927.

Lewis, Emmanuel Raymond. *Seacoast Fortifications of the United States: An Introductory History.* Washington, D.C.: Smithsonian Institution Press, 1970.

Logel, Jon Scott. *Designing Gotham: West Point Engineers and the Rise of Modern New York, 1817–1898.* Baton Rouge: Louisiana State University Press, 2016.

Lomask, Milton. *The Biographer's Craft.* New York: HarperCollins, 1987.

Longacre, Edward G. *The Early Morning of War: Bull Run, 1861.* Norman: University of Oklahoma Press, 2014.

———. *Fitz Lee: A Military Biography of Major General Fitzhugh Lee, C.S.A.* Cambridge, Mass.: Da Capo Press, 2005.

Luvaas, Jay. *The Military Legacy of the Civil War.* Lawrence: University Press of Kansas, 1988.

MacDonald, Rose Mortimer Ellzey. *Mrs. Robert E. Lee.* New York: Ginn, 1939.

Magnet, Myron. *The Founders at Home: The Building of America, 1735–1817.* New York: W. W. Norton, 2014.

Majewski, John. *Modernizing a Slave Economy: The Economic Vision of the Confederate Nation.* Chapel Hill: University of North Carolina Press, 2006.

Marvel, William. *Burnside.* Chapel Hill: University of North Carolina Press, 1991.

———. *Lee's Last Retreat: The Flight to Appomattox.* Chapel Hill: University of North Carolina Press, 2002.

———. *A Place Called Appomattox.* Chapel Hill: University of North Carolina Press, 2000.

Mason, Emily V. *Popular Life of Gen. Robert Edward Lee.* Baltimore: John Murphy, 1874.

Masur, Louis P. *Lincoln's Hundred Days: The Emancipation Proclamation and the War for the Union*. Cambridge, Mass.: Harvard University Press, 2012.

Maurice, Frederick. *Robert E. Lee the Soldier*. Boston: Houghton Mifflin, 1925.

McCabe, James Dabney. *Life and Campaigns of General Robert E. Lee*. Philadelphia: National, 1866.

McClintock, Russell. *Lincoln and the Decision for War: The Northern Response to Secession*. Chapel Hill: University of North Carolina Press, 2008.

McMurry, Richard M. *Atlanta 1864: Last Chance for the Confederacy*. Lincoln: University of Nebraska Press, 2000.

Mead, Edward C. *Genealogical History of the Lee Family of Virginia and Maryland from A.D. 1300 to A.D. 1866*. New York: University Publishing, 1871.

Meade, G. G., Jr. *Life and Letters of George Gordon Meade: Major-General United States Army*. 2 vols. New York: Charles Scribner's Sons, 1913.

Means, Howard B. *The Avenger Takes His Place: Andrew Johnson and the 45 Days That Changed the Nation*. New York: Harcourt, 2006.

Meredith, Elisha E., and Samuel Pasco. *Memorial Addresses on the Life and Character of William H. F. Lee*. Washington, D.C.: Government Printing Office, 1891.

Merk, Frederick. *Manifest Destiny and Mission in American History: A Reinterpretation*. New York: Knopf, 1963.

Moore, Gay Montague. *Seaport in Virginia: George Washington's Alexandria*. Charlottesville: University Press of Virginia, 1949.

Morgan, Edmund S. *American Slavery, American Freedom: The Ordeal of Colonial Virginia*. New York: W. W. Norton, 1975.

Morphis, J. M. *History of Texas: From Its Discovery and Settlement, with a Description of Its Principal Cities and Counties, and the Agricultural, Mineral, and Material Resources of the State*. New York: United States Publishing, 1875.

Morrison, James E. *"The Best School": West Point, 1833–1866*. Kent, Ohio: Kent State University Press, 1986.

Morton, Oren F. *A History of Rockbridge County, Virginia*. Baltimore: Regional, 1980.

Mullin, Robert Bruce. *Episcopal Vision/American Reality: High Church Theology and Social Thought in Evangelical America*. New Haven, Conn.: Yale University Press, 1986.

Murfin, James V. *The Gleam of Bayonets: The Battle of Antietam and Robert E. Lee's Maryland Campaign, September 1862*. New York: Bonanza Books, 1965.

Myers, William Starr. *A Study in Personality: General George Brinton McClellan*. New York: D. Appleton–Century, 1934.

Nagel, Paul C. *The Lees of Virginia: Seven Generations of an American Family*. New York: Oxford University Press, 1990.

Nelson, John K. *A Blessed Company: Parishes, Parsons, and Parishioners in Anglican Virginia, 1690–1776*. Chapel Hill: University of North Carolina Press, 2001.

Nesbitt, Mark. *Saber and Scapegoat: J. E. B. Stuart and the Gettysburg Controversy*. Mechanicsburg, Pa.: Stackpole Books, 1994.

Newell, Clayton. *Lee vs. McClellan: The First Campaign*. Washington, D.C.: Regnery, 1996.

———. *The Regular Army Before the Civil War, 1845–1860*. Washington, D.C.: Center of Military History, 2014.

Newton, Steven H. *The Battle of Seven Pines, May 31–June 1, 1862*. Lynchburg, Va.: H. E. Howard, 1993.

———. *Joseph E. Johnston and the Defense of Richmond*. Lawrence: University Press of Kansas, 1990.

Nichols, James L. *General Fitzhugh Lee: A Biography*. Lynchburg, Va.: H. E. Howard, 1989.

Nolan, Alan. *Lee Considered: General Robert E. Lee and Civil War History.* Chapel Hill: University of North Carolina Press, 1991.

Nolan, Cathal J. *The Allure of Battle: A History of How Wars Have Been Won and Lost.* New York: Oxford University Press, 2017.

Norris, Walter Briscoe, Jr. *Westmoreland County, Virginia.* Marceline, Mo.: Walsworth, 1983.

Oates, Stephen B. *To Purge This Land with Blood: A Biography of John Brown.* New York: Harper & Row, 1970.

O'Harrow, Robert, Jr. *The Quartermaster: Montgomery Meigs, Lincoln's General, Master Builder of the Union Army.* New York: Simon & Schuster, 2016.

O'Reilly, Frank A. *The Fredericksburg Campaign: "Stonewall" Jackson at Fredericksburg: The Battle of Prospect Hill, December 13, 1862.* Lynchburg, Va.: H. E. Howard, 1993.

———. *The Fredericksburg Campaign: Winter War on the Rappahannock.* Baton Rouge: Louisiana State University Press, 2003.

Ossman, Laurie. *Great Houses of the South.* New York: Rizzoli, 2010.

Ossman, Laurie, and Debra A. McClane. *The Gentleman's Farm: Elegant Country House Living.* New York: Rizzoli, 2016.

Page, Thomas Nelson. *Robert E. Lee, the Southerner.* New York: Charles Scribner's Sons, 1909.

Paret, Peter, ed. *Makers of Modern Strategy from Machiavelli to the Nuclear Age.* Oxford: Clarendon Press, 1986.

Patchan, Scott. *Second Manassas: Longstreet's Attack and the Struggle for Chinn Ridge.* Washington, D.C.: Potomac Books, 2011.

Perry, John. *Lady of Arlington: The Life of Mrs. Robert E. Lee.* Sisters, Ore.: Multnomah Press, 2001.

Peskin, Allan. *Winfield Scott and the Profession of Arms.* Kent, Ohio: Kent State University Press, 2003.

Pfarr, Cory M. *Longstreet at Gettysburg: A Critical Reassessment.* Jefferson, N.C.: McFarland, 2019.

Piston, William G. *Lee's Tarnished Lieutenant: James Longstreet and His Place in Southern History.* Athens: University of Georgia Press, 1987.

Plum, William R. *The Military Telegraph During the Civil War in the United States.* 2 vols. Chicago: Jansen, McClurg, 1882.

Pollard, Edward A. *Lee and His Lieutenants: Comprising the Early Life, Public Services, and Campaigns of General Robert E. Lee and His Companions in Arms.* New York: E. B. Treat, 1867.

Power, J. Tracy. *Lee's Miserables: Life in the Army of Northern Virginia from the Wilderness to Appomattox.* Chapel Hill: University of North Carolina Press, 1998.

Preston, Walter Creigh. *Lee: West Point and Lexington.* Yellow Springs, Ohio: Antioch Press, 1934.

Primm, James Neal. *Lion of the Valley: St. Louis, Missouri, 1764–1980.* St. Louis: Missouri Historical Society Press, 1998.

Pryor, Elizabeth Brown. *Reading the Man: A Portrait of Robert E. Lee Through His Private Letters.* New York: Viking, 2007.

———. *Six Encounters with Lincoln: A President Confronts Democracy and Its Demons.* New York: Viking, 2017.

Quarstein, John V. *C.S.S.* Virginia: *Mistress of Hampton Roads.* Lynchburg, Va.: H. E. Howard, 2000.

Quarstein, John V., and J. M. Moore. *Yorktown's Civil War Siege: Drums Along the Warwick.* Charleston, S.C.: History Press, 2012.

Quarstein, John V., and Dennis P. Mroczkowski. *Fort Monroe: The Key to the South.* Charleston, S.C.: Arcadia, 2000.

Rable, George C. *The Confederate Republic: A Revolution Against Politics.* Chapel Hill: University of North Carolina Press, 1994.

———. *Fredericksburg! Fredericksburg!* Chapel Hill: University of North Carolina Press, 2002.

———. *God's Almost Chosen Peoples.* Chapel Hill: University of North Carolina Press, 2010.

Rafuse, Ethan S. *Antietam, South Mountain, and Harpers Ferry: A Battlefield Guide.* Lincoln: University of Nebraska Press, 2008.

———. *McClellan's War: The Failure of Moderation in the Struggle for the Union.* Bloomington: Indiana University Press, 2005.

———. *Robert E. Lee and the Fall of the Confederacy, 1863–1865.* Lanham, Md.: Rowman & Littlefield, 2008.

Rankin, Richard. *Ambivalent Churchmen and Evangelical Churchwomen: The Religion of the Episcopal Elite in North Carolina, 1800–1860.* Columbia: University of South Carolina Press, 1993.

Rasmussen, William M. S., and Robert S. Tilton. *Lee and Grant.* London: Giles, 2007.

Reeves, John. *The Lost Indictment of Robert E. Lee: The Forgotten Case Against an American Icon.* Lanham, Md.: Rowman & Littlefield, 2018.

Reid, Brian Holden. *Robert E. Lee: Icon for a Nation.* Amherst, N.Y.: Prometheus Books, 2007.

Reynolds, David S. *John Brown, Abolitionist: The Man Who Killed Slavery, Sparked the Civil War, and Seeded Civil Rights.* New York: Vintage, 2005.

Rhea, Gordon C. *The Battle of the Wilderness, May 5–6, 1864.* Baton Rouge: Louisiana State University Press, 1994.

———. *The Battles for Spotsylvania Court House and the Road to Yellow Tavern, May 7–12, 1864.* Baton Rouge: Louisiana State University Press, 1997.

———. *Cold Harbor: Grant and Lee, May 26–June 3, 1864.* Baton Rouge: Louisiana State University Press, 2002.

———. *On to Petersburg: Grant and Lee, June 4–15, 1864.* Baton Rouge: Louisiana State University Press, 2017.

———. *To the North Anna River: Grant and Lee, May 13–25, 1864.* Baton Rouge: Louisiana State University Press, 2000.

Rister, Carl Coke. *Robert E. Lee in Texas.* Norman: University of Oklahoma Press, 1946.

Robertson, James I. *General A. P. Hill: The Story of a Confederate Warrior.* New York: Random House, 1987.

———. *Robert E. Lee: A Reference Guide to His Life and Works.* Lanham, Md.: Rowman & Littlefield, 2019.

———. *Soldiers Blue and Gray.* Columbia: University of South Carolina Press, 1988.

———. *Stonewall Jackson: The Man, the Soldier, the Legend.* New York: Macmillan, 1997.

Robertson, William Glenn. *River of Death: The Chickamauga Campaign.* Vol. 1, *The Fall of Chattanooga.* Chapel Hill: University of North Carolina Press, 2018.

Robinson, W. Stitt. *Mother Earth: Land Grants in Virginia, 1607–1699.* Williamsburg: Virginia 350th Anniversary Celebration Corporation, 1957.

Rogin, Michael Paul. *Fathers and Children: Andrew Jackson and the Subjugation of the American Indian.* New York: Knopf, 1975.

Roland, Charles P. *Albert Sidney Johnston, Soldier of Three Republics.* Lexington: University Press of Kentucky, 2001.

Roman, Alfred. *The Military Operations of General Beauregard in the War Between the States, 1861 to 1865.* 2 vols. New York: Harper & Bros., 1884.

Royster, Charles. *The Fabulous History of the Dismal Swamp Company: A Story of George Washington's Times.* New York: Knopf, 1999.

———. *Light-Horse Harry Lee and the Legacy of the American Revolution.* Baton Rouge: Louisiana State University Press, 1981.

———. *A Revolutionary People at War: The Continental Army and American Character, 1775–1783.* Chapel Hill: University of North Carolina Press, 1979.

Rudy, William George. "Interpreting America's First Grecian Style House: The Architectural Legacy of George Washington Parke Custis and George Hadfield." Master's thesis, University of Maryland, College Park, 2010.

Sanborn, Margaret. *Robert E. Lee: The Complete Man, 1861–1870*. Philadelphia: J. B. Lippincott, 1967.

———. *Robert E. Lee: A Portrait, 1807–1861*. Philadelphia: J. B. Lippincott, 1966.

Schaff, Morris. *The Battle of the Wilderness*. Boston: Houghton Mifflin, 1910.

Scharf, John Thomas. *History of Baltimore City and County, from the Earliest Period to the Present Day*. Philadelphia: Louis H. Everts, 1881.

Sears, Stephen W. *Chancellorsville*. New York: Houghton Mifflin, 1996.

———. *Controversies and Commanders: Dispatches from the Army of the Potomac*. New York: Houghton Mifflin, 1999.

———. *George B. McClellan: The Young Napoleon*. New York: Ticknor & Fields, 1988.

———. *Landscape Turned Red: The Battle of Antietam*. New York: Ticknor & Fields, 1983.

———. *To the Gates of Richmond: The Peninsula Campaign*. New York: Ticknor & Fields, 1992.

Semple, Robert Baylor. *A History of the Rise and Progress of the Baptists in Virginia*. Richmond: John O'Lynch, 1810.

Settles, Thomas Michael. *John Bankhead Magruder: A Military Reappraisal*. Baton Rouge: Louisiana State University Press, 2009.

Shackelford, George Green. *George Wythe Randolph and the Confederate Elite*. Athens: University of Georgia Press, 1988.

Shepard, Elihu Hotchkiss. *The Early History of St. Louis and Missouri: From Its First Exploration by White Men in 1673 to 1843*. St. Louis: Southwestern Book and Publishing, 1870.

Shultz, David L., and Scott L. Mingus. *The Second Day at Gettysburg: The Attack and Defense of the Union Center on Cemetery Ridge, July 2, 1863*. El Dorado, Calif.: Savas Beatie, 2015.

Simpson, Brooks D. *Let Us Have Peace: Ulysses S. Grant and the Politics of War and Reconstruction, 1861–1868*. Chapel Hill: University of North Carolina Press, 1991.

Simpson, Craig M. *A Good Southerner: The Life of Henry A. Wise of Virginia*. Chapel Hill: University of North Carolina Press, 1985.

Simpson, Harold B. *Cry Comanche: The 2nd U.S. Cavalry in Texas, 1855–1861*. Hillsboro, Tex.: Hill College Press, 1988.

Skelton, William B. *An American Profession of Arms: The Army Officer Corps, 1784–1861*. Lawrence: University Press of Kansas, 1992.

Slotkin, Richard. *The Long Road to Antietam: How the Civil War Became a Revolution*. New York: Liveright, 2012.

———. *No Quarter: The Battle of the Crater, 1864*. New York: Random House, 2009.

Smith, M. R., ed. *Military Enterprise and Technological Change: Perspectives on the American Experience*. Cambridge, Mass.: MIT Press, 1985.

Snow, William P. *Lee and His Generals*. New York: Richardson, 1867.

Sodergren, Steven E. *The Army of the Potomac in the Overland and Petersburg Campaigns: Union Soldiers and Trench Warfare, 1864–1865*. Baton Rouge: Louisiana State University Press, 2017.

Spruill, Matt. *Decisions at Second Manassas: The Fourteen Critical Decisions That Defined the Battle*. Knoxville: University of Tennessee Press, 2018.

Stahr, Walter. *Stanton: Lincoln's War Secretary*. New York: Simon & Schuster, 2017.

Stampp, Kenneth M. *America in 1857: A Nation on the Brink*. New York: Oxford University Press, 1990.

Styple, William B. *McClellan's Other Story: The Political Intrigue of Colonel Thomas M. Key, Confidential Aide to General George B. McClellan*. Kearny, N.J.: Belle Grove, 2012.

Swanson, Drew A. *A Golden Weed: Tobacco and Environment in the Piedmont South*. New Haven, Conn.: Yale University Press, 2014.

Symonds, Craig L. *Joseph E. Johnston: A Civil War Biography*. New York: W. W. Norton, 1992.

Tanner, Robert G. *Stonewall in the Valley: Thomas J. "Stonewall" Jackson's Shenandoah Valley Campaign, Spring 1862*. Garden City, N.Y.: Doubleday, 1976.

Tate, Thad W., and David L. Ammerman, eds. *The Chesapeake in the Seventeenth Century: Essays on Anglo-American Society*. New York: W. W. Norton, 1979.

Thomas, Emory M. *Bold Dragoon: The Life of J. E. B. Stuart*. 1986; Norman: University of Oklahoma Press, 1999.

———. *The Confederate Nation, 1861–1865*. New York: Harper & Row, 1979.

———. *Robert E. Lee: A Biography*. New York: W. W. Norton, 1995.

Thomason, John William. *Jeb Stuart*. 1929; Lincoln: University of Nebraska Press, 1994.

Thompson, Jerry. *Cortina: Defending the Mexican Name in Texas*. College Station: Texas A&M University Press, 2007.

Thorp, Willard. *The Lives of Eighteen from Princeton*. Princeton, N.J.: Princeton University Press, 1946.

Tillson, Albert H. *Accommodating Revolutions: Virginia's Northern Neck in an Era of Transformations, 1760–1810*. Charlottesville: University of Virginia Press, 2010.

Trudeau, Noah Andre. *Bloody Roads South: The Wilderness to Cold Harbor, May–June 1864*. Boston: Little, Brown, 1989.

———. *The Last Citadel: Petersburg, Virginia, June 1864–April 1865*. Boston: Little, Brown, 1991.

———. *Robert E. Lee*. New York: Palgrave Macmillan, 2009.

Tsouras, Peter G. *Major General George H. Sharpe and the Creation of American Military Intelligence in the Civil War*. Philadelphia: Casemate, 2018.

Tucker, Glenn. *Chickamauga: Bloody Battle in the West*. 1961; Dayton: Press of Morningside Bookshop, 1976.

Turk, David S. *A Family's Path in America: The Lees and Their Continuing Legacy*. Westminster, Md.: Heritage Books, 2007.

Tyler-McGraw, Marie. *An African Republic: Black and White Virginians in the Making of Liberia*. Chapel Hill: University of North Carolina Press, 2007.

Vance, Margaret. *The Lees of Arlington: The Story of Mary and Robert E. Lee*. New York: E. P. Dutton, 1949.

Varon, Elizabeth R. *Appomattox: Victory, Defeat, and Freedom at the End of the Civil War*. New York: Oxford University Press, 2014.

———. *Armies of Deliverance: A New History of the Civil War*. New York: Oxford University Press, 2019.

———. *Disunion! The Coming of the American Civil War, 1789–1859*. Chapel Hill: University of North Carolina Press, 2008.

Venter, Bruce M. *Kill Jeff Davis: The Union Raid on Richmond, 1864*. Norman: University of Oklahoma Press, 2013.

Villard, Oswald Garrison. *John Brown, 1800–1859: A Biography Fifty Years After*. Boston: Houghton Mifflin, 1910.

Wallenstein, Peter, and Bertram Wyatt-Brown, eds. *Virginia's Civil War*. Charlottesville: University of Virginia Press, 2005.

Ward, Harry M. *George Washington's Enforcers: Policing the Continental Army*. Carbondale: Southern Illinois University Press, 2006.

Waters Sander, Kathleen. *John W. Garrett and the Baltimore and Ohio Railroad*. Baltimore: Johns Hopkins University Press, 2017.

Watson, Harry L. *Liberty and Power: The Politics of Jacksonian America*. New York: Hill and Wang, 1990.

Wawro, Geoffrey. *The Austro-Prussian War: Austria's War with Prussia and Italy in 1866*. New York: Cambridge University Press, 1996.

Weaver, John R. *A Legacy in Brick and Stone: American Coastal Defense Forts of the Third System, 1816–1867*. Missoula, Mont.: Pictorial Histories/Redoubt Press, 2001.

Weigley, Russell F. *History of the United States Army*. New York: Macmillan, 1967.

———. *Quartermaster General of the Union Army: A Biography of M. C. Meigs*. New York: Columbia University Press, 1959.

Weingardt, Richard. *Engineering Legends*. Reston, Va.: American Society of Civil Engineers, 2005.

Weitz, Mark A. *More Damning Than Slaughter: Desertion in the Confederate Army*. Lincoln: University of Nebraska Press, 2005.

Wert, Jeffrey D. *General James Longstreet: The Confederacy's Most Controversial Soldier*. New York: Simon & Schuster, 1993.

West, Thomas. *The Political Theory of the American Founding: Natural Rights, Public Policy, and the Moral Conditions of Freedom*. New York: Cambridge University Press, 2017.

Wilentz, Sean. *No Property in Man: Slavery and Antislavery at the Nation's Founding*. Cambridge, Mass.: Harvard University Press, 2018.

———. *The Rise of American Democracy: Jefferson to Lincoln*. New York: W. W. Norton, 2005.

Wilson, Ben. *Heyday: The 1850s and the Dawn of the Global Age*. New York: Basic Books, 2016.

Wilson, Robert. *Mathew Brady: A Biography*. New York: Bloomsbury, 2013.

Winders, R. B. *Mr. Polk's Army: The American Military Experience in the Mexican War*. College Station: Texas A&M University Press, 1997.

Winner, Lauren F. *A Cheerful and Comfortable Faith: Anglican Religious Practice in the Elite Households of Eighteenth-Century Virginia*. New Haven, Conn.: Yale University Press, 2010.

Wittenberg, Eric. *The Battle of Brandy Station: North America's Largest Cavalry Battle*. Charleston, S.C.: History Press, 2010.

Wittenberg, Eric, and D. T. Davis. *Out Flew the Sabres: The Battle of Brandy Station, June 9, 1863*. El Dorado, Calif.: Savas Beatie, 2016.

Wolf, Thomas A. *Historic Sites in Virginia's Northern Neck and Essex County*. Warsaw, Va.: Preservation Northern Neck and Middle Peninsula, 2011.

Wood, Gordon S. *The Radicalism of the American Revolution: How a Revolution Transformed a Monarchical Society into a Democratic One Unlike Any That Had Ever Existed*. New York: Knopf, 1991.

Woodward, Colin E. *Marching Masters: Slavery, Race, and the Confederate Army During the Civil War*. Charlottesville: University of Virginia Press, 2014.

Woodworth, Steven E. *Davis and Lee at War*. Lawrence: University Press of Kansas, 1995.

Wooten, Mattie L. I., ed. *Women Tell the Story of the Southwest*. San Antonio: Naylor, 1940.

Wright, Gordon. *The Cavalry Manual of Horsemanship and Horsemastership*. New York: Doubleday, 1962.

Wyatt-Brown, Bertram. *Southern Honor: Ethics and Behavior in the Old South*. New York: Oxford University Press, 2007.

———. *A Warring Nation: Honor, Race, and Humiliation in America and Abroad*. Charlottesville: University Press of Virginia, 2014.

Wycoff, Max. *A History of the Second South Carolina Infantry, 1861–65*. Wilmington, N.C.: Broadfoot, 2011.

———. *A History of the 3rd South Carolina Regiment: Lee's Reliables*. Wilmington, N.C.: Broadfoot, 2008.

Yates, Bernice-Marie. *The Perfect Gentleman: The Life and Letters of George Washington Custis Lee*. 2 vols. Xulon Press, 2003.

Young, Alfred C. *Lee's Army During the Overland Campaign: A Numerical Study*. Baton Rouge: Louisiana State University Press, 2013.

Young, John Russell. *Around the World with General Grant*. New York: American News, 1879.
Young, Rogers W. *Robert E. Lee and Fort Pulaski*. Washington, D.C.: National Park Service, 1941.
Zambone, Albert Louis. *Daniel Morgan: A Revolutionary Life*. Yardley, Pa.: Westholme, 2018.

Articles

Abshire, J. Patten. "The History of the Boyhood Home of Robert E. Lee." *Alexandria Chronicle* 3 (Winter 1995/96).
Adams, Francis R. "Robert E. Lee and the Concept of Democracy." *American Quarterly* 12 (Autumn 1960).
Ambler, C. H. "General R. E. Lee's Northwest Virginia Campaign." *West Virginia History* 5 (Jan. 1944).
Arbery, Glenn C. "General Lee and the Siren: Allen Tate's Failed Biography." *Mississippi Quarterly* 64 (Winter/Spring 2011).
Barksdale, Kevin T. "Our Rebellious Neighbors: Virginia's Border Counties During Pennsylvania's Whiskey Rebellion." *VMHB* 111 (2003).
Berman, Russell. "The Nation's Official Memorial to Robert E. Lee Gets a Rewrite." *Atlantic,* Aug. 18, 2017.
Bickel, Karl A. "Robert E. Lee in Florida." *Florida Historical Quarterly* 27 (July 1948).
Blair, William. "Friend or Foe: Treason and the Second Confiscation Act." In *Wars Within a War: Controversy and Conflict over the American Civil War,* edited by Joan Waugh and Gary W. Gallagher. Chapel Hill: University of North Carolina Press, 2009.
Bradford, Gamaliel. "The Social and Domestic Life of Robert E. Lee." *South Atlantic Quarterly* 10 (April 1911).
Bragg, William Harris. "Our Joint Labor: W. J. De Renne, Douglas Southall Freeman, and *Lee's Dispatches,* 1910–1915." *VMHB,* Jan. 1989.
Bridges, Hal, ed. "A Lee Letter on the 'Lost Dispatch' and the Maryland Campaign of 1862." *VMHB,* April 1958.
Brown, Russell K. " 'An Old Woman with a Broomstick': General David E. Twiggs and the U.S. Surrender in Texas, 1861." *Military Affairs* 48 (April 1984).
Burton, William L. "The Life and Death of Bloody Island: A Ferry Tale." *Western Illinois Regional Studies* 11 (Spring 1988).
Bushman, Richard L. "The Genteel Republic." *Wilson Quarterly* (Autumn 1996).
Campbell, Edward D. C. "The Fabric of Command: R. E. Lee, Confederate Insignia, and the Perception of Rank." *VMHB,* April 1990.
Cassell, Frank A. "The Great Baltimore Riot of 1812." *Maryland Historical Magazine* 70 (Fall 1975).
Chase, Enoch Aquila. "The Arlington Case: George Washington Custis Lee Against the United States of America." *Virginia Law Review* 15 (Jan. 1929).
Clary, David A. " 'I Am Already Quite a Texan': Albert J. Myer's Letters from Texas, 1854–1856." *Southwestern Historical Quarterly* 82 (July 1978).
Coffey, David W. "Reconstruction and Redemption in Lexington." In *After the Backcountry: Rural Life in the Great Valley of Virginia, 1800–1900,* edited by Kenneth E. Koons and Warren R. Hofstra. Knoxville: University of Tennessee Press, 2000.
Coffman, Edward M. "The Army Officer and the Constitution." *Parameters: The U.S. Army War College Quarterly* 17 (Sept. 1987).
Connelly, Thomas L. "Robert E. Lee and the Western Confederacy: A Criticism of Lee's Strategic Ability." *Civil War History* 15 (June 1969).

Cornwall, Robert. "The Rite of Confirmation in Anglican Thought During the Eighteenth Century." *Church History* 68 (June 1999).

Crimmins, Martin L. "Colonel George Croghan and the Indian Situation in Texas in 1847." *Southwestern Historical Quarterly* 56 (Jan. 1953).

———. "Colonel J. F. K. Mansfield's Report of the Inspection of the Department of Texas in 1856." *Southwestern Historical Quarterly* 42 (April 1939).

———. "An Episode in the Texas Career of General David E. Twiggs." *Southwestern Historical Quarterly* 41 (Oct. 1937).

Cunningham, H. H. "The Confederate Medical Officer in the Field." *U.S. Armed Forces Medical Journal* 9 (Nov. 1958).

Curtis, Robert I. "Confederate Classical Textbooks: A Lost Cause?" *International Journal of the Classical Tradition* 3 (Spring 1997).

Dahlinger, Charles. "The *New Orleans,* Being a Critical Account of the Beginning of Steamboat Navigation on the Western Rivers of the United States." *Pittsburgh Legal Journal* 59 (Oct. 1911).

Daniel, Frederick S. "A Visit to a Colonial Estate." *Harper's New Monthly Magazine,* March 1888.

Dederer, John Morgan. "In Search of the Unknown Soldier: A Critique of 'The Mystery in the Coffin.'" *VMHB,* Jan. 1995.

———. "The Origins of Robert E. Lee's Bold Generalship: A Reinterpretation." *Military Affairs* 49 (July 1985).

———. "Robert E. Lee's First Visit to His Father's Grave." *VMHB,* Jan. 1994.

Delay, Brian. "The Wider World of the Handsome Man: Southern Plains Indians Invade Mexico, 1830–1848." *Journal of the Early Republic* 27 (Spring 2007).

Dirck, Brian. "Posterity's Blush: Civil Liberties, Property Rights, and Property Confiscation in the Confederacy." *Civil War History* 48 (Sept. 2002).

Drum, Stella. "Robert E. Lee and the Improvement of the Mississippi River." *Missouri Historical Society Collections* 6 (Feb. 1929).

Dudley, Edgar S. "Was 'Secession' Taught at West Point?" *Century Magazine,* May 1909.

Forman, Sidney. "Why the United States Military Academy Was Established in 1802." *Military Affairs* 29 (Spring 1965).

Gaines, William H. "The Forgotten Army: Recruiting for a National Emergency (1799–1800)." *VMHB,* July 1948.

Gignilliat, John L. "A Historian's Dilemma: A Posthumous Footnote for Freeman's *R. E. Lee.*" *Journal of Southern History* 43 (May 1977).

Gilje, Paul A. "The Baltimore Riots of 1812 and the Breakdown of the Anglo-American Mob Tradition." *Journal of Social History* 13 (Summer 1980).

Glatthaar, Joseph T. "A Tale of Two Armies: The Confederate Army of Northern Virginia and the Union Army of the Potomac and Their Cultures." *Journal of the Civil War Era* 6 (Sept. 2016).

Good, Cassandra. "Washington Family Fortune: Lineage and Capital in Nineteenth-Century America." *Early American Studies* 18 (Winter 2020).

Gorman, Michael D. "Lee the 'Devil' Discovered." *Battlefield Photographer* 3 (Feb. 2006).

Grimsley, Mark. "Robert E. Lee: The Life and Career of the Master General." *Civil War Times Illustrated* 24 (Nov. 1985).

Gudmestad, Robert H. "The Troubled Legacy of Isaac Franklin: The Enterprise of Slave Trading." *Tennessee Historical Quarterly* 62 (Fall 2003).

Hacker, Barton C. "Engineering a New Order: Military Institutions, Technical Education, and the Rise of the Industrial State." *Technology and Culture* 34 (Jan. 1993).

Harrison, Fairfax. "The Proprietors of the Northern Neck: Chapters of Culpeper Genealogy." *Virginia Historical Magazine,* Jan. 1926.

Heidler, Jeanne T. "'Embarrassing Situation': David E. Twiggs and the Surrender of United

States Forces in Texas, 1861." In *Lone Star Blue and Gray: Essays on Texas and the Civil War,* edited by R. A. Wooster and Robt. Wooster. Austin: Texas State Historical Association, 1995.

Hickin, Patricia. "John C. Underwood and the Antislavery Movement in Virginia, 1847–60." *VMHB,* April 1965.

Holloway, Kali. "Unpaid Debts." *Nation,* April 6, 2020.

Hopkins, Donald A. "A Portrait of Lee We Were Not Supposed to See." *Military Images* 32 (Winter 2014).

Hsieh, Wayne Wei-Siang. "'I Owe Virginia Little, My Country Much': Robert E. Lee, the United States Regular Army, and Unconditional Unionism." In *Crucible of the Civil War: Virginia from Secession to Commemoration,* edited by E. L. Ayers, G. W. Gallagher, and A. J. Torget. Charlottesville: University of Virginia Press, 2006.

Jervey, Byrd Pendleton. "Derwent in Powhatan County and General Robert E. Lee's Sojourn There in the Summer of 1865." *VMHB,* Jan. 1950.

Kearney, Kevin E. "Autobiography of William Marvin." *Florida Historical Quarterly* 36 (Jan. 1958).

Kelbaugh, Ross J. "The Swedish Nightingale and the Baltimore Daguerreians." *Daguerreian Annual* (1991).

Kukla, Jon. "A Spectrum of Sentiments: Virginia's Federalists, Antifederalists, and 'Federalists Who Are for Amendments,' 1787–1788." *VMHB,* July 1988.

LaFantasie, Glenn W. "The Confederate We Still Don't Know." *Salon,* July 31, 2011.

Lawton, Christopher R. "Constructing the Cause, Bridging the Divide: Lee's Tomb at Washington College." *Southern Cultures* 15 (Summer 2009).

Lee, Sarah L. "War Time in Alexandria, Virginia." *South Atlantic Quarterly* 4 (July 1905).

Lemon, Laura. "The Foundation of American Horsemanship Lies in Fort Riley." *Chronicle of the Horse,* Feb. 10 and 17, 2020.

Littlefield, Douglas R. "The Potomac Company: A Misadventure in Financing an Early American Internal Improvement Project." *Business History Review* 58 (Winter 1984).

Main, Jackson Turner. "The One Hundred." *WMQ* 11 (July 1954).

Mainwaring, Richard D., and Harris D. Riley. "The Lexington Physicians of General Robert E. Lee." *Southern Medical Journal* 98 (Aug. 2005).

Mainwaring, Richard D., and Curtis G. Trible. "The Cardiac Illness of General Robert E. Lee." *Journal of Surgery, Gynecology, and Obstetrics* 174 (March 1992).

Moger, Allen W. "General Lee's Unwritten 'History of the Army of Northern Virginia.'" *VMHB,* July 1963.

———. "Letters to General Lee After the War." *VMHB* 64 (1956).

Monroe, William H. "The Battle of Antietam: A Military Study." *Journal of the Military Service Institution of the United States* 49 (Sept.–Oct. 1911).

Mudd, Aloysius I. "The Theatres of Washington from 1835 to 1850." *Records of the Columbia Historical Society* 6 (1903).

Musser, Ruth, and John C. Krantz. "The Friendship of General Robert E. Lee and Dr. Wm. Beaumont." *Bulletin of the Institute of the History of Medicine* 6 (May 1938).

Nelligan, Murray H. "American Nationalism on the Stage: The Plays of George Washington Parke Custis (1781–1857)." *VMHB,* July 1950.

O'Connell, Kim A. "Arlington's Enslaved Savior." *Civil War Times* 54 (Feb. 2015).

Parker, Elmer Oris. "Why Was Lee Not Pardoned?" *Prologue* 2 (Winter 1970).

Parker, Franklin. "Robert E. Lee, George Peabody, and Sectional Reunion." *Peabody Journal of Education* 78 (2003).

Paullin, Charles O. "Early Landmarks Between Great Hunting Creek and the Falls of the Potomac." *Records of the Columbia Historical Society* 31/32 (1930).

Pellicer, Juan Christian. "'I Hear Such Strange Things of the Union's Fate': Charles Carter Lee's Virginia Georgics." *Early American Literature* 42 (2007).

Pickett, Lasalle. "The Wartime Story of General Pickett." *Cosmopolitan,* Jan. 1914.

P.J.K. "The Gratiot Portraits by Thomas Sully." *Record of the Art Museum, Princeton University* 20 (1961).

Pryor, Elizabeth Brown. "The General in His Study." *New York Times,* April 19, 2011.

———. "Rediscovered: Robert E. Lee's Earliest-Known Letter." *VMHB,* Jan. 2007.

———, ed. "'Thou Knowest Not the Time of Thy Visitation': A Newly Discovered Letter Reveals Robert E. Lee's Lonely Struggle with Disunion." *VMHB,* Sept. 2011.

Reese, Thomas H. "An Officer's Oath." *Military Law Review* 25 (July 1964).

Reidy, Joseph P. "'Coming from the Shadow of the Past': The Transition from Slavery to Freedom at Freedmen's Village, 1863–1900." *VMHB,* Oct. 1987.

Reinhart, Richard A. "Robert E. Lee's Right Ear and the Relation of Earlobe Crease to Coronary Artery Disease." *American Journal of Cardiology* 120, no. 2 (2017).

Reinhart, Theodore R., and Judith A. Habicht. "Shirley Plantation in the Eighteenth Century: A Historical, Architectural, and Archaeological Study." *VMHB,* Jan. 1984.

Riley, Harris D. "General Robert E. Lee: His Medical Profile." *Virginia Medical Monthly,* July 1978.

———. "Robert E. Lee's Battle with Disease." *Civil War Times Illustrated* 18 (Dec. 1979).

Risjord, Norman K. "The Virginia Federalists." *Journal of Southern History* 33 (Nov. 1967).

Roach, Catharine. "Robert E. Lee's Financial Impact on Washington College." *Washington and Lee Spectator* (Fall 2014).

Robert, Joseph C. "Lee the Farmer." *Journal of Southern History* 3 (Nov. 1937).

Ross, Michael A. "The Commemoration of Robert E. Lee's Death and the Obstruction of Reconstruction in New Orleans." *Civil War History* 51 (June 2005).

Rozear, Marvin P., et al. "R. E. Lee's Stroke." *VMHB,* April 1990.

Ryan, Edward L. "Imprisonment for Debt: Its Origin and Repeal." *VMHB,* Jan. 1934.

Scheer, George F. "Henry Lee on the Southern Campaign." *VMHB,* April 1943.

Sears, Stephen W. "The Curious Case of the Lost Order." *Civil War Monitor* 6 (Winter 2016).

———. "McClellan and the Peace Plank of 1864: A Reappraisal." *Civil War History* 36 (March 1990).

Smith, Bruce R. "Benjamin Hallowell of Alexandria." *VMHB,* July 1977.

Smith, Mark A. "A Crucial Leavening of Expertise: Engineer Soldiers and the Transmission of Military Proficiency in the American Civil War." *Civil War History* 66 (March 2020).

Smith, Stanley Phillips. "The Northern Neck's Role in American Legal History." *VMHB,* July 1969.

Smith, Thomas T. "U.S. Combat Operations in the Indian Wars of Texas, 1849–1881." *Southwestern Historical Quarterly* 99 (April 1996).

Sullivan, Robert. "A Confederate General in Brooklyn." *New Yorker,* June 19, 2017.

Sweig, Donald M. "The Importation of African Slaves to the Potomac River, 1732–1772." *WMQ* 42 (Oct. 1985).

Swift, Eben. "The Military Education of Robert E. Lee." *VMHB,* April 1927.

Thomas, Emory M., ed. "'The Greatest Service I Rendered the State': J. E. B. Stuart's Account of the Capture of John Brown." *VMHB,* July 1986.

Thompson, Mary V. "'A Sacred Duty': Mt. Vernon During the Years of the Civil War." *Alexandria Chronicle* (2003/2004).

Thomson, J. A., and C. M. Santos. "The Mystery in the Coffin: Another View of Lee's Visit to His Father's Grave." *VMHB,* Jan. 1995.

Trudeau, Noah Andre. "Unwritten History: The War Memoirs Robert E. Lee Chose Not to Write." *Civil War Times* 49 (Aug. 2010).

Woods, Michael E. "The Compromise of 1850 and the Search for a Usable Past." *Journal of the Civil War Era* 9 (Sept. 2019).

Wyrick, Connie H. "Stratford and the Lees." *Journal of the Society of Architectural Historians* 30 (March 1971).

Zwelling, Shomer S. "Robert Carter's Journey: From Colonial Patriarch to New Nation Mystic." *American Quarterly* 38 (Autumn 1986).

Index

ALSO BY

Allen C. Guelzo

GETTYSBURG

The Last Invasion

The Battle of Gettysburg has been written about at length and thoroughly dissected in terms of strategic importance, but never before has a book taken readers so close to the experience of the individual soldier. Two-time Lincoln Prize winner Allen C. Guelzo shows us the face, the sights, and the sounds of nineteenth-century combat: the stone walls and gunpowder clouds of Pickett's Charge; the reason that the Army of Northern Virginia could be smelled before it could be seen; the march of thousands of men from the banks of the Rappahannock in Virginia to the Pennsylvania hills. What emerges is a previously untold story of army life in the Civil War: from the personal politics roiling the Union and Confederate officer ranks to the peculiar character of artillery units. Through such scrutiny, one of history's epic battles is given extraordinarily vivid new life.

History